The Science of Religion and the Religion of Scientism

The Science of Religion and the Religion of Scientism

A Neuroscientist's Perspective on Consciousness, Morality, and the "New Atheism"

BRUNO G. BREITMEYER

The Catholic University of America Press
Washington, D.C.

The paper used in this publication meets the minimum requirements of American National Standards for Information Science—Permanence of Paper for Printed Library Materials, ANSI Z39.48–1992.

∞

Cataloging-in-Publication Data is available from the Library of Congress

ISBN (paper): 978-0-8132-4140-1
ISBN (ebook): 978-0-8132-4141-8

Contents

PART 3: BEYOND THE ATHEISTIC RELIGION OF SCIENTISM

APPENDICES

Preface

During my undergraduate studies, I majored in mathematics; yet, having enrolled in several philosophy, history, and literature courses (and having read a good number of books related to these topics on the side), I all along felt like an unfulfilled humanities major. My love and study of the humanities continued throughout my graduate career, although, then too, the focus of my studies lay elsewhere, on visual perception and neuroscience. Thereafter, my interest in, and study of, the humanities continued during my many years as an academic researcher in the area of visual cognition and of the allied field of visual consciousness studies. Fortunately, my academic and research careers were, timewise, not all-absorbing. So, while fulfilling my academic teaching and research obligations, a good portion of the free time I enjoyed was spent pursuing scholarship in the humanities that spanned the histories of science, philosophy, and religion, and more than a smattering of literary studies. After I retired from academia, my interests in visual cognition, consciousness, and neuroscience, and in the humanities, remained unchanged.

Consequently, by now I can claim to be a seasoned expert in the fields of visual cognition, consciousness, and neuroscience. Although I cannot claim to be an expert in my avocational areas of the humanities, I have acquired sufficient knowledge from their study so as to also have acquired informed opinions and assessments of topics covered in them. Combined, my expert and avocational studies have led me to an appreciation of the history of ideas and, in particular, on various relations between science and religion. Of these, two feature in the current book. One of them can be stated as the conflict thesis, according to which science and religion are irreparably at each other's throats. As explained in the following chapters, it turns out that the conflict thesis is closely tied to another controversial thesis, that of scientism—dear to many a scientist and philosophical supporter—which maintains that the only valid truth claims about the world we inhabit are those culled from the empirical researches of modern science. As a practicing Roman Catholic, I have always been quite comfortable with my career as a visual scientist; and, like many other theistic scientists, I never felt an irresolvable conflict between my religious faith and science that many an atheist scientist does, nor have I subscribed to scientism. In fact, my scientific expertise and well-informed scholarly opinions have led me to be quite critical toward scientism, yet favorably disposed toward science.

The 1st millennium BCE encompassed what is known as the Axial Age, which lasted from roughly 800 to 200 years BCE. During this time period, several pivotal (hence "axial") cultural changes arose in Eurasia that are of historical consequence and interest to this day. Exactly what these epoch-making changes were, and when and how they arose during the pre-Christian millennium, is not clear.[1] However, what we can summarize for the purposes of the present book is the following. (i) Prior to the Axial Age and especially going back as far as the prehistoric periods of human cultural evolution, most practicing religions relied on a mostly immanentist view of reality—that is to say, a view in which both humans and the many mythical gods they believed in were confined to the everyday mundane and natural world, the lifeworld defined by the local ecological niches inhabited by humans. For that reason, religions, besides being immanentist and polytheistic, were by and large geographically limited. (ii) In contrast, near the middle of the 1st millennium BCE new religions emerged in different regions of the world that adopted the following important characteristics: (a) belief in a divine realm that transcended the mundane and natural world; (b) a critique of pluralistic polytheism that resulted in an adoption of monotheism; and (c) despite originating in different regions of the world, the new religions subscribed to a similar universal ethic.

These world-transcending religions took on an additional characteristic that differed from the previous world-immanent religions. Since the divine gods in the latter religions were clearly bound to the natural world also inhabited by humans, the divine realm was not separated from the mundane realm. In contrast, in the religions of the Axial and post-Axial Age, the divine realm, as noted, transcended the mundane and natural realm. A major consequence of these historic processes was (iii) a separation or split between the divine realm and the worldly and natural realm.

Very important to note is that near the middle of the Axial Age, very significant changes also occurred in ancient Greece. Philosophy, after gradually emerging from its ties to the prior period in the Homeric mythic realm, adopted an increasingly rational and naturalistic view of the world. Rationalism featured most prominently in the writings of the Athenian philosophers Socrates, Plato, and Plato's student Aristotle. But it also impacted the natural philosophy of the pre-Socratic Ionian philosophers Thales, Anaximander, and Anaximenes. The rational philosophy of the Athenian philosophers and the additional naturalism of the Ionian philosophers played key roles in the historic emergence of the modern physical sciences and subsequently the biological and the human sciences. All three sciences deal exclusively with those phenomena found in the world around us that can be empirically observed, measured, and then explained in a theoretical and coherent body of interpretations. Consequently, by their nature, *modern sciences are embedded in, and reinforce, a naturalistic and immanentist realm that can (but need not) clash with the transcendental*

1. Hans Joas, *The Power of the Sacred: An Alternative to the Narrative of Disenchantment* (Oxford University Press, 2021), chapter 5; and Karl Jaspers, *The Origin and Goal of History* (Routledge, 2021), chapter 1, provide reviews and analyses of the characteristics attributed to the Axial Age.

realm (of primary concern to current monotheistic religions) in which the divine realities dwell. It follows that since the advent of modern science, and especially since the 18th-century Enlightenment, the monotheistic Abrahamic faiths (Judaism, Christianity, and Islam)—with which I will be mainly concerned—have increasingly had to deal with novel cultural and ethical problems that the methods and findings of modern science (which of course includes the science of religion) have posed.

A basic assumption of modern science is the methodological and epistemological principle that all aspects of nature must be fully explainable by recourse only to other well-known natural phenomena. Hence, the role of any extranatural explanatory influences is ruled out. This restriction is highly compatible with a limiting view which I refer to as *epistemological scientism*. In turn, it refers, as noted, to the belief that any true knowledge of the world must consist necessarily of scientific knowledge, i.e., knowledge that is characterized by the following criteria: it is (i) obtained through empirical observation of objects and processes and (ii) subjected to logical scientific analysis (iii) that preferably is supported by mathematical formulations. This all seems fine and good—as long as we ignore or suppress two significant facts. Fact 1: true knowledge about the world can be obtained in ways other than the scientific ones; Fact 2: all human knowledge including scientific knowledge that is taken to be *objective* knowledge depends first and foremost on each of our everyday *subjective* experiences made available to us by our conscious mind. In denying this, one denies also the truths revealed to us by science.

From the limiting worldview of epistemological scientism, it follows that only the naturalistic scientific study of religions can reveal their real nature. Neglecting or denying the possibility that true knowledge about the world can be obtained otherwise leads me to one of the main themes running throughout the book. It is summarized as follows: Science, yes! Scientism, no!

For many a scientist, their devotion to an epistemological scientism is premised additionally on either an explicit or else at least an implicit *ontological* scientism. In its milder form, it states that the world as *methodologically* carved out by epistemological scientism—namely, the causally closed physical world—is the only world that can really exist. In its bolder form, it states that the cosmos, the world of physics and nature, is entirely self-contained and self-sufficient. In this ontological form, here once more my theme is: Science, yes! Scientism, no! Ontological scientism rules out (i) any extranatural and extraphysical causal influences determining what happens in the world and (ii) any extranatural and extraphysical cause of the world's very being. In other words, the universe we inhabit is not only self-contained but it is also self-sufficient; hence, being self-contained and self-sufficient, it must also be the cause of its own existence!

What follows below, in the introduction of the book, is how the very practice of science and its scientistic interpretations are premised on prescientific metaphysical assumptions that are realized, implicitly or explicitly, in the study of any science, as well as in the study of religion. The conclusion there is that scientism undergirds a belief—a faith if you will—that in the hands of some atheists is expressed in an antitheistic ersatz-religion. Part 1 of the book, dealing with the scientific study of religion, consists of the first five chapters. Some of these studies, as shown in chapters 1 and 2, can be motivated by clear scientistic—in particular, purely naturalistic and reductive—biases, while other studies question these purely scientistic approaches to the study of religion. In addition to the scientific study of religion, part 1 also contains the scientific study of two of religion's connatural allies: the good (ethics and morality), covered in chapters 3 and 4; and the beautiful (art and aesthetics), covered in chapter 5.

Chapters 6 and 7 of part 2, and chapter 8 of part 3, explicitly narrate the deeper conceptual and historical roots of the scientistically-inspired, atheistic ersatz-religion. Chapter 9 might be considered a standalone, in that it reprises—in contrast to the aforementioned atheistic ersatz-religion—a theistic religion that is informed by a theology of nature and of science and is founded on two key tenets of the Abrahamic religions—namely, (i) that only a world-transcendent God is self-sufficient, and therefore (ii) that He is the Creator, the Cause and Sustainer, of the universe that contains us and every other entity, property, and process in it.

Acknowlegments

Preparing the manuscript that led to the publication of the book was a labor of love. Whom should I acknowledge and thank for seeing it published? The list could be long, because I could individually thank all the scholars and scientists, some known to me personally, regardless of their agreeing or disagreeing with any of the book's contents. Their contributions are listed in the endnotes and in the bibliography of the book. My thanks go to the following editorial staff of The Catholic University of America Press. John Martino, acquisitions editor, to my delight accepted my book proposal and guided me, during the course of slightly over two years, toward improving the final version of my manuscript. I moreover thank the several individuals selected by John to review the initially submitted manuscript. Their critical and supportive comments improved it as it progressed through several revisions to its penultimate version. John Martino also enlisted University of Notre Dame theologian Christopher Baglow to contribute a foreword to my book. I thank both for making this contribution possible. Many thanks also to copy editor James Reilly, whose helpful comments, suggestions, and revisions added numerous improvements of grammar and diction to a later version of my manuscript. This was further improved by the input from CUA Press's editor-in-chief Trevor Crowell, and I duly thank him. Last but not least, my gratitude also to graphic illustrator Ivy Johnson, who prepared and improved the image quality of figures 1.1 and 1.2 of the book, and especially to her mother, Laurel Johnson, my partner in the "senior" phase of my life. Her love, peppered as it was with her youthful, demonstrative, and quirky humor, renewed and energized my efforts throughout all stages preparatory to the book's publication.

Introduction

This book explores some of the ways in which science and religion can relate to each other. Several decades ago, the religious scholar Ian Barbour proposed an influential set of four relations that range from incompatibility and conflict at one end, through two intermediate ones, independence and dialogue, to compatibility and accord on the other end.[1] In the last three decades, a body of avid neoatheists composed of various scientists and scholars who are quite hostile to religion have made efforts to disseminate and perpetuate the conflict thesis. During this time, ardent efforts also have been expended by theistically inclined scientists and scholars in neutralizing the conflict thesis and finding a way to reconcile, if not harmonize, science and religion. And of course there have also been more moderate scientists and scholars on both sides of the theism and atheism divide who have advocated the independence and the dialogue theses. Although the present book covers, in chapters 6 and 8, some of the historic roots of the conflict thesis, overall it tends to accent the dialogue thesis. The following material will explore the connection between science and religion somewhat differently than the relational typology that Barbour proposed. Instead of hewing to his approach, the current approach to exploring how science and religion relate to each other is akin to a stroll along a winding scholarly road that reveals some anticipated but also some unexpected and interesting similarities and differences between science and religion. The section and subsection headings that the reader will encounter below can be taken as road signs near major and minor turns as we amble along the scholarly road.

A look at the historic roots of science and religion and at the definitions and etymologies of "science" and "religion" hint at some key characteristics shared by, and others distinguishing between, the beliefs and practices found in the two domains. While additionally looking at what can be designated as religious and epistemic impulses, an elaboration and refinement of the concepts of the supramundane or divine is offered that expands, no doubt controversially, the ambit of religion and theology. Given this expanded scope, we will also see how the shared and distinctive features of science and religion bear on the relation between theism and its apparent contrary, atheism. What will become apparent is that atheism, especially when wedded to a distortion of science known as scientism, can qualify as a nontheistic ersatz-religion.

Before we proceed, however, it is useful to insert the following brief excursus. We currently regard religion and science as well-established sociocultural realities, each with its identifiable histories and traditions. And each can be

1. Ian Barbour, *Religion in an Age of Science* (HarperCollins Publishers, 1990).

regarded as products of a lengthy biocultural evolution of human consciousness that goes at least as far back as the dawn of anatomically modern humanity, when *homo sapiens* developed brain powers sufficient for them to subject concrete sensory experiences to the scrutiny of more abstract cognitive, emotional, imaginative, and symbolic mental faculties. This critical prehistoric period is thought to have occurred between roughly 80 and 50 thousand years ago (Kya), during the transition from the Middle to the Upper Paleolithic period.[2] I agree with scholars that current *concepts* of religion cannot apply universally to many prior manifestations of religion.[3] Nonetheless, in view of extensive paleontological, anthropological, and cross-cultural evidence, one can conclude that ancient proto-religion in the form of ritualized practice or of cosmological perspective has evolved as a *sociocultural reality* over many more tens of millennia.[4] Religion and its practices, as we shall see in chapter 1, rely heavily not only on human thought but also on expressive, imaginative, and symbolic faculties. It therefore may be more than coincidence that during human biocultural evolution, symbolic and imaginative mental faculties—for instance, those underlying animism, the concepts of extra- and supernatural realms, shamanism, and ancestor worship[5]—appeared some 60 Kya, converg-

2. Matt J. Rossano, "Supernaturalizing Social Life: Religion and the Evolution of Human Cooperation," *Human Nature* 18, no. 3 (2007): 272–94, https://doi.org/10.1007/s12110-007-9002-4.

3. William T. Cavanaugh, *The Myth of Religious Violence* (Oxford University Press, 2009); Brent Nogbri, *Before Religion: A History of a Modern Concept* (Yale University Press, 2013).

4. I base this assertion on the following arguments. The first is analogical. Consider the modern *word* and *concept* of an electron that is a manifestation of physical *reality*. According to current estimates by physical cosmologists, the physical reality of electrons has been around no later than sometime between 10^{-10} and 1 second after the Big Bang, i.e., for over 14 billion years, whereas the scientific word and concept has a brief history of only about a dozen decades. A socially evolved or constructed word and concept of an electron among modern physicists does not confer physical reality on whatever it is that the word "electron" refers to. I therefore endorse the proposal that the evolution of *religion as a sociocultural reality* preceded its evolution as a modern word or concept. In contrast, take, for instance, the following two assertions from Brent Nongbri: "I have argued that the idea of religion is not as natural or universal as it is often assumed to be. Religion has a history. It was born out of a mix of Christian disputes about truth, European colonial exploits, and the formation of nation states." Therefore, as a second point, while I agree that the *concept* of religion has a relatively limited history, I disagree with the claim that religion, as such, emerged from a mix of events that transpired at most during the last two millennia. Religion as a *sociocultural reality* has a history that, as noted, goes back several tens of millennia, when the evolutions of imaginative, symbolic mental capacities fortuitously coincided and converged with the evolution of linguistic capacities.

5. David Lewis-Williams, *Conceiving God: The Cognitive Origin and Evolution of Religion* (Thames & Hudson, 2010); Peoples et al., "Hunter-Gatherers and the Origin of Religion," *Human Nature* 27, no. 3 (2016): 261–82; Rossano, "Supernaturalizing Social Life"; Matt Rossano, "The African Interregnum: The 'Where,' 'When,' and 'Why' of the Evolution of Religion,"

ing then with the nearly simultaneous appearance of fully developed linguistic capacities.[6]

Definitions and Etymologies of "Science" and "Religion"

Modern definitions of science and religion are not applicable to all places and all times. If one were to ask people on the street how they understand and define science, they might mention disciplines of it like physics, astronomy, chemistry, and biology. Similarly, if asked what religion is, they might mention notions such as belief in God, sacred rituals, or examples such as Hinduism, Judaism, and Islam. However, for more useful and definitive conceptions of religion and science and problems attending them, if the reader were to search the internet, she or he would find that there are way too many to cover adequately here. For that reason, I suggest that the reader interested in workable definitions of science and religion consult Helen De Cruz's entry on religion and science in the *Stanford Encyclopedia of Philosophy*.[7]

I have found it profitable, in forming concepts of science and religion, to go back to the possible roots of the words that linguistically express their semantic range. Such a look proves to be useful, since it reveals some of the properties shared by, as well as distinctive to, the two cultural practices throughout their long history. The word "science" derives from the Latin *scientia* meaning knowledge or knowing, which for centuries applied broadly to any area of systematic study, such as theology, philosophy, mathematics, law, or history, and was not confined to the current empirically-based physical, natural, and human sciences. Its etymology likely goes back to the proto-Indo-European root *skei-* (to cut or split) and thus may be related more closely to the Greek word σχίζειν (*skhizein*: split, rend, or cleave) than to the word επιστήμη (*epistími*: science). Modern science is both a body of knowledge and, indeed, a method of splitting or slicing off and isolating, from countless others, a particular worldly phenomenon for study. It is thus a way to systematically "carve nature at its joints" with increasingly precise "scalpels" that allow making progressively finer distinctions among natural processes, objects, and their properties. Such detailed approaches to the study of nature are a necessary (but not sufficient) feature of doing science. For some sensitive souls of the Romantic period, this analytic feature was bemoaned;

---

in *The Biological Evolution of Religious Mind and Behavior*, ed. Eckart Voland and Wulf Schiefenhövel (Springer, 2009).

6. Robert C. Berwick and Noam Chomsky, *Why Only Us: Language and Evolution* (MIT Press, 2016); Jean Clottes, *What Is Paleolithic Art?: Cave Paintings and the Dawn of Human Creativity* (University of Chicago Press, 2016).

7. Helen De Cruz, "Religion and Science," in *The Stanford Encyclopedia of Philosophy*, ed. Edward N. Zalta & Uri Nodelman (Fall 2025), https://plato.stanford.edu/archives/fall2025/entries/religion-science.

note William Wordsworth's sentiment in the seventh stanza of his poem "The Tables Turned": "Sweet is the lore which Nature brings;/ Our meddling intellect/ Mis-shapes the beauteous forms of things: —/ We murder to dissect."

However one wants to interpret this doleful poem in relation to the human(e) intellect and heart, analytic probing into nature is at the core of scientific method. This is not to deemphasize the way that an insightful, creative, and integrative mind, making full use of logic, imagination, and intuition, contributes to scientific theorizing that seeks to conceptually reunite into a coherent and far- and wide-reaching body of knowledge what the meddling intellect has rent asunder. However, there is no conceptual integration without things to integrate. And in modern empirical science, a thing is not a thing and a fact not a fact unless it can be separated methodologically, experientially, and conceptually from other things or facts. Besides being a huge body of knowledge with enormous social and cultural impact, science is a method of subjecting theoretical thinking about nature to the test of empirical observations of events and objects in the world. Another key mandate of the scientific method is that a scientist's theoretical concepts, research design and procedures, and observed results be specified with a sufficiently high clarity and exactness so as to (i) allow subjecting any hypothesized theoretical entities to the test of empirically observed results and (ii) allow other scientists, especially when deeply skeptical of these findings, to see whether or not they can replicate them using the same or similar research designs and procedures. However, the emphasis on clarity and exactness comes at a linguistic price: the terms and words of scientific discourse have very narrow, domain-specific applications, and the concepts that they apply to can be highly technical and abstruse, their specific scientific meaning often expressible only via abstract mathematical symbols and therefore way beyond the conceptual grasp of the nonexpert. Besides its requirements for clarity and empirical testability, the scientific method as currently understood also insists that theoretical explanations of newly discovered objects, properties, and processes in the world of nature do not invoke extranatural principles. To paraphrase a popular adage, "What plays in nature explanatorily stays in nature." Yet despite this methodological ban on inserting extranatural, specifically supernatural entities into scientific explanations, the scientific method does not proscribe a person's inspirations motivating his or her scientific enterprises from being traced to sundry metaphysical and theological sources.

In contrast to the concept of science, the conceptual roots of religion are not as readily traceable.[8] Some suggest that one root is related to the Latin word *relegere*, whose meaning is to repeatedly read, go over, focus on, or carefully consider a thing. This certainly may apply to one of the practices introduced to Christianity

8. Sarah F. Hoyt, "The Etymology of Religion," *Journal of the American Oriental Society* 32, no. 2 (1912): 126–29.

by St. Benedict, that of *lectio divina*, a prayerful meditation on scriptural readings so as to elucidate their deeper spiritual meanings, or to the communal scripture studies common among some contemporary Christian denominations. Analogous practices in Judaism might be contemplative Torah or Talmud studies; in Islam, the fivefold daily prayer practices, or the devotional studies of the Koran's surahs; in Buddhism and Hinduism, the Tantric sadhanas. Humans are celebratory and ceremonial social creatures. And in contemporary practice of their religious faiths, worshippers gather regularly, typically at least once a week, in a church, synagogue, or temple, for ritualized ceremonies and celebrations. Of course, in such communal gatherings the repetitious prayers, rituals, and other practices contribute in important ways to religious life. When performed individually and especially communally, they reinforce and recertify the bond of trust relating each member to God and to other members of the religious community.

Besides this communal aspect of religion, a second commonly cited conceptual root of religion may be found in the Latin *religare*, meaning to bind, join, or bond. Like the integrative theoretical task of science, religion emphasizes a synthetic putting together, a uniting of realities not only because of their shared characteristics but also because of their shared sources. Another way that *religare* is relevant is that religion is conceived in terms of covenant, a commitment that explicitly *binds* one member of a religious community to other members and that binds the community as a whole to a larger, transcendent reality. In theistic religions the covenant is between a human community and a divine agent. In the Abrahamic religions in particular, the covenant is between humans and God. It is a bond based on faith, expressed perhaps best as the fidelity with which God relates to humans and with which they in turn relate to each other and to God. As such, faith is more a matter of interpersonal commitment, loyalty, and trust than it is a matter of mere belief in the contents of doctrinal propositions. In contrast, while there may be an implicit covenantal relationship among scientists in that each shares a commitment to seek the truths about the natural world with other scientists, scientists as such need not, and generally refrain from, making explicit covenantal commitments to divine agents.

However, as a form of trust, belief remains a key feature not only of religion but also of science. To commit to and trust something one must believe that it is real, that it impacts one's life, and that one can concretely relate to it. Without this belief, any avowed relationship to it is sheer madness. A scientist, for instance, commits—even if only implicitly or unconsciously—to a belief in a relationship between the reality and the intelligibility of the world, for otherwise she or he would be mad or foolish to devote time and effort to the study of something that is unreal or unintelligible. (Even illusions—I am thinking especially of what in my specialty area are known as optical or visual illusions—are real and intelligible, insofar as they can and have become objects of study in the human sciences.) In contrast to scientists who study the physical or natural world, most religionists commit relationally to a more encompassing reality than the empirically observable world of modern science, in other words, a reality that is divine and usually is taken to transcend, without excluding, the world of physics and nature.

Science and religion are practices that in their own ways seek to find meaning in the world. It is therefore also important to note that the word "meaning" can have very different applications in science and religion. Later in this chapter, we shall see that the language of science seeks clarity and preciseness of expression and therefore relies on highly specific and at times very arcane meanings of the terms of its discourse. In contrast, the meanings or words used and expressed in religion are not so much strictly linguistic as they are *existential*. In other words, they address concerns about the meaning of life, of death, of values expressed through the arts and morality, of the cosmos, and of human existence in it. Moreover, the words used in the related discipline of theology (which is the modern "science" of religion) sometimes have an analogical meaning conveyed in terms of likeness or similarity; or at other times they may have some anagogical meanings that in some arcane way point to ultimate or higher spiritual and divine realties. In either case, such words convey meanings that are connotative and less focused and specific than the words that convey highly focused denotative meanings used in modern science.

The Pervasiveness of the Transcendental Motive

One thing that courses through most any religion is a desire to experience the sublime, the wondrous, the awesome, and the holy. Throughout history, humans have sought the meanings of objects, events, and processes occurring in nature, of nature and the universe, and of their own individual existences within the larger natural and cosmic realms. A nearly universal way of finding such meaning is to experientially encounter something, vague to strikingly clear, that transcends our mundane existence. The drive to find meaning in a transcendent realm—the "religious impulse," as the philosopher Tim Crane calls it—spurs the "systematic and practical attempt by human beings to find meaning in the world and their place in it, in terms of their relationship to something transcendent."[9] Consistent with the fact, discussed in chapter 1 below, that human religious sensibilities are informed by belief in the existence of an unseen order, a belief that provides meaningful content to the religious impulse is the belief in an unseen transcendent realm, a realm beyond that of our quotidian experiences. The search for meaning and how that search may be satisfied by a transcendent order is a reasonable start at a generously inclusive definition of religion that

9. Tim Crane, *The Meaning of Belief: Religion from an Atheist's Point of View* (Harvard University Press, 2017), 6.

will be elaborated below. Humans indeed seek and discover meaning in the things around them, in objects and events they encounter within the world. Yet, despite Crane's useful insight, the "something transcendent" is somewhat troubling: the meanings both of "something" and of "transcendent" allow a lot of interpretive latitude.

Crane, an atheist philosopher, maintains that religious belief need not be in anything like a supernatural deity, since "it is certainly possible for someone to have the religious impulse and not believe that God is a 'superhuman, supernatural intelligence.' The unseen [transcendent] order need not involve any idea of something superhuman or any claim about intelligence."[10] For Crane, as for others who have dispensed with a supernatural order, it is also a sacred order. What Crane appears to be articulating is found in recent movements, especially appealing to many contemporary scientists, philosophers, and some theologians, that go by the names of "religious naturalism" and "scientific pantheism." Among them, Chet Raymo claims—as the title of one of his books suggests—that without [a supernatural] God everything is holy.[11] Such naturalistic holiness, sacredness, and transcendence may motivate the quest for meaning among many a scientist and among thoughtful atheist philosophers like Crane.[12] Even Richard Dawkins, the most vocal among the recent tribe of neoatheists, can romanticize that "science can be spiritual, even religious in the non-supernatural sense of the word."[13] For instance, the cosmological realm reaches far outside, yet includes, the realm of our earthly existence; and one may wonder what may transcend the bounds of the workaday world or even of the scientifically studied cosmos. As the history of astronomy shows, the boundaries of the observable cosmos expand whenever new, more powerful methods of observation are devised. Hence it is quite proper—and here one can agree with scientists and atheists alike—to admire and be awed by the wondrous splendor, breathtaking expanse, and mysterious existence of the universe. Even the Afro-American theologian, mystic, and preacher Howard Thurman, aptly describes how in a "glorious and transcendent moment, *it may seem* . . . that all there is, is God"[14] (emphasis added). And if, as some scientists and the neoatheist Christopher Hitchens claim, the "all there is" is corralled into the natural order, one could seriously adopt a bona fide tran-

10. Crane, *The Meaning of Belief*, 59.

11. Chet Raymo, *When God Is Gone Everything Is Holy: The Making of a Religious Naturalist* (Sorin Books, 2008).

12. Surprisingly, the neoatheist Daniel Dennett considers the natural world to be sacred. Despite not believing in supernatural transcendence, he may be under the sway of the religious-naturalism impulse. See Daniel C. Dennett, *Darwin's Dangerous Idea* (Touchstone, 1995), 520.

13. Richard Dawkins, *A Devil's Chaplain* (Houghton Mifflin, 2003), 31, quoted in Gregory W. Dawes, *Galileo and the Conflict Between Religion and Science* (Routledge, 2016), 185.

14. Howard Thurman, *Temptations of Jesus* (Friends United Press, 1978), 46.

scendent standpoint such as Spinozian pantheism or, in Christopher Hitchens's case, what might be called "panatheism." In either case, the natural order and the sacred order are deemed to be identical, as expressed aptly by Spinoza's phrase, *Deus sive Natura* (God or Nature).

From the religious naturalist and Spinozian standpoints, one can see that Crane's claims about a sacred and transcendent order, or Raymo's claim that everything is holy, imply that the holy is strictly—and strangely—within rather than beyond the natural order that exists *in* the universe. The non-supernatural religious impulse toward the holy—and the godless natural "everything that is, is holy"—therefore issues from a religion of nature, a return to a more sophisticated, scientifically informed type of nature worship. This clearly is at odds with the views of theologians in the Abrahamic traditions, who take God to be the Creator of the natural cosmos, but not equivalent to it and, thus, participating in it only by virtue of his creation of it. In contrast, a pantheist or a religious naturalistic interpretation would appeal, for example, to someone like Richard Dawkins and fellow neoatheist and physicist Victor Stenger. As with Pierre Laplace some two centuries ago, it allows them to treat God as a scientific hypothesis.[15] Unlike Laplace, however, who merely expressed that his physical theory of the then-known universe had no need of the God hypothesis, Dawkins and Stenger make the stronger claim that extant scientific findings positively debunk the hypothesis.

Yet another way to interpret Crane's claim is that the transcendent order reaches beyond the physically evolving universe. What kinds of things could exist that transcend the physical cosmos? An example of unseen transcendent orders or realms, other than the divine or godly, are mathematical entities like the positive integers. The positive integers are nonphysical entities. None of our bodily senses have ever seen, heard, touched, smelled, or tasted any number.[16] The intellectual graspability of the system of numbers, such as the logical ordering of the positive integers, inheres, as many a mathematician believes, in a Platonic-like realm that transcends the observable natural/physical cosmos without

15. As a popular legend goes, Newton's theory was left with the problem of mathematically not guaranteeing the stability of our solar system, perhaps requiring that God periodically adjust the orbits of the planets so that they would not eventually spiral into the sun. Laplace mathematically eliminated this problematic aspect of Newton's theory. Once, when discussing astronomy with Napoleon Bonaparte, he was asked if God was needed to explain the dynamics of the solar system. Laplace answered Napoleon's query by stating that he had no need for that hypothesis. This anecdote is a wonderful example of confusing God with a deist demiurge.

16. The concept of number therefore should not be confused with that of a numeral designating it. Several visually perceivable distinct numerals like "4," "iv," "IV" (or their Braille tactile version) concretely signify or point to a single abstract number, but none of them is the abstract number itself.

denying, however, that this cosmos can materially instantiate quantitative and numerical properties. Should we therefore accord the status of the divine to number, as the ancient Pythagoreans have? Or instead, should the horizon of the cosmos be expanded to include also nonphysical, abstract, but mentally graspable entities like number? And if we allow the more expansive cosmos to contain number, then, as a pantheist might argue, why not also allow it to contain God? If we do, then do we thereby not simply reprise the immanentism of a Spinozian God? If yes, would this not render the Transcendent and Supreme God of the Abrahamic religions—the God who comprehends all realities, including those in the natural order and who is, via his supreme comprehension, immanent to it—obsolete?

Regarding the natural order that is the cosmos, Crane furthermore holds that a belief in an unseen sacred and transcendent order is a claim about the universe and therefore a cosmological claim.[17] However, this claim holds only if the physical cosmos exceeds anything that science can possibly observe. That, as explained below and elsewhere, could very well be the case. Such explanation requires us to ask: What is the universe, or rather, what is it not? The cosmos, what physicists take to be the universe, is a spacetime manifold within which all physical entities exist; yet, since it, after all, is the *UNI*verse, it cannot contain itself as one of its existing entities. In the same way that a set-theoretic universe is "incomplete" by not containing itself as an element, so, as the mathematician William Weiss phrases it, "the physical universe fails to have a physical existence. The things that have a physical existence are exactly the things *in* the universe, but the universe itself is not an object in the universe."[18] Consequently, if the things that have physical existence are what can be referred as natural entities, then the totality of all natural things is transcended by the universe, which contains—but itself cannot be within the collection of—all natural things.[19] If so, then the universe itself is indeed an extranatural thing that tran-

17. Crane, *The Meaning of Belief*, 54.

18. William A. R. Weiss, "An Introduction to Set Theory," course notes (2014), accessed June 29, 2022, https://www.math.toronto.edu/~weiss/Set_Theory.pdf. In set-theoretic terms, this follows from the Zermelo-Fraenkel (ZF) set theory, whose axioms provide a logical basis for the development of modern mathematics. Moreover, analogous to this "physical" incompleteness of the universe, Kurt Gödel's metamathematical proof of the incompleteness of formal mathematical systems proved that for any such system there are valid mathematical propositions that cannot be proved within that system. For an account of Gödel's proof, see Panu Raatikainen, "Gödel's Incompleteness Theorems," in *The Stanford Encyclopedia of Philosophy*, ed. Edward N. Zalta (Spring 2022), https://plato.stanford.edu/ archives/spr2022/entries/goedel-incompleteness.

19. For a related point, see Richard Pendergast, *The Cosmic Hierarchy: God's Plan for the Evolution of the Universe* (Crossroad Publishing Co., 2020), 67, where he discusses quantum cosmology as an application of "quantum theory [beyond entities *within* the universe but also] to the *universe as a whole* (emphasis added). Since the universe comprises all finite

scends nature, conceived as all physically specifiable entities. Taking the universe to be supernatural in this extranatural sense, if God is the creator of the universe and therefore of all that is natural in it, a theist can readily conclude that God who transcends the universe is not only superuniversal but also ultra-supernatural. This God, by transcending the extranatural universe, is transcendence nonpareil in that—to adapt St. Anselm's phrasing—he is Transcendence any greater of which cannot be thought.

A belief in some lesser transcendent order, be it found in number, nature, or the universe, might drive the religious impulse of a present-day religious naturalist, agnostic, or atheist. But it fails to satisfy the religious impulse energizing the theist seeking meaning in a source that transcends yet comprehends all natural, cosmological, logical, mathematical, and other intellectually conceivable entities. So, if there is no room or place in the universe for the universe itself, what is it that so providentially makes room for it and thereby endows it with existence? Spinoza's answer to this puzzle—logically inadequate in my opinion—is that there is no need to make such room since the Universe's essence, considered as *Deus sive Natura*, is its existence. Akin to Thomas Aquinas's *Ipsum Esse Subsistens* (*Summa Theologiae*, I, q. 4, a. 2), Spinoza's nature shares God's attributes in being necessarily eternal and subsisting in and of itself. However, in contrast to Spinoza's view, Aquinas maintained that nature exists contingently, since it is the result of God's freely willing the creation of the universe. Spinoza's *Deus sive Natura* thus fits quite well (i) with the belief in an eternal universe and (ii) with religious naturalism. Regarding (i), we shall see in chapter 9 that recent cosmological models point out that, unlike God's eternity, the quasi- or sempiternal universe is infinite in the future temporal direction but not the past one; and regarding (ii), that, at bottom, religious naturalists like Tim Crane and Chet Raymo also are, even if unawares, pantheists. Yet, despite this feature of Crane's and Raymo's approaches to religion, their views are appealing for two reasons. First, they run counter to that of neoatheists, such as Daniel Dennett, who singled out the supernatural element as a *sine qua non* in religious belief. Second, as we shall see in chapter 1, they allow agnostics and even atheists to have experiences of a realm transcending the mundane one, i.e., experiences that are religious in nature.[20]

---

beings, there cannot be any physical or natural cause outside it that would make the wave function of the universe collapse. Therefore, the explanation that the wave function of a system under observation collapses because of the influence of the experimental apparatus being used and the environment with which it is connected cannot apply in the case of the universe as a whole."

20. Alexander A. Fingelkurts and Andrew A. Fingelkurts, "Is Our Brain Hardwired to Produce God, or Is Our Brain Hardwired to Perceive God? A Systematic Review on the Role of the Brain in Mediating Religious Experience," *Cognitive Processing* 10, no. 4 (2009): 293–326.

The importance of the above discussions allows us to arrive at a working concept of religion. First, recalling our brief look at the biocultural evolution of religion (which will be explored more thoroughly in chapter 1), along with Crane we can define religion foremost as the impulse and quest for an *unseen transcendent realm.* Second, while the atheist Crane (and Raymo) claim that the innerworldly transcendent has the attribute of being *sacred, holy,* or *quasi-divine,* we maintain that the supramundane transcendent is the *truly divine.* In either case, this comports well with William James's general definition of religion as that by which humans "apprehend themselves to stand in [experientially moral, physical, or ritual] relation to *whatever* they may consider the divine"[21] (emphasis added). It is of utmost importance to note that this definition allows some leeway in *what* an individual or group of individuals considers to be the divine. To be remembered for later is that not only theists but also atheists like Crane, and especially scientistic atheists like the biologists Richard Dawkins and Jerry Coyne—though they deny the Supreme Reality of a supernatural God—practice some form of religion, a claim discussed further below and in chapter 7. In the interim, however, we turn to:

Transcendence Beyond Religious Naturalism, Within Reason

> There are two general methods of theology that are self-consciously critical. One of them is the general method of correlation, a method both empirical and critical, which seeks to discover compatibility, even integration, between science and [theistic] religious thought. The other is the general postmodern approach, a method that is hypercritical, which seeks to exempt religious belief from criteria of scientific or perhaps any other rationality.
>
> Michael Horace Barnes, *Stages of Thought*, p. 221

Yet in contrast to the scientifically inspired Crane and Raymo, theologians representing the Abrahamic faiths, who generally do not reject science and reason, hold that the in-and-of-itself-subsistent is the nonphysical, truly supertranscendent Reality that is God. In this regard, Stanley Jaki aptly reasons that modern "science, modern scientific cosmology, especially when recourse is made to Gödel's incompleteness theorem, assures us that those two points [referring here to the specificity and contingency of physical entities] are true about that of 'everything' or the universe. If, however, such is the case, then it can be shown that the universe is that supreme reality that [being the 'everything' containing 'all physical things,' therefore] cannot have within itself the reason for its own existence. Beyond the universe—which is the totality of consistently interacting things—there can, however, be only one being, God, the Creator. This is all that

21. William James, *The Varieties of Religious Experience* (Random House, 1936), 31.

one needs in order to reach the conclusion that the universe had to be created out of nothing, an act of which only a truly transcendental God is capable."[22]

Where theologians engage in *rational talk about* God as self-subsistent spiritual substance, mystics as well as everyday religious practitioners might well agree with the theologians' rational thoughts, while additionally *intimately experiencing* God as an inexpressible mystery to be lovingly contemplated rather than merely a being whose attributes can be expressed and explored rationally or logically. This ineffable mystery, which at long last "we cannot speak about" and "must pass over in silence,"[23] apophatically points to an awesome and fascinating source that from its incomprehensible transcendence manifests as a prodigal streaming forth of, and in its equally wondrous immanence as the flowing into, all created entities that exist in the cosmos. It is for this reason that, as noted by Vincent Miceli, "the Transcendent becomes present and communes with man *from within* as well as from without."[24] And this streaming forth from beyond and flowing into creation allows St. Augustine to prayerfully commune with a transcendent God who mysteriously also is most intimately present to us, in fact more so than we are to ourselves.[25]

22. Stanley L. Jaki, *The Savior of Science* (Regnery Gateway, 1988), 198.

23. The quotes are taken from p. 74 of Ludwig Wittgenstein, *Tractatus Logico-Philosophicus* (Routledge & Kegan Paul, 1974), published originally in 1921, during the heyday of scientific and philosophical positivism. For positivists, they might be read as saying that one must remain silent about what cannot be expressed in precise scientific language or logic, lest one utters something that, from the positivist viewpoint, is meaningless and nonsensical. However, along with others, I can interpret these quotes as expressions of a crypto-mystic, a mystic in the guise of an analytic philosopher whose religious impulses were complex yet strong and placed his philosophical need for clarity in conflict with his religious impulses. The complexity and conflict is evident the brief foreword to Ludwig Wittgenstein, *Philosophical Remarks* (University of Chicago Press, 1975), completed only nine years later, in 1930. In the foreword, he says: "I would like to say 'This book is written to the glory of God,' but nowadays [the days of logical positivism's ascendency] that would be chicanery, that is, it would not be rightly understood. It means the book is written in good will, and in so far as it is not so written, but out of vanity, etc., the author would wish to see it condemned. He cannot free it of these impurities further than he himself is free of them." It is perhaps by reason of this untimeliness that the first German edition of the *Remarks* was not published until 1964, 13 years after Wittgenstein's death. By 1964 logical positivism and its offshoot, behaviorism, were approaching their cultural demise. The quote from the foreword of Wittgenstein's *Philosophical Remarks* was downloaded from Terence Blake, "Empiricism vs. Hermeneutics," Agent Swarm, accessed September 28, 2024, https://terenceblake.wordpress.com/2013/09/23/empiricism-vs-hermeneutics-3-latour-and-wittgenstein-on-the-primacy-of-the-religious-spirit/.

24. Vincent Miceli, *The Gods of Atheism* (Sophia Institute Press, 2022), 20.

25. St. Augustine, *Confessions* (Oxford University Press, 2008). The attempts to corral the Divine entirely into the world in order to assure its immanence seem to be misguided and unnecessary in view of several recent proposals made by various religious practitioners and theologians working from a panentheistic viewpoint. See Phillip Clayton, "How Radically Can

The Pervasiveness of the Epistemic Motive

Besides searching for meaning that transcends mundane existence, in their passage through reality, religionists and scientists, atheists and theists are alike in another respect; they are motivated to seek an understanding, to seek the knowledge, truth, and meaning of reality. It follows that they share at least one common element: a need to explore, explain, and comprehend their world and their existence in it. This need drives not only the religious impulse but also what can properly be referred to as the epistemic impulse and passion. As we will see below and in chapter 5, even in the infantile stages of our lives, the delight of satisfying the epistemic is as important as mother's milk, for without it our affective and cognitive development stalls in a state of mental torpor. As adults, we subjectively feel this basic need as curiosity, driven by a cognitive and affective lack, which can be satisfied, much like sensations of hunger are by ingesting food, only by intellectual and emotional nourishment. Imagine, if you will, an existence without a minimal satisfaction of the desire that this indomitable epistemic impulse elicits; or, so to speak, without now and then scratching the itch to experience, know, and understand the meaning of the world you inhabit. Your life would be spiritually vacuous, at best one filled with an insipid lassitude, indolent ignorance, instead of vibrant engagement.

As so carefully described by the philosopher and theologian Bernard Lonergan in his masterful treatise *Insight*, the epistemic passion, the need to know, to explain and understand the world and us in it, is unbounded in its scope and aim and thus never completely or permanently satisfied. Yet it seeks to transcend the limits imposed by nature or society. Viewed this way, it is a Faustian impulse; for we want to know and experience *all* there is to know and experience, despite realizing that we will ever fall short of the desired goal. How is it that we shall fall short of this goal? An answer to his question is that scientific and scholarly research create islands of knowledge within a huge, perhaps limitless, sea of ignorance. There are far too many things about the world that

God Be Reconceived Before Ceasing to Be God? The Four Faces of Panentheism," *Zygon* 52, no. 4 (2017): 1044–59; Phillip Clayton and Arthur Peacocke, *In Whom We Live and Move and Have Our Being: Panentheistic Reflections on God's Presence in a Scientific World* (William B. Eerdmans Publishing Co., 2004); John W. Cooper, *Panentheism: The Other God of the Philosophers* (Baker Academic, 2006); David Ray Griffin, *Panentheism and Scientific Naturalism: Rethinking Evil, Morality, Religious Experience, Religious Pluralism, and the Academic Study of Religion* (Process Century Press, 2014). According to panentheism, God created and enfolds the universe, so that all of nature is in God yet; in contrast to pantheism, nature does not exhaust all that God is. Insofar as nature is in God and thereby is "divinized" by God's presence, panentheism can do justice to Crane's and Raymo's views of nature as part of the divine realm, without negating, as does pantheism, God's transcendence beyond the natural realm investigated by science.

science or scholarship as yet does not know but that are in principle knowable. Yet, scientific and scholarly research is choosy and therefore limited about what it seeks to know, and a choice to follow a given avenue of research leaves other potentially interesting and informative avenues untraveled. Moreover, although one can expand the frontier of the knowable, it is highly likely that it cannot be expanded forever. The physicist and cosmologist Lawrence Krauss notes that humans may be living in a Goldilocks zone of scientific research and may continue to live in it for some time, but eventually, if the universe continues to expand at ever increasing rates as it does now, the paradoxically stark possibility exists that the expansion of knowledge in the fields of astrophysics, astronomy, and cosmology, dependent as they are on detecting information conveyed in the medium of electromagnetic or gravitational waves, cannot be sustained beyond a certain point of the universe's expansion.[26] Moreover, even now it seems that the how and what concerning the universe and its coming into existence may be not only unknown but also unknowable in principle. Along lines echoing those expressed by Stanley Jaki above, the physicist Steven Weinberg aptly recognized that although there may be a final theory of physics—a grand unifying theory that harmoniously unites quantum physics with relativistic physics—there can be no physical theory of everything existing in the universe,[27] let alone, as noted by William Weiss above, of the universe itself. Similarly, the most ardent theologian lives with the sad fact that, at least in this world, the infinite and eternal essence of God is, and will remain forever, unknowable.

Yet simultaneously, despite and because of these limits, the epistemic impulse persists. Whence or why this insatiable impulse? I suggest that it may derive from a more primal, prerational drive to assimilate or interiorize, in one way or another, all worldly things with which we come into contact. There is evidence from studies of neonatal development that even a one-day old infant already seems to differentiate—if ever so crudely—between self and the world.[28] Most every object in the world that contacts the side of its mouth elicits an instinctive rooting or sucking response, as though the object aroused the sensation of touching one of its mother's teats. And it is common knowledge among new parents that almost every external object graspable by an infant is brought

26. Lawrence M. Krauss, *A Universe from Nothing: Why There Is Something Rather Than Nothing* (Free Press, 2012).

27. Steven Weinberg (in "The Future of Science, and the Universe," *New York Review of Books*, November 15, 2001) notes that "this theory, although I call it a final theory, will not be the end of the road for science. It will not be what is sometimes called a theory of everything, a theory that solves all scientific problems. We already have many scientific problems that will not be illuminated at all."

28. Phillipe Rochat, "Five Levels of Self-Awareness As They Unfold Early in Life," *Consciousness and Cognition* 12, no. 4 (2003): 717–31; Phillipe Rochat et al., "Perceived Self in Infancy," *Infant Behavior & Development* 23, no. 3 (2000): 513–30.

toward its mouth, a primitive gesture of trying to interiorize objects existing in their tiny world. Only through a period of growth and development, aided by a deep interpersonal bonding with a loving and supporting adult, does the infant learn to disengage from this primal, omnivorous other-absorption by coming to realize that not just any object in the external world can be ingested and interiorized. Gradually it acquires the more explicit and refined distinctions between self and world, a realization that most everything in the world can be incorporated only indirectly, as object and event of wonder and of delight; and as that which can be handled, seen, heard, smelled, or tasted, then laid away or ignored, and which, as many developmental studies of object-constancy have shown, continues to exist for the toddler even when the object lies hidden, inaccessible to his or her immediate sensory experience. With the further acquisition of linguistic competence, symbols mediate this more "objective" engagement of the now growing toddler with the world. And years later, the child-become-adult can engage the world with an experiential and epistemic appetite that can be just as insatiable and eclectic in its reach as the infant's appetite to take into its being all that the world proffers. The epistemic insatiability can impel us incessantly onward, inward, and outward as we quest to know and understand all, the entire reality, that which surrounds us as well as that which resides in us. Yet, because we are finite, mortal beings, our knowledge about the world we inhabit affirms partial, fragmentary, and provisional truths, ever approaching but never reaching a fully certain or final truth.

Epistemic Groundlessness?

Claims based on our partial truths are therefore moot, potentially open to endless arguments, debates, and criticisms. This, as noted by the pancritical rationalist William Bartley, can engender a disconcerting experience, where one senses, as he phrased it, an uncomfortable feeling of floating, of being without a secure epistemic foundation.[29] Bartley's way of dealing with this uncomfortable feeling is to get used to and live with it. However, for questers not resigned to a free-floating existence (and the free-floating anxieties to which it often leads), the desire for some sort of fundamental knowing can stimulate their

29. W. W. Bartley, "Theories of Rationality," in *Evolutionary Epistemology, Rationality, and the Sociology of Knowledge*, ed. Gerald Radnitzky and W. W. Bartley (Open Court, 1987). Bartley follows this apt description by the claim that there are no such foundations. Among others, I disagree with Bartley, because in his pancritical rationalism one can detect an intellectual oroboros, a circularity of argument that is unending, and that, among post-modern scholars, has fashionably devolved, or at least contributed, to the rampant *irrational* critiques of foundations. Moreover, a careful reading of Bartley's *Rationality in Science and Politics* (Springer, 1984) reveals that from a logical standpoint pancritical rationalism must rely on, in fact be *founded* on, the law of noncontradiction and the law of excluded middle.

seeking some hold on, some supportive grasp of, a more secure way of knowing. This still provisional way of knowing is accomplished most readily by adopting or constructing informal or formal theories that make sense of the world and of ourselves in it. But no matter how far and wide the conceptual web is spun by theory alone, the web itself does not attach to anything that itself is epistemically attached to a firm ground. The entire web, no matter how extensive, remains an untethered, free-floating structure within what remains an infinite space of ignorance. Usually and fortunately, we are not aware of that fact, since each one of us lives at the center of a personal epistemic web, while its margins are at such epistemic distance that we are all but unaware that they are not tethered to any moorings. But when, as Bartley has, we occasionally take stock and become aware of our untethered epistemic web, the awareness can have an exciting and dizzying effect. Yet it pays to remember that, like levity in physical space, levity in mental space ultimately pays its dues to gravity. Hence, a second and more durable step, avoided by Bartley and by many a postmodern philosopher (see the epigraph above), can be taken. It is a step, as we will see below, that is taken toward a commitment to preconceptual and pretheoretical suppositions—akin to axioms in different branches of mathematics—firmly grounded in a metaphysical intuition. Such epistemic foundations need not be explicitly acknowledged. Many scientists, for instance, do not bother to interrogate the metaphysical grounding of their research pursuits, yet their theoretical and empirical work nevertheless proceeds unimpaired. Metaphysical presuppositions can well serve their role implicitly as unobtrusive background, while yielding to theoretical and empirical research the explicitly and distinctly experienced foreground.

To some extent, all of us entertain theories based on and tied to pretheoretical suppositions and understandings of the nature of existence, ours and the world's. The pretheoretical understandings are part and parcel of distinct worldviews that shape the interpretations we make of our shared mundane as well as our more sophisticated experiences. For that reason, shared experiences can give rise to different intellectually satisfying interpretations made by practitioners of science and religion. In contrast to theistic religion, a key feature of science is that it, by presupposition, dwells in a world composed only of those entities and properties that are objectively observable and measurable, i.e., that exist in the natural world and are explainable entirely by other natural entities and processes. Theistic religions, however, dwell not only in the natural world studied by science but also in a more encompassing world that includes existential values such as justice, love, and friendship, the abstract nonphysical entities of mathematics, logic, and philosophy, and more importantly, beyond these, the spiritual realities transcending the natural ones. The world of theistic religion, in this sense, does not deny the world of science (despite the historically conflicted relation that existed between the two that is covered in chapter 6);

besides encompassing the world of value, philosophy, logic, and mathematics, it also accommodates the natural world and its scientific study. In this more expansive view, theological research takes on an ontology and a metaphysics that modern science neither does nor is qualified to take on as objects of its research. Without denying the fruits of scientific research and indeed sometimes benefitting from it, theology can take off when and where scientific research has landed.

Expanding the Scopes of Science and Theology

> In the intellectual climate of our times, respectability is reserved to such avenues of reason as are meticulously free not only of theological connotations but of even the least touch of metaphysics. What is novel in this climate is not its antitheological and antimetaphysical character. The novelty lies in the resolve to restrict rational discourse to the pattern set by the method of physics. This is the essence of present-day reductionism. Its protagonists are physicalists known by such names as operationists, behaviorists, and logical positivists.
>
> Stanley Jaki, *The Roads of Science and the Ways to God*, p. 214

> . . . no one engages in philosophy without being influenced by their extra-philosophical allegiances, religious, political, and otherwise. What is important here is twofold: first, not to disguise such allegiances as philosophical and, secondly, to make their influence on one's philosophical work explicit. The first is a danger that threatens those who fail to recognize, for example, that atheism requires an act of faith just as much as theism does and that physicalism is as liable to be held superstitiously as any religious view.
>
> Alasdair MacIntyre, *The Tasks of Philosophy*, p. xii

Enlarging the Compass of Science: Scientism, A Misguided Attempt to Turn Science into a Religious Worldview

Keeping in mind the notions of religious and epistemic impulses and that Alasdair MacIntyre's epigraph applies not only to philosophers but also to scientists and theologians, we have reached the point of asking if and how science can fall within the ambit of religion, and vice versa. In a seemingly tautological manner, above we referred to *theistic* religion. A reader living in a Western country may think it is obvious that religion is theistic, since to be religious is to believe in a divine entity, a god. However, several of the major world religions, Confucianism and Daoism, for example, are deemed nontheistic by religious scholars. One therefore can ask if other belief systems, especially ones in which atheism is inspired and supported by a worldview known as scientism, can be viewed as a religion. As the philosopher Michael Mitchell well defines it, "Scientism is the idea [and belief] that scientific inquiry is the only legitimate means of knowing what is true and real. It is the notion that if something can't be understood through empirical observation, scientific analysis, or mathematical calculation [used in scientific description and theory building], it is either unknowable or not worth knowing. It is rooted in the philosophy of naturalism which holds that all of reality is reducible to matter and energy so that the idea of immaterial reality is an oxymoron."[30]

This view or belief paradoxically claims to be all encompassing, while at the same time being exclusionary. The exclusion is a result of one of modern science's prime directives, namely the methodological ban on inserting extra-natural, specifically supernatural entities or processes into scientific explanations. One can therefore ask if scientism, and its particular branches such as naturalism and Darwinism, can therefore be viewed as types of nontheistic religion, as several scholars have proposed.[31] To address this question, the reader should recall the above discussion of the religious impulse, an impulse that is directed toward and realized in some form of religion.

Using reasoning akin to that used in the Turing test that is applied to so-called artificial intelligence, here I propose an additional route that is marked by features characterizing religions. In computer science, a criterion known as the Turing test is used to see if a computer program that attempts to simulate the intelligent behavior of humans can itself qualify as an intelligent agent. The Turing test rests on the logic of abductive reasoning by which, from a set of observations, one draws the most likely conclusion that adequately explains the observations. Thus, should a trained observer—who is naïve as to whether responses to questions are typed out by a human or a computer program—be unable to differentiate between a program's and a human's responses, then the program passes the Turing test and is therefore deemed to display intelligence; and in contrast, when the observer can detect a difference, the program fails to pass the Turing test and is not so deemed. That said, let me quote from two sources, the biologist Richard Lewontin's *Biology as Ideology* and the introduc-

30. Michael B. Mitchell, *Truth Before Logic: Finding Wisdom with G. K. Chesterton in a World Blinkered by Scientism* (Wipf & Stock, 2024), 2.

31. William Franke, *On the Universality of What Is Not: The Apophatic Turn in Critical Thinking* (University of Notre Dame Press, 2020), 361; John F. Haught, *Christianity and Science: Toward a Theology of Nature* (Orbis Books, 2007), 110, 186; Michael Heller, *The New Physics and New Theology* (Vatican Observatory Foundation, 1996), 3; Stanley L. Jaki, *The Road of Science and the Ways of God* (University of Chicago Press, 1978b), 288, 329; R. C. Lewontin, "Facts and the Factitious in Natural Sciences," *Critical Inquiry* 18, no. 1 (1991): 40–153; Mary Midgley, *Evolution as a Religion: Strange Hopes and Stranger Fears* (Routledge, 1985); Mary Midgley, *Science as Salvation: A Modern Myth and Its Meaning* (Routledge, 1994); and see below. I also consider scientism to be a type of religion as, I suspect, many other scientists and scholars do.

tory chapter of the physicist Ian Hutchinson's *Monopolizing Knowledge.* As to the first source, Lewontin states that one of the main purposes that modern science serves, "irrespective of the practical truth of scientific claims . . . is that of [sociocultural] *legitimation*."[32] He continues that

> for an institution [like science or religion] to explain the world so as to make the world legitimate, it must possess several features. First, the institution as a whole must appear to derive from sources outside of ordinary human social struggle. . . . Second, the ideas, pronouncements, rules and results of the institution's activity must have a validity and a transcendent truth that goes beyond any possibility of human compromise or human error. . . . And finally, the institution must have a certain mystical and veiled quality so that its innermost operation is not completely transparent to everyone. It must have an esoteric language, which needs to be explained to the ordinary person by those who are especially knowledgeable and who [like priests or theologians] can intervene between everyday life and mysterious sources of understanding and knowledge. . . . Revealed religion fits these three requirements perfectly, and so religion has been an ideal institution for legitimating society. . . . But this description also fits science and has made possible for science to replace religion as the chief legitimating force in modern society. Science claims a method that is objective and non-political, true for all time. Scientists truly believe that except for unwanted intrusions of ignorant politicians, science is above the social fray. . . . Not only the methods and institutions of science are said to be above ordinary human relations but, of course, the product of science is claimed to be a kind of universal truth. The secrets of nature are unlocked. Once the truth about nature is revealed, one must accept the facts of life. When science speaks, let no dog bark. Finally, science speaks in mysterious words. No one except an expert can understand what scientists say and do and we require the mediation of special people . . . to explain the mysteries of nature because otherwise there is nothing but undecipherable formulas [and technoscientific jargon]. . . . Despite its claim to be above society, science, like the Church before it, is a supremely social institution, reflecting and reinforcing the dominant values and views of society at each historical epoch."[33]

One thing to take away from Lewontin's appraisal of modern science as a social and cultural institution is that in our increasingly secular times it can be viewed as not only mimicking but actually supplanting the mystique and roles of organized religion. In this sociocultural sense it appears, based on the passages quoted above, that science, having passed the "Turing test" for religion,

32. R. C. Lewontin, *Biology as Ideology: The Doctrine of DNA* (Harper Perennial, 1993), 5–6.

33. Lewontin, *Biology as Ideology*, 7–9.

behaves like and thus can therefore legitimately assume the mantle of a religion. In fact, on the back of Lewontin's book jacket we find the following: "Many people now believe that science is the religion of the 20th century [and beyond]—that the authority of its clergy (scientists) is beyond question or challenge and that its rules and findings can indisputably explain the past and predict the future of human existence and of our individual behaviors." However, I, along with the philosopher and historian Gregory Dawes, would slightly but significantly amend Lewontin's thesis by claiming that it is not science per se, even in its institutional veneer, that is a religion. Instead, science has been transmogrified into an ersatz-religion known as scientism, ideologically and dogmatically adopted by some scientists and scholars.[34] Since Lewontin speaks as a geneticist, what is described in this promotional ad (presumably authored by him or approved by him) is applicable apropos a belief system known as Darwinism, a particular form of scientism. Darwinism, as well documented by the philosophers and historians of science Mary Midgley and Michael Ruse, can be considered a secular form of religion, a particular sect or expression of scientism, one that has become attractive to atheists and especially to the scientifically savvy neoatheists.[35] As to what I mean by Darwinism as a sect of scientism, the following, second quoted source clarifies as follows.

> Scientism is many-faceted. It is, first of all, a philosophy of knowledge. It is an opinion about the way knowledge can be obtained and justified. My single sentence definition of scientism focuses on this underlying and foundational aspect: "Scientism is the belief that all [and therefore the only] valid knowledge is science." However, the repercussions of this viewpoint are so great that scientism rapidly becomes much more. It becomes an all-encompassing world-view; a perspective from which all the questions of life are examined; a grounding presupposition or set of presuppositions which provide the framework by which the world is to be understood. . . . In so far as scientism is an overarching world-view, it is fair to regard it as *essentially a religious position*. Its advocates are unhappy with this assertion and argue that because scientism does not entail the belief in the supernatural, and does not entail ceremonials and rituals, it cannot be regarded as a religion. But that is hair-splitting. There are religions that don't involve a belief in God, and religions do not require participation in ceremonies. What's more, as we will see, several of the historic forms that scientism has taken [referring here to the nineteenth-century positivism

34. See Gregory Dawes, *Galileo and the Conflict Between Religion and Science* (Routledge, 2016), chapter 10.

35. Mary Midgley, *Evolution as a Religion: Strange Hopes and Stranger Fears* (Routledge, 1985); Mary Midgley, *Science as Salvation: A Modern Myth and Its Meaning* (Routledge, 1994); Michael Ruse, *Darwinism as Religion: What Literature Tells Us About Evolution* (Oxford University Press, 2016).

> of Auguste Comte and his mentor Henri Saint-Simon] *do* involve ceremonials and rituals of religious intent. In any case, the key aspect of religious conviction that scientism shares with most organized religions is that it offers a comprehensive principle or belief, which itself cannot be proved (certainly not scientifically proved) but which serves to organize understanding and guide our actions.[36] (emphasis added)

As we will see in chapter 7, advocates of scientism would be unhappy with such a definition. However, one can take what is made explicit by both quoted sources as valid and as applicable to not only scientistic but also atheistic belief systems inspired by science. As a prime example, one can list the biologist Richard Dawkins, who holds that Darwinism allows him to live as an intellectually satisfied atheist. Yet, despite such examples, one might regard the wordings of Lewontin and Hutchinson as stretching the definition of "religion" too far. However, the stretch is defensible, since it is supported by sociological observations as well as metaphysical assertions once, as MacIntyre in the above epigraph states, they are made explicit. So, beyond the context of Lewontin's and Hutchinson's quotes it is possible to go even deeper, to strengthen and give further substance to this assertion that science itself can transmute into a type of religion when it is taken to be the sole determiner of true and authentic knowledge and of the deepest understanding about the world.

Enlarging the Compass of Religion: Science's Pretheoretical, Metaphysical, and Theological Underpinnings

Here I am not arguing that theistic religion should explicitly intrude either methodologically or theoretically into the practice of modern science, as some creationists, young earthers, and their sympathizers would have it. Instead, the argument for enlarging the compass of religion is to show how pretheoretical, metaphysical, and theological concepts bear foundationally, even if only indirectly or implicitly, on the empirical and theoretical practices of science. To that end, let us explore a line of reasoning that to my knowledge was first proposed by the philosopher Roy Clouser, but was also expressed somewhat later and differently by the philosopher of science Michael Hanby. In his essay *The Myth of Religious Neutrality,* Clouser describes the ubiquitous role that religious belief plays in theoretical enterprises, including of course scientific ones.[37] This is so,

36. Ian Hutchinson, *Monopolizing Knowledge: A Scientist Refutes Religion-Denying, Reason-Destroying Scientism* (Fias Publishing, 2011), 2–3.

37. Roy A. Clouser, *The Myth of Religious Neutrality* (University of Notre Dame Press, 1991) is referring to high-level and abstract cognitive schemata that encompass and explain a considerable number and variety of observations and data. The subject matter of theories can be the natural world, in which case we are dealing with scientific theories that describe and explain observations and measurements based on empirical research; and the subject

he claims, because every working theory that is capable of not only explaining extant scientific observations but also predicting novel, theory-testing observations, is a theory that—with due respect but contrary to William Bartley—rests on foundational presuppositions that are neither part of that theory nor subject to scientific empirical test. These pretheoretical presuppositions, as noted, support beliefs about the constitution of reality, the world, and of our minds within it, that invariably have their source in metaphysics and theology, in that they either affirm (theistically), modify (deistically), or else deny (atheistically) God's role in creating and sustaining the universe. This may sound dubious to scientists who, following the example of positivist philosophers, believe that they have freed themselves from supposedly senseless metaphysical and theological beliefs.[38] Of these pretheoretical underpinnings, the most offensive to atheistic scientists is that God is the Creator, the First Cause of all other causes and the Sustainer of the universe (more on this in chapter 9). As Hanby has duly remarked, "not only does science always already presuppose a theology which is tacitly operative in its conception of its objects, but also it requires a true theology to be adequate to its own nature and to the world . . . [since] the content of this true theology—[based as it is on a Creator of the universe]—is already operative to some extent within scientific reason despite the best efforts to deny it, because science and its objects are *creatures*."[39] According to Clouser and Hanby, fashionable claims regarding scientists' liberation from metaphysical and theological presuppositions are therefore questionable, if not outright false. This espoused freedom is based not on scientific evidence itself but on an *a priori* fiat, which in turn is based on an active forgetting of—a suppression of, rather than a liberation from—metaphysical underpinnings of the scientific enterprise. Excepting the more subjectivist quantum physicists, ask reality-oriented, objective scientists (i) if the world they study exists separately from their observations and studies of it, and (ii) if this world is intelligible and therefore invites rational scientific investigation. If they answer "yes" to these questions, they are (at least implicitly) expressing a trust in, a pretheoretical metaphysical belief about, a reality beyond their personal existence and subjective experience, yet accessible to scientifically based observations and therefore empirically knowable. For as

---

matter of theories also can be the world of ideas, examples of which are mathematical, logical, philosophical and theological theories dealing with either existing or newly proposed conceptual entities.

38. Exception to the general neglect of philosophical and foundational issues among scientists is found in Carlo Rovelli, *The Order of Time* (Riverhead Books, 2018); and Lee Smolin, *Einstein's Unfinished Revolution: The Search for What Lies Beyond the Quantum* (Penguin Press, 2019).

39. Michael Hanby, *No God, No Science?: Theology, Cosmology, Biology* (Wiley-Blackwell, 2017), 2.

pointed out by Christopher Mooney, without such an implicit or explicit belief, the enterprise of science, consisting of experimentation, empirical observation, and explanatory theories cannot take off.[40] Moreover, ask them further what warrants such metaphysical, pretheoretical beliefs. Some will candidly answer that the warrant lies with the God who is the Creator of all realities. Others will probably answer with stumped silence, a pragmatic indifference, or with vigorous rejection of such metaphysical and theological claims. Nonetheless, despite such indifference and protests, when daring to probe the metaphysics underlying their profession, the protesting scientists and scholars unwittingly yet theologically transpose Anselm of Canterbury's *fides quaerens intellectum* (faith in search of reason) to read, as expressed in one of Bernard Lonergan's apt insights, *intellectus quaerens fidem* (reason in search of faith).[41]

This brings us to a more controversial thesis—namely, that the quest for scientific truth is at bottom a religious or theological undertaking. How so? Agreeing with Hanby (and with Hutchinson) that science is *a* way of understanding the world, Clouser's thesis, presented in the following summary, goes as follows:

> There is a deeper level of understanding which humans have always sought, the level at which the nature of our world and ourselves is interpreted and explained. In our culture, that level has long been thought to be attained through theories. It is by the theories of philosophy and sciences that we try to explain all that we experience. . . .[42] [And] it is through theories of reality that the influence of religious belief is conveyed to scientific theories: scientific theories necessarily presuppose an overview of reality, while overviews of reality necessarily *presuppose some religious belief.* Religious belief . . . regulates overviews of reality directly, and through the mediation of overviews regulates scientific theories indirectly.[43]

What is noteworthy here is how Clouser's and Hanby's theses state that overviews of reality, also known as worldviews, presuppose some religious beliefs that regulate scientific theories. Furthermore, notes Stanley Jaki, "insofar as science is not merely a tool but intellectual creativity it is intertwined with [worldview] presuppositions that [can] have [a] distinctly ideological character."[44] This resonates with Hutchinson's noted claim that scientism, an ideology

40. Christopher F. Mooney, SJ, *Theology and Scientific Knowledge; Changing Models of God's Presence in the World* (University of Notre Dame Press, 1996), 10.

41. Bernard Lonergan, *Insight: A Study into Human Understanding* (University of Toronto Press, 1992), 731.

42. Clouser, *The Myth of Religious Neutrality*, 2.

43. Clouser, *The Myth of Religious Neutrality*, 66.

44. Stanley L. Jaki, *The Savior of Science* (Regnery Gateway, 1988), 3.

based on the metaphysical belief that all valid knowledge is science, can transmute into a religious, all-encompassing worldview. Hutchinson's simple definition of scientism, as the belief that all valid knowledge is science, finds resonance in the dogmatic assertion, made by Nobel laureate physicist Isidor Isaac Rabi, that "science is the *only* valid underlying knowledge that gives guidance to the *whole* human adventure [and that] those who are not acquainted with science do not possess the *basic* human values that are necessary in our time."[45] Scientism can claim such an exclusive yet universal reach of science because it rests on a tacit metaphysical worldview that itself is already religious in nature. Why such belief is religious follows from what Clouser explicitly means by religious belief and from what was implicit and therefore inferable from Tim Crane's views of religion and the religious impulse. We might have a firm practical handle on the meaning of "belief" since we explicitly entertain a few of them daily. But the handle on the meaning of "religion" is quite slippery; we do not entertain religions daily, although at least once a week we might, even if only perfunctorily, participate in specific religious ceremonies and rituals. And just as most scientists do not reflect on the metaphysical underpinnings of science, so most of us do not spend hours reflecting on the meaning of religion.

Insofar as the supramundane transcendent order is divine, we can initiate a deeper meaningful and interesting discussion of religion and its relation to science. Philosophically extracting from theology two of God's essential attributes, Clouser explicitly defines the divine as *that which is self-subsistent*, i.e., as not being created and thus not depending on anything else for its existence, and therefore as also *that which has everything else depend on it*. Thus, for secular and scientifically minded materialists, naturalists, or pantheists like Tim Crane and Chet Raymo, physical matter and nature, being sacred and holy in their all-encompassing cosmological sense, can stand as a make-do for the divine. As the historian Eugene McCarraher phrased it, ". . . nature assumes a luminous grandeur with the disappearance of the supernatural; the world and its inhabitants were now a beloved community of earthly beatitude."[46] Although Clouser's definition is philosophically stripped down, it is, despite its incompleteness, a theologically correct definition of the divine. Hence, Clouser is justified in defining religious belief as belief in what is considered to be divine. For a Christian, Muslim, or Jew, only God is recognized as the Divine, since his preeminent "I AM" transcends the cosmos, exceeds in perfection—as Anselm of Canterbury posited almost a millennium ago—anything that can be thought, is unencumbered by dependence on any of its created entities, and has all these entities

45. *Time* Magazine, May 26, 1967, 48, quoted in Stanley L. Jaki, *The Road of Science and the Ways of God* (University of Chicago Press, 1978), 329.

46. Eugene McCarraher, *The Enchantments of Mammon: How Capitalism Became the Religion of Modernity* (Harvard University Press, 2019), 97.

depend on it. Yet, as Clouser also correctly points out, divinity conceived as self-existent and independent from everything else (and on which everything else depends for its existence) has in past pagan culture also been attributed to other realities—for example, to number, more broadly to mathematics, by the Pythagoreans. Along similar lines, from reading the popular books of the cosmologist and physicist Stephen Hawking or of the idealist Bernardo Kastrup,[47] one can get the impression that the universal law of gravity or universal consciousness might qualify as divine in Clouser's sense. Insofar as number, gravity, and consciousness are regarded in this way, Pythagoreans, physicalist cosmologists, and radical idealists willy-nilly hew to some sort of religious creed, although they might protest and profess otherwise.

Summarizing Clouser's thesis, one can say that a creedal system emanating from what is taken to be a foundational, self-subsistent source on which all else depends, can be regarded as a religion. This line of reasoning allows identifying religions that subscribe to a transcendent supernatural realm and agency as theistic ones and distinguishing them from nontheistic ones, those religions that do not subscribe to a supernatural realm and agency. Following Hutchinson, scientistic atheism can therefore rightly be viewed as a specific form of nontheistic religion, one that I have already referred to as an ersatz-religion.[48] If still in doubt that scientistic atheism is an ersatz-religion, it would be useful to recall Tim Crane's claims—rightly or wrongly—that (i) the religious impulse spurs humans to find meaning in the world they inhabit in terms of their relationship to something transcendent, (ii) the transcendent need not be identified with the supernatural, and (iii) the sacred can be discovered in the natural realm. Together these claims, in turn, lend credibility to the claim that (iv) scientistic atheism, by dwelling in and on the worldly, natural realm, can be viewed as a nontheistic ersatz-religion inspired and motivated by religious naturalism.

Comparing Scientific Empirical and Theistic Mystical Experiences

> [Adequately addressing the problem of personal consciousness requires] removing it from the metaphysical realm (that is, as reflected from the

47. Stephen Hawking and Leonard Mlodinow, *The Grand Design* (Random House, 2010); Bernardo Kastrup, *The Idea of the World: A Multi-Disciplinary Argument for the Mental Nature of Reality* (Iff Books, 2019). On p. 180, Hawking and Mlodinow claim that "because there is a law such as gravity, the universe can and will create itself from nothing." The claim intended to say that not God but instead the law of gravity is the *raison d'etre* of the universe's creation.

48. I do this out of deference to those scientists who may vigorously disagree with Lewontin's and Hutchinson's characterization of science transmuted into a (presumably) "genuine" religion.

> "outside") and placing it into an existential context, that is, as reflecting the essential feature of the lived experience which must be placed at the foundation and beginning of all further reasoning. Such an approach accentuates two, usually separate, directions of research about embodied consciousness (naturalistic and theistic) without giving priority to one at the expense to the other, and treating both as equally contributing to the open-ended hermeneutics of the human condition. Yet, such an attitude implies the recognition of lived experience as the ultimate presupposition of any form of investigation. The lived experience is understood widely as forming the life-world in the context of Husserl's attempt to ground all experience, included that of the [natural and theological] sciences.
>
> Alexei V. Nesteruk, *Consciousness and Matter*, p. 47

Once having carefully read the following chapters 1–5, the reader will recall that religion, and its connatural partners, morality and art, depend heavily on experience, on consciousness and its contents. Of course, the same can be said of science. Scientific experiences derive from the empirical observations and measurements made of the properties of objects and events in the world. Theistic religions also are based on experiences of and about the world. So, what's the difference between these two types of experiences? It all depends on what the term "world" refers to. The German philosopher Edmund Husserl some hundred years ago talked about the *Lebenswelt* (lifeworld) to distinguish it from the world of science, what in German is referred to as the *Naturwelt* (nature-world). The lifeworld of every human is experientially realized through personal, phenomenological contact with everyday objects and events in our normal, everyday habitat that are revealed via varied subjective sensory, cognitive, and emotional states. In its unfiltered form, it is a private world, a world-for-me,[49] yet spared from solipsism by being filtered through a wider sociocultural milieu that each human shares with others. Because the modern natural sciences, as the qualifier "modern" suggests, are of relatively recent provenance, the phenomenologically accessible lifeworld enjoys temporal and experiential priority over the nature-world. The latter world is accessible only via highly specialized and methodologically sophisticated scientific investigations. In other words, the scientifically investigated nature-world has culturally evolved from what is regarded as the first-person subjective lifeworld into what is regarded its intersubjectively validated, third-person world of objective science (see appendices 1 and 2 for details). Because the lifeworld provides the general context of our everyday existence, one can conceptually distinguish the world of science from the lifeworld as something special, special to the extent that the world investigated and experienced by scientists is by and large not iden-

49. Antti Revonsuo, *Inner Presence: Consciousness as a Biological Phenomenon* (MIT Press, 2006) elaborates how the conscious awareness of the world is a life world for each of us.

tifiable with—to the point of sometimes contradicting—our everyday lifeworld experiences. Like the world of magic or the occult, the scientific world, as noted by Richard Lewontin, can be relatively exotic. In contrast, the lifeworld is rather mundane. Yet, it is the communal matrix from which, since ancient times, the practical and fine arts, morality, philosophy, politics, and religion emerged and from which, in more recent times, science also emerged. It is also within the lifeworld's matrix that all the above cultural practices continue to flourish and find their home.

Able to make room for the nature-world that science investigates, the phenomenal lifeworld, being more capacious, can also accommodate the world of religious experiences. Though affected by the external nature-world of science, such experiences are often more powerfully influenced by what transpires in an individual's interior world. Not confined to mystics or the spiritually adept, and well documented by scholars, the interior world of religion is accessible to a large segment of humanity.[50] As pointed out by Tim Crane and as documented in chapter 1 by Alexander and Andrew Fingelkurts, even atheists can be endowed with the ability to have transcendent and religious experiences, despite their "theistic unmusicality" relative to the religious experiences reported by practitioners of theistic religions. As previously noted, atheists no doubt experience the sublimities, wonders, and beauties of nature and the awesome immensity of the heavens and an unbounded cosmos and can derive joy and perhaps even solace from such experiences.[51] However, from a theistic viewpoint, the want of attunement of most atheists to God could be regarded as an unfortunate lack for two reasons. For one, very many if not most atheists are missing out on religiously "musical" experiences that in their everyday forms can be consoling, supportive, peacefully blissful, and in their most sublime form can be encounters with what Rudolf Otto termed the *Mysterium Tremendum et Fascinans*, the holy or divine.[52] Second, besides being religiously unmusical, neoatheists such Richard Dawkins and Christopher Hitchens can also be strident antitheists hypercritical of religion and judge it in extremely virulent terms. Yet whether benign or virulent, atheists—in Thomas Dubay's slightly adapted words—"commonly make the fatal error of assuming that they have the capacity and right to [harshly] judge religious truth without preparation [or reparation] of their hearts. . . . This is like a tone-deaf critic claiming to pass judgement on a Mozart concerto or symphony."[53]

50. Fingelkurts and Fingelkurts, "Is Our Brain Hardwired?"; Bill Underwood and Bert Moore, "Perspective-Taking and Altruism," *Psychological Bulletin* 91, no. 1 (1982): 143–73.

51. I say "perhaps" because for others, including the 17th-century mathematician and scientist Pascal, a devout theist, the awesome immensity and "the eternal silence of these infinite spaces fill me with dread." Blaise Pascal, *Pensées* (Penguin Books, 1966), 95.

52. Rudolf Otto, *The Idea of the Holy* (Oxford University Press, 1958).

53. Thomas Dubay, SM, *The Evidential Power of Beauty* (Ignatius Press, 1999), 271.

That said, it is important to note that a distinction needs to be made between what are considered to be genuine, theistic religious experiences and other profound but nonreligious experiences. Examples of the latter are known as extrovertive experiences. Like religious experiences, they tend "to be characterised by one or more of the following: profound sense of unity, profound sense of knowledge or profound sense of contact with reality. However, this experience is distinguished from religious experience by its orientation towards the natural world. In extrovertive experience, such features as unity, knowledge, reality, love, luminosity and so forth, characterize experience of the natural world, but not the experience of something beyond the natural world such as a transcendent God, soul, or divine realm."[54] For atheists and religious naturalists like Tim Crane and Chet Raymo, a naturalized religious impulse toward transcendence may be satisfied by extrovertive experiences; however, they would not satisfy a theist's religious impulse directed toward the supernatural, transcendent divine.

Religious Theism Versus Religious Scientistic Atheism

Moreover, when considered as a type, a scientistic atheists' experiences of transcendence are what one might call experiences of penultimate or, somewhat paradoxically, immanent transcendence. For them, experiences of absolute, ultimate transcendence are something to be dreaded, in the sense of being mistrusted and aversive. The experience of the holy, we noted above, can take the form of not only the *mysterium fascinans* but also the *mysterium tremendum*. While the former might evoke a graceful and trustful attraction; the latter can provoke a fear of, a distrustful aversion to, an awesome, overwhelming, and controlling power that transcends every natural and human power. Despite this, a majority of humans usually suspend their personal preferences and submit to the authoritative power, knowledge, and discernment of all sorts of trusted human experts—teachers, medical doctors, lawyers, expert technicians, to name just a few—sometimes quite willingly, at other times with some misgivings and resentments. Yet there are many humans who refuse to trustfully rely on God's omniscience, although in his transcendence, God is the cosmic authority figure. Paul Lakeland describes this distrust as follows:

> Prior to faith we recognize the [Ultimate] Transcendent but we do not trust it. This is "natural religion," and in this moment our task is Promethean. . . . [Commenting on Bertrand Russell's *The Scientific Outlook*, Lakeland continues that] Russell's conviction of the absence of divine purposes spares us "the necessity for that [Promethean] attitude of impotent hatred which every brave and humane man would otherwise be called upon to adopt

54. Fingelkurts and Fingelkurts, "Is Our Brain Hardwired?," 308.

> towards the Almighty Tyrant." So, if we believe in this God of natural religion, we fear this God. The contrast is between Prometheus and Job, whose "honest questioning" is "without fear oppressed by guilt." [And quoting the American theologian H. Richard Niebuhr's *Faith on Earth,* Lakeland continues that] "the brave man of the Promethean type confronts a distrusted transcendent reality with courage; [whereas] the brave man trusting stands before God like Job asking for an answer; the fearsome man [lacking trust] confronts the distrusted [Ultimate] Transcendent with trembling; the fearsome man full of trust is awed but not cowed and there is joy in his awe."[55]

This appraisal of an atheistic as compared to a theistic faith is noteworthy in several respects. For one, it identifies theistic faith more with a trusting love and awe of God rather than, as for example some atheists would have it, with belief in or intellectual assent to some doctrinal proposition propagated as true. Second, one's stance toward God is not one of groveling acceptance of anything and everything that occurs but one of gratitude, praise, and joy for the gifts of blessing and life, yet also one that is emboldened to question God (like Job asking for an answer)—with impassioned complaint and protest, as several biblical prophets did—in the face of pain, confusion, injustice, and, yes, tremendous loss and suffering.[56] Third, one can grant the atheist the virtue of courage in distrustfully confronting the Ultimate Transcendent. The atheistic fear or distrust, as noted, engenders an aversion to it, or in terms of the philosopher J. P. Moreland, a *pneumatophobia* compounded by the "cosmic authority problem" that the existence of a personal God poses.[57] The atheist philosopher Thomas Nagel speaks to the aversion to God in fittingly exemplary terms that are representative of most scientific and philosophic naturalists, in that he, like other atheists, would very much like *not* to live in a world governed by a God who, akin to the Almighty Tyrant à la Bertrand Russell, cannot but be viewed aversively. Nagel's fear of reli-

55. Paul Lakeland, *The Wounded Angel: Fiction and the Religious Imagination* (Liturgical Press, 2017), 28–29.

56. The Jewish theologian Arthur A. Cohen, in *The Tremendum: A Theological Interpretation of the Holocaust* (Continuum, 1993), addresses the theological problem raised by the sheer immensity of human suffering brought on by the Holocaust. Immense human suffering as well as the suffering of sentient creatures has been a constant in human and evolutionary history. They pose now, as ever, one of the severest impediments to belief/trust in a good and just God.

57. J. P. Moreland, *Consciousness and the Existence of God: A Theistic Argument* (Routledge, 2008), 178. Regarding the cosmic authority problem, the physicist Angelo Tartaglia (in *A Physicist's Journey Between Science and Faith: Friends or Foes?* [Cambridge Scholars Publishing, 2023], 97) pointed out that the "idea of an impersonal divine essence, whether immanent or transcendent, assumed in the Age of Enlightenment a rationalist connotation which set a new type of religiousness against the traditional one, considered *oppressive* and obscurantist" (emphasis added).

gion is not based merely on his recognition of "the objectionable moral doctrines, social policies, and political influence [of institutionalized religions nor on] the association of many religious beliefs with superstition and the acceptance of evident empirical falsehoods. [What] I am talking about [is] something much deeper—namely, the fear of [theistic] religion itself. I speak from experience, being strongly subject to the fear myself: I want atheism to be true and am made uneasy by the fact that some of the most intelligent and well-informed people I know are religious believers. It isn't just that I don't believe in God and, naturally, hope that I'm right in my belief. It's that I hope that there is no God! I don't want there to be God; I don't want the universe to be like that. My guess is that this *cosmic authority problem* is not a rare condition and that it *is responsible for much of the scientism and reductionism of our time*"[58] (emphases added). Should the distrustful aversion soften and be replaced gradually by trustful love of the Ultimate Transcendent—the Author of the created order who thereby wields Ultimate *Author*ity over it—one is on the way to a conversion from atheism to theism. Of course, the converse can also occur, particularly when one confronts the immensity of past and present suffering in the world.

Theistic Concepts of Religion and God

In view of the above reflections on the divine, a telling question to pose here is: *What* or *who* is your god? A standard definition of religion as it is practiced now includes a set of beliefs about god as a supernatural entity.[59] Such a definition is broad enough to include the Christian God, the Hebraic YHWH, the Muslim Allah, the Sikh Waheguru or the Hindu Brahman. However, we noted that although some major religions are theistic, others, such as Confucianism, Buddhism, and arguably Jainism, Shintoism, and Daoism, are nontheistic in outlook. We also noted that Clouser's (partial yet necessary) definition of the divine characterizes it as that which is taken to be self-subsistent and to have the existence of all other entities depend on it. One could argue on the one hand that this definition is too inclusive and indiscriminate to be useful. While listing two necessary attributes, the self-subsistence of the divine and our ultimate dependency on it, the definition leaves out much that a fuller theistic definition encompasses. On the other hand, one can claim the partial definition to be useful precisely because it is generously inclusive, since, while not specifying

58. Thomas Nagel, *The Last Word* (Oxford University Press, 1997), 130–31.

59. For a look at the difficulty of pinning down a transhistorical valid definition of religion, see Cavanaugh, *The Myth of Religious Violence*, chapter 2, "The Invention of Religion"; and Nogbri, *Before Religion*. A mirthful yet trenchant look at the difficulty of conceptually cornering religion is given in David Bentley Hart's review—"Daniel Dennett Hunts the Snark," *First Things*, January 1, 2007—of Daniel Dennett's *Breaking the Spell*. Dennett defines religion simply as belief in a supernatural God.

them, it doesn't exclude any of the other attributes such as loving, omniscient, omnipresent, or divine. Its generality is its virtue; for, by bracketing but not eliminating the distinctive particularities of, say, the Christian and the Hindu God or the particularities that distinguish the theistic divine and the nontheistic divine, it notes their important commonality. Clouser's "catholic" definition, therefore, while broad in application, nevertheless focuses on what we take to be of ultimate significance, that at which our philosophical, metaphysical, and religious bucks stop.

For those (like me) insufficiently schooled in theology or philosophy of religion to discourse competently on the full conceptual territory over which notions of God range, let's go to the following compact yet rich list of classical theistic ways to think and speak about Him offered by the religious scholar, David Bentley Hart:

> To speak of "God" properly, then—to use the word in a sense consonant with the teachings of orthodox Judaism, Christianity, Islam, Sikhism, Hinduism, Bahá'í, a great deal of antique paganism, and so forth—is to speak of the infinite source of all that is: eternal, omniscient, omnipotent, omnipresent, uncreated, uncaused, perfectly transcendent of all things and for that very reason absolutely immanent to all things. God so understood is not something posed over against the universe, in addition to it, nor is he the universe itself. He is not a "being," at least not in the way a tree, shoemaker, or a god is a being; he is not one more object in the inventory of things that are, or any sort of discrete object at all. Rather, all things that exist receive their being continuously from him, who is the infinite wellspring of all that is, *in whom* (to use the language of Christian scriptures) all things live and move and have their being. In one sense he is "beyond being," if by "being" one means the totality of discrete, finite things. In another sense he is "being itself," in that he is the inexhaustible source of all reality, the absolute upon which the contingent is always utterly dependent, the unity and simplicity that underlies and sustains the diversity of finite and composite things. Infinite being, infinite consciousness, infinite bliss, from whom we are, by whom we know and are known, and in whom we find our true consummation.[60]

Let's unpack some of these concepts. Many theologies and religious traditions speak of God by way of (cataphatically) affirmative statements of what he is like while, all along, aware that one must speak of Him in a way that is not comprehensible in an entirely exhaustive, clear, and rational way. Other theologians therefore prefer to speak of God in (apophatically) negative terms by noting what he is not, or they speak suggestively by relying on ways of expressing his ineffable reality that are more poetic than prosaic or literal. So, when we

60. David Bentley Hart, *The Experience of God* (Yale University Press, 2013), 30.

speak of God as omniscient or omnipresent, we mean that in the positive sense that he knows all there is to know and that in and through his creation of the world his immanence is present to every existing thing, regardless of its spatiotemporal locus. Additionally, when we affirm that God is Love or the Font of Life and Light, we are making again an affirmative assertion; but here we are using an associatively rich anagogical and figurative manner of speech, akin to a spiritually elevated form of poetic metaphor. However, when we speak of God as the infinite and ineffable source of all that is, we are, in one sense, affirming one of God's attributes—but notice also that the words "ineffable" and "infinite" are negations of "effable" and "finite." In other words, to speak of God as ineffable and infinite is to speak of him as *not* being just another of the world's readily definable and finite entities—say, a tree or a scientist. When we positively attest that God is eternal, we mean that he is without a beginning and an end, that he transcends time, that he is, in negating terms, *non-* or *a*temporal. And when we say that God is absolute, we mean, again by use of negative terms, that he is *un*restricted by and *in*dependent of all things, while all things, being created entities, are fully dependent on him for their contingent existence.

Rational Conundra in Religion and Science

Let us now turn from these theological distinctions between God and God's created beings to some puzzling questions arising from our concepts of God. How can God both be transcendently beyond and additionally be immanently present to the world and everything in it? The terms "transcendent" and "immanent" exemplify a dichotomy, a mysterious antinomy that seems to be a self-contradictory affirmation, a *reductio ad absurdum*. The classic logic on which human reason depends takes the principles of noncontradiction and the excluded middle as fundamental. The assertion that God transcends the world seems to contradict his being immanent to it (and vice versa), since the assertion of the one (transcendence or immanence) logically excludes the other. How can we, then, reconcile the two? We cannot rationally do so, without ascribing to a distinct *theo*-logic, much like the Danish philosopher Søren Kierkegaard did. It allows us to think of God more inclusively but in paradoxical ways.[61] A skeptic might rightfully think that this is an unwarranted and cheap copout. But consider the following examples taken from one of the securest branches of physics, known as quantum mechanics, all the many predictions of which have been confirmed up to now without exception. Beyond acknowledging that quanta exist, their existence poses various conundra to even the best quantum physicists. To paraphrase the humbling paradox posed by the physicist Richard Feynman, any claim of ours that we understand quan-

61. Søren Kierkegaard, *The Sickness unto Death* (Penguin Books, 1986); Søren Kierkegaard, *Fear and Trembling* (Penguin Books, 1989).

tum mechanics is proof that we really don't understand it. This is the quantum physicist's version of the quandary posed apophatically to many a philosopher and theologian by St. Augustine in his Sermon 117: *si enim comprehendis, non est Deus* (if you think that you have grasped him through your intellect, it is not God you have grasped). Regarding the quantum quandary, let's use two examples. First, according to the quirky *quantum*-logic, two massless photons (massless particles of light) emanating from the same source and separated in space need not obey locality, since the measurement of the physical properties of one can instantaneously influence the measurement of the properties of the other. This contravenes the logic of classical and relativistic physics—and of our so-called nonexpert "folk physics" based on observing cause-effect relations—stating that such influence cannot occur instantaneously. Similarly, how can a subatomic entity with mass, such as the electron, paradoxically display, on the one hand, the properties of a point-like particle and, on the other, of a wave spread out in space?

So, if in our perplexed cognitive state, we allow ourselves—along with most practicing physicists and without too much protest or reservation from them—to scratch our heads and live with these logical conundra in the natural sciences, can we on rational grounds disallow analogous conundra in theology? Much like the peculiar quantum-logic, *theo*-logic also requires that we allow paradoxical thinking. All we can do in quantum physics and theology is try to resolve paradoxes by eventually developing accounts that delve into deeper ontological levels of reality, some so deep that they border on the realm of metaphysics. Currently, physicists are attempting to resolve these quandaries by producing an entirely new theory that unifies quantum mechanics and general relativity or by adopting entirely new metaphysical assumptions about the foundational properties of the cosmos.[62] But even if they are successful, the primal mystery of being—the fact that nothing, the lack of anything, by definition cannot exist, and therefore that anything exists at all—will remain. In the face of that mystery, a Christian like St. Augustine can hold, and even experience, the paradox of a transcendent God's relation with, or immanence, to us that is more deeply intimate than our intimacy with ourselves. Such intimate contact with the transcendent Divinity is not unique to Christianity; it has been attested to in other major theistic religions.[63]

Moreover, how can God be simple? And how can he be one? The answers to both questions, given by theologians and philosophers of religion, are related: He is not composite, not made up of parts or attributes, although he comprehends all of them. Here the word "comprehend" means to grasp, hold together,

62. Rovelli, *The Order of Time*; Smolin, *Einstein's Unfinished Revolution*.

63. See, for example, the treatise on the three Abrahamic faiths by Roger Arnaldez, *Three Messengers for One God* (University of Notre Dame Press, 1994).

and unify all in God's single and simple act of being. Along the lines of reasoning taken by Michael Augros and Robert Spitzer, an analogical proposal for the answer to these questions can here also be given in terms of scientific theories.[64] Below I consider two examples. First are Faraday's intuitive and Maxwell's formal mathematical theories of electromagnetism. Because they *unify* two forces, electricity and magnetism, Faraday's and Maxwell's theories transcend and are simpler than prior, separate theoretical accounts of electricity and magnetism in that both are comprehended (unified) as attributes of a single electromagnetic force. In doing so, the theories can additionally and comprehensively explain why various electromagnetic sources of radiation such as infrared and visible light, radar, and microwaves can be applied in telecommunication of information, in mapping the cosmos, and much more. Serving as a second example are the theories of space, gravity, and motion that Newton proposed. They are arguably simpler from the standpoint of understanding the underlying principles and their mathematical expressions than Einstein's theory of general relativity is. However, we should not confuse subjective difficulties, limits, and frustrations posed to our understanding with the difficult yet elegant and simple mathematical formulations of theories. Of the two theories, Einstein's is the simpler one, in that (i) it has no need of relying on ad hoc assumptions and conditions in order (ii) to elegantly comprehend and unify many more observed phenomena than Newton's theory can. Some of the explanatory difficulties of Newton's theory, arising from phenomena such as the precession of the perihelion of Mercury and gravity's "action at a distance," or from assumptions such as absolute space and time, are simply resolved as nonproblems in Einstein's more unified theory of a geometrically curved space-time manifold that is subject to warping by large material objects like the sun. Moreover, Einstein's theory was also able to account for the finite speed of light, which prior theories of electromagnetism such as Faraday's did not account for.

So, again taking greater simplicity as that which comprehends and unifies more and excludes less, we can analogously extrapolate and go a step further by noting that God *is* the simplicity that comprehends and unifies all his seemingly complex attributes. Unlike feathering and bipedality that birds *have* as attributes, God does not so much have each of his attributes as simply in his unity being all of them. In this sense, God's simplicity "suffers" the ultimate poverty of "having" no attributes, since he comprehensively *is* all of them. In other words, God is his simplicity, which is his unity, which in turn is his eternity, his love, consciousness, bliss, omniscience, omnipresence, transcendence, immanence—in short, in God all these attributes are ultimately united, because his

64. Michael Augros, *Who Designed the Designer?: A Rediscovered Path to God's Existence* (Ignatius Press, 2015), chapter 9; Robert J. Spitzer, *New Proofs for the Existence of God* (William B. Eerdmans Publishing, 2010), 121–32.

oneness unifies, comprehends, and *is* all of them. It is important to note that this way of addressing God's simplicity and unity deviates immensely from how, for example, the neoatheist Richard Dawkins addresses it. Like the atheist philosopher J. J. C. Smart,[65] he dismisses God's simplicity in favor of His complexity as necessarily compositional and at least as great and therefore as improbable as the compositional complexity of the biological world.[66] Such a seemingly rational dismissal is neither obvious nor straightforward, for it implicitly assumes the scientistic premise, noted above by Hutchinson, that all legitimate knowledge and knowability is confined to scientific rationality.

So, apropos God's simplicity, is it more than coincidental that the sciences of physics and physical cosmology strive to develop a single theory that comprehends and unifies the currently disparate theories of quantum mechanics and general relativity? If such development of the single theory of the universe's existence is achieved, it will, to paraphrase Stephen Hawking, come as close as we can to understanding the (simple) mind of God.

And how can God both be and not be? Answering this fundamental question allows us to better understand the answer to the other questions posed. One way to answer them can be expressed as follows (additional ways are considered in chapter 9). God's chief attribute is his aseity, an uncaused and uncreated existence. His essence is necessarily his existence; he is, in St. Thomas's words, *Purus Actus*, pure act of existence. In agreement with Roy Clouser, what this logically entails is that God is uniquely self-sufficient, in that he does not depend on anything else, i.e., on any creature, for his existence. So, in the *a se* (from and in itself) sense, he is; however, in the sense that creatures have being *ab alio* (from something other), he is not. Aseity is the attribute that logically is prior to the other attributes that God is; for if he did not exist from and in himself, i.e., if he were not self-subsistent but created *ab alio* like all finite and contingent creature, he could not be omniscient, omnipresent, uncaused, or eternal.

Religion in Secular Humanistic and Divine Godly Realms

In current Western societies, secularism is practically coterminous with atheism, and therefore theistic religions tend to be viewed as oppositional to the secular world and to the natural sciences. What should be kept in mind is

65. J. J. C. Smart and J. J. Haldane, *Atheism and Theism*, 2nd ed. (Blackwell Publishing, 2003), 23.

66. Richard Dawkins, *The God Delusion* (Houghton Mifflin, 2006), 147, 153–55. But is it more than coincidental, yet paradoxical, that physics and physical cosmology strive to develop a single theory that simplifies, unifies, and comprehends the currently disparate and complex physical facts explained by quantum mechanics and those explained by general relativity?

that the notions of the religious, the secular, and the scientific have co-evolved in Western history and at one time were not oppositional notions. Centuries ago, priests who addressed the needs of their parish flocks were known as secular priests (nowadays they are more commonly referred to as lay or parish priests). In contrast, those who were members of a religious order—e.g., a monastic one like the Trappists—were known as religious priests. Moreover, what is not widely known is that the religious-secular split is a recent historical phenomenon, inextricably tied to the rise of nation-states and the concomitant shift of power—in particular regarding the sanctioning of force/violence—from religious to state authority.[67] Additionally, the transcendent humanism of the 16th-century Renaissance and the personal and qualitative essayistic style of its representative writers, such as Michel de Montaigne, Desiderius Erasmus, and Thomas More, was in short order followed by Francis Bacon's thoroughly this-worldly humanistic and utilitarian view and promotion of experimental science, and by the rigorously quantitative and mathematical style advocated by Galileo Galilei and Johannes Kepler in their investigations of the dynamic and inertial systems of nature. The revolutionary scientific enterprises of the late 16th and early 17th centuries motivated the formalization of physically reductive methodological and theoretical innovations proposed by René Descartes and developed mathematically by Isaac Newton. The innovations were taken to be universally applicable, in the cosmological as well as cosmopolitan senses. They were also taken to be based on an equally universal and cosmopolitan reason, best exemplified by its application to the budding natural sciences and by proponents of the Enlightenment,[68] and subsequently were appropriated by the stalwarts of 20th-century and today's scientism.

Scientific reasoning, concerned with explaining the workings and attributes of the *res extensa*, the physical and material entities, only recently excluded the direct agency of God from causal explanations of natural phenomena. Indeed, Newton himself believed that his theory was true to physical reality; yet he nonetheless conceded that God not only pervaded the cosmos (absolute space was His sensorium) but also sustained it, for example by periodically adjusting the solar system so that the planets would not crash into the sun. Full scientific acceptance of the methodological constraint that keeps the Deity from interfering with the workings of nature was accelerated, if not initiated,

67. Stephen Toulmin, *Cosmopolis: The Hidden Agenda of Modernity* (University of Chicago Press, 1990); Cavanaugh, *The Myth of Religious Violence.*

68. Immanuel Kant's treatise on the significance of the Enlightenment (see his *Beantwortung der Frage: Was ist Aufklärung?* [Henricus Edition Deutsche Klassik GmbH, 2019]), was written in the wake of the historical impact of Newtonian physics. In it, the success of reason in the natural sciences is taken also to promise its successful application in the human sciences, on which an autonomous ethics and politics, freed from religious tradition and authority, could be established.

in physics by the likes of Laplace and in biology by Darwin's theory of natural selection, both finding God's role in the efficient causal processes of nature as unnecessary and thereby excluding it. And along with the impressive theoretical, empirical, and technological advances of the natural sciences, this constraint, by also dispensing with formal and final causes, did much to reinforce a cultural movement from a transcendent humanism to a purely immanent, secular one, to which most of us are willy-nilly exposed today. As summarized in the introduction of his magisterial opus, *A Secular Age*, Charles Taylor's main thesis is ". . . that the coming of modern secularity . . . has been conterminous with the rise of a society in which for the first time in history *a purely self-sufficient humanism* came to be a widely available option. I mean by this a humanism accepting no final goals beyond human flourishing, nor any allegiance to anything else beyond human flourishing"[69] (emphasis added). Taking Taylor at his word, if the current humanism is self-sufficient, it practically heightens the rank of humanity to that of a demigod.

A thoroughly secular, nontheistic humanism might happily coexist with certain expressions of Daoism or Buddhism[70] and be quite compatible with atheism, but it poses some major points of contention with theistic religions. Six to seven centuries ago, belonging to a theistic religion was not so much a viable option as it was the only way of life. But belonging to such a religion nowadays, ascribing to its view of the world, and adopting its practices is, in our pluralistic culture, viewed as just one lifestyle option among many. For many atheists, as explained above, the natural world is taken as the be-all and the end-all of reality. This, an illegitimate extension of epistemological scientism (all knowledge is necessarily scientific knowledge) to an ontological and metaphysical view of reality (matter and energy is all there is), supports a belief system based on an airtight this-worldly immanence. In it, every entity—even the sacred, conceived of as merely one entity among innumerable others—is of and in the natural cosmos. And insofar the philosopher Tim Crane is correct, in some sense the transcendent can be found in it. It is therefore an immanent transcendence and not the absolute transcendence that characterizes, for instance, the theistic Abrahamic religions.[71] In such a world the promoters of nontheistic, secular ersatz-religions, prominently present on both sides of the Atlantic, are the apostles whose mission is to convert humankind to their tenets and creeds, an effort that will surely be thwarted by the missionaries of the genuine theistic religions.

Looking back on the walk along our winding scholarly road, we can see that the relation between science and religion is characterized by their noticeably

69. Charles Taylor, *A Secular Age* (Harvard University Press, 2007), 18.

70. Stephen Batchelor, *Buddhism Without Beliefs: A Contemporary Guide to Awakening* (Penguin Group, 1998).

71. Franke, *On the Universality of What Is Not*, 222–25.

overlapping as well as their distinctive features. Unfortunately, because the nature of the so-called cultural clashes over the past three decades has raised confrontational temperatures in theists and atheists alike, center stage among the possible relations between science and religion has been assumed by the conflict thesis. Although theists like me are open to dialogue, any talk among the most ardent neoatheists of accommodation between science and religion based on independence or dialogue, let alone compatibility or harmony, is heresy. For them, religion is the avowed enemy of science, reason, and cultural progress. The evidence indicating that neoatheist scientism in particular perpetuates this conflict marks the following three parts of the book. The nature of the conflict is not ascribable to a single cause. It has various roots, some of them historical, others philosophical or metaphysical, still others theological. On the side of modern science, the single factor that most contributes to the conflict between science and religion appears to be the adoption—for purely methodological reasons—of a metaphysics of a nontheistic naturalism. On the side of religion, the single factor that most contributes to the same conflict appears to be an insistence on the metaphysical stance of a theistic extra- or supernaturalism. Given this ongoing oppositional cultural impact of science and religion, it will be the task of an ever-updatable theology of nature, such as the one outlined in chapter 9, to dwell in the space opened between these two metaphysical stances and there take on the role of mediator in the conflict between scientistic atheists and religionist theists. The hard-core neoatheists like Richard Dawkins and Jerry Coyne and the hard-core, scripturally literalist, young-earthers notwithstanding, the hope is that the introduction of the best rationally defensible facts that science and theology have to offer will—in the metaphysical space opened up between immanent naturalism and transcendent supernaturalism—promote in the purveyors on both sides of the current science religion conflict a less contentious and more dialogical relationship.

PART 1

The Science of Religion and the Science of Religion and Its Partners, Morality and Art

The spell that I say *must* be broken is the taboo against a forthright, scientific, no-holds-barred investigation of religion as one natural phenomenon among many.

Daniel Dennett, *Breaking the Spell*, p. 17

When scientists purport to treat religion in the same way that they treat heat or electricity, there is every reason to suspect that they are constructing monuments to their own stupidity.

Jean-Pierre Dupuy, *The Mark of the Sacred*, p. 91

CHAPTER 1

Neuroscientific, Developmental, and Evolutionary Sciences of Religion

Theists and atheists alike can agree on what at first sight seems to be a less contentious relation between religion and science—namely, that religion was and is a topic of scientific investigation. Yet, as is evident from the above two epigraphs and from what follows below, some contentiousness still plagues this relation.

The roots of the modern scientific study of religion reach back into the 19th century.[1] Contributors to the study of religion consisted of philosophers, historians, anthropologists, archaeologists, folklorists, ethnographers, philologists, sociologists, and psychologists. Most of these disciplines contribute to religious studies to this day. Covering the vast literature accumulated over the many decades by these disciplines is beyond the scope of the present book. For that reason, I will focus on developments in the scientific study of religion beginning in the 1990s. Since then, four areas of research that have become particularly prominent are evolutionary anthropology, evolutionary psychology, developmental psychology, and cognitive neuroscience. Jointly, they comprise the mainstay of current sciences of religion.

Since the beginning of the 20th century, when scholars like Max Weber, Émile Durkheim, and William James made their sociological, anthropological, and psychological studies, the scientific studies of religion have largely assumed a *methodological* atheism. This need not imply that modern scientists are necessarily atheistic; in fact, many are theists. Yet to qualify as modern, a science (such as physics, chemistry, and biology) must subscribe to the *methodological constraint* that supernatural influences have no place in explanations of natural phenomena. It follows that current scientific studies of religion generally follow suit by adopting this methodological constraint. This *naturalizing* of scientific studies of religion is expressed in Dennett's epigraph above. However, as the epigraph of the French philosopher Jean-Pierre Dupuy indicates, such naturalizing may not do justice to a more comprehensive study of religion. Dupuy places his brief epigraph in the following longer passage.

> I now turn to the following question: is it possible to imagine a science concerned with the universal phenomenon of religion in human societies

1. Kwame Anthony Appiah, "What Is a Science of Religion?," *Philosophy* 93, no. 4 (2018): 485–503; Marjorie Wheeler-Barclay, *The Science of Religion in Britain, 1860–1915* (University of Virginia Press, 2010).

> that is nonetheless completely freed of any connection with religion, in the manner of astronomy, for example, developed by detaching itself from the belief that the stars exert an influence on human beings, and therefore, in particular, on astronomers . . . ? [Earlier] I likened the work of René Girard [which has contributed to our understanding of religion] to the Einsteinian revolution in physics. Yet Girard admits that his [anthropological] theory of religion is completely dependent on religion from which it derives its claims to knowledge. *Here we find the object of a science acting upon science itself.* The challenge this presents to the dominant positivism of the modern age can scarcely be underestimated. When scientists purport to treat religion in the way they treat heat or electricity, there is every reason to suspect that they are constructing monuments to stupidity. . . .
>
> One can speak of religion only by immersing oneself in it, by bringing to bear not only all the resources of the intellect but also the whole emotional range of one's being—in other words, by engaging one's convictions and beliefs as fully as possible. Our being is indissolubly bound up with religion, no less than it is bound up with society and history, even when we examine these things critically and seek to demystify them. As [Blaise] Pascal famously said to those who doubt God's existence "[I]l faut parier; cela n'est pas voluntaire, vous êtes embarqé [You have to wager; it's not voluntary, you have to climb on board]." There is no escaping uncertainty; whether we like it or not, we have to place our bets.
>
> This is why it is useless to speak of religion in the third person, adopting the sort of disinterested attitude that is appropriate to a scientific investigation on the positivistic model. Those who speak this way typically find that they cannot avoid betraying the hatred they feel toward religion. It is altogether natural, then, that they should hold it at arm's length, holding their noses against the stench it gives off—not out of a concern for scientific objectivity, but because of the stinking abuse and ridicule they themselves heaped on it. Understanding the least thing about religion in this case is quite obviously impossible.[2]

Despite Dupuy's cutting critique of positivist, third-person approaches to the study of religion, many scientists currently take a hard-line naturalistic approach to the study of religion, while some of them indeed hold religion "at arm's length, holding their noses against the stench it gives off. . . ."

The Peculiarity of Religion: An Object of Derision in Its Scientific Study

The combination of neuroscientific, cognitive-science, developmental, and evolutionary-science approaches to the study of religion took off auspiciously and confidently at the turn of the 21st century, promising to give us new, natural-

2. Jean-Pierre Dupuy, *The Mark of the Sacred* (Stanford University Press, 2013), 90–91.

science based explanations of religion. Among other scientists advocating and practicing this approach are the scientistically-inspired anthropologist and cognitive scientist Pascal Boyer—who, keeping religion at arm's length, holds his nose against stench he has heaped on it—and the evolutionary psychologist and anthropologist Scott Atran who, more cautious than Boyer, avoids explicit denigration of religions. However, in their respective 2001 and 2002 publications, *Religion Explained: The Evolutionary Origins of Religious Thought* and *In Gods We Trust: The Evolutionary Landscape of Religion*, neither was shy about criticizing approaches to the study of religion that were not naturalized like their pet approach, cognitive evolutionary psychology. Equally wedded to a scientistically-inspired worldview, the philosopher Daniel Dennett, who, as a prominent neoatheist advocates the elimination of religions from the public sphere, somewhat belatedly hopped on the Boyer-Atran train with his 2006 publication of *Breaking the Spell: Religion as a Natural Phenomenon*, and advocated to the larger reading public a purely naturalistic approach to the scientific study of religion. Of course, not all practitioners of the human and natural sciences are as brazen as Boyer and Dennett in their contempt or animus towards religion. Yet to highlight this anti-religious, scientistically inspired antipathy to religion, it's worthwhile to cite the additional comments made by Dupuy:

> The literature I wish to examine, a rather unappetizing one it must be said, is a by-product of attempts made by cognitivists in biology, psychology, and anthropology to account for religion in terms of evolutionary theory. Religion stands revealed instead as their stumbling block, their *skándalon*. . . . The ethologist and evolutionary biologist Richard Dawkins argues that religious beliefs are irrational, nonsensical, and pathological; that they spread like a virus, infecting the brains they attack; that they have spread like parasites, vermin, and cockroaches, infesting human populations; and that we should be ashamed of holding them. [Blaise] Pascal's Wager is the wager of a coward, we are told. As for the Gospels, the only thing that separates them from *The Da Vinci Code* is that this is modern fiction, whereas they are an ancient fiction. The cognitive anthropologist Pascal Boyer, even if he has a less vulgar way of putting things, will not be outdone when it comes to ironic derision and facile humiliation. Rituals are nothing more than "gadgets." More than this, because there is "something dramatically flawed *in principle* about religion as a way of knowing things," it is unsurprising that the Church should have lost the war of ideas: in its long competition with science to explain "what happens in the world . . . every battle has been lost [by the Church] and conclusively so. . . ."[3]

3. Dupuy, *The Mark of the Sacred*, 91–93. What Dupuy is saying here is that, without a prior adequate understanding of religion and of God, the anti-theistic scientific study of religion cannot be adequate to a thorough scientific understanding of religion. Regarding the hostile anti-theistic view of religion and God, Henri de Lubac, SJ (*The Drama of Atheist*

> [Moreover,] Boyer recounts a personal anecdote that Dawkins finds especially revealing, so much so that he quotes from it and then devotes almost a page to commenting on it. The challenge these authors have set for themselves is to understand how human beings, people like you and me, can believe unbelievable things, such as the existence of a mountain that is alive and feeds on animals that are sacrificed to it. Explaining this challenge, and his method of meeting it, to a prominent Catholic theologian, Boyer was "dumbfounded" when the divine turned to him and said: "That is what makes anthropology so fascinating and so difficult too. You have to explain *how people can believe such nonsense*."
>
> Fearing that the reader will fail to understand why, Dawkins hastens to list the nonsensical beliefs that a Christian is supposed to entertain, none of them less absurd than stories of flying witches who cast spells on their victims or invisible dragons that wear cologne [and more]. . . .[4]

However, what seemed to fly over Boyer's and Dawkins's atheistically disposed heads was the possibility that the Catholic theologian was ironically referring not to Catholic doctrine but instead to the beliefs of the Fang people that Boyer had been studying and to the beliefs in flying witches, invisible dragons, or orbiting teapots. By stirring dragons, witchcraft, and the Catholic religion and theology in the same kettles, the likes of Dawkins and Boyer imply that the latter is also no more than such witchcraft nonsense. I contend that this denigration and hostility toward particularly the Christian religion is a natural—in the sense of a readily deducible—consequence of an atheistic scientism, an ersatz-religion discussed at greater length in the introduction and in chapter 7. Going beyond the naturalistic, *non*theistic approach to the scientific study of religion adopted by Atran, Dawkins's and Boyer's encounter with religion and theology is negative and *anti*theistic. Ironically, they hold religious and theological approaches to the study of religion at arm's length while all along their views are indebted and tied to the very things, religion and theology, that they denigrate. For, in referring to such antitheists, the philosopher and theologian David Alcalde states insightfully that "Their engagement in the very enterprise [of religion and theology] that they reject, albeit in the negative form of an intellectually lazy atheism with a cartoon God, is evident to everyone but themselves."[5] That is to say, even antitheists like Boyer and Dawkins cannot escape their metaphysically negative religious and theological presuppositions.

Humanism [Ignatius Press, 1995], 181) notes the following: "The anti-theist—the militant atheist—claims to know God, otherwise he could not oppose him. But by that very fact, and whatever he may say, he in not really opposing God. For God [and the religions he inspires] cannot be known in that [oppositional] way."

4. Dupuy, *The Mark of the Sacred*, 94.

5. David Alcalde, *Cosmology Without God? The Problematic Theology Inherent in Modern Cosmology* (Wipf & Stock, 2019), x.

That noted, it is also important to add that, only a year after the publication of Dennett's book, the experimental psychologist Justin Barrett, who seems to be kindly disposed to religion, responded to such anti-religious developments by noting that the religious spell bemoaned by Dennett was by no means broken by the new cognitivist science of religion and that believers had no reason, based on this new science, to empty the church pews.[6] Moreover, as Barrett pointed out, the use of cognitive- and evolutionary-science findings and conclusions to critique religion can in several cases also apply to the new science of religion itself. After all, from an evolutionary-psychology perspective, new developments in the cognitive-science study of religion are themselves cultural products that, like religions, can be viewed as mere byproducts of natural evolutionary developments. Consequently, if we apply the naturalist approach to the scientific study of not only religion but also science itself, then even worse, as pointed out by the theologian John Haught, "The naturalistic view of reality, if taken consistently, leads to self-subverting of all truth claims, including those of science."[7]

What the above illustrates clearly is that what motivates the neurocognitive and evolutionary approaches of some scientists to the study of religion is premised on varieties of scientistic worldviews that are vocally hostile to the very object of their study. While other natural scientists such as atheist physicists might also share scientistic worldviews that deride religion, they do not denigrate their own objects of study such as subatomic, astrophysical, or biological phenomena. Yet, as noted above by Haught and apparently going unrecognized by these scientists, their religiously hostile, naturalistic worldviews they hold, as well as the natural sciences they practice, are also philosophically self-defeating. Therefore, they too are open to the derision that they heap on religious phenomena. Included in scientistic worldviews are, among others, reductionism, positivism, physicalism, naturalism, and Darwinism (I will henceforth refer to all of these as physicalism or naturalism, unless other nomenclature is contextually called for). What should be noted here is that none of these variants of scientism adequately accounts for several inscrutable aspects of existence, especially the existences of the universe, of the origin of life in its myriad manifestations, and of consciousness as an immaterial entity.

Setting the Stage: The Importance of Consciousness in Religious Experiences

What will become evident below (see additionally appendices 1–2) is that, among other things, the existence of consciousness poses an irresolvable problem to any of the above reductively motivated approaches to research, not only in the physical and natural sciences but also, especially, in the scientific study of reli-

6. Justin L. Barrett, "Is the Spell Really Broken? Bio-Psychological Explanations of Religion and Theistic Belief," *Theology and Science* 5, no. 1 (2007): 57–72.

7. Haught, *Christianity and Science*, 18.

gion. Regarding a concept of reality more capacious than the physical and material ones, the philosopher Daniel Robinson pointedly remarks, ". . . there is no more a 'problem' of consciousness than there is a 'problem' of bivalent atoms; *it is simply one of the constituents of reality*. That is, it is not problematic in and of itself. Rather, it becomes problematic only on the further assumption that (i) all really existing items are physical and (ii) mental properties as such do not exist at all or, if they exist, they exist dependently on [and as mere byproducts of] physical properties"[8] (emphasis added). It only turns into a problem under metaphysically reductive, physicalist presuppositions. Consciousness, therefore, as has additionally been argued by several other philosophers[9] and as I have pointed out in appendix 1, constitutes a *sui generis* fact, item, or constituent of a reality that is distinct from any material or natural constituent of purely physical reality. And in line with Daniel Robinson's comments, the philosopher Benedikt Göcke equally tersely notes "that not all facts are physical facts, and that physical facts do not entail all facts," leading him to further emphasize that this "*is what dualists said all along*."[10] In other words, according to Göcke the reality accessible to our senses and intellect has an irreducible dual—perhaps even a plural—quality. And I claim that any scientist or scientifically cognizant philosopher who denies this does so, as the philosopher J. P. Moreland has pointed out, either (i) because of his or her deep-seated fear and aversion to physicalism's or naturalism's alternative (namely, the supernatural realm—more on this later),[11] or (ii) because his or her intellect, fully and pre-reflectively immersed in its phenomenal world, takes no explicit note of consciousness at all. For, in our daily lives the fact that consciousness is so extremely important, so basic to what we are and do, is lost in our occasional daydreams or is buried under the reflective cogitations that dominate and occupy the intellect while it is focusing on the demands posed by mundane or professional problems.

A Crucial Question and Its Implications

To preface what follows in the (sub)sections below, let's pose an important question asked by Alexander and Andrew Fingelkurts in the title of their article: Is our brain hardwired to produce God, or is our brain hardwired to perceive God?[12] The question raises a crucial point. What humans refer to as God either is merely an invention or product of the human mind that is projected onto

8. Daniel N. Robinson, *Consciousness and Mental Life* (Columbia University Press, 2008), 19.

9. Benedikt Paul Göcke, introduction to *After Physicalism*, ed. Benedikt Paul Göcke (University of Notre Dame Press, 2012), 1–24; Moreland, *Consciousness and the Existence of God*; Howard Robinson, "Qualia, Qualities, and Our Conception of the Physical World," in *After Physicalism*, ed. Benedikt Paul Göcke (University of Notre Dame Press, 2012), 234–37.

10. Göcke, *After Physicalism*, 5.

11. Moreland, *Consciousness and the Existence of God*, 157.

12. Fingelkurts and Fingelkurts, "Is Our Brain Hardwired."

some aspect of reality or else God constitutes the Supreme Reality that is revealed to and, thus, perceived and discovered by the human mind. For some atheistically inclined scientists and philosophers, just as consciousness is nothing but a nonreal epiphenomenon of the brain's biophysical activity, God and religion are not *sui generis* realities but merely byproducts of the human intellect. For others, however, consciousness, God, and religion are taken to be valid realities per se.

In the last several decades, the number of journals devoted to the study of religion and of its positive and negative effects on the well-being of humans has increased immensely. By now the number of research studies and reviews of such scientific studies of religion that have appeared in these journals and in other journals that are not devoted specifically to the study of religion runs into many hundreds. Presenting an in-depth overview of all this literature is beyond the task and the scope of this book. Nevertheless, we will see below how the human intellect deploys several key research strategies and programs directed at exploring religion as a natural, biocultural fact, and therefore subject to investigation by the natural and human sciences. Only some of the most relevant published findings obtained by neuroscientific, developmental, and cognitive-evolutionary research approaches will be reviewed.

Over the past few decades, the neuroscience of many mental functions and capacities has increasingly relied on sophisticated, noninvasive brain-imaging techniques such as magnetic resonance imaging (MRI), single-photon emission computed tomography (SPECT), positron emission topography (PET), electroencephalography (EEG), and magnetoencephalography (MEG). Other, more invasive techniques rely on the study of patients—of course with their permission—whose brain structures are exposed during brain surgery (since surgical intervention in the brain itself does not result in pain, patients can remain calm and fully conscious during surgery).

Here, let's begin with a brief description of several regions in the human brain, very schematically depicted in figure 1.1. The left panel of figure 1.1 depicts the major subdivisions of the brain's cerebrum, including the neocortical frontal and temporo-parietal regions, and the subcortical thalamic regions, all of which play supporting roles in spiritual and religious cognitions and experiences.[13] Inspection of the left panel also shows, in very schematic, abbreviated form, that visual neural activity initiated in the occipital region travels up the cortical visual hierarchy, terminating eventually in the prefrontal/frontal areas. Important to note also is the fact that the long-range upward, feedforward projections to higher levels are in turn accompanied by a downward feedback projection to prior lower levels of processing. Also accompanying the long-range

13. Fingelkurts and Fingelkurts, "Is Our Brain Hardwired"; Dimitrios Kapogiannis et al., "Cognitive and Neural Foundations of Religious Belief," *Proceedings of the National Academy of Sciences USA* 106, no. 12 (2009): 4876–81; Andrew B. Newberg, "The Neuroscientific Study of Spiritual Practices," *Frontiers in Psychology* 5 (2014): 215.

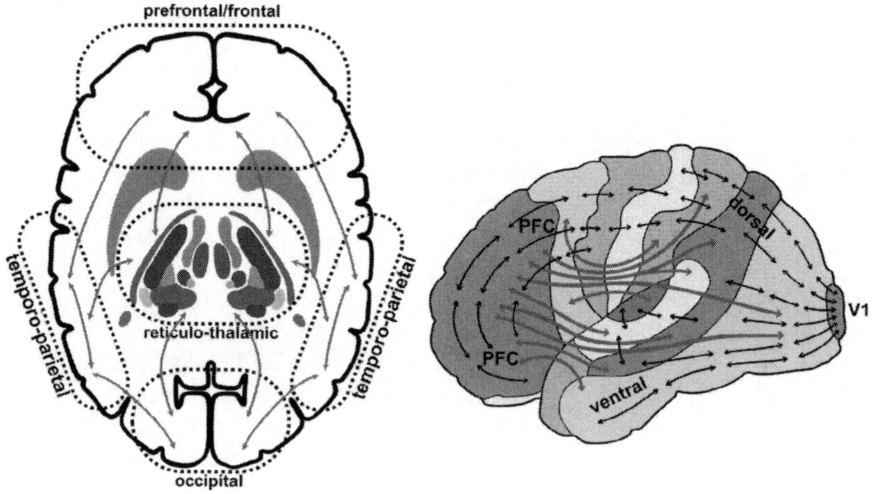

Figure 1.1. Neuroscientific Approaches to the Study of Religious and Spiritual Phenomena. ***Left***: Depiction of major subdivisions of the human brain involved in conscious visual perceptions. The region labeled "reticulo-thalamic" is located in the midbrain, below the neocortex, and its activity is crucial in supporting and maintaining a *global* conscious *state*. The grey two-ended arrows designate the feedforward-feedback connections between the major subdivisions. Given that a global conscious state is attained, *local* neural activities in the depicted neocortical (occipital, temporo-parietal, and prefrontal/frontal) areas of the neocortex are necessary for conferring on the manifold visuo-cognitive contents their important *trait* of consciousness. ***Right***: Schematic of a lateral view of the human visual neocortex with its numerous feedforward-feedback connections, beginning with area V1 (the primary visual cortex). The thinner black, two-ended arrows depict the shorter feedforward-feedback connections within areas of the dorsal and ventral cortical visual system all the way up to the PFC, the prefrontal cortex; the thicker grey, two-ended arrows depict, as the left panel does, the longer feedforward-feedback connections across different regions of the cortical visual system. The dorsal cortical pathways encode the locations of visual stimuli in the visual field; the ventral pathways encode various inherent features (color, shape, size, etc.) of the same stimuli. See text for additional information. Adapted from Fig. 1.1 in Bruno G. Breitmeyer, *The Visual (Un)Conscious and Its (Dis)Contents*, © Oxford University Press 2014, reproduced with permission of the Licensor through PLSclear.

interactions depicted in the left panel of figure 1.1 are a local, short-range feedforward-feedback organization shown in the right panel by the shorter two-ended black arrows. As in the left panel, the right panel of figure 1.1 also depicts, via the larger grey two-ended arrows, the global, long-range feedforward-feedback projections. In both cases of feedforward-feedback neural networks, the feedback connections are deemed essential supports of conscious visual per-

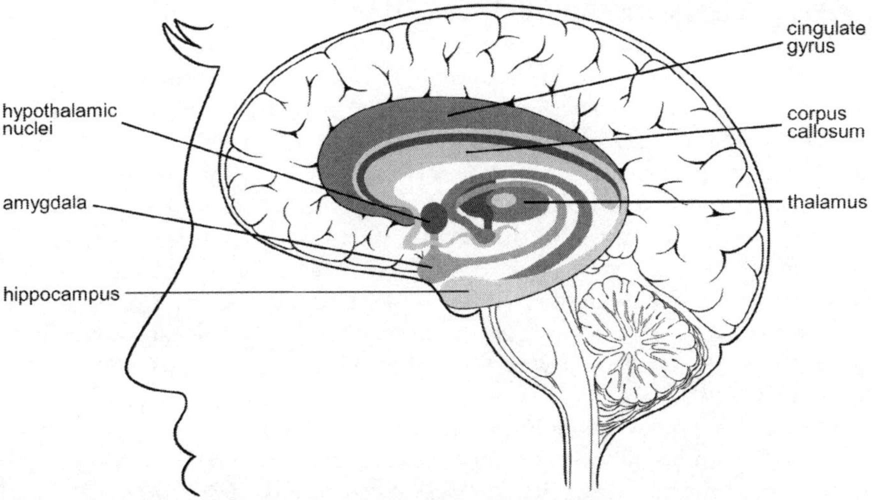

Figure 1.2. Depiction of the Human Brain's Limbic System. The limbic system, important for supporting mental imagery, memory, and the experience of basic emotions, is heavily connected with regions located in the neocortex lying above it. See text for additional information. Adapted from Wikimedia Commons [https://commons.wikimedia.org/wiki/File:1511_The_Limbic_Lobe.jpg], with permission.

ception (it may also be important to note here that the downward feedback projections significantly outnumber the upward feedforward ones). Of course, similar organization characterizes the conscious perceptions supported by other sensory systems such as the auditory, tactile, and somesthetic senses.

Figure 1.2 shows the essential components of the phylogenetically older and more primitive limbic system, a part of the brain that plays an important supporting role in memory and mental imagery, and in the emotional valences accompanying religious cognitions and experiences.[14] The reader not informed about cognitive neuroscience is encouraged to refer to these diagrams as we look at the ways that these brain areas relate to religious cognitions and experiences.

Several scholars and neuroscientists have provided thorough reviews of empirical studies of the biochemical and neuronal brain signatures associated with religious, spiritual, and mystical experiences (RSMEs).[15] Such experiences can arise spontaneously, without intent or preparation, but are more frequently elicited in settings specifically employed to induce these experiences, such as

14. R. Joseph, "The Limbic System and the Soul: Evolution and the Neuroanatomy of Religious Experience," *Zygon* 36, no. 1 (2001): 105–36; Newberg, "The Neuroscientific Study."

15. Fingelkurts and Fingelkurts, "Is Our Brain Hardwired?"; Newberg, "The Neuroscientific Study"; David Bryce Yaden et al., "Neuroscience and Religion: Surveying the Field," in *Religion: Mental Religion*, ed. Niki Kasumi Clements (Macmillan Publishers, 2016).

meditative and contemplative practices, private or communal prayer, and spiritual and religious rituals involving rhythmic chanting, music, and dance. Their induction during sacred rituals also can be assisted by ingestion of several psychoactive substances such as psilocybin (found in the psilocybin mushroom) or mescaline (found in the peyote cactus), and they additionally can be a side effect of brain pathologies such as epileptic seizures, usually originating in the temporal cortex, and brain lesions produced accidentally or incidentally during a required neurosurgery. The regions of the normal, healthy human brain most heavily implicated in RSMEs are the prefrontal, frontal, temporal, parietal, limbic, and thalamic areas.[16] It should be pointed out that although these interconnected and interactive areas constitute an extensive neural network, each component of the network may be activated (or deactivated) differentially by the RSMEs associated with variable types of religious cognitions and experiences.[17] To illustrate this, let's look at the limbic system illustrated in figure 1.2. As the neuroscientist Rhawn Joseph explains, the "ancient limbic system includes the hypothalamus, amygdala, cingulate gyrus, septal nuclei, and hippocampus . . . , [and] these limbic nuclei are primary in regard to memory, the production of visual imagery, and the expression and perception of most aspects of emotion, including love, sadness, grief, depression, fear, aggression, rage, pleasure, happiness, elation and even sexual and religious ecstasy."[18] Since memory, visual imagery, and emotions are common experiential constituents of participants engaged in religious services, rituals, and contemplative practices, it is expected that the limbic system plays a prominent role in supporting the experiences elicited in these settings. For example, according to what the 16th-century Carmelite St. John of the Cross describes in his *Dark Night of the Soul*, it is common for novices and even some advanced contemplative practitioners to have feelings of spiritual dryness, of no longer feeling the consoling presence of God, and of divine abandonment, all of which can resist any effort to be rid of them. At an emotional level, such experiences can take on various shades of sadness, grief, desolation, depression, and fear. Within the limbic system, for example, one would expect that these emotions would activate neuronal nuclei supporting these experiences. Yet, if the novice (or advanced) practitioner persists through this "purgative" phase, these experiences eventually can be replaced by those of utter elation, love, and ecstatic union with God, so evocatively expressed in Gian Lorenzo Ber-

16. Fingelkurts and Fingelkurts, "Is Our Brain Hardwired?"; Newberg, "The Neuroscientific Study"; Yaden et al., "Neuroscience and Religion."

17. Fingelkurts and Fingelkurts, "Is Our Brain Hardwired?"; Newberg, "The Neuroscientific Study"; Yaden et al., "Neuroscience and Religion"; Berkovich-Ohana et al., "Alterations in the Sense of Time, Space, and Body in the Mindfulness-Trained Brain: A Neurophenomenologically-Guided MEG Study," *Frontiers in Psychology* 4 (2013): 912; Joseph, "The Limbic System"; Urgesi et al,. "The Spiritual Brain: Selective Cortical Lesions Modulate Human Self-Transcendence," *Neuron* 65, no. 3 (2010): 309–19.

18. Joseph, "The Limbic System," 112.

nini's sculpture of St. John's Carmelite friend, St. Teresa of Avila. Here, one would expect that these latter emotions would activate other limbic nuclei supporting these ecstatic experiences. As a second example, brain areas that are activated by experientially rich, concrete, and imageable religious knowledge differ from the areas activated by experientially poor, abstract, and doctrinal religious knowledge.[19] Finally, as a third example, prayer practices tend to activate more strongly those brain regions associated with processing social, interpersonal relations than do most practices, such as meditation, that tend to focus more on individual intrapersonal aspects of religious experience.[20] Although one could go on listing additional nuanced experiences that are correlated with specific activation patterns in the brain's neural networks, I will forego such listing and hope the above examples give the reader an idea of how variations of religious and spiritual experiences and cognitions tend to correlate with differences in the brain's neural activation patterns.

No doubt, by employing the various brain-imaging methods noted above and perhaps newer and more sophisticated ones, future studies of the neural and even the neuropharmacological correlates may reveal ever clearer differences among the variable aspects of religious knowledge and experience. However, it is not clear whether such increase of knowledge will answer the question posed just prior to the beginning of this section: Is our brain wired to produce God, or is our brain wired to perceive God? The next section further addresses this question.

Developmental Approaches to the Study of Religion and Spirituality

As noted by the developmental psychologist Paul Bloom, the developmental acquisition of religious beliefs and cognitions is as natural a phenomenon as is the acquisition of language.[21] Both may rely on innately given but underdeveloped predispositions priming and supporting their development. However, because religion is regarded worldwide by most of its practitioners, including of course some developmental psychologists, as a sacrosanct domain, developmental studies of religion may be regarded by some of them as hands-off, taboo endeavors. In particular, religious individuals may "react negatively . . . [especially] to the claim made by many cognitive scientists that religious belief is an evolutionary accident, an unexpected by-product of cognitive systems that have evolved for other purposes."[22] That issue put aside for the time being, let's briefly explore some of the key concepts and findings regarding the developmental acquisition of religion.

19. Kapogiannis et al., "Cognitive and Neural Foundations."
20. Yaden et al., "Neuroscience and Religion," 289.
21. Paul Bloom, "Religion Is Natural," *Developmental Science* 10, no. 1 (2007): 147–51.
22. Bloom, "Religion Is Natural," 148.

It should be obvious that a good proportion of religious practices and cognitions, especially those practices and doctrinal beliefs expressed in a particular religion, are acquired via culturally transmitted information obtained from parents, peers, schoolteachers, and religious instructors. Being culturally distinct, these practices and doctrinal beliefs cannot be considered as religious universals. Nonetheless, there is evidence that such universals do exist.[23] As noted by Alexander and Andrew Fingelkurts, it "is striking that people from different religions (and cultures) experience certain *common* religious phenomena, for example, the feeling of timelessness, divine love, and being at one with the universe or divine being . . . , [and that these] religious experiences exist in all stages of individual development: from infancy through adolescence into adulthood. . . . Indeed, the literature in this field [of developmental psychology] attests to the profound religious experience in children. . . . This experience in children may be conditioned by children's 'intuitive theism' (a default theory of the world) which is independent on [sic] cultural-environmental input from parents' religiosity (atheism/theism), story books and family conversations. . . . Religious experience is a fundamental and universal characteristic of human being [*sic*]."[24]

Largely seconding this assessment of the universal aspects of religious experience are the reviews of developmental research on religious cognitions and experiences provided by Tyler Greenway and Justin Barrett and, separately, by Pamela King and Chris Boyatzis. The former two reviewers maintain that cognitive scientists studying religion "have argued that religious beliefs and practices are common and persistent because they are natural . . . [in the sense that they] refer to ways of thinking or abilities that are a normal part of development . . . [such that] these natural cognitive structures facilitate pancultural beliefs in superhuman beings, some kind of afterlife, and other religious ideas. . . . In this way, evolved cognitive systems undergird [religious] cultural evolution."[25] Additionally, the extensive review of life-span religious and spiritual development from infancy through adolescence into adulthood provided by the second pair of reviewers notes that "a spiritual propensity in very young children presupposes that children are spiritual beings first and then are acculturated (or not) within a religious tradition that channels inchoate spirituality into particular institutional expressions (rituals, creeds, etc.). . . . Children possess powerful inference mechanisms for intuitively sorting out [physical] reality and the supernatural. Such intuition is integrated with increasing reflection and is

23. Bloom, "Religion Is Natural," 148; Fingelkurts and Fingelkurts, "Is Our Brain Hardwired?"

24. Fingelkurts and Fingelkurts, "Is Our Brain Hardwired?," 296. See also Deborah Kelemen, "Are Children 'Intuitive Theists'?: Reasoning About Purpose and Design in Nature," *Psychological Science* 15, no. 5 (2004): 295–301.

25. Tyler S. Greenway and Justin L. Barrett, "Evolutionary Developmental Psychology of Children's Religious Beliefs," in *The Oxford Handbook of Evolutionary Psychology and Religion*, ed. James R. Liddle and Todd K. Shackelford (Oxford University Press, 2021), 69.

supported and scaffolded by cultural practices that orient the child to cultural modes of spiritual knowing and being."[26]

Let us now examine some of the more important developmental milestones believed to naturally mark children's reliance on these powerful inference mechanisms and the religious cognitions and beliefs they can yield. I take the "naturalness" of inferential thinking to mean something like what Justin Barrett refers to as "its degree of fluency, ease, automaticity, and reflexivity."[27]

Agency Detection

Why do cognitive scientists regard agency detection as important to our understanding of religion? Watching any of several nature programs on the PBS television network can give a hint to an answer. Consider hungry predators such as lions or leopards in the African Serengeti, continuously on alert for so-far unseen and undetected prey such as gazelles; or, vice versa, gazelles feeding on the shrubs and grasses, continuously on alert for so-far unseen and undetected predators. For individuals of these mammalian species, it is important to be continuously on the alert and on the lookout for the potential presence of their prey or predators. Regardless of whether an animal is prey or predator, it is clear that it acts accordingly. Since humans also belong to a mammalian species, when they went hunting tens of thousands of years ago for prey in the wild, they too had to be not only watchful for their prospective prey but also especially alert for potentially dangerous predators that they might encounter along the way. For both types of alertness, cognitive psychologists have suitably invented the acronym HADD, which stands for hyperactive agency-detection device.[28] Now consider the fact that nearly all religions, past and present, subscribe to beliefs in unseen spirits, gods, or a God. With HADD in mind, cognitive psychologists could readily hypothesize that belief in unseen spiritual agents to be *merely a natural byproduct* of the evolved human tendency to be hyperalert for unseen prey or predator (see further below).

Theory-of-Mind Formation

Along with the development of agency detection, most toddlers can eventually also develop, if ever so gradually, what is known as a theory of mind. A "fully developed theory of mind allows a normal human being to consider the goals, preferences, desires, emotions, visual perspectives, and beliefs of

26. Pamela Ebstyne King and Chris J. Boyatzis, "Religious and Spiritual Development," in *Handbook of Child Psychology and Developmental Science: Socioemotional Processes*, vol. 3, ed. Michael E. Lamb and Richard M. Lerner (John Wiley & Sons, 2015), 979.

27. Justin L. Barrett, "The Relative Unnaturalness of Atheism: On Why Geertz and Markússon are Both Right and Wrong," *Religion* 40, no. 3 (2010): 169.

28. Justin L. Barrett, "Exploring the Natural Foundations of Religion," *Trends in Cognitive Sciences* 4, no. 1 (2000): 29–34.

others. . . ."[29] Very young children, under the age of 3 years, have not yet developed a workable theory of mind. To measure children's ability to "read" other people's minds, developmental psychologists present children with what's known as the false-belief task. As described by Tyler Greenway and Justin Barrett, in an example of this task, the Sally-Anne task, a

> child observes Sally [an adult experimenter] leaving a toy somewhere in a room, perhaps in a toy chest. Sally leaves the room. Anne [another adult experimenter] enters [the room] and moves the toy somewhere else, perhaps a drawer. Anne then also leaves. Sally returns and the children are asked to indicate where Sally will look for the toy. If children believe Sally will look for the toy where Anne left it (e.g., the drawer) they [toddlers that are 3 years old or younger] fail the task because they do not distinguish between reality (e.g., the toy is in the drawer) and Sally's belief about reality (e.g., the toy is still in the toy chest). If, however, [somewhat older] children indicate that Sally will look for the toy where she left it (e.g., . . . the toy chest) they pass the task because they demonstrate that they are capable of distinguishing between reality and Sally's belief about reality.[30]

It follows that, since the older but not the younger children have the ability to correctly infer the contents of agents' minds, only the older children can then transfer their theory of mind to supernatural agents such as ghosts, spirits, and gods or God.

Teleological Thinking

Children develop teleological or teleofunctional thinking and apply such thinking to all sorts of objects early in their lives.[31] The development of teleofunctional ideas, when coupled to the development of the theory of mind, can naturally lead to children's notion that creators of these objects intended and designed them with their functional purposes in mind.[32] Combined with developing notions of a god, these creator notions can readily attach to the further notions of purpose and design in a world fashioned by a Creator God.[33]

29. Greenway and Barrett, "Evolutionary Developmental Psychology," 72.

30. Greenway and Barrett, "Evolutionary Developmental Psychology," 72.

31. Deborah Kelemen, "The Scope of Teleological Thinking in Preschool Children," *Cognition* 70, no. 3 (1999): 241–72; Kelemen, "Are Children 'Intuitive Theists'?"; Deborah Kelemen and Cara DiYanni, "Intuitions About Origins: Purpose and Intelligent Design in Children's Reasoning About Nature," *Journal of Cognition and Development* 6, no. 1 (2005): 3–31.

32. E. Margaret Evans, "Cognitive and Contextual Factors in the Emergence of Diverse Belief Systems: Creation Versus Evolution," *Cognitive Psychology* 42, no. 3 (2001): 217–66; Kelemen, "Are Children 'Intuitive Theists'?"; Kelemen and DiYanni, "Intuitions About Origins."

33. Kelemen, "Are Children 'Intuitive Theists'?"; Kelemen and DiYanni, "Intuitions About Origins."

Dualistic Thinking

Children tend to be natural, intuitive dualists.[34] Accordingly, the tendency toward mind-body dualism can lead to early beliefs that individuals can exist in two separate realities, the material and corporal and the immaterial mental and spiritual. This in turn can lead to beliefs in an afterlife, as indicated in both young (4–6 years old) and older (10–12 years old) children's beliefs that mental entities survive biological death.[35] Mental or spiritual entities that are believed to be immortal can take on strange, counterintuitive characteristics. In some cultures, older children and adults believe ghosts (e.g., of deceased ancestors) and spirits to be agents that not only are invisible but also can pass through walls to monitor a person's private actions and conduct, abilities that violate children's intuitive ideas of physical impermeability of solid substances. Strangely, such *minimally counterintuitive ideas* about ghosts and spirits are thought to increase their memorial salience and may facilitate the spread of religious ideas.[36]

In summary, except for the formation of counterintuitive ideas, the abilities to apply theory of mind, teleological thinking, and dualistic thinking develop naturally, intuitively, and early in children. Children's acquisition of religious beliefs may be facilitated by such natural developmental tendencies, thus accounting for the naturalness of religious belief and for children being natural believers.[37]

I return now to the question posed by Alexander and Andrew Fingelkurts: Is our brain hardwired to produce God, or is our brain hardwired to perceive God? A positive answer to the first alternative is highlighted in the neuroscientific work of Kapogiannis and coworkers, when they conclude that their "findings support the view that religiosity is integrated in cognitive processes and brain networks used in social cognitions rather than being *sui generis*. . . ."[38] Again, implicit in this conclusion is the idea that religion is merely a byproduct of naturally acquired cognitive processes. However, other neuroscientists (I included) are open to considering religious and theological implications of their findings. We shall see in the next section that endorsing or opting for the inference that religion is merely and nothing but a cognitive byproduct of the brain—while dominant in the cognitive and evolutionary sciences—is itself merely a

34. Bloom, "Religion Is Natural"; Chudek et al., "Do Minds Switch Bodies? Dualist Interpretations Across Ages and Societies," *Religion, Brain & Behavior* 8, no. 4 (2018): 354–68.

35. Jessie M. Bering and David F. Bjorklund, "The Natural Emergence of Reasoning About the Afterlife as a Developmental Regularity," *Developmental Psychology* 40, no. 2 (2004): 217–33.

36. Barrett, "Is the Spell Really Broken?"; Pascal Boyer, *Religion Explained: The Evolutionary Origins of Religious Thought* (Basic Books, 2001).

37. Justin L. Barrett, *Born Believers: The Science of Children's Religious Belief* (The Free Press, 2012).

38. Kapogiannis et al., "Cognitive and Neural Foundations," 4879.

reflection and example of a pretheoretical bias. In other words, the second alternative, that our brains are hardwired to form *sui generis* religious conceptions and perceptions of God, cannot be ruled out.

Evolutionary Approaches to the Study of Religion and Spirituality

The present section explores at greater length evolutionary accounts of consciousness and mind and how they might add to our understanding of religion. In the following discussion, the term "evolutionary epistemology" will come up. It refers to a widely used approach to epistemology, with roots traceable to Darwin's speculations of how the human mind's capacity to explore and acquire information about the world evolved. It was subsequently adopted and refined by psychologists, philosophers, and ethologists, among them most notably James Mark Baldwin (1861–1934), Jean Piaget (1896–1980), Konrad Lorenz (1903–1989), Karl Popper (1902–1994) and Donald T. Campbell (1916–1996). The term has been applied in two meaningful ways. It can mean either (i) the acquisition, through biological evolution, of human traits that allow us to perceive, know, and act in the world; or, (ii) the use of key notions found in the theory of biological evolution as conceptual tools to explore how analogously various types of knowledge and other cultural products arise, develop, proliferate, and go extinct in the course of sociocultural evolution. Regarding the latter meaningful application, novel ideas, intuitions, explanatory hypotheses, theories, artistic styles, religious sects, or some other entities trying to make a lasting sociocultural impact compete, survive, flourish, or eventually become passé and perish within the larger social and cultural environs, much like biological species competing for survival in their natural environments.[39] In the

39. According to Karl Popper (*Objective Knowledge: An Evolutionary Approach* [Oxford University Press, 1979], chapter 4) these cultural products reside in World 3. Although World 3 transcends and is independent of the physical World 1 and the subjective World 2 of individual minds, all three worlds can interact with each other. World 3 includes a vast number of human cultural products. On page 38 of Karl R. Popper and John C. Eccles's book, *The Self and Its Brain: An Argument for Interactionism* (Springer, 1977), Popper elaborates as follows: "By World 3 I mean the world of the products of the human mind, such as stories, explanatory myths, tools, scientific theories (whether true or false), scientific problems, social institutions, and works of art [and the list could go on]." Any content of World 3 clearly predates the similar notion of a "meme," a neologism coined by Richard Dawkins (*The Selfish Gene* [Oxford University Press, 1976]), a notion that has caught the attention of students of cultural evolution (e.g., Susan Blackmore, *The Meme Machine* [Oxford University Press, 1999]; Daniel C. Dennett, *Consciousness Explained* [Little, Brown & Co., 1991]) and more recently has found a busy niche in the internet. Although Dawkins sparingly devotes only a single sentence to Popper, it seems to me that memes are renamed residents of Popper's World 3 that have also found residence in the individual subjective minds constituting World 2. Is it any wonder that

following, the term "evolutionary epistemology" will be applied only in the second sense; whereas the term "evolutionary cognition" or "evolutionary psychology" will be used only when applying the first sense, i.e., when, as De Cruz et al. aptly put it, ". . . biological evolutionary forces, in particular natural selection, are important in shaping [human] cognition."[40]

Evolutionary psychology has, so to speak, branched off from the main trunk of psychology in an attempt to study and offer explanations for how human psychological traits and their behavioral expressions may have evolved via natural and sexual selection. In contrast to neuroscience, evolutionary psychology is of more recent provenance and more speculative.[41] For that reason, in the study of human cognition and behavior, evolutionary psychology relies heavily on developments and findings in the well-established discipline of neuroscience, as well as the broad field of cognitive and behavioral science composed of several subdisciplines: cognitive psychology, social psychology, anthropology, economics, artificial intelligence, and philosophy.

Evolutionary Psychology: Its Birth, Program, and Limits

The fields of evolutionary cognition and psychology are themselves still evolving and thus, in the second sense of evolutionary epistemology, face the struggle for survival among competing, at times highly critical, conceptual schemes and theories (see note 39 above). Combined, both disciplines claim to contribute to the understanding of a variety of human practices and the mental traits and functions that motivate and support them. Included among these are sensory perception, memory, reasoning, imagination, choice appraisal, decision-making, social (interpersonal) cognition, visual and performing arts, literary studies, criminology, sociopathy, sexuality, altruism, morality, science, and religion. In the present and following chapter, discussion will be limited to the studies of conscious mind and how they in turn relate to evolutionary-psychology studies of religion and one of its value-laden consociates, art[42] (The relation between art, morality, and religion and science are explored further in chapters 3–5).

---

a notion or practice that makes its entry into culture (like the neologism "meme" itself) can, via sundry World 1 communication channels, mimetically "replicate," spread, and catch on?

40. Helen De Cruz et al., "Evolutionary Approaches to Epistemic Justification," *Dialectica* 65, no. 4 (2011): 518.

41. For a précis of evolutionary psychology and a source of references useful to the reader interested in further study of the topic, see J. C. Confer et al., "Evolutionary Psychology: Controversies, Questions, Prospects, and Limitations," *American Psychologist* 65, no. 2 (2010): 110–26.

42. More extensive accounts of the explanatory roles that evolutionary and cognitive science play in the studies of mind, religion, and theology are found in Helen De Cruz and Johan De Smedt, *A Natural History of Natural Theology: The Cognitive Science of Theology and Philosophy of Religion* (MIT Press, 2015).

No longer in its naked infancy, evolutionary psychology is experiencing the youthful and troubled exuberance of an adolescent. Like the conceptual reach of its older, sociobiological kin, the scope of evolutionary psychology is ambitious, since, like neuroscience, it attempts to cut broad swaths through many scholarly and scientific fields of study. For some of its critics, it is too ambitious and in need of trimming its imaginative and speculative narratives. Regarding the speculative nature of evolutionary psychology, one can quote Daniel Dennett's qualification that the "power of the theory of [evolution by] natural selection is not the power to prove exactly how (pre)history was, but only the power to prove how *it could have been* [emphasis added, given what we know [*not of how things actually were, but*] about how things are [now]."[43] Such conceptual "reverse engineering," consistent with the theory of biological evolution, of how something could possibly have become what it now is, leaves a lot of just-so, it-could-have-been leeway to imaginative faculties and their powers to speculate on how things might have come about. According to the philosopher Stephen Downes,[44] the basic theoretical tenets behind the reverse-engineering approach of evolutionary psychology, as outlined by the evolutionary psychologists John Tooby and Leda Cosmides,[45] are:

1. The brain is a computer designed by natural selection to extract information from the environment.
2. Individual human behavior is generated by this evolved computer in response to information it extracts from the environment. Understanding behavior requires articulating the cognitive programs that generate the behavior.
3. The cognitive programs of the human brain are adaptations. They exist because they produced behavior in our ancestors that enabled them to survive and reproduce.
4. Some of the cognitive programs of the human brain may not be adaptive now, although they were adaptive in ancestral environments.
5. Natural selection produced a brain composed of many different special purpose programs and not a domain general architecture.
6. Describing the evolved computational architecture of our brains "allows a systematic understanding of cultural and social phenomena."

Yet this ambitious, but debatable, set of tenets is confronted with a problem that applies to many theoretical scientific enterprises—namely, the problem of

43. Daniel C. Dennett, *Darwin's Dangerous Idea* (Touchstone, 1995), 319.

44. Stephen M. Downes, "Evolutionary Psychology," in *The Stanford Encyclopedia of Philosophy*, ed. Edward N. Zalta, Spring 2021, https://plato.stanford.edu/archives/spr2021/entries/ evolutionary-psychology.

45. John Tooby and Lea Cosmides, "Conceptual Foundations of Evolutionary Psychology," in *The Handbook of Evolutionary Psychology*, ed. David M. Buss (John Wiley & Sons, 2005).

the underdetermination of theory by evidence. Theoretical underdetermination occurs whenever scientific observations are not decisive in selecting the best of several possible theoretical explanations. Such explanatory looseness can give rise to what Raymond Tallis calls "Darwinitis,"[46] the facile and simplistic overreach of scholarly and popularly espoused explanations of human traits and behaviors, resulting in a proliferation of just-so stories that comprise evolutionary psychology. A similar assessment was also expressed some years ago by the ecological biologist Jerry Coyne, who otherwise is a fan of neo-Darwinian evolution.[47] Although Coyne's scathing criticism of the early, cruder evolutionary-psychology storytelling has softened somewhat in light of what he considers to be more sophisticated stories found in recent works, others (I included) still find these accounts too speculative.[48] Explicit examples of such storytelling and of the underdetermination of theory by evidence are left for discussions in chapter 2, where the fruits of the evolutionary-psychology approach to the study of religion are sorted and evaluated.

A well-thought-out article regarding the evolutionary-psychology approach was published in 2010 by Jamie Confer and colleagues. Although the article is quite informative, for a non-specialist it nevertheless raises some troubling questions. One can readily agree with Confer et al. that "understanding the evolved function of a psychological mechanism, or *why* it exists (often referred to as an **ultimate explanation**) provides a complementary level of analysis to that of understanding the details of *how* the mechanism works (often referred to as a **proximate explanation**). Both types of explanation are required for a complete understanding, and indeed they mutually inform one another."[49] The basic explanation in evolutionary psychology therefore rests on a combination of mechanistic (how) as well as teleofunctional (why) thinking. Within the larger Darwinian research program, the mechanistic explanation is provided by the *natural selection* of psychological and behavioral traits that promote the teleofunctional end results, the *survival* and *reproductive fitness* of species. Within this naturalistic framework, Confer et al. add the following points regarding hypothesis testing in evolutionary psychology.

> Often a hypothesis is embedded within a larger theoretical network. For example, one evolutionary *prediction* is that women will prefer men as potential mates who express a willingness to invest in them and their off-

46. Raymond Tallis, *Aping Mankind: Neuromania, Darwinitis and the Misrepresentation of Humanity* (Acumen, 2011).

47. Jerry A. Coyne, "Of Vice and Men: The Fairy Tales of Evolutionary Psychology," *The New Republic*, April 3, 2000.

48. As to the questionable claims made by evolutionary psychologists, see Robert C. Richardson, *Evolutionary Psychology as Maladapted Psychology* (MIT Press, 2007). His overall assessment of evolutionary psychology, based on methodological and evolutionary considerations, is that it is a speculative just-so storytelling.

49. Confer et al., "Evolutionary Psychology," 111.

> spring. . . . This is derived from the [proximate] *hypothesis* that in paternally investing species, females will use cues to a [male's] willingness to invest as a criterion for mate selection. In turn, this hypothesis is derived from [the intermediate] *parental investment theory*, which posits that the sex that invests more in its offspring will be the choosier sex when selecting mates. . . . Finally, the logic behind parental investment theory is derived from [the ultimate] *inclusive fitness theory*. . . , the modern [neo-Darwinian] formulation of evolution by natural selection. As in all realms of psychological science, the evaluation of each evolutionary psychological hypothesis, as well as the broader theories within which they are embedded, rests with the cumulative weight of the empirical evidence.[50]

Confer et al. go on to say that "although evolutionary psychology is a relatively young field, hundreds of empirical studies have been conducted to evaluate a variety of evolutionary-psychology hypotheses. Some have been confirmed; others have been falsified; and others have not yet been subjected to enough empirical tests to render a firm scientific conclusion."[51] All these—the confirmations, falsifications, and generation of reasonable hypotheses and their prospective subjection to tests—are consistent with regarding evolutionary psychology as a science.

It is important to note that scientific research hypotheses are, by definition, speculative and in that sense also just-so propositions that must be assessed by empirical observations. Note also that in the above example, inclusive fitness, based on the modern theoretical formulation of evolution by natural selection, is the comprehensive master theory on which parental-investment theory is logically based, which in turn is the sub-theory on which the research hypothesis regarding a female's selection of a mate is based. A way to frame this is as follows: an evolutionary research prediction (ERP) is true **if** the evolutionary research hypothesis (ERH) also is true, and the ERH is true **if** the parental investment theory (PIT) also is true, and the PIT is true **if** the CFT (acronym for "comprehensive fitness theory," alternately referred to as the inclusive fitness theory) in turn is true. The actual empirical finding may either confirm or disconfirm the truth of the ERP. In cases in which the outcome of the research project matches and confirms the ERP, we can be reasonably confident that the ERH, PIT, and CFT also are also valid. The problem arises when the outcome fails to confirm the ERP, since that raises the possibility that the ERP is false. If

50. Confer et al., "Evolutionary Psychology," 113.

51. Confer et al., "Evolutionary Psychology," 113. It would have been helpful to have an exact count of the then-extant studies whose evolutionary hypotheses were confirmed and of those studies whose hypotheses were falsified. For, if these two numbers were nearly equal, the entire program offers no more than an a priori probability of 0.5 that it can discriminate true from equally probable false hypotheses. From a statistical stance, one would like the likelihood ratio of confirmed hypothesis relative to disconfirmed ones to be substantially higher than 0.5/0.5 = 1.0.

so, then—given that the logical reasoning going from all prior **if** premises to their respective conclusions was sound—one can now reasonably ask (i) whether the ERP's **if**-premise and therefore its following conclusion are false; or for that matter whether any one or more of the preceding—the ERH, PIT, and CFT—**if**-premises and their conclusions are false. Alternatively, one can ask (ii) whether the logical reasoning connecting any preceding **if**-premise to its consequent conclusion was unsound. An additional possibility is that all the intermediate theories/hypotheses and the reasoning connecting them are sound but that the instrumental and methodological implementations of the research design are seriously flawed. As many a scientist's experience can attest, the sorting out of which possibility or combination of possibilities is responsible for the failure to confirm a research prediction can pose a daunting task. Despite these problematic aspects of the evolutionary-psychology research program, *what currently no evolutionary psychologist seriously dares to question is the veracity of the CFT*. But more on that question later.

Evolutionary Psychology, Its Neuroscience Companion, and Their Limitations

For now, consider the fact that the "neuromania" that has infected neuroscience has been criticized on the grounds that brain neurons only do two things: they, like other neurons in the human nervous system such as those in the spinal cord, respond to and emit electrochemical signals. Hence, singly or collectively, they neither think, ponder ethical dilemmas, have conscious experiences, make aesthetic, moral, or juridical judgments, or evaluate and optimize economic decisions; nor do they love or talk of God.

Similarly, with the above-noted evidential problems set aside, those critics who find fault with too liberally and thoughtlessly applying evolutionary-psychology theory in the social sciences and humanities might justifiably claim that mutating genes, which play an essential role in current neo-Darwinian accounts of evolution, may regulate the roles played by other genes; yet, collectively, regulatory and expressive genes code for proteins and not for artistic, sociopathic, altruistic, musical, religious, intellectual, or any other traits and behaviors. However, such a response may be too ungenerous, since genes, via their indirect regulatory and the direct expressive roles in coding for proteins, contribute to an organism's structural organization, i.e., its anatomy. And since function depends on structure, genes can also impact an organism's functional and behavioral traits. However, this is far from claiming that there is, for example, anything like "God genes" or genes for religious faith, which some geneticists have proposed.[52] Such claims or arguments may

52. An example of such scientific overreach is found in Dean Hamer, *The GOD Gene: How Faith Is Hardwired into Our Genes* (Doubleday, 2004). There he claims that there is a GOD gene; i.e., that religious faith is hardwired into our genetically controlled makeup. (One

make for brisk book sales, but current research offers next to nothing to substantiate them.

A reasonable interpretation of evolutionary psychology is that its evolutionary component refers to several concepts important to neo-Darwinian theory of biological evolution by natural (or sexual) selection: (i) adaptations; (ii) exaptations, i.e., adaptations that are co-opted to serve functions other than the ones for which they originally were selected[53]; and (iii) fortuitous byproducts of adaptations. Since the human mind and human behavior are so intimately tied to neuroanatomy and neurophysiology, the psychology component, at least for now, is informed far more richly and directly by neuroscience than by evolutionary science. We already noted that during the last four decades neuroscience has made impressive advances in its research methods and findings. During the 1980s, an influential, broadly defined computational approach to sensory and cognitive information processing proposed by David Marr conjoined neuroscientific findings and their functional significance—their behavioral purposes—within a wider ecological scope[54]; and in my opinion, this conjunction implicitly rested on an eco-coupling that in turn provided a major conceptual platform for the new discipline of evolutionary psychology.

Turning briefly from natural to human design, exemplified by architecture, it has repeatedly been noted that the design of arches supporting the ceilings of cathedrals create spandrels, the small niches resulting supposedly as mere nonfunctional leftovers or byproducts. These nonetheless often did find an incidental function—for example, serving as surfaces that can be filled with decorative ornamentations or sacred paintings. For that reason, ancillary byproducts of biological adaptations have been referred to as "evolutionary spandrels."[55] As to human behaviors, examples of such byproduct spandrels

---

might add here that since instincts are described as innate stereotyped patterns of behavior that result from biological factors under genetic control, there is no such thing as an "art instinct" in other than a metaphoric sense; see Dennis Dutton, *The Art Instinct: Beauty, Pleasure, and Human Evolution* (Bloomsbury Press, 2009)).

53. It is difficult to distinguish exaptations from adaptations (Dennett, *Darwin's Dangerous Idea*; Larson et al., "Exapting Exaptation," *Trends in Ecology and Evolution* 28, no. 9 (2013): 497–98). For instance, the feathers that covered some dinosaurs evolved originally to conserve body warmth, and later they also served to support flight (natural selection). Nonetheless, they still retain their function as thermal insulation or as mate attraction (a form of sexual selection evident in the plumage displays of male birds such as the peacock or great argus pheasant). As these cases exemplify, the use of feathers to support aerodynamical flight maneuvers can be a partial cooptation rather than a full one, and it therefore may count as an additional adaptation.

54. David Marr, *Vision: A Computational Investigation into the Human Representation and Processing of Visual Information* (W. H. Freeman, 1982).

55. Stephen Jay Gould and Richard Lewontin, "The Spandrels of San Marco and the Panglossian Paradigm: A Critique of the Adaptationist Programme," *Proceedings of the Royal Society London B* 205, no. 1161 (1979): 581–98.

would be the fear of poisonous spiders (an adaptation) generalizing to harmless ones (a byproduct). That is not to say that evolutionary spandrels don't contribute to biological survival and reproductive functions. That they *can* contribute to such functions is evident from the following reconsideration of Donald Hoffman and collaborators' proposal (see appendix 1 for details) that perception's truth-tracking function—a function necessary for arriving at scientific explanations regarding the properties and processes of nature—is outdone by its biological reproductive-fitness function. Recent history, however, has shown that the truth-tracking function of scientific research has in fact contributed immensely to the survival and reproductive fitness of the human species. For this research not only yielded an enriched scientific understanding of nature; it also was instrumental in stimulating the development of many technologies that, over the last two centuries, resulted in the steep geometric growth of human population, a reproductive-fitness event that signaled what is now taken to be the start of the Anthropocene era of evolution.

While, in this way, spandrels could contribute to reproductive fitness, it is nevertheless important to note that spandrels, though they free-ride on evolutionary adaptions, *need not be* adaptive in the sense of promoting the reproductive fortunes of individuals; some can also be biologically counteradaptive.[56] That said, an important question arises for scientific research in the field of evolutionary psychology. Since our brains and our cognitive, motivational, affective, and behavioral capacities are evolutionary adaptations, the question is: Are phenomena like religion also adaptations, or are they mere byproducts of such adaptations? Before providing answers, let's remind ourselves that evolutionary psychology is a merger of principles and findings derived not only from the fields of biological evolution and psychology but also from neuroscience and its allied fields.

Relevance of Ecological, Developmental, and Evolutionary Aspects of Conscious Mind to the Science of Religion

> The baby, assailed by eyes, ears, nose, skin, and entrails at once, feels it all as one great blooming, buzzing confusion. . . .
>
> William James, *Principles of Psychology,* Vol. 1, p. 488

The aim of this section is to provide an understanding of the human mind not only when its capabilities are deployed with fully conscious awareness but also when it is able to function at unconscious levels of processing. The last four

56. For example, humans generally seek sexual satisfaction in the reproductive act (an adaptation). Yet some humans are addicted to onanistically watching pornography (a byproduct), to the exclusion of his or her tying sexual satisfaction to furthering the reproductive success of his or her kind.

decades have witnessed the burgeoning of new, extended approaches to biological research, one called "evo-devo" and more recently, one called "eco-devo-evo." Eco-devo-evo extends the study of the evo-devo relation, by dealing with the three-way interactive relations between ecological, pre- and postnatal developmental (ontogenetic), and evolutionary factors.[57] We focus here on the eco-devo portion, which deals with the two-way interactive relation between ontogenetic development of organisms from the fetal to the adult stage and the structures and events found in the organisms' environment. It is this developmental context to which James's above epigraph applies.[58] It describes the post-birth feel, the what-it-is-like-to-be, of an infant's mind confronting its strange, new external environment. The what-it-is-like-to-be aspect relates to the internal, private, and subjectively experienced qualitative aspects, referred to as qualia, that, as noted by the philosopher Thomas Nagel, accompany and characterize consciousness.[59] Along with speculating on the nature of a human infant's qualitative mental state, James pointed out that there also can be different quantitative intensities of consciousness. As to both the quantitative and qualitative types of consciousness, a healthy human being is endowed with sensory consciousnesses that are directed in various modalities (e.g., visual, auditory, tactual, gustatory, and olfactory) toward external sources of stimulation but also those consciousnesses directed toward internal and bodily sensations such as hunger or thirst and the proprioceptive and kinesthetic sensations produced when moving one's legs, arms, and hands. Helen Keller, for instance, lacked visual and auditory consciousness but compensated for this lack by enhancing her conscious awareness of her surroundings through the olfactory, gustatory, tactual, proprioceptive, and kinesthetic senses. Turning from distinguishable qualitative types to quantitatively measurable ones, conscious experiences can vary quantitatively from nearly none (when, for instance, one is in a state of very deep anesthesia or very deep sleep), through an intermediate state governing normal everyday life, up to a maximally aroused waking state (when, for example, one's well-being or one's very survival is threatened).

The Eco-Devo Approach to the Study of Consciousness as State and Consciousness as Trait

These examples, illustrating a distinction between qualitative types and quantitative levels of consciousness, allow us to distinguish further between

57. Eva Jablonka and Marion J. Lamb, *Evolution in Four Dimensions: Genetic, Epigenetic, Behavioral, and Symbolic Variation in the History of Life* (MIT Press, 2014); Kevin N. Laland, *Darwin's Unfinished Symphony: How Culture Made the Human Mind* (Princeton University Press, 2017).

58. William James, *The Principles of Psychology*, vol. 1 (Dover Publications, 1950).

59. Thomas Nagel, "What Is It Like to Be a Bat?," *The Philosophical Review* 83, no. 4 (1974): 435–50.

consciousness as a trait, henceforth referred to as trait consciousness, and consciousness as state, henceforth referred to as state consciousness.[60] The philosopher John Searle characterized consciousness as that which one's mind loses when one is in a coma or under general anesthesia and which one regains when one recovers from either.[61] Here he was referring to both the *mental* state-consciousness and an underlying *biological* state that depends on the existence of what is referred to as the neural-activation or -arousal system. This system consists of various regulatory subcortical sites, whose collective neural output is relatively high during the waking state and all but eliminated during the state of deep sleep or anesthesia. In the normal, daily cycle of life, the subcortical activation/arousal system is under the influence of neurohormonal changes that in turn are influenced by diurnal body rhythms. During the waking state, the output of the subcortical arousal system projects globally to the brain's neocortex, where it activates the various local and regional interactive neural networks specialized to process specific types of sensory information and to generate and guide appropriate responses to the processed information.

It is also here, at the cortical level, that the interactive processing of sufficiently aroused neural networks supports the existence of trait-consciousness. That is to say, the local and regional interactive networks are known to support the processing of distinct types of information that are consciously expressed as distinct types of phenomenal experience. As an example of the coarsest types of qualitative differences, visual experience supported by its regional interactive neural networks is obviously qualitatively different—different in its experienced qualia—from other sensory experiences, such as the olfactory one, which is supported by its own neural networks that overlap little if at all with the visual networks. Across *different* sensory systems, the associated sensory qualia in one system simply don't "feel" the same as those of another. As another example, in normal humans the experienced color of a rose blossom is nothing like its experienced scent. Furthermore, *within* a sense modality like vision, we can make even finer sensory discriminations in that we can experientially distinguish between different sensations or qualia such as the color, shape, and motion of, say, a bouncing ball. In this example, trait-consciousness allows the mental content of the ball to have its distinct conscious properties; the experience of motion, for example, is qualitatively different from that of its shape or color. Correspondingly and even more diversely, in the cortical visual system that supports these distinct qualitative experiences there are even more distinct neural networks that can respond to (i) the subtle variations of the shape or form of a

60. For adoption of this nomenclature, see Bruno G. Breitmeyer and Petra Stoerig, "Neural Correlates and Levels of Conscious and Unconscious Vision," in *The First Half Second: The Microgenesis and Temporal Dynamics of Unconscious and Conscious Visual Processes*, ed. Haluk Öğmen and Bruno G. Breitmeyer (MIT Press, 2006).

61. John R. Searle, "Consciousness," *Annual Review of Neuroscience* 23, no. 1 (2000): 557–78.

stimulus, (ii) the rich variety of colors and shadings, (iii) the many speeds and directions of motion, and many other variable properties of a stimulus. It is these aspects of a consciously apprehended, seen stimulus that give rise to the nearly endless number of qualia comprising the qualitatively rich diversity of visual trait-consciousness (regarding the perception of color alone, for example, when taking into account all the possible combinations and variations of the wavelength, the intensity, and the saturation of visual stimuli, the number of colors that a human with normal color vision can distinguish runs into several millions). From an *objectively neutral, scientific* information-processing standpoint, the diversity with which the world superabundantly proffers its distinct visual aspects represents merely the superabundance of the world's informational content that can engage the mind. But from an *everyday subjectively experiential* standpoint, it is trait-consciousness that adds a bonus property to cognitive contents by rendering them visible, thus revealing the qualitative and multidimensional richness of the world in its full splendor and beauty. The upshot of this supports my claim that while state-consciousness, necessarily supported by the subcortical activation system, is in turn the *necessary* precursor to and supporter of trait-consciousness, trait-consciousness *per se* is comprised of its qualia-rich experiential contents that are *necessarily* supported by the neocortex—and it above all.[62] This claim applies not only to the sense-based consciousnesses but most likely also to the qualia-rich what-it-is-like-to-be aspects of any other types of trait-consciousness, be it emotional, memorial, cognitively reflective, fantasy-filled, dream-filled, and whatever else, which also requires the brain's aroused neocortex.

One might ask—as an anonymous reviewer of the present book's initial manuscript did—what evidence supports this assertion about the dependence of state-consciousness on the neocortex? Recent neuroscientific investigations of human vision not only support the assertion but show additionally that the highest levels of visual cortical processing are absolutely necessary for qualia-rich consciousness.[63] A particular study conducted by Michael Cohen and coworkers[64] showed that the qualia-rich experience characterizing visual consciousness relies necessarily on activation of high-level frontal areas of the visual cortex that are activated about 250 to 300 milliseconds after stimulus onset. It did so by comparing the visual evoked response using standard cortical EEG recordings (i) when the stimulus was clearly seen to (ii) when the conscious vis-

62. I emphasize the importance of the neocortex, because, as I'll argue below, only it can support the superabundant and qualia-rich experiences that humans can have.

63. Mikko Hurme et al., "Early Processing in Primary Visual Cortex Is Necessary for Conscious and Unconscious Vision While Late Processing Is Necessary Only for Conscious Vision in Neurologically Healthy Humans," *Neuroimage* 150 (2017): 230–38; Michael A. Cohen et al., "Neural Signatures of Visual Awareness Independent of Postperceptual Processing," *Cerebral Cortex* 34, no. 11 (2024): 1–15.

64. Cohen et al., "Neural Signatures of Visual Awareness."

ibility of the stimulus was suppressed by what is known as a visual mask.[65] Activation of the high-level frontal areas of visual cortex was recorded only when the stimulus was visible in the unmasked condition but not when its visibility was suppressed in the masked condition. That is to say, although the lower levels of cortical (and subcortical) processing were activated by the stimulus when it was masked, their activities alone were not sufficient to support the conscious visibility of the stimulus. Only the unimpaired activation of the frontal areas of the visual cortex in the unmasked condition (when added, of course, to the necessary activation of lower visual areas going as far down as the retinal level) resulted in the qualia-rich conscious perception of the stimulus.

In view of the distinction between state-consciousness as a globally aroused condition and trait-consciousness as a property of local and specific perceptual and cognitive contents (and their correlated neural activations in the frontal visual cortex), let's try to reconstruct the developmental characteristics of these two types of consciousness. I tend to be cautious about what the mental life of an infant is like. Nonetheless, concurring with William James's epigraph, I assume that a human infant's mental life most likely has a feel to it of a "great blooming, buzzing confusion." In other words, when awake, the infant clearly is aroused and alert and therefore avails itself of state-consciousness. However, it is largely, if not totally, devoid of the trait-consciousness necessary for distinct, qualia-rich mental contents.

To understand why this is so, we must consider several important properties characterizing the infant's brain.

1. At and shortly after birth, much of an infant's development that is necessary for the acquisition of cognitive and behavioral skills, allowing it to thrive in its immediate environment, is maturational and largely guided by genetic factors.
2. The newborn is born with a brain whose neurons exceed greatly in number those that will eventually populate the fully developed adult brain. These two properties constitute the foundation given at birth on which postnatal cognitive development is based.
3. Some of the immediate maturational post-birth growth, being genetically guided, can proceed without environmental influences.
4. Yet the development of all sorts of subsequently acquired perceptual, cognitive, affective, and behavioral skills depends not only on rapid growth of billions of the brain's activated neurons, but also on the

65. For details of visual masking, see Bruno G. Breitmeyer and Haluk Öğmen, *Visual Masking: Time Slices Through Conscious and Unconscious Vision*, 2nd ed. (Oxford University Press, 2006). Visual masking is an experimental procedure in which the visibility of one briefly flashed stimulus, known as the target, is suppressed or degraded when a second briefly flashed stimulus, known as the mask, is located in space and time at or near the spatio-temporal location of the target.

sprouting of their axonal and their dendritic branchings, all of which eventually become part of the adult brain.

5. It also and somewhat counterintuitively depends on the gradual pruning and elimination of the remaining, nonactivated billions of neurons. It seems as though the tremendous variety of behavioral and ecological niches that our world could possibly present to the infant is miraculously matched by the infant's brain that, at birth, is endowed with overabundant billions of neurons, of which fewer billions survive as a result of the infant's active engagement with the objects and events of its particular behavioral and ecological niche. In other words, the end result is that the infant's brain seems to have been tailor-made for whichever of the world's tremendous variety of behavioral and ecological niches in which the infant finds itself.
6. Hence, the growth and sprouting of the billions of neurons activated during the infant's exposure to its environmental inputs (and the simultaneous pruning of the billions of nonactivated neurons) provide the basis for selecting, from the superabundant potential given at birth, the optimal match of sensory, cognitive, and behavioral skills needed to thrive in a particular ecological niche.

Thus, the environmental factors present in the infant's lifeworld, via their physical, behavioral, social, and cultural manifestations, exert an influence equal to or greater than nature alone does on its post-birth development. Shortly after birth and lasting from several months to several years, all sorts of nurturing encounters with objects and events in its lifeworld powerfully influence, on one hand, which of the billions of the infant brain's neurons survive and sprout exuberantly and thus form complex neural networks while, on the other hand, the remaining billions of neurons (along with their axonal and dendritic sproutings) are eliminated by being converted, so to speak, into the brain's material "food for thought." This process implies, moreover, that distinct cultures, with their correspondingly different visual ecologies, may induce developmental differences that in turn cause differences in the visual perceptions and cognitive styles of individuals in these cultures. Scientific evidence for such cross-cultural differences has been mounting for many decades. Experimental and observational research shows that there are cross-cultural differences between part-whole perception of visual stimuli, between ambient and focal styles of visual information processing, and between the perceptions of colors, of depth or distance, of visual illusions, and of pictorial or photographic stimuli.[66] Since different cultures pose to their inhabitants physically

66. Marshall H. Segall et al., *The Influence of Culture on Visual Perception* (Bobbs-Merrill, 1966); William L. Phillips, "Cross-Cultural Differences in Visual Perception of Color, Illusions, Depth, and Pictures," in *Cross-Cultural Psychology: Contemporary Themes and Perspectives*, ed. Kenneth D. Keith (Wiley-Blackwell, 2019).

and therefore visually different ecologies, cross-cultural differences of perception point to the importance of the eco-component of development that contributes to these differences. *Viva les differences*!

Sadly, however, the selective growth and pruning of neurons can have serious and long-lasting consequences. It is important to note that persons raised in any culture, from infancy through childhood, under unfavorable conditions of severely deprived physical, emotional, social, and cultural nurturing, will most likely acquire a set of stunted perceptual, cognitive, and behavioral skills, as well as stunted motivational and aspirational desires, resulting in an overall early developmental enfeebling that can continue to manifest in various ways throughout their later lives.

But even a normally nurtured, unimpeded course of early development must await the infant brain's neural sprouting and the subsequent, environmentally influenced formation of complex neural networks. These include the networks that eventually support the processing of the distinct features of external objects and events in each of equally distinct sensory modalities, but also those that in a healthy adult integrate those distinctive features and modalities to form a unified and qualia-rich conscious experience of the world. However, like an anonymous reviewer of the present book's initial manuscript did, the reader can ask what the evidence-based reasons are for awaiting this normal, time-consuming postnatal developmental process. For one, as developmental studies of the human visual system show, the visual acuity of newborn infants is very poor, yielding values of 20/600 or worse, relative to 20/20 acuity of the average healthy human child and adult.[67] These facts indicate that even when a one-week-old infant directs its eyes toward a stimulus, its very poor acuity would result in very blurry, indistinct vision, so much so that objects qualitatively experienced as distinct by a visually healthy adult would appear so blurred or smudged together as to yield a single indistinct fuzzy quale (singular of qualia). Second, as noted above, the newborn infant has a very underdeveloped neocortex. This of course includes the visual frontal cortex, which, as demonstrated by Cohen and coworkers' aforementioned study, is essential for supporting any conscious vision at all. It is therefore not until the development of the distinctive, yet increasingly integrative, cortical neural processing occurs that a unified consciousness of the world can in turn develop. Only after it has fully developed does it allow for the emergence of the distinct qualia-rich experiences characterizing a similarly fully developed trait-consciousness. Given these two reasons, the underdeveloped functional neuroanatomy of the human visual cortex, even in a healthy newborn infant, is in my opinion inadequate for supporting the qualia-rich experiences characterizing a full-blown trait-consciousness, thus leaving the newborn infant with a sense of "one great blooming, buzzing confusion."

67. Susan J. Leat et al., "Development of Visual Acuity and Contrast Sensitivity in Children," *Journal of Optometry* 2, no. 1 (2009): 19–26.

That said, the question that needs addressing is: What allows the innately given but mentally confused state-consciousness to "prime" the development of its complement, the distinctive trait-consciousness? A preliminary short answer is that, at birth, state-consciousness is supported by *innate* neural mechanisms that respond to highly salient, attention-grabbing stimulation. Implied by James's epigraph is that state-consciousness is innately able, via these innate attention-grabbing brain processes, to prime other brain processes that eventually can support development of the highly differentiated, and therefore qualia-rich, trait-consciousness. After James's speculative contributions to consciousness research, this progression from a global but confused state-consciousness to a highly distinct and differentiated trait-consciousness became a central theme in the theorizing of developmental psychologists Heinz Werner and Eleanor Gibson, and neuropsychologist Donald Hebb.[68]

Merging the Eco-Devo- with the Evo-Approach to the Study of Human Consciousness

We can extend the above eco-devo approach to the study of human consciousness to also include its evolutionary component in a broader eco-devo-evo approach. Here it is important to note again the claim that trait-consciousness depends crucially on a (fully developed) neocortex. Based on findings from paleontological studies, studies of ontogenetic prenatal development, and studies tracking the recovery of consciousness from deep sleep and anesthesia, George Mashour and Michael Alkire proposed that the necessary global and local neural substrates of consciousness first manifest along the following timelines of phylogenetic development: on the evolutionary time scale, a rudimentary, proto-consciousness arose no earlier than about 315 million years ago (Mya), shortly after vertebrate mammals and reptiles began their evolutionary journey; and on the ontogenetic timeline, it arises between weeks 26 and 30 of human development.[69] However, based on what I have proposed above, I venture to modify Mashour and Alkire's views by arguing that while the evolutionary origins of something like conscious experiences in vertebrates may be dated about 315

68. Eleanor J. Gibson, *Principles of Perceptual Learning and Development* (Appleton-Century-Crofts, 1969); Eleanor J. Gibson, "Exploratory Behavior in the Development of Perceiving, Acting, and the Acquiring of Knowledge," *Annual Review of Psychology* 39, no. 1 (1988): 1–41; Donald O. Hebb, *The Organization of Behavior: A Neuropsychological Theory* (Wiley and Sons, 1949); Heinz J. Werner, "The Conception of Development from a Comparative and Organismic Point of View," in *The Concept of Development: An Issue in the Study of Behavior*, ed. Dale B. Harris (University of Minnesota Press, 1957). On Werner's contribution, see also Jaan Valsiner, "Heinz Werner: A Differentiation Theory of Development," in *Portraits of Pioneers in Developmental Psychology*, ed. Wade E. Pickren et al. (Psychology Press, 2012).

69. George A. Mashour and Michael T. Alkire, "Evolution of Consciousness: Phylogeny, Ontogeny, and Emergence from General Anesthesia," *Proceedings of the National Academy of Sciences USA* 110 (Suppl 2) (2013): 10357–64.

Mya, when reptiles and mammals first climbed onto the phylogenetic tree, their consciousness qualitatively did not approach anything like that of, say, a monkey, let alone that of a human. As I—tongue in cheek—often told my students, the human brain is made of a chimp's brain sitting on top of a reptile's brain. What distinguishes the chimpanzee's from the reptile's brain is not the existence of cortical areas of neural processing (reptilic brains have rudimentary, three-layered cortical structures known as the archicortex and/or paleocortex) but instead that reptiles are missing the additional, six-layered neocortex characterizing the mammalian brain. The visual system of reptiles—like that of their evolutionary neighbors, the amphibians—is geared to respond more or less instinctively, in an automatized manner, to a limited number of stimuli, including prey, predator, and various movements occurring in the environment. These types of reflexive visually guided behaviors need not be accompanied by consciously generated experiences or decisions. For instance, rattlesnakes wait until after sunset, when the desert's ambient temperature can eventually fall to less than 40° Fahrenheit, before they can begin to detect and pursue the small mammals whose warm bodies radiate infrared heat waves. It is very doubtful that rattlesnakes consciously experience anything even approximating the distinct, detailed images that we can experience with the aid of an infrared night-vision device. In contrast, bats flying in the dark can echolocate their prey, flying insects, with an astounding speed and accuracy and, being mammals, might have some primitive form of consciousness, some vague phenomenal experience of the insects.

Like reptiles such as snakes, monkeys that are missing the part of their neocortex known as the primary visual cortex lack conscious, qualia-rich visual experiences. Nonetheless, they can still master what is known as an open field test, by avoiding and negotiating around obstacles as they locomote through their behavioral field.[70] In other words, without being consciously aware of the obstacles, they evince a visual capacity that has been oxymoronically named "blindsight,"[71] an anomalous kind of ability to detect the presence and location of stimuli and objects in the field of view without being accompanied by a clear, conscious experience of them. Blindsight has also been observed in humans who have incurred damage to their primary visual cortex.[72] In humans it is a distinct capability devoid of conscious experience rather than a merely degraded form of normal, conscious vision.[73] Moreover, like a monkey lacking its primary

70. N. K. Humphrey, "Vision in a Monkey Without Striate Cortex: A Case Study," *Perception* 3, no. 3 (1974): 241–55.

71. Larry Weiskrantz et al., "Visual Capacity in the Hemianopic Field Following a Restricted Occipital Ablation," *Brain* 97, no. 1 (1974): 709–28.

72. Weiskrantz et al., "Visual Capacity"; Paul Azzopardi and Alan Cowey, "Is Blindsight Like Normal, Near-Threshold Vision?," *Proceedings of the National Academy of Sciences* 94, no. 25 (1997): 14190–94.

73. Larry Weiskrantz, "Is Blindsight Just Degraded Normal Vision?," *Experimental Brain Research* 192, no. 3 (2009): 413–16.

visual cortex, by relying on neural activity originating in subcortical anatomical sites, humans with damage to the primary visual cortex can locate moving objects and avoid obstacles while locomoting through the environment, again without being able to consciously perceive and recognize them.[74]

Do these facts suggest that one can extend James's epigraph from ontogenetic development to evolutionary phylogenetic development? Here, we will reasonably assume that hominins, who appeared as early as 6–7 Mya, had a fully functioning state-consciousness and a functionally adequate trait-consciousness. From this evolutionary line emerged the genus *homo* that lived from about 2.5 Mya in the Lower Paleolithic period until the Middle Paleolithic period beginning around 300 Kya, when anatomically "modern" *homo sapiens* began their evolutionary journey. Mastery of stone tool making by *homo habilis* around 2–3 Mya, which was subsequently refined during the Acheulean period starting about 1.7 Mya, most likely had to involve at least the following abilities, all of which relied on an existent, highly differentiated consciousness:

1. The ability to perceptually recognize the small flintstone that could be worked into a tool.
2. This relied in turn on the ability to imagine the appropriately to-be-finished tool as somehow existing inside the small-sized flintstones. In turn, this would require
3. The ability to access this idealized image of the to-be-fashioned stored in long-term visual memory.
4. This in turn required the ability to transfer the idealized image stored in long-term visual memory into visual working memory during the process of knapping the flintstone toward the desired end result, such as a blade, scraper, or spearhead.
5. The lengthy knapping process also required the ability to attentively refresh and maintain in visual working memory the tool's idealized mental image.
6. It also required the ability to implement an intuitive physics that is applied throughout the knapping process, thereby guiding how forcefully and at what angle the shaping tool must strike the flintstone.
7. The gradual shaping of the flintstone in turn relied on the ability to periodically compare the perceived intermediate product with the idealized mental image in visual working memory.
8. Finally, it also required the ability to recognize the desired end result, the satisfactory match between the perceived final product and its stored ideal mental image activated in visual working memory.

74. Christopher L. Striemer et al., "'Real-time' Obstacle Avoidance in the Absence of Primary Visual Cortex," *Proceedings of the National Academy of Sciences USA* 106, no. 37 (2009): 15996–16001; Lawrence Weiskrantz, *Consciousness Lost and Found: A Neuropsychological Exploration* (Oxford University Press, 1997).

In my opinion, these proto-artistic sculpting skills depend on a well-developed and well-articulated consciousness in its sensory-perceptual, intellective-cognitive, and visuomotor manifestations. Moreover, these proto-artistic skills indicate the existence of corresponding proto-symbolic behavior. A form of "genuine" symbolic behavior may not have developed until the Upper Paleolithic period around 50–60 Kya, when human language also came into play. However, recent archeological studies indicate that such symbolic behavior was already present during the prior Middle Paleolithic period.[75] Pertinent here is the previously noted fact that the beginning of the Middle Paleolithic period dates to as early as 300 Kya, when modern homo sapiens first appeared and by which time Neanderthals had already thrived since about 200 K years earlier and continued to thrive along with homo sapiens until the Upper Paleolithic period. During the Middle Paleolithic time, prehistoric humans already created hollowed out stones and stone spheroids that, according to the philosophical anthropologist Marie König, may have—however compactly and crudely—symbolized the heavenly vault and the cosmic sphere.[76] The appearance of more refined and highly differentiated symbols would have to await the later, Upper Paleolithic period of homo sapiens evolution around 60 Kya. Meanwhile, Neanderthals may have been engaging in less differentiated symbolic behavior from their emergence 500 Kya until they became extinct roughly 25 Kya.

Much earlier, many of the most ancient hominid artifacts, going back to between 2.5 and 3.0 Mya, were primarily utilitarian rather than symbolic; they were used, for example, to chop open bones of hunted prey to extract their nutritious marrow. Yet the very fact that they were *manu*factured (manually worked) *creations* already indicates an incipient appreciation for something resembling an aesthetic, if not yet a symbolic, sense. In either case, the creation of aesthetically pleasing utensils or symbolically charged objects by ancient humans requires that human trait-consciousness already went through an appreciable period of development during human evolution. As indicated above, by the time of the Upper Paleolithic some 60 Kya, the prior lengthy interactive influences of phylogenetic, ontogenetic, and environmental developments had made possible a sophisticated trait-consciousness and symbolic thought processes in modern humans and contemporaneous Neanderthals. The impor-

75. Africa Pitarch Martí et al., "The Symbolic Role of the Underground World Among Middle Paleolithic Neanderthals," *Proceedings of the National Academy of Sciences USA* 110, no. 33 (2021): e2021495118; Antonio Rodríguez-Hidalgo et al., "The Châtelperronian Neanderthals of Cova Foradada (Calafell, Spain) Used Imperial Eagle Phalanges for Symbolic Purposes," *Science Advances* 5, no. 11 (2019): eaax1984; Alison Tripp et al., "Art, Paleolithic," in *Encyclopedia of Global Archaeology*, vol. 1, ed. Claire Smith (Springer, 2018); Genevieve von Petzinger and April Nowell, "A Place in Time: Situating Chauvet Within the Long Chronology of Symbolic Behavioral Development," *Journal of Human Evolution* 74 (2014): 37–54.

76. See chapter 2 of Barry Cooper, *Paleolithic Politics: The Human Community in Early Art* (University of Notre Dame Press, 2020).

tance of this for the evolutionary study of religion covered in the present chapter is, for one, that symbolic *religious* thought such as that expressed in beliefs of ancestral afterlife and in sacred rituals could already have existed not only in homo sapiens but also in the older line of Neanderthal hominins.[77] And secondly, it is highly likely that, without prior conscious experiences of something like such primitive thoughts, beliefs, and rituals, a subsequent discovery of a divine spiritual realm that transcends ordinary, day-to-day experiences could not have developed into the more sophisticated monotheistic High-God religions that arose in human history many millennia later during the Axial Age.

77. Thomas Hughson, SJ, *Neanderthal Religion? Theology in Dialogue with Archeology* (Wipf & Stock, 2024).

CHAPTER 2

Assessing Key Concepts of the Evolutionary-Psychology Approach

As we saw in the prior chapter, evolutionary psychology provides a broad context that encompasses the developmental, cognitive, and evolutionary sciences. In such an evolutionary-psychology approach to the study of religion, several key notions undergird explanatory accounts of religion. Below, we will focus on five key notions that have been employed by cognitive evolutionary psychologists. As described in chapter 1, they are the generally accepted notions of hyperactive agency detection, theory-of-mind formation, teleological thinking, dualistic thinking, and counterintuitive thinking. To these we will add the sixth, somewhat controversial, notion of costly and hard-to-fake commitments. These six notions comprise the core notions of the evolutionary cognitive approach to the scientific study of religion. Below, besides discussing these core notions, we will address two additional topics: the cultural rarity supposedly unique to the natural sciences, and research findings that point to what is known as the underdetermination of theoretical explanations as it applies to the evolutionary-psychology approach to the scientific study of religion.

Of these first six central notions, hyperactive agency detection appears to be the cornerstone of the evolutionary account of religion. Humans must first have the notion of unseen agents (such as gods, spirits, and souls of the deceased) in place before they can apply a theory of mind, purposeful behavior, and counterintuitive attributes to them. Agency detection is hypothesized to be an evolutionary adaptation that finds its survival- and reproduction-enhancing function by discriminating between prey and predator and between conspecific and allospecific creatures. It therefore also is closely tied to approach and avoidance behaviors and to evaluations of good vs. bad, same vs. other, friend vs. foe. Moreover, detection of agents does not depend on their perceived presence. For instance, tracks or scent marks made by one animal are traces left for other animals to detect, and these traces can signal an absent but potential friend or foe, predator, or prey. As a generalization of these binaries, evolutionary psychologists assume that primitive humans could have formed concepts of gods and spirits, not by directly sighting them but instead, via the traces of their actions, thinking of them as intelligent anthropomorphic agents displaying one or more traits similar to those of humans. According to Pascal Boyer,

> gods and spirits are not represented as having *human* features in general but as having *minds*, which is much more specific. . . . Indeed, anthropologists know that the only feature of humans that is always projected onto supernatural beings is the mind. So it is quite likely that concepts of gods and spirits are mostly organized by our intuitive notions of *agency in general* (the abstract quality that is present in animals, persons, and anything that appears to move of its own accord, in pursuance of its goals) rather than just human agency. . . . People do not so much visualize what supernatural agents must be like as detect traces of their presence in many circumstances of their existence. . . . It is part of our constant, everyday humdrum cognitive functioning that we interpret all sorts of cues in our environment, not just events but also the way things are, as the result of some agent's actions. . . . This "naturalness" results from the fact that agency-detection systems are biased toward overdetection. . . . *Our evolutionary heritage is that of organisms that must deal with both predator and prey. In either situation it is far more advantageous to overdetect agency than to underdetect it . . . [since] the cost of not detecting agents when they are actually around (either predator or prey) could be very high.*[1] (emphases added)

And the evolutionary psychologist Scott Atran largely seconds the above by noting that "agent-based interpretations of complex events . . . appear to represent a default strategy of the human mind, that is, an evolved strategy that is universal, innate, [and, due to the aforementioned overdetection bias embedded in the HADD,] easily triggered by the appropriate input, and difficult to inhibit. . . ."[2] In this way, evolutionary psychologists believe that God concepts are extensions from "a more encompassing *evolutionary program for avoiding and tracking predator and prey*. It is an *innate module for detecting agency and intention, whether good or bad*."[3]

The second important notion in the evolutionary account of religion proposed by Boyer is that some religious concepts are minimally counterintuitive by violating our everyday understanding of physical, biological, and psychological properties. Like other organisms, humans cannot walk through walls, cannot live forever, and cannot directly read minds; yet gods and spirits, endowed as they are with supernatural qualities, can pass through walls, be immortal, and know the most hidden intentions of humans. According to Boyer, counterintuitive notions are striking in their salience and therefore find potent lodging in our memories. Once formed, such memories can have their staying power furthered by prayer, contemplative practices, and regular participation in religious rituals, celebrations, and ceremonies.

1. Boyer, *Religion Explained*, 144–45.

2. Scott Atran, *In Gods We Trust: The Evolutionary Landscape of Religion* (Oxford University Press, 2002), 49.

3. Atran, *In Gods We Trust*, 78.

Among others, the evolutionary-cum-neurocognitive approach makes plausible but—as pointed out below—limited contributions to our understanding of religion. As to its plausibility, if we take the notion of agency detection beyond that of possible predator and prey to include, for example, that of ingroup friend and outgroup foe, it becomes understandable that the agency of God—e.g., as depicted in the more ancient Biblical accounts—can on the one hand come across as providential, loving, merciful, and protective; but on the other as unkind, angry, punitive, and cruel. So if, as Boyer argues, the minds of gods are universally anthropomorphized via theory-of-mind formation, then, since we are on some occasions loving and at other times unkind, sometimes forgiving and sometimes punitive, one should not be surprised that such contraries are found in divine characteristics. However, as to their limits, the evolutionary and (neuro)cognitive accounts leave many significant blanks to be filled in, and several problematic issues to be resolved. (Here, it pays to recall [i] the research rationale underlying evolutionary-psychology carefully outlined above by Jamie Confer et al. but also [ii] the many inferential steps and therefore possible reasoning errors—let alone additional methodological flaws—that can occur between research findings that confirm or disconfirm an evolutionary research prediction [ERP] and its fundamental inferential basis, the comprehensive fitness theory [CFT] underlying evolution by natural selection.)

The Hyperactive Agency-Detection Device (HADD)

As observed by the theologian Ilkka Pyysiäinen, the evolutionary HADD "has . . . become one of the core *hypotheses* in the standard model of the cognitive science of religion [referred to, in in its acronym form, by CSR] . . ."[4] (my emphasis). It, like any other scientific hypothesis, should be regarded, in a real sense, as a just-so story. As a just-so explanatory device, the HADD's utility could readily—perhaps too readily—apply to many phenomena besides religion. For example, as Boyer and Atran describe HADD above, it could explain the experience of watching motion pictures, especially the watching of suspenseful crime or horror movies—perhaps even more effectively than it explains the religious experiences and the formation of religious thoughts that the two evolutionary psychologists/anthropologists intended to explain. Regardless of its wider range of explanations, only when the HADD just-so story is confirmed by scientific observations does it move from being a just-so story to a scientific fact. But that cannot happen because, as an explanatory device, it remains ever hypothetical instead of factual. At best, in a wider explanatory context, obtained scientific

4. Ilkka Pyysiäinen, "The Cognitive Science of Religion," in *Evolution, Religion, and Cognitive Science: Critical & Constructive Essays*, ed. Fraser Watts and Léon Turner (Oxford University Press, 2014), 28.

observations can be consistent with the HADD hypothesis; but an observation's being consistent with a hypothesis is not to be confused with the empirical confirmation of its truth. That said, instead of this hypothetical, oft-applied and -cited account of supernatural agency detection, based as it is on rather stark and violence-evoking notions of primitive predator-prey relations, one can offer another, milder account of supernatural agency detection, *for which direct observational and experimental evidence already exists.* It therefore offers an alternative explanatory scenario—*without need* of the evolutionary HADD hypothesis—that is based on natural factors playing out developmentally in early postnatal infants.

The ability to infer the existence of agents that can move on their own and to distinguish them from passive objects that cannot move on their own begins early in life, within a year of an infant's birth. An infant is normally exposed to agents as soon as they are born. The agent may be a kind caretaker, for example, a nurse in a hospital's neonatal care unit, its own mother recovering from labor in the maternity ward, or a midwife, if birth occurs at home. The mother (or another nurturing individual such as a nanny), who is the primary attachment figure for the infant, continues to be an interactive agent during the postnatal development of the infant, as typically also are, to somewhat lesser degree, the father, older siblings, and grandparents, among others. Objects such as dolls, toys, or mobiles suspended above the infant's crib, do not move on their own. They must be moved by an agent, who can be the infant itself. Consequently, even self-produced motion of, for instance, the arms of an infant could contribute to a natural acquisition of agency detection. It is no surprise, therefore, that an infant, developing normally into childhood, can distinguish between active agents and passive objects in the first year of their lives.

On its own, this *natural* ability to detect agents does not readily transfer to the experience or knowledge of *unseen* supernatural agents such as spirits or gods. How, on the basis of an ontogenetic as opposed to an evolutionary phylogenetic account, might this transfer occur? Since the 1960s, numerous developmental studies have demonstrated a phenomenon known as object-constancy or object-permanence.[5] (This ability must rely on a kind of primitive visual short-term memory that becomes progressively sharpened and elaborated as the infant develops through childhood and adolescence into adulthood, where, along with other sensory short-term memories, it is an extremely important component in a human's cognitive and imaginative toolkits.) I myself had the

5. T. G. R. Bower et al., "The Development of the Object Concept as Manifested by Changes in the Tracking Behavior of Infants Between 7 and 20 Weeks Of Age," *Journal of Experimental Child Psychology* 11, no. 2 (1971): 182–93; M. Keith Moore et al., "Visual Tracking in Young Infants: Evidence for Object Identity or Object Permanence?," *Journal of Experimental Child Psychology* 25, no. 2 (1978): 183–98.

pleasure of watching an infant behaviorally demonstrate the object-constancy phenomenon in two interesting ways in a developmental psychology lab. In the first way, the infant, a bit older than half a year, sat on its mother's lap and faced a table on which was placed a tiny toy figure within its arm's reach that captured the infant's attention. The infant grasped and inspected the object for a brief while before the experimenter gently took the toy figure from the infant, placed it on the table, and then covered it with a cylindrical cup so that it was no longer visible. Unbeknownst to the infant, the toy figure rested on a trapdoor that was swung open by a lab assistant hidden underneath the table, causing the figure to drop into another container below the table before the assistant shut the trapdoor. After ten or so seconds elapsed, while the infant's eyes were still fixated on the inverted cup on the table, the experimenter lifted the cup. An audio-video recorder captured the infant's response to the "disappearance" of the toy figure. The response of the infant clearly revealed facial gestures of surprise and of visually scanning back and forth along the table as though it was searching for the toy figure (in other infants whose responses were recorded, besides behavioral signs of surprise and visual search, there also were behavioral signs of confusion and consternation). What this experiment, and similar ones, showed is that even a six months-old infant expected the toy figure to still be under the cup, where the experimenter had placed it.

In the second demonstration, an infant of similar age and her mother were playing a game of peek-a-boo, in which the mother, facing her infant at a distance of a few feet, would disappear behind a screen for a short while and then, taking a peek, her face would appear from behind the screen. Playing this game through several cycles delighted the infant to no end. However, if on the following cycle an adult confederate whose appearance differed significantly from the mother peeked from behind the screen, the child showed various signs of surprise, consternation, or even distress, since this was a violation of the object-constancy attributed by the infant to the mother. Now, in normal extra-laboratory life, a mother or else some other agent can frequently also go briefly out of the infant's sight—for instance, when the mother leaves the infant in the crib for the kitchen to see if the cookies she is baking are ready to take from the oven—without upsetting the infant, since, with the help of a functioning object-constancy system, it senses that the mother, though unseen, is still nearby. By having mastered object-constancy, the infant can thus transfer its appreciation of the agent's visual presence to instances of its *unseen* presence. Consequently, regarding the HADD hypothesis, one need not necessarily rely on evolutionary, biologically inherited tendencies to be *hyperactively* alert for predator or prey in order to developmentally transfer this type of agentive "object" permanence to unseen supernatural agents. An infant's attachment to an object that is its nurturing mother (or mother-figure) can later in the child's life be transferred to an imagined, unseen nurturing agent such as a supernatural God-like being.

The mother, no matter how nurturant, may at times also gently scold the infant and thus, later on, the child may transfer this scolding and punitive aspect of its otherwise nurturant mother to its unseen God-like being. Unfortunately, if the mothering figure is unable to form a loving attachment with its infant or is overly neglectful or punitive, the later development of a supernatural agent can be one of a predominantly distant or punitive God-like being.

What is demonstrated here is that evolutionary cognitivists, like Pascal Boyer and Scott Atran, who too readily, uncritically, and repeatedly take recourse to the evolutionary HADD accounts of agency detection (and perhaps other cognitive inferential devices important to understanding religious thought and behavior), are prone to make an explanatory-confound error. This error rests on the fact that, particularly in the human sciences—including my specialty area of visual perception and cognition—the validity of a theoretical model and thus also the range of the explanatory accounts it can generate are often underdetermined by a particular finding. (I can remember many professional conferences where, after talks presented by a vision researcher explaining his or her findings via a preferred theoretical model, several attendees of the talk raised objections to the offered interpretation of the findings and gave equally valid accounts based on their preferred, alternative theoretical models.) In other words, recalling my prior caution that scientific hypotheses are reasonable, yet just-so, conjectures, a particular finding can be consistent with the hypotheses formulated by several competing theories. For example, an empirical research observation of children reporting their belief in the existence of unseen supernatural agents can be consistent with (i) the evolutionary HADD hypothesis, (ii) the postnatal development in infants and children of object permanence, or (iii) both. (Indeed, there may be additional valid explanations, e.g., [iv] children's developmental tendency to establish relationships with an unseen imaginary friend or play pal whom they cannot see or hear may later transfer later to the notion of God as friend.) Therefore, it appears that the validity of the explanatory range of evolutionary cognition—to use Daniel Dennett's phrasing—"to prove how *it could have been*" cannot be accepted lightly. The point is not that the HADD hypothesis is wrong; it may very well be correct. However, unlike the object-permanence hypothesis—for which hard hypothesis-testing experimental evidence exists, thus moving it from a mere hypothetical to an established factual explanatory device—*there is no hard, directly observed experimental evidence that can support the validity of the HADD hypothesis.* In other words, the HADD hypothesis, while consistent with experimental findings, simply cannot be confirmed directly by experiment and therefore ever remains strictly hypothetical. It will always depend on an indirect inferential process that, as noted in chapter 1, is inherent to the evolutionary-psychology approach. So, I pose to evolutionary cognitivists studying religions the following question: Why rely on the questionable evolutionary HADD hypothesis, for which there is no direct observational evidence, when there is an object-permanence hypothesis, for which directly observed evidence exists and therefore is preferable? In summary, the observationally unconfirmable HADD hypothesis, in contrast an observationally confirmed object-permanence hypothesis, is an example of not only (i) a just-so story but also (ii) the underdetermination of an explanatory theory based on that story.

Moreover, regardless of how (phylogenetically or ontogenetically) the notion of unseen agents is acquired by human infants, the validity and importance of agency detection, as an account of how things could have been, has been questioned on the basis of recent empirical findings reported by psychologist and neuroscientist Anthony Jack and coworkers. From extensive research on why people believe in God, one of their main conclusions is that their reported results

> present a challenge to a number of theoretical accounts of religious belief, especially those which emphasize a link between religious and spiritual beliefs and the perception of agency. . . . The present findings put religious and spiritual beliefs in a new light by suggesting that they are not so much linked to the perception of agency as they are broadly to moral concern, and in particular empathic concern. In line with this view, a number of theologians and religious scholars have claimed that compassion is a central theme that unites many religions. . . . While further work is needed to establish causal links, it is plausible both that religious thinking increases moral concern, and that individuals who possess greater levels of moral concern are more inclined to identify with religious and spiritual worldviews.[6]

I agree with Anthony Jack and his coworkers, but only partly. For the challenge that their results pose to the agency-detection hypothesis is not so much that they oppose or disconfirm it; instead, their results merely point out that several causal factors, such as moral empathic concerns, could contribute more strongly than the HADD to something as complex as religious belief.

Minimally Counterintuitive Ideas

Outside of the current cognitive science of religion (CSR), a good example of a minimally counterintuitive idea is found in the study of the mythologies of ancient Greece, in which the creature Pegasus, the winged horse, appears. Perhaps the oddity of Pegasus is not the fact that the vast majority of winged animals can fly but rather that *a horse can have wings*—and therefore can fly. The notion that horses can have wings is therefore a minimally counterintuitive.

6. Anthony I. Jack et al., "Why Do You Believe in God? Relationships Between Religious Belief, Analytic Thinking, Mentalizing and Moral Concern," *PLOS ONE* 11, no. 3 (2016): 15.

Returning to the evolutionary science of religion (CSR), a second of its key features is the role of minimally counterintuitive ideas in promoting and maintaining religious beliefs. From a cognitive-science standpoint, these indeed are key features of religious belief since they are minimally counterintuitive and therefore may enhance their consolidation in long-term memory. However, the scholar Fraser Watts points out the following problematic assumption implicit in cognitive scientists' talk of counterintuitive ideas: "In CSR studies of how counterintuitive information is processed, judgments of what is counterintuitive are often those of contemporary CSR researchers, most of whom are naturalists. My point is that what is counterintuitive for contemporary naturalists may not have been counterintuitive for emerging humanity. The distinction between naturalism and supernaturalism that seems so obvious to us may not have been obvious at all for primitive *homo sapiens.* The distinction between the ontological categories of agents and non-agents may have been a hard-won cognitive achievement that was reached only gradually. Before that conceptual distinction was achieved, it may not have been counterintuitive to think in animistic or religious ways."[7] In other words, Watts cautions against the use of presentist thinking, which assumes that what is taken to be true in the present was also taken to be true in the very distant past. Moreover, the fact that the evolving cognitions of prehistoric humans may have developed and differentiated gradually implies that, in Watts's slightly amended words, "just as emerging humanity may have made no clear distinction between agents and non-agents, so there may initially have been no clear distinction between . . . material and psycho-spiritual realities. In both cases, I suggest, it is at least possible that the world was perceived in a relatively undifferentiated way by emerging humanity."[8] This view comports well with William James's similar idea that the less gradual post-natal development of human consciousness also proceeds from an initial compact and undifferentiated state to an increasingly more capacious and differentiated state. Furthermore, both James's and Watts's reasoning comports well with Eric Voegelin's similar proposal that prehistorical consciousness went through a gradual progression from an initial compact and undifferentiated state to an increasingly capacious and differentiated state.[9] What all the above illustrates is that what counts as the official interpretation along evolutionary CSR-hypothesized lines is determined more by pretheoretical presentist and naturalist assumptions of cognitive-evolutionary scientists than by any putative facts. In the candid words of philosopher Michael Ruse, "the extent to which

7. Fraser Watts, "Religion and the Emergence of Differentiated Cognitions," in *Evolution, Religion, and Cognitive Science; Critical and Constructive Essays,* ed. Fraser Watts and Léon P. Turner (Oxford University Press, 2014), 125.

8. Watts, "Religion and the Emergence of Differentiated Cognitions," 127.

9. Cooper, *Paleolithic Politics,* 51–60, 157.

one is going to be inclined to take one or another of these various [evolutionary CSR] proposals seriously is going to depend less on [the factual content of] the proposals themselves and more on one's background commitments."[10]

Watts's and Ruse's constructive criticisms aside, there are other features of human cognition that also pose a problem for the minimally-counterintuitive-idea hypothesis. For instance, our intuitive "folk physics" relies on the principle of sufficient reason—namely, that effects have causes or reasons for occurring; for instance, all human-made things (e.g., artistic or technological ones) have as the reason for their existence the prior productive and creative actions of humans. From the above discussions we can assume that, like adults, children have a sufficiently developed teleofunctional mode of thinking. If so, is it not downright pro-intuitive for these children—since, according to cognitive scientists, they have a built-in or developmentally acquired cognitive inference-making device—to teleofunctionally infer from the impressively bountiful appearances of design in nature, as William Paley did, that nature as a whole was designed and created by the intelligent agency of a Designer and Creator God? One can protest, following Richard Dawkins, that evidence for such intelligent and intentional and purposeful design is specious, since the appearance of biological design supposedly can be explained within a neo-Darwinian account by the totally nonintentional, chance (random) genetic mutations whose viabilities are subjected to an equally nonintentional necessity, the future-blind process of natural selection.[11] But even if Dawkins's explanation of biological design were correct, his protest misses the point in two ways. One, the facts on the ground indicate that even children exposed to natural-science courses prefer to use teleofunctional as compared to objective scientific thinking to explain natural and especially biological phenomena; and two, this tendency is not lost in adulthood.[12] This not-outgrown tendency persisting into adulthood indicates that the intuitive belief in intentional and purposeful design, supported as it is by numerous instances during a child's development into adulthood, can be just as important a feature of religious cognition—e.g., the belief that God is the designer of nature—as can the counterintuitive beliefs noted by Boyer and Atran. Hence, here again the role of a powerful memorability and transmissibility of minimally counterintuitive information is not the only hypothesis explaining the cultural adoption, maintenance, and spread of religious beliefs; a *very pro-intuitive teleofunctional thinking* can equally account for the vivid memorability and transmissibility of religious beliefs.

10. Ruse, *Darwinism as Religion*, 49.

11. Richard Dawkins, *The Blind Watch Maker: Why the Evidence of Evolution Reveals a Universe Without Design* (W. W. Norton, 1986).

12. Greenway and Barrett, "Evolutionary Developmental Psychology"; Kelemen, "Are Children 'Intuitive Theists'?"; Kelemen and DiYanni, "Intuitions About Origins."

Religion as Mere Byproduct of Evolutionary Adaptive Traits

Boyer and Atran's message is that from an evolutionary standpoint religion is not a real, *sui generis*, entity and thus cannot be an adaptation; instead, by merely complying with and appropriating several innately available cognitive inference systems that are adaptations, it is merely a spandrel-like byproduct of such adaptations.[13] There are two objections to this view of religion. One is based on the results reported by Hervey Peoples and coworkers.[14] These investigators' extensive study of hunter-gatherer societies, coupled with sophisticated statistical methods, allowed them to temporally sequence the most likely historical appearance of the following seven traits of hunter-gatherer religions: animism, belief in an afterlife, shamanism, ancestor worship, the presence of high gods, worship of ancestors who are active in human affairs, and worship of high gods who are active in human affairs. They concluded that the oldest trait to emerge in the prehistory of religion was animism; it was followed by belief in an afterlife, which in turn was followed by shamanism and ancestor worship. In contrast to this clear sequencing of traits, the presence of high gods, the worship of ancestors who are active in human affairs, and the worship of high gods who are active in human affairs were found to be absent in early humans. Nonetheless, an interesting finding was that although statistical tests of pair-wise correlations between most religious traits indicated that there was a consistent sequence in the co-evolving development of these traits, the later emerging trait of high gods was a standalone, indicating *that it can emerge in society regardless of other traits of religion*. In other words, emergence of religious belief in a supreme high god, evident in the worship of Aten (Sun God) as early as the short-lived Egyptian Amarna Period of 14th-century BCE and the High Gods that arose later during the 1st millennium BCE, falls into a *sui generis* category.

Here it is important to turn to the period dating from about 800 to 200 years BCE, known as the Axial Age, which introduced several major changes in how humans experience and think about reality. During this period, notes the scholar Michael Barnes, "it was bold for thinkers in Greece, India, China, Persia, and Palestine to claim that in spite of the disorderly complexities of life and nature there is a *single* Being or Force that rules everything at once. This was a new belief; it was a new kind of belief; it accompanied a new style of thought. . . . [T]here was a search for the *single* Ultimate Reality in terms of which it would be possible to make sense of everything else. . . . [And this] belief in an ultimate unity to nature and the Power that lies behind nature took science

13. Pascal Boyer, "Religious Thought and Behaviour as By-Products of Brain Function," *Trends in Cognitive Sciences* 7, no. 3 (2003): 119–24.

14. Peoples et al., "Hunter-Gatherers and the Origin."

to a new level . . . , [and it] sometimes also included a severe perfectionism. This appears most often in religious theories of salvation"[15] (emphases added). I emphasized the word "single" deliberately because it importantly points out that this new way of thinking—whether motivated by philosophy, politics, or religion—was monistic. Monism, as exemplified by Paul Feyerabend's second epigraph at the head of chapter 7, characterizes not only the thinking in most sciences, but ever since the Axial Age has also given religion a distinct character identified as *mono*theism.

This comports with the philosopher Henri Bergson's hypothesis that the prehistoric polytheistic religions, that he referred to as "static outer religion," were transformed—perhaps rather rapidly during the Axial Age—into dynamic "inner religions" and their modern monotheistic offshoots.[16] As such, humans did not create God, as Boyer proposes.[17] Instead they discovered the God who creates all real entities, including us and, by revealing it to us, our religion. That said, we can now answer Alexander and Andrew Fingelkurts's question: Is our brain hardwired to produce God, or is our brain hardwired to perceive God? The answer is that our brains or, rather, our cognitive inference system, do not create God. Neither God nor religion are airy nothings, mere byproducts or naturally evolved cognitive biases. Instead, since God is the God of history, our brains allow us to perceive and thus discover the reality of God revealed to us through his creations in the natural world and through the course of historical events.

A second objection to the byproduct hypothesis is that other evolutionary approaches argue that religion clearly is an adaptation rather than merely a byproduct of biologically evolving traits. For example, the personality trait of religiosity has a significant genetic loading that, in turn, has been associated with significantly higher survival fitness as measured by longevity and with significantly higher reproductive fitness as measured by fertility rates.[18] On the basis

15. Michael Horace Barnes, *Stages of Thought: The Co-evolution of Religious Thought and Science* (Oxford University Press, 2000), 92–94. For further characterizations of the Axial Age, see Joas, *The Power of the Sacred*, chapter 5; and Jaspers, *The Origin and Goal*, chapter 1.

16. Henri Bergson, *The Two Sources of Morality and Religion* (University of Notre Dame Press, 1977).

17. Pascal Boyer, "Gods and Mental Instincts That Create Them," in *Science, Religion and the Human Experience*, ed. James D. Proctor (Oxford University Press, 2005).

18. Candace S. Alcorta and Richard Sosis, "Ritual, Emotion, and Sacred Symbols: The Evolution of Religion as an Adaptive Complex," *Human Nature* 16, no. 4 (2005): 323–59; Fingelkurts and Fingelkurts, "Is Our Brain Hardwired?"; Kevin N. Laland, "The Niche Construction Perspective: Implications for Evolution and Human Behavior," *Journal of Evolutionary Psychology* 5, no. 1 (2007): 51–66; Lynda H. Powell et al., "Religion and Spirituality: Linkages to Physical Health," *American Psychologist* 58, no. 1 (2003): 36–52; Robert Rowthorn, "Religion, Fertility and Genes: A Dual Inheritance Model," *Proceedings of the Royal Society B* 278, no. 1717 (2911): 2519–27; Richard Sosis and Jordan Kiper, "Religion Is More Than Belief: What Evolutionary Theories of Religion Tell Us About Religious Commitments," in

of satisfying these two fitness criteria, one therefore can consider it a *sui generis* and bona fide evolutionary adaptation.[19]

The Role of Costly Hard-to-Fake Commitments

Regarding religion, one can think of hard-to-fake commitments as referring to obligations, vows, and loyalties whose fulfillments require very time- and effort-consuming actions that are too costly to be performed insincerely. Examples are the rigorous adherence of heart and mind to religious practices and beliefs that demand a high degree of self-denial such as might be found, for instance, in Trappist or Carthusian monks and nuns. Hence, another important notion in the evolutionary account of religion, according to Boyer and other evolutionary psychologists, are such costly, hard-to-fake commitments made by religious individuals.[20] However, along with still other evolutionary psychologists, Atran holds that they are not essential features. He maintains that the "criterion of costly commitment appears to rule out *purely cognitive theories of religion as sufficient.* Such [commitment] theories are *motiveless.* In principle, they can't distinguish cartoon fantasy from religious belief. The criterion of belief in the supernatural rules out commitment theories of religion as sufficient. Such theories are *mind-blind,* in that they ignore the cognitive structure of the mind and its causal role. In principle, such theories can't distinguish strong secular ideologies from religious belief"[21] (emphases added). But these negative evaluations of costly com-

Disagreement and Evolution, ed. Michael Bergmann and Patrick Kain (Oxford University Press, 2014); Mark Townsend et al., "Systematic Review of Clinical Trials Examining the Effects of Religion on Health," *Southern Medical Journal* 95, no. 12 (2002): 1429–34.

19. For in-depth discussions and critiques of adaptation and byproduct-of-adaptation approaches to religion, see Joseph Bulbulia, "The Cognitive and Evolutionary Psychology of Religion," *Biology and Philosophy* 19, no. 5 (2004): 655–86; Ilkka Pyysiäinen and Marc Hauser, "The Origins of Religion: Evolved Adaptation or By-Product?," *Trends in Cognitive Sciences* 14, no. 3 (2010): 104–9; Richard Sosis, "The Adaptationist-Byproduct Debate on the Evolution of Religion: Five Misunderstandings of the Adaptationist Program," *Journal of Cognition and Culture* 9, no. 3 (2009): 315–33. Regarding these approaches, Dominic Johnson, "What Are Atheists for? Hypotheses on the Functions of Non-Belief in the Evolution of Religion," *Religion, Brain & Behavior* 2, no. 1 (2012): 48–99, discusses the possible ways in which non-belief and atheism may be adaptive as well as non-adaptive in cultural and biological evolution.

20. Pascal Boyer, "Religion: Bound to Believe?," *Nature* 455, no. 7216 (2008): 1038–39; Pascal Boyer and Brian Bergstrom, "Evolutionary Perspectives on Religion," *Annual Review of Anthropology* 37, no. 1 (2008): 111–30; William Irons, "Religion as a Hard-to-Fake Sign of Commitment," in *Evolution and the Capacity for Commitment,* ed. Randolph Nesse (Russell Sage Foundation, 2001); Matt J. Rossano, *Supernatural Selection: How Religion Evolved* (Oxford University Press, 2010).

21. Atran, *In Gods We Trust,* 264. I argue in the introduction and in chapter 7 that some ideologies can be viewed as religions, albeit ersatz-religions.

mitment explanations can be read in several ways. For one, in what sense ought purely cognitive theories to be sufficient? Here Atran's answer is (circularly and self-servingly) quite correct in the sense that the criterion of commitment costs and their offshoots does not predict the peculiarities of religions that he attempts to account for on cognitive grounds. However, one response is: But so what? For if by "sufficient" is meant that, indeed, a *purely cognitive theory* is sufficient (i.e., no other explanation is needed) to account for the phenomenon of religion, then clearly this possible reading of his claim is questionable. For, even Atran himself acknowledges that other, noncognitive theories can add to our conceptual grasp of religion.[22] Therefore, they can contribute to a *fuller* scientific understanding of religion that incorporates noncognitive factors. Such fuller understanding would be lacking if a purely cognitive theory were sufficient. One might also add that making costly and hard-to-fake commitments calls on several cognitive capacities such as conscious choice appraisals, weighing of costs and benefits, and making likelihood estimates, all of which are involved not only when making religious commitments but also when making commitments to staying single or, in contrast, to a marriage, to having and raising children, or to follow one of several other desirable vocations.

In a sense perhaps not meant by Atran and to which he might be mindblind, commitment-based theories are not motiveless since costly religious commitment *can* have clear motives. "By requiring members to engage in costly ritual behaviors and to profess belief in unverifiable supernatural claims," notes evolutionary psychologist Matt Rossano, "religion effectively filters out uncommitted, less trustworthy group members. . . . Furthermore, the most enduring of religious communes were those that made the greatest personal demands on their members."[23] So clearly, we do have a motive, but one that is corporate and communal in addition to being private or individual. Another clear motive for costly commitment is the experience of the presence and love of God and steadfast obedience to his will, as evidenced, for instance, in the strongest way by Jesus and by his many followers who devoted and offered the highest price, their lives, to the service of creation and its Creator God.[24] Finally, the fact that, as

22. Atran, *In Gods We Trust*, 13–15.

23. Rossano, *Supernatural Selection*, 168.

24. Such supreme costly commitment of heartfelt and free-willed persons does not negate but instead greatly exceeds in *moral* depth and breadth the so-called "altruistic" self-sacrificial behavior that is mindlessly and amorally regulated by genetically formed mechanisms to benefit the reproductive fitness of one's nearest kin by promoting the furtherance of that subset of one's genes that is also found in the kin's genomes. Among biologists of a naturalist bent, such as Richard Dawkins, the so-called "altruistic genes" are sometimes taken to be the sole factors contributing to self-sacrificial behavior (the classic example, that of soldier ants protecting the queen ant, the sole final vehicle of genetic reproduction), to the exclusion of ethical or religious factors that motivate altruistic self-sacrifice regardless of kinship relations.

Atran claims, a high-cost commitment approach cannot distinguish religion from secular ideologies—Marxism, for example, for which many have willingly given their lives—can be viewed from a perspective quite different from Atran's narrow one focusing on *supernatural* religion. As was discussed in the introduction, two philosophical and theological considerations that are crucial to explicating religion are the concept of *transcendence* and of the *self-subsistent divine* (that which does not depend on anything else for its existence but has everything else depend on it).[25] As also explained in the introduction and further elaborated in chapter 7, these notions can readily apply to descriptions of many secular ideologies—such as physicalism, naturalism, and atheist scientism—that effectively act as nontheistic ersatz-religions. In contrast to theistic religions based on beliefs in world-transcendent divine powers, generally these ersatz-religions tend to espouse an inner-worldly, natural transcendence.

The Rarity of Modern Science vs. the Ubiquity of Religion?

A somewhat ancillary yet significant point is what can be taken to be Boyer's approbative characterization of scientific activity. He maintains that ". . . scientific activity is both cognitively and socially very *unlikely*, which is why it has only been developed by a very small number of people, in a small number of places [e.g., Italy, France, England], for what is only a miniscule part of our evolutionary history. As philosopher Robert McCauly concludes on the basis of similar arguments, science is every bit as 'unnatural' to the human mind as religion is 'natural.'"[26] Up to a point, this is a valid assessment. But this description does not serve as a sound criterion for distinguishing scientific from religious practice. The essential criterion of distinction is not their respective "unnaturalness" and "naturalness." Instead, it is that science is based on a metaphysical presupposition of a worldly, immanent reality, whereas theistic religion, while not denying the worldly reality, is based additionally on a metaphysics of a world-transcending reality. But despite this distinction, from a methodological and procedural viewpoint, as more fully explained in appendix 2, there are some strong parallels between the scientific and religious quests for truth. More telling still is that major religions, e.g., the Abrahamic, Buddhist, and Hindu ones, were, like science, developed by a small number of "elite specialists" such as Moses and several Biblical prophets, Jesus and his few selected apostles, Mohammed and his designated immediate successors, Gautama Buddha and his closest disciples. And the practices and characteristics of these religions have flourished to this day, in no small part because of the disciplined practices of these small groups of elite practitioners several tens of centuries ago—namely,

25. Clouser, *The Myth of Religious Neutrality*.
26. Boyer, *Religion Explained*, 322.

the Christian, Jewish, and Muslim mystics, the Buddhist bodhisattvas, and the Hindu yogis. For these important historic reasons—to which Boyer's cognitive-evolutionary approach appears to be mindblind—current world religions, like modern science, are, to paraphrase his words, also cognitively and socially very unlikely, which is why they were founded and first promulgated by only a very small number of people (e.g., Abraham, Jesus, Mohammed, Gautama Buddha), in a small number of places (e.g., the Levant, the Arabian peninsula, the Asian subcontinent), for what is only a miniscule part of our evolutionary history (the combined duration of which is roughly 1.5K years, marked by the beginning of the Axial Age, 800 BCE; followed by the beginning of Christianity, 1st century CE; in turn followed by Islam, early 7th century CE). The fact that they are still promulgated and practiced by millions of humans also is not a telling criterion of demarcation, since the practice of modern science, founded by a few creative and daring innovators, also has spread widely throughout earth and is now no doubt promoted and practiced not only by hundreds of thousands, if not several millions, of scientists, but worldwide also has a following of science enthusiasts in the tens if not hundreds of millions.[27]

The above, point-by-point assessment of only some of the problems with the cognitive-evolutionary studies and accounts of religion is generally in agreement with that made by Barbara Herrnstein Smith. Referring specifically to Boyer's book, but readily extendable to other published cognitive-evolutionary accounts, her summary states that the evolutionary psychologists' attempts to give a "hard-nosed, comprehensive explanation of religion based on up-to-date, established 'evolutionary' and 'cognitive' scientific knowledge is better described as an array of more or less *speculative accounts of selected features* of religious belief and practice based on a set of still highly controversial theories developed in fields at some distance from evolutionary biology and empirical neuroscience"[28] (emphasis added; also, see notes 41 and 43 in chapter 1). This conceptual distance between evolutionary psychology on one hand and biology and cognitive neuroscience on the other creates an epistemological space that allows imaginative narratives within a framework provided by the latter two disciplines to be too readily taken as established science rather than as an imaginative and conjectural undertaking. Moreover, selective accounts like Atran's and Boyer's

27. According to data from S. Schneegans, T. Straza, and J. Lewis, eds., *UNESCO Science Report: The Race Against Time for Smarter Development* (UNESCO Publishing, 2021), accessed May 8, 2022, https://www.unesco.org/reports/science/2021/en/statistics, the worldwide number of full-time equivalent (FTE) scientific researchers in 2018 was 8.854 million. That number has most likely increased somewhat, since scientific research has been steadily increasing over the years. No doubt the number of amateur scientists and science buffs runs into many additional millions.

28. Barbara Herrnstein Smith, *Natural Reflections: Human Cognition at the Nexus of Science and Religion* (Yale University Press, 2009), 37.

focus on cognition (the subtitle of Boyer's book is *The Evolutionary Origins of Religious* Thought) and thus exclude additional, noncognitive sources of evidence that are relevant and important. There are and have been many other accounts of religion with which evolutionary theory must contend.[29]

We noted above that costly, hard-to-fake religious commitments can be as much a matter of spiritual experiences of God—i.e., of the "heart's" feelings and emotions, and of the urgings of the will and desire—as they are of cognitive thoughts. The philosopher Hugh McCann emphasizes that the importance of religious experience lies in the fact that its mental contents are far richer and far wider than simply having religious thoughts and concepts. McCann explains that

> a believer may feel that [religious] experiences are veridical, but a skeptic might think they are simply a common illusion to which religious people are in certain circumstances subject.
>
> At present, I don't see how to resolve this issue in a way that is usefully scientific. It is, for example, no good treating claims of encounters of the divine as hypotheses. Those who have such experiences are not offering us a claim that there is a God as a hypothesis. They are not inferring that there is a God any more than a person looking at her hand infers that there is a hand before her. They are reporting what they allege to be their *direct experience*. What then are we to say? Should such reports be declared uniformly illusory? Surely not on the basis that ordinary empirical experience—experience with the usual five senses [the exteroceptors that acquire information about the external world]—has shown that so-called mystical experience cannot be veridical. Such claims would be straightforwardly question-begging as to what kinds of experiences we may trust. . . .
>
> [This is] important because the broader range of religious experience constitutes the heart of the matter when it comes to explaining the phenomenon of religion. What holds religion in place is not arguments for the existence of God, . . . external signs and wonders, . . . the childlike tendency to believe parents or Sunday school teachers, [or] the Kantian sense of the sublime. . . . Rather, it is the compelling nature of religious experience that holds [religious] things in place.[30] (emphasis added)

29. Smith, *Natural Reflections*, 41. Here Smith also notes that Boyer, along with "other New Naturalists tend to exaggerate the revolutionary character of their ideas and, in the course of promoting them, produce distorted accounts of the history and current state—and, indeed, existence—of a long naturalistic tradition in the study of religion." One need only mention Émile Durkheim, Max Weber, Sigmund Freud, Carl Jung, Claude Lévi-Strauss, and James George Frazer among the ethnologists, historians, psychologists, anthropologists, and sociologists who were interested in comparative and cross-cultural studies of religion.

30. H. J. McCann, "Getting Scientific About Religion," in *The Future of Atheism: Alister McGrath & Daniel Dennett in Dialogue*, ed. Robert B. Stewart (Fortress Press, 2008), 124–25.

Moreover, based on pertinent discussions of consciousness in appendices 1 and 2, we can see that attempts to deal with the many religious phenomena without accounting for the fundamental importance of human consciousness, on which such experiences depend, are in my opinion doomed to be insufficient. The question posed to (incomplete) evolutionary-cognitive theories of religion, then, is: How did the rich gamut of religious experiences, commitments, and practices supporting them come about? For an answer we have to go . . .

Beyond Neo-Darwinian Accounts of Religion

We noted above that up to now no credible evolutionary-psychology account of religion has seriously dared to question the veracity of the comprehensive fitness theory, as expressed in the neo-Darwinian concept of inclusive fitness. The currently insufficient and incomplete explanations from a neo-Darwinian evolutionary standpoint of the many religious phenomena suggest that what, among other things, may be needed is a more complete, comprehensive theory of evolution, a theory that includes explanatory components of not only the processes of random genetic variation and natural (and sexual) selection that the neo-Darwinian synthesis subscribes to, but also other important components. This wider evolutionary approach calls for inclusion of (i) additional genetic factors that are attributable to ontogenetic and epigenetic developmental factors and (ii) the ability of humans to construct symbolically and experientially rich cultural niches as factors contributing to genetic inheritance. To that end, several evolutionary scientists have proposed an extended evolutionary synthesis, a more comprehensive, eco-devo-evo approach, that includes these additional hereditary influences,[31] although the explanatory necessity of the extended synthesis has not gone unchallenged.[32]

The anthropologist Augustín Fuentes seconds the need to consider evolutionary accounts of human nature that include, beyond the pale of the current neo-Darwinian paradigm, the roles played by the additional inheritance factors, especially niche construction and epigenesis, that are found in the extended synthesis.[33] Not only is it widely known that genetic factors can influence human niche constructions that have fostered the culturally evolving linguistic and symbolic abilities (including of course those supporting religious and artistic

31. See Luis Oviedo, "'Self-Organizing Personhood' and Many Loose Ends," in *Verbs, Bones, and Brains*, ed. Augustín Fuentes and Aku Visala (University of Notre Dame Press, 2017).

32. Among supporters of an extended evolutionary synthesis are Eva Jablonka and Marion J. Lamb, *Evolution in Four Dimensions*; Laland, *Darwin's Unfinished Symphony*; Kevin Laland et al., "Does Evolutionary Theory Need a Rethink?," *Nature* 514, no. 7521 (2014): 161–64.

33. For a critique of the synthesis, see Laland et al., "Does Evolutionary Theory Need a Rethink?"

expressions). It is also known that these culturally evolving abilities within a cultural niche constructed by humans in turn can influence the genetic factors that contribute to the very continuation of human niche constructions. And since cultural and genetic influences can interact and coevolve,[34] the likelihood that cultural niche constructions affect genetic selection indicates that the influences on gene selection of experiences aroused by religious rituals and practices cannot be ruled out. Human symbolic abilities and practices that contribute to the development of religious experiences and practices no doubt depend on a repertoire of mental faculties far richer than the agency detection, theory of mind, teleofunctional thinking, dualistic thinking, and counterintuitive ideas that cognitive evolutionary psychologists have so far proposed. To name just a few: planning for future events and contingencies, short-term as well as long-term memory, a number of imaginative abilities, and generating the nearly inexhaustible agential possibilities whose mental pruning results in the action that is implemented. These mental faculties, in turn, are made possible by complex neural structures and networks of the human brain that interacted and coevolved with correspondingly complex cultural niches. How did these mental faculties and their expressions manifest in human history? An answer can be found by more closely examining the results of anthropological, paleontological, and archeological studies of some of . . .

The Importance of Experiential Dimensions

One of the outliers is religious experience. Here again, along with McCann, let us be mindful of the primacy of religious experience relative to religious (after)thought. In his commentary on Ara Norenzayan's book *Big Gods,* Augustín Fuentes perceptively concurs with McCann when he states that "a core aspect missing from Norenzayan's book, and in much of the literature on this topic [i.e., the cognitive-evolutionary approaches to religion], is . . . the individual believers' experiences of religious faith and their interpretation of what that faith [experience] means. The cognitive, physiological, and perceptual realities of people who believe in Big-God religions [religions in which a moralizing High God, e.g., YHWH of the Israelites, exercises the supernatural enforcement of a

34. Augustín Fuentes, "Putting Evolutionary Theory to Work in Investigating Human Nature(s)," in *Verbs, Bones, and Brains: Interdisciplinary Perspectives on Human Nature,* ed. Augustín Fuentes and Aku Visala (University of Notre Dame Press, 2017). For discussions of such co-evolution, see Nicole Creanza et al., "Cultural Evolutionary Theory: How Culture Evolves and Why It Matters," *Proceedings of the National Academy of Sciences USA* 114, no. 30 (2017): 7782–89; Maciej Chudek and Joseph Henrich, "Culture-Gene Coevolution, Norm-Psychology and the Emergence of Human Prosociality," *Trends in Cognitive Sciences* 15, no. 5 (2011): 218–26; Peter J. Richerson et al., "Gene-Culture Coevolution in the Age of Genomics," *Proceedings of the National Academy of Sciences USA* 107 (Suppl 2) (2010): 8985–92.

society's morals] vary and in that there might be an evolutionarily relevant complexity that is missed in large-scale functional treatment of what religion does."[35] Heartfelt religious experiences, as Alexander and Andrew Fingelkurts have defined them and pointed out, consist of the lived encounter with a transcendent God and a divine realm. They are furthermore characterized by (i) a profound sense of reality, a reality "even more real than the baseline reality of everyday life; and (ii) "intense memorability,"[36] a memorability perhaps stronger than the memorability of the counterintuitive concepts and thoughts so important to Boyer's and Atran's cognitive accounts of religion. Additionally, religious experiences and the semiotics of faith depend not only on the exercise of linguistic skills but also, crucially, on the exercise of playful and symbolically fluent and fertile imaginative skills, both of which were present some 50–70 millennia ago or even earlier.[37]

Big-God religions probably appeared as early as the transition from the Pleistocene to the Holocene era, about twelve millennia ago,[38] as indicated by the recent archeological evidence obtained at Göbekli Tepe, Cata Höyük, Asikli Höyük, and other prehistoric sites in present-day Turkey.[39] Yet much earlier, the first inklings of spiritual experiences may have been associated with Paleolithic mortuary practices[40] and with Paleolithic cave and rock art. Paleolithic mortu-

35. Augustín Fuentes, "Hyper-Cooperation Is Deep in Our Evolutionary History and Individual Perception of Belief Matters," *Religion, Brain & Behavior* 5, no. 4 (2015): 23.

36. Fingelkurts and Fingelkurts, "Is Our Brain Hardwired?," 294, 312; David Lewis-Williams, *Conceiving God: The Cognitive Origin and Evolution of Religion* (Thames & Hudson, 2010), 129, 135.

37. Robert N. Bellah, *Religion in Human Evolution: From the Paleolithic to the Axial Age* (Harvard University Press, 2011); Robert C. Berwick and Noam Chomsky, *Why Only Us: Language and Evolution* (MIT Press, 2016); Augustín Fuentes, "Human Evolution, Niche Complexity, and the Emergence of a Distinctively Human Imagination," *Time & Mind* 7, no. 3 (2014): 241–57; Robert K. Logan, "The Extended Mind Model of the Origin of Language and Culture," in *Evolutionary Epistemology, Language and Culture*, ed. Nathalie Gontier et al. (Springer, 2006); Rossano, *Supernatural Selection.*

38. See Ara Norenzayan, *Big Gods: How Religion Transformed Cooperation and Conflict* (Princeton University Press, 2013), chapter 7.

39. Andrew Collins, *Göbekli Tepe: Genesis of the Gods* (Bear & Company, 2014); Klaus Schmidt, *Sie Bauten die Ersten Tempel: Das Rätselhafte Heiligtum der Steinzeitjäger* (Verlag C. H. Beck, 2006).

40. For the influence of Paleolithic mortuary practices, see Bellah, *Religion in Human Evolution*; René Girard, "Animal Scapegoating at Çatalhöyük," in *How We Became Human: Mimetic Theory and the Science of Evolutionary Origins*, ed. Pierpaolo Antonello and Paul Gifford (Michigan State University Press, 2015); David J. Lewis-Williams and Jean Clottes, "The Mind in the Cave—The Cave in the Mind: Altered Consciousness in the Upper Paleolithic," *Anthropology of Consciousness* 9, no. 1 (1998): 13–21; David Lewis-Williams and David Pearce, *Inside the Neolithic Mind: Consciousness, Cosmos, and the Realm of the Gods* (Thames & Hudson, 2009); Rossano, *Supernatural Selection.*

ary practices, which go back 100 millennia, could have facilitated a belief in an afterlife (or vice versa). And despite contrary views of naturalists like R. Dale Guthrie and Pascal Boyer,[41] Paleolithic cave art very likely served to express, among other things, an incipient religiosity. However, there seems to be a frankly scientistic, naturalistic bias among many researchers in the cognitive science of religion; the consequence is, as Fraser Watts has pointed out, that "many of those advocating the CSR [cognitive science of religion] story . . . make materialist, naturalist assumptions, from which it is congenial to find support for the assumption that religion is a cognitive mistake [i.e., merely a misapplication of an otherwise adaptive cognitive system]."[42] Guthrie and Boyer are hard-nosed scientists[43] and therefore, being devotees of research approaches based on these naturalistic assumptions, they prefer to interpret such cave art as naturalistic and figurative representations of this-worldly phenomena. Regarding such a naturalist, materialist bias in the (especially human) sciences, it bears to once more read Jean-Pierre Dupuy's comments that

> it is useless to speak of religion in the third person, adopting the sort of disinterested attitude that is appropriate to a scientific investigation on the positivist [i.e., the reductive naturalist] model. Those who do speak this way typically find that they cannot avoid betraying the hatred they feel toward religion. It is altogether natural, then, that they should hold it at arm's length, holding their noses against the stench it gives off—not out of a concern for scientific objectivity, but because of the striking abuse and ridicule they themselves have heaped upon it. Understanding the least thing about religion in this case is quite obviously impossible.[44]

While I find that this assessment to be fitting overall, I also find that this passage and especially the last sentence may seem to be too harsh an indictment of the naturalist approach to the science of religion. For as was noted above, there are neuroscientists and cognitive scientists who neither discount nor demean the favorable implications of their findings for religious life and theological study.[45]

Granting such sympathetic accord, a positivist natural-science approach to the study of the evolution of human cultural beliefs and practices would be, as

41. Pascal Boyer, "Paleolithic Art: Awesome—but Not Religious," International Cognition and Culture Institute, February 24, 2009, accessed June 5, 2022, https://www.cognitionandculture.net/blogs/pascal-boyer/paleolithic-art-awesome-mdash-but-not-religious/index.html. R. Dale Guthrie, *The Nature of Paleolithic Art* (University of Chicago Press, 2005).

42. Fraser, "Religion and the Emergence," 127.

43. For instance, from a naturalist perspective, Guthrie, *The Nature of Paleolithic Art*, believes that the cave paintings were made by testosterone-high male adolescents, a belief also consistent with his views that statuettes of females served as a form of prehistoric pornography.

44. Dupuy, *The Mark of the Sacred*, 91.

45. As an example, see Lewis-Williams, *Conceiving God.*

the British philosopher of history Robin G. Collingwood argued, a study of the *natural past* and not of the *historical past*. The study of biological evolution, after all, is a historical as well as a natural science. Seen this way, evolutionary psychology considered as a purely natural science cannot do full justice to the history of poignant religious experiences on which religious ideas and practices rest. As Collingwood pointed out in his treatise *The Idea of History*, the proper study of the historical past can be aided by study of the natural past. Yet, to minimize the influence of presentist thinking and interpretation, that study requires use of a distinct historical method consisting of a sympathetic reenactment of past thought, by which the historian feels her- or himself immersed as much as possible in the full cognitional context and ambience characterizing a particular period in the past.[46] To this I would that, when researching the natural history of religion, the historian even more importantly immerses her- or himself sympathetically as much as possible in the full *experiential* context and ambience characterizing a particular period in the past.

That said, much of Paleolithic cave art consists, alongside the more figurative naturalistic representations, of nonrepresentational "abstract" and symbolic images found in deep passages many hundreds of meters from the caves' entrances. Symbolic expressions of Neanderthal origin have even been found recently in caves as early as the Middle Paleolithic period, which predates the Upper Paleolithic period, ranging from roughly 55 to 15 Kya.[47] What sort of conscious experiential contents would motivate Neanderthals and early *homo sapiens* some 50 millennia ago or earlier to invest so much effort to produce nonfigurative, *symbolic* expressions in caves, especially in chambers at the farthest reaches of the caves? From the viewpoint of a religiously sympathetic and informed historian, is it not reasonable to see that symbolic art expressions found in the farthest depths of the cave reflect a desire to physically distance oneself, and thus spiritually retreat, from the mundane, natural world outside the cave into an extra-natural sacred realm that is as experientially rich as it is profound? And could the experiences associated with such a retreat from everyday reality possibly serve as a precursor to deeply emotion-laden, ecstatic experiences of transcendence and the holy that were attested to in much later times by the likes of Teresa of Avila, John of the Cross, or Julian of Norwich? Based on the extensive archeological and anthropological evidence reviewed and examined by David Lewis-Williams and by Gregory Wightman,[48] a credible

46. As advocated by R. R. Collingwood, *The Idea of History* (Oxford University Press, 1956).

47. Marti et al., "The Symbolic Role"; A. W. Pike et al., "U-series Dating of Paleolithic Art in 11 Caves in Spain," *Science* 336, no. 6087 (2012): 1409–13; Rodríguez-Hidalgo et al., "The Châtelperronian Neanderthals."

48. Lewis-Williams, *Conceiving God*; Gregory J. Wightman, *The Origins of Religion in the Paleolithic* (Rowman & Littlefield, 2015).

answer is that the depths of the caves served not merely as canvases for this-worldly figurative art but also as portals to otherworldly realms. Entry into these spiritual realms by shamans was facilitated via ritualistically-induced visions and other "ur-religious" experiences, many of which were depicted on the walls and ceilings of the caves. It is likely that the cultural memory of such primal experiences was kept alive over millennia and expressed in symbolic versions of caves such as those that are found, among other cultures, in the sacred earth lodges of American Plains Indians and in the kivas of New Mexico's Pueblo communities, both of which contain altars and sipapus, the latter serving as symbolic portals from and to the depths of a subterranean spiritual realm.[49]

Although I hazard to venture into the field of prehistoric shamanic religious experiences, I will nonetheless do so, since such experiences may be key to understanding how the emergence of a personal, private, and privileged access to them by a shaman transmuted these experiences in a politically and economically meaningful way by endowing the shaman with a claim to his or her personal ownership of them. In other words, it's the personal privilege claimed by the shaman to *mediate* his or her experience of the transcendent, extra-natural realm to the spiritually unpracticed community. This, I speculate, resulted in the eventual formation of a hierarchical top-down power structure *governing* the communal lives of the Paleolithic, ur-religious community. Preserved in the later priestly mediation practiced ritualistically, for example, in Biblical times, this governing body eventually adopted a sanctioning of violence directed at those deemed to be offenders against the religious community. Much later still, in the 17th century CE, the religious governance sanctioning use of violence against the community's offenders was transferred to secular authority, characterizing the modern nation-state that occasionally has to deal with offenders against the secular social community.[50] Although this may sound like farfetched fantasy, it finds support in the study by the political scientist Barry Cooper of "Paleolithic politics." Referring to the work of Jean Clottes and David Lewis-Williams,[51] he notes that a

> novel conclusion the authors drew from their understanding of the caves as ritual centers and of the art as shamanic was that, to put it bluntly, a big, lavishly decorated cave was an expression of *spiritual and material power.* Their conclusion seemed to combine a Durkheimian view of religious experience with a contemporary notion of the major caves as [communal] "aggregation sites." A large cave that combined both decorated "public"

49. Lewis-Williams, *Conceiving God*, 129, lists numerous other examples of sipapus, hole-like entries into the spiritual realm.

50. Toulmin, *Cosmopolis*; Cavanaugh, *The Myth of Religious Violence.*

51. Clottes, *What Is Paleolithic Art?*; Jean Clottes and David Lewis-Williams, *The Shamans of Prehistory: Trance and Magic in the Painted Caves* (Harry N. Adams, 1998).

> spaces and decorated hidden nooks, such as Lascaux or Chauvet, could also combine a ritual space for social groups larger than extended families and as "sanctuaries" to which initiates might repair for ASC [altered states of consciousness] experiences. Such chambers "were—paradoxically—conspicuous yet hidden displays of religious, and no doubt economic, power and influence." Moreover, such unequal power relations "were probably underwritten by different degrees of exploitation of the shamanic cosmos."[52] (emphasis added)

Although this shamanistic hypothesis has not gone uncontested,[53] it does make sense in the context of prehistoric communal religious experiences and ritual practices. Governance of these experiences and practices may have evolved into the exclusive sanction of violence to protect and preserve the communal and social structures of prehistoric and later of historic humans.

Mimetic Desire and Sacrifice

Another outlier of the cognitive evolutionary approach to the scientific study of religion is found in the French literary and anthropological scholar René Girard's notions of mimetic desire and its cultural consequences. While most rituals practiced in the prehistoric shamanic settings may have been benign insofar as they merely induced ASCs, the rituals that were adopted in later religious and social practices were far from benign; for these later sacrificial rituals and practices could take on very violent forms. It is this violence evident in ritualistic sacrifice that has captured the attention of René Girard. Extrapolating from his comparative literary studies of novels, Girard formulated an idea that is the foundation of his anthropological, social, and cultural theorizing—namely, that of mimetic desire.[54] As is typical of overly ambitious builders of theoretical systems, he promoted this interesting concept as the

52. Cooper, *Paleolithic Politics,* 283. See also David Graeber and David Wengrow, *The Dawn of Everything: A New History of Humanity* (Farrar, Straus and Giroux, 2021), 124, 157–58.

53. Cooper, *Paleolithic Politics,* 294–97.

54. For development of Girard's views on mimetic desire, see René Girard, *Deceit, Desire, and the Novel: Self and Other in Literary Structure* (Johns Hopkins University Press, 1966); René Girard, *The Scapegoat* (Johns Hopkins University Press, 1986); René Girard, *The Girard Reader* (Crossroads Publishing Co., 1996); and René Girard, "Animal Scapegoating at Çatalhöyük," in *How We Became Human: Mimetic Theory and the Science of Evolutionary Origins,* ed. Pierpaolo Antonello and Paul Gifford (Michigan State University Press, 2015). For the relevance of mimetic-desire theory to religion and theology, see Pierpaolo Antonello and Paul Gifford, eds., *How We Became Human: Mimetic Theory and the Science of Evolutionary Origins* (Michigan State University Press, 2015); Grant Kaplan, *René Girard, Unlikely Apologist: Mimetic Theory and Fundamental Theology* (University of Notre Dame Press, 2016).

foundation of an all-encompassing explanation of the origin and dynamics of human social order, culture, and religion. Despite Girard's peremptory style of presentation, the mimetic-desire approach is credible as a *partial* explanation of how rivalrous violence that can arise within and among social groups is mitigated by sacrificial scapegoating. According to Girard, desire in humans living in social settings rarely, if ever, arises spontaneously, but instead is generated foremost by observing and then mimetically appropriating the behavioral expression of the desires of others. (The immediately evident problem here is that some ur-persons must have experienced their desire spontaneously before others could mimetically appropriate it.) At any rate, such social contagion of desire leads not only to the "Jacksons competitively keeping up with the Joneses" but eventually also to the "Jacksons outdoing the Joneses," which in turn leads to the Joneses mimetically upping their desires in a perpetuating a cycle of competition ever spiraling upward. According to Girard, given limited resources for satisfying the relentlessly amplified desires, on a massive group scale such a positive feedback loop results in a mimetic crisis of heightened interpersonal and social stress and tension that portends a catastrophic breakup of the very interpersonal fabric that, up to that point, bound all members the group to each other.

Girard further proposed that to avert or respond to this disastrous crisis, which is misinterpreted—and here the religious element is inserted—as caused by the displeasure of a god or gods, the members of the social community, blind to the actual internal cause of their troubles, look to an external source, in short, to a human scapegoat. The scapegoat's sacrifice, believed to appease the gods, restores social calm. Examples of the consequences of this sort of mimetic rivalry are portrayed in the Biblical account of Cain's murder of Abel and in Sigmund Freud's imaginative accounts of religion's founding murder of the primal father (or father figure) by his sons.[55] The sacrifices reduce the accumulated

55. With due respect but contrary to Cavanaugh, *The Myth of Religious Violence*, religious violence is a real phenomenon and danger. Here, see James K. Wellman, Jr., ed., *Belief and Bloodshed: Religion and Violence Across Time and Tradition* (Rowman & Littlefield, 2007); Pierpaolo Antonello and Paul Gifford, eds., *Can We Survive Our Origins: Readings in René Girard's Theory of Violence and the Sacred* (Michigan State University Press, 2015); and Jonathan Sacks, *Not in God's Name: Confronting Religious Violence* (Schocken Books, 2015). Cavanaugh's claim that religious violence is a myth, for one, rests greatly on his emphasis that historically "religion" was not clearly defined or identified and on the questionable assumption that religion (whatever it is) and the politics of the modern state, which now controls and authorizes the power of violence, are separable. One should note again (see note 4 of the introduction) that many physical concepts, e.g., that of the electron, also defied clear specification for some time. Nonetheless, physicists do not deny that whatever our current concept of electron refers to, it existed several billion years ago. For similar reasons, to say that religions did not exist until recent times denies the historic facts that religious practices such as sacrifice, prayer, ritual, worship, and others clearly existed in antiquity, even though the words and

stress and tension and thus function as powerful sources of drive reduction, which in turn acts as a powerful reinforcer of scapegoating behavior. This prompts further scapegoating behavior when a subsequent crisis of mimetic desire eventually arises and thus the violent cycle of sacrificial rituals is continued, either with humans serving as scapegoats (e.g., child sacrifices and the massive human sacrifices found in past Meso-American Indian cultures) or, to spare humans, with animal scapegoats (e.g., animals used in the Biblical temple sacrifices). According to Girard, the ignorance or suppression of the actual reason for the sacrifices is facilitated by the creation of religious myths and by substituting the primal sacrificial events with more agreeable, symbolic ones. The emphasis here is not on religious thought—as emphasized in the evolutionary accounts of Pascal Boyer or Scott Atran—nor on practices per se, but on the myths' roles in hiding or suppressing aggressive, violent motives and drives within humans' individual and collective psychologies. Mythical elaborations of religious experiences and practices are a cultural veneer that serves to hide or suppress knowledge of deeper violent mimetic motives and their horrific consequences.

Girard therefore argues that a thorough demythification is required in order to contain or eliminate the other-directed violence that has been and continues to be practiced in the name of religion.[57] The demythification rests on exposing the underlying cause of scapegoating, i.e., the rivalrous mimetic desire that requires sacrificing a chosen victim, and on realizing through an act of conversion that, instead of sacrificing the other, the sacrificing of self or of self-centered desires can facilitate the attainment of nonviolent societal structures and norms of behavior. Such conversion is exemplified, for instance, in Christianity and Buddhism. In Christianity, Jesus's death on the cross can be seen not merely in terms of sacrificial ransom, atonement, or substitution for a sinful and fallen humanity, but also as the epitome and the freely chosen realization of self-sacrifice performed in solidarity with all humans striving for the Kingdom of God, where they can live with minimal violence done to each other. Similarly, in Buddhism, in addition to renouncing any violence done to sentient beings, bodhisattvas commit themselves to unselfishly foregoing the personal attainment of nirvana, the highest attainable state of well-being, until less enlightened sentient beings are liberated from the violence and suffering done to themselves and others.

However, as all-encompassing as Girard's account of scapegoat- or other-sacrifice may seem, other accounts of religious sacrifice are equally valid. In contrast to the other-sacrifice emphasized by Girard's account of the mimetic-

---

concepts for whatever religion referred to then might not have been clearly defined. That said, like the elite officials of the modern state, the religious elite in past societies also wielded political power, sometimes violently.

desire crisis, a key notion in chapter 1 of Terry Eagleton's book *Radical Sacrifice* is that "one must take a remarkably indulgent view of humankind, as many a liberal does, to assume that the self can come into its own without that fundamentally breaking and refashioning of which sacrifice has been one traditional sign. It would be the equivalent of claiming that the forms of political life we see around us could evolve into a state of justice without any notable degree of turbulence. Those who oppose sacrifice to the mutuality of love forgot that any durable version of the latter involves the self-giving of the former."[56] It is therefore the sacrifice of the self, and not the sacrifice of the other, that features prominently in many religions. This may mean voluntarily foregoing, at the near end of sacrifice, much of self-interest and self-pleasuring for the sake of benefitting and pleasing others and, at the remote end of sacrifice, offering up for the benefit of others, and to the glory of God, the pains attending torture, martyrdom, or crucifixion.

Yet one cannot forget that even self-sacrifice can partake of symbolic, substitute sacrifice that is part of religious rituals and practices. Describing ancient religions, the Jewish biblical scholar Abraham Heschel commented that "the distinction between the holy and the profane, between the divine and mundane, is the basis of religious thinking. A line is drawn between the interests of man and the demands of God. . . . The sacrificial act was [and still is] a form of personal association with God, a way of entering into communion with Him. In offering an animal, *a person was offering himself vicariously* [to God, since] it had the power of atonement [for sins]. . . . In offering [vicarious] sacrifice, man mingled with mystery, reached a summit of significance: sin was consumed, self [was] abandoned, [and] satisfaction was bestowed on divinity."[57] What held for the Hebrew religion, still holds for the other Abrahamic religions.[58] Especially in the Eucharist celebrated in Christian liturgies, wine and bread are offered to God in observance of Christ's offering to Christians his body, blood, and life.

What can the reader and I conclude from all the approaches to the study of religion discussed above? The cognitive-based approaches taken by evolutionary psychologists are sufficient within the realm of human intellect and thought. Costly commitment-based approaches are sufficient within the realms of the human heart, will, and motivation. Mimetic-desire approaches are sufficient within the realm of human desires and the aggressive drives and rivalries often associated with them. Religious impulses inspired by any of these realms, even if they are evoked at nonconscious levels, are inevitably accompanied by

56. Terry Eagleton, *Radical Sacrifice* (Yale University Press, 2018), 2.

57. Abraham J. Heschel, *The Prophets* (Harper & Row, 1962), 250–51.

58. David L. Weddle, *Sacrifice in Judaism, Christianity, and Islam* (New York University Press, 2017); Meir Hatina and Meir Litvak, eds., *Martyrdom and Sacrifice in Islam: Theological, Political and Social Contexts* (I. B. Tauris, 2017).

some phenomenal qualities, by some kind of conscious experience, be it that of merely a thought, of an unseen agent, of the sacred dimension of existence, of righteous anger and judgment or, in contrast, of self-giving charity and compassion. The historic and cultural evolution of human consciousness and the phenomenal experiences that manifest mind's sensuous, intellectual, and emotional contents go hand in hand with whatever strictly naturalistically evolved endowments might promote religious beliefs and practices. Collectively, these approaches play a role in fashioning a somewhat richer understanding, one that in its full existential and spiritual import is experientially richer and more comprehensive than the partial, cognitive, and neo-Darwinian evolutionary explanations of religion. Getting to know the empirical findings of, and the different theoretical approaches to, the scientific study of religion can be a wonderful scholarly adventure of the intellect. However while this intellectual adventure can add to one's religious sensibilities, it might do so, as it did for me, by not a whole lot more than a smidgen.

CHAPTER 3

The Science of Morality, Religion's Partner

The reader may wonder why morality is considered a partner to religion. One reason for the partnership is the fact that, historically, the doctrines of every major world religion have been accompanied by evident ethical and moral principles. The reason for this may lie in a natural inclination to view morality and religion as inseparable. In discussing mystical knowledge in his book *Degrees of Knowledge*, Jacques Maritain sheds light on this connatural relation between religion and morality by asking and answering the following question: "Where in the natural order do we find at every turn knowledge by inclination? In that vast realm of judgments about action: practical judgments. That is the field par excellence of knowledge by connaturality, for such knowledge necessarily intervenes in prudential judgments wherein the intellect has to judge with conformity with right will. . . . [And] let it be noted that the moral virtues—and even the natural beginnings of such virtues within us—create a certain affinity in the soul with the *spiritual order*. . . ."[1]

This chapter, then, addresses two additional questions: What does scientific research contribute to our understanding of morality? And what part does religion play in our understanding of morality? The answer to the first question might be: Not much at all; for according to what by now is a platitude, science can inform you about what in our conduct *is* or *can be* the case, but not about what in it *ought to be* the case. To confuse the facts of morality revealed by scientific research—which can inform us about how we arrive at specific decisions that guide our moral actions—with the *wherefore* that grounds the oughtness of moral choices is, as pointed out by the 18th-century Scottish philosopher David Hume and by the early 20th-century English philosopher G. E. Moore,[2] to commit what is known as the naturalist fallacy. Although empirically garnered facts explain *that* certain moral principles, strategies, and decisions are applied in morally fraught situations, one must not too readily conclude they establish scientific foundations for what choices of action *ought to be made* in such situations. Yet despite the caution, in recent

1. Jacques Maritain, *The Degrees of Knowledge* (University of Notre Dame Press, 1998), 298–99.

2. David Hume, *An Enquiry Concerning Human Understanding* (Hackett Publishing, 1993); G. E. Moore, *Principia Ethica* (Dover Publications, 2004).

years one of the ambitious aims of the science of morality was to explore and find natural foundations of morality.

An important concern addressed in what follows below is whether scientific investigations of human nature can disclose something akin to a natural-law basis—the what-is of nature, specifically the what-is of human nature—that underwrites the regulative ought-to-be of human conduct. This concern is as ancient as the philosophic thinking about the nature of matter and the nature of the good life addressed in the 5th and 4th centuries BCE by Greek philosophers.[3] To address the concern, let's first explore what in nature might motivate scientific research strategies aimed at revealing the ethical principles and rules underlying moral choices and behaviors.

A Practical Reason for Distinguishing Ethics from Morality

Although ethics and morality are sometimes considered to be identical, for practical reasons discussed below the meaning of "ethics" is herein reserved for the abstract principles or standards that can provide *general* guidelines for *specific* moral conduct. Besides natural-law principles, several other influential examples of such principles for guiding conduct are (i) virtue ethics (achieving human excellence; advocated by Aristotle), (ii) consequentialist ethics (judging the morality of actions only by their consequences), (iii) utilitarian ethics (a type of consequentialism: achieving maximal happiness and minimal unhappiness for the maximal number of humans, advocated by Jeremy Bentham and Adam Smith), (iv) pragmatic ethics (adapting the methods of science to incrementally discover the moral good; advocated by Charles Sanders Peirce and John Dewey), (v) the deontological duty ethics (the obligation to regard humans as ends rather than means and to do the right thing for its own sake, advocated by Immanuel Kant), and (vi) the emotivist/expressivist ethics relying purely on personal preference.[4] In contrast to these general principles, "morality" will refer to the specific choice of conduct of individual humans in the changeable, at times tangled, and conflict-ridden settings to which the more general principles are meant to apply.

3. See Kenneth James Dover, *Greek Popular Morality in the Time of Plato and Aristotle* (University of California Press, 1974). Besides the Greek and Christian moral traditions, those of Buddhism and Taoism also espouse something akin to a natural-law basis of ethical conduct, where the aim is to conduct one's life according to a way/path (the Tao) that is in harmony with human nature.

4. For explanation and critique of emotivist/expressivist ethics, see Alasdair MacIntyre, *After Virtue* (University of Notre Dame Press, 1984); Alasdair MacIntyre, *The Task of Philosophy* (Cambridge University Press, 2006); Alasdair MacIntyre, *Ethics in the Conflicts of Modernity: An Essay on Desire, Practical Reasoning, and Narrative* (Cambridge University Press, 2016).

This choice of meanings of, and distinction between, ethics and morality is not based on substantive reasons but is instead for strictly practical reasons when conducing scientific research into moral decision-making. In these research settings, the difference between ethical systems is often considered to be the *independent variable* from which the researcher ideally is free to choose two or more, and the behavioral and neuroscientific responses that accompany the moral choices of research participants are the *dependent variables* (since a participant's choice of action is thought to depend on which ethical principles guide his or her choice of actions). As will become evident below, of the ethical principles that could be implemented in research on moral decision-making, the utilitarian and the deontological have featured nearly exclusively in the current science of morality. From my perspective, the reason for this is that they are conceptually easy to distinguish and thus easily implemented in behavioral and neuroscientific research on how moral choices are made. In contrast, although the behavioral and neuroscientific recordings of the dependent variable would present next to no problem, the subtle distinctions between, say, utilitarian ethics and consequentialist ethic would be harder to implement methodologically as distinct independent variables.

Moral Alchemy: Can the Moral "Ought" Be Distilled from the Factual "Is"?

What does science, specifically evolutionary science, neuroscience, and human sciences such as cognitive science, anthropology, and developmental psychology have to offer to our understanding of the basis of morality? One answer, as noted above, is: Not much at all. Yet, I believe that there is a moral precept that applies in any ethic and that we can take as a minimal given: When painful suffering, be it corporal or psychological, is experienced by humans and other sentient creatures, it is not experienced as an *intrinsic* good.[5] On the contrary, in the evolution of sentient creatures and particularly in humans whose consciousness is most highly developed, it is experienced as intrinsically aversive, an *intrinsic* bad, to be instinctively avoided[6]; this, despite its ability to occasionally serve a good. Consider, for example, the physical sensation of pain when touching a hot object with one's fingers; it serves two goods, the instinctive withdrawal of the fingers so as to minimize tissue damage and the knowledge that one should avoid such painful and potentially destructive contacts in the future. Given the

5. There are the rare cases of masochism in which pain, though aversive, is nonetheless sought and experienced as a desirable sensation and thus as a good.

6. Timothy Anders, *The Evolution of Evil* (Open Court, 1994). Mara Van der Lugt, *Dark Matters: Pessimism and the Problem of Suffering* (Princeton University Press, 2021), 248, notes that the 18th-century philosopher Jean-Jacques Rousseau also considered physical (bodily) evils as intrinsic to sentience or consciousness.

universally aversive nature of pain and suffering, a prime natural, instinctive directive governing human conduct negatively is that we eliminate or at least minimize undue or unnecessary pain and suffering to ourselves and others before we and others can even consider and promote the positive pursuit a happy and flourishing life.

Whether and under what circumstances we ought to avoid pain and suffering in ourselves and others or tolerate them or under what circumstances we ought to increase the enjoyment of our and their lives ultimately comes down to a judgment issuing from our practical and moral senses. That science can inform our understanding of ethical and moral judgments and the pursuant behavior is no more controversial than its also informing our understanding of other value-laden practices like our enjoyments of hobbies and the arts. In this purely instrumental way, the neurosciences, evolutionary sciences, and life-span sciences may shed some light on how the study of brain processes, genes, cognition, emotions and motivations, and human postnatal development influence or support moral choices and the actions that behaviorally ratify them.

A Scientistic Proposal for Scientific Study of Morality

Yet in his book *The Moral Landscape*, Sam Harris, basically reprising a combination of the utilitarian ethics of Jeremy Bentham and John Stuart Mill and the pragmatic, science-derived ethics promoted by Charles Sanders Peirce and John Dewey noted above, seems to go beyond such merely descriptive accounts of the isness of morality's necessary supports by endorsing a naturalistic, scientific framework for understanding the foundational oughtness of morality. As the subtitle of the book, *How Science Can Determine Human Values*, suggests, Harris's aim is more ambitious in claiming that science, particularly human brain science, is now in the position to inform us not only descriptively how we arrive at decisions that affect our moral choices of behavior but also prescriptively determine what humans *ought to* value and, thus, how they *ought to* act in morally fraught situations. One can readily agree, for instance, with Harris's premise that the aim of ethics and morality is to promote human well-being. That agreement itself, however, does not require a "scientific" imprimatur. Through centuries spanning from, say, the Axial Age (800–200 years BCE) to present times, it has been accepted by ethicists throughout the world that human physical, mental, and spiritual well-being is a good to be promoted and pursued, and their opposite, physical, mental, and spiritual miseries, are to be minimized. An account of science consistent with these pre-scientific truths sounds reasonable insofar as it describes the moral landscape filled with desirable goods and undesirable bads. But among others, I argue that science ultimately cannot give us a foundational account that *determines* or augments in any measurable way the reason for the oughtness underlying our pursuit of goods and avoidance of bads produced by individual humans or communally by sociocultural structures.

Harris, like the rest of us, subscribes to a complex set of views on what constitutes a morally aware human person. Touting his expertise in human brain science, he asserts that "the more we understand ourselves at the level of the brain, the more we will see that there are right and wrong answers to questions of human values. . . . [This claim supports his premise that] human well-being *entirely* depends on events in the world and on states of the human brain"[7] (emphasis added), claiming further that "human experience shows every sign of being determined by, and realized in, states of the human brain."[8] So far, we see that Harris's approach to morality is conditioned by a combination of pragmatic, behavioral, naturalistic, and neuro-reductive perspectives. When he adds to his scientific-pragmatic ethics the belief that "science can help us find a path leading away from the lowest depths of misery and toward the heights of happiness for the greatest number of people,"[9] one can additionally conclude that his approach to understanding the ethics behind human morality also includes a hefty share of utilitarianism/consequentialism.[10] One can moreover infer that Harris's search for a scientific basis of morality is motivated not only by purely scientific reasons but also by the aim of promoting a scientistic belief system that in turn supports his militant neoatheist and anti-religious belief system, a system that seeks to destroy any trace of religion in human society. Harris explains that he has "made the case elsewhere [referring to one of his prior books, *The End of Faith*] that religion and science are in a zero-sum conflict with respect to facts. Here I have begun to argue that a division between facts and values is intellectually unsustainable, especially from the perspective of neuroscience."[11] The final phrase in the quoted passage is *especially* astounding. I for one fail to see how the perspective of neuroscience in particular renders a division between presumably scientific facts and human values unsustainable. There is no line of philosophical or logical reasoning, beginning from the perspective of neuroscience, that supports this bold and bald claim.

Elsewhere, Harris makes the additional claim "that consciousness is the only intelligible domain of value"[12] (emphasis added). I chose this particular claim two reasons. First, as a positive note and in light of the discussions in

7. Sam Harris, *The Moral Landscape: How Science Can Determine Human Values* (Free Press, 2010), 2.

8. Harris, *The Moral Landscape*, 8.

9. Harris, *The Moral Landscape*, 28.

10. Utilitarian ethics is guided by the principle that human pain and misery should be minimized and that human pleasure and happiness should be maximized. But because, as noted by MacIntyre, *After Virtue*, 64, both pleasure and happiness come in a wide variety of forms, utilitarianism suffers from the lack of specificity as to *which* pleasure and which happiness one should pursue.

11. Harris, *The Moral Landscape*, 24.

12. Harris, *The Moral Landscape*, 32.

chapters 1 and 2 and in appendices 1–2 of the importance of consciousness to science, religion, art, and other cultural practices, one can heartily agree with Harris that consciousness is, if not the only, then certainly one of the highest ranking human values. Second, however, when one assesses Harris's praise of consciousness more deeply, using Harris's own scientistically inspired neuroreductive view of consciousness, one can come to a very different conclusion regarding consciousness. From Harris's reductive neuroscientific perspective, human experiences are realized in brain states (see note 8 above). There are various meanings that can be attached to "realize." The meaning that I assume Harris intends is found in the words "actualize" and "materialize," or in the phrase "make real." If so, then according to Harris, consciousness is actualized, materialized, or made real in a brain state. However, based on the meaning of these words and phrasing, which perhaps was not intended by Harris, one can easily go on to conclude—as the psychologist Nicholas Humphrey did[13]—that consciousness is, without remainder, nothing but pattern of neuronal activity in the brain. In other words, the consciousness by which your, the reader's, and my mental contents become subjectively and most immediately and intimately manifest to each of us is not a *sui generis* real entity. Instead, consciousness is, as many scientistically leaning neuroscientists believe, nothing but an epiphenomenal illusion, a mere insubstantial shadow and sideshow of what's actually going on in the brain. In either view—consciousness reduced to a mere brain state or as a mere illusion—Harris might just as well have claimed that a brain state or else an illusion is the only intelligible domain of value. There are many other such anomalies one can identify that follow from a neuroreductive view of consciousness and therefore of conscious mental functions such as deliberately reasoning about, judging, choosing, and planning courses of action.

What should be an obvious fact to the reader is that non-sentient creatures, those without any consciously experienced well-being or suffering, lack any moral concerns about the oughtness regarding good and bad conduct. Hence, one can readily agree with Harris that, since consciousness has evolved to the highest degree in humans and is closely tied to the neuronal activity in the human brain, neuroscience and evolutionary psychology can provide some insights into human ethical and moral conduct.[14] Yet all of this is uncontroversial and consequently, in and of itself, it fails to justify Harris's prescriptive extrapolation "that morality *should* be considered an undeveloped branch of science"[15] (emphasis added). This claim is somewhat ambiguous. It could simply

13. Nicholas Humphrey, *Soul Dust: The Magic of Consciousness* (Princeton University Press, 2011).

14. Boyer, "Gods and Mental Instincts," 248; Rossano, *Supernatural Selection*, 20; Norenzayan et al., "The Cultural Evolution of Prosocial Religions," *Behavioral and Brain Sciences* 39 (2016): e1.

15. Harris, *The Moral Landscape*, 4.

mean that morality can, and therefore *should*, be considered an undeveloped branch of science insofar as scientific research may reveal previously unknown facts that could provide insights to other disciplines such as philosophy and theology when they deal with ethics and morality. But as stated, the claim could also be understood from a scientistic perspective—to which science-informed atheists like Harris too readily subscribe—that the study of ethics and morals will be entirely subsumed under natural science. For once the science of morality is sufficiently developed, it may serve—as the sociobiologist E. O. Wilson would have it—as the primary and ultimate and thus the fully sufficient understanding of morality.[16] Harris goes on to claim that since "the well-being of conscious creatures *is bound to be* a product of natural laws, we must expect that this space of possibilities—the moral landscape—will increasingly be illuminated by science"[17] (emphasis added). From a natural-science viewpoint—and I believe that is the standpoint that Harris assumes—the phrase "natural laws" here means the physical laws of nature rather than the moral laws that can be derived philosophically from an anthropological view of human nature and the nature of the social world that humans inhabit.

This scientistic naturalizing of ethics goes at least as far back as the utilitarianism of Jeremy Bentham, who according to Stephen Gaukroger "initiated the naturalization of moral reasoning, arguing that the morality of behaviour was to be assessed in terms of observable consequences."[18] Bentham was enthralled by the burgeoning quantifiable empirical sciences and even went so far as to "quantify" the moral consequences—at least on an ordinal scale—along a continuum of greater or lesser good. This consequentialist naturalization program was adopted by John Stuart Mill, who extended it "to all forms of reasoning, construing logical inference in terms of a combination of naturalistic psychology and empirical generalization."[19] The generalization went so far as to include not only moral but also political and economic discourse, allowing Mill to unify "ethics and political economy into a single scientifically inspired utilitarian project."[20] In line with natural-law views of morality, one can fully agree that there can be a natural science of ethics and morality. But need it unnecessarily exclude the influence of factors that are not the natural laws explored by science, e.g., ethical principles that have been painstakingly studied and rationally—but not necessarily scientifically—appraised through careful philosophical reflections and

16. Edward O. Wilson, *Consilience: The Unity of Knowledge* (Vintage Books, 1999); Edward O. Wilson, *Sociobiology: The New Synthesis* (Harvard University Press, 2000); Edward O. Wilson, *The Social Conquest of Earth* (W. W. Norton, 2013).

17. Harris, *The Moral Landscape*, 13.

18. Stephen Gaukroger, *The Failures of Philosophy: A Historical Essay* (Princeton University Press, 2020), 256.

19. Gaukroger, *The Failures of Philosophy*, 256.

20. Gaukroger, *The Failures of Philosophy*, 256.

analyses? By all means, science can illuminate the moral landscape, a landscape that, however, has existed for millennia prior to its scientific illumination.

That said, doesn't the additional danger exist that science will reshape and thereby change the moral landscape by flattening it to suit scientific methods of studying it, or conform it to the scientistic credo in an ultimately naturalistic, all-encompassing scientific landscape in its stead, which would be the case if our understanding of morality, according to the wishes of E. O. Wilson, is absorbed *tout court* by the natural sciences? Along with others,[21] one can reply with an emphatic "Yes, these dangers exist!" While factually illuminating and adding to the moral landscape, science *cannot replace* but *can displace*—by shoving aside—the additional moral knowledge and insights garnered from philosophy, religion, and even the literary arts (see below). Limited to a natural-science approach to morality, it is difficult if not impossible to explain how Jesus's moral injunction to love and forgive not only your friends and neighbors, but additionally your adversaries, could have been uttered by him.

Even Harris agrees that natural science "cannot tell us why, *scientifically*, we should value [our] health [and well-being, and that of other creatures]."[22] However, although science cannot tell us *why* we *ought to* value human health and well-being, it does inform us *that* and *how* we *do* value them, as Harris believes. But again, that leaves science merely confirming a fact that most humans in the world have (unscientifically) taken for millennia as obviously granted. That science cannot tell us *why* is because, to paraphrase Stanley Jaki, science can deliver only the patterns of nature [the *that*] but it cannot deliver ethical principles on which moral conduct is based.[23] As to why one *ought to* value health and well-being of oneself and of others, a straightforward and satisfactory scientific answer is not forthcoming; for just like the child that responds to every factual answer their parent gives with another "but why . . . ?" so also an answer given by the wisest scientist in terms of, say, the flourishing of bodily, psychological, or spiritual life, only provokes further why-questions. So, if science can tell us *that we naturally do* but ultimately cannot tell us *why we should* value our health and well-being, then the same applies to additional values; for science can't tell us why forgiving our neighbors and even our enemies is to be valued, why refraining from tormenting a child emotionally or physically is valuable, why a beautiful painting deserves admiration, or why a musical composition is valuable, and similarly with innumerable additional whys and values. It therefore follows, as Michael Polanyi and his fellow philos-

21. See Hutchinson, *Monopolizing Knowledge*; Tallis, *Aping Mankind*; Curtis White, *The Science Delusion: Asking Big Questions in a Culture of Easy Answers* (Melville House, 2013).

22. Harris, *The Moral Landscape*, 37.

23. Stanley L. Jaki, *Patterns or Principles and Other Essays* (Intercollegiate Studies Institute, 1995), 17.

opher Harry Prosch have noted, that it's as unlikely for objective—and presumably value-free—science to extract values from its factual research observations as it is to square a circle or construct a perpetual-motion machine.[24] Regarding the issue of objective, value-free science, Harris argues that the "categorical distinction between facts and values has opened a sinkhole beneath secular liberalism—leading to moral relativism. . . ."[25] Presumably he believes that the distinction ought to be eliminated, if only to save secular liberalism. Yet Harris would have to agree that *why we should* value and therefore save secular liberalism cannot be answered by science.

One can forgive Harris for any scientific overreaching—a characteristic of scientism—in trying to give what presumably is an objective grounding of moral and ethical values. This is particularly evident when contrasted with views held by a the biologist and fellow atheist Jerry Coyne, who claims, in response to his own question as to whether there are objective moral truths to be discovered, "I think not, for ultimately morality must rest on preferences . . . [and though these preferences] are often nearly universal ('It is immoral to kill an innocent person'), . . . they often diverge among cultures . . . [and therefore] their justification is invariably subjective."[26] That nearly universal preferences can often also diverge substantially among cultures is a somewhat baffling conclusion. I believe that what Coyne may have wanted to convey is not so much that such basic moral principles, e.g., "It is morally wrong to kill an innocent person," do not express objective moral truths—as opposed to a subjectively preferential one—but instead that among cultures there can be noticeable variance in the specific interpretation and application of such principles. For instance, rape is universally deemed to be a morally deplorable and evil act.[27] In most cultures, a raped woman is not deemed culpable; instead, she is regarded as a victim of violence done to her body and person. So, in those cultures one generally does not add to the harm already done to her by blaming, shaming, or punishing her. Instead, the culpability, social stigma, and punishment are meted to the perpetrator. However, in cultures in which, for instance, misogyny prevails, the woman, by some perverse reasoning, is regarded as adulterous and complicit and therefore also blamable and punishable for her rape. What differs among cultures here is not the basic principle that rape is an evil act to be abhorred but rather the spe-

24. Michael Polanyi and Harry Prosch, *Meaning* (University of Chicago Press, 1975).

25. Harris, *The Moral Landscape*, 46.

26. Jerry A. Coyne, *Faith vs. Fact: Why Science and Religion Are Incompatible* (Viking Press, 2015), 189.

27. The philosopher Luke Russell, *Evil: A Very Short Introduction* (Oxford University Press, 2022), makes a distinction between the classes of morally evil acts and morally bad acts. Accordingly, not all bad acts, e.g., filching candy from a dime store's counter, are necessarily evil ones; only the most heinous ones such as rape, torture, and murder are truly morally evil acts. Analogous to this is the Catholic doctrinal distinction between venial and mortal sins.

cific definitions of, and confusions about, cultural norms—which are not to be confused with moral norms—as to what differentiates victim from perpetrator, honor from dishonor, innocence from complicity, and how to differentially assign these attributes to the rapist and his victim.

Further Explorations of the Scientistic Approach to the Science of Morality

Harris's emphasis on health and well-being as a guiding moral principle that allows science's deterministic and largely utilitarian insertion into the moral landscape poses other foreseeable problems. Some contemporary ethicists and scientists[28] argue on utilitarian or personal grounds that it is morally permissible to euthanize, much like the ancient Spartans did, genetically or congenitally "defective" infants. Now, infants are, by definition, innocent. Hence the moral principle that no innocent person should be killed applies also to infants—unless, of course, as these same scientists and ethicists, "enlightened" as they are by science, argue that infants do not qualify as persons or that the suffering caused by their defect once they have attained bona fide personhood poses not only a possibility but instead also a probability nearing certainty that they and their loved ones will be subjected to greater harm than the definite harm done to them by euthanizing them shortly after birth.

But then, what of those documentable cases in which adults disabled by birth defects (Down's syndrome, cerebral palsy, cystic fibrosis, for instance) as well as their caretakers lived productive, meaningful, and otherwise flourishing and satisfying lives? Shall we have also sacrificed these impaired individuals at their birth to the finality of death? Many of us are likely aware of cases of individuals who, despite being afflicted with a serious birth defect, lead productive and flourishing lives. So, the future flourishing life of a disabled infant is not necessarily precluded by the handicap. In addition to these considerations are the ones applicable to cases where the defect is acquired after birth. Examples are the traumatically (open- or closed-head) brain injured, for example victims of strokes or inoperable brain tumors, war injuries, gun violence, and traffic, industrial, or sports accidents.[29] They, when comparing their current afflicted

28. Examples are the ethicist Peter Singer and the scientist James Watson. On Singer's ethics, see Jeffrey A. Schaler, *Peter Singer Under Fire: The Moral Iconoclast Faces His Critics* (Open Court, 2009). James Watson, Nobel laureate and co-discoverer with Francis Crick of the double-helical structure of DNA, maintains that only an infant older than 3 days merits being called a "person." For his view that an infant with disabilities should be euthanized at birth, see his online comments, accessed March 24, 2022, https://www.catholicleague.org/james-watson-fan-of-infanticide-resigns.

29. I was personally acquainted with two individuals afflicted with paraplegia and one, a former student, with quadriplegia. The quadriplegic student retained a buoyant, optimistic,

state to their past healthy state, perhaps suffer even more than those who have been afflicted by a defect since birth. How should we deal with these individuals and the burdens that they and their families and friends bear?

No one desires to carry such burdens and surely would rather be rid of them. In cases such as these, following St. Claire of Assisi's dictum that a love that does not know suffering is not worthy of the name, we are called on one hand to expend efforts unselfishly and lovingly—and suffer, if need be, discomforts and pains to ourselves—to rehabilitate these victims to the greatest extent possible, given whatever resources are available. On the other, less compassionate hand, a starkly contrasting calculus—based, for instance, on Ayn Rand's personalist and "objectivist" ethics that exalts the "virtue" of selfishness to the status of a straightforward prime directive[30] or on Jeremy Bentham's consequentialist utilitarian ethics that cooly calculates overall costs and benefits—might lead you to justify neglecting or even euthanizing them. If so, you might be spared having to deal with the problematic question raised in Dostoyevsky's novel, *The Brothers Karamazov*, by one of the brothers, Ivan: Can a great evil done to one innocent child be justified by the greater good for you or the rest of us? If you, however, have even a trace of the moral "heart" of Ivan's brother, Alyosha, and answer "no!," you might be affirming the minimizing calculus consistent with deontological principles that oblige one to commit no evil.

Conflicting considerations such as these (deliberately heightened by me) illustrate that deciding what moral course of action to take in ethically fraught situations, though sometimes straightforward, very often can be problematic. They also point out that the oughtness of moral action cannot be and should not be decided by science alone. Nevertheless, scientific approaches to the study of morality can be informative and provide some answers regarding how humans acquire a sense of morality and decide on what courses of moral action to take. That noted, the following sections deal with scientific approaches relevant to our moral understanding of human behavior.

Developmental Studies of the Acquisition of Moral Capacities

It is important, before appraising the postnatal acquisition of moral capacities, to spell out that the acquisition of any postnatal mental capacity depends on

---

and hopeful attitude; however, the paraplegic nursed a bitterly resigned, plaintive, and depressive attitude. The latter's attitude also seemed to resist efforts of psychological/spiritual counseling. In the very recent past, prosthetically aided physical therapies have produced promising rehabilitative results, allowing paralytics to regain some use of their lower limbs. The virtue of hope can be bolstered by the beneficent fruits of science-based technology.

30. Ayn Rand, *The Virtue of Selfishness* (Signet Classics, 1963).

the contribution of three key factors: (i) genetically inherited endowments already in place at or very shortly after birth, (ii) normal postnatal maturational processes that complete unfinished prenatal maturation, and (iii) postnatal exposure to environmental informational inputs. Examples from my specialty arise from the study of visual capacities. First, since at latest the1960s, it has been repeatedly shown that the visual systems of higher mammals such as cats and primates are not blank slates but instead are endowed at birth with a genetic, preorganized visual cortical anatomy that functions, if ever so crudely, as the necessary platform for the subsequent development of their more refined visuobehavioral capacities. Since humans are members of the primate species, their neocortices (as well as their subcortical structures) also are endowed at birth with an analogous functional neuroanatomy necessary for the maintenance and refinement of visual capacities during subsequent development. Second, like many other higher mammals, the human infant is born somewhat "prematurely" in that its visual and motoric systems continue to develop during a maturational period *ex utero* that continues along the genetic and ontogenetic trajectory begun during *in utero* development. This initial postnatal, maturational development, while obviously depending on sufficient nutritional sources available in the external environment, can proceed with little, if any, visual input from that environment. Third, in contrast to the postnatal maturational stage, it also has been repeatedly shown that the infant's subsequent development of the visual system's capabilities is very much influenced by the informational input available to the infant in the specific environment in which it is raised. In other words, during infancy, the environment in all of its visual complexity and richness must provide the stimulation necessary for the maintenance and further development of a healthy visual system. In summary, in humans the postnatal development of a normal, healthy visual system depends on the contribution of all three—the genetic, maturational, and environmental—factors. Hence, it's neither "nature," in its genetic or maturational form, or environmental "nurture" alone that is required for proper postnatal development; it is both.

These three factors no doubt also shape the postnatal development of human moral capacities. Developmental research on these capacities requires what by now are standard, cleverly applied experimental procedures and criteria. Of these, one of the most important is the use of an appropriate "indicator response" that an infant is capable of generating. Meant by that term is a response available to an infant before or at latest at the time the assumed presence of a moral sensibility is experimentally measured. Among such responses are (i) an innate orienting response elicited by sensory stimuli; (ii) an innate heart-rate habituation to repeated presentations of the same stimulus followed by dishabituation when a novel stimulus is presented; maturational acquisition of binocularly coordinated eye movements allowing infants to show (iii) preferential looking, indicating that infants are directing their attention toward some stimuli to the exclusion of others; somewhat later (iv) the acquisition of preverbal reaching-for and pointing-to responses, and later still, (v) responses like verbal indicators. For example, if developmental studies of infant vision were to rely strictly on verbal responses, one could conclude only that, for instance, two-year old toddlers can discriminate between assorted colors or wavelengths of stimuli. Fine and good as far as two-year old toddlers are concerned; however, it does not allow one to make any claims regarding the possibility that the same infants could have discriminated between them much earlier. In fact, with use of the visual orienting response that is present very few days after birth, developmental vision research has shown that even such young infants can already discriminate between long (red) wavelengths and medium (green) wavelengths of light, leading the researchers to conclude that this capability is most likely present at birth.

Behavioral Approaches to the Study of Postnatal Moral Development

The rationales and principles discussed above regarding the study of visual development apply also to the study of moral development. The following discussion of the postnatal development of moral sensibilities (but not of full-blown morality) relies heavily on the thorough research reviews published by several developmental scientists[31] who are more expert in this area of study than I am. Before turning to the conclusions drawn from the reviewed studies, two further aspects of these studies need to be listed. First, most of these studies relied on infants' viewing attention-eliciting "puppet shows" that displayed various behaviors of one puppet, the actor puppet, in relation to several other puppets; while simultaneously recording age-appropriate indicator responses to behaviorally assess the extent to which the infants could discriminate the favorability from the disfavorability of the actor puppet's behaviors. Second, I agree with Lawrence Kohlberg, one of the first psychologists to experimentally study the development of morally relevant behaviors,[32] that infants have not attained sufficient high-level reasoning powers to exercise genuine moral judgements. However, as the social psychologist Jonathan Haidt has pointed out, during

31. See Jean Decety, "The Neuroevolution of Empathy and Caring for Others: Why It Matters for Morality," in *New Frontiers in Social Neuroscience*, ed. Jean Decety and Yves Christen (Springer, 2014); J. Kiley Hamlin, "The Origins of Human Morality: Complex Socio-Moral Evaluations by Preverbal Infants," in *New Frontiers in Social Neuroscience*, ed. Jean Decety and Yves Christen (Springer, 2014); Julia W. Van de Vondervoort and J. Kiley Hamlin, "Evidence for Intuitive Morality: Preverbal Infants Make Sociomoral Evaluations," *Child Development Perspectives* 10, no. 3 (2016): 143–48.

32. Lawrence Kohlberg, *Stages in the Development of Moral Thought and Action* (Holt, Rinehart & Winston, 1969).

human development proceeding even into adulthood, "higher-level [rational] human thinking is accompanied, permeated, and influenced by affective reactions [feelings of like and dislike that already manifest during infancy by an infant's indicator response] which push us gently toward approach or [or not so gently toward] avoidance."[33] Despite infants' lacking higher-level reasoning abilities, these affective likes and dislikes can be easily elicited in preverbal infants. Hence, just as the developmental psychologist Deborah Kelemen thought of children as "intuitive theists" (see chapter 1, notes 26 and 28), one might want to refer to infants as "intuitive moralists."[34] However, in spite of the fact that developmental psychologists might refer to toddlers' "moral judgements," I believe that the best one can infer from these infant studies, for instance, of simulated inter-puppet relations, is that infants evince pre- or proto-rational inferences and therefore pre- or proto-moral sensibilities. For instance, confronted with the claim that "recent evidence indicates that infants are already capable of sophisticated mentalistic reasoning and can attribute to agents not only motivational states (e.g., goals) and epistemic states (e.g., ignorance) and counterfactual states (e.g., false beliefs) . . . ,"[35] one can pause and question exactly how *sophisticated* the *reasoning* of infants can actually be. No doubt, infants can behaviorally indicate their making some sort of mental inference, but it can be of a mostly primitive, intuitive, or emotional, i.e. irrational, nature than a sophisticated rational one.

That said, let's now present in summary form—with minimal experimental methodological and procedural details—several pertinent findings regarding the developmental trajectory of moral sensibilities.

1. With infants' preferential looking as an indicator response, Hamlin and co-workers used a puppet show where in one condition, a puppet helped another puppet accomplish a challenging task, and in a second condition hindered the same task. The results showed that a majority of 3-month infants preferred to look at a helper for a longer period time than at a hinderer. Thus, infants as young as three months old can already discriminate between prosocial and antisocial behaviors. However, these "early preferences [for helpers] appeared driven by a negative evaluation of the hinderers rather than a positive evaluation of the helpers: The 3-months-olds looked longer at a neutral [puppet] character than at the hinderers but looked equally often at the neutral

33. Jonathan Haidt, "The New Synthesis in Moral Psychology," *Science* 316, no. 5827 (2007): 998.

34. See Van de Vondervoort and Hamlin, "Evidence for Intuitive Morality."

35. Reneé Baillargeon et al., "Infant Social Cognition: Psychological and Sociomoral Reasoning," in *The Cognitive Neurosciences*, 5th ed., ed. Michael S. Gazzaniga and George R. Mangun (MIT Press, 2014), 7.

characters and the helpers."[36] However, when using reaching-for as a preferential indicator response, somewhat older infants between 4.5 and 6.5 months of age preferred to reach for helpers over hinderers, but additionally they preferred to reach for helper puppets over neutral puppets. And importantly, by 6 years of age, children's preference was characterized by a definite positive evaluation of helpers (choosing to reach more for helper puppets than neutral puppets) and a definite negative evaluation of hinderers (choosing to reach more for neutral puppets than hinderer puppets).

2. Hamlin was also able to show, in several experiments controlling for possible other explanations, that by 8 months of age infants were able to incorporate perceived intention of an agent in their evaluations of helper and hinderer regardless of the outcome of their actions. In these experiments, despite equating for outcomes of helpers' and hinderers' actions, the preferences of 8-month-old infants indicated that they distinguished puppet characters based on intention. In the positive-outcome condition, 8-month-old infants preferred helpers who succeeded in assisting a puppet accomplish its task over hinderers who failed to hinder the accomplishment of the same task. Similarly, in a negative-outcome condition, 8-month-old infants preferred helpers who failed in their helping efforts over hinderers who succeeded in their hindering efforts.
3. Employing these kinds of experimental setups, several studies also showed that infants between roughly 6 and 12 month of age required that the actions of helpers and hinderers be directed toward what was perceived to be a social agent when making their behavioral evaluations of helpers and hinderers. When neutral, nonsocial objects were substituted for the puppets, the infants showed no differential responses to helpers vs. hinderers.
4. Additional similar studies conducted by Hamlin and coworkers showed that preverbal infants were able to make knowledge-based evaluations. The infants differentially evaluated those puppet helpers and hinderers that the infants knew were deliberately acting to help or hinder, but did not differentially evaluate those that, to the infants, appeared to merely incidentally happen to help or hinder.[37] In other words, infants evaluated the helpers and hinderers favorably vs. unfavorably only when the helpers and hinderers *knowingly* (intentionally) helped vs. hindered an agent in achieving a goal but not when they *ignorantly* (unintentionally)

36. See Van de Vondervoort and Hamlin, "Evidence for Intuitive Morality," 144–45.

37. J. Kiley Hamlin et al., "The Mentalistic Basis of Core Social Cognition: Experiments in Preverbal Infants and a Computational Model," *Developmental Science* 16, no. 2 (2013): 209–26.

helped vs. hindered an agent in achieving a goal. This is analogous to what morally mature adults do when they respectively praise vs. blame those who knowingly commit morally good vs. bad actions but fail to praise or blame those who just happen to commit the same actions out of ignorance.

5. Infants also are able to take into account variations in the contextual setting when making evaluations of an agent's behavior. In one experiment, for example, infants positively evaluated a puppet that took goods away from a second puppet that had antisocially hindered others in achieving their goals; in contrast infants did not evaluate positively a puppet that took goods from second a puppet that that had prosocially helped others in achieving their goals. In other words, it appears that infants favor "punishing" wrongdoers. In another experiment examining the effects of varying contextual settings, two experimental conditions were implemented that equated for the outcomes of helpers' and hinderers' actions. Here, even infants as young as 4.5 months who selectively reached more for puppets that prosocially helped others did so more often than 4.5-month old children who selectively reached for puppets that also prosocially hindered antisocial others.[38]
6. Besides infants' abilities to intuitively manifest the above nuanced prosocial evaluations of the actions of others, unfortunately—as I see it—even young infants also appear to manifest biases towards positively evaluating the behaviors of an in-group (friend) vs. an out-group (stranger). But because the evidence supporting such a differential in-group vs. out-group biases seem less than strong to me and because such a finding about moral intuitions might have profound moral implications, I believe that more investigations confirming this possibility need to be forthcoming.
7. As humans progress from preverbal infancy into childhood, adolescence, and adulthood, they can eventually develop a more differentiated (see the bottom of point 1 above) and mature moral sense. Although the proto-moral sensibilities of the youngest toddlers may depend on inherited, built-in intuitive processes, the later developmental processes rely on higher-level cognitive capabilities that depend increasingly on environmental factors expressed in familial and social settings. In line with Kohlberg's assessment of infants' "moral judgments" noted above, it is therefore important to note, as Van de Vondervoort and Hamlin have, that

38. J. Kiley Hamlin, "Context-Dependent Social Evaluation in 4.5-Month-old Human Infants: The Role of Domain-General Versus Domain-Specific Processes in the Development of Evaluation," *Frontiers in Psychology* 5 (2014): 614.

> while we have presented evidence that infants evaluate others' morally relevant behaviors in complex ways, we do not claim that infants' moral evaluations are sensitive to all the factors adults consider when making moral judgments. Rather, the development of mature moral systems require experience, the maturation of cognitive abilities (executive functioning, problem solving, counterfactual reasoning), interactions with parents and peers, and socializations within the family and community. . . . We simply claim that these [later] developmental processes may be shaped by the [inherited predispositions that make possible the] early-emerging evaluations of cooperative and uncooperative others that are surprisingly consistent with certain aspects of mature moral systems.[39]

While all the above developmental trends in preverbal infants have relied on behavioral indicators, some of them are also corroborated by neuroscientifically obtained findings. These and other findings in the brain sciences relevant to our understanding of the brain substrate supporting moral intuitions and reasoning are covered below.

Neuroscientific Approaches to the Study of Moral Postnatal Development

It should be obvious that how humans respond to the physical and social distress and pain of others is very relevant to their acquisition of a properly functioning moral sense. As above, I rely on the extensive review provided by Jean Decety, but the focus here are the neurodevelopmental findings as opposed to the behavioral.

1. Neonates, even as young as 3- to 7-day olds, possess built-in neural mechanisms tuned to emotional vocalizations of others. For instance, their hearing sad vocalizations of others increases neural activity in brain regions involved in processing emotional stimuli.
2. Neonates also contagiously cry when nearby conspecifics are distressed. Such contagious crying depends on subcortical neural pathways that connect the thalamic nuclei and the primitive limbic system (see chapter 1, figures 1.1 and 1.2). Since these pathways show up very early in prenatal fetal development, contagious crying most likely depends on inherited emotional predispositions.

Compared to the mainly affective reactions evident in very young infants, cognitive components such as the ability to understand facially expressed emotions

39. Van de Vondervoort and Hamlin, "Evidence for Intuitive Morality," 146.

and the ability to take the emotional perspective of others play increasing roles in the first 3–5 years of life.

3. Thus, in children 4 years old and older the perception of harm done to others correlates with "age-related increase of neural activity . . . in the ventromedial prefrontal cortex (vmPFC), as well as increased functional connectivity between this region and the amygdala [in the subcortical limbic system]. In all participants, irrespective of their age, perceived intentional harm to people (as opposed to accidental harm) was associated with increased activation in brain regions sensitive to the perception, prediction, and interpretation of others' intention. . . ."[40] The vmPFC as well as many other neocortical areas responding to the physical and social pain of others are associated with these higher-level cognitive abilities, abilities that characterize the presence of rational cognitive powers not available to preverbal infants. These higher-level cortical activities can modulate, via downward-projecting neural connections, the affective, intuitively generated neural activities present in the subcortical limbic sites of preverbal infants.
4. One can be impressed by the neuroscientific findings associated with the prosocial feelings and behaviors found already in young children. However, in a normally maturing human neocortex, one finds that, for instance, the recorded response of the anterior cingulate cortex (ACC) depends on whether the victim of the pain is differentially recognized as an in-group member or an out-group member by the subject whose brain activation is being recorded. In particular, the response recorded from the ACC when the harm was done to an out-group member was significantly lower compared to when the harm was done to an in-group member. Like the previously noted suggestive findings observed from preverbal infants, these findings are important since they may reflect an emotionally primitive, intuitive response already present during preverbal infancy that persists even into adulthood (see note 32 above), when all the higher-level cognitive control processes have been acquired.

The Neuroscience of Matured Moral Development

Near the beginning of this chapter, we listed several types of ethics that possibly contribute to a foundational basis of morality. We also noted that such a basis for the oughtness of moral actions, despite claims made to the contrary, cannot be provided by science alone. Consequently, we looked subsequently at scientific studies that abandoned the quest for establishing such a foundational basis, and pragmatically focused their efforts on *how* different ethical principles

40. Decety, "The Neuroevolution of Empathy," 138.

affect the choice of moral actions rather than on *why* they ought to. Leaving aside ethics based on personal preferences and emotions, one can arguably make a case for noticeable functional overlap of the virtue ethics of Aristotle and the deontological ethics of Immanuel Kant, but for a lesser overlap of either one of these two with the utilitarian ethics of Jeremy Bentham. Regarding this functional overlap, the philosopher Walker Trimble remarks that "there are four ways by which the contrast between deontology and aretology [from ἀρετή (aretḗ, "virtue")] *can be reconciled* if conceived as having a relationship to what goes on in the brain: (1) rules of behavior are encoded in the brain (deontology), (2) the organism has a particular disposition that shapes its behavior (virtue ethics), (3) dispositions are the collective expressions of encoded rules occurring at various levels of functioning (deontology), (4) rules and dispositions together work to shape sets of habits and choices (virtue ethics)"[41] (emphasis added). In other words, the overlap consists in the two ethics reinforcing each other.

That noted, let's look at available scientific evidence, apropos utilitarian and deontological ethics, obtained from research on the *what* and the *how* factors that might be involved when we engage in moral decision-making and behavior. By focusing on cognitive-science and evolutionary approaches, we can at least get a glimpse of some interesting and philosophically significant implications for how we understand not only religion but also ethics and morality.

The articles published on human morality and religion over the past three decades by social and cognitive psychologists, evolutionary psychologists, and cognitive neuroscientists no doubt runs into hundreds, too many to adequately review in this book. Therefore we proceed with this limitation in mind. But several cautions are in order before we proceed. First, most of the findings obtained in this vast set of studies were obtained from research participants recruited from the student bodies of universities in WEIRD (Western, Educated, Industrialized, Rich, and Democratic) countries; hence, it is not clear that the inferences drawn from these results are universally valid. Second, many studies are performed in laboratory settings where moral dilemmas are simulated and resolved by role-playing rather than in real settings. Therefore, their generalization to real life situations, what researchers refer to as their ecological validity, may be limited. Moreover, our focus on utilitarian and deontological principles limits us to considering a small fraction of the research results that deal with the nature of moral decisions and behaviors and how religion contributes to them. These things noted, it is my opinion that one can briefly summarize some of the extant scientific findings as follows. Research evidence indicates (i) that

41. Walker Trimble, "Seed and Law: Neuroscience and Virtue Ethics in Christian Anthropology," in *Consciousness and Matter: Mind, Brain, and Cosmos in the Dialogue Between Science and Theology*, ed. Kirill Kopeikin and Alexei V. Nesteruk (Wipf & Stock, 2024), 197.

a combination of utilitarian and deontological principles applies in many, if not most, cases of moral decision-making; (ii) that application of utilitarian principles is often associated with activation of neural networks underlying conscious (explicit) rational processes, while application of deontological principles is often associated with networks underlying unconscious processes involved in intuitive/emotional evaluations;[42] and (iii) that social norms and religion, as one would expect, need to be taken into account to understand how human morality is expressed in these experimental settings.[43] What is additionally intriguing and relevant here is the following. In contrast to religious knowledge based on religious doctrine, which depends on neural networks supporting abstract, semantic processing, concrete religious knowledge based on personal experiences relies more on underlying neural networks associated not only with memory, much of it taken up by prior concrete visual experiences, but also with imagery, especially the visual kind.[44] This is very likely due to the fact that such imagery may facilitate the ability of empathic or compassionate perspective-taking involved in moral decision-making.[45] While doctrinal religious knowledge may be associated with neural activity supporting reliance on utilitarian decision-making as well as with separate neural activity supporting reliance on deontological moral decisions, it is likely that experiential religious knowledge may be important primarily in activating brain sites underlying reliance on only deontological moral principles.[46]

42. Joshua D. Greene, "Beyond Point-and-Shoot Morality: Why Cognitive (Neuro)-Science Matters for Ethics," *Ethics* 124, no. 4 (2014): 695–726; Joshua D. Greene, "The Cognitive Neuroscience of Moral Judgment and Decision-Making," in *The Cognitive Neurosciences*, vol. 5, ed. Michael S. Gazzaniga (MIT Press, 2014); Joshua D. Greene et al., "Cognitive Load Selectively Interferes with Utilitarian Moral Judgment," *Cognition* 107, no. 3 (2008): 1144–54; Joseph M. Paxton et al., "Reflection and Reasoning in Moral Judgment," *Cognitive Science* 36, no. 1 (2012): 163–77; Renata S. Suter and Ralph Hertwig, "Time and Moral Judgment," *Cognition* 119, no. 3 (2011): 454–58.

43. See Bergson, *The Two Sources*; Matt J. Rossano, "Supernaturalizing Social Life: Religion and the Evolution of Human Cooperation," *Human Nature* 18, no. 3 (2007): 272.

44. Greene, "Beyond Point-and-Shoot"; Greene, "The Cognitive Neuroscience"; Jonathan Haidt, "The Emotional Dog and Its Rational Tail: A Social Intuitionist Approach to Moral Judgment," *Psychological Review* 108, no. 4 (2001): 814–34; Amitai Shenhav et al., "Divine Intuition: Cognitive Style Influences Belief in God," *Journal of Experimental Psychology: General* 141, no. 3 (2012): 423–28.

45. C. Daniel Batson et al., "As You Would Have Them Do unto You: Does Imagining Yourself in the Other's Place Stimulate Moral Action?," *Personality and Social Psychology Bulletin* 29, no. 9 (2003): 1190–1201. Underwood and Moore, "Perspective-Taking and Altruism."

46. Elinor Amit and Joshua D. Greene, "You See, the Ends Don't Justify the Means: Visual Imagery and Moral Judgment," *Psychological Science* 23, no. 8 (2012): 861–68.

Connections Between Religious Belief, Empathic Moral Concerns, and Critical Thinking

The results of several additional studies support the need for further neuroscientific examinations of deontological and utilitarian modes of making moral decisions. But before discussing these studies, we must consider important recent findings revealing the existence of intrinsic, concurrent, and anticorrelated changes (increases and decreases) of brain activity when engaged in a given attention-demanding cognitive task, such as the task, for instance, of searching for a hard-to-find target item embedded in visual display containing also a clutter of non-target distractor items. In such tasks a few localized task-relevant cortical brain regions are activated while simultaneously other task-irrelevant brain regions are deactivated. This asymmetry of regionally specific positive and negative activation patterns increase as the difficulty of the task increases.[47]

Taking advantage of this phenomenon, the psychologist and neuroscientist Anthony Jack and his colleagues asked to what extent, if any, two different experimental cognitive tasks relate to each other in terms of the respective brain-activation patterns that they produce. One task relied on accurate interpersonal social cognitions such as recognizing the facially expressed emotions of others or applying theory of mind to others by inferring their mental states, while the other relied on nonsocial, physical/mechanical cognitions. Using functional magnetic resonance imaging (fMRI) to record brain activity, Jack and his colleagues found evidence for concurrent anticorrelated activities between brain regions devoted, on one hand, specifically to the social cognition tasks and, on the other hand, to other brain regions devoted specifically to the physical cognition tasks. That is, the social-cognition task deactivated regions associated with the analytical thinking used in physical-/mechanical-reasoning, whereas the analytical-thinking task deactivated regions associated with the social-reasoning tasks.[48]

Why this is of interest, as further findings of Anthony Jack and coworkers indicate, is because (i) prosocial cognition, i.e., cognitions related to empathic moral concern for others, is positively linked to belief in God[49] whereas analytical thinking is negatively linked, at both the correlational and causal level,[50] to

47. Michael D. Fox et al., "The Human Brain Is Intrinsically Organized into Dynamic, Anticorrelated Functional Networks," *Proceedings of the National Academy of Sciences USA* 102, no. 27 (2005): 9673–78.

48. Anthony I. Jack et al., "fMRI Reveals Reciprocal Inhibition Between Social and Physical Cognitive Domains," *Neuroimage* 66 (2013): 385–401.

49. Jack et al., "Why Do You Believe."

50. Will M. Gervais and Ara Norenzayan, "Analytic Thinking Promotes Religious Disbelief," *Science* 336, no. 6080 (2012): 493–96.

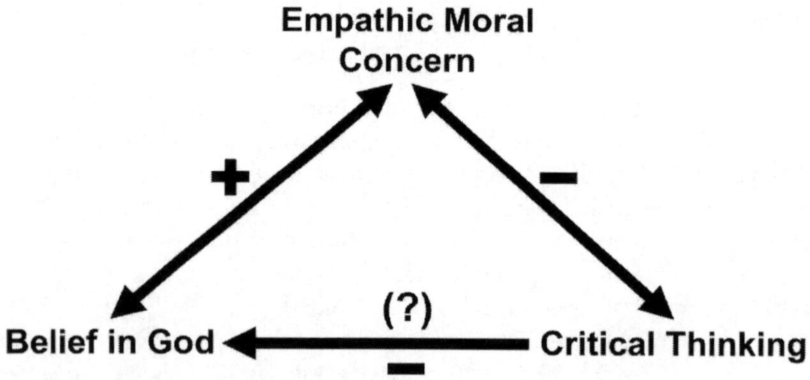

Figure 3.1. Depiction of two-way correlational (double-arrowed lines) and causal (single-arrowed lines) relations between empathic moral concern, belief in god, and critical thinking. Causal relations are also correlational ones; correlational relations may or may not be causal ones. The question mark indicates the fact that some recent studies have failed to replicate the findings of prior studies originally reporting the existence of a causal relation (see text).

belief in God. Importantly, moreover, as Jack and coworkers' findings also indicated, there is a significant negative correlation between analytical thinking and empathic moral concerns. As depicted in figure 3.1, this negative relation can therefore account for a sizable portion of the negative association between reflective analytical thinking and belief in God. A pooled analysis of results found that even after statistically factoring out the negative relationship between empathic moral concern and critical thinking that partially mediated the negative correlation between analytic thinking and belief in God, a somewhat reduced yet significant negative correlation between analytic thinking and belief in God remained.[51]

Despite the informative relations depicted in figure 3.1 among critical thinking, empathic moral concern, and religion, several things need further clarifying in future research. As depicted by the bidirectional arrows in figure 3.1, (i) the negative correlation between critical thinking and empathic moral concern found by Jack et al. and (ii) the positive correlation between empathic moral concern and belief in God found by them do not allow us to draw firm causal inferences in either case. This is due to the fact that the existence of correlations as such only tell us that *a* relationship exists between two variables without telling us that it definitely is a causal one. For that reason, the possibilities that belief in God and empathic moral concern can interact in a

51. Jack et al., "Why Do You Believe," 13.

mutually positive causal way requires further research. Similarly, the possibility that empathic moral concern can interact in a mutually negative causal way with analytic thinking also requires further research. Furthermore, whether or not disbelief in God is a causal factor contributing to critical thinking also awaits further research. In contrast to these uncertainties, from Gervais and Norenzayan's finding that experimentally induced critical thinking increased disbelief in God, we could *hypothetically* infer as depicted by the unidirectional arrow at the bottom of figure 3.1, that critical thinking contributes causally to disbelief in God.[52]

However, finally returning to the effects of deontological and utilitarian thinking on moral decision-making, additional research conducted by Conway and Gawronski has shown that critical thinking and empathic moral concern also *might* cause changes, dissociatively and respectively, in the extent to which utilitarian thinking, on one hand, and deontological thinking, on the other, are applied in moral decision-making. That is to say, experimentally interfering with the ability to use reflective critical thinking reduces the reliance on utilitarian thinking, without any appreciable effect on deontological thinking; whereas experimentally enhancing empathic moral concern causes increases reliance on deontological thinking, without any appreciable effect on utilitarian thinking.[53]

Yet, despite the wealth of informative facts such as the above garnered from scientific research, which only point out *that* certain moral principles, strategies, and decisions are applied, one must not too readily conclude they establish scientific foundations for what courses of action *ought to be taken* in morally fraught cases. Here we again must be cautious about committing what G. E. Moore referred to as the naturalistic fallacy of mistaking a scientific fact about moral behavior for a moral ought.[54] Additionally, we must note that in some cases the interpretation of scientific findings can be intrinsically ambiguous. Consequently, much like interpretations of religious scriptures, these interpretations are prone to cherry picking. Take, for instance, altruism, which generally is taken to be virtue. The justification for willingly and unselfishly,

52. Gervais and Norenzayan, "Analytic Thinking." However, the inference is questionable, because more recent studies reviewed by Omid Ghasemi et al., "Reflective Thinking Predicts Disbelief in God Across 19 Countries," *Psychonomic Bulletin & Review* 32, no. 4 (2025): 2220–29, have failed to replicate the findings of Gervais and Norenzayan.

53. Paul Conway and Bertram Gawronski, "Deontological and Utilitarian Inclinations in Moral Decision Making: A Process Dissociation Approach," *Journal of Personality and Social Psychology* 104, no. 2 (2013): 216–35; see also Shenhav et al., "Divine Intuition." But here any inference as to clear causal influences again is hypothetical, because more recent studies reviewed by Ghasemi et al., "Reflective Thinking Predicts," have failed to clearly replicate the findings of Shenhav et al.

54. Moore, *Principia Ethica*.

sometimes even sacrificially, giving up part or, in extreme cases, all of our well-being or lives for the good of others could clearly be explained, at least in part, by Darwinist evolutionary science in terms of kin relationships and group survival serving the transmission and preservation of uniquely shared genes from one generation to the next. On the other hand, and again along Darwinist lines, explanations of facts that include resource scarcity, competition for these limited resources due to population growth, and reproductive success (survival of the fittest) also can support the "objectivist" libertarian philosophy of Ayn Rand, in which, as we noted above, the "virtue" of selfishness takes precedence over concern and care for others.[55] Accordingly, if one takes Rand's selfishness virtue to heart, the concern for the welfare of your neighbor, the elderly, the infirm, infant with birth defects, and other at-risk persons can be overruled, with little if any moral compunction, by egotistic concern and preference for one's individual flourishing. This should illustrate that, from a standpoint of moral guidance, science and reason each offer a double-edged sword, not the clean single-edged scission separating good from evil and right from wrong.

What Do Evolutionary Approaches to the Study of Morality Tell Us?

The Evolution of Basic Interindividual and Prosocial Moral Sensibilities

Our understanding of morality is aided by the knowledge we have acquired through the study of biocultural evolution. On our planet, morality did not preexist the evolution of life. Only with the evolutionary advent of advanced primates like our hominin ancestors could anything like morality, the knowledge of good and evil governing human behavior, exist on Earth. There was nothing moral, nothing virtuous or evil, in the lifeless physical objects and processes that formed the earth some 4.5 billion years ago, although they all were God's creation and, in that sense, good, indeed very good (Gen. 1:31). And in hindsight they can be seen as necessary and beneficial to the eventual creation of sentient beings. Since many of these creatures, including of course humans, evolved to live in social settings, morality, as several evolutionary psychologists have pointed out, is built on and, in turn, supports social organization and therefore depends on and fosters interindividual cooperation.[56] Social life is found in all mammal species. Since it is especially evident in primates, a rudimentary form of morality, a proto-morality—observed for instance in a recognition of unfair-

55. Rand, *The Virtue of Selfishness.*

56. Nicolas Baumard and Pascal Boyer, "Explaining Moral Religions," *Trends in Cognitive Sciences* 17, no. 6 (2013): 272–80; Rossano, "Supernaturalizing Social Life."

ness or injustice—is expressed by our non-human cousins.[57] However, along with the philosophers John Fischer and Mark Ravizza,[58] I hold that animal species other than humans cannot be truly moral, and therefore they cannot be held morally accountable for their actions.

My limited readings of the scientific literature dealing with the development and neuroscience of moral and proto-moral capacities[59] of, respectively, human adults and infants lead me to believe that some of the postnatal development and some brain processes are not only influenced by postnatal environmental factors but also by prenatal, naturally endowed, and phylogenetically inherited properties acquired via evolution. In view of this, claims have been made by some evolutionary cognitivists (see chapter 1) that human infants are "natural theists," and I can agree with that statement. I am even more confident in stating that, as with nature's foundational contribution to postnatal development of religions, its contribution to postnatal development of human moral capacities can be traced back to prehistoric, phylogenetic/evolutionary developments. Concurring with this assessment, Jean Decety summarizes his reviews of the neuroevolution of empathy and caring for others by stating that

> Overall, many of the basic components of empathy, such as emotion contagion, empathic concern, and caring for others, are deeply rooted in our evolutionary history and their neural and endocrine mechanisms are highly conserved across species. . . .
>
> One significant difference that must be taken into account in human research is the fact that high-level cognitive abilities such as executive function, language, and theory of mind, which are largely implemented in the prefrontal cortex, are layered on phylogenetically older social and emotional capacities. These evolutionarily newer aspects of information processing expand the range of behaviors that can be motivated by empathy beyond kin, such as caring for and helping out-group members and even members of different species. . . .[60]

This summary assessment is supported by several cross-species findings.

1. Several studies with rodents such as rats, that are relatively low on the phylogenetic scale, have shown that, for instance, empathic arousal in

57. Jessica C. Flack and Frans B. M. de Waal, "'Any Animal Whatever': Darwinian Building Blocks of Morality in Monkeys and Apes," *Journal of Consciousness Studies* 7, no. 1–2 (2000): 1–29.

58. John Martin Fischer and Mark Ravizza, *Responsibility and Control: A Theory of Moral Responsibility* (Cambridge University Press, 1998).

59. The number of such articles published in the last three decades runs into the many tens if not over a hundred, and I have read at most several dozens of them.

60. Decety, "The Neuroevolution of Empathy," 134.

unrestrained rats leads them to alleviate the distress of other restrained rats by freeing them—even when reward is withheld from the empathic rats. Additionally, when experimenters pitted liberating a restrained cagemate against obtaining highly desired chocolate chips located in a second restrainer, the experimental rats generally opened both restrainers and shared the chocolate chips with the freed rats. These helping gestures involving some "self-sacrifice" indicate the presence of altruistic and generous-sharing behaviors.

2. Similarly, rhesus monkeys have been shown to refrain from operating a food-delivering device if operating it would cause another monkey to receive an electric shock. Again, this provides evidence for a form of altruistic self-restraint and care for the other.
3. The many studies of chimpanzees conducted by the primatologist Frans de Waal also found that chimpanzees show similar "prosocial" behaviors, respond empathically and compassionately to other distressed chimpanzees, and spontaneously console and provide comfort to other chimpanzees who were victims of aggression. One could list additional behaviors found in de Waal and his coworkers' behavioral studies of animals that can be interpreted as evidence for prosocial altruism, empathy, consolation, and care of the other.[61] Nonetheless, one might want to be cautious about overinterpreting and overgeneralizing these results. All the above-listed findings obtained from experimental and observational studies use animals that are raised in captivity. For instance, experimental animals like rats and rhesus monkeys generally interact with human caretakers who feed them, clean their living quarters, or otherwise address their needs; and in many cases they are held or manipulated by the experimenters themselves. Therefore, in addition to the explicit experimental manipulations, prior interactive contact with humans may have affected the animals' behaviors in unknown ways. This even holds for the chimpanzees who are given free rein in their more spacious outdoor enclosure, in which, still, there is plenty of interaction with human caretakers and researchers. In all cases this interactive contact with humans could pose some threats to the validity and generalizability of the conclusions drawn by researchers, especially when generalizing their findings to animals living in the wild. To offset this concern, one may consider that the primatologist

61. Frans B. M. de Waal, "Putting the Altruism Back into Altruism: The Evolution of Empathy," *Annual Review of Psychology* 59, no. 1 (2008): 279–300; Frans B. M. de Waal and Stephanie D. Preston, "Mammalian Empathy: Behavioural Manifestations and Neural Basis," *Nature Reviews Neuroscience* 18, no. 8 (2017): 498–509; Flack and de Waal, "'Any Animal Whatever.'"

and anthropologist Jane Goodall, in her many decades of observing chimpanzees in the wild in Gombe, Nigeria, observed not only cases of intergroup and ingroup hostility and aggression among chimpanzees but also of empathic and compassionate behaviors.

4. As further noted by Decety, in the context of parental care the entire evolutionary line of mammals appears to have developed a sense for the distress and suffering of conspecifics, and have developed the accompanying caring behavior, both of which are supported by activation of cortical and subcortical neuronal networks. The involvement of subcortical sites like the phylogenetically older limbic system (see chapter 1, figure 1.2), suggests that the propensity for activating altruistic, empathic, caring emotions and their resultant behaviors is, if not instinctive, then at least a fundamental feature built into mammalian creatures.[62]

How Does the Biocultural Evolution of Religion Affect the Morality of the Highest Primate?

As the title of this chapter indicates, morality and religion form a partnership. So, let's now explore its properties. Although further on we will see that the social psychologist Jonathan Haidt is no fan of religion, he does present some information relevant to understanding the partnership between religion and morality. He remarks that

> the most useful contrast for moral psychology is between two kinds of cognition: moral intuition and moral reasoning. . . . Moral intuition refers to fast, automatic, and (usually) affect-laden processes in which an evaluative feeling of good-bad or like-dislike (about the actions or character of a person) appears in consciousness without awareness of any steps of search, weighing evidence, or inferring a conclusion. Moral reasoning, in contrast, is a controlled and "cooler" (less affective) process; it is conscious mental activity that consists of transforming information about people and their actions in order to reach a moral judgment or decision. . . . Moral reasoning, when it occurs, is usually a post-hoc process in which we search for evidence to support our initial intuitive reaction."[63]

62. Frans B. M. de Waal and Stephen A. Sherblom, "Bottom-Up Morality: The Basis of Human Morality in Our Primate Nature," *Journal of Moral Education* 47, no. 2 (2018): 250, remark on instinct as follows: "*Instinct* is a term we barely use anymore because instinct has this implication of something that is inflexible and genetic. In both . . . primates and humans very few behaviors are purely like that. So, we usually don't use that term because everything is modified by learning, environment, and culture. But, I do think . . . [that some primate behaviors are] deeply ingrained."

63. Haidt, "The New Synthesis," 998.

Moreover, the evolutionary research strategy discussed in the prior section proceeded on explicitly stated assumptions[64] that (i) human morality and religion evolved separately, with morality playing the primary role of promoting prosocial behaviors in order to bind humans into a unified group or society and (ii) religion playing the ancillary role of consolidating and reinforcing this social cohesion. The biologist Donald Broom proposes that "[t]he religious framework makes it easier for the average person, or perhaps more importantly for the likely transgressors of the moral codes, to understand what should and should not be done. . . . In the course of the evolution of religion in humans, much of the moral code would have been established early on but the extent of observance of this code would have varied among individuals. The religion would have developed in order to provide a [reinforcing] structure which encouraged the widespread observance of the moral code."[65] One can agree that this explanation aptly encapsulates the evolutionary-cognitive perspective in the study of religion and that one can take it as implicitly saying that religion served as a mere handmaiden to or a byproduct of an earlier evolved morality. In my opinion, however, this inference would be mistaken. Although empathic and other moral concerns and behaviors may be good predictors of religious belief, it should be noted that religion has a culturally evolved structure that is only partially filled with moral concerns. Therefore the historically prior existence of moral concerns cannot be the sole source of a historically evolving religion. Moreover, the inference does not consider the possibility that religious concerns provide feedback to moral concerns.

That said, regarding how religion relates to human morality, several especially pertinent distinctions made by Henri Berson about a century ago are still relevant today.[66] In his concern for communal, social living, Bergson clearly differentiated between the purely instinctive, rigid, and thoughtlessly organized society of insects such as ants and that of ancient, prehistorical humans. Since the thoughtlessness of insects finds its human analog in the moral intuitions described above by Haidt, the social behaviors of humans as described by Bergson, though in some part also controlled by instinct, are in much larger part influenced by the conscious mind's ability to generate religious myths, which increasingly do the job of consolidating the foundations of human societies, a task that instincts alone perform in consolidating the foundation of insect societies. However, common to both ways of specifying normative behavior is their goal of establishing and preserving a smooth-running, cohesive social structure. So, the moral norms in human societies are not only specified by but

64. See Baumard and Boyer, "Explaining Moral Religions"; Donald M. Broom, *The Evolution of Morality and Religion* (Cambridge University Press, 2003); Haidt, "The New Synthesis."

65. Broom, *The Evolution of Morality*, 176.

66. Bergson, *The Two Sources*.

also subordinated to this goal. In this way, morality can be regarded as a necessary and naturally emergent property of the organization of human societies, something that current evolutionary psychologists and anthropologists can agree with.

Furthermore, according to Bergson, the formation of myths and the religions associated with them did not so much create as they reinforced the structural integrity of human societies already supported by social norms. Concurring with this appraisal of religion, Broom argues that the evolutionary basis of religion lies in morality: "If morality has evolved and morality is [at] the core of religions then the basis of religions has evolved. All human societies have a propensity for religion because religion provides a valuable structure or the moral code which is valuable in all of those societies. . . . [The] societies which formed such a framework were more likely to remain stable because anti-social, disruptive actions would have been less likely to occur."[67] And seconding both Bergson and Broom, J. Wentzel van Huyssteen—commenting on Nicholas Wade's approach to the study of religion—notes: "As to the crucial and defining role of *morality* in religion, Wade thinks religion and morality share a common feature that reflects their origins as evolved behaviour: both are rooted in the emotions . . . , and both religious knowledge and moral intuitions appear in the mind as strong convictions, not as neutral facts. Wade argues that morality is older than religion, since we know of its roots in primate behaviour. In this sense we can say that religious behaviour was engrafted on top of the moral sense in the human lineage alone. . . ."[68]

In other words, at least this type of social morality can be regarded to have a natural basis in the biocultural evolution of humans, with supernatural religions playing a subsequent but very important supportive role. As noted by the anthropologist Matt Rossano, since scrutiny of a person's conduct by his or her social confreres is a powerful way of counteracting his or her excessively individualistic, dishonest, or free-riding behaviors, religion, by introducing the belief in spiritual agents such as ever-vigilant deceased ancestors or supernatural gods, can additionally reinforce such moral monitoring of a person's conduct in the absence of his or her social companions.[69]

It follows that although God can be regarded as the ultimate source of morality, one can nonetheless hold that a flourishing moral life can be led without religion or an explicit belief in God. For, in matters of morality, religious

67. Broom, *The Evolution of Morality*, 176.

68. J. Wentzel Van Huyssteen, "From Empathy to Embodied Faith? Interdisciplinary Perspectives on the Evolution of Religion," in *Evolution, Religion, and Cognitive Science: Critical and Constructive Essays*, ed. Fraser Watts and Léon P. Turner (Oxford University Press, 2020), 143.

69. Rossano, "Supernaturalizing Social Life," 272; Francesca Gino et al., "Contagion and Differentiation in Unethical Behavior: The Effect of One Bad Apple on the Barrel," *Psychological Science* 20, no. 3 (2009): 393–98; Haidt, "The New Synthesis."

traditions can intersect with what is known as the natural-law tradition. According to this tradition, morality relies not only on divine revelation for its foundation but also on reasoning about the basic attributes found in human nature, endowed as it is especially with consciousness and uniquely with a normative conscience; for they, via our conscious awareness and our conscientious rational faculties, regulate the collective interindividual dependencies characterizing social life. Consequently, all sorts of nonbelievers and nontheists act morally whenever their actions accord with moral precepts inscribed in their communal life and in their individual consciences.

That acknowledged, Bergson nevertheless argues that a transformation occurred in what he calls a "static religion" whose myths function primarily—like instincts do in insect societies—to preserve the cohesion of human societies, each in their own way. The transformation of the so-called static religion occurred, as noted briefly in chapter 1, during the "religious awakening" of the Axial Age lasting from about 800 to 200 BCE, resulting in what he calls "dynamic religion" that includes its modern offshoots found in the Abrahamic tradition as well as in Confucianism, Hinduism, and Buddhism. All of these religions are therefore examples of what is designated as "dynamic moral religion." In the prior static religious traditions, as Nicolas Baumard and Pascal Boyer explain, "the gods were generally construed as unencumbered with moral conscience and uninterested in human morality. That [also] is the case for the gods of classical antiquity, Sumerian, Akkadian, Egyptian, Greek, and Roman. . . ."[70] One can conclude therefore that the dynamic moral religions rely on the existence of supernatural agents, on a High God that, unlike the gods of static religions, cares about and can monitor human moral and immoral activities.

Bergson, however, adds importantly that the transformation of static into dynamic moral religions was additionally accompanied by a "mystic" thrust away from metaphysical questions that preoccupy philosophers or theologians as to why "underneath Being lies nothingness, that *de jure* there should be nothing, that we must explain why there is *de facto* something . . . , questions which are the main origin of metaphysical anguish. . . . Now, [in contrast to metaphysically inclined philosophers or theologians,] for the mystic these questions simply do not exist."[71] The mystic rejects the "'metaphysical' attributes of Deity: he has nothing to do with properties which are mere [apophatic] negations and can only be expressed negatively [for example that God is *in*finite, *un*caused, and *im*mortal]; he believes that he sees what God is, for him there is no seeing of what God is not. . . . [For the mystic,] God is love, and the object of love: herein lies the whole contribution of mysticism. About this twofold love the mystic will never have done talking. His description is interminable because

70. Baumard and Boyer, "Explaining Moral Religions," 272.

71. Bergson, *The Two Sources*, 251.

what he wants to describe is ineffable. But what he does state clearly is that divine love is not a thing of God: it is God Himself."[72]

This mystic "vision" of God was emphasized in the lives of many mystics in the Eastern Orthodox tradition and Western tradition of Christianity. In the Western tradition, with which I am more familiar, the 16th-century mystics, St. Teresa of Avila, and her companion Carmelite St. John of the Cross, whose chief concern was to promote the "spiritual science of love," stand out. These mystics did nothing but obey their Divine Teacher, Jesus Christ, to follow Him and a renewed morality that exhorts and strives toward a vision of God as *Abba* who, before all else, is Merciful Love. It is Christ's inaugural act that elevates *religious* morality—a morality also found in Buddhism—to a level beyond that of the old morality, which is based on love toward in-group others vs. indifference or animosity toward out-group others. Based as it is on Christ's new vision of God, the new religious morality is a universal instead of a local morality, exhorting people everywhere to compassionately love not only their friends and neighbors but also their rivals and enemies. It is well-nigh impossible to explain such a morality on the basis of research findings reported by the evolutionary and neurocognitive sciences. The reality that these sciences study is what we might refer to as natural morality. To paraphrase Henri Bergson, this old morality was only the first half of morality; the other half had no place in nature's plan.[73] That is why, as stated previously, the old naturally evolved morality only partially fills the complete structure of religion, whereas the complete structure of religion fully incorporates or absorbs Christ's new morality. It is for this reason that—thanks again to the insight of an anonymous reviewer of this book's prepublication manuscript—a theist can ask: If by finding evidence in their research that the morality of love is adaptive and produces uplifting experiential effects such as positive emotions and prosocial empathic behavior,[74] can scientists have learned something—even if only inadvertently and implicitly—about the nature of the God who is the Love that embraces all of humanity, including of course all atheists? And in view of this, considering the partial (in both the biased and quantitative senses of the word) evolutionary and neurocognitive approaches to the study of morality, a thoughtful theist can ask if a fuller explanation of the scientific study of morality is needed. The answer is addressed in the following chapter.

72. Bergson, *The Two Sources*, 251.

73. Bergson, *The Two Sources*, 56.

74. See Rett Diessner et al., "Who Engages with Moral Beauty?," *Journal of Moral Education* 42, no. 2 (2013): 139–63. Anthony Jack et al., "fMRI Reveals Reciprocal Inhibition between Social and Physical Cognitive Domains," *Neuroimage* 66 (2013): 385–401; Anthony Jack et al., "Why Do You Believe in God? Relationships Between Religious Belief, Analytic Thinking, Mentalizing and Moral Concern," *PLOS ONE* 11, no. 3 (2016): e0155283; Rico Pohling and Rhett Diessner, "Moral Elevation and Moral Beauty: A Review of the Empirical Literature," *Review of General Psychology* 20, no. 4 (2016): 412–25.

CHAPTER 4

Further Scrutiny of the Neuroscience of Morality

[The German philosopher] Max Scheler . . . adopted a similar outlook [to that adopted by the British philosopher Richard Price], articulating in a nuanced form the idea of there being a normative order of love (*ordo amoris*). The moral life consists, in part, of affective responsiveness. This idea can also be found in Pascal's work in his description of the order of the heart, *l'ordre du coeur*.

Charles Taliaferro, *Consciousness and the Mind of God*, p. 326

Since we are the one kind of animal that is not governed [merely] by instinct, but one that has to discover and choose its defined good, we must have appropriate habits of action (i.e., virtues) that form our desires and actions toward our perfection as rational, political, and moral animals. . . .

Benjamin Wiker, *God's Grandeur: The Catholic Case for Intelligent Design*, p. 188

We noted at the end of the prior chapter that the chief concern of the religious mystic St. John of the Cross was to promote the spiritual science of love. There we also saw that the natural science of morality can inform us about the facts regarding how humans—predominantly those studied in Western societies—arrive at moral decisions that inform their conduct. Yet, despite initial optimism that it would provide a foundation for morality, the science of morality so far has failed to do so. Therefore, we can ask:

Is a Look Outside of Science for Foundations of Morality Needed?

The short answer to the title of this section is that the basis of morality must be sought elsewhere, notwithstanding the fact that moral behavior is scientifically relatable to our neurocognitive capacities and our biological inheritance. To explain, however, that these facts are insufficient to ground morality, let's start with the pertinent cross-species examples. For one, capuchin monkeys, in rejecting unequal fruits for their labor, appear to have a rudimentary sense of fairness, equity, or justice, as do 10-month-old human infants.[1] Combining this with the observation that a capuchin monkey is also capable of offering assistance adapted to the specific need or situation of another conspecific, their rudimentary sense of justice may be based on more than merely self-serving motives[2]—motives that perhaps deserve to be called altruistic or empathic and compassionate, qualities that, as noted in the previous chapter, also exist in preverbal human infants. Despite the similarity between nonhuman proto-morality and human morality, a closer look is warranted at, among other things, the possibility that religion can be a significant contributor to the historic development of human morality rather than the converse possibility, as also noted in the prior chapter, that morality is not influenced by religion but merely serves as a prior platform for the historic development of religion.

Yet, religion and moral conduct are not the only phenomena influenced by our neurocognitive architecture and biological inheritance. Therefore, cognitive neuroscience and evolution can also impact our understanding of the historic appearance of our consciousness and intelligence; of our abilities to reason rigorously and analytically, to understand, and to imagine; and thus of our ability to engage in the humanities, in the arts, and in doing science. In this larger sphere of human interests, one can ask what influences besides those of cognitive neuroscience and evolutionary science play a role not only in our understanding and pursuit of the good but also of the true and the beautiful. Does a question like this point to an abiding explanatory conundrum that pushes the limits of science's abilities alone to solve it?

Regarding a focus on the morally relevant pursuit of the good, a reading of James Hunter and Paul Nedelisky's *Science and the Good* can nudge a reasonable answer to what is found in the latter part of the question above—namely, the limits of science's abilities alone. These authors, who respectively are a sociologist of knowledge and culture and a philosopher, present a critique of what they call "the new moral science" that is the synthesis of cognitive, evolutionary, and neuroscientific research strategies discussed above. These strategies are purported to give a strictly scientific account of not only the facts but also the scientific foundations of morality. In short, what Hunter and Nedelisky conclude

1. Sarah F. Brosnan and Frans B. M. de Waal, "Monkeys Reject Unequal Pay," *Nature* 425, no. 6955 (2003): 297–99; Marek Meristo and Luca Surian, "Infants Distinguish Antisocial Actions Directed Towards Fair and Unfair Agents," *PLOS ONE* 9, no. 10 (2014): e110553.

2. Sarah F. Brosnan, "Why an Evolutionary Perspective Is Critical to Understanding Moral Behavior in Humans," in *Challenges to Moral and Religious Belief: Disagreement and Evolution*, ed. Michael Bergmann and Patrick Kain (Oxford University Press, 2014); Frans B. M. de Waal, *Good Natured: The Origins of Right and Wrong in Humans and Other Animals* (Harvard University Press, 1996); de Waal and Preston, "Mammalian Empathy"; Megan Van Wolkenten et al., "Inequity Responses of Monkeys Modified by Effort," *Proceedings of the National Academy of Sciences USA* 104, no. 47 (2007): 18854–59.

is that "the idea of morality—as a mind-independent reality—has lost plausibility for the new moral scientists, [who initially] sought to discover the good . . . [but] abandoned that quest and now, at best, [inform us about] . . . how to get what we want."[3] The new moral scientists have settled on an approach to the study of morality in which the question of what "courses of action are 'better' [and therefore *ought to be* followed] is . . . ultimately a question of utility, and utility is best approached empirically and instrumentally as a sort of practical human engineering project."[4] One can here add, to this assessment of a pragmatically driven utilitarianism ethic, the following possibility. Since we generally want what we like, the question of what choices of action are "better" could readily be resolved by relying on an emotivist ethic of personal preference. Within either the utilitarian of the emotivist ethic, the fact is that, in our commodified culture, what we want is heavily influenced by commercial interests expressed in our neoliberal economy, by social forces conducive to conformity, and by science that is joined to technology, so to speak, at the hip. It should therefore not be a surprise, as Hunter and Nedelisky put it, that the "idiom and sensibilities of the new moral science are also the idiom and sensibilities of the managerial elite of the dominant technocratic [and the dominant economic] regimes . . . [and although] the new moral science is marginal to mainstream philosophy, . . . it provides an intellectual legitimation for the unspoken technocratic [and commercial] hopes found everywhere in contemporary public culture."[5] And what seems to be increasingly hoped for in our contemporary culture is the creation and satisfaction of ever more personal preferences. Fully in step with the techno-managerial elite, this hope is therefore closely allied to the marketing by the corporate elite of ever-new technologies that appeal to our consumer-driven sensibilities. Left, therefore, to rely largely on personal as well as socially and economically engineered objectives as guides to what we "ought" to want, the danger here is that the new moral science "is incapable of either critiquing the distortions of power and privilege or affirming higher moral ends that draw us to the possibility of greater human flourishing—for everyone, but especially for those without power and privilege."[6] These encapsulated but far-reaching conclusions regarding the prioritization of pragmatic, utilitarian, and emotivist principles call for some elaboration.

It is not clear what, besides aligning with current socioeconomic and political trends (discussed below), impels the new science of morality to focus on the role that the utilitarian principle plays at the cost of considering the roles

3. James Davison Hunter and Paul Nedelisky, preface to *Science and the Good: The Tragic Quest for the Foundations of Morality* (Yale University Press, 2018), xv.

4. Hunter and Nedelisky, *Science and the Good*, 91.

5. Hunter and Nedelisky, *Science and the Good*, 16–17.

6. Hunter and Nedelisky, *Science and the Good*, 22.

played by other ethical principles. A reasonable answer offered by Hunter and Nedelisky is the following. The cultural logic of the new moral science plays out in terms of the historically longstanding problem of religious, social, and moral conflict and the belief that past "societies were governed by various 'deontological' moral beliefs—those that placed duties to friends, family, or god(s) over those to humanity in general. These, it is argued, were necessary to help humans cope with life in small tribes. For that reason, they long shaped our intuitive judgments. The problem is that, in modern society, those intuitions, beliefs, and judgments often provoke or justify conflict."[7] Contrary to the universal *religious* morality noted at the end of the prior chapter, the new science of morality is premised on what it believes is a more universalizable and less conflict-prone basis of morality residing in a *utilitarian* ethic instead of a deontological one. By focusing on the utilitarian ethic, the new moral scientists are (wittingly or unwittingly) following one of the prime directives of the Enlightenment's modernist project—namely, to establish a cosmopolitan basis of morality that is founded on universal reason, a reason in turn supported by a scientific, evidence-based moral calculus, and thus one that all of right-thinking humanity can (or ought to?) endorse. However, such a research strategy leaves unaddressed the following questions for enlightened modernists: Like reason, aren't religion, intuition, emotion, and virtues also universal and cosmopolitan traits? And if so, how, other than neglecting or defocusing from them, shall we cope with their nagging intrusions into our mental, intellective, and moral spheres? Moreover, the same scientists seem to avoid the problem, raised by René Girard (see chapter 2), of mimetic desire that is so evident in, and props up, the capitalist consumer-oriented economies in advanced industrialized nations. As technological progress that supports consumer-driven economies spirals upward at an ever-increasing pace, one can expect that the economic, social, and political crises that accompany the ever upward-spiraling mimetic desires of consumers will correspondingly become more frequent and devastating.

These pesky sociocultural questions and problems aside, a more pertinent question is: Has the new moral science succeeded in its goal of finding evidence that could serve as grounds for morality? Hunter and Nedelisky's answer is more complex than a simple yes or no. My reading of relevant research concurs with their trichotomous assessment of the new science of morality. The trichotomy follows from the fact that scientific research could inform us about morality in at least three ways. In what Hunter and Nedelisky call the "Level One" way, "the most interesting way—always the highest aspiration of those who have sought a scientific foundation for morality—would be if science could settle longstanding moral questions."[8] That is, Level One refers to scientific evidence supporting or

7. Hunter and Nedelisky, *Science and the Good*, 93.
8. Hunter and Nedelisky, *Science and the Good*, 99.

contradicting the existence of a moral doctrine that could conclusively differentiate good from bad and right from wrong and that therefore could serve as a foundation for our moral conduct. Less ambitiously, Level Two ways do not yield findings that demonstrate a moral doctrine but instead yield evidence for or against some extant moral claim or theory. An example of this is a social psychological finding by Darley and Batson. At first glance, their work seems to support moral "situationism" and thus puts morality based on virtue ethics at risk.[9] Assuming theoretically, as the new moral scientists do, that virtues are *stable* character traits that should *invariably* lead to consistent behavior across different situations, the results showed that virtues, so conceived, do not motivate consistent moral choices across variable situations. Ergo, it was concluded that virtue ethics has no empirical justification. However, from the standpoint of psychologists who also view virtue itself as a personality trait, but as one that, like other personality traits, is supple rather than rigid, the ruling out of virtue ethics on the basis of evidence disconfirming a simple, rigid cross-situational stability is questionable on methodological, interpretational, and conceptual grounds.[10]

In contrast to the first two levels, the Level Three findings cannot resolve the validity of moral theories nor prescribe moral precepts. Failing to prescribe moral behaviors, they instead merely describe them, for example by showing how moral decisions are supported by underlying functional architecture of the brain, and how personal, social, and cultural factors influence them. Many of these descriptive findings are not to be dismissed as trivial, despite the fact that some of them confirm what we already know and take for granted in our everyday moral behavior. So, I concur with Hunter and Nedelisky's assessment that while findings such as these have little bearing on the foundations and substantive content of morality, they nonetheless have something important and interesting to say about the cognitive capacities engaged during moral decision-making of humans. Yet, despite the gradual realization that the empirical

9. John M. Darley and C. Daniel Batson, "From Jerusalem to Jericho: A Study of Situational and Dispositional Variables in Helping Behavior," *Journal of Personality and Social Psychology* 27, no. 1 (1973): 100–108.

10. For the pros and cons regarding the bearing of social psychological research on virtue ethics, see Rachana Kamteka, "Situationism and Virtue Ethics on the Content of Our Character," *Ethics* 114, no. 3 (2004): 458–91; Maria Merritt, "Virtue Ethics and Situationist Personality Psychology," *Ethical Theory and Moral Practice* 3, no. 43 (2000): 65–83; Christian Miller, "Social Psychology, Mood, and Helping: Mixed Results for Virtue Ethics," *Journal of Ethics* 13, no. 2 (2009): 145–73; Gopal Sreenivasan, "Errors About Errors: Virtue Theory and Trait Attribution," *Mind* 111, no. 441 (2002): 47–68. Here, it is also important to note that, according to Robert P. Tett and Hal A. Guterman, "Situation Trait Relevance, Trait Expression, and Cross-Situational Consistency: Testing a Principle of Trait Activation," *Journal of Research in Personality* 34, no. 4 (2000): 397–423, variable situations can interact with or activate (presumably latent) personality traits. This interactionist perspective may provide a way to reconcile situationism with virtue ethics.

findings produced by the tribe of new moral scientists miss the mark of providing a scientific foundation of morality, one can wonder why they nonetheless persist in advocating an instrumentalized and utilitarian version of morality.[11] An answer, I suggest, is that ontologically the new moral scientists are prone to affiliate with naturalism; epistemologically, to scientism; and practically, to technologism. This is so because a naturalist approach to morality can be made methodologically accessible to science and because a scientifically endorsed morality is well suited to being implemented throughout society and culture by way of ever new individually and socially applicable technologies. Ever newer developments of such technologies are the prime drivers, in an amenable consumer-oriented society, of what is deemed to be genuine societal and cultural progress.

But the failure of science to secure a foundation for moral values and practices bodes ill also for its attempts to provide foundations for other valued cultural practices such as the arts, humanities, and religion. For that reason, I furthermore agree with Hunter and Nedelisky, not only that science has useful knowledge to offer to our understanding of morality (and other social and cultural practices), but also—as they say in their ending note—that "there is finally no substitute for history, literature, poetry [and the other arts], philosophy, sociology and the world's great religious traditions—no substitute for understanding morality on its own terms—as we struggle to achieve a more just, inclusive, and humane world."[12] Faced with the lack of Level One findings supporting a naturalistic basis of universal moral precepts, the new moral scientists' persistent embrace of such a basis resulted in a pragmatic turn away from the insurmountably difficult search for a scientific foundation of morality. The turn was realized in less ambitiously adopting a retailored, customized research strategy in which the utilitarian research program, readily implementable in neuroscientific and behavioral research into all sorts of human decision-making, takes center stage in the study of moral choices and conduct. The utilitarian approach, by also being readily quantifiable—a characteristic taken to be a highly preferable, if not essential, methodological feature of "true" science—displaces the less easily implemented and quantifiable approaches offered by a virtue ethic and a deontological ethic. Yet, besides being readily translatable into scientific research programs, utilitarian thinking can equally readily morph into an individualistic, emotive, and relativistic morality in which maximizing the sum of human pleasures and satisfactions of desires, influenced as they are by ever changing social pressures and norms, become the moral *sine qua non.*

11. The tribe is too large to name all its members; its chiefdom features stellar elites Edward O. Wilson, Steven Pinker, Sam Harris, Patricia Churchland, Joshua Greene, Michael Shermer, and Marc Hauser.

12. Hunter and Nedelisky, *Science and the Good,* 215.

This problem is further and more deeply analyzed in Jeffrey Bishop and coauthor's book, *Biopolitics after Neuroscience.* Placing their book in a wider cultural context, the authors call attention to "a striking characteristic of both neuroscientific and popular rhetoric on morality, namely, the ways they are perfused with economic language and concepts. . . . [A] key aspect of this rhetoric . . . [is] its laser-like focus on intervening in human bodies to improve not only individual performance but [also] economic productivity—in other words, its biopolitics. . . . [Our] book, then, is about the neuroscience of morality; or, more specifically, it is about *what one has to believe* about human morality *in order for the findings of the neuroscience of morality to be true.* Put differently, in this book, we will argue that [current] neoliberal political economy shapes what it is possible to say about the neuroscience of morality"[13] (emphases added). Focusing their critique on the published works of three public intellectuals, John Haidt, Sam Harris, and Paul Zak—none of them a trained or practicing neuroscientist[14]—the authors go on to say that the writings of these intellectuals tend to follow a common storyline in which "science is beginning to prove that morality is less about rationality and more about moral tastes or preferences, based in neurologically generated experiences of pleasure and pain. Rooted in our evolutionary biology, these moral tastes served to bind social groups together for the purpose of survival. Biologically grounded, these moral tastes give rise to human behaviors that are more instinctual or automatic and unconscious than we have normally understood, with rational deliberation, conscience, or choice. . . ."[15] Accordingly, one can thus readily add to a cognitive utilitarian calculus the more primitive and instinctive emotional inputs (see in the prior chapter the discussion of proto-moral sensibilities in infants) that, now, jointly comprise a neuroscientific basis of morality. Without fully engaging the mind's ability to engage in rational discourse, such a basis perforce supports an emotivist ethic that, as the rational virtue-ethicist Alisdair MacIntyre has pointed out, panders to individual preferences[16] or, in the words used by Hunter and Nedelisky above, to our getting what we want. In this naturalistic neuroscientific scheme, rational deliberation, conscience, or conscious choice are "merely the post hoc operations of our cerebral cortex working to understand or justify our actions. As such, our moral or

13. Jeffrey P. Bishop et al., *Biopolitics After Neuroscience: Morality and the Economy of Virtue* (Bloomsbury Publishing, 2022), 4.

14. Johnathan Haidt is a social psychologist, Sam Harris was trained in neuroscience but no longer practices it, and Paul Zak is an economist.

15. Bishop et al., *Biopolitics After Neuroscience*, 78.

16. MacIntyre, *After Virtue*, 11–12. By my reading, on p. 273, MacIntyre advocates a return to virtue ethics, wherein virtues refer to "qualities necessary to achieve the goods internal to practices; . . . [the] qualities contributing to the good of a whole life; . . .[and] the pursuit of a good for human beings the conception of which can only be elaborated and possessed within ongoing social traditions."

immoral actions are largely not under our control."[17] In other words, we are not free to consciously deliberate and decide on the moral choices that guide our actions. Our sense of conscious control is a mere illusion. Therefore, this unconscious, automatic "bottom-up account of morality combined with the continuing importance of morality for society's well-being suggests, in the end, that the political and economic order must necessarily function as the regulative locus for the possibility of moral behavior, or, in other words, help us control our animal [instincts and] emotions."[18]

As we shall see, this neuromanic and neuroreductive account raises several concerns. For now, I will address the following three important points. First, if our consciously guided decisions to act morally are mere after-the-fact, illusory confabulations, then any consciously planned, decided, and guided actions simply do not really exist, including those of the above three public intellectuals to write and publish their opinions. If so, then any of their published writings are merely the outcome of unconscious, biophysical brain processes. If that's the case, why should I or any attentive reader of my book take these opinions seriously? What endows these brain processes and the lengthy paragraphs they presumably generate with even a semblance of truth? Without a reasonable truth-bearing warrant provided by them, can one them seriously? The answer is: Hardly.

Second, in an ethic perfused with instinctual and emotive inclinations, the many differences among individuals' personal preferences and assessments of what maximizes his or her pleasures and satisfactions can easily morph into a pervasive moral individualism, and from there further into a moral nihilism emptied of any objective moral standards. Taking seriously the implications of Nietzsche's febrile musings, nihilism cuts the last fibrils restraining the assertions of individual human will-to-power from becoming the ultimate arbiter of values, a gloomy prospect to be sure.[19] Moreover, decisions on how to morally conduct one's life that are based on individual feeling and self-interest can, when collectively activated via social and political consensus, lead to particularly destructive long-term results. For, as the biologist Christian de Duve has pointed out, evolution by natural selection tends to favor traits that govern immediately useful behaviors, with little or no regard for their future consequences.[20] For that reason, despite my overall misgivings concerning Freudian

17. Bishop et al., *Biopolitics After Neuroscience*, 78.

18. Bishop et al., *Biopolitics After Neuroscience*, 78.

19. Although current popular notions of nihilism are generally associated with the 19th-century Nietzschean will-to-power, according to Jacques Ellul, *The Subversion of Christianity* (William B. Eerdmans Publishing Co., 1966) and Michael Allan Gillespie, *Nihilism Before Nietzsche* (University of Chicago Press, 1995), the nihilistic will-to-power as a cultural phenomenon preceded the 19th century by several centuries.

20. Christian de Duve, *Genetics of Original Sin: The Impact of Natural Selection on the Future of Humanity* (Yale University Press, 2010).

psychodynamics, I concur with Freud that the (utilitarian) pain-minimizing and pleasure-maximizing behaviors, many of which are governed by human instinctual emotions and passions, need to be reined in by the reality principle governed by the mind's use of reason—whose voice, as Freud also correctly noted, is not loud but, on the contrary, soft. However, rationally assessing and making decisions to act on the basis of long-term consequences is often an onerous task; in a quick-profit—I am thinking here of the computerized algorithms used to make super high-speed trades in stock markets—and consumer-oriented society, governed as it is by the principle of short-term or immediate satisfaction, such strenuous mental labor tends to be assiduously avoided. As the writer Mark Edmundson observes when addressing the banes of short-term self-interest, the modern, acquisitive self, overwhelmed as it is by instinctual drives and desires, becomes unhinged from the reality principle and, filled "with fear of the future, . . . believes if it could only get to the next rung of wealth, the next tier of society, the next level of recognition and success, then all would be well. So the [self] pushes on [compulsively] in its impossible task, creating [vicious cycles of] sorrow for others and anxious fear for itself."[21] Puny and fearful as it is, the modern self, plagued as it is with an insistent will-to-power, is nonetheless powerless against the onslaught of its drives and desires, and therefore compensates by confusing belligerence with power. For these reasons, I agree also with Andrew Steane's recent caution that, to stave off a bleak moral future dominated by unsatiable avarice, aggressive power, and abject oppression, the standard of moral truth must be sought outside the human sphere, a sphere that of course includes the wizardries of science and technology.[22] But how do we find evidence supporting such a standard? My best bet is that the evidentiary enterprise will not succeed unless it expands beyond the confines of science to include also sound philosophically, theologically, and historically informed anthropology. Such an anthropology must have an eye especially on the long-term and ultimate ends motivating human action. Additionally, it must look to the core moral precepts that have been appropriated and put into practice by the world's major religious traditions that, over the past three millennia, have mitigated the problems posed by human failures and miseries and additionally posed by the stifling of not only the material but also the spiritual flourishing at the individual and the communal levels.[23]

The third concern raised by the idea that the political and economic order must regulate moral behavior is a tendency among many neuroscientists and

21. Mark Edmundson, *Self and Soul: A Defense of Ideals* (Harvard University Press, 2015), 190.

22. Andrew Steane, *Faithful to Science: The Role of Science in Religion* (Oxford University Press, 2014), 105.

23. See Jacques Maritain, *Science and Wisdom* (Charles Scribner's Sons, 1940), 137–220, for such an approach to morality from specifically the Catholic religious tradition.

their popularizers to minimize, if not reject, the importance of religious influences in their research. While part of their underlying motive is the methodological rule proscribing supernatural explanations in the natural sciences, another part is their vivid antipathy to religion. As an example, the three public intellectuals, Haidt, Harris, and Zak, popularizing the findings of practicing neuroscientists, "share a common objective: to reject or reconfigure the relationship between morality and religion. [Along with other neoatheists such as Daniel Dennett], Harris . . . sides with the [outright] abolition of religion. Haidt and Zak are more subtle, both narrating religion as simply a [byproduct] manifestation of biological processes that bind people together."[24] Short of forceful sociopolitical prohibitions—in the United States, for instance, by restricting or rescinding the constitutional First Amendment's free-exercise clause—it is doubtful that religions will be entirely abolished. Any such prohibitions would be resisted in the United States by a majority of citizens. The chances of this occurring are therefore slim. Moreover, the chances are equally slim elsewhere. In the United Nations's Universal Declaration of Human Rights, Article 18 proclaims that everyone has the rights to freedom of thought, freedom of conscience, and freedom of religion. Except in a few cases, this latter right is acknowledged internationally. The free exercise of religion makes the worldwide phenomenon of religion one of the most powerful sociocultural phenomena, which in my opinion promises to continue as such even in our increasingly secularized society. Additionally, by simply observing its powerful sociocultural impact around the world, one can see that it is much more than a mere expression of evolved biological processes that binds a small tribe of humans together. As noted by the religious scholar William Franke, there is

> the problem of deficient solidarity in secular [i.e., nonreligious] reason and its natural morality. Practical reason is strong in its appeal to individuals and to their autonomous moral judgment and conscience, but it cannot compare with religious communities in motivating solidarity and collective commitment and action. Religions are oriented to communitarian praxis, whereas practical reason is based primarily on individual judgment. Its starting point seems to bias it toward an individualistic outlook and approach to the world. [Quoting the philosopher Jürgen Habermas, Franke continues that] "in contrast, religious consciousness remains bound up with ongoing life practices within a community, and in the case of the major world religions with the worldwide communities united in common rites of all the faithful. From this universalistically structured communitarianism, the religious consciousness of the individual can receive even in a purely moral perspective stronger impulses to solidarizing action."[25]

24. Bishop et al., *Biopolitics After Neuroscience*, 98.
25. Franke, *On the Universality of What Is Not*, 231–32.

Thus conceived, religion provides the solidarizing ingredient that unites small communities of faithful, such as parishes, into a major religious movement that magnifies its collective moral impact in the world, something that a purely secular, individualistic morality cannot compete with. In today's world of climate change, rampant exploitive capitalism, massive economic inequalities, regional wars, and all these forcing the most disadvantaged peoples of the world to relocate or migrate in their search for a better life elsewhere, it is religion that most powerfully raises the moral concern and action of humans everywhere to respond to the worldwide suffering of others. That said, ultimately it is nevertheless up to the moral choices made willingly and freely by each individual in a community of the faithful to collectively realize such a broad impact on improving the lives of especially the most marginalized people around the world.

Hence, a fourth problem raised by the neuromanic and neuroreductive focus and account of morality is that of individual free will, which is addressed below.

Morality and the Exercise of Free Will

> A human being feels . . . [a moral] obligation only if he is free, and each obligation, considered separately, implies liberty. But it is necessary that there should be obligations; and the deeper we go, away from those obligations which are at the top, towards obligation in general, or, . . . towards obligation as a whole, which is at the bottom, the more obligation appears as the very form assumed by necessity in the realm of life, when it demands, for accomplishment of certain ends, intelligence, choice, and liberty.
>
> Henri Bergson, *The Two Sources of Morality and Religion*, p. 29

> The only option for the physicalist is to assume that as a matter of metaphysical contingency the actual world is in fact causally closed. To adopt this assumption is attractive only for those who already assume that there is not room for genuine mental causation, which is to say that it is convincing for those who already accept the conclusion of the argument.
>
> Benedikt Paul Göcke, *After Physicalism*, p. 3

> . . . the subject of freedom and responsibility has never been separable from the subject of consciousness.
>
> Ted Honderich, *Exploring the Illusion of Free Will and Moral Responsibility*, p. 60

The above epigraphs encapsulate the roles that the topics of necessity, freedom, intelligence, choice, conscious mind, and mental causation play in our understanding of moral conduct. Choice in morally significant cases is not comparable to the trivial or whimsical exercise of our "consumer rights" to choose between purchasing Levi's or Dior blue jeans. In exercising consumer rights, we largely rely on personal, subjective preferences, preferences that are exercised *chacun à son gout* and free of moral scruples. But even these cases reveal a philosophically weighty issue regarding to what extent, if any, choices of action—even morally trivial ones—are made freely. In morally and juridically fraught cases, the issue of freely willed choices is accompanied by another issue, the bearing of responsibility for choosing actions that affect other people's lives and, as previously noted, of assigning praise and blame for a person's conduct.[26] Although the concept of the will was not foreign to Hellenistic philosophy, it was not until the turn of the 4th century CE that St. Augustine's theodicy introduced the notions of human *free* will and *original* sin to prominence in order to spare an omniscient and omnibenevolent God from taking responsibility and blame for the existence of evil in the world. According to Augustine, free will and original sin are, so to speak, joined at the hip. The world's evils, particularly human evil, were a consequence of a transgenerational, inherited flaw in human nature, the original sin committed by Adam and Eve in the Garden of Eden, where they exercised their free will in defiance of God's command. Given the existence of free will, should we be held morally responsible for actions and inactions chosen to harm others as well as for actions and inactions chosen deliberately that benefit them? If so, then in the former case do we justifiably merit blame, censure, and loss of respect from our peers, and in the latter case, their praise, approbation, and respect? If yes to both, the level of blame or praise and of respect or disrespect befitting our conduct reflects a judgment about a person's moral integrity and dignity.

Beyond Freedom and Dignity?

Nearly fifty years ago the behaviorist psychologist B. F. Skinner already proclaimed that we must move beyond not only human freedom but also human dignity.[27] The two concepts, he notes, are intimately related. The sense of freedom is the sense that we enjoy autonomous control of at least some aspects of our lives, i.e., that these aspects are not entirely controlled only by internal organic factors or by externally determined environmental factors. When our actions are forced to conform to unjust external controls and circumstances, as in slavery or under oppressive political regimes, we regard this as an affront to our dignity and to our sense of being autonomous humans fully worthy of respect and fair treatment. Skinner proposed that although the concepts of human freedom and dignity have served useful purposes in the past, in the future—the brave new world of his novel *Walden Two*—we must no longer rely

26. A thorough treatment of these questions and related concerns can be found in Daniel N. Robinson, *Praise and Blame: Moral Realism and its Applications* (Princeton University Press, 2002).

27. B. F. Skinner, *Beyond Freedom & Dignity* (Alfred A. Knopf, 1972).

on our inner feeling, sense, or conscious experience of freedom and dignity, but instead place our faith in various installations of behavioral technology that will guide the conduct of our personal and social lives. Skinner premised his proposal that we move beyond freedom and dignity on the claim that our actions are determined by our inherited genes and by our history of reward (positive reinforcement) and punishment (negative reinforcement), and therefore that human freedom and dignity are illusory (here we have a symptom of rampant panillusionism; see below and appendix 1).

Eventually, the influence of Skinner's extensive research waned, and since then most cognitive scientists have moved beyond Skinnerian operationalism and behaviorism, without jettisoning some of its more palatable features. However, the metaphysical leanings toward naturalism and physical causal closure of the universe among many current scientists and science-informed scholars led, as with Skinner, to a negative answer regarding the question concerned with the reality of human freedom. Over the past few decades, these assumptions have received putative confirmation from results of neuroscientific and psychological research. Here I will not contest the interpretations of such results made by scientists and scholars on the basis of their deterministic presuppositions. Instead, I will deal with the evidence of scientific research that supposedly confirms their choice of interpretations. As will be illustrated below, several influential scientists, scholars, and free-will skeptics have taken the scientific-fact bait hook-line-and-sinker, that is offered as evidence of research on human control of actions to justify dismissing free will as an illusion.[28] The problem is that the research is highly flawed conceptually and methodologically. Ironically, this justification relies at best on an what is known as the confirmation bias, a bias in reasoning that "objective" scientists presumably are trained to avoid, demonstrating that scientists can hold non-objective, metaphysical views that bias their acceptance and interpretation of research findings. Contrary to what Jerry Coyne claims, the absence of confirmation bias—a bias that is the willingness, as he defines it, to accept positive results and neglect negative ones—does not clearly distinguish science from religion. When scientific findings are published and widely advertised in popular culture, such biased justifications based on questionable research findings do a disservice to the public that for the most part respects science and relies on it as a source of credible information. Psychologists and neuroscientists who claim that our sense of having conscious control of our actions is an illusion, that we have no free will, make that claim because humans have a tendency to confabulate and fabricate

28. Among these scientists, scholars, and free-will skeptics are: Coyne, *Faith vs. Fact;* Mark Hallett, "What Does the Brain Know and When Does It Know It?," in *Exploring the Illusion of Free Will and Moral Responsibility*, ed. Gregg D. Caruso (Lexington Books, 2013); and Harris, *The Moral Landscape*; Sam Harris, *Free Will* (Free Press, 2012).

(we do not truly know the motives regulating our moral choices) or because our choices of action are made at an unconscious and, therefore, non-deliberated level.[29] For them, psychological or neural determinism is the fashionable dogma *du jour*.

In an attempt to salvage an acceptable semblance of free will from the rubbish heap piled up by determinists, some present-day scholars and scientists adapt a questionable strategy that is similarly used by Spinoza in his *Ethics*,[30] where he proposes that humans have the freedom to act but without also having a true, libertarian free will. Accordingly, these scholars claim that while human actions are the determined effects of a complex causal nexus, they nonetheless can be *interpreted* as being freely chosen, on the questionable pretext that no *external* force coerces them not to act.[31] A refinement added to this Spinozian strategy is to think of free will in terms of a similarly unencumbered exercise of moral competence, the capacity to appropriately discern and act in morally significant settings. However, this refinement leaves intact the problem of Spinoza's compatibilist notion of free will vis-à-vis the libertarian notion of free will. The latter notion posits that a truly free act is unblemished by *any* sort of deterministic influence. Yet from a purely physical or naturalist viewpoint, the human brain is nothing but complex neuronal machinery. The successful execution of any human action is therefore *necessarily* determined/constrained by the mechanistic biophysical properties of the brain. Because the brain's own biophysics comprises a deterministic mechanism, it seems impossible to reconcile a philosophically factitious compatibilist notion of free will

29. Examples of such psychologists and neuroscientists are Susan Blackmore, "Living Without Free Will," in *Exploring the Illusion of Free Will and Moral Responsibility*, ed. Gregg D. Caruso (Lexington Books, 2013); and Daniel Wegner, *The Illusion of Conscious Will* (MIT Press, 2002); Daniel M. Wegner, "The Mind's Best Trick: How We Experience Conscious Will," *Trends in Cognitive Science* 7, no. 2 (2003): 65–69.

30. In Spinoza's *Ethics*, "Part I. Concerning God, Definition 7," accessed on May 30, 2024, https://www.marxists.org/reference/subject/philosophy/works/ne/ethics.htm, 202, the following claim is made: "That thing is said to be free [*liber*] which exists solely from the necessity of its own nature, and is determined to action by itself alone. A thing is said to be necessary or rather, constrained [*coactus*], if it is determined by another thing to exist and to act in a definite and determinate way." Rephrased in human terms, it reads: "That human is said to be free who exists solely from the necessity of her/his own nature, and is determined to acti by her-/himself alone. A human is said to be necessary or rather, constrained, if she or he is determined by another entity (e.g. a physical obstruction or another human) to exist and to act in a definite and determinate way."

31. Daniel C. Dennett, *Freedom Evolves* (Viking Press, 2003); Michael S. Gazzaniga, *Who's in Charge?: Free Will and the Science of the Brain* (Harper Collins Publishers, 2011); Daniel C. Dennett, *Breaking the Spell: Religion as a Natural Phenomenon* (Penguin Books, 2007); Joshua Greene and Jonathan Cohen, "For the Law, Neuroscience Changes Nothing, and Everything," *Philosophical Transactions of the Royal Society B* 359, no. 1451 (2004): 1775–85.

with the notion of a true, libertarian free will. Hence, since the former notion is compatible with determinism, it seems to fit with some sort of quasi- or ersatz-freedom. Compatibilism seems more plausibly to show not so much that freedom evolves, as Daniel Dennett would have it (see previous note), but instead that paradoxically our crafty brains have evolved deterministically by chance and necessity so as to flout both by a clever ruse. We more fully discuss libertarian free will below.

In place of this ersatz, as-if, form of free will, the true free will that is denied by determinists is what I, along with others, refer as to incompatibilist free will, i.e., a free will that is incompatible with determinism. Can such free will be denied by currently available scientific findings? Along with Susan Pockett, I believe it cannot.[32] The reasons are given below. Turning first to philosophy and addressing the philosophical conundrum of accommodating determinism *and* free will, Daniel Robinson argues that the deterministic

> line of reasoning suffers from the self-refuting nature of the parent theory [of determinism]. For to accept the deterministic theory is to accept further that, whether or not one does accept such a theory—whether or not one is disposed to advance such a theory—is also determined by constitutional factors over which one has no control. In the end, we have no means by which to subtract out, as it were, the genetic predispositions to accept or reject propositions of a certain kind from their intrinsic truth or epistemic worth. The determinist who implores us to accept determinism on the strength of the arguments favoring it implicitly ascribes to us the power to choose one argument over another, and to do so solely *on the basis of the quality of the argument.* Thus, to argue for the adoption of such a theory is to deny its validity.[33] (emphasis added)

In other words, like Gödel's incompleteness theorem applying to mathematics, a theory of determinism can be regarded as valid insofar as it applies, for example, to the constitution of causal brain processes, but as an internally consistent theory applying to free moral choices it is either incomplete, thus in need of additional axiomatic postulates, such as the existence of a conscious human mind that can propose rational arguments; or, if it is complete, then as Robinson has argued, it is internally inconsistent.

32. Susan Pockett, "If Free Will Did Not Exist, It Would Be Necessary to Invent It," in *Exploring the Illusion of Free Will and Moral Responsibility*, ed. Gregg D. Caruso (Lexington Books, 2013), presents analyses and arguments concluding (on p. 271) that "neither neuroscience nor physics has yet killed a form of incompatibilist free will. . . . And of course nothing can kill compatibilist free will." See also Manuel Vargas, "If Free Will Doesn't Exist Neither Does Water," in *Exploring the Illusion of Free Will and Moral Responsibility*, ed. Gregg D. Caruso (Lexington Books, 2013).

33. Robinson, *Praise and Blame*; Harris, *Free Will*, 100.

Consciousness and Its Relation to Free-Will Deniers and to Free-Will Defenders

Hereafter, turning to empirical and scientific approaches to the free-will problem, our second turn is to philosophical musings of Sam Harris, a denier of free will. He is correct in saying that the "popular conception of [incompatibilist] free will seems to rest on two assumptions; (1) that [counterfactually] each of us could have acted differently than we did in the past, and (2) that we are the *conscious* source of most of our thoughts and actions in the present"[34] (emphasis added). In contrast to these assumptions, the gist of his thesis on free will is expressed by the immediately following assertion that "as we are about to see, both of these assumptions are false."[35] And further on, he claims rather casually that "acts of volition merely arise spontaneously (whether caused, uncaused, or probabilistically inclined, it makes no difference) and cannot be traced to a point of origin in our conscious minds."[35] These claims, especially the one that acts of volition merely arise spontaneously, are highly questionable when seen in light of a wider spectrum than that provided by determinism.

Under such light, I turn first to an analysis of the second assumption of the standard conception of free will—namely, that each of our conscious minds is the source of many of our thoughts and actions, an assumption that Harris declared to be false. For one, denial of the validity of this assumption rests importantly on highly *questionable interpretations of* results, reported originally by Benjamin Libet and his collaborators and subsequently by others, that brain signatures, especially ones known as readiness potentials, of our putative free decisions to perform an action as simple as moving a finger occur from several hundreds of milliseconds—to, according to other investigators, a truly astounding several full seconds—*before* the conscious registration of the decision to act occurs.[36] Second, such denial is based on highly questionable and overgeneralized interpretations of results reported by the social psychologist Daniel Wegner.[37] Wegner, who took the validity of anti-free-will interpretations of Libet

34. Harris, *Free Will*, 6.

35. Harris, *Free Will*, 6.

36. Benjamin Libet, "Unconscious Cerebral Initiative and the Role of Conscious Will in Voluntary Action," *Behavioral and Brain Sciences* 8, no. 4 (1985): 529–39; Benjamin Libet et al. "Time of Conscious Intention to Act in Relation to Onset of Cerebral Activity (Readiness-Potential)," *Brain* 106, no. 3 (1983): 623–42; Itzhak Fried et al., "Internally Generated Preactivation of Single Neurons in Human Medial Frontal Cortex Predicts Volition," *Neuron* 69, no. 3 (2011): 548–62; Chung Sion Soon et al., "Unconscious Determinants of Free Decisions in The Human Brain," *Nature Neuroscience* 11, no. 5 (2008): 543–45.

37. Wegner, *The Illusion of Conscious Will*. For a response to his critics, see Daniel M. Wegner, "Précis of *The Illusion of Conscious Will*," *Behavioral and Brain Sciences* 27, no. 5 (2004): 649–92

et al.'s results for granted, presented additional experimental findings showing that we can be fooled by our sense of free agency. However, as others—e.g., the neuroscientist Peter Tse and the philosopher Julian Baggini—have noted,[38] to claim on that basis that free-will agency does not exist and that our sense of it is illusory *all* the time is like inductively claiming (falsely) on the basis of several well-known visual illusions that all our perceptions are fundamentally nonveridical.[39] It is understandable that some scientists, including several top-notch neuroscientists, have adopted or fortified their own naturalistic and deterministic biases on the basis of these questionable neuroscientific and behavioral studies of human agency. Even scientists are prone to contagions of "groupthink" or of neglecting to question the results of these studies seriously and skeptically in a methodologically and conceptually fine-tuned manner.

Recently, however, other scientists and philosophers, more apt to be free-will defenders, have questioned the interpretations of these studies, both on methodological grounds and on deeper, conceptual grounds.[40] Among others, Peter Tse and John Kihlstrom argue and show that the Libet et al. experiments are so flawed methodologically that their findings, resulting largely from extraneous artifacts that confounded the experimental method, ought to be allocated to science's dustbin.[41] Kihlstrom notes a similar flaw in another study of free

38. For example, Peter Ulric Tse, *The Neural Basis of Free Will: Criterial Causations* (MIT Press, 2013); Peter Ulric Tse, *A Neurophilosophy of Libertarian Free Will* (Oxford University Press, 2024); Baggini, *The Possibility of Free Will.*

39. That all our perceptions are illusory is something, as noted in appendix 1, that the cognitive neuroscientist Donald Hoffman and co-workers also subscribe to.

40. Julian Baggini, *The Possibility of Free Will: Freedom Regained* (University of Chicago Press, 2015); Mark Balaguer, "Free Will, Determinism, and Epiphenomenalism," *Frontiers of Psychology* 9 (2019): 2623; Bruno G. Breitmeyer, "What's All the Free-Will Ado About?," *Psychology of Consciousness: Theory, Research, and Practice* 4, no. 3 (2017): 330–33; George Ellis, *How Can Physics Underlie the Mind?: Top-Down Causation in the Human Context* (Springer, 2016), 369–84; Adrian G. Guggisberg and Anais Mottaz, "Timing and Awareness of Movement Decisions: Does Consciousness Really Come Too Late?," *Frontiers in Human Neuroscience* 7 (2013): 385; Han-Gue Jo et al., "Spontaneous EEG Fluctuations Determine the Readiness Potential: Is Preconscious Brain Activation a Preparation Process to Move?," *Experimental Brain Research* 231, no. 4 (2003): 495–500; John F. Kihlstrom, "Time to Lay the Libet Experiment to Rest: Commentary on Papanicolaou," *Psychology of Consciousness: Theory, Research, and Practice* 4, no. 3 (2017): 324–29; W. R. Klemm, "Free Will Debates: Simple Experiments Are Not So Simple," *Advances in Cognitive Psychology* 6 (2010): 47–65; Christian List, *Why Free Will Is Real* (Harvard University Press, 2019); Alfred R. Mele, *Free: Why Science Hasn't Disproved Free Will* (Oxford University Press, 2014); Jeff Miller et al., "Effects of Clock Monitoring on Electroencephalographic Activity: Is Unconscious Movement Initiation an Artifact of the Clock?," *Psychological Science* 22, no. 1 (2011): 103–9; Andrew C. Papanicolaou, "The Myth of the Neuroscience of Will," *Psychology of Consciousness: Theory, Research, and Practice* 4, no. 3 (2017): 310–20.

41. Tse, *The Neural Basis*; Kihlstrom, "Time to Lay."

choice[42]—and, I would add, in a still further study.[43] In addition, Kihlstrom, Andrew Papanicolaou, and Mark Balaguer wonder, as I do, what in these studies went on in the minds of the experimental subjects during the interval—which can last up to an astounding 10 seconds—between the neural signal putatively specifying their supposedly unconscious decision to act and the execution of the following act itself.[44] It is hard to interpret such findings without knowing, and experimentally controlling for, the many sorts of uncontrolled, extraneous mentation that most likely went on during that interval.

Moreover, the movement of one's finger *arbitrarily* or *spontaneously* in a laboratory setting like that of Libet et al. is a behavior that, noted by me several decades ago and recently as well by psychologist and neuroscientist Uri Maoz and collaborators, is purposeless, require no deliberation or reasoning, and is existentially inconsequential.[45] In contrast, many choices that humans make in their day-to-day lives, such as personally, financially, or morally weighty ones, are deliberate and consequential. Just like late-19th-century structuralist psychologists, following the example of their chemist confreres in the physical sciences, attempted to establish the existence of "sensory atoms" from which more complex "perceptual compounds" could be realized, Libet et al.'s goal likewise seemed to be one of establishing the simplest "free-will atoms" from which more complex "free-will compounds" could be realized. Both ventures failed, since neither simple sensory atoms nor simple free-will atoms succeeded in giving real-life, ecologically valid accounts of perceptions on the one hand or of more complex, real-life behavioral choices on the other. Maoz et al. found that in an experimental situation resembling the one used by Libet et al., that is, one that requires no deliberation or weighing of consequences, readiness potentials (RPs) did precede the conscious registration of the decision to act. However, in a more life-like, ecologically valid situation where decisions to act had to be deliberated and weighed as to their possible consequences, no RPs were observed. These combined findings clearly show that unlike Maoz et al.'s findings, Libet et al.'s findings, by the very fact that they were methodologically limited and necessarily bound to the presence of RPs, are also severely limited in their relevance to interpretations of free-will decisions as they occur in real-life settings.

42. Soon et al., "Unconscious Determinant."

43. Fried et al., "Internally Generated Preactivation."

44. Balaguer, "Free Will, Determinism"; Kihlstrom, "Time to Lay"; Papanicolaou, "The Myth of the Neuroscience."

45. Bruno G. Breitmeyer, "Problems with the Psychophysics of Intentions," *Behavioral and Brain Sciences* 8, no. 4 (1985): 539–40; Bruno G. Breitmeyer, "In Support of Pockett's Critique of Fried's Studies of the Time Course of Consciousness," *Consciousness and Cognition* 11, no. 2 (2002): 280–83; Uri Maoz et al., "Neural Precursors of Decisions That Matter—an ERP Study of Deliberate and Arbitrary Choice," *eLife* 8 (2019): e39787.

This conclusion concurs with that of the philosopher Julian Baggini, who additionally raised the following conceptual problem. The fact that prior investigators of free-will decisions concluded that conscious thoughts and decisions have no causal efficacy locally, e.g., when subjects are in an experimental laboratory, cannot be legitimately overgeneralized to show that they have no causal efficacy everywhere (and everywhen). In other words, the mere fact that some motives, intentions, and decisions to act are generated unconsciously cannot be taken as evidence that globally all actions proceed without prior consciously assessed motives, intentions, and choices. Such overgeneralization, Baggini notes, is like claiming that since people's conscious religious beliefs do not affect their choice of laundry soap when shopping, they also do not affect their choice of a place of worship, say, after moving from one city and settling down in a new one.[46] In contrast to Baggini's cautionary appraisal, Harris gladly (and unconsciously?) takes to heart these highly questionable overgeneralizations when he asserts that there "is no question that our attribution of [conscious] causal agency *can be* gravely in error. I am arguing that it *always is*"[47] (emphases added).

The above discussions illustrate that timing is an important variable in experimental studies of how and when decisions to act are made, even in cases where the actions are morally trivial. What proponents of the free-will illusion fail to take into account is that time also is of the essence when making weighty decisions. When we make nontrivial, morally (or, say, economically) important decisions, we generally don't act arbitrarily, impulsively, or whimsically. We spend sufficient time weighing alternative decisions and actions, the possible means by which we can actualize them in the future, and their possible consequences to our short-term and long-term well-being. Sometimes these deliberations are emotionally painful because our decisions may negatively affect not only us but also loved ones. As the philosophers William James and Mark Balaguer and the neuroscientist Peter Tse fully appreciate, such future-directedness of human thought and agency—particularly for those decided-upon actions that may be postponed for a long time due to unforeseen events or further deliberations—characterize morally weighty actions.[48] Like Balaguer, Tse attempts to present a case for a strong free will, i.e., an incompatibilist, libertarian type of free will,[49] which assumes physical indeterminism—at least at the level of quantum physics—and relies on what Tse refers to as neuronally realized *criterial-information causation*. At the microneural level, the latter can

46. Baggini, *The Possibility of Free Will*.

47. Harris, *Free Will*, 25.

48. James, *The Principles of Psychology*; Balaguer, "Free Will, Determinism"; Tse, *The Neural Basis*.

49. Tse, *The Neural Basis*.

be deployed by the conscious mind in a top-down manner when prior physically implemented, postsynaptic informational criteria "select," from among the many possible presynaptic information-bearing inputs—due to the many possible presynaptic quantal states—only those that meet these preset informational criteria. Here free will is premised on the reasonable assumptions (i) that criterial information is realized physically in the brain's neural-activity patterns (much like genetic information for constructing proteins is realized in the structures of DNA's molecular sequences), (ii) that this criterial information, call it Info1, is preset by prior conscious decision, and (iii) that a human agent must have been counterfactually able to choose and decide to act otherwise, i.e., by vetoing Info1 and replacing it with a new criterial information, call it Info2, and therefore to act in a way other than she or he initially intended.

Without going into the details of Tse's thesis, I find it an admirable attempt to neuroscientifically defend the existence of free will. However, I am not satisfied that the attempt has satisfactorily succeeded. The reason for my dissatisfaction is that the problem of incompatibilist free will is, as Tse agrees, inextricably linked to the mind-body or consciousness-brain problem. In the introductory chapter of his book *The Neural Basis of Free Will*, Tse, like many other neuroscientists, confidently expresses that neuroscience will solve the mind-body problem, although up to now it has not done so. Along with others, I am not as confident as Tse that neuroscience will ever solve the problem. I agree with Tse that there can be no incompatibilist free will unless there also is a conscious being who exercises it. But the problems posed by mind and consciousness (without them, incompatibilist free will is wish rather than reality) remain far from having been solved satisfactorily by either philosophy or by science. How much more work must be done or what sort of conceptual breakthrough must occur in philosophy and science before the problem is ever solved is an open question. Thus, here I again agree with Susan Pockett that current science cannot resolve decisively whether incompatibilist free will exists or not.[50] Within the current scientific perspective of naturalism, the ontological problem of such free will is unsolved. So, for now as before, the choice between adopting an ersatz compatibilist vs. an incompatibilist free will, while not arbitrary, rests more on the metaphysical presuppositions one takes as fundamental and rationally defensible than on any decisive scientific evidence.

That noted, I will briefly outline Tse's scheme of accounting for free will, by again stating my ontological claim that existence of consciousness is as real as, say, that of a segment of DNA that we refer to as a gene. On that basis, I venture to offer the following possibility for reconciling free will with the existence of microneural processes going on in the brain. Recall from above that Tse's incompatibilist, libertarian free will assumes (i) physical indeterminism—there-

50. Pockett, "If Free Will Did Not Exist."

fore many realizable physical possibilities—and (ii) neuronally realized criterial-information causation. Unlike Tse, who maintains that science will eventually be able to give a reductive material account of consciousness, one can argue instead (see chapter 1: Setting the Stage: . . .) that consciousness is an *immaterial* mental substance for which such an account cannot be given.[51]

Then, how can consciously generated information cause physical, neuronal realized changes? Two reasonable answers can be given. One answer regarding mental causation was proposed by the philosopher Stephen Priest as follows: "The existence of mental causation is, however, no threat to . . . [the first law of thermodynamics]. If something physical causes something physical, then energy is displaced or transferred from cause to effect. There is no reason why mental causation should not merely displace energy and neither add to nor subtract from the quantity of energy in the universe [as the first law of thermodynamics demands]."[52] Although Priest's proposal is reasonable, a skeptic might ask for a fuller explanation of *how* the mind causes such energy displacement.

A second, more telling, answer lies with the fact that information and energy are, via the second law of thermodynamics, intimately related to each other.[53] In an intriguing recent study that employs a rationale analogous to that of Tse's indeterminacy- and information-based explanation of free will, the physicist Shoichi Toyabe and collaborators have demonstrated that an *information-to-energy conversion* is possible without contradicting the second law of thermodynamics, which states that in thermodynamic processes the total entropy (a measure of the disorder in interacting thermodynamic systems) never decreases.[54] In other words, in their experiment, a physically implemented crit-

51. When I maintain that consciousness is an immaterial mental substance, I am not also claiming that human consciousness is a supernatural entity, but only that it is some sort of nonphysical, extranatural entity, a claim that will be clarified and defended in later discussions in the main text.

52. Stephen Priest, "The Unconditioned Soul," in *After Physicalism*, ed. Benedikt Paul Göcke (University of Notre Dame Press, 2012), 330.

53. Myron Tribus and Edward C. McIrvine, "Source Energy and Information," *Scientific American* 225, no. 3 (1971): 179–90. The second law of thermodynamics states that in any spontaneous physical process, the entropic, low-quality, disordered energy will never decrease. Such a process can theoretically be counteracted locally by the high-quality free energy made available by the information supplied by what in physics is known as Maxwell's demons. Theoretically it turns out that this information-based process does not contradict the second law of thermodynamics.

54. Shoichi Toyabe et al., "Experimental Demonstration of Information-to-Energy Conversion and Validation of the Generalized Jarzynski Equality," *Nature Physics* 6, no. 12 (2010): 988–92. Translated in terms of the thermal energy, the second law of thermodynamics states that heat always moves from higher-energy hotter objects or states to lower-energy colder objects or states, unless another process is made available to reverse the direction of heat flow.

erial information could be employed to create an amount of what is known as high-quality, free energy (energy available to do useful work) that is larger than the amount of energy expended in work done to physically implement the criterial information. The effect of this information-based procedure was to yield a positive amount of high-quality, free energy.[55] By analogy, this finding suggests that at least one critical role of an immaterial conscious mind is to provide, in a top-down manner, the criterial information involved in the same information-to-energy conversion that results in the most efficient use of free energy made available to do work in the human cerebral cortex at the microneural level.

The vital role of criterial information is not limited to arriving at existentially important, freely willed decisions to act in one way or another. It is also found to play a role whenever a freely chosen, conscious decision to act counters any unfree, unconsciously triggered impulses that would cause or maintain contrary actions. An example of such a role is found in the supramodular interaction theory proposed and explored by Ezequiel Morsella and coworkers.[56] In this theory, the primary role of consciousness is to control human behavior whose underlying neural processes, though in themselves nonconscious, are nonetheless consciously penetrable. An example of conscious penetrability is the following. Carrying a dish held by hand to the dinner table is a simple voluntary action. Imagine, however, that the dish you're transporting to the dinner table is painfully hot. While carrying the dish in your bare hands, your instinctively protective and unconsciously triggered response is to terminate the pain by dropping the plate. However, here, much like in Tse's case of executing a freely chosen course of action, the nonconscious neural processes supporting your

55. It also plays a role in normal visual behavior generated when we sequentially scan a scene to, so to speak, visually forage for its task-relevant informative content. An apt example is my perusing a textbook whose thematic contents may help my thinking about and composing the present book's final draft. As I am attentively reading the words in a current fixation, the peripheral (non-fixated) words that are anticipated to occur at the next, to-be-fixated, location are automatically and preconsciously processed by the brain. This automatically processed contextual word-information constitutes the brain's anticipatory criterial information that will or else will not match the information conveyed by the words that actually appear at the next fixation location. When there is a match, the reading proceeds smoothly without a hitch. However, when a mismatch occurs—as has happened very, very infrequently in my past readings—between the brain's anticipated word-information and the word-information actually processed attentively during next fixation location, further reading might be interrupted. During such infrequent pauses, my eye moved to view the words fixated previously so as to give me a hint about the contextual mismatch.

56. Ezequiel Morsella, "The Function of Phenomenal States: Supramodular Interaction Theory," *Psychological Review* 112, no. 4 (2005): 1000–1021; Ezequiel Morsella et al., "The Primary Function of Consciousness in the Nervous System," *Annual Review of Biomedical Sciences* 9 (2007): 37–40; T. Andrew Poehlman et al., "Adaptive Skeletal Muscle Action Requires Anticipation and 'Conscious Broadcasting,'" *Frontiers in Psychology* 3 (2012): 369.

instinctive tendency to drop the dish are penetrable by consciously directed processes, which, via criterial information, counteract and neurally suppress the instinctive response tendency long enough to place the dish on the table.

Combined, Tse's and Morsella and coworkers' theoretical approaches indicate that consciousness, as a conveyor of information, can freely and causally influence neurophysiological activity that proceeds at unconscious levels of processing. Without higher cortical brain processes, such as those found in higher mammals, consciousness and its control over human behavior would not exist. As pointed out in chapter 1, organisms lower on the phylogenetic scale, for example reptiles or amphibians, have a primitive paleocortex but lack the complex functional neural anatomy found in the mammalian neocortex that in humans supports consciousness. It therefore is no wonder that their sensorimotor behaviors are nearly completely instinctive and stereotyped, in that they are determined largely by "hard-wired" neural networks that are all but impenetrable to higher-level conscious control.[57] Such primitive, instinctive sensorimotor behaviors can even be found in humans. An example of such an instinctive, consciously impenetrable neural response mechanism in humans is the eye's pupillary reflex caused by an increase or decrease in the ambient light level. Under normal circumstances, our conscious free will cannot penetrate the unconscious processes underlying this involuntary response.

Nonetheless, the findings supporting conscious penetrability of unconscious neural activity imply that the human agent, by consciously deciding on a course of action, can exercise free will as argued by Tse. It therefore supports the views (i) that humans can be held morally accountable for the consequences of such action and (ii) that, as stated by the philosopher Alasdair MacIntyre, conscious "[e]valuative judgments [such as moral judgments] are a species of *factual* judgments concerning final and formal causes of activity of members of a particular species [such as humans]"[58] (emphasis added). Consequently, one also has support for the type of moral realism defended by Daniel Robinson.[59]

What constitutes human freedom is not only the possibility of consciously countermanding the reflexive actions in response to human instinctual needs or in response to unconsciously and insistently aroused desires (see note). Unfortunately, there also is the possibility of consciously countermanding the evaluative, consciously deliberated judgments dictated by the intellect and

57. R. W. Sperry, "The Problem of Central Nervous Reorganization After Nerve Regeneration and Muscle Transposition," *The Quarterly Review of Biology* 20, no. 4 (1945): 353–55, presents evidence of the absence, in all but nonconscious amphibians, of conscious penetrability of instinctive reflexes.

58. Alasdair MacIntyre, *Three Rival Versions of Moral Enquiry: Encyclopaedia, Genealogy, and Tradition* (University of Notre Dame Press, 1991), 134.

59. Robinson, *Praise and Blame.*

reason.[60] It is therefore one thing to consciously penetrate and suppress actions prompted by unconscious instinct and desire to, for instance, drop a hot plate carried to the dinner table, but entirely another thing to *consciously subvert* a chosen action that effects a moral good in order to promote another *consciously chosen* action effecting what is morally deplorable. It is in this latter case, where both courses of action (subverting the good so as to promote the bad) are consciously chosen, that the problems of sin, guilt, and responsibility arise.

60. I owe this distinction, hidden by its very obviousness, to the following remarks made by Hannah Arendt, *The Life of the Mind*, vol. 2: *Willing* (Mariner Books, 1978), 130: "It is the possibility of resistance to the needs of desire, on the one hand, and the dictates of intellect and reason, on the other, that constitutes human freedom." This high-level philosophical remark finds its apt analog in Ezequiel Morsella's Supramodular Interaction Theory, which describes the low-level, sensori-motor interactions during conscious control of unconscious, instinctive needs and drives.

CHAPTER 5

The Science of Beauty, Religion's Other Partner

> . . . beauty is one of the divine names. God is beautiful. He is the most beautiful of all beings, because, as set forth by Denys the Areopagite and St. Thomas, His beauty is without change or vicissitude, without increase or diminution; and . . . it is not like that of things, which all have a particularized beauty. . . . He is beautiful by Himself and in Himself, beautiful absolutely. . . . He is Beauty itself. . . .
>
> Jacques Maritain, *Art and Scholasticism*, pp. 44–45

> In the visible, the artist seeks the invisible.
>
> Louis Dupré, *Religion and the Rise of Modern Culture*, p. 25

On the basis of the above epigraphs, it is easy to see that beauty is intimately tied to religion. Since God, Beauty itself, created the world, the beautiful, along with the good and the true, abound in our world and reflect his splendor. In their perfection, the Beautiful, the Good, and the Truth are transcendental attributes united in God's Being. As pointed out by an anonymous reviewer of the prepublication book manuscript, "in my understanding, truth as an attribute of God refers to transcendental truths, such as his mercy and love—not to worldly realities. In this understanding, truth is consistently beautiful." And the same statement can apply to goodness as an attribute of God. Yet within these-worldly realities, the attributes of truth and goodness disclose themselves to us as realities within—and despite—their imperfect realizations in matter and nature and in our hearts and minds. The gap between their perfections in God and their imperfect manifestations in our world is not a void; it is instead a portion of freedom's space in which—unfortunately—falsity, ugliness, and evil can also find their realizations. So, in our world the true does not completely overlap the good and the beautiful. To deny this is to do a disservice to the facts of human history and to our intellect. Not every truth, in its historic context, is good or beautiful. As the many world-shattering events—especially those of the last century still fresh in our memory—have demonstrated, truths can be downright ugly and evil. The human-wrought wars, genocides, tortures, indiscriminate killings, and environmental degradations are subjectively experienced as inherently (and thus objectively) ugly and evil effects produced when human desire and power have been corrupted and decoupled from any moral constraint. Moreover, there are too many natural events, pestilences, famines, floods, and earthquakes that in the recent and more remote past have wrought ill and ugly effects. While inner-worldly facts and truths can be ugly and evil, the beautiful, by definition, cannot be ugly.[1] Yet it too can, in some circumstances, be associated with ill effects. In the natural realm, the purely physical grace of the sinewy and lithe bodies of a running African antelope or a running leopard pursing it can be seen as a thing of beauty. But these beautiful bodies within the context of pursuit and escape are all momentary prelude to and part of a biologically necessitated, natural end. The death of the antelope and the furtherance of the leopard's life are a mix of good and ill within the clawed and throat-piercing hold of the leopard, the sight of which we instinctively would rather be spared. In the human realm, the ivory carvings displayed for sale by morally ignorant or unscrupulous traders at a market can express an intricate beauty, yet not without the ever increasing and unnecessary loss of elephants' lives caused by the equally ignorant or corrupted behaviors of poachers. Such human evils are deplorable and regrettable; however, they are often committed not for the sake of evil per se but instead for lucrative ends and thus fail to measure up to the level of horrific evils that humans are capable of committing.

Regarding such heinous types of malevolence that grips some humans, Claire Ortiz Hill, in her book *The Roots and Flowers of Evil in Baudelaire, Nietzsche, and Hitler*, describes the influence of evil in art, literature, and life and shows how sinister, raw evils found in human nature have featured in celebratory and glorified garb in the poetry or literary works of Baudelaire, Nietzsche, and Hitler. All three men, each in his own way, expressed the seductive power of evil in their writings, in which "evil was depicted, beautified, glamorized, justified calmly at their desks to lay bare its roots and romanticize its horrors [that are its flowers]. . . . [Indeed,] Baudelaire, the author of *Flowers of Evil*, labored 'to extract beauty from evil' and to express it in poetic form."[2] Anticipating Ortiz Hill's appraisal by over a century, the Russian philosopher Vladimir Soloviev noted that poetry, like all art, "in itself is neither good nor bad. It is a *flowering* and *radiance* of spiritual powers—good or evil. Hell has its own fleeting flower and its own deceptive radiance."[3] In the creative human arts, there

1. In my younger days I read an article on the relation between art and science, in which a scientist—if I recall correctly, it was Albert Einstein—responded to someone's praising the beauty of a piece of visual art by asking, "But is it good?"

2. Claire Ortiz Hill, *au lecteur* to *The Roots and Flowers of Evil in Baudelaire, Nietzsche, and Hitler* (Open Court, 2006), xv. It is, however, important to note that when Jacques Maritain, in his book *Art and Scholasticism*, quotes Baudelaire, he seems to do so approvingly. Baudelaire was not so much consumed *by* evil, as was Hitler, but more so *with* evil by exposing the moral underside of humanity in his poetry.

3. Vladimir Sergeyevich Soloviev, *The Heart of Reality: Essays on Beauty, Love, and Ethics* (University of Notre Dame Press, 2003), 169.

nevertheless is something fraudulent about evil's beauty. Baudelaire's and Nietzsche's inspired but pained attempts to mimic nature by forcibly, and thus unnaturally, extracting beauty from evil, or conversely by foisting evil on beauty, were expressions of a broader movement in the literary, visual, and musical arts of the 19th-century Romantic period. To this day the legacy of this Dark Romanticism is its demonic mark stamped on artistic, societal, economic, and political developments.

It is because of this moral ambiguity in the relation between truth and the beautiful in nature and in human art that, in a theistic understanding, truth as an attribute of God refers to transcendental truths, such as his goodness, his mercy, and his love, and not to this-worldly realities. In this understanding, truth is consistently beautiful. The moral ambiguity present in worldly beauty was also apparent to the theologian Hans Urs von Balthasar, who cautions "that what is beautiful in this world—being spirit as it makes its appearance—possesses a total dimension that also calls for a moral decision."[4] Von Balthasar adds that "the total dimension carries in it the possibility of evil as well as good. If this is so, then from the beautiful the way must also lead [via morality] into the religious dimension which itself includes man's definitive answer to the question about God and, indeed, his answer to the question God poses to *him*."[5] One of other possibly reasonable ways to pose God's question to humanity is: Your crafts, creations, and actions, are they as moral, as just and as good, as they are beautiful? If they are, then, as David Bentley Hart states it, "ethics [the principles guiding human moral conduct] is an aesthetics: an optics, that is, in an unequivocal sense, an order of seeing that obeys a *story* of being according to which the other [person affected by one's actions] is delineated with the radiant proportions of the other, who elicits the infinite regard of God and compels an infinite awe and even love from the one who looks on (an awe that is, necessarily, a recognition of the other's beauty as other). The secret of the ethical is that it is a certain aesthetic convention, a certain kind of aesthetic theme."[6] The close relation between beauty and morality at a theological level, noted by von Balthasar and Hart, is also found at the level of human psychology. Research findings reported by Rett Diessner and coworkers speak to this relation.[7] Their research and their review of relevant literature indicate that humans have a distinct sense of moral beauty. Besides giving rise to feelings of delight, it arouses in them also what Diessner et al. call "moral elevation," defined as the emotional response to

4. Hans Urs von Balthasar, *The Glory of the Lord: A Theological Aesthetics*, vol.1, *Seeing the Form* (Ignatius Press, 2009), 34.

5. Balthasar, *Seeing the Form*, 34.

6. David Bentley Hart, *The Beauty of the Infinite* (William B. Eerdmans Publishing Co., 2004), 343.

7. Rett Diessner et al., "Who Engages with Moral Beauty?"; Pohling and Diessner, "Moral Elevation and Moral Beauty."

witnessing acts of moral beauty. Being perceived as pleasant, the emotional response motivates interpersonal bonding and social affiliation with others, as well as moral behavior tendencies.

While the moral good can partake of the aesthetic dimension and, by definition, cannot be a moral evil, can it nevertheless be false or ugly? Or can the good be neither? On one hand, a good compromised by a falsity is a lie, and as such—even when posing as the only "good" solution to a moral dilemma requiring a choice between two equally deplorable, undesirable actions—is not a good. As so movingly depicted in one of William Styron's novels, *Sophie's Choice*, the resolution of such moral dilemmas can only be an imperfect one of opting for one of equally evil actions. On the other hand, a good that is or has become ugly is a good defiled, and therefore not a good at all. For example, ingesting nourishment is a life-maintaining activity and thus a good. However, a gourmand's gorging food excessively, needlessly resulting in his ill health and unsightly obesity to the point of his bare mobility, is a good defiled to the point of having become an evil. Moreover, it is morally repulsive in view of millions of humans, especially children, throughout the world who suffer from starvation every day. The good life, as Aristotle pointed out, is a life of virtue, the most important of which is prudence, the cognizance of a moderate life between abject lack and debauched excess.

The good, then, is untainted by evil and therefore true and beautiful. Akin to Plato's view, the good is the unifying principle at the heart, at the intersection of the three transcendentals properties of being. The good, from which the true and beautiful flow beyond its purview and establish their creative autonomy in the sciences and the arts, is the primary referent. Therefore, when we ponder the wondrously beautiful theories and discoveries made in the many natural and human sciences and the marvelous achievements in the visual, literary, musical, and performing arts, it is always proper for us also to ask (see notes 2–5 above): But are they good? Do they serve the good? The fact that they can be and do good is expressed by the contemporary painter Makato Fujimura, in his book *Art and Faith*. In it, art, the practice of co-creating, of making visible and audible God's goodness that otherwise remains invisible and inaudible—blinded and deafened as we are by the excessive clutter and noise of contemporary audio-visual media—has inspired Fujimara's theology of making,[8] a theology that potentially addresses not only the fine, literary, musical, and performing arts but also the artful world of ideas, as well as the practical crafts such as carpentry, pottery, weaving, and woodwork.

8. Makoto Fujimura, *Art and Faith: A Theology of Making* (Yale University Press, 2020).

What Does Science and Theology Reveal About Beauty and Its Delights?

The human realm of the beautiful presupposes that beauty exists in the world and that we have an adequate sense for experiencing it. The beautiful abounds in nature in various forms. On a grand physical scale, a star-filled night sky, the aurora borealis, a sunrise over secluded shores, the panoramas of Arizona's painted desert or of Colorado's snow-capped Rockies are all beauties and sublimities that can arouse in us joy, wonder, serenity, and awe. And on a smaller scale, a multitude of gemstones and minerals exhibit nature's trove of beautiful crystalline shapes and coruscating colors. In the kingdom of plants, the commonest fern illustrates nature's art in its fractal designs, and the rarest orchid does so in its floral design and color. And in the animal kingdom, nature advertises its vast array of colors and shapes throughout the invertebrate (e.g., cuttlefish, beetles, butterflies), and vertebrate (e.g., tropical fish, birds) all the way up, through graceful felines and gazelles, to humans gifted with classic, athletic physiques and physiognomies. Moreover, natural beauties, available not only to sight but also to hearing, are found in the murmur of brooks flowing down mountain meadows, in the nightingale's nocturne, and of course in the melodies of human vocalists. The above, a mere résumé, testify to the tremendous catalogue of beauties that are on display in nature. Since prehistoric times, the visually and manually gifted have depicted the natural visual beauties on cave walls, rock faces, wood, canvases, or have shaped them from antlers, seashells, crystals, clay, wood, or stone. And the acoustically and vocally gifted have reworked the aural beauties of nature into music, song, and poetry. Culture augments nature's bounty of beauty.

Yet despite this natural and cultural exorbitance, there are individuals who have eyes, ears, and minds that are not receptive to the beautiful. In a minority (around five percent) of individuals, some of these shortcomings, such as amusia (tone deafness) and color blindness, are genetically inherited or congenital defects; others, including acquired amusia and achromatopsia (cortical color blindness) are caused by localized brain damage. Adding to that the minority of individuals who suffer from congenital or else acquired anhedonias (deficiencies in enjoying various experiences), one realizes that a noticeable number of individuals, through no fault of their own, are unable to experience beauty in its full splendor and delight. The sense of beauty of individuals who are totally blind from birth is no doubt limited; yet their delight in perceiving beauty found in environmental sources of stimulation via their remaining senses, remains just as intense, and may even be heightened, relative to that of normal, sighted individuals. Illustrated here is the difference between the objective existence of the beautiful per se and the subjective sense of beauty, not to mention the challenge posed to (Berkeleyan) idealist claims that what is not or cannot be perceived does not exist. Just as the reality of a snow-peaked mountain can elicit in an observer a subjective sense of its objective existence, so can the splendor of the mountain elicit in an observer a subjective sense of its beauty. For if the beautiful is not an out-there reality to which an unimpaired human is attuned, how can he or she ever acquire an in-here sense or an appreciation of beauty?

Even when limited by some organic anomaly, our sense of beauty, our ability to appreciate the beautiful—the variegated and well-formed objects of sight, sound, smell, and taste—is a connatural gift. In a rudimentary form, it might even exist in nonhuman creatures. For humans, however, the maintenance, refinement, and amplification of these natural senses in the cultural realm and the realm of the spirit calls for cultivating a discernment that demands lengthy training and reflective thought to bear on the products of our sensory and imaginative apparat.[9] Here nature and nurture cooperate to increasingly reveal a plenitude of beauty. The connatural response to the gift of beauty varies; it manifests on some occasions in surprise, or awe, or serenity, and most importantly in some form of delight. Delight, delectation, or rapture is an emotion that animates the spirit as much as it gratifies it. Once roused in its primal pure form, the emotion is a cycling of affect and motive, a self-perpetuating exploration and celebration of the world and our life in it. One need only observe kittens or pups at play, expressing a desire satisfied and simultaneously stimulated by delight as they repeatedly practice their skills in exploring, discovering, and getting to know the richness and the newness of world around them. And when they tire from play, we delight in their peaceful slumber. And what holds for kittens and pups holds more so for human infants. Delight satisfies and arouses their desire to perceptually explore their world and develop their mastery of skills needed to live and thrive in it. In the presence of a loving and lovable caretaker, someone who acknowledges and reciprocates the infant's own experience of delight, it provides the emotional space for developing the infant's connatural sense of beauty within a larger personal, social, and cultural context. Throughout life, our perceptual and cognitive takes of the world and the affective experience of delight it elicits are heightened and refined as is, along with them, our sense of beauty.[10]

What is the source of such vital delight? It would not be mistaken to say that it is a divine gift, a freely flowing source of joyful and life-cultivating energy—the divine sparks (Göttersfunken), as the philosopher and poet Frie-

9. For the role of high-level cognitive functions in aesthetic experience, see Edward A. Vessel et al., "The Brain on Art: Intense Aesthetic Experience Activates the Default Mode Network," *Frontiers in Human Neuroscience* 4 (2012): 66; Aenne A. Brielmann and Denis G. Pelli, "Beauty Requires Thought," *Current Biology* 27, no. 10 (2017): 1506–13.

10. As Aenne A. Brielmann and Denis G. Pelli, "Intense Beauty Requires Intense Pleasure," *Frontiers in Psychology* 10 (2019): 2420, have established, the refinement and intensification of our sense of beauty requires an intensification of our delight in experiencing beauty.

drich Schiller put in in his *Ode to Joy* (*An die Freude*), that also inspired Beethoven to compose his Ninth Symphony. It is what energizes the pursuits, and realizes the rewards, of culture.[11] At a deep emotional level, the perceptual experience of the world is accompanied by an experience of joy. For that reason, according to Hans Urs von Balthasar, the "doctrine of perception always includes implicitly a doctrine of ecstasy. For, even in the realm of worldly beauty, form cannot really be perceived without the beholder being taken [ecstatically] into it."[12] David Bentley Hart aptly amplifies that "a God whose very being is love, delight in the glorious radiance of his infinite Image, seen in the boundless love of his Spirit, and whose works are then unnecessary but perfectly expressive signs of this delight, fashioned [the world] for his pleasure and for gracious sharing of his joy with creatures for whom he has no need (yet loved even when they were not), is a God of beauty in the fullest imaginable sense."[13] And referring to the Trinitarian writings of the 13th-century Italian theologian Bonaventure, he adds that, therefore, "the principal term of the analogy between the Trinity and the world is aesthetic: the sensual apprehension of and delight in beauty leads to a sharing in that authentic delectation that belongs to the Trinity, in whose measure the creature participates through grace."[14] In contrast to Hart's ebullience, even the deep-seated pessimism of the philosopher Arthur Schopenhauer, says fellow pessimist philosopher Mara van der Lugt, "is yet a measured pessimism, one that speaks to the brokenness of existence as well as to its fullness; and that delves deeply into the darkness to find therein the frailest openings for beauty and rapture, as well as for redemption, compassion, and consolation."[15] Perhaps because the measure of my occasionally experienced pessimism is not as deep and bleak as Schopenhauer's, I find that experiences of beauty and its delights point to God's redemptive, compassionate, and consoling love.

Among the most important and impactful cultural pursuits are art, religion, and science. One can only wonder what unites them in their stirring effects on culture. How are these three cultural pursuits related to each other? The short answer is that all three are pursuing something about and within reality that at

11. Kent C. Berridge and Morton L. Kringelbach, "Pleasure Systems in the Brain," *Neuron* 86, no. 3 (2015): 646–64; Morten L. Kringelbach and Kent C. Berridge, "A New Understanding of How The Brain Generates Pleasure Could Lead to Better Treatment of Addiction and Depression—and Even to a New Science of Happiness," *Scientific American* 397, no. 2 (2012): 40–45; Jocelyn M. Richard et al., "Mapping Brain Circuits of Reward and Motivation: In the Footsteps of Ann Kelley," *Neuroscience and Biobehavioral Reviews* 37, no. 9/Pt A (2013): 1919–31; Balthasar, *Seeing the Form*, 587.

12. Balthasar, *Seeing the Form*, 587.

13. Hart, *The Beauty of the Infinite*, 131.

14. Hart, *The Beauty of the Infinite*, 308.

15. Van der Lugt, *Dark Matters*, 392.

its core is beautiful, good, and true. This is as much a statement of fact as of faith, and of hope. In his novel *The Idiot*, Dostoyevsky expresses this hope by claiming that beauty will save the world. Dostoyevsky always regarded the beautiful, good, and true as constituting a perfectly unified whole.[16] Why, then, did he give this prophetic and soteriological priority to beauty and not to the good—or the true? For now, a plausible answer (elaborated in a later section) can be given as follows. In our worldly lives the true, the good, and the beautiful are not on equal experiential footing. As the history of science has shown, separating the true from the false and thus uncovering and understanding the deeper truths about nature—for example the existence of dark matter and dark energy believed to make up most of the cosmos's entire matter and energy—is a difficult and arduous task. And as the history of religions has shown, revealing the depths of the good has also been an equally arduous and, unfortunately too often, a conflict-ridden task. Experientially, these difficulties pose nearly insurmountable obstacles to all but a few especially gifted and enlightened individuals. Inner-worldly beauty is, in contrast, more readily and generally accessible to human experience. The reason is that the conscious, perceptual apprehension of properties and objects of the world is superficial (as explained in appendix 2). Beauty, as David Bentley Hart describes it, "does not 'essentialize' (essences are supremely anaesthetic), but remains always at the surface: in closely wrought detail, elaborate devices, suavities of style, immensities and fragilities, grandeurs and graces. . . ."[17] Experientially, inner-worldly beauties and their delightful rewards can thus serve as foundational stones, as steppingstones, and as marker stones on the more difficult road toward the true and the good. It seems, then, that beauty, joined as it is as preface and postscript to the true and the good and by way of the joy it arouses, allows one to at least glimpse reality's less readily apprehended truth and goodness. I believe that therein, as Dostoyevsky also claims, lies beauty's power of salvation, once this power permeates, and takes effect in, the spiritual realm.

Human Developmental Science: Taking Delight in Beauty, Truth, and Goodness

Let's now briefly explore how the disciplines of developmental psychology and neuroscience can shed a bit of light on the roles that the sense and the delight of beauty play in science and theology.[18] By way of introduction to this section and cognizant of the immoderate neuromania, pointed out by the philosopher

16. For this assessment of Dostoyevsky, see Soloviev, *The Heart of Reality.*

17. Hart, *The Beauty of the Infinite*, 141.

18. I have left out art, since it is beauty that obviously still informs and inspires most of the creative arts.

Raymond Tallis,[19] that has afflicted the science of the human mind, I ask the reader's forbearance as I attempt to explain how neuroscientific and psychological research findings bear relevantly on our refining the sensory, affective, and cognitive tuning to the beautiful. These findings can serve as developmental markers pointing to how our sensory, affective, and cognitive faculties are thereby also tuned to the good and the true. I believe that my explanation will be useful, especially to those not familiar with important research in neuroscience and developmental psychology. So, patiently tuned to exploring relevant and, what may turn out to be, latest ideas, let's proceed.

Several interesting and important aspects characterize the psychological and behavioral development of neonates.

1. Already noted in chapter 1 is the fact that the number of neurons in the infant's brain exceed greatly in number those that will eventually make up the adult brain. So, the development of all sorts of cognitive, affective, and behavioral skills depends not only on growth and sprouting on the part of the neurons and their filaments that eventually become part of the adult brain but also on the pruning and elimination of the remaining neurons. It is as though our world, endowed as it is with a tremendous variety of behavioral and environmental niches, is matched, in a seemingly miraculous coincidence, by the infant's corresponding endowment, at birth and shortly thereafter, of a more than sufficient potential to adapt to and thrive in most any of these niches. Adding to and exploiting the infant's genetically innate potential, the multifaceted natural, sociocultural, and behavioral niche comprising its lifeworld in its superabundant supply of stimulation and gratification, also exerts an equal, if not greater, influence on its development than does its genetic endowment. Exposure to the myriad objects and events encountered by the infant in its environmental niche winnows those bountiful neurons that respond to these myriad external inputs from those that do not respond to them. Only those that do respond survive, and only their axonal and dendritic terminals sprout exuberantly to form complex neural networks supporting the infant's ability to perceive, know, and act on its environment. The many unresponsive neurons are eliminated.

   This selective growth and pruning has serious and long-lasting consequences. On one hand, under favorable conditions an infant growing up in the local culture of a small, tribal village in, say, the Amazon basin or Papua New Guinea will acquire a set of neurocognitive and neurobehavioral skills, likings, and aspirational desires suited to its social and physical ecology that will differ in significant ways from that of an infant

19. Tallis, *Aping Mankind*.

growing up in the metropolitan setting of, say, Paris or Singapore. On the other hand, under unfavorable conditions, infants who are raised in severely deprived physical, emotional, social, and cultural environments will likely acquire a set of stunted neurocognitive and neurobehavioral skills, likings, and aspirational desires, a stunting that can persist and manifest in several ways throughout their later lives.

2. Another interesting fact is that the adult mammalian brain's neocortex is organized in such a way that its most posterior (back) regions of the brain are devoted to the registration of simple aspects of sensory inputs, e.g., visual, auditory, and tactile ones, while progressively more anterior (forward) regions of the cortical sensory hierarchy are devoted to associative functions that underly the formation of more complex and integrated perceptual, cognitive, and behavioral processes, such as the identification of objects and events in the environment that inform the choice of behaviors elicited by them.
3. Correlated with this fact is an additionally important one—namely, that as one progresses from the posterior to the more anterior regions of the brain, one finds a corresponding progressive increase in the concentration of endogenous opiate receptors, otherwise known as endorphin receptors, that in part modulate how we respond affectively and attentively to environmental inputs. One might call these "feel-good" or "reward" receptors.[20] This dual posterior-to-anterior brain arrangement is found throughout the higher mammalian—including, of course, the human—brain.[21] Findings such as these motivated the cognitive neuroscientists Irving Biederman and Edward Vessel to propose, in their article entitled "Perceptual Pleasure and the Brain," a theory of what I would call aesthetic delight.[21] As the subtitle of their article—"A Novel Theory Explains Why the Brain Craves Information and Seeks It Through the Senses"—indicates, one can think of the human brain as supporting a self-rewarding information-seeking behavior—as proposed decades ago by the developmental psychologist, Elizabeth Gibson[22]—that is especially tuned to, and thus driven towards seeking the new, the

20. Jacob M. Hiller and Li-Quin Fan, "Laminar Distribution of the Multiple Opioid Receptors in the Human Cerebral Cortex," *Neurochemical Research* 21, no. 11 (1996): 1333–45; Michael E. Lewis et al., "Opiate Receptor Gradients in Monkey Cerebral Cortex: Correspondence with Sensory Processing Hierarchies," *Science* 211, no. 4487 (1981): 1166–69; J. M. Walker et al., "Distribution of Opiate Receptors Within Visual Structures of the Cat Brain," *Experimental Brain Research* 73, no. 3 (1988): 523–32.

21. Irving Biederman and Edward A. Vessel, "Perceptual Pleasure and the Brain: A Novel Theory Explains Why the Brain Craves Information and Seeks It Through the Senses," *American Scientist* 94, no. 3 (2006): 247–53.

22. Gibson, *Principles of Perceptual Learning*; Gibson, "Exploratory Behavior."

unexpected, and the diversiform sensory inputs available in the environment.

4. When we combine the three above facts, we note further that self-rewarding behavior is particularly instrumental in the development of the infant's cognitive, affective, and behavioral repertoires. For, from the perspective of the infant, the world, the environment outside its mother's womb, is strikingly new, unexpected, and varied in the richness of inputs to which it can respond. And this gratuitous richness of information available in the environment is exposed even more once the infant become a toddler, is able to crawl and waddle about on its own. It can now more actively and thoroughly explore its surroundings and make increasingly more delightful discoveries—or, in much fewer cases, some painful discoveries activated by endogenous feel-bad receptors—about the amiable and adverse feedback that its environment can afford.
5. This increasing fund of information about the external world becomes internalized in memory and imagination, and though initially dependent on the external world's input, both memory and imagination (the mind's eye) become increasingly autonomous, mental faculties. As the child grows into adulthood, it can explore this interior domain in various transformative and combinatorial ways and make novel and insightful discoveries within and about it. Of course, although the imagination and the memory on which it depends can function independently of the external world, the child (and the adult that was the child) all along spends most of its life in the real, external world and therefore retains and sharpens its ability to engage with and make novel and insightful discoveries within and about its external environment. In both the imaginative and the perceptual domain, much of our *joie de vivre* thrives on being surprised by the insightful discoveries of the new, the different, and the unexpected that arrest the routines of our bland, day-to-day lives. Our state of well-being depends on such surprises. This holds especially so in the creative arts, but also in the fields of science, religion, and theology. In all three disciplines, our full conscious experience of the world depends on superficial sensory information flowing into and thus being enriched by the increasingly deeper levels of cognitive processing.[23] And this threesome marriage of the sensory, cognitive, and imaginative mental functions is where the rewards of the beautiful attain a correspondingly deeper and richer level.[24]

23. Hillary Putnam, "The Depths and Shallows of Experience," in *Science, Religion, and the Human Experience*, ed. James D. Proctor (Oxford University Press, 2005).

24. My focusing on the importance of the rewarding and motivating effects of delight in the acquisition of cognitive and behavioral skills is not meant to exclude the equally

Science and the Sense of Beauty

> The beautiful is that which gives joy—not just any joy, but joy in knowing; not the joy proper to the act of knowing, but a joy abounding and overflowing from this act because of the object known. . . . Beauty is essentially an object of intelligence, for that which *knows* in the full sense of the word is intelligence, which alone is open to the infinity of Being. The birthplace of Beauty is the intellectual world wherefrom it comes down. But in a certain manner also it falls under the grasp of the senses, in the measure in which with man they serve the intelligence, and are themselves capable of enjoying knowledge. . . . The share of the senses in the perception of beauty is even made unmeasurable with us by the fact that our understanding is not intuitive . . . ; it sees doubtless[sic] but on condition of abstracting and discoursing; in man sensitive knowledge alone possesses in perfection the intuitiveness necessary to the perception of the beautiful. Thus man may doubtless enjoy pure intellectual beauty, but the beauty connatural to man is that which touches the understanding with delight through the senses and their intuition.
>
> Jacques Maritain, *Art and Scholasticism*, pp. 33–34

It's of course a truism that beauty inspires and thus informs all kinds of art. However, it also inspires and informs much of science. For example, in some sciences, such as geology or botany, the prospect of discovering a new type of geode hiding in its interior a beautiful crystalline structure, or of a unique fractal structure found in the branchings of a newly discovered plant species, could inspire a geologist or botanist. In these cases the beauty of the scientific discovery is twofold. On the one hand, it is a sensory, on-the-surface type of beauty that only hints, on the other hand, at a deeper structure of beauty hidden from direct

---

connatural ability to experience physical and emotional distress (see Siri Leknes and Irene Tracey, "A Common Neurobiology for Pain and Pleasure," *Nature Reviews Neuroscience* 9, no. 4 (2008): 314–20). Such distressful sensations and feelings do not promote the "approach" responses that are vital to exploring and getting to know the infant's and toddler's world. Nonetheless they, too, play a very important role in an individual's development from infancy to old age. Objects and events that cause physical or emotional distress, a sensation that signals threat to an individual's welfare, are instinctively avoided and counteracted. Such avoidance very often is learned after a single experience of such pain, referred to by psychologists as one-trial learning. However, it can become dysfunctional in later life. For example, a toddler bitten by a dog may develop a life-long aversion to all dogs, even though most dogs are very playful, friendly, and approachable. Similarly, an infant or toddler exposed to an emotional trauma caused by an uncaring adult can develop emotional and interpersonal problems that affect them throughout life. However, even in a loving environment, experiences of emotional and physical pain serve a very useful function. The evidence for this is provided by infants born with congenital analgesia, a rare but very dangerous insensitivity to pain. Painful sensations serve a vital survival function.

access by the senses. This hidden beauty, a beauty discovered by and accessible to only the intellect, is so far removed from the senses that its existence is found only, via increasing levels of abstraction, in the more arcane mathematical formulae of the physical sciences. At this level of abstraction, the beauty is that of a theoretical gem that, much like an object of art, is fashioned by the intellect. While the beauty of the geode's interior or the fractal structure of a plant is accessible not only to the geologist or the botanist but also to the average human, it is very doubtful that the beauty of intellectual gems found in the physical sciences can be fully appreciated by humans other than specially trained mathematicians and physicists. Physicists often speak of the beauty of their abstract mathematical theories in terms of their elegance, clarity, and distinctiveness,

In his book *The Cosmic Landscape*, Leonard Susskind, a leading figure in attempting to develop a final theory of physics known as string theory, summarily defines beauty in science; it is the "combination of elegance, uniqueness, and the power to answer all [scientifically] answerable questions [that] makes a [scientific] theory beautiful." Elegance is akin to simplicity of theoretical expression, because "physicists like their axioms to be simple and few in number. Any more than is absolutely essential is inelegant. An elegant theory should be expressible in terms of a small number of equations, each of which is simple to write." Closely related to elegance and simplicity, the uniqueness of a theory refers to the fact that it "should predict [and explain] all that is possible to predict [and explain] and no more . . . [and, especially in reference to a final physical theory,] that it is the *only* possible theory."[25] And the power of a scientific theory is, of course, its ability to provide answers to all scientifically answerable questions—and no more.

As described by the astrophysicist Subrahmanyan Chandrasekhar, beauty has been considered a key element in the motivation for, and the appreciation of, scientific breakthroughs, from the late 16th-century beginnings of mathematical theorizing in celestial physics to the 20th-century theoretical developments in general relativity and quantum mechanics.[26] Ever since Johannes Kepler's publication of *Harmonices Mundi* in the early 17th century, theoretical physicists have been motivated by the guiding principle of the harmonious unification of seemingly disparate and hard-to-reconcile phenomena. Harmonious mathematical unification was also a key factor in the 20th-century developments of general relativity theory and quantum mechanics. Paul Dirac, who had a deep understanding of quantum mechanics as well as relativity theory,

25. Leonard Susskind, *The Cosmic Landscape: String Theory and the Illusion of Intelligent Design* (Little, Brown & Co., 2005), 113–14.

26. S. Chandrasekhar, "The General Theory of Relativity: 'Why It Is Probably the Most Beautiful of All Existing Theories,'" *Journal of Astrophysics and Astronomy* 5, no. 1 (1984): 3–11; see also Gideon Engler, "Aesthetics in Science and in Art," *British Journal of Aesthetics* 30, no. 1 (1990): 24–34; Ian Stewart, *Why Beauty Is Truth* (Basic Books, 2008).

placed a premium on the role of beauty, not as a substitute for, but as a propaedeutic to and a post-hoc imprimatur of, establishing sounder criteria of truth. In fact, when developing mathematical theories of physics, Dirac promoted these roles of beauty even to the point of suspending or bracketing relevant data.[27] For, in the words of the philosopher Frederick Turner, "the beauty experience is as much more constructive, as much more generous, to the outside world, as much more holistic and more exact and particularizing than ordinary perception, as ordinary perception is than mere sensation. Beauty-perception is not a vague and touchy-feely thing relative to ordinary perception; quite the reverse. That is why, given an infinite number of theories that will logically explain the facts, scientists will sensibly choose the most beautiful theory. For good reason: because this is the way the world works."[28] And how does the world work? It works in the simplest way it can, that is, by expending the least amount of energy required to maintain the spatiotemporal configuration, the form, of its physical entities, its objects, and its processes. As noted above by Leonard Susskind, simplicity also plays a leading role in scientific epistemology. For it is a prime aesthetic criterion governing the organization of a conceptual Gestalt (but, as we shall explore more fully in the following section, also of a visuo-perceptual one). A Gestalt is a single, unified organization of diverse parts. Pertinent here is Geoffrey Vickers's appreciation "that the human mind has available to it at least two different modes of knowing and that it uses both in appropriate and inappropriate combinations in its endless efforts to understand the world in which it finds itself, including its fellow human beings and itself. One of these modes is more dependent on analysis, logical reasoning, calculation, and explicit description. The other is more dependent on synthesis and the recognition of pattern, context and the multiple possible relations of figure and ground. The first involves the abstraction and manipulation of elements, irrespective of the forms in which they are combined. The other involves the recognition or creation of form, irrespective of the elements that compose it. . . . Both are needed and both are used in most normal mental operations."[29]

27. P. A. M. Dirac, "The Evolution of the Physicist's Picture of Nature," *Scientific American* 258, no. 5 (1963): 45–53, expressed the premium placed on mathematical beauty as follows: "I think there is a moral to this story, namely that it is more important to have beauty in one's equations than to have them fit experiment. . . . If there is not complete agreement between the results of one's work and experiment, one should not allow oneself to be too discouraged, because the discrepancy may well be due to minor features that are not properly taken into account and that will get cleared up with further developments of the theory." See also chapter 7 of Dubay, *The Evidential Power of Beauty*, on the importance of beauty in evaluating scientific theories.

28. Frederick Turner, *Beauty: The Value of Values* (University of Virginia Press, 1991), 58.

29. Geoffrey Vickers, "Rationality and Intuition," in *On Aesthetics in Science*, ed. Judith Wechsler (MIT Press, 1978), 145.

Consistent with these figure-ground, Gestalt-like notions, Werner Heisenberg, a key contributor to quantum mechanics who was more amenable to hewing to experimental data than Dirac, held that "beauty is the proper conformity of the parts to one another and to the whole."[30] To Heisenberg, this included his elegant conceptual, Gestalt-like approach to quantum mechanics via a highly abstract, non-imageable mathematics. His classical definition of beauty in terms of such harmonious relation between parts and their composite Gestalt still holds today in the sciences and in the arts, despite some rather garishly dissonant developments in the arts that have been introduced since beginning of the 20th century. The drive from discordance toward harmony in science is currently evident especially in the attempts of theoretical physicists—so far unsuccessful—to unify, to go beyond the incompatibilities between, the mathematical formulations of general relativity on one hand and those of quantum mechanics on the other. Should they succeed, the physicists might rightly claim that they have found a most beautiful intellectual gem, its glow reflecting, for the theists among them, the resplendent unity of creation and the mind of its Creator God. It is ironic that in the last century and a half this centripetal search for harmony and unity in theoretical science has been accompanied by centrifugal diffusion of myriad novelties not only in empirical and applied sciences but, in a wider cultural setting, also in philosophy and, through it, in the arts. Similar to the prodigal diffusion and dissipation of energy in the physical cosmos, culturally the extravagant dispersal and waste of the diverse and the novel has the potential of increasingly obscuring the mind's search for, and discovery of, a harmonious, unifying power underlying them.

The sense of beauty *guiding, but not determining,* the scientific search for the truths about our physical world,[31] reprised in Heisenberg's "proper conformity of its parts to one another and to the whole," holds also for the psychological science aimed at describing and explaining visual perception. In the discipline of scientific psychology, a good example is the *holistic* phenomenological approach to the study of perception adopted by Gestalt psychologists.[32] The approach was influential in continental Europe during the first half of the last century and has uncovered interesting and puzzling findings of phenomenal sensory organization that are still motivating very active areas of research in visual cognition. By claiming that the dynamic structural organization of visual

30. Quoted in Chandrasekhar, "The General Theory of Relativity," 5.

31. Sabine Hossenfelder, *Lost in Math: How Beauty Leads Physics Astray* (Basic Books, 2020).

32. To some physical scientists who are obsessed with facts, and to confirmed ontological and epistemological reductionists like Sabine Hossenfelder, holistic thinking is anathema. Sabine Hossenfelder, *Existential Physics: A Scientist's Guide to Life's Biggest Questions* (Viking Press, 2022), 83, expresses her sentiments regarding holism bluntly and somewhat crudely as follows: "If you say 'holism,' I hear 'bullshit.'"

perception maps isomorphicly onto the brain's dynamic structural organization, Gestalt psychologists could also claim to be brain scientists. Moreover, they saw their integrative approach as guiding not only a scientific program but also an aesthetic one. The approach relied on numerous factors of phenomenological organization, including symmetry, good curve and continuation, closure, and others, all of which fell under the umbrella concept of Prägnanz, the superordinate factor of factors also known as good form. "Good" is not precisely defined; it designated a somewhat fuzzy concept that implied the simplicity of sensory and phenomenological organization, yet it clearly carried aesthetically evaluative import. One can see why the perception of symmetry and good curve characterizing, for example, human faces and bodies and those of other mammals, can arouse experiences of beauty in scientist and artist alike. Moreover, the Gestalt approach was also of ontological import. As much as the simplicity of phenomenal sensory organization was assumed to map isomorphicly onto the simplest, least energy-expending organization of brain dynamics, it thereby also mapped onto the simplest, least energy-expending organization of the material world—and vice versa. That is why raindrops, for instance, come in the simple, least energy-expending shape of spheres rather than the complex shapes of a tetra- or octahedron. In other words, according to the tenets of Gestalt psychology, external physical reality maps isomorphicly onto the internal physical reality of the brain, which in turn maps onto the phenomenal experience which it supports. Expressed in its simplest form, beauty (or its lack) is therefore as much a property of the objective, external world as it is of the subjective phenomenal realm.

Beauty in the Cognitive Neurosciences

Regarding more recent developments on the relation of aesthetics and the brain sciences, Vilayanur S. Ramachandran and William Hirstein's approach to the neuroscience of art is of diagnostic interest in that it is symptomatic of the neo-Darwinist and neuromanic overreach of cognitive neuroscientists noted previously by Raymond Tallis. In the abstract of their article, they claim that "*any* theory of art (or, indeed, *any* aspect of human nature) *has to* ideally have three components: (a) The logic of art: whether there are universal rules or principles; (b) The evolutionary rationale: why did these rules evolve and why do they have the form that they do; (c) What is the brain circuitry involved?"[33] (emphasis added). Note especially the immoderate use of "any" (ergo "all") and "has to" (or "must") that is typical of many a scientist's inflated rhetoric directed not only to experts but to a wider academic and lay public. In line with such scientistic

33. Vilayanur S. Ramachandran and William Hirstein, "The Science of Art: A Neurological Theory of Aesthetic Experience," *Journal of Consciousness Studies* 6, no. 6–7 (1999): 15.

hyperbole, Ramachandran and Hirstein espouse an eight-law, neuroscientific theory based on effects of supernormal stimuli in activating behaviors.[34] As an example, they list a number of supernormal stimuli exaggerating certain features, such as the slim waist, wide hips, firm breasts and thighs, and nearly perfect facial and body symmetry that play a key role in aesthetic appreciation of the artful depiction of a female, presumably via some titillation aroused by such a caricatured female body—at least in males who, in the instinctual arousal of their evolutionary, biological imperative, unconsciously take such features as signs of reproductive fertility. Closely related ideas have been around for some time. Over a century ago, the English naturalist Charles Darwin, the Spanish philosopher George Santayana, and the Russian philosopher Vladimir Soloviev already noted that the arousal of human sexual instinct contributes to our sense of beauty.[35]

In his book *Inner Vision,* neuroanatomist Semir Zeki proposes that a similar, yet more chaste, neural titillation is aroused by some varieties of abstract, minimalist, and expressionist art (like that of the Dutch painter Piet Mondrian or the Russian painter Wassily Kandinsky), wherein optimally designed stimuli falling on the retinal receptive fields of neurons in the human visual cortex elicit from them supercharged responses. Zeki has aptly named such art the "art of the [visual] receptive field."[36] Although somewhat overstated, one can admit that Zeki's as well as Ramachandran and Hirstein's neuro-speculations have added a bit to an understanding of artistic sensibilities. A look at any good political cartoonist's work (think of how the nose of Richard Nixon and the ears of Barak Obama were caricatured) gives the gist of their theoretical speculations quite well. Yet the degree to which knowledge of the effects of supernormal stimuli impact one's phenomenal, experiential, and aesthetic appreciation and understanding of art remains questionable. One can wonder how a trained art critic, initially unaware of Ramachandran and Hirstein's and Zeki's neuroscientific theorizing, would appraise, for instance, Vincent van Gogh's earthy paintings *Irises in a Vase, Peasant Woman Binding Sheaves,* and *Sunflowers Gone to Seed,* compared to how she or he would appraise them after having been familiarized with this theorizing. It is doubtful that much would change. For, besides exaggeration of visual features, art and aesthetics also call on a sense of realism (surreal art notwithstanding, since it is parasitic on a prior sense of realism), subtlety, balance, and restraint; hence, a theory of visual art and aesthetics based

34. Niko Tinbergen, *The Herring Gull's World* (Collins, 1953), amply covers the role of supernormal stimuli in animal behavior.

35. Charles Darwin, *The Descent of Man* (Penguin Classics, 2004); George Santayana, *The Sense of Beauty* (Dover Publications, 1955); Soloviev, *The Heart of Reality.*

36. Semir Zeki, *Inner Vision: An Exploration of Art and the Brain* (Oxford University Press, 1999).

on exaggerated or deformed visual features can be problematic. Extreme hyping of such features can create depictions that border on ridiculous or grotesque distortions. But to be fair, insofar as Zeki's and Ramachandran and Hirstein's neuroscientific approaches can add to a conceptual understanding of artistic sensibilities, familiarity with these approaches can increase somewhat the purely conceptual appreciation of art. And as was also noted in chapter 1 regarding, similarly, the influence that empirical and theoretical scientific studies of religion can have on the appreciation of religious sensibilities, the engaging of higher-order intellective functions like reflective thought, discernment, and evaluation can also influence the delight associated with the experience of beauty (see above, Maritain's epigraph and note 10) and thereby amplify somewhat the direct experiential appreciation of beauty.

The Sense of Beauty in Religion and Theology

Except for perhaps Ramachandran and Hirstein's and Zeki's speculations, as a whole the above scientific accounts of our sense of beauty are a far cry from the summary dismissal and devaluation made by evolutionary psychologist Steven Pinker, of art, beauty, and aesthetic delight as mere titillations of the dopaminergic reward system.[37] For if Dirac, Einstein, and Heisenberg were correct in allowing their conceptual researches to be influenced by their aesthetic sense, then beauty, in all its particular on-the-surface manifestations and our delight in it, *can serve as a sign pointing to* but—as emphatically noted by the physicist Sabine Hossenfelder (see note 32 above)—*not as a criterion of* deep truths in the physical sciences. And if there, why could the sense of beauty not also guide the search for still deeper truths in our religious and theological pursuits? Centuries ago, Anselm of Canterbury thought of theology as religious faith in search of intellectual understanding (*fides quaerens intellectum*). Within this Anselmian context, religion, and religious practices, are attempts to fathom the truths of the divine world. In chapter 1 we saw that the connection between religion and the arts may be primeval, extending from their archetypal expressions in Paleolithic times to the later and current expressions in the literary, musical, performing, and fine arts. Our understanding of religion and religious experiences is thus tied to our understanding of artistic and aesthetic experiences, and thus to beauty. Hence, as described below, the relevance of the above scientific understandings of beauty to religion and theology.

37. See Curtis White, *The Science Delusion: Asking Big Questions in a Culture of Easy Answers* (Melville House, 2013), 104–5. To be fair, Steven Pinker, "Science Is Not Your Enemy: A Plea for an Intellectual Truce," *The New Republic*, August 6, 2013, correctly points out the tit-for-tat, unsophisticated, and equally philistine disregard with which some scholars in the arts and humanities express their criticism and disdain of science.

Besides the obvious, readily apparent way that the experience of beauty contributes to religious liturgy, ritual, ceremony, and celebration, a more studious look at how and why beauty is relevant to theology is particularly found in von Balthasar's multivolume series *The Glory of the Lord: A Theological Aesthetics*, where he expounds extensively on how beauty and its experience contribute to theological understanding. In the first volume of this series, subtitled *Seeing the Form*, he remarks that

> we may . . . distinguish and relate to each other . . . two elements in the beautiful which have traditionally controlled every aesthetic and which, with Thomas Aquinas, we could term *species* (or *forma*) and *lumen* (or *splendour*)—form (*Gestalt*) and splendour (*Glanz*). . . . The form as it appears to us is beautiful only because the delight that it arouses in us is founded upon the fact that, in it, the truth and goodness of the depths of reality itself are manifested and bestowed, and this manifestation and bestowal reveal themselves to us as being something infinitely and inexhaustibly valuable and fascinating. The appearance of the form, as revelation of the depths, is an indissoluble union of two things. It is the real presence of the depths, of the whole of reality, *and* it is a real pointing beyond itself to these depths. . . . [Together and inseparable from each other] both aspects . . . constitute the fundamental configuration of Being. . . . We see form as the splendour, as the glory of Being.[38]

He augments his definition of form by noting further that

> *species* [*forma* (*Gestalt*)] and *lumen* [*splendor* (*Glanz*)] in beauty are one, [but only] if the species truly merits that name [i.e., only when it is a pleasing, radiant form]. . . . Both natural and artistic form has an exterior which appears and an interior depth, both of which, however, are not separable in the form itself. The content (*Gehalt*) does not lie behind the form (*Gestalt*) but within it. Whoever is not capable of seeing and "reading" the form will, by the same token, fail to perceive the content. Whoever is not illumined by the form will see no light in the content either. . . .[39]

These are passages rich in cognitive goods that call for unpacking. First, one notes a similarity in the importance accorded to form by von Balthasar and by the Gestalt psychologists. Form as the splendor and glory of Being (von Balthasar) is readily relatable to the Gestalt psychologists' basic aesthetic principle of Prägnanz or good form discussed above. Neither von Balthasar nor the Gestalt psychologists regarded form (*Gestalt*) as separated from its content (*Gehalt*). Moreover, for both, the content (*Gehalt*) conveys the *lumen* (*splendor/Glanz*) of

38. von Balthasar, *Seeing the Form*, 115–16.
39. von Balthasar, *Seeing the Form*, 147.

form. The beauty of a flower's blossoms, for example those of a rose or carnation, is found in the luminescent colors contained within the contours, the forms, their petals, which in turn are beautifully arranged into an even more complex form of the blossom. Without this splendorous content within the form, the form itself could not appear as a visual phenomenon (see appendix 1), let alone be aesthetically appreciated.[40] Yet what in theological aesthetics corresponds to the splendorous, beautiful form in sensory aesthetics? Von Balthasar, a theologian hewing closely to time-honored doctrine, claims the corresponding equivalent—aptly praising it as the "form of forms"[41]—to be found in Christ. Accordingly, von Balthasar attests that God has revealed the form of forms' content (*Gehalt*) and its splendor (*Glanz*) through his historically unique incarnation in Jesus of Nazareth. Without this down-to-earth, human content in Christ's form, the Word of God, made visible to Jesus's contemporaneous disciples as the splendorous beauty of God, would not ever have been revealed to humankind. That revelation of God's beauty is summarized succinctly in the apostle John's gospel where (in John 14:9) Jesus says, "Anyone who has seen me has seen [God] the Father." The contents of a form disclosed in our perceptual, cognitive, and spiritual apprehensions render them not only beautiful but also significant—in both senses of the word: meaningful and important.

Everything we experience and know exists in and by virtue of a contextual background. What modern physics has taught us is that subatomic particles and objects composed of them do not exist as autonomous pointlike entities in a spatial vacuum, but instead are inextricably linked to a background of forces whose fields extend infinitely throughout space. It was for this reason that the physicist Paul Dirac could claim that whenever we pick a flower, we also move distant stars. And correspondingly, what every Gestalt psychologist knows is that the perceived form or figure of an object does not exist in a phenomeno-

40. For details of how this interplay between content and form relates also to sensory perception, see Stephen Grossberg, "Filling-In the Forms: Surface and Boundary Interactions in Visual Cortex," in *Filling-In: From Perceptual Completion to Cortical Reorganization*, ed. Luiz Pessoa and Peter De Weerd (Oxford University Press, 2003); Vilayanur S. Ramachandran, "Foreword," in *Filling-In: From Perceptual Completion to Cortical Reorganization*, ed. Luiz Pessoa and Peter De Weerd (Oxford University Press, 2003); Bruno G. Breitmeyer, *The Visual (Un)Conscious & Its (Dis)Contents* (Oxford University Press, 2014), chapter 4. What holds for sensory perception may hold for non-sensory cognitive apprehension. But in the latter case it is more difficult to construct an abstract representation of a cognitional form devoid of its content. Hence, as with a sensorily perceived form, it is not possible to apprehend the formal structure of a cognition without its content. While a complex cognition may be condensed in the good form of a simple formula, for example a mathematical one, its cognitive content consists of the myriad of conceptual entities that, once arduously compiled and organized into a compact form, led to discovery of the formula. For the cognoscenti, Paul Dirac for instance, the splendor of the compact cognitive form is in the wealth of its conceptual contents.

41. von Balthasar, *Seeing the Form*, 165.

logical void.[42] A sensorily perceived form takes on the property of foreground within a larger totality that includes the background, the context, in which it is embedded. This larger context establishes a phenomenologically explicit-implicit, figure-ground relation. You, the reader, can play Gestalt psychologist by looking at some object, perhaps as I am doing now, viewing a cat dozing on a chair next to you. Now, return to reading your book. While your attention was explicitly centered on visually focusing on the cat, the many unfocused objects in the rest of the visual field were all implicitly processed and went all but unnoticed. For if I were to ask you to describe in detail what you attentively processed, you could give an explicit description of the object: that was an orange tabby curled up, with legs tucked to its underside, tail curled and pointing to its head, eyes closed, all on a chair next to you. But if you were asked to describe what you saw in the surrounding background, all you could say is that other things were indeed present, but indistinctly so, in your field of view, so that their explicit, detailed description would mostly elude you.

Such explicit-implicit relation between figure and ground, as Michael Polanyi has argued,[43] also characterizes our cognitive apperception, our knowledge, of the world. We know much more than we can explicitly say or understand. At any moment, our focal, explicit knowledge is *embedded* in a much broader context of implicit knowledge; and this context is made possible by our bodily embeddedness in our extensive behavioral environment. In this external milieu, our bodies (and our brains in them) get exposed to the world around us through our engagements and active explorations of it; and there our bodies become the instruments of fully *embodied* cognitions,[44] which overcome a strict body-mind dualism that since the 16th century has haunted our philosophical world with mindless zombies and mental specters. Some of the embodied knowledge of the world, for example a tourist's knowledge that Chicago's Hancock Tower is

42. Gestalt psychology developed shortly after the turn of the 20th century and was influenced heavily by Michael Faraday's intuitive understanding of physical force fields given explicit mathematical representation in the latter half of 19th century by James Clerk Maxwell's equations governing the electromagnetic force. One of the key founders of Gestalt psychology, Wolfgang Köhler, had studied at the Humboldt University of Berlin. While there, under the influence of the psychologist Carl Stumpf and the physicist Max Plank, he focused his theoretical research on the connection between psychology and physics. By analogy to *physical* force fields, the Gestalt approach eventually morphed into the study and interpretation of cognitive, perceptual, and motivational findings in terms of *phenomenological* force fields.

43. Michael Polanyi, *Personal Knowledge: Towards a Post-Critical Philosophy* (University of Chicago Press, 1958); Michael Polanyi, *The Tacit Dimension* (Doubleday, 1966).

44. For embedded and embodied cognition, see Lawrence Shapiro and Shannon Spaulding, "Embodied Cognition," in *The Stanford Encyclopedia of Philosophy*, ed. Edward N. Zalta and Uri Nodelman, Fall 2024, https://plato.stanford.edu/archives/fall2024/entries/embodied-cognition.

located on North Michigan Avenue, not far from Lake Shore Drive, is factual and explicit. But this impersonal, abstract knowledge exists in a much greater field of embodied implicit and personal knowledge that cannot always be explicitly or linguistically articulated. Nonetheless, for example, a tourist's procedural knowledge underlying her ability to amble—without explicitly thinking about each step or each turn—generally northward along Lake Shore Drive until she arrives at her goal relies largely on such embodied and implicit contextual knowledge. After years of extensive experience ambulating about and learning to easily interpret traffic symbols and signs, the use of these abilities, once automatized and embodied, is consigned to background knowledge that implicitly also is in use while her attention is simultaneously taking in specific sights and sounds of interest to her.

Recalling that Gestalt psychology grew out of aesthetic as well as scientific concerns, we can say that the perceived Gestalt (form) exists only in relation to a more extensive ground of embedded and embodied knowledge, in which its beauty exists and through which it is revealed to our senses and cognitive faculties. That said, it merits to return to von Balthasar's theological aesthetic by way of noting two things. First, being incomprehensibly awesome, God's appearance to humans prior to his incarnation in Jesus of Nazareth was not face to face but mediated either through natural signs (e.g., a cloud, a burning bush) or through deflected vision (e.g., of his backside as he passed Moses). Second, "God's invisibility and his visibleness in his historical revelation are not connected by necessity that he reveal himself: [whereas] such is the relation that exists in inner-worldly aesthetics . . . between 'ground' and 'form.' This general [inner-worldly] relation is surpassed in a singular and wholly underived manner, and only in this way does it [God's revelation] yield a foundation for a theological aesthetics."[45] This singular and underived manner is expressed and evident in God's "form of forms" revealed to humans through his incarnation in Jesus of Nazareth. Jesus, Christ incarnate, is not only the splendorous content of the revelation but also, to his historic contemporaries, its body-to-body, palpable, and face-to-face, visible form. But one can ask: How is the worldly form-ground relation surpassed in a singular and underived form of Christ Incarnate? Well established by Gestalt phenomenologists, in inner-worldly aesthetics the form-ground relation is not symmetric. In other words, the perceived form of an entity is always explicitly and directly imbedded in a surrounding background, whereas the ground is only implicitly and, therefore, indirectly present in the form. Based on that analogy, and arguably in agreement with what von Balthasar expounds at great length, one can say that if in theological aesthetics there is anything like a "ground," it is the implicit, eternal, and unchanging Godhead, within which a perfect love is shared equally and symmetrically among the

45. von Balthasar, *Seeing the Form*, 303.

explicit forms that are the triune Persons of the Father, the Son, and the Spirit; a sharing finding its inner-worldly counterparts expressed less than perfectly in the relations among our sensory renditions of the true, the beautiful, and the good.

No doubt, since religious experiences (von Balthasar devotes nearly two hundred pages to them) are the medium of religious revelations, then like artistic experiences, they partake of perceptual, conceptual, and affective dimensions. It follows that knowledge of the brain areas that may be activated by these dimensions can shed *some* light on how religious experiences affect us. Insofar as the supremely good, beautiful, and truthful—i.e., the trinitarian transcendental properties of Being—are perfectly overlapping manifestations in and of the One, their inner-worldly instantiations, while doing so only imperfectly, do overlap to a significant extent. If so, then in agreement with even the most reductionist neuroscientist, if brain activity underlies and supports every living human's experience, and at bottom if religious, aesthetic, and scientific sensibilities and the experiences aroused in them overlap, then a psychological and neuroscientific research program like that proposed by the neuroscientist Anthony Jack (see chapter 3) could in principle measure the degree to which they do so.[46] In that way one could, using neuroscientific methods, potentially home in on the neuro-cognitive *whats* that not only distinguish the subjective experiences of the good, the beautiful, and the truthful but also can reveal the *what* of the overlap, the core common to their experiences. Nonetheless, as noted, one ought to be mindfully cautious and circumspect as to the intent, the possible overreach, and the misuse of psychological and brain-based explanations to the scientistic exclusion of all other explanations.

Beauty in art and other creative activities can arouse positive emotions and intense pleasure (see notes 20 and 21 above). Yet one cannot dismiss their total impact or importance cynically and disparagingly, as Pinker has done for art, by asserting from a reductive neurobiological and evolutionary standpoint that they are frivolous and vain activities used merely to enhance social status and to titillate the brain's dopamine reward system of the artist and that of the appreciator of his or her art. One could surmise that such cavalier assessment of aesthetic sensibility would also apply to the assessment of religious sensibility. According to some cognitive and behavioral neuroscientists, aesthetic and religious sensibilities, like all others, are nothing but merely illusory, epiphenomenal byproducts of the brain's organized neural activity. Yet not only mystics but many other religiously "musical" individuals have now and then experienced an ecstasy, a bliss that surpasses all description and understanding, including scientific ones. In their state of ecstatic rapture, such individuals no doubt hyper-arouse their brains' reward systems. But that is a mere scientific fact, not

46. Jack et al., "Why Do You Believe."

an insight that furthers a deeper and wider understanding of these memorable experiences. Such intense experiences are not only emotionally gratifying, but they also fortify and deepen faith, despite their eluding the intellect's efforts to fully understand them.

In contrast to such stunning experiences, some religious encounters with, and experiences of, the divine are blissfully tranquil and less dramatic, yielding a delightful sense of serenity that also deepens faith and likewise, as St. Paul phrased it (Phil. 4:7), surpasses understanding. If so, and if, as Anselm stated it, faith seeks understanding, then it follows that one can seek assiduously yet never attain the full understanding of that which one's faith is seeking. The evidence provided by reports of rapturous or serene religious experiences throughout the centuries attests to the fact that their understanding will ever lack the intellect's full conceptual and linguistic grasp of a purely subjective event. There will always remain a purely experiential residue no matter how far the intellect abstractly probes that event. In this apophatic gap itself, experienced as devoid of all words and concepts—the *nada* as St. John of the Cross calls it—the purely subjective residue of the mystical state attests to the cognitively unfathomable splendor of God. To use Polanyi's terminology, a mystic's faith as well as ours—what we know, trust, and live—is embedded in a non-understood, implicit background, the knowledge of which from a theological standpoint is fully and explicitly accessible only to the Godhead.

And Yet . . .

In contrast to these saints and mystics, there is a minority of individuals whose religious and spiritual sensibilities are deficient. For if the religious impulse is ultimately grounded in the love of and striving toward the ultimate and the transcendent, there are some individuals who suffer from developmental or constitutional impairments—over which they have no control—that may dampen their religious impulse. Anthony Jack and coworkers[47] provide two examples. First, as discussed in chapter 3, since moral concern and religiosity are positively correlated, they argued that psychopathic individuals, who are deficient in moral concerns, may also have a deficient religious sense. And second, since moral concern and analytic thinking are negatively correlated, they suggest that analytic thinkers may also have acquired a deficient religious sense. It therefore seems likely that psychopaths and analytic thinkers suffer from a deficiency in experiencing the beauty of religion and its delights. Having a deficient sense for the transcendently sacred, their meager experience of the sacred dimension is accompanied by little if any sense of joy. They are akin to those constitutionally or neurologically afflicted individuals, noted above, who suffer from congenital

47. Jack et al., "Why Do You Believe."

or, per accident or disease, from acquired amusia.

Then also, there are those individuals whose disinterest in the question and topics of religion and of God is not due to a congenital or acquired deficiency but instead due to lack of sufficient exposure to religious and spiritual experiences. Their religious amusicality can be overcome by exposure to such experiences, much like intermittent exposures to previously unfamiliar musical genres can develop a strong liking for them.[48] At the other end, however, are individuals who, in several ways having gone beyond the banal, casually indifferent disregard of God, suffer from what one could diagnose as misotheism. Instead of being indifferent to the question of God, they are quite taken by it. Yet they have developed a displeasure, to the point of intense hate and aversion, toward God.[49] Misotheists are not necessarily atheists (those atheists, like some of the neo-atheists, who also are misotheists, seem to be very obsessed with the very notion, if not the existence, of God). In fact, most misotheists may be theists; yet their spiritual relationship to God and their views of God have been severely damaged, in some cases by a cruelly punitive religious upbringing or in other cases by traumatic life experiences that are extremely difficult to reconcile with belief in a personally caring God. Believing nonetheless that there is a God, they, unlike Job, are painfully alienated from him. Having been exposed to evils—including the evils committed by those teaching and preaching in the name of God—misotheists pose a dual problem to religion: the pastoral problem of how to deal with their hate of God and the moral problem posed by natural and human evils that give rise to it.

48. This was my experience in my freshman year at university studies. Before that year, I was rarely exposed to any sort of music other than, now and then, listening to the pop music regularly broadcast on the radio. My roommate came from a cultured Jewish family living in Chicago. For free-time relaxation and during our evening homework and studies in our dorm room, he regularly played classical music. Ever since then, I have been a lover of classical music, and by way of classical music my taste expanded to include the classical Afro-American music genre of jazz, as well as those of folk music and rhythm & blues.

49. For different causes and types of misotheism, see Bernard Schweizer, *Hating God: The Untold Story of Misotheism* (Oxford University Press, 2011).

PART 2

Scientism, the Ersaz-Religion of Science

Sober naturalists seem willing to swallow what they take to be the poisonous implications of their creed, and they want no part of sunny naturalism's facile compromises. They frankly acknowledge that science in all its splendor can never make the universe responsive enough to satisfy the human longing for meaning. . . . Sunny naturalists . . . officially endorse scientism and (usually) materialism, and they admit to the finality of death and the perishability of the cosmos, but their general outlook on life remains one of resilient sanguinity. As such, they are the kind of skeptics that a Nietzsche or a Sartre would have denounced for the timidity of their atheism. If the universe is meaningless, and ethics groundless, then truthfulness demands that one pass through the fires of nihilism before finding a post-religious comfort zone. But sunny naturalists have not yet looked down into the bottom of the abyss they have opened up. Instead, they have nestled into the cultural and ethical worlds nurtured for centuries by worshippers of God.

John F. Haught, *Is Nature Enough: Meaning and Truth in the Age of Science*, pp. 194–95

CHAPTER 6

Historic Roots of the Science–Religion Conflict Thesis

On this new champion, Galileo, the whole war was at last concentrated.

Andrew Dickson White, *A History of the Warfare of Science with Theology in Christendom*, p. 130

In the introduction, we saw that while science and religion share some characteristics, they differ significantly in others. We saw also that in the hands of extreme religionists and atheists the differences can transform into a staunch belief that there is an irresoluble conflict between science and religion. Regarding such conflict, Philip Clayton begins his recent article on panentheism as follows: "God and science are at war. Or at least this is standard narrative, usually with New Atheists placed on the one side and Intelligent Design defenders dropped on the other. The roots of the war metaphor have grown deep into Western consciousness, influencing thought and action more strongly than many realize. Although many authors deny that it is a battle to the death, it certainly has that appearance in the many combative publications that have appeared over the last several decades."[1] The past three decades especially have seen the thesis of war or conflict between science and religion raised to a new pitch, exploited as a hostile agitprop against religion by a small tribe of neo-atheists: several scientists, philosophers, and popular literati. In contrast, a defensive reaction has been stoked also by defenders of theism, especially those at odds with interpretations of research findings in evolutionary, geophysical, and cosmological sciences. As an anticipatory note to the contents of the following chapter, the point I wish to make here is that the supposedly irresolvable science–religion conflict thesis serves as merely a tactical ploy. That is to say, the conflict is not between science and religion *per se* but rather a war of words perpetuated on one hand by the promotion of the so-called creation science of a minority of theists who hold to a literalist interpretation of sacred scripture, and on the other by the scientism of skeptics and atheists. That said, historically, the explicitly formulated source of the thesis that conflict prevails between science and religion is two tractates appearing in the latter half of the 19th century: the 1874 publication of John William Draper's *History of the Conflict*

1. Clayton, "How Radically Can God."

Between Religion and Science and the 1896 publication of Andrew Dickson White's *A History of the Warfare of Science with Theology in Christendom.* The books contrasted the progress made in the understanding of astronomy, geology, medicine, and biology in the worldview of modern empirical science with their prior understanding, supposedly inspired by a theological worldview that favored the authority of tradition over that of empirical evidence.

By the beginning of the 17th century, religions with longstanding doctrinal and ritualistic traditions had been around for millennia, whereas the modern empirical sciences were just beginning to develop, especially in the fields of physics and astronomy. The above epigram from White's book highlights the unparalleled significance of the Galileo affair in defining the historic religion–science conflict at that juncture. Galileo had adopted the Copernican heliocentric hypothesis as a realistic worldview. Questioning the then-reigning Aristotelean/Ptolemaic cosmology, the so-called revolutionary Copernican worldview also questioned the earth's and, with it, humans' centrality in God's creation. Two and a half centuries later, advances in the geological and biological sciences, culminating in Charles Darwin's theory of biological evolution by natural selection, gave a further stinging blow to those Christians who had assured themselves that, of all living creatures, humans enjoyed a supreme status in God's creation. Among scientists, Darwin's champion, the biologist Thomas Henry Huxley, still believed in the special status of humans, but one conferred on them not so much by God as by their ethical stance in the face of the imperfections of and tremendous suffering found in creation and human society. Despite this promotion of secular humanism, Huxley, who coined the word "agnostic" to describe his uncertainty regarding the existence of God, was wary of endorsing the science–religion conflict theses that were promoted by White and Draper. He dismissed the conflict thesis as a mere sideshow to the main historic developments: the cultural ascendency of science and the concomitant decline of organized religion. Nevertheless, as Sheridan Gilley and Ann Loades have pointed out, Huxley "could dismiss the antagonism between science and religion as 'purely factitious-fabricated'—effectively by reducing religion to a nonscientific realm of imagination, hope, and ignorance—and yet [despite his agnosticism] remain obsessed about religion."[2] Huxley's combination of agnosticism and religious sensibility was, in historic hindsight, mere prelude. For during the three to four decades spanning the 20th and 21st centuries, a similar obsession

2. Sheridan Gilley and Ann Loades, "Thomas Henry Huxley: The War Between Science and Religion," *The Journal of Religion* 61, no. 3 (1981): 307. Huxley's, Draper's, and White's dealings with the conflict thesis are not merely factual historic accounts. As noted by Lindberg and Numbers in their edition *God & Nature: Historical Essays on the Encounter Between Christianity and Science*, all three rendered polemical accounts biased, each in its own way, by clear anti-Church and anti-theological stances.

with religion has appeared, especially in the publications of neoatheists, which was fueled no longer by an agnosticism filtered through profound religious feelings but instead by an unrestrained anti- or misotheistic reaction formation against any such feelings that neoatheists may experience.[3]

An Introduction to the Galileo Affair

The Generally Accepted Preconditions of a Harmonious Relation

Prior to the Galileo affair, the general belief held among theologians and scientists alike was that God's plan for his creation was to be found in two books, Holy Scripture and the Book of Nature. God disclosed his plan to humans via revelations found not only through study and interpretation of scriptural passages but also via the study of natural philosophy. Based on reason rather than revelation, natural philosophy had already been adopted and adapted—from Latin translations of prior Islamic translations of Aristotle's *Physics*—by Thomas Aquinas in the 13th century. Aquinas, a Doctor of the Church, promoted the harmonious relation between divine revelation and natural philosophy. He relied on natural philosophy to present several reasoned arguments that bolstered, but in themselves did not replace, the Holy Scripture's revelations pointing to the existence of God.

By the time Aquinas published his *Summa contra Gentiles*, mechanical clocks had been around for over a hundred years. Their widespread use in Europe made credible, to the burgeoning scientific community of the 12th- to 15th-century medieval renaissance, the metaphor of the universe as a *machina mundi*; the universe was a clocklike mechanism whose components worked in coordinated fashion according to physical laws. As argued by Stephen Meyer, three theologically-motivated metaphors—the book of nature, the clockwork of nature, and the laws of nature[4]—fit harmoniously into the wider scheme of 12th- and 13th-century natural philosophy, which evolved into modern physical science three to four centuries later. Near the turn of the 17th century, the troubling relations between Galileo, who advocated the mechanistic helio-centric model of the solar system, and the Church's authorities who opposed it, eventually lead to his trial in 1633. A bit later, Rene Descartes's proposed the new physical dynamics of the solar system, published in his 1644 *Principia Philosophiae*. About four decades later still, in 1687, the mathematically elaborated physical theory of the solar system was published by Isaac Newton in his *Philosophiæ Naturalis Principia Mathematica*. In Newton's book, the new science—the *novum organum* advocated by Francis Bacon—had found its secure methodological, conceptual, and physical footing.

3. For misotheism (hating God), see Schweizer, *Hating God*.

4. Stephen C. Meyer, *Return of the God Hypothesis: Three Scientific Discoveries That Reveal the Mind Behind the Universe* (Harper Collins, 2021).

Historic Precursors to the Troubling Science–Religion Relations at the Turn of the 17th Century

Among Greek pre-Socratic philosophers, the love of knowledge and wisdom already leaned heavily on rational arguments instead of myth or common lore, a consequence, according to Werner Jaeger, of the premise and "demand that the universe shall have a rational meaning."[5] The Ionian/Milesian philosophers of the 6th century BCE were the first Western thinkers to adopt not only a rational but also a naturalists' viewpoint of the cosmos. Although they had not yet formalized the explicit hypothetico-deductive method of research used in modern science,[6] they already rejected supernatural explanations to account for objects and events occurring in the world. In their stead they applied, along with reason, the observational method to understand the processes believed to inhere in natural objects, thus rendering an empiricist, naturalistic account of the world. The rejection of supernatural explanations and emphasis on empirical observations have become methodological standards governing the modern physical, natural, and human sciences. Yet, as pointed out by Jaeger, the Ionian/Milesian project was accomplished without necessarily casting aside religious or theological interests. Even the radical atomism and materialism espoused by Epicurus existed compatibly with his interests in the gods. In other words, there was no overt conflict in ancient Greece between science and theology. Such harmonious relation was not to characterize the dawning of the modern era during the 16th century CE.

While the work of Galileo played a pivotal role (as did Darwin's subsequent work) in the creation and perpetuation of the science–religion conflict thesis, some of the troubling relations between science and religion can be traced to events much earlier—even as far back as the medieval renaissance of the 12th to 15th centuries.[7] Intellectual developments in these four centuries put in place the foundations of what is now the modern scientific worldview. These developments were spurred by recovery of ancient texts translated into Arabic by notable Islamic scholars such as Al-Kindi, Al-Khwarizmi, Avicenna, and Averroës. These works, in turn translated into Latin, influenced notable medieval

5. Werner Jaeger, *The Theology of the Early Greek Philosophers* (Wipf & Stock, 2003), 23.

6. The hypothetico-deductive method rests on developing an experimental hypothesis (deduced either from prior observations or from theory) which, if true, correctly predicts expected outcomes. It must be subjected to experimental test designed to see whether or not the actual, obtained outcomes conform to its expected outcomes. When the actual outcomes conform to the expected ones, one can with confidence accept the truth of the hypothesis.

7. Philip Ball, "Triumph of the Medieval Mind," *Nature* 452, no. 7189 (2008): 816–18; Hanby, *No God, No Science?*, 108–12; Jaki, *Patterns or Principles*, chapter 4; Olaf Pederson, *Two Books: Historical Notes on Some Interactions Between Natural Science and Theology* (Vatican Observatory Foundation, 2007), chapters 5 and 6.

scholars like Adelard of Bath, Peter Abelard, Bernard of Chartres, William of Conches, Thierry of Chartres, Thomas Aquinas, and Nicolas of Cusa. During that time period, Nicole Oresme, Jean Buridan, and William of Ockham proposed novel properties of moving objects—importantly including the earth's diurnal rotation—and their mathematical relation to time. The two most important properties of moving bodies were their impetus and inertia. All of these proposals anticipated the later developments in Copernican cosmology and Galileo's astro- and geophysics.

As to the foundations of science that were put into place during the medieval renaissance, four traits are particularly noteworthy. One trait eventually enshrined into modern scientific method is healthy senses of skepticism and criticism, an attitude toward authoritative claims advocated by Peter Abelard in his book *Sic et Non*, which "is something of a sceptic manual: 'We seek through doubt,' Abelard wrote, 'and by seeking we perceive the truth.'"[8] A second trait is the application of rational/logical investigation of nature, an approach practiced and advocated especially by the Platonist Chartres scholars, William of Conches and Bernard and Thierry of Chartres.[9] According to historian of religion David Albertson, thinking among theologically minded scholars, beginning in late antiquity with Anicius Manlius Severinus Boethius at the turn of the 6th century CE, was substantially influenced by ancient mathematics. Consequently a third trait was an emphasis on mathematical thinking, which was increasingly incorporated by medieval scholars in the form of mathematical theologies that took in—along with the qualitative sciences of the trivium: grammar, logic, and rhetoric—the four quantitative disciplines of the quadrivium: arithmetic, harmonics (music), geometry, and astronomy.[10] These three traits stood in the shadow of the fourth trait, namely, the separation of the mathematical sciences from theology. Already in the 12th-century Chartrean School, ideas were floated which prefigured this separation, a separation that was more evident in the 13th-century writings of Albertus Magnus, and which two centuries later played a major role in contributing to Nicolas of Cusa's dilemma: trying to harmonize mathematical theology and Christology.[11]

Throughout this time, the reigning approach to natural philosophy, assiduously worked out by Aquinas in the 13th century, was Aristotelean. As pointed out by Stephen Gaukroger, Aristotle regarded mathematics and natural philosophy (physics) as separate disciplines, and therefore the former played little, if

8. Ball, "Triumph of the Medieval Mind," 816. See also Dawes, *Galileo and the Conflict*, 39–42.

9. Ball, "Triumph of the Medieval Mind," 816.

10. David Albertson, *Mathematical Theologies* (Oxford University Press, 2014).

11. Albertson, *Mathematical Theologies*, see especially pp. 95–100, 116, 142, 205. See also Gaukroger, *The Failures of Philosophy*, 63, 120–21.

any, role in the latter.[12] Aristotelean science, by not incorporating mathematics, was thus qualitative in nature, relying mostly on a system of descriptive observation that furthered the categorization and classification of natural entities. According to the historian Michael Hobart, from a methodological standpoint Aristotelean science was based at best on what can be referred to as thing-numeracy. Although allowing for categorization of entities into distinct numerically-based classes, thing-numeracy could account at most for ordinal differences between natural entities based on observable relational properties such as their relative sizes, weights, speeds of motion, and other variables.[13] But as such it could never quantitatively describe or explain the spatiotemporal dynamics of swinging pendula, moving projectiles, or the orbiting of planets around their sun. The new science of physics, terrestrial and celestial mechanics, that Galileo was intent on developing could account for these dynamics, since it was based on what Hobart designates as a totally new, more sophisticated relational numeracy, by which the language of mathematics functionally relates, say, the abstract quantitative dimension of space along which an object's location can vary, to changes along another abstract quantitative dimension of time. By adopting the quantitative, relational-numeracy approach, Galileo perforce broke the tie to the prior Aristotelean science (and its thing- or innumeracy) that had supported, over several centuries, if ever so frailly, the harmonious relation between faith and reason, science and theology. It was this break with the prevailing Aristotelean approach to science that created or at least played a significant role in creating—as the title of Hobart's book, *The Great Rift*, proclaims—the revolutionary break of the new, modern science of physics from the tethers of religion and theology.

12. Gaukroger, *The Failures of Philosophy*, 61; Stephen Gaukroger, *The Emergence of a Scientific Culture: Science and the Shaping of Modernity 1210–1685* (Oxford University Press, 2006), 79, 401.

13. In the sciences, observations/measurements of an entity's properties rely on successively more informative scales: nominal, ordinal, interval, and ratio. Nominal scales are used to categorize properties by name or class; examples are classifying celestial objects in terms of planet, asteroid, comet, star, or galaxy. Ordinal scales allow one to order properties of objects along relative gradations of magnitude; examples are aligning the planets of the solar system from the largest, Jupiter, to the smallest, Pluto. While ordinal scales do not contain information about the exact numeric differences of magnitude, interval scales do; example, on the Fahrenheit temperature scale, normal body temperature is 98.6 degrees, whereas its temperature in a fevered state, say, 101 degrees, is not only higher but, additionally, higher by an interval of 2.4 degrees. The most sophisticated and informative scale is the ratio scale, which is characterized by the existence of a naturally defined null or zero point; for example, the radius of a planet cannot be smaller than zero mile. So, if the planet Mercury has a radius of (roughly) 1,500 miles and Jupiter (roughly) 45,000 miles, then Jupiter's radius is (i) nominally large, (ii) ordinally larger, (iii) with an interval difference of 43,500 miles, and (iv) in a ratio of (roughly) 45,000/1,500 (=30/1) with Mercury's.

Although this separation may account in objective, historical terms for the break between science and theology, it cannot account for the hostility, the subjective animus of Aristotelians toward Galileo and vice versa, that prevailed near the turn of the 17th century. Perhaps Galileo's overly arrogant and pushy personality was, or those of the Aristotelians were, at fault. Either way, it was the great rift's historic aftermath that, two centuries after the lesser rift between Galileo and his Aristotelean rivals, accentuated and "flavored" the accounts of hostile relations described by John Draper and Andrew White in the latter half of the 19th century, and that to this day is still expressed by neoatheists like Jerry Coyne and Richard Dawkins.

According to Philip Ball, the Chartres rationalism, endorsing the intelligibility of divinely created nature, can be stated as follows: by posing reasonable questions of nature, we can expect to get reasonable answers,[14] an anticipation of a key feature of scientific method reiterated some four centuries later by Francis Bacon in his *Novum Organum*. Such an attitude toward nature, though necessary, is not sufficient. Therefore, a fifth trait characterizing the medieval renaissance was the careful attention to empirically observed details advocated by Robert Grosseteste and Roger Bacon. This emphasis on detail anticipated a fourth trait, the methodological stress on quantification of precise and accurate observations that characterizes modern science.

However, these nascent intellectual progressions from scholastic *philosophia naturalis* toward what would become the modern empirical, experimental, and hypothetico-deductive sciences were not met without resistance from practitioners of theology, the *scientia divina*. Referred to by Ball as "a kind of medieval Counter-Reformation,"[15] theological opposition to the medieval renewal of empirical and rational natural science culminated in the Church's reassertion of authority, when the Archbishop of Paris, Étienne Tempier, issued the Condemnation of 1277, which targeted the assimilation of the works of Aristotle into the theology that was taught at the University of Paris. As Gregory Dawes notes, even earlier in the 13th century, around 1234, the Dominican Theologian Roland of Cremona stated [that] "philosophy is the handmaid [*ancilla*] of theology; theology is the ruler and queen of the sciences which must wait upon it as servants. . . . Theology is the science of sciences which is raised above all philosophical speculation and surpasses all others in dignity."[15] Condemnations and remarks such as these, which subordinates natural philosophy to theology, led some recent scholars, e.g., Étienne Gilson, to take a dual-truth approach to the religion-science relation, according to which scientific truths and theological truths are different species of truth that need to

14. Ball, "Triumph of the Medieval Mind," 816.

15. Dawes, *Galileo and the Conflict*, 42.

accommodate each other.[16] Exactly how the accommodation, if any, is to be realized still poses problems today.

Regarding such troublesome relations between natural philosophy and theology, a reasonable case can be made that nascent forms of harmony theses, and their counterpart conflict theses, were expressed even centuries earlier than the 13th century. On one hand, the early Church Fathers Clement (150–215 CE) and Origen (185–254 CE) of Alexandria regarded pagan philosophy as a worthy handmaiden to theology, though not of value on its own.[17] In contrast, their nearly contemporary Church Father and theologian Tertullian of Carthage (155–220 CE) was more contemptuous, if not hostile, toward philosophy, despite being conversant in the writings of Greek philosophers. Tertullian decried the notion that philosophy could compete with or enlighten theology. He associated Greek rational philosophical thought practiced in Athens with heresy, famously scoffing in chapter 8 of his *Prescription against Heretics*, "What has Jerusalem to do with Athens, the Church with the Academy, the Christian with the heretic?" Not long after, Tertullian's dismissive attitude toward philosophy was still found in less contemptuous, yet somewhat belittling terms, in the writings of later Church Fathers like Basil the Great (329–379 CE), Ambrose of Milan (340–397 CE), and St. Augustine (354–430 CE).[18] These views of Greek philosophy by such as Tertullian were forerunners of what, thirteen centuries later, analogously erupted into a dramatic and momentous altercation between natural philosophers promoting the Copernican heliocentric worldview and theologians representing the then-authoritative geocentric worldview of the Church.

Contemporaneous Factors Contributing to the Galileo Affair

It is also important to note that the troublesome relations around the turn of the 17th century between Christian theology and natural philosophy—the latter of which became modern science—played out and was amplified in the context of another cultural upheaval in Christendom: the struggles between Protestant reformers and the Roman Church. By challenging her scriptural, religious, and political authority in the early decades of the 16th century, Martin Luther, John Calvin, Huldrych Zwingli, and Thomas Münster, among others, rejected the doctrinal authority of the Roman Church. The Counterreformation, the Church's response to the Protestant reformers' challenges to her authority, was well under way when Galileo adopted Copernican heliocentrism. Within these intra-Christian clashes, the conflicts between natural philosophers' espousal of the Copernican doctrine and the Church's authority in matters of

16. Étienne Gilson, *History of Christian Philosophy in the Middle Ages* (Sheed and Ward, 1980), 218.

17. Dawes, *Galileo and the Conflict*, 36.

18. Dawes, *Galileo and the Conflict*, 36.

scriptural interpretation were sorely compounded. Although today the conflictual relations between the Roman Church and the many other reformed Christian denominations have been mitigated in an atmosphere of mutual ecumenical respect and dialogue, especially during the decades following the Second Vatican Council, the conflict between Christianity and science still simmers and, as Clayton pointed out, now and then flares up even to this day.

Among natural philosophers at the turn of the 17th century, neither Johannes Kepler nor Tycho Brahe, both Protestants pursuing astronomical research, were severely troubled by or troubling to their fellow Protestants, including the reformers Martin Luther, Philip Melanchthon, and John Calvin, who, though opposed to the Copernican heliocentric worldview, were more distracted than sorely perturbed by it. The role of gravely troubled and troubling middleman negotiating between loyalties to the truths of natural philosophy and those of the Roman Catholic Church was shouldered by Galileo Galilei. Ultimately, his polemical and combative negotiating style was doomed to failure and to severe rebuke from the Church authorities.

In the eyes of many current scientists and scholars, by condemning Galileo's promotion of the Copernican worldview, the Church inadvertently canonized Galileo as a saint of free-thinkers and of science. As one of my colleagues once exclaimed during a discussion on the science–religion relation, "Look what they [the Roman Curia] did to him!"[19] Behind such exclamations by scientists like my colleague, who tend toward off-the-shelf, clichéd sloganeering without appreciating the complexity of the Galileo affair, is the false belief that Galileo was wholly blameless, thereby rendering the Church entirely at fault. Following Maurice Finocchiaro's caution against such oversimplification,[20] my aims, therefore, in what follows are (i) to correct such simplistic reduction of the Galileo affair, (ii) to render an overview of how, according to recent historians of science, the conflict between Galileo and the Roman Church played out in the late 16th and early 17th centuries, and thus (iii) to refute any one-sidedness, arising from a dearth of historical context, in attributing blame in the contentious case of Galileo vs. the Roman Church.

19. This exclamation typifies the summary, unthinking response expressing many a scientist's antipathy toward religion, an antipathy that, in light of thoughtful and historically informed reflection, may not be justified. My following brief discussion of the Galileo affair summarizes what I have garnered from my readings concerning the case. The complex nature of the case, which involves multiple influences of temperament and personal polemics, of theological, philosophical, and exegetical controversies, and of historical upheavals in religion and worldviews, merits book-length treatments than cannot be provided here. The reader interested and motivated in pursuing the details of this case can consult the many Galileo-related references in the bibliography.

20. Maurice A. Finocchiaro, "Science, Religion, and the Historiography of the Galileo Affair: On the Undesirability of Oversimplification," *Osiris* 16 (2001): 114–32.

Regarding the history of the Galileo affair, among the several types of religion–science relations that have been proposed,[21] the conflictual relation seems to me the most relevant one. Contemporary antireligious scientists and philosophers promote it passionately, since it relies on what is itself a mythical account of how the worldviews of rational, free-thinking science and an irrational, dogmatic religion inevitably and unalterably conflict. Recent hardline expressions of the conflict thesis can be found in the writings of biologists Richard Dawkins and Jerry Coyne.[22] Such expressions and understandings of the conflict thesis, informed by events that transpired over the last five centuries, thrive partly on facts but partly also on myths that have circulated in intellectual and academic communities ever since the 16th-century Copernican revolution.[23] The conflict thesis supports a central feature of current atheistic scientism: a thoroughly anti-religious outlook.

The Galileo affair takes us back to the radical change in worldview that emerged with Copernicus's (re)introduction of heliocentric cosmology to mid-Renaissance Europe.[24] The publication of his *On the Revolutions of the Celestial Spheres* in 1543 was, compared to Galileo's later publications, relatively uneventful in the eyes of the Roman Church. The intellectual stir it caused was not yet forcefully opposed by the Church; instead, the Church's intellectual armory was directed at the far greater cultural turmoil initiated a few decades earlier by the Protestant Reformation. Among others like the Protestant Johannes Kepler, the Catholic Galileo began to promote Copernican heliocentrism toward the end of the 16th century. In contrast, many contemporaneous natural philosophers continued to reject heliocentrism in favor of Aristotelian geocentricism; or else, like Tycho Brahe, the most famous astronomer of the time, they entertained a hybrid, geo-heliocentric view that combined aspects of the Copernican and the pre-Copernican Ptolemaic approaches. That concern found expression in the Tridentine Counterreformation initiated by the Council of Trent (1545–1563) and ending about a century later. Among a list of Protestant doctrinal "heresies," the council condemned the Protestant doctrine of *sola scriptura*, according to which not only authoritative theologians and clerics but any literate and pious Christians were qualified to read and interpret Holy Scripture. In contrast, for Roman Catholics the source of authoritative interpretation of the Bible lay solely within the domain of the Roman Curia and its theologians.

21. Barbour, *Religion in an Age of Science*; Arthur Peacocke, *Theology for a Scientific Age: Being and Becoming—Natural, Divine, and Human* (Fortress Press, 1993).

22. Dawkins, *The God Delusion*; Coyne, *Faith vs. Fact*. More balanced views, yet defending Galileo's over the Church's cause, have been expressed by Dawes, *Galileo and the Conflict*.

23. See Ronald L. Numbers, ed., *Galileo Goes to Jail: And Other Myths About Science and Religion* (Harvard University Press, 2009).

24. The heliocentric model of the solar system was proposed as early as the third century BCE by Aristarchus of Samos, a Greek mathematician and astronomer.

A Brief Interlude Regarding Institutional Competencies and Boundaries

Since the beginning of the 17th century and particularly in the past century and a half, the natural sciences have provided the reigning paradigm for study and understanding of the properties and workings of the natural and physical world. Concomitantly, science has also become heavily institutionalized by the founding of various scientific societies (e.g., in the Anglo world, the Royal Society of London in 1660, the British Association for the Advancement of Science in 1831, and their American counterparts, the American Association for the Advancement of Science in 1848, and the National Academy of Sciences in 1863). These broadly inclusive scientific organizations were supplemented by less inclusive professional societies representing the interests of specialists in more narrowly defined areas of science such as physics, chemistry, biology, and psychology. The institutionalization of science was additionally expressed when scientific organizations and individual scientists began to offer their advisory and consultative services in a variety of legal, political, technological, and industrial settings. For instance, in the USA, the National Academy of Sciences provides advisory input to governmental, educational, industrial, and technological organizations. Scientists or a group of scientists comprising such advisory boards have acquired a prominent level of competence in their specialty areas of research, qualifying them to render expert opinion on the way particular branches of science apply to these and other organizations. In recent years, biologists and geologists have rendered expert testimony in legal cases regarding topics that properly belong to high school science courses. An example is the 2005 trial of Kitzmiller (plaintiff) vs. Dover Area School District (defendant). Kenneth Miller, a Brown University cell biologist, served as expert witness for the plaintiff, and Michael Behe, a Lehigh University biochemistry professor, served as expert witness for the defense.

In such cases, only the opinions of practitioners within a pertinent scientific or scholarly discipline are deemed sufficiently informed to offer competent expert opinions. In our present scientifically informed culture, their opinions carry much greater weight than those of concerned parents, teachers, and others not trained in the relevant sciences or scholarly disciplines. In its explanations and methods, science as practiced today takes recourse only to natural entities and processes subjected to empirical investigations; recourse to divine or supernatural influences and powers are therefore excluded from scientific explanations. Consequently, it is expert scientific judgments that currently provide authoritative assessments of what topics properly constitute a particular science and what topics do not. On one hand, the opinion of most expert theologians would not carry much, if any, legal weight in these cases. On the other hand, when evaluating the niceties of Christian doctrine, a theologian's expert opinion would outweigh that of a theologically unlearned scientist. What, then, is important to note is that although an expert can render competent judgment on issues germane to her or his specialty area, in other specialty areas she or he typically defers to the expert judgment of individuals deemed competent in those areas. As a slight alteration of a popular saying goes, competent-expertise boundaries foster good neighbors.

Returning to Contemporaneous Factors Contributing to the Galileo Affair

That said about the discipline-specific limitations of expert testimony, let's transport ourselves to Rome during the five decades or so bracketing the turn of the 17th century. The Roman Church had by then a centuries-long tradition of theological and scholarly expertise in doctrinal matters, and for that reason it was left to the Church's expertise to assess how passages in Holy Scripture ought best to be interpreted. Science as we now know it was then still in its nascent state. We therefore cannot fault the Church for calling on its theological experts to render their assessment of contentious issues affecting the meaning of Scripture. That, after all, was their proper purview. A lay person like Galileo was considered an unwelcome intruder onto theological turf, despite his well-argued theological claims.

Like some other bright polymaths, Galileo could at times be pushy and cocksure in his promotion of ideas outside the limits of his expert fields of mathematics and astronomy, including his interpretations of biblical Scripture that, he believed, would not conflict with the Copernican worldview. However, in its overly zealous and resolute response to the Protestant Reformation, the Roman Church claimed to be the sole and final arbiter regarding any interpretation of Holy Scripture. Galileo nonetheless confidently expressed his opinions on theological matters dealing with scriptural interpretations. Additionally, he dismissed, either with overweening bitterness or with belittling ridicule, the then fashionable and dominant Aristotelians who criticized the scientific ideas he proposed. By 1615, in the wake of the Protestant Reformation, the Church's authority in Christendom was at stake. The Church therefore not only opposed any private scriptural interpretation but also declared the Copernican heliocentric doctrine to run counter to Holy Scripture. Consequently, as William Shea and Mariano Artigas relate it, in 1616 Galileo was given friendly advice (or a not-so-friendly warning) by Cardinal Bellarmine, Prefect of the of the Holy Office of the Index (otherwise known the Holy Inquisition), (i) not to instruct theologians (most of whom were Aristotelians) on how to correctly read the Bible and (ii) not to hold or defend the Copernican doctrine.[25]

25. William R. Shea and Mariano Artigas, *Galileo in Rome: The Rise and Fall of a Troublesome Genius* (Oxford University Press, 2003). A document signed by Bellarmine was issued in 1616 to protect Galileo from public defamation by possible false rumors, floating around

The fragile status *ante bellum* governed by this admonition prevailed until 1632, when Galileo published his *Dialogue Concerning the Two Chief World Systems*. In it, he clearly advocated Copernican heliocentrism, not merely as an instrumentally useful hypothesis but as a truth-affirming theory of physical reality. This clearly contravened the earlier advice that Cardinal Bellarmine—who in 1632 had been deceased for eleven years—gave to Galileo in 1615. Moreover, in the *Dialogue*, the Aristotelians, among whom can be counted many Church officials, including the then Pope Urban VIII, were for rhetorical reasons represented by the character of the credulous Simplicius, a staunch defender of Aristotelian thought opposed to the Copernican system. Of course, as one can imagine, to be regarded by association to such a simpleton may have offended and alienated a man like Urban, who felt compelled to defend the Church's doctrines and authority. Moreover, the Jesuits, who were bound not only by traditional vows of poverty, chastity, and obedience to their superior general but additionally by a special vow of obedience to the pope, followed suit and distanced themselves from Galileo. Although up to that time the pope and several of the Jesuits had supported him, Galileo now faced the inquisitors of the Holy Office alone, in whose presence he solemnly forswore Copernican heliocentrism. He was placed under house arrest near Florence, where he spent the rest of his productive life publishing less controversial scientific treatises.

In the centuries-long aftermath of Galileo's trial, these regrettable events were interpreted in inherently conflictual terms by many scholars and scientists. A leading interpretation, adopted for instance by Andrew Dickson White, was to regard the Galileo affair as the signal event highlighting the perpetual conflict between science and religion. But is this interpretation justified? Answering this question depends on looking more closely at how Galileo and the Church respectively presented their cases.

A Critical Look at the Soundness of Galileo's Arguments and Evidence

In his book *The Tasks of Philosophy*, Alasdair MacIntyre comments that the "old mythological empiricist view of Galileo saw him as appealing to the facts against Ptolemy and Aristotle: what he actually did was to give a new account of what an

---

in 1616, that he abjured any of his opinions or doctrines in the presence of the Sacred Congregation of the Index. However, also issued was a written yet unsigned admonition to Galileo—the use and legal status of which, seventeen years later in the 1633 trial of Galileo, is for that reason very problematic. Why this document was not signed by the parties involved and why its explicitly stated restrictions imposed on Galileo were more severe than those implied in a signed document is not clear. Detailed coverage of this problematic injunction can be found in Annibale Fantoli, "The Disputed Injunction and Its Role in Galileo's Trial," in *The Church and Galileo*, ed. Ernan McMullin (University of Notre Dame Press, 2005).

appeal to facts had to be. Wherein lies the superiority of Galileo to his predecessors? The answer is that he, for the first time, enables the work of his predecessors to be evaluated by a common set of standards."[26] While this may be a valid assessment of Galileo's long-term legacy as a methodological innovator—combining mathematical hypothetico-deductive reasoning with precise and quantifiable observations—it fails to account for the fact that, when it suited his bumptious and contentious nature, Galileo failed to abide by this common set of standards. To demonstrate this, let's first consider some of the evidence and argument presented by Galileo for the earth's motility. Its motility is twofold: a daily axial rotation and an annual revolution around the sun. Was the evidence Galileo presented for both types of motility clear and conclusive, and were his arguments sound? Or were they, just after the turn of the 17th century, ambiguous and inconclusive? The emphasis on this historical context is extremely important because the case that Galileo presented for the Copernican doctrine seems less clear-cut and conclusive than the praise of Galileo a century and a half ago by both Draper and White might suggest. The time around 150 years ago, during which Draper and White published their books, constituted their present time. And living in any historic period designated as the now—for example by the phrase "in our present times"—raises the possibility of presentism, the tendency to evaluate past events in terms of present cultural values and criteria. Historical works more recent than Draper's and White's, and more aware of the dangers of presentism, tend neither to bury nor to praise Galileo, but instead to offer an overall balanced appraisal of his contentious affair with the Roman Church.

After learning of the invention of the telescope, Galileo, with help of Venetian lens manufacturers, fashioned several of his own, progressively improving their clarity and their powers of magnification. They allowed him to discern, for instance, something akin to the ring of Saturn and the phases of Venus. The latter could be taken to support Copernican heliocentrism, but at the time they were only an equivocal support, since the phases were also reconcilable with Tycho Brahe's rival, hybrid geo-heliocentric model of the solar system. We have here an example of what in philosophy of science is referred to as the underdetermination of a theory's validity by the observed data. It turns out, moreover, that the Tychonic approach accounted more adequately for additional contemporaneous astronomical observations than could the Copernican approach, a fact that, besides being irksome, turned Tycho Brahe into Galileo's *bête noire.* I concur with recent appraisals of Galileo's case that the evidential support he offered for the Copernican system in his *Dialogue* was neither as conclusive as he believed it to be nor as cleanly presented as he promoted it to be. These, among others, were sound reasons for the Church's skeptical and theologically negative appraisal of the Copernican doctrine, a view expressed insistently by Cardinal Bellarmine. I

26. MacIntyre, *The Task of Philosophy*, 10.

will approach the shortcomings of Galileo's promotion of Copernican heliocentrism in his *Dialogue* in terms of what I will refer to as lapses, mistakes, or sins.[27]

Humans are finite, fallible, and morally flawed creatures, ranked superior to beasts yet inferior to angels. Despite best intentions, we tend to miss the mark in many of our endeavors, and theologically the rational and moral limitations and flaws afflicting us might be taken as manifestations of "original sin." However, commissions of mistakes can be regarded more charitably, especially since in scientific research one is allowed to make mistakes—and, at times, even encouraged to risk making them. Making mistakes can serve the greater good of advancing knowledge, and therefore one cannot invariably fault Galileo for making mistakes. That acknowledged, what were some of the fault-imputing fallacies committed by Galileo? For his worldview, Galileo relied on his reading of two books, both of which he regarded as revealing to mankind God's plan for creation: Holy Scripture and the Book of Nature. Regarding the former, after consulting and following the writings of St. Augustine, he read it in a faithful but nonliteral sense. Augustine, an early 5th-century bishop in the North African city of Hippo, taking exception to his predecessor Tertullian's hard-line distrust of philosophy, thought of reason as a divine gift presented, among all of God's earthly creatures, uniquely to humans. In a letter to a faith-oriented individual named Consentius, in which Augustine explains the Church's soteriological doctrine, he commented as follows:

> You say that truth is to be grasped more by faith than by reason. . . . Therefore, according to your rule you ought in this matter . . . to follow only the authority of the saints and not seek understanding by asking me for reasons. For when I begin . . . to lead you to an understanding of so great a mystery, . . . I will simply be giving you reasons, insofar as I am able. But if it is reasonable for you to beg me or some other teacher to help you understand what you believe, then you ought to correct your rule—not to the point of overturning faith, but of permitting you to discern in the light of reason what you already firmly hold by faith.
>
> Heaven forbid that God should hate in us that by which he made us superior to the other animals! Heaven forbid that we should believe in such a way as not to accept or seek reasons, since we could not even believe if we did not possess rational souls. Therefore, in certain matters pertaining to the doctrine of salvation that we cannot yet grasp by reason—though one day we shall be able to do so—faith must precede reason and purify the heart and make it fit to receive and endure the great light of reason; and this is sure something reasonable.[28]

27. A harsher reference would be to sins of omission and sins of commission.

28. Quoted in David C. Lindberg, "Science and the Early Church," in *God and Nature: Historical Essays on the Encounter Between Christianity and Science*, ed. David C. Lindberg and Ronald L. Numbers (University of California Press, 1986).

So, while giving priority to faith in matters pertaining to the revealed doctrine of salvation, Augustine confidently expresses the proper role of reason, for without a rational soul we could not come to believe anything or anyone. Additionally, in his book *De Genesi ad Litteram* (*The Literal Meaning of Genesis*), Augustine states that

> even a non-Christian knows something about the earth, the heavens, and the other elements of this world. . . . Now [in view of this] it is a disgraceful and dangerous thing for an infidel to hear a Christian, presumably giving the meaning of Holy Scripture, talking nonsense on these topics, and we should take all means to prevent such an embarrassing situation, in which people show up vast ignorance in a Christian and laugh it to scorn. The shame is not so much that an ignorant individual is derided, but that people outside the household of faith think that our sacred writers held such opinions, and, to the great loss of those for whose salvation we toil, the writers of our Scripture are criticized and rejected as unlearned men.[29]

Unlike biblical literalists and young-earthers some sixteen centuries later, Augustine advocated a middle ground between reason and faith in matters of doctrine but also between a strictly literal and a nonliteral, figurative interpretation of Holy Scripture.[30] Galileo adopted a hermeneutical approach to Holy Scripture similar to Augustine's. But this was to no avail in his 1633 trial, not only because of historical context—the Reformation and Counterreformation discussed above—but also for factual reasons given below.

Let us now look at the evidence that Galileo presented—and neglected or dismissed—in defense of the Copernican heliocentric system. As noted, a key feature of the system was the motility of the earth, realized by its daily axial rotation and its annual revolution around the sun. Galileo, aided by his modifications of the newly invented telescope with the best lenses he could obtain from Venetian lens makers, was clearly an observational innovator, revealing, as noted above, many celestial phenomena—heretofore invisible heavenly bodies, new stars, Jupiter's moons, Saturn's rings, the phases of Venus—that were as novel as they were perplexing within the then-reigning Ptolemaic geocentrism. Among them also were the discoveries of craterous and irregular

29. Lindberg, "Science and the Early Church." Eight centuries later, St. Albert the Great and his most famous student, Thomas Aquinas, concurred completely with Augustine's admonition.

30. This was not only the opinion of Christian theologians such as Augustine, but also of the 12th-century Jewish philosopher Maimonides. For this, see Daniel Davies, "Reason, Will, and Purpose," in *Creation ex nihilo: Origins, Development, Contemporary Challenges*, ed. Gary A. Anderson and Markus Bockmuehl (University of Notre Dame Press, 2018), 217.

features on the moon's surface and of sunspots, both of which seemed at odds with the Aristotelian view of the incorruptible heavens.[31]

In contrast to these breakthrough observations of the heavens, Galileo's observations supporting the earth's diurnal rotation on its axis were not as clear-cut and directly evident as he proposed them to be. This is important because the diurnal rotation of the earth gives the strong appearance of the sun, moon, stars, and planets moving across the sky, relative to what is concomitantly the appearance of a stationary earth, appearances that could on their face be taken—as they were by the Aristotelians of Galileo's time—as equally direct evidence supporting Ptolemaic geocentrism. Hence, it was incumbent on Galileo to present strong and convincing evidence for the earth's rotation on its axis. Yet two key examples point out how controversial his evidence was. One concerns the ebb and flow of tides, which depends on the earth's daily axial rotation. According to the historians William Shea and Mariano Artigas,

> . . . Galileo received a letter from . . . the Tuscan ambassador to Spain, to whom he had written . . . requesting information about the period of the tides on the Spanish coast and elsewhere. What motivated this inquiry was Galileo's belated discovery that in the Mediterranean there were two high tides and two low tides each day, and not only one high tide and one low tide as his own theory demanded. [The ambassador] . . . made enquiries and confirmed that the flow and ebb of the sea followed a 12- and not a 24-hour cycle. This was devastating news for Galileo's explanation of the tides, which postulated one high tide at noon and one low tide at midnight. . . . [He] concluded that these discrepancies could be explained [away] by the odd shapes and varying depth of the ocean's floor. He was so convinced of the validity of his truth of the Earth's motion that he continued to believe, *in the face of [contradicting] evidence*, that the diurnal period in the ocean followed a 24- and not a 12-hour cycle. His faith in his theory [of the tides] was greater than his trust in what sailors [observed and] reported.[32]

This insistent conceptual scheme of tides, as further noted by Shea and Artigas, was nevertheless taken by Galileo as key physical evidence for the earth's rotation, despite the contraindicative evidence that the conceptual scheme was as

31. Galileo interpreted the sunspots as inherent features of the sun's surface. However, his contemporary, the Jesuit Christopher Scheiner, also observed the spots and argued that they signified planets moving around the sun. Although Scheiner's argument was meant to counter the corruptibility of the heavens implied by Galileo's interpretation, it inadvertently implied that other bodies could feasibly revolve around the sun, thus opening the possibility that the earth also revolves around the sun. This illustrates just how messy arguments and counterarguments regarding Aristotelian incorruptible heavens or Copernican motion of earth around the sun could be in Galileo's time.

32. Shea and Artigas, *Galileo in Rome: The Rise and Fall*, 132.

false as it was ingenious. It is important to note, for one, Galileo's confusing a conceptual scheme with decisive evidence. Second, Galileo interpreted the natural occurrence of two daily tides *via ad hoc hypotheses* regarding the influences of the contours of seabeds as well as those of seashores, influences for which there was no observational evidence. Consequently, as pointed out by the philosopher and historian of science Paul Feyerabend, Galileo's theory of tides proceeded largely on counterinductive argument rather than inductively on the basis of convincing observational evidence.[33]

Christopher Graney provides a second troublesome example concerning the fall of a body, say, a metal ball, from the top of a tower to its base.[34] According to Galileo's theory, the earth's axial rotation plays a key role in explaining the spatiotemporal path of the ball's descent after it is dropped from an elevated location. However, as shown by Galileo's near contemporary, the Italian Jesuit astronomer Giovanni Battista Riccioli (1598–1671), Galileo's theory predicted the falling ball's downward acceleration to be significantly smaller than was actually measured. Moreover, it predicted that the downward acceleration should decrease as the locus of the measurements shifts progressively from the earth's equator to one of its poles. Here again, Galileo's counterinductive theory, in which the earth's rotation plays a crucial role, did not square with the critical evidence provided by actual measurements of the falling ball made by Galileo himself and replicated by Riccioli. Although one can praise Galileo for his ingenious ideas and his careful observations and measurements, one also can find fault with one of his lapses—the *failure to check* and admit when and how *his own measurements* did or did not square with implications of his explanatory models.

As to the orbit of the earth around the sun, here again what Galileo took to be conclusive evidence was far from convincing in the context of astronomical knowledge at the time. With the aid of his refined telescopes, Galileo, as noted, was able to discern phases of Venus as well as Jupiter's moons. Regarding the phases of Venus, he took them to be conclusive evidence that Venus, instead of orbiting around the earth, orbits around the sun. However, as again noted, Tycho Brahe's competing hybrid approach could equally well account for and thus interpret Galileo's observations without recourse to the Copernican version of heliocentrism, a fact that Galileo was aware of. So, within this competitive theoretical nexus, Venus's phases could not be taken as conclusive evidence supporting Copernican heliocentrism *to the exclusion of other theories*, the latter a requirement for deciding between the validities of competing physical models, only one of which is to be accepted and preferred over the others.

33. Paul Feyerabend, *Against Method* (Verso, 1984), chapters 6–8.

34. Christopher M. Graney, *Setting Aside All Authority: Giovanni Battista Riccioli and the Science Against Copernicus in the Age of Galileo* (University of Notre Dame Press, 2015), chapter 7.

Regarding another neglect, Graney additionally raised the problem for the Copernican cosmos posed by the size of distant stars recorded during Galileo's telescopic observations.[35] Tycho Brahe had argued, on credible mathematical grounds—grounds that Galileo, occupying the chair of mathematics at the University of Pisa, could readily understand—that, if the Copernican system were valid, the sizes of distant stars would have to be absurdly large, with a diameter larger than, for instance, that of earth's orbit around the sun. Despite these egregiously absurd sizes, Galileo failed to address this unpleasant implication of the Copernican cosmos pointed out by his troublesome *bête noire*.

Moreover, taking note of Galileo's unreceptive obstinacy, Shea and Artigas take Galileo to task on several additional accounts. For one, they claim that "[to] the end of his life, Galileo held to a simplified version of the Copernican system in which all the planets moved in perfect circles [around the sun]. Although he preached open-mindedness, he never lent an ear to Kepler's arguments about [the planets'] elliptical paths."[36] Additionally, Kepler, a Copernican himself who therefore opposed Tycho Brahe's non-Copernican geo-heliocentric hypothesis, complained in all fairness about Galileo's not addressing the Tychonic hypothesis.[37] Elsewhere, Shea and Artigas state that Galileo "had been asked . . . to prove that the Earth really moved before expecting everyone to reinterpret the Scriptures. Instead of making a gesture to comply, he became increasingly annoyed at the pig-headedness of the academic world."[38] Additionally, the orbits of three new comets discovered in the fall of 1618 were found to be much larger than the Copernican universe allowed. Galileo again countered with a dismissive ad hoc postulate "that comets were just atmospheric phenomena caused by sunlight bouncing off high-altitude vapors."[39]

One can only surmise Galileo's reasons for deliberately discounting Kepler's evidence contrary to his firmly held belief in the perfectly circular planetary orbits around the sun; for the rejection of evidence regarding the two diurnal ebbs and flows of tides; for the rejection of counterarguments regarding the phases of Venus or the satellites of Jupiter; for not subjecting his theoretical predictions to the test of his own observations; for his ad hoc rejection of the reality of comets; and for several other ways of stacking the deck in favor of his version of the Copernican system. However, whatever the reason, one can interpret these lapses as evidence that Galileo, like some unscrupulous trial lawyers,

35. Christopher M. Graney, "Stars as the Armies of God: Lansbergen's Incorporation of Tycho Brahe's Star-Size Argument into the Copernican Theory," *Journal for the History of Astronomy* 44, no. 2 (2013): 165–67.

36. Shea and Artigas, *Galileo in Rome*, 26.

37. Dawes, *Galileo and the Conflict*, 72n21.

38. Shea and Artigas, *Galileo in Rome*, 71.

39. Shea and Artigas, *Galileo in Rome*, 99.

willfully committed sins of omission by not being entirely forthcoming in fairly presenting and weighing the evidence that thwarted his arguments for the Copernican system nor, later, in presenting his case at his trial.[40] In view of this, it may not be surprising that Cardinal Bellarmine (and the Aristotelians of his time), for lack of clearly conclusive evidence, were epistemologically justified in responding with marked skepticism to Galileo's case made in defense of Copernican heliocentrism. Commenting in summarized fashion on all these evidentiary problems posed by Galileo's defense of Copernican heliocentrism, Guy Consolmagno and Christopher Graney recently concluded that "Galileo's scientific argument was fallacious. The science of the day—the observable evidence, the most correct reasoning—was against him and his theory. And his opponents knew that. Francesco Ingoli, a Theatine priest, who played a role in the Church's censoring of Copernicus's work in 1616, cited the star-size problem and the problem of falling bodies. The Jesuit Melchoir Inchofer, who played a role in the rejection of the *Dialogue*, noted the star-size problem; the Rev. Zaccaria Pasqualigo, also involved in that rejection, noted the [additional] issue of tidal periods. Thus when churchmen . . . argued against Galileo, they were not denying science. They had science on their side."[41]

Yet despite this lack of conclusive evidence, Richard Westfall offers an important critique of Bellarmine. In it, he notes that "[Bellarmine's personal skepticism] may all be well and good if we restrict ourselves to parts of Bellarmino's letter [to Galileo], but if we are discussing science, we need to recall other parts of it, which were also parts of Bellarmino's position—to wit, that the word of Scripture, which speaks the truth of God, outweighs the hypothetical conclusions of science, not just in questions of theology, but also in questions of science."[42] However, Galileo did not present his conclusions as mere hypothesis but, as noted, as a convincing, evidence-supported and therefore truth-affirming theory of God's creation, the physical cosmos. Nonetheless, the issue of concern raised by Westfall, and also raised above by Gregory Dawes, is that Bellarmine's magisterial standpoint regarding the relation of the truth of God and the truth of science was ill-informed as to what qualifies as authoritative evidence for or against claims made by scientists. Bellarmine did not understand the significance of the new science as Galileo understood it. This misunderstanding

40. For Galileo's self-serving argumentative style, see Feyerabend, *Against Method*, chapters 6–12, and Paul Feyerabend, "Galileo and the Tyranny of Truth," in *The Galileo Affair: A Meeting of Faith and Science. Proceedings of Cracow Conference*, ed. George V. Coyne et al. (Vatican Observatory Foundation, 1985). Yet some of Feyerabend's accusations against Galileo are sufficiently derisive as to amount to character assassination, thus raising the suspicion that Feyerabend in turn was less than neutral when assessing Galileo's flaws.

41. Guy Consolmagno and Christopher M. Graney, "The Galileo Myth," *America*, September 18, 2020, 55.

42. Westfall, *Essays on the Trial of Galileo*, 19.

poses the question of the validity of Bellarmine's and Church's counterarguments. Moreover, it goes against the subsequent, generally accommodative tenor of the Church's relation to the newly emerging natural sciences. As we noted above, the intellectual stirrings toward the separation of science from theology began as early as the 11th century, was furthered in the 13th century, and was well-nigh completed by the 15th century. In view of the subsequent Galileo affair, it is noteworthy here that according to Stephen Gaukroger this historic separation of natural science from theology, which allocated to science primary, if not exclusive, epistemic access to the properties and processes inherent in nature, allowed Christianity to *eventually* take on "a unique feature: *a fundamental [nonhostile] engagement with science*, which set it apart from all other religions, transforming it radically and giving it a distinctive identity."[43] (emphases added).

A Critical Look at the Roman Church's Response to Galileo's Arguments

Given the Church's generally nonhostile accommodation of science, in addressing the issue of extra-scientific authority I take recourse to the official motto of the Royal Society of London regarding its directive for improving natural knowledge: *Nullius in Verba* (take nobody's word for it). In matters of natural science, that motto of course applies to the words of Scripture and of ecclesial officials who vouch for the authority of Scripture. Richard Blackwell has made the following appraisal. In the wake of the Protestant Reformation and the Roman Church's subsequent Council of Trent (Session 4, April 8, 1546), the Galileo case can be viewed as pitting the authority of the Church in matters of scriptural interpretation against any individualistic interpretation, be it that of Luther or of Galileo.[44] From that perspective, the case throughout became primarily one not of contesting scientific facts and observations as of testing Galileo's obedience to the authority of the Church, with Bellarmine acting as the chief advocate representing the Church. According to Blackwell, the main issue for Bellarmine was not how Scripture is interpreted but rather who is to determine what its true meaning is; in other words, "for Bellarmine the protection of the Church's interpretive authority was a separate and more basic issue than the specific question of whether the motion of the sun and the stability of the earth should be taken

43. Gaukroger, *The Failures of Philosophy*, 122. It was unique because, as Gaukroger, on the same page, further states, "Islam was the only other religion which had had a full-scale engagement with science, and Aristotelianism had also provided the route for this engagement: indeed the scholars of 13th-century Paris were deeply indebted to the Arabic Aristotle tradition, always realizing it. But the commitment to theocracy in medieval Islamic culture resulted in the Arab engagement coming to an end just as the Christian one was beginning."

44. Blackwell, *Galileo, Bellarmine, and the Bible.*

as literal or as figurative truth."[45] And still further, Blackwell notes that "the Church's failure in 1615–16 to use its own exegetical inheritance from Augustine, even after having this pointed out by Galileo, can be understood only as an aberration due to the excessively defensive mind-set of the Counter-Reformation. The Principle of Interpretive Authority so strongly focused attention against private interpretation that it overshadowed a much more complex situation. There was no way that the Church would have granted to Galileo what it had denied to Luther."[46] In line with Blackwell, Westfall adds that Bellarmine's role in the Galileo affair led to "[t]he tragedy of his Church in the fact that he [Bellarmine] saw the rise of modern science on the analogy of Protestantism and failed to recognize that it was instead a fundamental reshaping of the intellectual landscape [a massive, scientific and cultural paradigm shift of worldview, as Thomas Kuhn much later described it][47] within which Christianity, Catholic and Protestant alike, would have henceforth to proceed."[48] Bellarmine was a member of the Society of Jesus (in short, a Jesuit), and several of its members were avid practitioners of astronomical and other sciences. In light of this, a further unintended and regrettable consequence, according to Blackwell, was that "Jesuit science thus died on the vine, just as the first blossoms had appeared."[49] This assertion, however, exemplifies a mythic hyperbole more than historic fact. The Church's contentious position regarding Galileo's promotion of the heliocentric model of the solar system coexisted with its overall positive attitude toward contemporaneous science evidenced by Jesuit science flourishing during and after the Galileo affair pretty much as it had prior to it.[50]

Yet like most of us, Galileo and the officials who spoke for the Church each played all the roles: villain and sinner, hero and saint. Few, if any, historians would deny that in 1633, in the presence of the Inquisitors of the Vatican's Sacred Office of the Index, Galileo, officially charged with disobedience to the Church, abjured his Copernican views under perceived threat of possible torture or, worse, his

45. Blackwell, *Galileo, Bellarmine, and the Bible*, 36.

46. Blackwell, *Galileo, Bellarmine, and the Bible*, 84. This may be too harsh an assessment of Bellarmine, for as seen by Thomas Woods, *How the Catholic Church Built Western Civilization* (Regnery Publishing, 2005), 72, Bellarmine was open to figurative reinterpretation of Scripture but only if there were proof (in the sense of incontestable empirical evidence) that the earth moved around the sun. To the end of his life, Bellarmine, like today's healthily skeptical scientists, was still awaiting such proof.

47. Thomas S. Kuhn, *The Copernican Revolution: Planetary Astronomy in the Development of Western Thought* (Harvard University Press, 1992).

48. Westfall, *Essays on the Trial of Galileo*, 23.

49. Blackwell, *Galileo, Bellarmine, and the Bible*, 142.

50. As noted by Woods, *How the Catholic Church*, 100–104, and by Agustín Udías, *Jesuit Contribution to Science: A History* (Springer, 2014), Jesuit science of astronomy continued unimpeded and, subsequently, Jesuits contributed significantly to several other natural sciences as well as mathematics.

execution. However, although so threatened and placed under house arrest, he was neither jailed nor physically tortured, as some popular myths have claimed. Yet one can surmise fairly confidently that he was mentally tormented while waiting for his upcoming trial and perhaps even more so during the several days that elapsed from beginning to end of his trial. No doubt, by today's standards, his arrest and trial, as pointed out in Annibale Fantoli's recent account,[51] were unjust, to the shame and chagrin of today's many Catholic scientists, especially physicists and cosmologists. Concurring with this appraisal, Consolmagno and Graney further concluded that, despite the many problems blighting Galileo's defense of heliocentrism, and although "Galileo's story is certainly not one of church versus science. . . , Galileo's trial was indeed a terrible injustice. [Moreover, of the many factors that may have contributed to it,] none justified a heresy trial."[52]

The "Sorry" Aftermath to the Galileo Affair

In response to such embarrassment, at the behest of Pope John Paul II the Vatican acted, first in 1979, by reconsidering the Galileo affair, followed by a final declaration and apology in 1992. Pope John Paul II noted in his address to the Pontifical Academy of Science that things were different in Galileo's time. Indeed, they were that; but they also were very deplorable. And as noted by the Jesuit George Coyne, the pope, speaking for the Vatican, officially apologized—for many scientists, no doubt, too late and too warily—for the Galileo affair and admitted that, in contrast to his Aristotelian adversaries, Galileo had indeed been the better theologian.[53] It is true, at the same time, that Galileo did not present clear and conclusive evidence for the Copernican system, and Bellarmine was justified in questioning the validity of his arguments. But that does not justify the harsh treatment meted out by the Church, especially the fatal threat—burning at the stake—enforced against Giordano Bruno 33 years earlier in 1600 Rome.[54]

51. Annibale Fantoli, *The Case of Galileo: A Closed Question?* (University of Notre Dame Press, 2012).

52. Consolmagno and Graney, "The Galileo Myth," 55.

53. George V. Coyne, SJ, "The Church's Most Recent Attempt to Dispel the Galileo Myth," in *Church and God*, ed. Ernan McMullan (University of Notre Dame Press, 2005).

54. Compelling a rational adult's conscience to comply under threat of extreme measures lacks justification. Yet Augustine, Aquinas, and other theologians supported the death penalty in cases of heresy. Aquinas argued, for instance, that much like a diseased part of a body might be removed to save a human from fatal septicemia, a heretic must be expunged from the body of the Church to protect its life. But what Aquinas apparently failed to consider when arguing the case for the death penalty is that acting on this premise takes recourse to the sacrificial scapegoat mechanism, which according to René Girard, *The Scapegoat* (Johns Hopkins University Press, 1986) and René Girard, *The Girard Reader* (Crossroads Publishing Co., 1996), has haunted religions since prehistoric times. The scapegoat rationale used by the Pharisee high priest Caiaphas in John 11:50, viz., that ". . . it is better for you that one man should die

Who knows? Despite Galileo's sins and personal foibles, is it too far-fetched to expect that someday he might be canonized by the Church, as J. L. Heilbron whimsically predicted?[55] After all, saints are repentant sinners. A century and half ago, Andrew Dickson White, by uniformly lauding a by-and-large sinless, struggling Galileo and fully blaming the Church, had already elevated him reverently to champion of science and all but sainthood in the name of science;[56] while nearly a century later Paul Feyerabend fully canonized Galileo, albeit mockingly, as saint of science.[57] Heliocentrism, once regarded as a heresy, today prevails as accepted fact in the Roman Church. After the discovery of stellar parallax in 1838 provided hard evidence for the earth's revolution around the sun and the discovery in 1851 of the precession of the rotational axis of Foucault's pendulum provided evidence for the earth's axial rotation, it was—again much too belatedly—no longer possible for the Church not to officially accept the motion of the earth.

Yet the above multifaceted treatment of the historic conflict, aroused by Galileo's astronomical and cosmological science and the Roman Church's response, contrasts with the straightforward assessment of the conflict made by a scholar like Gregory Dawes. Dawes argues that the Galileo affair is a clear example of a conflict between epistemic attitudes espoused by *scientism*, on the one hand, and a scripture-based, authoritarian *religionism*, on the other, that has persisted to this day.[58] Such a view, based as it is on a hard-set essentialist reading of conflicting epistemic attitudes and norms, rests not on historic evidence in its entirety but instead those selective parts of it that highlight Dawes's assessment of supposedly irreconcilable epistemic differences. One must be careful, therefore, that Dawes's assessment and similar ones are not used as blunt instruments in the battle waged by "enlightened" or "progressive" science against "benighted" and "retrogressive" religion, and vice versa. Historically simplified and ideologically motivated approaches such as these, as also exemplified by the polemics of biologists Richard Dawkins and Jerry Coyne, keep stoking embers in the hopes of inflaming and perpetuating a mostly factitious conflict between science and religion.

Other views on the relation between science and religion are much more nuanced and mixed. For example, as pointed out in the introduction, Ian Barbour

---

instead of the people, so that the whole nation may not perish," presumably justified the execution of Jesus, Christ Incarnate. What Aquinas appeared not to realize is that when he himself applied the scapegoat rationale to heretics—like Caiaphas did to Christ—it did not differentiate between innocence and guilt.

55. John L. Heilbron, *Galileo* (Oxford University Press, 2010), 365.

56. Andrew Dickson White, *A History of the Warfare of Science with Religion in Christendom* (Prometheus Books, 1993).

57. Feyerabend, "Galileo and the Tyranny of Truth," 164.

58. Dawes, *Galileo and the Conflict.*

developed a typology of relations ranging from conflict at one end, through two intermediaries, independence and dialogue, to integration and compatibility at the other end.[59] Among scientists promoting the independence thesis are two biologists, Francisco Ayala and Stephen Jay Gould.[60] Here religion and science are viewed as two separate and, in Gould's terms, "nonoverlapping magisteria," in that science claims authority over empirically investigating and explaining the physical and natural world while religion and theology attend to how aspects of the supernatural world relate to such things as religious faith, spirituality, and values. Despite or because of their nonoverlap, these two authorities can coexist in an atmosphere that varies from a chilly détente to warm and cordial dialogue. Among scientists who have promoted the dialogue and/or integration thesis are the mathematician John Lennox, the biochemist Arthur Peacocke, and the particle physicist John Polkinghorne.[61] And as was noted above, the default position on the relation between theology and the natural sciences that was assumed by the initiators of the scientific revolution, such as Copernicus, Tycho Brahe, Johannes Kepler, and, yes, even Galileo Galilei, was one of possible harmony. It was, as noted by Stephen Meyer, only after the historic developments wrought by the Enlightenment, the rise of scientific materialism and physicalism, and the historic revision of epistemic attitudes and norms, that the conflicts came to a pitch in the 18th and 19th centuries.[62] In the spirit of not oversimplifying the science–religion relation, Maurice Finocchiaro points out that there are numerous additional ways of classifying the relation and that each way itself is nuanced and multifaceted. Conflict, for example, "can take the form of either open warfare or peaceful competition," and harmony "can involve influence by science on religion and also by religion on science."[63]

But even if an irresolvable conflict persists, its deeper and persisting source is not epistemic incompatibilities between science and religion, as Gregory Dawes or Jerry Coyne claim. For, in line with Stephen Meyer's and my own his-

59. Barbour, *Religion in an Age of Science.*

60. Francisco J. Ayala, *Darwin's Gift to Science and Religion* (Joseph Henry Press, 2007); Stephen Jay Gould, "Nonoverlapping Magisteria," *Natural History* 106, no. 2 (1997): 16–22.

61. John Lennox, *God's Undertaker: Has Science Buried God?* (Lion Hudson, 2009); Peacocke, *Theology for a Scientific Age*; John Polkinghorne, *The Interaction of Science and Theology* (Princeton University Press, 1986); John Polkinghorne, *Theology in the Context of Science* (Yale University Press, 2009).

62. Meyer, *Return of the God Hypothesis,* chapter 3. Since the Enlightenment project promised, besides interminable intellectual progress, an ever-progressive morality, it also spurred a metaphysical revolt against what was perceived to be the morally reprehensible evils found in humanity's finite and troubled existence. This revolt, grounded in Promethean and Gnostic myths, had the unfortunate effect of transforming from an intellectual and cultural revolution into unintended violent political revolutions, side effects that were neither anticipated nor promoted by most of the 17th- and 18th-century proponents of the Enlightenment.

63. Finocchiaro, "Science, Religion, and the Historiography," 132.

toric perspective, Finocchiaro raises several additional important points regarding the science–religion conflict thesis by noting that

> we need to distinguish sharply between two controversies: the original one, which climaxed with Galileo's condemnation in 1633, and the subsequent one, which began then and continues down to our own day. *Although it is probably not the case that the trial exemplifies the conflict between science and religion,* the subsequent controversy may very well do that, since the latter is defined primarily by the way the original trial was perceived, and the traditional and most common perception (whether correct or incorrect) has been one of a conflict between science and religion. To undermine the perception of such a conflict (in the historiographic of the affair), it is not enough to criticize the factual correctness of the corresponding interpretations. I *believe the most promising way is not to deny or explain away the conflict, but to regard it as the surface manifestation of something deeper* [than a conflict based on epistemic criteria, attitudes, and norms]. Nor do I think that that the deeper structure is the same one underlying the original controversy, namely the dialectic between conservation and innovation. *That deeper structure lies, I would suggest, in the phenomenon of the origin, diffusion, and development of cultural myths.*[64] (emphases added)

In line with the third aim of the present chapter—to demythologize the Galileo affair, and now also its historic aftermath—I endorse Finocchiaro's assertion that the deep structure of the science–religion conflict lies not in the perennially incompatible epistemic norms but instead in the phenomenon of the origin, diffusion, and development of cultural myths. *The Oxford Dictionary of English Grammar* summarizes definitions of deep and surface structures as follows: "Deep and surface structure are often used as terms in a simple binary opposition, with the deep structure representing meaning, and the surface structure being the actual sentence we see."[65] While this dictionary definition of deep structure refers to linguistic meaning, one can additionally ask if it applies to even deeper historic and existential meanings.

Regarding the search for deeper meanings, the thoughts of existential psychotherapist Viktor Frankl and of the literary humanities scholar William Franke are relevant. According to Frankl, human existence is fundamentally a meaning-seeking endeavor.[66] If so, then viewed from the perspective of an inevitable and unmitigated science–religion conflict, our understandings of the Galileo affair and, following it, the historic dissemination of the conflict thesis only scratches the surface of what at greater depth is a search for its deeper meaning.

64. Finocchiaro, "Science, Religion, and the Historiography," 132.

65. *Oxford Dictionary of English Grammar* (Oxford University Press, 2014), 108, under "deep and surface structure."

66. Victor Frankl, *Man's Search for Meaning* (Beacon Press, 1984).

But among postmodern scholars and many scientists who have given up on searches for profound meaning, a belief prevails that such ventures are in vain; that therefore, instead of seeking a rock-bottom or ultimate source of meaning, ever revisable meanings can be created or constructed at will. Perhaps for that reason, what distinguishes religions from science and postmodern humanities is that religions, as Viktor Frankl further realized, are inherently quests for ultimate meaning and truth.[67] Regarding such quests, not only in religion but also in science, Franke maintains that "[t]he real difference between science and religion is not that they have separate domains or are grounded in separate epistemological faculties. Such distinctions are always artificial wherever the essential human vocation and drive to know as such is at issue. What separates science and religion—and even then, not in their essential core, but only in their most common manifestations—is simply that their interests are different. Science is interested in what can be objectively known and manipulated, whereas religion is interested in what transcends our control and what we can relate to only through means other than objective knowing, for example, by worship, ritual devotion, love, commitment, and engaged action."[68] What separates science and religion at their core, is that on one hand, religion, as was noted in the introduction, is a quest for transcendent truths that render life existentially, spiritually, and personally substantive and meaningful; on the other hand, science is a description and explanation of empirical observations that are rendered impersonally in objective language conveying—as Ian Hutchinson also pointed out in the introduction—very focused, clear, and precise meaning. Noting that science mainly searches for physical causes while theology is mainly in search of more inclusive meaning and values, Christopher F. Mooney explains that the tensions between theology and science exist

> at the points of their [meaning-seeking] overlap because we all want our understandings of causes and meanings to cohere. [Mooney goes on to say, by quoting the philosopher Holmes Rolston, that] "the warfare between science and theology is often a struggle to clarify to what extent causal explanations are compatible with or antagonistic to meaning explanations." Sometimes "precursors of meaning" may even appear in biological and sociological explanations, but a religious explanation is usually needed to provide a full account of meaning. Nor do such full accounts of meaning compete with [the scientific meaning provided by recourse to] causes. Rather, there is a "causal looseness" in matter itself, an unfinished openness and indeterminacy well documented by science. It is here that meaning is to be found, not in some "perforation of the natural by a supernatural order. . . ." For the universe that science studies

67. Victor Frankl, *Man's Search for Ultimate Meaning* (Perseus Books, 2000).
68. Franke, *On the Universality of What Is Not*, 357.

> is not a mere sequence [of facts] but a story, a struggle upward through matter, life, thought, history, and culture. Only a narrative can really capture what is going on. And it is precisely this need of humans for meaningful narrative [e.g., a literary, historical, philosophical, or religious narrative, as Franke has pointed out][69] that allows theology to complement the causality of science.[70]

Whatever goes beyond the impersonal, precise meaning offered by scientific causal explanations is to be found in extrascientific realms such as philosophy, poetry, the various arts, and spirituality, in which personal and deeper meanings regarding the universe's existence and the existence of humans in it can be discovered. But according to science-infatuated extremists—like the neo-atheist Richard Dawkins and most likely some other scientistically inclined and antitheistic scientists and scholars—no such deeper meaning is to be found in the universe's, and in human, existence. Dawkins and some of his confreres are, to slightly rephrase a portion of John Haught's above epigraph, "sober naturalists who seem to be willing to swallow what they take to be the poisonous implications of their creed, and they want no part of sunny naturalism's facile compromises. They frankly acknowledge that science in all its splendor can never make the universe responsive enough to satisfy the human longing for meaning." Especially when coupled with Dawkins et al.'s desire to culturally enshrine the provisional nature of the truths and meanings of science, their disclaimers of any meanings at all that are deeper than the meanings attending scientists' explanations of their findings are therefore deeply and intrinsically at odds—and in conflict—with the human desire to seek an ultimacy of truth and meaning, even if such ultimacy may perpetually elude our experiential grasp. It therefore is here, in the quests for ultimate meaning of the universe and of us humans in it—and not in the different epistemic stances taken in science and religion—that the conflict between science and religion actually is to be found. The following chapter deals with the drama attending the quests for ultimate truths and meanings when the implications of epistemic and ontological scientism adopted by some atheist scientists and scholars are followed to their ultimate limit.

69. Franke, *On the Universality of What Is Not*, chapter 12.
70. Mooney, *Theology and Scientific Knowledge*, 27.

CHAPTER 7

The Drama of Atheist Scientism, an Idolatrous Religion of Science

> . . . theories are not direct images of a real world, they are *fictions*, and only a deep belief, a *strong religiosity* can consider them useful representatives of the real world; the creativity of the scientist is closely related to his religious attitude.
>
> Paul Feyerabend, *Wissenschaft als Kunst*, p. 112

> . . . reality, so goes the thought underlying the [scientistic] argument, is *one*, and only *one* mode of its representation can suffice.
>
> Paul Feyerabend, *Wissenschaft als Kunst*, p. 38

> Science can be popularly and naively supposed to be one in its methods or structures and to constitute the only valid or the most fundamental and comprehensive form of knowledge. Under such persuasion, it sometimes subsumes the function of religion, at other times it provides the foundations for religion, and still at other times religion is excluded as illusion or myth.
>
> Michael J. Buckley, *Denying and Disclosing God*, p. 22

Whatever misunderstandings and incompatibilities exist between science and religion, they are greatly exacerbated when science is misused to promote scientistic worldviews, and religion is misused to promote pseudoscientific religionist worldviews. The latter problem manifests when, for instance, religionists try to deny or reinterpret scientifically obtained and interpreted findings to suit literalist readings of scriptural creationist passages. As a scientist, I find their mental acrobatics ad hoc, tortuous, and inelegant, when they are responding to scientific discoveries that may clash with scriptural claims regarding nature and the cosmos. Accepting such claims would require a scientist to jettison much of the painstakingly acquired knowledge of fundamental physics and of chemistry, biology, geology, and the human sciences. Additionally, although presenting lengthy critiques, mainly of scientific methodology, religionists offer little, if any, empirical and theoretical value that advances scientific research. Hence, I concur with Richard Dawkins's loss of patience regarding their tiresome mental antics that call into question their intellectual integrity. And therefore I agree with the Christian philosopher Michael Augros's assessment that "some of the 'creationist science' books do more to destroy the credibility of theism than any atheist could ever do."[1] I will simply dismiss the tangled dramatics of the scriptural literalists as religion's overreach into the research and explanatory domains proper to science. Nonetheless, scientists, I included, can be creationists without being scriptural literalists.[2] That said, it is also important to address at some length the overreach of science, especially when atheist scientists and scholars use it to espouse a scientistic worldview, doing so typically by recruiting and weaponizing scientific facts against religion.

In the prior chapter, I suggested that the most likely candidate for the deep structure underlying the conflict between science and religion can be found in the human quest for existential and spiritual meaning. Theistic religion and its understanding of the world deals with ultimate meaning, whose source is in the divine realm transcending humans' finite understanding. In contrast, the innerworldly scientific understanding of the known facts about nature is limited to semantically and (ideally) mathematically precise descriptions and explanations that are offered in most scientific research articles. Although such descriptions and explanations are very desirable within the scope of science, in themselves they also are very impoverished in their ability to address or express broader issues concerning the existential and spiritual significance of our place in the cosmos. And though physics and biology are relevant to addressing some of the profoundest questions posed to humanity about the origin and fate of the universe, and the place of life, consciousness, human minds, free will, and good and evil in it,[3] some of these questions such as the *why*—the end or purpose of it all—may ever lie outside the scope and the ability of science to address, let alone answer. For scientists like Steven Weinberg and Stephen Hawking, two of the most cerebral theoretical and mathematical physicists, the physical understanding of the cosmos can leave them rather cold. For something emotionally warmer and spiritually more meaningful and satisfying, Hawking, for instance, preferred instead to turn to human companionship or to the music of Mozart; a quite understandable preference, since Mozart's compositions have been described as conveying to the musically attuned human spirit an otherworldly, celestial quality.

The aims of the present chapter are to explore the purported conflict between the practices of science and religion, how that conflict is affected by our search for existential and spiritual meaning, and to see if that search is realized within some sort of religious or ersatz-religious belief system. Achieving

1. Augros, *Who Designed the Designer*, 136.

2. Most scientists who are faithful practitioners of the Abrahamic religions no doubt believe scriptural claims that God created the universe, without also believing that he literally did so in six successive earth-days between 6,000 and 10,000 earth-years ago.

3. Hossenfelder, *Existential Physics*.

these aims relies on a subsidiary aim of also exploring further the metaphysical position of scientism. From a theistic viewpoint, it can be regarded as an idolatrous belief system adopted, as we saw in the introduction, by many an atheist scientist and scholar. As noted by the Jesuit scholar Vincent Micelli, historically and still presently it attempts to transform science into a new religion—and humanity, especially the scientist, to the level of its god.[4]

The title of the present chapter is adapted from the 20th-century theologian Henri de Lubac. In his book *The Drama of Atheist Humanism*, de Lubac investigates the influential works of 19th-century critics of Christianity, most notably Ludwig Feuerbach, Karl Marx, Auguste Comte, and Friedrich Nietzsche, and how their views contrasted with Christian advocates and sympathizers, notably Søren Kierkegaard and Fyodor Dostoyevsky. In de Lubac's words, "man is getting rid of God in order to regain possession of the human greatness that, it seems to him, is being unwarrantably withheld by another. In God he is overthrowing an obstacle in order to gain his freedom. . . . Modern humanism, then, is built upon resentment and begins with a choice. It is, in Proudhon's word, an 'antitheism.'"[5] It therefore is an expression not only of the very *ressentiment* attributed by Nietzsche to a servile Christianity[6] but also of the militant and needlessly shrill hostility directed toward religion by neoatheists like Richard Dawkins and Christopher Hitchens.[7]

Not covered by de Lubac was the antitheology promulgated by the 19th-century champions of Darwin's theory of evolution, most prominent among them Thomas Huxley. In the late 19th century, British promoters of science like Huxley worked to advance a thoroughly secularized science and its broader impact on culture and society. As expressed by the historian Frank Turner, "secularization was their goal; science, their weapon."[8] This strand of Darwinism has found its enamored and inspired admirers to this day. Currently, it belongs to a class of scientistic worldviews that additionally incorporate, under the rubric of scientific naturalism, materialist and physicalist pretensions. Scientistic naturalism, however, subscribes not only to *epistemological* but also to *ontological* naturalism, the latter of which confuses the *all there is to explain in nature* with the claim that the *nature of the all is that which can be so explained.* However, as J. P. Moreland summarizes, "it is not science that says that the world

4. Vincent Micelli, *The Gods of Atheism* (Sophia Institute Press, 2022).

5. De Lubac, *The Drama of Atheist Humanism*, 24–25.

6. Friedrich Nietzsche, *On the Genealogy of Morals: A Polemic* (Oxford University Press, 1996).

7. Dawkins, *The God Delusion*; Christopher Hitchens, *God Is Not Great* (Hachette Book Group, 2007).

8. Frank Miller Turner, *Between Science and Religion: The Reaction to Scientific Naturalism in Late Victorian England* (Yale University Press, 1974), 16. This assessment may actually exempt Huxley.

[i.e., reality] consists entirely of aggregates of particles standing in fields of force. It is the [scientists and scholars assuming the role of] philosophical naturalists who are making claims about the limits of ontology and epistemology, and whose claims are themselves philosophical, not scientific."[9] Hence it is not surprising that especially prominent over the last three to four decades were the dramatics of atheist scientists and scholars flexing their intellectual muscles in print, debates, and interviews, and Christian theists similarly flexing theirs in response. On both sides, the dramatics—an expression of what Francis Bacon called the idols of the market and idols of the theater—has made for brisk book sales and histrionics.

A key tenet of atheistic scientism is that there is an abiding, inherent incompatibility to the point of conflict between science and religion that, as expressed in the Feyerabend's second epigraph above, must be resolved in favor of science. For antitheistic neoatheists, the desired end of the conflict is the destruction of religion.[10] Despite such extreme views, there is, however, significant disagreement among them and their entourage about the impact of their scientistic Darwinian worldview.

Scientism: Shallow and Nice or Deep and Bleak?

Rather than describing scientism in greater detail, I instead juxtapose and contrast its characterizations described by atheists and theists. To begin, I need not make apologies for science other than my cautioning that science ought not be confused with scientism. I say this in response to the opinions of the priest, theologian, and scientist David Alcalde, who in his recently published book *Cosmology without God?* claims that

> modern science cannot get rid of its scientism *because it is inherent to it.* This so because modern science has reduced the understanding of being from actuality to facticity. As a consequence, there is a new concept of positive quantitative matter, free of form, and free of the distinction between act and potency. There is also a new functionalist notion of truth: truth is equated with usefulness and verified by results. As a result, modern science is incapable of being integrated into a more comprehensive order of knowledge or recognizing any access to truth other than via the scientific method. It is, then, not surprising when scientists, e.g,, Hawking, consider

9. Moreland, *Consciousness and the Existence of God*, 166.

10. Dennett, *Darwin's Dangerous Idea*; Sam Harris, *The End of Faith* (W. W. Norton & Co., 2004). While Dennett seems to be content with awaiting the elimination of religion by the increasing secularization of civilization, Harris appears to be less patient in actively advocating its destruction by science. Harris, "Science Must Destroy Religion," *Huffington Post*, January 2, 2006, accessed on July 22, 2025, www.huffingtonpost.com/sam-harris/science-must-destroy-reli_b_13153.html.

> science, especially physics, as the first philosophy, and claim that science should expand itself in order to conquer every possible area of human knowledge, dismissing everything that cannot be subjected to the self-imposed rigor of the scientific method. . . . Because the ontology of modern science precludes the integration of scientific reason into a more comprehensive understanding of reason, *the distinction between science and scientism is facile and untenable*. . . .[11] (emphases added)

This is a peculiar assessment of modern science. It is inspired as much by a religionistically motivated fervency as is a zealous atheist's scientistically-inspired negative assessment of religion. For one, Alcalde's assessment rests on philosophical notions such as the metaphysical distinctions between actuality and facticity, form and matter, and act and potency; all of which are notions that are very dear to theology but not so much to science, nor to most practicing scientists. Second, Alcalde's argument is that modern *science* is blighted in several ways. For example, it has reduced the understanding of being and it has introduced a new functionalist and pragmatic notion of truth—but despite these blights, Alcalde believes, it will expand itself in order to conquer every possible area of human knowledge. Only by heaping the blame on modern science per se, whose historic beginnings can be dated to the turn of the 17th century, instead of on scientism, which appeared subsequently *by appropriating later philosophical interpretations* of science, can one come to the conclusion that scientism is an essential feature of science. Third, Alcalde's conflating of science and scientistic science does not do justice to the numerous theistic scientists, including me, who by choice do not subscribe to scientism and who instead fervently oppose it. Consequently, fourth, by claiming that science is by nature scientistic, he also places himself in a position as extreme as that of scientistic atheists, who simply wish to perpetuate the present cultural conflicts between science and religion.

That said, as a retired nonscientistic scientist, I can reasonably concur with the theologian John Haught's critique of scientism in that he and I are

> not speaking here . . . of science as such. *Science is an authentic and fruitful unfolding of the desire to know.* Moreover, science appropriately employs a reductive *method* in order to focus its inquiry on a manageable set of data. But at times the [purely] *methodological* reduction characteristic of scientific method can be taken hostage by the will to mastery [a manifestation of Nietzsche's will-to-power]. Whenever this takeover occurs, the world shrinks in size and complexity. Thought loses touch with the native wildness and elusiveness of the knowable world, and Occam's razor

11. Alcalde, *Cosmology Without God?*, 45. Stephen Hawking's elevation of physics to first philosophy, was preceded five centuries by his English compatriot, Francis Bacon, who, in his *Novum Organum*, had already elevated the new science to first philosophy.

> becomes a weapon of destruction. *Once it has been taken prisoner by scientism,* science has the goal no longer of expanding knowledge but instead of putting arbitrary limits on what can be taken as true or real. And so nature gets fictionalized as manipulable machinery, or a set of mindless particles-in-motion, subject in principle to complete scientific and technological control. Here the humble and inherently vulnerable desire to know has been shoved aside by an aggressive impulse to subject *all reality* to complete scientific hegemony.
>
> The outcome of this assault is a new, *quasi-religious* dogmatism known as materialism (or physicalism), the belief that *the physical world,* as made intelligible by scientific method, *is really all there is.*[12] (emphases added)

The emphases I have added stress several important points. For one, they demonstrate how a rigorous methodological rule of scientific practice can segue readily into an ontological and metaphysical assertion about reality. Second, as covered in the introduction, they point out the quasi- or ersatz-religious belief system that underlies atheistic scientism. It is this religious aspect of scientism that is explored more fully below. Regarding the first point, the philosopher John Cottingham correctly states that "scientism, the claim that science is the measure of *all* reality, or *all* truth, is a claim that could not possibly be established by scientific means, and therefore, if truly asserted [as a valid view of science], would be self-refuting."[13] Such self-contradicting consequences are evident to many an intelligent and questioning mind. For example, in a rephrasing of Cottingham's quote, the mystical, yet rational, mind of the Jewish nonscientist and theologian Abraham Heschel can correctly understand that "the claim that there are no significant questions so profound that they cannot be solved by the exact sciences raises a question that seems to defy solution: How does one account [scientifically] for the dogmatic and monstrous presumption implied in such a claim?"[14] The presumption is found not in science itself but in a *prescientific belief* in a scientistic worldview. The failure of many scientists and scholars to plainly see and address the pretentious hubris behind scientism and their attempts to mitigate the potential consequences of its much-less-than-nice versions reflects an irritating sore spot in the scientistic worldview.

Shallow and Nice Scientism

Here, before taking an in-depth look at the darker underside of scientism (and its specific avatars in the form of materialism, physicalism, and Darwi-

12. Brague, *The Kingdom of Man,* 186.

13. John Cottingham, *In Search of the Soul: A Philosophical Essay* (Princeton University Press, 2020), 26.

14. Heschel, *The Prophets,* 522.

nism), I first take note of some of its mild and modest versions that the atheist biologist Jerry Coyne lists. According to Coyne,

> scientism usually denotes one or more of the following four claims. First, science is the sole source of reliable facts about the universe, that is, it is the only "reliable way of knowing." Alternatively, scientism could mean that the humanities should be *subsumed* under the rubric of science. That is, areas like history, archeology, politics, morality, art, and music should be viewed *only* through a scientific lens. And when possible should adopt the methods of science. [Third], scientism could also refer to the idea that questions that can't be answered by science aren't worth considering or discussion. Such questions include those involving morality, ways to live, beauty, emotions, and, of course, religion. The [fourth and] most damning definition of scientism is the idea that scientists are arrogant, lack humility, and are reluctant to admit that their findings might be wrong.[15]

Coyne goes on to develop an apologetic for each of these more and less mild versions of scientism. I can agree with him on several points. I agree that, up to now, science has proven to be the soundest way to obtain *objective* knowledge about nature and the physical universe. But it is not the only way to gain every type of knowledge whatsoever. I challenge you, the reader, to look around and take in what you observe in your immediate setting. Does not your *subjective* apprehension of the informational contents experienced in your (and only your) conscious here-and-now constitute knowledge? If not, then how, by what warrant, can a thousand such observations, such *private* and *subjective* apprehensions in the conscious minds of each of a thousand scientists in the same or similar research settings, sum up to be *objective* knowledge? By the assent of a majority or, better yet, by a unanimous assent? Indeed, such consensual agreement is a necessary feature of a truth accepted by the scientific community, but it is not sufficient. For, without the concurrent *trust* or *faith* that truth, as Thomas Aquinas put it, is conformity of thing (fact) and intellect (cognition) ("*Veritas est adaequatio rei et intellectus.*")—that is, without a prior trusting that the private phenomenal experience of the same setting in each of the scientists will render a subjective perceptual and cognitive apprehension that is true to the reality and intelligibility of the setting—the unanimous *post hoc* consensus by itself is an ineffective guarantor of objective truth. Leaving aside, for now, the source of that trust, if the communal and publicly acknowledged perceptual and cognitive apprehension is true to the scientific setting at hand, then the private apprehension of the world in each scientist must also constitute knowledge that is true. Contrast this with Coyne's facile claim that "'knowledge' is *simply* the public acceptance of facts," and therefore that private, personal knowledge

15. Coyne, *Faith vs. Fact*, 198.

isn't factual, "for it is missing the crucial ingredients of verification and consensus."[16] To wit, it seems that Coyne is putting the cart before the horse. He fails to realize or refuses to acknowledge that any public consensual agreement (the cart) about observed states and affairs in the world (i.e., the facts) cannot occur unless first and foremost there is the private subjective apprehension of facts by each scientist (the horse) contributing to the consensus. Without prior trust in the truth-seeking capacity of each scientist's subjective experience, how can simply a consensus among—i.e., the summation of—many scientists' private first-person subjective apprehensions generate bona fide scientific "third-person" objective knowledge about the physical and natural states and affairs in the world? How, except by another observed consensus that such consensus constitutes genuine, scientific knowledge; and how, except by an additional observed consensus, can the consensus on consensus, and continuing recursively *ad infinitum*? In other words, consensus-building as a guarantor of truth is ultimately groundless. So, the more important and crucial question is: Whence the unstated *trust/faith* that in human knowledge (private or public) a thing (fact) conforms to intellect (cognition)? What underwrites this conformity? Here, for centuries, Christianity has provided a readily accessible answer: God's creative Logos establishes both the rational intelligibility of the physical world and the human intellect's ability to grasp this worldly intelligibility.

Despite this disagreement with Coyne, I also agree with him that, as we saw in part 1 above, scientific study can to some extent inform, for instance, our understanding of art and morality; and it is important to add that such study can also inform somewhat our understanding of religion and theology. In the human sciences, disciplines like anthropology, sociology, and psychology have studied religion for many decades. However, although I find largely unobjectionable Coyne's discussion of additional versions of scientism, what I do find objectionable is that the four versions he considers are rather mild and "nice" forms of it. A similar "benign" version of scientism was delineated by the neo-atheist fellow traveler, Steven Pinker, as follows:

> Scientism, in this good sense, is not the belief that members of the occupational guild called "science" are particularly wise or noble. On the contrary, the defining practices of science, including open debate, peer review, and double-blind methods, are explicitly designed to circumvent the errors and sins to which scientists, being human, are vulnerable. Scientism does not mean that all current scientific hypotheses are true; most new ones are not since the cycle of conjecture and refutation is the lifeblood of science. It is not an imperialistic drive to occupy the humanities; the promise of science is to enrich and diversify the intellectual tools of humanistic scholarship, not to obliterate them. And it is not the dogma that physical stuff is the only

16. Coyne, *Faith vs. Fact*, 186.

> thing that exists. Scientists themselves are immersed in the ethereal medium of information, including the truths of mathematics, the logic of their theories, and the values that guide their enterprise. In this conception, science is of a piece with philosophy, reason, and Enlightenment humanism. It is distinguished by an explicit commitment to [the] two ideals [of science's intelligibility and its rigorous practice], and it is these that scientism seeks to export to the rest of intellectual life.[17]

Perhaps so. But I remain unconvinced, because other than all the apologetics regarding what scientism is not or does not, a key missing ingredient is that this sort of nice and kind scientism, instead of being merely a benign attitude and set of commendable ideals adopted by scientists, is much more. First, as the philosopher Michael Mitchell notes, "the [impressive] success of talented scientific authorities in developing technology creates the illusion that they are moral authorities. Such is the propagating engine of scientism. The general outlook of scientism is well articulated by Steven Pinker, one of its giddiest proponents, [who claims the following on p. 394 in his book *Enlightenment Now*]: 'The moral worldview of any scientific literate person—one who is not blinkered by fundamentalism—requires a clean break from religious conceptions of meaning and value. . . . The worldview that guides the moral and spiritual values of a knowledgeable person today is the worldview given to us by science.'"[18] What is propagated here is not scientism's explicit commitment to the two aforementioned ideals of science that it seeks to export to the rest of the intellectual world. Instead, like the other neoatheists, Pinker is aiming a broadside specifically at theistic religions, and that in a supercilious and smug manner. Second, Pinker is, so to speak, preaching mainly to the scientistic, religiously amusical, and falsetto-pitched atheist choir. For there are many intelligent, thoughtful, and unblinkered theistic scientists who are not swayed towards atheism by Pinker's currently fashionable philosophical musings. Instead, they are musically attuned to a perennial philosophy that is shared by all major world religions.

In the end, Pinker's assessments of scientism, like Coyne's, come across as specious ploys, deliberately avoiding the heart of bleakness in atheistic scientism. Like the crafty offer of a seemingly conciliatory and attractive Trojan horse, the offer of a benign yet bumptious scientism hides deeply within it a hubristic lust for power.[19] As the theologian Richard Pendergast puts it, "scientism draws a great deal of its persuasiveness from a collective hubris that inclines its victims to scientific imperialism and to the delusory belief that

17. Steven Pinker, "Science Is Not Your Enemy: A Plea for an Intellectual Truce," *The New Republic*, August 6, 2013.

18. Mitchell, *Truth Before Logic*, 2–3.

19. See Leon Wieseltier, "Crimes Against Humanities," *The New Republic*, September 3, 2013.

science is the most important [if not the only true] kind of human knowledge."[20] Unfortunately many scientistically inclined scientists are not aware that their religious-like *faith* in science is a collective delusion.

Deep and Not-so-Nice Scientism

While, as Coyne sees it, the most damning element of scientism is that scientists are high on arrogance and low on humility, i.e., high on hubris, a more nuanced look at scientism ought to concern itself not merely with such mild and superficial definitions but also with its broader and deeper metaphysical bases and cultural consequences. Once that is done, the most damning aspect of scientism is not so much the hubris of arrogant scientists as it is their ignorance or denial of its condemnable nihilistic consequences. Agreeing with Coyne and Pinker on several points, Richard Williams, in the introduction to the book *Scientism: The New Orthodoxy*, presents the following less palatable assessment of a more assertive, muscular, and reductive version of scientism:

> Scientism entails a zealous metaphysical commitment and a requisite orthodoxy in method and in thought regarding the nature of the world and how understanding of the world is to be approached. Scientism entails also a commitment to naturalist, reductive, or emergent materialism and tries to define science in a way that includes not only a commitment to empirical methods, but also to this particular metaphysics. [Agreeing with Hutchinson's definition of scientism that I covered in my introduction, Williams continues that] it is a tenet of scientism that only certifiably scientific knowledge counts as real knowledge. All else is mere opinion or nonsense. [It follows] that the methods and assumptions underlying the natural sciences, including epistemological and metaphysical ones, are appropriate for all sciences, including, prominently, the social and human sciences. [A third tenet] is that scientism exudes and promotes an exaggerated confidence in science (i.e., natural science in all its avatars) to produce knowledge and solve the problems facing mankind. The fourth tenet of scientism articulates the heretofore implicit assumption underlying the other three. Scientism is not just an attitude about science and the power of science. *Scientism makes metaphysical claims* . . . [most notably] that the world must really be like the methods of contemporary natural science assume it to be. . . . [In short], scientism *assumes, and requires a naturalist, materialist, rather mechanistic metaphysics.*[21] (emphases added)

The bleak upshot of all this, as Williams notes further, is "a fundamental alteration of our understanding of our nature and ourselves. The very meaning of what

20. Pendergast, *The Cosmic Hierarchy*, 17.

21. Richard N. Williams, introduction to *Scientism: The New Orthodoxy*, ed. Richard N. Williams and Daniel N. Robinson (Bloomsbury Press, 2015), 3–7.

it is to be a human being, and the essence of human relatedness, are called into question."[22] Moreover, "at stake in the tension between scientism and the science it seeks to dominate, as well as the understandings it seeks to replace, is our very humanity—the nature of our existence, the meaning of our lives, and our understanding of the best to which we can aspire."[23] Thus, it is the ideological metaphysics of scientism, *not science itself*, that threatens to vacate the world of its *telos*, its solemn and sacramental motifs, and its existential and spiritual significance. And, as Williams further explains, by extending its influence "into the human sciences, the humanities, [the arts,] and even religion, [scientism] calls into question all transcendence along with the trans-situational values and morality generally, offering in return only a severely impoverished, strictly utilitarian, moral [and aesthetic] landscape."[24] In other words, from a theistic viewpoint it is and promotes a thoroughly atheistic, antireligious humanism, taken up with its own religious fervor in recent years, especially by the cult of strident neoatheists.

Above we noted that Coyne stresses, as does many a fellow scientist, that science is "merely" a method of epistemically exploring the universe, from its tiniest particles of matter, through our bodies and behaviors, to the entire cosmos itself. As such, the scientific method is not only a necessary but also a sufficient and universal way to attain to "genuine" truth and knowledge. Here I would like to contrast this simplistic view of the scientific method by returning to the historian and philosopher of science Paul Feyerabend, an apostate not only from the Christian Church but also from the Church of Scientism. In Feyerabend's book *Against Method* (as well as in his later books *The Tyranny of Science* and *The Conquest of Abundance*), he laments and lambasts the excesses of science that are scientism, and he asks if it is

> not possible that science as we know it today, or a "search for the truth" in the style of traditional philosophy, will create a monster? Is it not possible that it will harm man, turn him into a miserable, unfriendly, self-righteous mechanism without charm and humor? "Is it not possible," asks Kierkegaard, "that my activity as an objective observer of nature will weaken my strength as a human being [since we are human beings first, and then scientists]?" I suspect the answer to all these questions must be affirmative and I believe that a reform of the sciences that makes them more anarchistic and more subjective (in Kierkegaard's sense) is urgently needed.[25]

Further on, Feyerabend offers two theses. First, hard-core scientistic scientists (e.g., the sociobiologist Edward O. Wilson) "are not content with running

22. Williams, introduction to *Scientism*, 8.
23. Williams, introduction to *Scientism*, 16.
24. Williams, introduction to *Scientism*, 17.
25. Feyerabend, *Against Method*, 175.

their own playpens in accordance with what they regard as the rules of scientific method, [since] they want to universalize these rules, they want them to become part of society at large and they use every means at their disposal—argument, propaganda, pressure tactics, intimidation, [ridicule of their critics], lobbying—to achieve their aims."[26] And second, Feyerabend therefore maintains that it is detrimental to humanity that science can and therefore should be run in accordance with these universal rules. For thus conceived, science is "unrealistic and pernicious. It is *unrealistic*, for it takes too simple a view of the talents of man and of the circumstances which encourage, or cause, their development. And it is *pernicious*, for the attempt to enforce the rules is bound to increase our professional qualifications at the expense of our humanity."[27] However these theses are taken, one can agree that Feyerabend expressed a prophetic protest directed against those practitioners of science who are "*unable to understand*, and *unwilling to condone*, different ideologies, because they have the *power* to enforce their wishes."[28] To resist such power and thus to avert loss of the diverse humanistic, aesthetic, spiritual, and religious species of cultural expressions, Feyerabend, an atheist sympathetic to religion, is clearly airing an impassioned plea against an imperialistic and triumphalist overtake of cultural space, be it by scientism or by religionism.

Here, relevantly, let's cite, from the last chapter of Dennett's *Darwin's Dangerous Idea*, the following scientistic apologetic, rendered in somewhat moralizing and patronizing style, for science-driven cultural progress. No doubt referring to religion among other cultural practices, he says in paternalistic tone that

> there is certainly a treasury of ill-appreciated truths embedded in the endangered cultures of the modern world, designs that have accumulated details over eons of idiosyncratic history, and we should take steps to record it, and study it, before it disappears. . . . [We] should not expect this variety of respect to be satisfactory to those [i.e., the religiously faithful] who wholeheartedly embody the memes we honor with our attentive—but not worshipful—scholarship. On the contrary, many of them [the religionists among the religious] will view anything other than enthusiastic conversion to their own views as a threat, even an intolerable threat. We must not underestimate the suffering such confrontations cause. To watch, to have to participate in, the contraction or evaporation of beloved features of one's heritage is a pain only our species can experience, and surely few pains could be more terrible. *But we have no reasonable alternative*, and those whose visions dictate that they cannot peacefully coexist with the rest of us *we will have to quarantine* as best we can, minimizing the pain and damage, trying always to leave a path or two that may come to seem

26. Feyerabend, *Against Method*, 220.
27. Feyerabend, *Against Method*, 295.
28. Feyerabend, *Against Method*, 299.

> acceptable. . . . What will happen, one may wonder, if religion is preserved in cultural zoos, in libraries, in concerts and demonstrations? It is [already] happening.[29] (emphases added)

Although Christian theists can agree with much that Dennett states in the last chapter of his book, it is doubtful that they will take as gospel truth that "we have no reasonable alternative," nor will they anticipate and accept the realization of his desire to marginalize the cultural impacts of their religious traditions, in effect to the point of their elimination. This indeed is a *Dennettian* dangerous idea, but not one that follows necessarily from Darwinian evolution by natural selection. For there are plenty of Christian scientists, evolutionary scientists among them, who see neither the inevitable conflict nor the unavoidable danger that, as Dennett argues, Darwinian evolution poses to their religious faith. Referring to theistic religions, Dennett asks "hasn't there been a tremendous rebirth of fundamentalist faith in these creeds? Yes, unfortunately, there has been, and I think there are no forces on this planet more dangerous to us all than the fanaticisms of [religious] fundamentalism, of all the species: Protestantism, Catholicism, Judaism, Islam, Hinduism, and Buddhism, as well as countless smaller infections. Is there a conflict between science and religion? There most certainly is."[30]

I will take the liberty of rephrasing these questions by inserting different words: "Hasn't there been a tremendous rebirth of fundamentalist scientistic faith in these secular neoatheist creeds? Yes, unfortunately, there has been, and I think there are no forces on this planet more dangerous to us all than the fanaticisms of secular fundamentalism, of all the species: atheism, materialist and functional reductionism, scientific positivism, scientism, moral emotivism and relativism, and nihilism? Is there a conflict between scientism and religion? There most certainly is." Why? Because, as concluded in the introduction, the scientism and secularism of especially the neoatheists like Dennett are in effect nontheistic ersatz-religions militantly opposed to theistic religions. As correctly diagnosed by the mathematician Amir Aczel, the "New Atheism is combative, aggressive, and belligerent against people of belief [in God]. Its proponents hold that religion is evil, and they state *this [antireligious] belief* loudly and clearly. . . . And these neoatheists—Dawkins, Krauss, the late Hitchens, Harris, and Dennett—are bound together under a powerful common purpose, and [like members of any mutual admiration society] continually reinforce each other. The problem with the science described in the books and lectures of the neoatheists is that it is not pure science—the objective pursuit of knowledge about the universe. Rather, it is 'science with a purpose': the purpose of disproving the

29. Dennett, *Darwin's Dangerous Idea*, 519–20.
30. Dennett, *Darwin's Dangerous Idea*, 519–20.

existence of God."[31] This neoatheist goal is pursued so stridently and virulently that the more anti-religious views expressed by French Enlightenment figures, such as those of Baron D'Holbach and Denis Diderot, pale next to it. Some neoatheists—e.g., Richard Dawkins and Christopher Hitchens—evangelize along aggressive lines matching and perhaps even exceeding in their jangling the aggressive evangelization of some fundamentalist preachers of religion. The danger is not so much posed by religion or by atheism but by fundamentalist ideologies of any stripe that, as Feyerabend pointed out above, are "unable to understand, and unwilling to condone, different ideologies." So, I say to readers, "Beware the pushy fundamentalist ideologues of any stripe; for they vie for totalitarian control!"

Moreover, it may seem rather odd that in the case of theistic religions and other traditional ways of life, Dennett can readily tolerate their enforced zoo-like status, but that in the case of isolated Indian-Ocean islanders, he is righteously offended that their islands should be treated as a human zoo or sanctuary by anthropologists observing—and preserving—the islanders' cultures.[32] But it is not odd at all, once one considers that the promotion of personal ideological agendas by elitist intellectuals often is subject, wittingly or carelessly, to self-serving two-timing (I must admit that occasionally I have also been guilty of such lapse or sin). But however conflicted it is, can Dennett's enlightenment project, enforced as it is by scientistically weaponized science, constitute a threat to existing human cultures? Though in theory they need not be threatened, in practice they nonetheless may very well be; for as Dennett's claims—and many a practicing religionist would agree—they already show signs of being threatened.[33]

Given our current secular age, in which cultural diversity has attained something akin to celebrity status, it is ironic and chilling to consider the purely secular, scientistic neo-colonization of cultures, the anti- and miso-religious proselytizing, and the zoo-like marginalization, if not the veritable destruction so resolutely advocated by neoatheist Sam Harris, that may await religions.[34] And if we take into account the extreme scientistic sentiments expressed by the likes of Edward Wilson, Edward Slingerland, and Donald Wiebe,[35] the humanities and the arts also may suffer, short of elimination, their transformation beyond recognition, should the "enlightened" motives of secularist academics and scientists infected with the scientistic meme have their way. Here, recalling

31. Amir D. Aczel, *Why Science Does Not Disprove God* (Harper Collins Publishers, 2014), 18.

32. Dennett, *Breaking the Spell*, 324–26.

33. Dennett, *Darwin's Dangerous Idea*, 519–20.

34. For such threats, see Harris, *The End of Faith*.

35. Wilson, *Consilience*; Edward Slingerland, *What Science Offers the Humanities: Integrating Body and Culture* (Cambridge University Press, 2008); Donald Wiebe, *The Learned Practice of Religion in the Modern University* (Bloomsbury Academic, 2021).

Coyne's and Pinker's advertisements of benign scientism, a troubling note in Coyne's otherwise upbeat apologetic of scientism is his mentioning *en passant* that "[scientistically inclined] academics like Edward O. Wilson . . . have indeed argued that all areas of inquiry, including the humanities, will be not only united with science, but subsumed in it."[36] And as we saw in chapter 5 (note 38), Pinker, despite his specious plea for mutual understanding between science and the humanities and arts, holds less-than-neutral, contemptuous views of the arts. In view of such contradiction, it is no wonder that his views of benign scientism might not be taken at face value.

In the past century we have seen increasingly a turn made by Anglo-American philosophy away from a love of wisdom, the perennial philosophy, first toward the exertions of analytic and linguistic philosophy and then, in the present century, toward empirical investigations imitating the natural sciences. One should therefore not be surprised at recent proliferations of what Raymond Tallis refers to as neuromania and Darwinitis[37] that characterize such science-enchanted philosophies. Yet, adding scientistically-inspired reductive disciplines, such as neurophilosophy and neurotheology, to the humanities is, as perceptively pointed out by William Franke, another attempt to place the cart before the horse. For science is

> a quintessentially human activity, one that requires reflective awareness of its own affective and aesthetic motivations [and, as we saw in the introduction, its religious and theological ones]. So understood, science must also be aware of its moral [and religious] presuppositions in order to remain humanly responsible and culturally significant. This means that in order to be meaningfully and self-critically aware and complete, scientific knowledge has to be grounded in humanities wisdom rather than the other way around. However, in the university curriculum today, typically it is science that is accorded this foundational role of setting the standards and norms for whatever type of study and reflection. . . .[38] [Franke adds that] "there is surely a dialectic concerning the goals of human knowledge that needs to be worked over in debate between the sciences and the humanities. More than a shared conception of reality, the richness of our *different* conceptions in relating [apophatically] to the inconceivable is perhaps to be prized as the most important source of cross-fertilization. In any case, this irreducible disparity [between the sciences and the humanities] is not to be preempted or circumvented by any conception of consilience that conforms essentially to the scientific understanding of reality and human knowledge. This understanding has developed in the modern scientific age without critical awareness, and often with deliberate forgetting of the his-

36. Coyne, *Faith vs. Fact*, 198.
37. Tallis, *Aping Mankind.*
38. Franke, *On the Universality of What Is Not*, 315.

> torical conditions and [epistemological] limits of its paradigm in the much larger arc of human history.[39]

To preserve the ties to our historic past, to promote and cherish the best in the temporal continuity of cultural growth and development, and to prevent a gradual slide into a presentism and a futurism, it is this sort of deliberate forgetting that religions and the study of humanities attempt to forestall, and rightly so. For, besides the "amnesic" adumbration noted above, a scientistic conception of consilience, for example that of Edward O. Wilson,[40] also carries within it a totalitarian strain.

Currently a prime cultural trend is the protest against the shrinkage of wilderness, nature, and biodiversity. In view of this protest, should humans complacently condone living in a shrinkage of cultural diversities by their being assimilated into a scientistic high-tech monoculture? Should they allow modernity's elites like Daniel Dennett, Richard Dawkins, Edward Wilson, Steven Pinker, Edward Slingerland, and Donald Wiebe, who are afflicted with a secular scientistic fundamentalism—particularly one that pushily preaches that their enlightened way is *the* way to progress—to unleash their will to colonize or dismantle other cultural expressions and practices? Shouldn't they instead, as Paul Feyerabend and William Franke have done, at least protest, if not condemn such cultural coups? If so, why so? For the reason, I maintain, that under the guise of cultural progress, the coup's leaders advocate what at bottom is a destructive and totalitarian cultural nihilism.

Why this is so and not merely an exaggerated travesty is twofold. For one, as noted by St. Augustine, in every act of will there is a choice between *nolle* and *velle*, between nilling and willing, denying and desiring;[41] and for another, according to the philosopher Hannah Arendt, it is feasible that some type of nihilism, superficial or deep, inheres in every form of critical thinking.[42] Besides noting the danger of critical thinking in establishing a new intellectual orthodoxy that makes further thinking unnecessary,[43] Arendt offers neither what the possible dangers are nor how they vary from the trite to the profound. Her take on nihilism seems to be that it is merely a by-product of the inevitable advance

39. Franke, *On the Universality of What Is Not*, 345–46.

40. Wilson, *Consilience*.

41. Augustine, *Confessions*, 155, expressed it as follows: "The nub of the problem is to reject [*nolle*] my own will and to desire [*velle*] yours [i.e., God's]."

42. Hannah Arendt, *The Life of the Mind*, vol. 2, 89, endorses this possibility by noting that "what we commonly call 'nihilism' . . . is actually a danger inherent in the thinking activity itself. . . . All critical examinations must go through a stage of at least hypothetically negating [nilling] accepted opinions and 'values' by searching out their implications and tacit assumptions, and in this sense nihilism may be seen as an ever-present danger of thinking."

43. Arendt, *The Life of the Mind*, vol. 2, 179.

in any intellectual enterprise and seems also to be so general that it can apply not only to critical thinking in philosophy but also to all sorts of other critical thinking in the sciences, humanities, and arts. Like the version of scientism espoused by Jerry Coyne and Steven Pinker, the dangers of such a broadly applicable version of nihilism can also be given a benign veneer. Yet, consider the physicist Steven Weinberg's deep-felt grievance (see below) that from a purely scientific standpoint the existence of the universe—thus also of humans and their conduct in it—appears to be ultimately and utterly meaningless. This and similar beliefs constitute a truly profound form of nihilism arising from scientistically energized thinking concerning metaphysics, ethics, and morality. Seconding Weinberg's bleak appraisal, Richard Dawkins claims that "the universe we observe [scientifically] has precisely the properties we should expect if there is, at bottom, no design, no purpose, no evil, and no good, nothing but blind pitiless indifference."[44]

Such appraisals, if forthrightly and publicly propagated, could deeply affect the spiritual flourishing of individual and communal life in an adverse manner. Consequently, it is here that a true reckoning with scientistic nihilism's deepest consequences becomes evident from Tamler Sommers and Alex Rosenberg's observations made of the Darwinian sect of scientism.[45] They hold that Darwinist scientism, when its implications are drawn to their limit, entails more than a merely naturalist worldview in that it and other reductive versions of scientism also entail a metaphysically and morally nihilistic one. Along with Sommers and Rosenberg (as well as Coyne and Pinker), one hopes that, if moral nihilism ever attains cultural supremacy, it can be—according Sommers and Rosenberg—"nice." But what would they mean by a nice moral nihilism? They mean, as Sommers and Rosenberg further state, that "it treats morality as instrumentally useful—instrumentally useful for our nonmoral ends or perhaps the nonmoral ends of some other biological systems, such as our genes for example. . . . Nihilism can be, as one might say, 'nice,' provided that in its explaining away of ethics, it also shows that we are in fact disposed to behave nicely—to cooperate, be altruistic, show guilt and shame, anger and resentment in just the way we would if some morality were true, right, or real. *Darwinian* nihilism is the thesis that the theory of natural selection and its application to biological data explains why morality is at most an instrumentally useful illusion."[45]

But Darwinism, as pointed out by the geneticist Richard Lewontin (see my introduction, footnote 33), can too readily underwrite also the speculations made by the likes of sociobiologist Edward Wilson and his Harvard colleague,

44. Cited in Francis S. Collins, *The Language of God: A Scientist Presents Evidence for Belief* (Free Press, 2006), 195.

45. Tamler Sommers and Alex Rosenberg, "Darwin's Nihilistic Idea: Evolution and the Meaninglessness of Life," *Biology and Philosophy* 18, no. 5 (2003): 653–68.

the evolutionary psychologist Steven Pinker regarding other adaptive biological universals, such as spite and family chauvinism, tribalism, xenophobia, male dominance and superiority, all of which stimulate or aggravate morally deplorable activities and dispositions such as human warfare, sexual dominance and abuse, and idolatrous love of private property.[46] By adding to Lewontin's list racism, supremacism, imperialism, male violence, infanticide, and genocide, moral nihilism can also be very "ghastly." As Fyodor Dostoyevsky has so aptly described in several of his novels, the human will-to-power, accompanied as it is by a tendency to sin, expresses itself at the psychological level by commandeering nihilism *tout court*, the consequences of which can be downright "vile." To the service of atheists and theists alike, Alex Rosenberg, a hard-core scientistic and atheistic philosopher, has been willing to unflinchingly explore and expose the Darwinian scientistic worldview at its darker depths beyond anything that Pinker's, Coyne's, or Dennett's shilly-shally has done so far.[47] Perhaps moral nihilism is nice when confined to the cushy and abstract environs of academia; but as the last century has shown, when, like a miasma, it drifts into the public sphere outside the academy and tightens the deadly grip of a Hitler, Stalin, or Pol Pot, its consequences have been horrifically homicidal.

Darwinism as Universal Acid

The philosopher Daniel Dennett has metaphorically alchemized the theory of Darwinian evolution into a universal acid corroding and dissolving many a cherished cultural institution and tradition, including especially the religious faith practiced by Christians and other theists.[48] Unlike the complicated mathematics underlying much of fundamental physics, the basic principles underlying the "mechanics" of Darwinian evolution are relatively simple to grasp. Random genetic variations, blind to their phenotypic consequences, give rise to correspondingly blind variations of organisms' phenotypic traits that are subject to the equally mindless causal processes comprising natural selection. Organisms whose genetically endowed traits help them to withstand the winnowing process of natural selection, reproduce and pass these traits on to future generations; those that don't are destined for extinction. Less easily forthright, an implication of this conceptual framework, presumably in fatal conflict with Christian faith, is the secular worldview that humans are accidental inhabitants of a goalless cosmos, neither foreordained nor assigned a special niche in it. Accordingly, among all other species, humans just happen to have evolved along one of countless blood-stained branches of the tree of life via clueless algorith-

46. Lewontin, *Biology as Ideology*, 89–91.

47. Alex Rosenberg, *The Atheist's Guide to Reality: Enjoying Life Without Illusions* (W. W. Norton & Co., 2011).

48. Dennett, *Darwin's Dangerous Idea.*

mic processes governed entirely by natural laws. As Dawkins once described it, you and I at bottom are (quasi-autonomous) automatons, hefty robots programmed by and in the service of genes replicating to no grander end than their continuing replication.[49] Consequently, contrary to the Christian and other theistic worldviews, there is no ultimate meaning or purpose assigned to the cosmos or us in it; for the cosmos simply popped up spontaneously as it is, and past humans in it arose by pure happenstance to become what they now are. Hence, we had better brace up to these dreary and chilling realities and cope as best we can.

Is this picture of the meaninglessness of life and existence too dreary? Perhaps—but just perhaps, not. For according to the subtitle of Dennett's 1995 book, evolution does have something to say about the *meaning* of life and of the universe we inhabit. Although he offers a lengthy, dry account of the evolution of discursive meanings relevant to linguists, scientists, and philosophers, Dennett said little—and not until his closing chapter—about the *existential* and *spiritual* meanings of life and the universe, i.e., their value-laden significance to the lifeworld inhabited by enlightened scholars as well as benighted village clerks and laborers. In the final chapter, after some quasi-theological musings on Spinoza, pantheism, Nietzsche, and the affirmable magnificence of the (non-Edenic, evolutionary) Tree of Life, we find a compelling, nearly out of place, sentence: "This world is *sacred*."[50] Considering that Dennett's fellow atheist Sam Harris, the atheist philosopher Tim Crane, and the nature-religionist Chet Raymo warmly concur[51] that the world is sacred, how do they squeeze an affirmable sacred significance out of a world described by Nietzsche, by Darwinians, and by other natural scientists? To paraphrase Nietzsche,[52] how, after we have drunk up the sea and sponged—or corroded away by Dennet's universal Darwinian acid—the horizon of the meaningful and the holy, can we recover it? What underwrites holding on to meaning and sacredness? Following Nietzsche, Dennett's answer seems to be this: personal fiat, the ego's will to have it so, its wishful will-to-power. For, as we shall see below, when the Darwinian *aqua regia* is allowed to work its effects to their limits, to pervade and eat through all the meaning and sacredness of the universe and our lives in it, then both meaning and sacredness are not only dissolved but also destroyed. The source of the sacredness of the Tree of Life and of the physical cosmos that nourishes it does not inhere in either of them. As Somers and Rosenberg observe, sentiments like Dennett's instead find their source in a wishful welling up of a personal, idiosyncratic, and semi-religious craving for meaning and sacredness, and they

49. Dawkins, *The Selfish Gene.*

50. Dennett, *Darwin's Dangerous Idea*, 520.

51. Harris, *The End of Faith*, 17.

52. Friedrich Nietzsche, *The Gay Science* (Vintage Books, 1974), 181.

chasten Dennett for failing to go beyond his bathos and unflinchingly look into the abyss of Darwinian nihilism.[53]

The Tragedy of Scientistic Nihilism

Fully supporting this diagnosis are the following two sobering quotations, one from Dennett himself and a contrasting passage from another staunch foe of religion, the physicist Steven Weinberg. While heaping sacred praise on the world, Dennett more coolly declaims: "Love it or hate it, phenomena like this exhibit the heart of the power of the Darwinian idea. An impersonal, unreflective, robotic, mindless little scrap of molecular machinery is the ultimate basis of all the agency, and hence the meaning, and hence the consciousness, in the universe."[54] Include in this list of outcomes the sacredness in or ascribed to the universe, and you have an idea of how god-like a robotic scrap of molecular machinery portrayed by Dennett pretends to be. But why does the search for the basis of meaning stop at what in fact clearly is not the ultimate but instead the penultimate?[55] For if, as Dennett argues, the likes of Darwinian evolution extend not only all the way up to human culture but also all the way down to the quantum level, why not delve deeper than the impersonal, unreflective, robotic, mindless little scrap of molecular machinery and explore the mindless physical entities found at the submolecular and even the subatomic levels, as Steven Weinberg and other physicists have done?

Because, once having done so, one can juxtapose Dennett's paean to nanorobotics with the following sobering and bleak portrayal from Weinberg. Paying respects to Darwinian evolution in passing, Weinberg goes on to remark that "it is even harder to realize that this present universe has evolved from an unspeakably unfamiliar early condition, and faces a future extinction of endless cold or intolerable heat. The more the universe is comprehensible, the more it seems pointless."[56] One can translate the previous sentence as follows: The greater the purely *scientific* knowledge, understanding, and meaning of the uni-

53. Sommers and Rosenberg, "Darwin's Nihilistic Idea."

54. Dennett, *Darwin's Dangerous Idea*, 203.

55. Daniel Robinson, "Still Looking: Science and Philosophy in Pursuit of Prince Reason," in *Neuroscience & Philosophy: Brain, Mind, & Language*, ed. Maxwell Bennett et al. (Columbia University Press, 2007), 188. Robinson points out that Dennett is prone to making assertions that fall short of being philosophically rigorous when it comes to the ultimate, i.e., where the philosophic buck can no longer be passed on. Recourse to Dennett's proneness toward penultimacy also is found elsewhere in Dennett, *Breaking the Spell*, 244, where he states that the material world, as "we have seen, does perform a version of the ultimate bootstrapping trick; it creates itself *ex nihilo*; or at any rate out of something that is well-nigh indistinguishable from nothing at all." This lax, sort-of, almost, and "well-nigh" ultimacy might satisfy a for-all-intents-and-purposes pragmatist, but it smacks of sophistry instead of sound philosophy.

56. Steven Weinberg, *The First Three Minutes* (Basic Books, 1993), 154.

verse, the less *ultimate* meaning and significance appears in it. Every scientific hypothesis, claim, conclusion, or inference (e.g., "DNA strands have the structure of a double helix") is stated as a proposition that is intended to convey what is an impersonal, objective meaning. To the advantage of science, one of its criterial features is its communicating discursive meaning in unambiguous and clear ways, readily accessible to trained experts around the world.[57] But in line with Weinberg's dismal assessment, even when summed over the vast web of scientific knowledge, such meanings do not render the universe itself meaningful in the existential sense, that is, the universe and everything in it *has no point, no telos* toward which it evolves. So, from beginning to end, from the primal "Be!" that grants existence to subatomic particles, DNA molecules, miniscule viruses, humanity's admirable achievements, and the vast expanse of the heavens filled with countless stars and galaxies, the A and Ω, the *arche* and the *telos* of the cosmos and our lives, when exposed as they are to Dennett's universal scientistic acid, leave at best a scant stick-figure likeness of the "Big Picture." From a thoroughly atheistic and scientistic perspective, what we can point to is that the scientistic ransom of the meaning and significance of our existence as well as that of the universe we inhabit is ultimately paid not, as Dennett claims, by nanorobotics; but instead, as Weinberg correctly intuited, it is paid by *nothing.*

Weinberg is one of those sober naturalists described by John Haught in the epigraph introducing part 2 of this book. So, how can Weinberg's paradoxical meld of hope and despair deal with his—as Miguel de Unamuno aptly calls it—tragic sense of life?[58] Weinberg goes on to offer a semblance of an answer in the following: "But if there is no solace in the fruits of our research, there is at least some consolation in the research itself. . . . The effort to understand the universe is one of the few things that lifts human life a little above the level of farce, and gives it some of the grace of tragedy."[59] To such rare and rarified sources of solace one can perhaps add several other pursuits such as productive scholarly research, and creative endeavors in the performing, literary, and visual arts, engineering sciences, and technological research and development. However, since these are all limited to elite classes of individuals who are especially gifted in their vocations, one wonders how and where the clerk checking and rechecking his accounting, the farm laborer stooping to pick strawberries to meet his daily quota, and the worker in her humdrum repetitiveness on assembly lines or in outsourced sweatshops, find their solace. Here again, it is Christianity that offers far wider-embracing spiritual and practical answers, as it has for centuries, by providing spiritual as well as physical sustenance not only to the priv-

57. Hutchinson, *Monopolizing Knowledge.*

58. Miguel de Unamuno, *The Tragic Sense of Life* (Dover Publications, 1954).

59. Weinberg, *The First Three Minutes,* 154.

ileged few but also to the many who through no fault of their own are poor, uneducated, infirm, diseased, hungry, imprisoned, and otherwise deprived or societally marginalized.

A person like Dennett with a stolid constitution may be satisfied or resigned to the meanings afforded by dwelling in the philosophic or scientific tents set up on the outskirts of the ultimate. In fact, doing science is to dwell in them; for a scientist's good fortune is the fact that, not invariably, yet often enough, "on discoveries made, new problems are laid." It is the experience of most scientists that nearly any productive scientific research project can typically pose new questions, puzzles, and scientific problems to address and solve, and therefore it may well be a never-ending adventure, a pursuit of ever-elusive ultimate solutions. It is hard to imagine the scientific pursuit otherwise. We are finite beings blessed (or cursed) with a taste for the transcendent, the infinite, and the eternal. The downside of scientific research is that few of its fruits are of eternal—in the sense of everlasting—validity. Science thrives not only on what we currently know but also on what we do not yet know and on a tentativeness, if not doubt, about what we claim to know. The abilities to live with a great deal of ignorance and with a good measure of uncertainty are, as the physicist Richard Feynman put it, among the foremost virtues of a good scientist, virtues of intellectual humility that help many an unpretentious scientist to deal with frustrations and disappointments during his or her adventuresome pursuit of knowledge.[60] So, while musical compositions (think of Mozart's sonatas, Beethoven's late quartets) may, and logical and mathematical proofs (think of Gödel's proofs or of Fermat's last proof) do, partake of the eternal, scientific theories and findings are ever provisional, reinterpretable, modifiable, and ultimately dispensable when new findings and better theories arise. Moreover, the works of many scientists enjoy no longevity at all; once published, many are very rarely, or even never, cited. That is a built-in and somewhat sobering feature of scientific progress.

Spiting the Tragedy: A Blind and Blithe Buoyancy

Notwithstanding this rather pessimistic assessment, one can of course deal with the deeply troubling tragic sense of life by ignoring, suppressing, or denying it—by simply opting for optimism, as sunny naturalists are wont to do. Throughout his recent book, *Until the End of Time*, the string theorist Brian Greene exudes such an oblivious and sunny optimism in the name of science, claiming—in line with the physicist Freeman Dyson's similar reasoning, that "our entire chain of reasoning is forged in optimism,"[61] even as Greene explains at

60. Richard P. Feynman, *The Meaning of It All: Thoughts of a Citizen-Scientist* (Basic Books, 1998).

61. Brian Greene, *Until the End of Time: Mind, Matter, and Our Search for Meaning in an Evolving Universe* (Vintage Books, 2021), 277.

length throughout his book that the ultimate fate of everything in the cosmos looks very bleak—at least to a pessimistic and sober naturalist like Steven Weinberg. Yet, stoutly believing that physics will eventually explain everything in our world that there is to explain, Greene, outdoing the scientistic exuberance of Edward Wilson, even anticipates "that we will one day explain consciousness with nothing more than a conventional understanding of the particles constituting matter and the physical laws that govern them. That would yield its own variety of revolution, establishing a virtually unlimited hegemony for physical law, reaching arbitrarily far into the outer world of objective reality and arbitrarily deep into the inner world of subjective experience."[62] This patently hubristic optimism is further exemplified by taking recourse to the hypothetical existence of a multiverse made of infinitely many worlds, all of which entail "a peculiar conclusion; the reality that you and I and everyone else experiences is happening out there in other regions—in other universes—over and over again. Modify that reality in any manner that is not strictly forbidden by the laws of physics . . . and it is also out there, over and over again. [And then, overwhelmed by his optimism, Greene continues that it] tickles the mind to fathom realms where alternate realities play—Lee Harvey Oswald misfires, Claus von Stauffenberg succeeds, James Earl Ray doesn't. [In addition to the multiverse hypothesis,] quantum aficionados will recognize a similarity to the so-called Many Worlds interpretation of quantum physics, which envisions that every outcome allowed by it takes place in its own separate universe."[63] Greene's overwhelming optimism apparently blinds him to the fact that the existence of multiverses or a multitude of quantum worlds raises grievous ethical and moral problems. For as noted by the physicist Bernard Haisch (see below, chapter 9, note 35), one can equally be far, far less tickled, in fact be horrified, by the existence of universes in which one turns out to be a serial killer, or for there to be something more diabolical than the Holocaust that plays out again and again its horrific twists in a macabre Nietzschean eternal recurrence. So much for the sunny and sober sides of naturalistic thinking. As Jerry Coyne, Steven Pinker, and Brian Greene have done, one can whitewash and thus render "nice" and sunny one side of the naturalistic coin inspired by scientism; but, as pointed out by Sommers and Rosenberg above, one cannot thereby eliminate the through-and-through spiritual darkness of its existential and moral abyss.

Scientism, Scientific Method, and Truth

At the core of modern science is not only a body of theoretical and empirical knowledge but also a method, a technique, of acquiring such knowledge. Hence,

62. Greene, *Until the End of Time*, 120.
63. Greene, *Until the End of Time*, 307.

I can agree partly with Jerry Coyne when he says that science is "*a method for understanding how the universe (matter, our bodies, behavior, the cosmos, and so on) actually works.* Science is a set of tools, refined over hundreds of years, for getting answers [to questions] about nature. It is the set of methods we cite when we're asked 'How do you *know* that?' after making claims such as 'Birds evolved from dinosaurs' or 'The genetic material is not a protein, but a nucleic acid.'"[64] I partially agree with Coyne's definition because Coyne foregrounds science as method, while saying little abouts science as a body of knowledge summarized in theories that, if fruitful, raise the prospect of obtaining ever-novel empirical findings. His definition relies too heavily on the utilitarian/instrumental/methodological nature of science. Implicit in Coyne's definition, and clearly pointed out by Bernard Lonergan, is that doing successful empirical science indeed relies on clear empirical observations that in turn rely on the use of correct methods. But what is additionally required is the *discovery* of fruitful theoretical ideas; and these, as Lonergan additionally explained, emerge through creative imaginative insights that lead to deeper levels of understanding of the world we inhabit.[65] It is ultimately the deeper levels of understanding that make science a body of finely-honed cognitive gems as well as an archive of empirical observations and a set of methodological tools. That said, one can also agree with Coyne that naturalism *has become* a "guiding principle of science. Its use in all scientific studies is called *methodological naturalism* or—because it's used to explain observations—*methodological empiricism*."[66] (I stressed the phrase "has become" because methodological naturalism/empiricism is of relatively recent provenance, increasingly accepted among scientists only since the middle of the 19th century, in large part due to—especially in biology—the influence of Darwin's naturalized theory of evolution. (The relevance of this historic evolution of methodological naturalism/empiricism to David Alcalde's above claim [see note 11 above] that science is *inherently* scientistic should be obvious.) Coyne furthermore characterizes science as a way to find *truths* about the universe, and he underwrites this claim with what seemingly is the correspondence theory truth, the conformity of knowledge claims to facts or data derived from empirical observations.

Agreeing with Coyne on these points, one can nevertheless disagree with some of his other statements. To list two relevant ones: (i) he asserts, as does Richard Dawkins and Victor Stenger,[67] that existence claims about God are

64. Coyne, *Faith vs. Fact*, 28.

65. Bernard Lonergan, *Insight: A Study into Human Understanding* (University of Toronto Press, 1992).

66. Coyne, *Faith vs. Fact*, 92.

67. Dawkins, *The God Delusion*; Victor J. Stenger, *God: The Failed Hypothesis* (Prometheus Books, 2007).

clearly *empirical* claims, claims that require some kind of observational evidence; and (ii) despite the guiding principle of methodological naturalism, again agreeing with Dawkins, he claims that "nothing in science prohibits us from considering supernatural explanations."[68] The first point, an example of scientistic overreach, was already critiqued and dismissed in the introduction. It merits adding, however, that requiring that it be empirical, observational evidence that ultimately decides the truth or falsity of the "God hypothesis" already introduces a bias favoring science, since it does not allow consideration of evidence based on personal subjective experience, on solely the use of reason, or on supernatural, non-empirical revelation. It is only when, for example, one reads scriptural revelations literally, like biblical and scientistic literalists do, rather than analogically that such supernatural claims somehow qualify as "hypotheses" subject to "scientific" considerations. Regarding Coyne's second point, one can agree that nothing prohibits scientists from considering supernatural explanations, since methodological naturalism prohibits us not from *considering* such explanations but from *invoking them* to account for natural phenomena. But if atheist biologists like Dawkins, Stenger, and Coyne allow themselves, in the name of science, to consider hypothetical supernatural explanations, then why, again in the name of science, should creationists or proponents of intelligent design (ID) be vigorously prohibited by their philosophical and scientific critics from also considering such explanations? One does not need to subscribe to creationism or ID to see the patent selectivity and inconsistency inherent in Dawkins's and Coyne's antitheistic ploys.[69] Hence, insofar as ID-science comports well with theism, it could be argued that theism currently provides as good an, if not a better, explanation of several phenomena, such as the irreducibility and the hyper-ubiquity of consciousness, than respectively metaphysical physicalism and panpsychism do.[70]

One could go on to list several other questionable claims and downright bloopers made by many an atheist scientist. But what I shall simply do for now is to suggest that the very nature of the sciences needs reconsideration in view of its evolving nature. Both science and religion have evolved culturally and will

68. Coyne, *Faith vs. Fact*, 94.

69. I and other scientists, e.g., the particle physicist John Polkinghorne, the mathematician John Lennox, and the nuclear physicist Ian Hutchinson, to name just a few, are Christian theists, and as such we are creationists, in the sense that we believe it is God, the Uncaused Cause, who caused the physical universe to come into being, although as scientists we fully acknowledge the causal efficacy of inner-worldly natural processes. Here the ID-sympathetic computer scientist David Gelernter, accessed August 8, 2021, https://www.hoover.org/research/mathematical-challenges-darwins-theory-evolution-david-berlinski-stephen-meyer-and-david, notes the starkly large improbabilities attending the standard neo-Darwinian versions of protein evolution, let alone that of entire organisms.

70. Cottingham, *In Search of the Soul*; Meyer, *Return of the God Hypothesis*.

continue to do so.[71] Even now there are calls to free the pursuit of truth from currently entrenched practical limits and methodological strictures imposed in the name of science.[72] And as we saw, already over four decades ago Feyerabend explored and critiqued the role of scientific method,[73] especially when it overreaches into cultural domains other than science. Feyerabend, trained in physics and the philosophy and history of science, well understood that methodological naturalism, a feature of currently accepted scientific method, was a contingent, historically emergent convention rather than necessary attribute of scientific practice (more on this topic in chapter 8 below). For it cannot be denied that the earliest empirical and theoretical scientists—Copernicus, Kepler, Galileo, Newton, and Boyle, to name just a few—were guided and inspired in their research by a thoroughly transcendent, supernatural, and theistic worldview rather than a thoroughly immanent, natural, and antitheistic one. As we also saw above, it is Coyne's, Stenger's, and Dawkins's idiosyncratic methodological overreach into the issue of God's existence and his attributes—issues crucial to the Christian faith and properly addressed by philosophers and theologians—that cannot be justified by science, since science aims to attain truth and knowledge concerning the natural entities in the universe but not supernatural ones transcending the natural domain. A misappropriation of science's epistemology and methodological naturalism by a metaphysical, scientistic, and ersatz-religious worldview attempts, but fails, to justify such overreach.

What Truth, if Any?

Above we also noted that key notions in science, as well as other research disciplines, are "truth" and "fact," which have highly malleable meanings. To reduce ambiguity in their meaning, Jerry Coyne consults the *Oxford English Dictionary*,[74] noting that "truth" is defined as "conformity with fact; agreement with reality; accuracy, correctness, verity (of statement or thought)."[75] And if we look up "fact," we'll find it's defined as "something that has really occurred or is actually the case; something certainly known to be of this character; hence a particular truth known by actual observation or authentic testimony, as opposed to what is merely inferred, or to a conjecture or fiction; a datum of experience,

71. Steve Fuller, *Science* (Acumen Publishing Ltd., 2010); Susanna Schellenberg, "Experience and Evidence," *Mind* 122, no. 487 (2013): 699–747; Rodney Stark, *Discovering God: The Origins of the Great Religions and the Evolution of Belief* (Harper Collins Publishers, 2007).

72. Fuller, *Science*; Philip Sheldrake, *Spirituality: A Very Short Introduction* (Oxford University Press, 2012).

73. Feyerabend, *Against Method*.

74. *Oxford Dictionary of English Grammar* (Oxford University Press, 2014) under "truth" and "fact."

75. Coyne, *Faith vs. Fact*, 29.

as distinguished from the conclusions that may be based on it." Fine and good. But as a first response, since the above definitions hinge on what is meant by "real" and "reality," one might want to know what is meant by them. If here we again consult the *Oxford English Dictionary*, not much help is offered. We end up with definitions such as "The state of things as they actually exist, as opposed to an idealistic or notional idea of them." Then we head for the definition of "actual," which is: "existing in fact; real." We are back where we started. And then, to get out of this linguistic loop, we might perhaps go on to the definition of "exist," which is "have objective reality or being." So now the whole enterprise has become somewhat like the pre-Copernican, Ptolemaic account of the solar system; only here, instead of planets, definitions course around each other in cycles and epicycles.

Stopping here to catch our breath, let's proceed to a more philosophic—rather than vernacular—notion of reality that applies, beyond physical, to general realism. It is defined as follows: "*a*, *b*, and *c* and so on exist, and the fact that they exist and have properties such as *F-ness*, *G-ness*, and *H-ness* is (apart from mundane empirical dependencies of the sort sometimes encountered in everyday life) independent of anyone's beliefs, linguistic practices, conceptual schemes, and so on."[76] This definition would include not only tangible or measurable entities in the physical world but, for instance, also entities such as a specific number, say 4, since numbers like 4 exist as abstract intelligible entities that have properties such as being integral, positive, even or odd, prime or nonprime, all of which are "independent of anyone's beliefs, linguistic practices, conceptual schemes, and so on." Yet despite being abstract, numbers can be concretely instantiated in countless natural phenomena. Otherwise, how could one know as a fact that the group of Fuji apples in the bowl on the kitchen counter consists of four instances of a Fuji apple? One does so if the abstract concept of fourness finds a fitting correspondence in the sensorially ascertainable numerical distinctness of the apples in the bowl.

Such accord between concept and percept comports well with the notion of scientific truth, as the above dictionary definition emphasizes, that places priority on truth as *conformity* of mind with fact, as *agreement* between the intellect's judgment and perceived reality. Implicit in this definition is what is known in philosophy as the correspondence theory of truth.[77] Although the theory is problematic, it nevertheless is very successfully applied when a scientific theory or one of its implications is empirically appraised. Basically, what

76. Alexander Miller, "Realism," in *The Stanford Encyclopedia of Philosophy*, ed. Edward N. Zalta (Winter 2021), https://plato.stanford.edu/archives/win2021/entries/realism.

77. Miller, "Realism"; Marian David, "The Correspondence Theory of Truth," in *The Stanford Encyclopedia of Philosophy*, ed. Edward N. Zalta (Summer 2022), https://plato.stanford. edu/archives/sum2022/entries/truth-correspondence.

the correspondence theory says is that a scientific claim concerning some worldly entity or property is validated if the claim finds agreement with a corresponding observation of the predicted entity or property.

As noted above, this sort of scientific truth does not exhaust the scope of all truths. There are after all truths in other, nonempirical investigative realms, in the realm of mathematics and logic, for instance. Here the correspondence theory of truth is cashed in for a coherence *cum* consistency theory, according to which a given assertion does not contradict other assertions existing within the same coherently integrated conceptual system. Even the theory of biological evolution relies for its truth on its coherence and consistency with what is known in a wide array of other scientific disciplines. And what of the truths in the realms of art, poetry, and music? Are there any at all to speak of? Along with many scientists and scholars, one can maintain that truths are to be found in extra-scientific realms also, and with methods appropriate to each of them. In case the reader is skeptical, let's pose the following question: Did a serious and dedicated artist like Vincent van Gogh, a composer like Ludwig van Beethoven, or a poet like T. S. Eliot stake a claim on what constitutes reality that was affirmed by the evidence of their works? If the answer is "no," then either one is a borderline philistine or else the substance expressed in these works is nonreal, mere illusion, since they merely titillate our brains' dopaminergic reward systems, as Steven Pinker would have it. If the answer is "yes," then in these creative arts there is truth to be found in a coherent and consistent correspondence between their works and a world far richer than science alone can describe or explain. And we could venture to say that what applies to the arts equally applies to the theological truths inscribed in the Christian faith.

This chapter began with reference to de Lubac's assessment of antitheistic humanism. It seem appropriate, therefore, to offer an appraisal of all that was discussed above by returning to de Lubac's in-depth portrayal of the drama of atheist humanism. In it, of his many poignant remarks, two additional ones also apply to the drama of atheistic scientism. In the chapter entitled "The Search for a New Man," de Lubac recaps its contents as follows:

> Scientific intoxication, ontological rebellion, noetic [i.e., epistemological] reduction: such are, in sum, the three temptations by which the progress of our age is accompanied, temptations to which it has largely succumbed and which have opened the spiritual crisis in which we are struggling. Such are the three elements that, combining to have an effect in all of life, form what could be called the *organizing scientism*. [And then he adds that] the one who avoids a false conclusion does not come any closer to the truth if, at the same time, he closes himself from understanding the problem himself. . . .[78] Now is that not precisely what we are seeing happen?

78. De Lubac, *The Drama of Atheist Humanism*, 422.

> The whole of reality, of which man is an integral part, surrenders something of its meaning only to a loving and disinterested gaze. How could it be *understood* by someone who is seeking only to *explain* the phenomena with a view to submitting them to his manufacturing ends? Hypertrophied in one of its functions, human reason is thus, on the other hand, miserably atrophied.[79]

One of the "manufactured ends" to which scientific explanation is submitted can be, if some scientistic atheists have their way, the destruction of religion. What they seem to forget in carrying out their Promethean agenda, however, is that the proper task of science qua science is to explain the natural entities in our world, not to interpret it so as render the semblance of a universally comprehensible worldview, one that has been subjected to and severely damaged by—to use Daniel Dennett's phrase—the "universal acid" of scientism, a particular version of which is Darwinism.

The search for truth is as important to Christianity as it is to science. The drama that recently has been played out by the scientistic atheism and religionist theism is fortunately limited to the extreme fringes of atheism (e.g., the misotheistic neoatheists) and of theism (e.g., the ardent young-earth creationists). Both vie for an unbending universal, if not totalitarian, authority regarding the facticity and interpretation of scientific findings and theories. The "dramatic" choices offered by the two are, on the one hand, an abysmal epistemic and ontological naturalism that at its depths fails to find any existential and spiritual meaning, and, on the other, a rigid religionism whose strategy is to offer an equally unsatisfactory choice based, as it is, on a risibly twisted, tangled, and ad hoc reasoning. By not acceding to such extreme fringe elements of biblical literalism, a moderate Christianity's accommodation of scientifically validated facts and theories reflects a desire to accept theologically relevant truths whatever their source or cost. And potential costs there are; for, as expressed above by Stephen Weinberg, science's findings and theories can support a tragic interpretion of the world, a world vacated of any ultimate meaning, and in which we find little if any consolation for our finite, dispensible existence. However, Christianity is not a tragic drama; instead, in the finality of its eschatological promise, it is a tragicomedy.

Despite or because of this, rather than truncating theological, historical, spiritual, moral, and aesthetic truths as well as the truths of the natural sciences, now and in the future Christianity can welcome them into its comprehensive space that accommodates significantly more than the dimensionally limited space of reality laid out by scientistic atheism or creationist literalism. Toward the end of the introduction, we noted that, in contrast to science, Christianity

79. De Lubac, *The Drama of Atheist Humanism*, 424.

accommodates a most important aspect of our existence, the nonending quest, not for the ever-provisional meanings acquired by science, but for truly ultimate meaning. In the context of the present chapter, it is a meaning in which, according to religious scholar David Bentley Hart, even the stark contrast between an all-good and all-just God and the senseless suffering of innocent creatures is ultimately resolvable.[80] And therefore, in its ultimacy, it is in stark contrast to Dennett's claim that the ultimate source of meaning is an impersonal, unreflective, robotic, and mindless little scrap of molecular machinery, a machinery that has furthered, yes, the creation of new life forms, yet not without dealing out great creaturely suffering and death throughout the rather bloody course of biological evolution.

Despite his and others' muscular neoatheism, Dennett to his credit (see note 54 above) acknowledges the important connection between meaning and consciousness, which in turn points to meaning and consciousness as constituents of the lifeworld that humans inhabit. Without the *reality* of consciousness, we cannot seek and discover meaning in our and the world's existence. As rational, knowledge-seeking beings, we become consciously aware by way of many daily activities of our goal-directedness, and through it there arises also the awareness of, and the concern and quest for, an ultimate goal that endows our existence with correspondingly ultimate meaning, a telos to which, atheists notwithstanding, humans are called to dedicate their desires, energies, and efforts. As was noted in Part 1, since humans conduct science, their conscious minds are also necessary for achieving even its limited goals. And since science is the pursuit of truth and knowledge about the universe we inhabit, one of its prime goals—toward which its research is driven by the hope or promise of finding ultimate scientific meaning—is the yet undiscovered grand unifying theory of physics, which would underwrite our understanding of the physical basis of the world's natural phenomena. And so, human consciousness, without which also religious experiences and theological study would not exist, allows us to experientially encounter the Grand Unifier conferring meaning on all that is—including human science.

80. See David Bentley Hart, "The Devil's March: Creation *ex nihilo*, the Problem of Evil and a Few Dostoyevskian Meditations," in Anderson and Bockmuehl, *Creation ex nihilo*, 2018.

PART 3

Beyond the Atheistic Religion of Scientism

Was it really the sciences that bear the main responsibility for the origin of modern atheism? Or was it what religion did with the sciences, as [the Jesuit] Michael Buckley argued? After all, to the great pioneers of the physical sciences, Galileo, Kepler, and Newton, religion and science had appeared more than compatible. For Galileo, the Bible and physics merely spoke a different language. Kepler went even further and declared science a religious complement to Scripture. The latter is the tongue of God, the former the finger of God. According to Newton, science supports religion, by establishing a "fundamental religion" as ground for divine revelation of Scripture.

The real problem, according to Buckley, was that religion came to rely on scientific conclusions, thereby indicating that it possessed no resources of its own to defend itself. It thereby traded all that was specific and personal in the religious experience for the impersonal conclusions of modern physical cosmology.

Louis Dupré, *Religion and the Rise of Modern Culture*, pp. 48–49

Nothing is more dangerous than a religion that claims to have outdistanced reason; it can only lead to fanaticism, illuminism, obscurantism; it is lost in a jungle of superstition. Above all, it runs the risk of being an idle solution. Recourse to the supernatural easily turns into an escapist's paradise. It claims to find mystery where there may only be ignorance, and thus to justify the positivist critic for whom religion corresponds to a prescientific stage of thought. But the true religious mystery is quite different; it is concerned with what cannot be explained in any other way. Yet there is a danger of confusing the two regions. The function of scientific criticism is precisely that of clearing up this confusion.

Jean Daniélou, *God and the Ways of Knowing*, p. 47

CHAPTER 8

Scientism's Transition to Technoscientism

Atheistic scientism is a recent historical phenomenon. Like most other scientists living in the 16th and 17th centuries, the founders of modern physical astronomy such as Nicolas Copernicus, Galileo Galilei, Johannes Kepler, and Isaac Newton were solidly in the theistic fold, as were, among the 18th-century founders of modern chemistry, the French and British chemists Antoine Lavoisier and Robert Boyle. However, during the 18th century a revolutionary change in philosophic outlook occurred, away from a world of unshakable faith to one of increasing doubt, skepticism, agnosticism, and antireligious atheism, all of which marked especially the French Enlightenment. Modern atheistic scientism has its roots there.

Recalling from chapter 4 that science and technology have formed a happy, mutually supportive union, a union that is aptly known as technoscience, we shall see below that the more recent sect of the Enlightenment's scientism has become a very modern atheistic technoscientism, the belief among some scientists and technophiles that the combination of science and technology is sufficient for explaining and addressing humanity's concerns at the material, cultural, social, economic, political, and spiritual levels of existence. We shall explore how the Enlightenment was influenced by the advent of the modern period in the late Renaissance, which in turn was influenced by the still earlier union of the Promethean and Gnostic myths.

From Scientism to Technoscientism

How has modern technoscientism evolved from scientism? To answer this question, we need to distinguish between what is often referred to as speculative, basic, or pure science on the one hand, and practical or applied science on the other. Modern science is a way of discovering, explaining, and knowing the structure and workings of our natural world and our universe. And for many scientists, including myself, our primary interest or motivation in doing science is to get to know the *what* and the *how* of our natural world and our universe, simply for the sake of understanding them at a deeper, more basic level. Whether or not that knowledge and understanding has any practical applications is of secondary importance. When the scientifically acquired knowledge bears fruit in applications that address various mundane or urgent societal concerns, the gratification of the pure scientist may stimulate and further his or her efforts in doing basic research. Applied science, in contrast, deals with taking what is current scientific knowledge and applying it to solve practical problems. For instance, throughout my career as an academic research psychologist, I was interested in acquiring a basic understanding of the what and the how underlying visual cognition, without wondering if that understanding had any practical applications. In contrast, a scientist working in a university's school of optometry is interested in alleviating visual deficits in patients by investigating how the findings of basic visual research can be applied practically to the development of *techniques* for treating and improving the visual capabilities of individuals afflicted with various vision problems. Similar pure–applied research distinctions can be made in all other sciences.

Let's not forget from above that advances in applied scientific research, by promoting technological innovations, can, in turn, advance pure scientific research. Again, taking as an example my field of visual cognition and neuroscience, the use of brain scanning technology such as positron emission tomography (PET) and functional magnetic resonance imaging (fMRI), the developments of both resting on basic research in quantum physics, has proved immensely useful in medical diagnosis and in the equally basic and applied neuroscientific research of visual cognition. So, one answer to the above question as to how technoscientism has evolved from scientism is another question: Is it a wonder that technology and science, like two partners in a marriage, are united interdependently?

A Foreshortened Historic Introduction to Enlightenment Scientism

It is now believed that the evolution of the hominin species began with the upright locomotion of *Australopithecus afarensis* on the African savannah about 3.2 Mya and culminated stagewise in the appearance of our species, *homo sapiens*, about 300 Kya. The upright hominid body freed the hands around 2 Mya, making them available for stone tool making in *homo habilis* and, about 1 Mya, for controlled use of fire in *homo erectus*. It is important to note that although *homo habilis* and *homo erectus*, unlike modern scientists, had no explicit knowledge of the principles and laws governing the physical world, they no doubt had an intuitive, implicit knowledge of how to apply them. Much later in human prehistory, the more complex symbolic mental functions of *homo sapiens* became manifest, starting around 100 Kya, via linguistic and artistic skills; and much later, around 12 Kya, these functions were applied to agriculture and the development of agrarian societies. The discovery of agriculture may have marked a major transition, on a massive scale, from using technologies merely *to exploit what was already available* in nature, such as fire, to deliberately *acting into* and thus *altering* nature. A feasible scenario of this action into nature was accomplished by controlled burning of large areas of wilderness and then converting these burnt-off expanses of land into arable acreage used to plant and raise a variety of crops. Next to this acreage, groups of individuals created civilized settlements consisting of family dwellings, granaries, and other storage facilities, temples devoted to ceremonial celebrations and the worship of gods, and administrative structures from which priests and other select leaders issued and enforced rules of civic order. In these settled communities, artisans refined existing trades such as woodworking and pottery, and discovered new ones such as metal casting, smithing, wheelwrighting, writing, and accounting—all the way to modern technologies applied to the biomedical sciences, space explorations, and artificial intelligence (AI).

Viewed from a historic perspective, the upright posture of the human body freed its hands to become the preeminent manipulator of the objects, processes, and forces found in the natural world. In the 17th century, this manipulative view of the human body was explicitly laid out by Rene Descartes, in his *Traité de L'Homme* (*Treatise on Man*), in which he posited that anatomically the human body was merely a machine that could act into nature.[1] Within Descartes's mind-body dualism, the human soul, which supposedly controlled the mechanics of the body, was not subject to the mechanically deterministic principles governing the body. However, only a century later, the French Enlightenment figure La Mettrie dispensed with the Cartesian soul; and, within the monist and materialist worldview expressed in his treatise *L'Homme Machine* (*Man a Machine*), he argued that the soulless human being was nothing other than its physically governed mechanical body.[2] From this reductive perspective, everything in the world was in the last analysis reducible to matter in motion, physically determining not only the interior contents of the human mind but

1. In Descartes's own words: "I suppose the body to be nothing but a statue or machine made of earth, which God forms with the explicit intention of making it as much as possible like us." See Section 2.1, *The Treatise of Man*, of Gert-Jan Lokhorst, "Descartes and the Pineal Gland," in *The Stanford Encyclopedia of Philosophy*, ed. Edward N. Zalta (Winter 2021), https://plato.stanford.edu/archives/win2021/entries/pineal-gland.

2. To quote La Mettrie, "But since all the faculties of the soul depend to such a degree on the proper organization of the brain and of the whole body, that apparently they are but this organization itself, the *soul is clearly an enlightened machine*" (emphasis added). Accessed on January 6, 2022, https://www.gutenberg.org/files/52090/52090-h/52090-h.htm#pb128. The reductive mechanical view of mind and soul has prevailed to this day among materialist, behaviorist, and functionalist philosophers and scientists such as Danniel Dennet and Richad Dawkins. To update this view, Dennett considers the human mind not so much an enlightened machine as a chemo-electric one running complex algorithmic programs, and soul is nothing but an organized agglomeration of otherwise stupid, mindless micro-robots. In Dawkins's view, a human is a lumbering robot serving, and controlled by, selfish genes. Similar views are espoused by numerous neuroscientists and cognitive psychologists.

also its exteriorized technological products. This view of the world as a causally closed mechanical system had no need of God's presence. We see here an explicit example of a burgeoning atheistic scientism that was adopted by several other prominent thinkers of the French Enlightenment.

Despite this religiously barren picture of the natural world, the enlightened view held that scientific and technological reasoning could be deployed as intellectual and practical tools for bettering the material and spiritual estate of mankind, a view that had been taken for granted and espoused two centuries earlier by the British jurist and thinker Francis Bacon in his *Novum Organum*. It was subsequently adopted and propagated by modernist thinkers, especially, as noted, those who inaugurated the Enlightenment, as a way of liberating mankind not only from the unenlightened "medieval" religious, cultural, and social impediments to the use of reason and science but also from the constraints that a mechanized nature placed on humanity's progress.[3] And the physical and natural world, theoretically viewed by scientists as made of autonomous, self-regulating mechanisms, had, à la the French scientist Pierre Simon Laplace, no need of the God hypothesis to explain how they worked. This exclusionary ploy was adopted by most subsequent scientists as a leading methodological principle: all newly discovered objects and processes in the natural world must be explained without recourse to supernatural influences but instead only by other known natural objects, properties, and processes. From a scientific standpoint, everything stays or plays out within the closed causal nexus of nature. Here, as was noted above, God is again evacuated not only from the physical world of nature but also from the explanatory world of natural science.

Accordingly, at not only an explanatory but also a practical level, the gap left by a noninterventionist God was to be filled by humans whose ingenuity and toil incrementally intervened into nature's ability to regulate itself. Likewise, humanity, now also seen as autonomous and self-regulating, had, à la the deists, agnostics, and atheists of the 18th and 19th centuries, no longer a need for God's role in matters human. How humans ought to conduct themselves privately and socially was a question left to human will and reason. Along with not having to answer to God or to Church, humans—so the more radically enlightened scientists and philosophes of the 18th century thought—were no longer left hapless

3. The Enlightenment period of modernity spans two centuries and, beginning in the late 17th century, includes the thinker John Locke; 18th-century figures include David Hume, the French philosophes (e.g. Voltaire, Denis Diderot, and Jean-Jacques Rousseau), Benjamin Franklin, Thomas Jefferson, Immanuel Kant, Jeremy Bentham; its most notable 19th-century representative is John Stuart Mill. The spectrum of the Enlightenment was broad; England, the Continental regions, and the Americas each had their varied, nationally colored expressions. Contrary to what many believe, deists, agnostics, and atheists did not wholly "own the Enlightenment." Christian intellectual movements spanning the 18th and 19th centuries also were part of the Enlightenment.

and helpless in the face of nature's forces and constraints. From now on, the constraints imposed by nature on humans would be loosened by harnessing and controlling its forces with the aid of science. All this would be done in honor of the goddess of progress. Together with the Enlightenment's installation of the goddess of reason and her handmaiden, science, humanity would thus be freed from historically traditional and "outmoded" beliefs and practices. It was hoped that the Enlightenment would give humans increasingly powerful intellectual and technological tools to control and steer nature's powers toward useful purposes, with the bonus side effect of limiting, if not eliminating, the role of divine powers. While earlier scientific innovators like Kepler, Galileo, Newton, and Boyle ascribed to a belief that God's powers superintended those of nature, the more deistically and atheistically inclined scientists and philosophers of the Enlightenment adopted a methodological naturalist view of scientific practice, which eventually eliminated supernatural influence from any explanations of empirically observable phenomena.

A Deeper Historical Look at Modernity's Enlightenment Project

Whence this heightened expression of humanity's insistent but ever-thwarted mastery over nature and the unhinging from prior sociocultural traditions that defined the aims and limits of human ways of living? To answer these questions, my readings led me to focus, for a start, on two related sources: the striving to realize the Promethean and the Gnostic myths. The relation between the Promethean and Gnostic myths, in Eric Voegelin's words, can be summarized as follows:

> Prometheus [one of the Titans] is riveted to a rock by the sea. Below on the strip of beach stands Hermes [the messenger god] looking up at him. The fettered Prometheus gives his bitterness free reign, Hermes tries to calm him and urges moderation. Then, Prometheus crams his impotence and rebellion into the line [taken from Aeschylus's *Prometheus Bound*] . . . : "In a word, I hate all gods." But the line is not a part of a monologue. At this outbreak of hatred, the messenger of the gods replies admonishingly: "It appears you have been stricken with no small madness. . . ." The soul's rebellion against the order of the cosmos, hatred of the gods, and the revolt of the Titans are not, to be sure, unheard of in Hellenic myth. But the Titanomachia ends with the victory of Jovian justice (*dike*), and Prometheus is fettered. The revolutionary reversal of the [fettered] symbol—dethronement of the gods, the victory of Prometheus—lies beyond classical culture; it is the work of Gnosticism.[4]

4. Eric Voegelin, *Modernity Without Restraint*, vol. 5 (University of Missouri Press, 2000), 269–70.

Related accounts of the historic ties between the Promethean rebellious hate of the gods and Gnosticism can be found also in Albert Camus's *The Rebel*, where he discusses the roots of what he calls "metaphysical rebellion," a form of rebellion that appears in clear, crystallized form only at the end of the 18th century,[5] a time, not coincidentally, at which the Enlightenment finds its most radical feet. This radicalized metaphysical rebellion, against a tyrannical divine being who condoned humanity's exile into a world of pain and suffering, was subsequently given worldly expression, as Augusto Del Noce notes in his *The Crisis of Modernity*,[6] in the close relation between Gnosticism and the political violence—which was justified, paradoxically, not by improving humanity's spiritual lot but instead in the name of improving its earthly and bodily lot—that was wrought on tens, if not hundreds, of millions in the last two centuries.

What is the Gnostic source of such violent expressions that can result from the deep alienation from their lifeworld that humans are able to experience? For a plausible answer, I again quote Voegelin's slightly amended, insightful diagnosis, whose main concern and question is

> what causes Gnosticism to appear, and to become influential, precisely at the time when the consciousness of a pneumatic [i.e., spiritual] Beyond becomes intensely luminous in the various movements radiating from the epiphany of [Jesus] Christ, as well as such manifestations of pagan Gnosis as the *Poimandres*. If the question is formulated in this manner, it implies an answer: The intensely experienced presence of the Beyond [the Divine] brings the problem of the [worldly] Beginning to intense attentions. . . . [Hence, the] fallacy of the Gnostic answers to the question is the expansion of consciousness from the Beyond to the Beginning. In the construction of Gnostic systems, the immediate [i.e., intuitive] experience of divine presence in the mode of the Beyond is speculatively expanded to comprehend a knowledge of the Beginning that is accessible only in the [this-worldly] mode of mediated experience. In the imagery of the expansive speculation, the process of reality becomes an intelligible psychodrama, beginning with a fall in the pneumatic divinity, continuing with the imprisonment of parts of the pneumatic substance in a cosmos created by an evil Demiurge, and ending with the liberation of the imprisoned substance through its return to the pneumatic divinity. The knowledge, the Gnosis, of the psychodrama is the precondition for engaging successfully in the operation of liberating the pneuma in man from its cosmic prison. The imaginative game of liberation derives its momentum from an intensely experienced alienation and an equally intense revolt against it; Gnostic thinkers, both ancient and

5. Albert Camus, *The Rebel: An Essay of Man in Revolt* (Vintage Books, 1956). See especially the chapter entitled "The Son of Cain."

6. Augusto Del Noce, *The Crisis of Modernity* (McGill-Queen's University Press. 2014), chapter 2.

> modern, are the great psychologists of alienation, carriers of the Promethean revolt. . . . [And when the Gnostic thinker's] imagination invents the drama of the divine fall, in order to bring it to its redemptive end by [his] speculative action, [he] must be insensitive to the fact that he is indulging in his *libido dominandi.*[7]

The *libido dominandi,* according to St. Augustine, who coined the phrase (see his *City of God,* Book 1, p. 1), is the sin of sins, the human lust to rule, the desire for power and domination over everything beyond, and especially above, a human's self-centered and prideful existence. As we shall see below, its modern expression is the will-to-power celebrated by Friedrich Nietzsche.

Regarding on one hand the contributions of Promethean rebellion and Gnostic pride to the enlightened modern project, the French scholar Rémi Brague distinguishes crucially between two senses of humanity's superiority and dominance over nature, one found in Holy Scripture, the other in human hubris or pride. "The [biblical] realization of the superiority of man," Brague says, "entails a commandment to fulfill; it results from an order received from without, not from an enterprise freely assumed. It is a task, not a project. . . .[8] [And] thus, the [modern] project of [technologically] mastering nature is not found in the New Testament. It is found, however, in gnosticism."[9] Brague further elaborates that it "was with the radical Enlightenment that Prometheus arrived at the summit. According to Diderot, man is the 'child of Prometheus.' [To top that,] in his doctoral thesis, Marx makes Prometheus the 'first saint of the philosophical calendar.'"[10] One must admit that the Enlightenment project did have an ethical motivation, for it aimed "at the humanization of morals and manners"; but a second aim was "the empowerment of man vis-à-vis every external instance, whether it comes from the physical universe that accompanies him or from the divine that looks down upon him."[11] "[The] modern [Enlightenment] project [therefore] appears as *an emancipation vis-à-vis everything that presents itself above man,* as his inaccessible origin: a creator and/or legislator god, or a nature whose active character renders it divine"[12] (emphasis added). While the first aim is generally laudable for motivating positive and humane changes such as the reforms of penal, educational, and psychiatric and medical institutions, it is the Promethean pursuit of the second aim, the real-

7. Chares R. Embry and Glenn Hughes, eds., *The Eric Voegelin Reader: Politics, History, Consciousness* (University of Missouri Press, 2017), 347–49.

8. Rémi Brague, *The Kingdom of Man: Genesis and Failure of the Modern Project* (University of Notre Dame Press, 2018), 22.

9. Brague, *The Kingdom of Man,* 131.

10. Brague, *The Kingdom of Man,* 131.

11. Brague, *The Kingdom of Man,* 131.

12. Brague, *The Kingdom of Man,* 4.

ization of—in Charles Taylor's apt phrasing—"the tractability of the universe to human ends,"[13] that has proved to yield a problematic mix of constructive and destructive results not only in the natural and humanly constructed world but also in philosophy. Regarding such modern unleashing of Promethean impulses from the prior medieval synthesis of philosophy and spirituality, Jacques Maritain remarked several decades ago that, "henceforward philosophy became separated from the stream of truth and spirituality which came down to it from the heights of the soul. It became, as Descartes said, 'practical'; and its goal was to make us 'masters and owners of nature.'"[14]

Although the historic origin of ancient Gnosticism is not clearly known, what is known is that Gnostic sects competed with early Christian sects for religious orthodoxy.[15] Several key tenets held by Gnosticism were at odds with orthodox doctrines held by the Judeo-Christian traditions. Among Gnostic tenets was the belief that the material world, created by a mere demigod subordinate to the true, higher god, is corrupt and evil, whereas goodness resides exclusively in the spiritual world. We have here a matter-spirit dualism that contradicts the orthodox Judeo-Christian belief, expressed in Genesis 1:31, that "God looked at everything he had made, and he found it very good." Two other Gnostic tenets were at odds with the teachings found in the New Testament. According to a second Gnostic tenet, our spiritual problem was not so much due to sin, the tendency in us to defect from the word and will of God, but primarily due to human ignorance. From this follows a third Gnostic tenet, according to which human salvation depends on attaining gnosis, i.e., knowledge, rather than on repentance for one's propensity to commit evil acts that consequently requires the conversion to a life renewed by following the example set by Jesus Christ.[16] It should be apparent to the reader how the scientific pursuit of knowing and understanding the material or physical world fits in very neatly with especially the last two Gnostic tenets. Although from an ancient Gnostic standpoint the world is thoroughly evil, the modern version of gnosis has adopted Bacon's aspirations for science,[16] in an effort to at least mitigate the worldly evils by supporting and expanding the theoretical foundations provided by scientific research for technology's actions into nature. Who but a reactionary Luddite would decry the contributions of science-based technology to our individual and society's material and physical well-being?

13. Taylor, *A Secular Age*, 257.

14. Maritain, *Science and Wisdom*, 29.

15. Irenaeus, *Scandal of the Incarnation: Irenaeus Against the Heresies* (Ignatius Press, 1990).

16. As noted by Bishop et al., *Biopolitics After Neuroscience*, 182, Bacon's *Novum Organum* can be viewed "in light of [his being] the Renaissance Magus, the master, who seeks the secrets of nature, through astrology, alchemy, and necromancy, a form of Gnosticism that arose in the Renaissance."

Gnosticism's main concern, however, was never our material well-being. As far as our bodies were concerned, Gnosticism took an all but indifferent stance; our bodily well-being could be left to anything ranging from engaging in severe bodily ascesis to indulging the body in uninhibited libertine excesses. Its concern was focused nearly exclusively on the spiritual realm, for otherwise it would never have been the competitor in gathering disciples that it proved to be during the several centuries needed to clarify and consolidate orthodox Christian doctrine. In contrast to Gnostic doctrine, Christian doctrine positively valued the material as well as spiritual realm. So, the questions regarding modern, updated versions of Gnosticism, variously expressed via a mix of scientism, behaviorism, and a jaunty or blithe progressivism, are: To what extent has technoscience contributed to—besides human bodily and material well-being—the health and well-being of the human spirit? And, to what extent has it also contributed to modern bodily and spiritual ailments?

While the Prometheans expressed hate of any and all gods, the Gnostics sundered the unity that in orthodox Christianity identifies God with both the *deus transcendentis* and the *deus immanentis*. By crediting the creation of corrupt nature to an inferior demiurge, traditional Gnosticism severed the unitive relation between the Transcendent God—the Beyond—and the Creator God's Immanence—at the Beginning of the cosmos and during its subsequent evolution—and thus also between the human transcendent spirit and its immanence in nature. In combination with Spinozian pantheism, which erased the distinction between a transcendent God and nature,[17] and with Promethean hostility toward God, modern Gnosticism pretty much left it to disenchanted yet supposedly enlightened humans, now freed from divine intervention in human affairs, to do with nature more or less as they please. By assuming the authority to wrest from nature its secrets, modern sciences supported technology's action into nature pretty much as enlightened humans saw fit.[18]

17. The conjoining of Gnosticism and Spinozism is an immiscible blend, like that of oil and water. Gnosticism seeks to separate spirituality from any trace of matter, while in contrast, Spinozism, as Ulrich L. Lehner, *The Catholic Enlightenment: The Forgotten History of a Global Movement* (Oxford University Press, 2016), 5, points out, reduces the spiritual substance of God to the substance of matter, thus eliminating spirituality. But perhaps, by subjecting the two to the "agitation" and "chemistry" of the radical Enlightenment, an "emulsified" concoction resulted, in which the contradiction lay visibly clouded in its enlightened translucence. This strange union of Spinozism and Gnosticism, which I did not find discussed in my research into the history of ideas, might deserve a historic study of its own.

18. Barry Cooper, *Action into Nature: An Essay on the Meaning of Technology* (University of Notre Dame Press, 1991).

A Still Deeper Look: The Early Origins of Modernity

Let's here take a look a couple of centuries further back than the 18th-century Enlightenment, to the history of ideas that have shaped and motivated the "Ascent of Man."[19] By posing the following queries, Stephen Toulmin has suggested that the origins of modernity (which of course includes the Enlightenment) lay in two successive phases:

> Instead of focusing exclusively on the early 17th century, here we may therefore ask if the modern world and modern culture did not have two distinct origins, rather than a single origin, the first (literary or humanistic phase) being a century before the second. If we follow this suggestion, and carry the origins of Modernity back to the later Renaissance authors of northern Europe in the 16th century, we shall find the *second*, scientific and philosophical phase, from 1630 on, leading many Europeans to turn their backs on the most powerful themes of the *first*, the literary or humanistic phase. . . . [One can therefore ask further,] how far did the later scientists and philosophers positively *reject* the values of the earlier humanistic scholars [e.g., Desiderius Erasmus, François Rabelais, Michel de Montaigne, and William Shakespeare], and how far did they merely take them for granted? Further, to the extent that they truly turned their backs on those values, how far did the birth of modern philosophy and the exact sciences involve something of an actual *counter*-Renaissance?[20]

Developments in the scientific positivisms of the 19th and 20th centuries (August Comte, followed by the Vienna Circle) indicate that many of the values espoused by humanists, literati, and ethicists were indeed rejected as meaningless fluff by at least some scientists and many a philosopher. The consequences of the conflict between these values and the modern, 20th- and 21st-century scientistic outlooks were raised in a sharp and clear relief by Charles P. Snow in his *The Two Cultures*.[21] And the devaluation of, if not contempt for, the arts and

19. This phrase was the title of a popular BBC television series presented in the early 1970s by the Polish born mathematician, historian, and lover of poetry Jacob Bronowski. Like many others, I watched the 13 episodes "religiously" when I was in the early, exuberant stages of my scientific career. A lover of poetry and a Jew, Bronowski was aware that the poet's life cannot escape the melancholy awareness of human existence and that at the moral level the ascent of man was not characterized by uninterrupted progress. The wealth of ideas covered in the series was impressive, as was the gentle, humane, largely buoyant, but at times also tragic element in his presentation of the ascent of man. The television series was followed by a print version in 1973, one of many wonderful books that Bronowski published in his career and that are still worth reading.

20. Toulmin, *Cosmopolis*, 23.

21. Charles P. Snow, *The Two Cultures and the Scientific Revolution* (Cambridge University Press, 1959).

humanities can be found to this day in modern thinkers like Steven Pinker, who has not so much expressed regret for his prior remarks regarding the fine arts, as engaged in a questionable turn-around effort to sanitize his boorish scientism (see chapters 5 and 7).[22]

Pinker's Harvard colleague Edward O. Wilson strikes a more conciliatory tone. In his *Consilience*, he attempts to present a kinder, gentler, holistic or Gestalt version of the scientific enterprise that poses no threat to the hearts and minds of those who find a home in the arts, humanities, and religion. He suggests that

> the focus of the natural sciences has begun to shift away from the search for new fundamental laws and toward new kinds of synthesis—"holism," if you prefer—in order to understand complex systems. That is the goal, variously, in studies of the origin of the universe, the history of climate, the functioning of cells, the assembly of ecosystems, and the physical basis of mind. The strategy that works best in these enterprises is the construction of coherent cause-and-effect explanations across levels of organization. Thus the cell biologist looks inward and downward to ensembles of molecules, and the cognitive psychologist to patterns of aggregate nerve cell activity. Accidents, when they happen, are rendered understandable. No compelling reason has ever been offered why the same strategy should not work to unite the natural sciences with the social sciences and humanities. The difference between the two domains is in the magnitude of the problem, not the principles needed for its solution. The human condition is the most important frontier of the natural sciences. Conversely, the material world exposed by the natural sciences is the most important fron-

22. See Wieseltier, "Crimes Against Humanities," where he critiques Pinker's *The New Republic* article calling for a truce to the science-humanities culture war. Regarding Pinker's attempt at reconciliation, Wieseltier responds as follows:

> A few weeks ago this magazine published a small masterpiece of scientizing apologetics by Steven Pinker, called "Science Is Not Your Enemy." Pinker utters all kinds of sentimental declarations about the humanities, which "are indispensable to a civilized democracy." Nobody wants to set himself against sensibility, which is anyway a feature of scientific work, too. Pinker ranges over a wide variety of thinkers and disciplines, scientific and humanistic, and he gives the impression of being a tolerant and cultivated man, which no doubt he is. But the diversity of his analysis stays at the surface. His interest in many things is finally an interest in one thing. He is a foxy hedgehog. His essay, a defense of "scientism," is a long exercise in assimilating humanistic inquiries into scientific ones. By the time Pinker is finished, the humanities are the handmaiden of the sciences, and dependent upon the sciences for their advance and even their survival.

In his article, Wieseltier goes beyond a critique of Pinker and delivers a broadside counter to all forms of scientistically inclined thinkers who attempt decide on the truth or meaning of the humanities, the arts, and religion, as though science were the sole judge qualified to do so.

> tier of the social sciences and humanities. The consilience argument can be distilled as follows: The two frontiers are the same.[23]

Yet, one wonders how this conciliatory note on uniting the natural sciences with the social sciences and humanities at their common border squares with Wilson's less gentle and kind "central idea of the consilience world view . . . that all tangible phenomena, from the birth of stars to the workings of social institutions, are based on material processes that are ultimately reducible, however long and tortuous the sequences, to the laws of physics."[24]

For sure, Wilson does say "tangible phenomena." Does he mean by "tangible" the "physical" or, in the wider sense, the "real"? If the former, then one can ask how social institutions are "physical" in a sense other than, say, an educational institution such as Harvard University is indeed composed of a physical space encompassing physical structures. But, although I might be wrong, I don't think this is what Wilson intended to say. Hence, if the latter is meant, one can ask: Aren't the arts, humanities, and religion also tangible phenomena in the sense of being "graspable" and "touchable" by conscious human minds? And are these minds also "ultimately reducible, however long and tortuous the sequences, to the laws of physics?" If so, where is the consilience to be found in this assertion? For that reason, one can chime in with Toulmin—when referring to the two-culture conflict described by C. P. Snow—that if "the Two Cultures are still estranged [despite Wilson's shaky consilience], then, this is no local peculiarity of 20th century Britain: it is a reminder that Modernity had two distinct starting points, a humanistic one grounded in classical literature, and a [separate] scientific one rooted in 17th century natural philosophy."[25] After the estrangement, if not divorce, of the humanities and science, a true consilience, a reuniting of the two disciples, requires something other and deeper than the one encased in Wilson's scientistic and reductive aspirations, one that includes not only the humanistic and scientific but also the religious and theological disciplines.

Along with Voegelin, who sees the essence of modernity as the recrudescent growth of Gnosticism, one can go further back than the late Renaissance to the late 12th-century medieval period of Joachim di Fiore, an Italian abbot who proposed an interpretation of the Trinitarian concept of God in terms of three historic and eschatological periods: (i) the period of the Father, followed by (ii) the period of the Son, to be followed by (iii) the final, apocalyptic period of the Spirit in which eschatology and human history would coincide. Note here that the latter, spiritual phase nicely suits the Gnostic emphasis on spiritual as

23. Wilson, *Consilience*, 292–93.
24. Wilson, *Consilience*, 291.
25. Toulmin, *Cosmopolis*, 43.

opposed to material and incarnate, bodily concerns. This three-age eschatological structure was not lost to modernity. In fact, argues Voegelin, one saw its inner-worldly transformations continue during the 18th and 19th centuries, as exemplified in "the humanistic and encyclopedist periodization of history into ancient, medieval, and modern history; Turgot's and Comte's theory of theological, metaphysical, and scientific phases of humanity; Hegel's dialectic of the three stages of freedom and self-reflective spiritual fulfillment; the Marxian dialectic of the three stages of primitive communism, class society, and final communism. . . ."[26] From Comte to Marx, the arrival of a final age would herald the deliverance of mankind from its prior defective stages of development. Yet paradoxically, the "more fervently all human energies are thrown into the great enterprise of salvation through world-immanent action, the farther the humans who engage in this enterprise move away from the life of the spirit. And since the life of the spirit is the source of order in man and society, the very success of a gnostic civilization is the cause of its decline. . . . [For, a] limit is reached when an activist sect that represents the gnostic truth organizes the civilization into an empire under its rule. Totalitarianism [already evident in 20th-century Leninist/Stalinist communism and a variety of Fascist regimes], is the end form of progressive civilization."[27] If the reader wonders what all this has to do with science and religion, Voegelin raises the caution that "with the prodigious advancement of science since the 17th century, the new instrument of cognition [i.e., the *novum organum* à la Bacon] would become, as one is inclined to say inevitably, the symbolic vehicle of gnostic truth. In the gnostic speculation of scientism this particular variant reached its extreme when the positivist perfectors of science replace the era of Christ with the era of Comte. Scientism has remained to this day one of the strongest gnostic movements in Western society; and the immanentist pride of science is so strong that even the special sciences have each left a distinguishable sediment of the variants of salvation through physics, economics, sociology, biology, and psychology."[28]

In view of the fact that the avowed supremacy of the Gnostic spirit over matter goes back at least as far as the first two to three centuries CE, we can agree with Brague when he correctly concludes that "the *intention to dominate* nature [expressed so zealously by Francis Bacon] preceded the birth of the technology that allowed its realization"[29] (emphasis added). While the intention to dominate nature is an incontrovertible fact introduced into human history, such domination remains an imaginative yet ever-elusive fiction. For that reason, the Gnostic/Promethean hubris, manifested in the unholy union of an insatiable

26. Voegelin, *Modernity Without Restraint*, 179.
27. Voegelin, *Modernity Without Restraint*, 195.
28. Voegelin, *Modernity Without Restraint*, 191–92.
29. Brague, *The Kingdom of Man*, 59.

human *libido dominandi* and an unbounded human imagination, is an expression, as Augustine realized, of humanity's abiding tendency to err and sin.

The Failures and Fizzling Demise of Late Modernity's Enlightenment Project

Let's take stock of the present by examining the state of the modern human project, its accomplishments and its failures. One cannot but agree with Voegelin that the advancement of science since the 17th century has been prodigious. One can additionally agree that, since then, the advancement of technologies has been equally prodigious. Technology and science reinforce each other—one could almost say, become each other—in ever upward-spiraling positive feedback cycles. However, without some counterbalancing negative feedback, such cycles, as any competent cyberneticist knows, can destructively spin out of control. We are becoming increasingly aware of the fact that prodigious technoscientific advancement is accompanied by equally prodigious side effects that, contrary to what Francis Bacon had hoped but had not foreseen, do not promote the material or spiritual estate of humankind. There may be rare exceptions to the many unintended and unforeseen deleterious consequences of scientific discoveries and their technological applications. Yet, we are becoming increasingly aware of rising sea levels that threaten large numbers of humans, prevailing droughts leading to increases of human and animal starvation; extreme storms causing destructive flooding that results in private and public loss summing to many tens of billions of dollars; the increasing loss of biohabitat and biodiversity summing to species extinctions; the accumulation of plastic debris and chemical sludge that forms the Pacific trash vortex; and the summed overload of vapid, tawdry, sordid, and toxic information posted on internet sites, to name just a few nasty effects to which applied technologies contribute a significant share. These "collateral damages" demonstrate that even the unintended consequences of technoscience can be deleterious to body and spirit. Francis Bacon, were he alive today, would no doubt experience a mix of amazement and dismay. His dream of progressively modernizing society and civilization was not so much ill-conceived as the realization of its utopian vision was limited by unforeseeable problems inherent to the technological designs used to implement the dream.

But what can be said about the spiritual estate of modern humans? Here I can do no better as an introductory remark than Brague's following commentary:

> The modern project is perfectly fine when it comes to producing *goods*: material, cultural and moral goods, which it makes a point of providing to human beings; for that, it has no need of anything but the resources it finds in man. On the other hand, however, it seems incapable of explaining why it is *good* that there are human beings to enjoy the goods that are thus put at their disposal.

> Here I would borrow a thought from [the philosopher] John N. Gray. "At the period of late modernity in which we live, the Enlightenment project is affirmed principally because we fear the consequences that its abandonment would entail. . . . Our cultures are Enlightenment cultures not by conviction [except for a vocal minority (see below)], but by default." That is why we are so careful to maintain the specter of "obscurantism" and keep vigilant watch to ensure that credible "reactionaries" are around to play the role of foils that can justify an Enlightenment that is incapable of defending itself."[30]

Is this a true description of the current state of Modernity and its Enlightenment project? In his call for *Enlightenment Now*, one of its stoutest defenders and cheerleaders, Steven Pinker, clearly disagrees with Brague's and Gray's assessments[31] (despite the fact that his evangelizing and prolix espousal of the Enlightenment project can be summarized in large part by Brague's above statement that the "modern project is perfectly fine when it comes to producing *goods*: material, cultural and moral goods. . . ."). In contrast to Pinker's defense of, and cheering for, the Enlightenment, his former Harvard colleague, Edward O. Wilson, in a mixture of paean and eulogy, viewed the Enlightenment in the following, less buoyant way. "The dream of intellectual unity first came to full flower in the original Enlightenment, an Icarian flight of the mind that spanned the 17th and 18th centuries. A vision of secular knowledge in the service of human rights and progress, it was the West's greatest contribution to civilization. It launched the modern era for the entire world; we are all its legatees. *Then it failed. Astonishingly—it failed.* When does such a historical period come to an end? It dies when, for whatever reason, usually in the aftermath of war and revolution, its ideas no longer dominate."[32]

One can pass over Wilson's evangelical fervor when speaking of the Enlightenment's promises. For although the Enlightenment *has acquired* the reputation for reason, science, and humanistic morals, its *original form*, contrary to Wilson, also included, in its less luminous side, the praise of "pleasure-seeking" passions by the likes of Diderot and their more sordid tokens in the libertine writings of the Marquis de Sade.[33] Of course, one could view the praise of natural passions and their delights more benignly as seeds dormant in the Enlightenment's shal-

30. Brague, *The Kingdom of Man*, 214.

31. Steven Pinker, *Enlightenment Now: The Case for Reason, Science, Humanism, and Progress* (Viking Press, 2018).

32. Wilson, *Consilience*, 15.

33. For an account of Diderot's views on erotic passion, see Philipp Blom, *A Wicked Company: The Forgotten Radicalism of the European Enlightenment* (Basic Books, 2010), 186–200.

low soils.[34] One can also forgive Wilson's overgeneralized appraisal of the Enlightenment as a total failure. His idealized, empyrean *the*-version of it certainly did fail, but many of its on-the-ground laudable accomplishments attest to the fact that it was not entirely a failure. To that extent, one can justifiably join Pinker in defending the positive Enlightenment achievements and values.[35]

Some Corrections to the Excesses of the Modern Enlightenment Project

Yet from a present-day retrospective, the modern Enlightenment project was in several respects a failure, most notably in respect of reason (rationality), science, and morals, since these three were touted to be its key advocacies. The three cannot be treated as independent from one another. Regarding reason, Steven Toulmin correctly notes that, over the past two and a half millennia of human history, reason has played a vital role in speculative pursuit of knowledge in all sorts of human activities. No field of human investigation or speculation was dismissed as intrinsically unphilosophical. "From the mid-seventeenth century on, however, an imbalance began to develop. Certain methods of inquiry

34. It required only a few years before the seedlings sprouted to bear various delectable fruits when, during the early Romantic Counter-Enlightenment, literature and the arts explored the irrational, emotional, and creative side of human nature. Still bathed in the dimming glow of the Enlightenment, by the middle of the 19th century the explorations undertaken in literature and the arts during the later Dark Romantic period uncovered the darker, destructive side of human nature.

35. Given the reasonable desideratum of a wing- and claw-clipped and more inclusive Enlightenment, I can respond to Pinker's cry to man the barricades in defense of commonly shared Enlightenment values. The 19th century reckoned with the excesses of Enlightenment rationalism by countering with a Romantic irrationalism that pervaded and occupied, for instance, Schopenhauer's, Kierkegaard's, and Nietzsche's thoughts, and continued to flourish via various modifications throughout the 20th century, only to culminate in—forgive the mixed metaphor—a thoroughly post-modern "potpourri" of novelties to suit every individual's moral, literary, artistic, and philosophical "taste." Accordingly, it seems that we now have as many "sciences" as there are group-identity interests. Like music and art, true science is not limited to a particular nation, region, ethnicity, or other identity group. It is an undertaking with international and interpersonal (social) dimensions. However, unlike music and art, its "local productions" can be communicated in a standard, readily appreciable way to thousands of scientists and science aficionados regardless of national, ethnic, and other group affiliations. In contrast, the allures and charms of art and music lie in their ability to communicate in nationally, ethnically, and personally specific expressions that are not always readily appreciated by all artists and musicians and all art and music lovers. So, yes, when it comes to science, let's be cautiously traditional rather than postmodern; let's follow the sage advice of Alexander Pope, "An Essay on Criticism: Part 2," ll. 142–43, accessed January 11, 2026, https://www.poetryfoundation.org/poems/44897/an-essay-on-criticism-part-2: "be not the first by whom the new are tried, nor yet the last to lay the old aside."

and subjects were seen as philosophically serious or 'rational' in a way that others were not. As a result, authority came to attach particularly to scientific and technical inquiries that put those methods to use. Instead of a free-for-all of ideas and speculations—a competition for attention across all realms of inquiry—there was a hierarchy of prestige . . . so that the *reasonableness* of [e.g., humanistic and religious] narratives came to seem a soft-centered notion . . . , qualifying neither as philosophy nor as science."[36] The effect was to "inflict on Human Reason a wound that remained unhealed for three hundred years—a wound from which we are only recently beginning to recover."[37] The dreams of a universal rationalism supported by a clear rational method, an exact language, and a unified science "form a single project designed to purify the operations of Human Reason by *desituating* them: that is, divorcing them from the compromising association of their cultural contexts."[38]

One can readily admit that there are formal, logical methods for presenting valid scientific explanations and arguments. However, although there may be a rationally justifiable scientific method, the last century of thinking in the history and philosophy of science—ranging from the logical positivists' method of verification, through Karl Popper's method of falsification, Paul Feyerabend's methodological anarchism, Thomas Kuhn's revolutionary paradigm shifts, Imre Lakatos's emphasis on scientific research programs, to the postmodern relativist tussles—has failed to convincingly specify what exactly it is.

In addressing such confusions regarding "true" or most appropriate versions of scientific method, I rely on the approach of the physicist Ian Hutchinson who, in my opinion, cuts through these confusions by specifying essential characteristics not of scientific method but of scientific practice manifest throughout any in-the-lab and in-the-field research project. Two such characteristics are reproducibility, also referred to as replicability, and what he refers to as clarity. As Hutchinson describes them, "clarity can be thought of as the foundational requirement for the expression and communication of reproducibility; so these two scientific traits are partners. The [design, procedures, and] results of any scientific investigation have to be expressed in terms that are [linguistically] unambiguous."[39] Perhaps impressed by science's requirement for such linguistic

36. Stephen Toulmin, *Return to Reason* (Harvard University Press, 2001), 15.

37. Toulmin, *Return to Reason*, 13.

38. Toulmin, *Return to Reason*, 78.

39. Hutchinson, *Monopolizing Knowledge*, 49. Without linguistic clarity, scientists would not be able to replicate observational or experimental procedures in order to assess if a reported finding can itself be reproduced. Reproducibility plays a key role in confirming or disconfirming an especially strikingly new or counterintuitive reported finding. Findings that cannot be replicated do not become part of the scientific corpus of knowledge. Replication failures are particularly important in rare cases where scientific findings are reported fraudulently.

clarity, analytic philosophers like Bertrand Russell and Ludwig Wittgenstein attempted to develop a clear, exact language—based, for example, on Wittgenstein's use of first-order predicate logic—that would not be prone to the conceptual ambiguities of so-called "ordinary language."[40] This philosophic attempt was to be realized by applying the principles of formal logic to the analysis of linguistically expressed propositions. It is doubtful that the attempt has been successful, for formal logical languages tend to be high in clarity when applied to a very limited number of intellectual endeavors such as mathematics, but very impoverished when attempts are made to apply it to the linguistic discourse relevant in mundane human existence. This may be one of the reasons why Wittgenstein abandoned the project of finding the meaning of concepts in their logical and linguistic clarity and exactness. He subsequently turned his efforts to understanding language games (*Sprachspiele*) that are played within the speaker's form of life (*Lebensform*) embedded in the social context of his or her expressive actions.[41] So now, as Wittgenstein did, we can return to ordinary language, *resituated* in rich interpersonal and cultural contexts. This, as noted above, is not to say that the exact sciences, e.g., physics and chemistry, do not use a language that strives for disambiguation by approaching exactness of expression. They do, but such language is foremost the language of arcane mathematics and a terminology, whose meanings, for all intents and purposes, are undecipherable except to experts.

Yet the unification of all the separate sciences under some yet-to-be specified method and semantically univocal language, dear to the hearts of scientistically inclined philosophers, is far from realized. Repeated assurances have been made that it will eventually be achieved by reducing all observable phenomena to the language of physics, of matter in motion. But that is less a promise than a hope, a hope based on a resolute scientistic faith—an ersatz-religious faith, as we already noted—in the power of science to produce a theory of and for everything.[42] One could say that such faith is not only the realization of what is hoped for but also evidence of things not scientifically observed; and hope as such is a blessing, for it cannot disappoint.[43] But, based on the observation, made by St. Augustine already 16 centuries ago, that we know more than what

40. Wittgenstein, *Tractatus Logico-Philosophicus.*

41. Ludwig Wittgenstein, *Philosophical Investigations* (Blackwell Publishing, 2001).

42. An example of such faith that the basis of everything from subatomic particles, through conscious minds, to the entire cosmos rests ultimately on the unification of the physics of thermodynamics, quantum mechanics, and general relativity can be found in Brian Greene, *Until the End of Time*, 270–79.

43. I render this description of scientistic faith and hope tongue-in-cheek and at the risk of profaning holy Scripture. St. Paul's scriptural passages read "Faith is the realization of what is hoped for and evidence of things not seen" (Hebrews 11:1), and "hope does not disappoint" (Romans 5:5).

we can clearly express, a non-scientistic scientist can subscribe to a humbler yet more encompassing claim. To wit, the unity of knowledge is not achieved as a post-hoc end result, an apical achievement, of the scientific quest for knowledge and clarity; rather, it is ever present—in Michael Polanyi's sense—in the tacit dimension of knowledge that is prior to, and contextually supports the many intellectual efforts that are exerted in every scientific and scholarly research paradigm that tries to make explicitly evident to the human mind as much as is possible about the world we inhabit.[44]

One of the "sins" of modernity was and still is, to use Toulmin's phraseology, the wound inflicted on human reason by the scientistic/rationalistic confiscation of it from domains of study falling outside that the rationality of the natural sciences. "Hard" scientists should therefore not respond with surprise or with self-righteous indignation to the accusation that one of the long-term effects of this extraction of reason from the "soft" social sciences, arts, humanities, and theology was the burgeoning postmodern irrationalism that has crept into these disciplines. Indeed, while much of this irrationalism can rightly be regarded as an aftereffect of the 19th-century Romantic Counter-Enlightenment, the unwitting complicity of scientism in causing and furthering such irrationalism cannot be denied. This, besides what I consider to be an inherent worthiness of these "soft" disciplines, is a primary reason that I am not a scientistic scientist. Let's grant that the thinking and doing that is applied *rationalistically* in science does allow one to pursue the truth about the physical and natural world. Yet, besides the truths of nature, there are many other truths to be explored and discovered. And if one takes Toulmin seriously, then rational thought can be returned to *reasonable* areas of study outside of natural science, for example to the purely philosophical or theological studies of ethics and morality in pursuit of the good.[45] And if we unfetter reason from its scientistic servitude and widen its ambit still further, we can restore it also to the *reasonable* study, if theologians and philosophers are so inclined, of the metaphysical transcendental values of Being, Truth, Goodness, and Beauty.[46]

Such a pluralistic and robust reason goes hand in hand with the correspondingly *pluralistic robust realism* advocated recently by Hubert Dreyfus and Charles Taylor. Reality is more complex and more capacious than the physical and material reality explored by a science that pretends to adopt "a view

44. This tacit dimension is referenced by Saint Augustine, *Confessions*, 230, when he expresses the puzzling nature of time as follows: "What, then, is time? If no one asks me, I know what it is. If I wish to explain it to him who asks me, I do not know." That we know more than we can clearly articulate is central also to Michael Polanyi's philosophy. See Michael Polanyi, *Personal Knowledge*; Michael Polanyi, *The Tacit Dimension*.

45. See Toulmin, *Return to Reason*, chapter 9.

46. Montague Brown, *Restoration of Reason: The Eclipse and Recovery of Truth, Goodness, and Beauty* (Baker Academic, 2006).

from nowhere," a perspective from which the rational intellect, detached as it is from the wider context of the everyday world, ideally mediates knowledge of the natural world's objects and properties that are accessible only to scientific observational methods of investigation. According to Dreyfus and Taylor, pluralistic robust realism meets the following stipulations: "(1) multiple ways of interrogating reality (that's the 'plural' part), which nevertheless (2) reveal truths independent of us, that is that require us to revise and adjust our thinking to grasp them (and that's the robust realist part), and where (3) all attempts fail to bring the different ways of interrogating reality into a single mode of questioning that yields a unified picture or theory [of everything] (so they are plural)."[47] Note that there is no talk of individually or socially constructing the truths of reality, as many postmodernists claim, but rather of conforming our thoughts and beliefs to these real truths. Although one can regard the scientific method as detached from the wider context of living (i.e., from Husserl's *Lebenswelt*), it is nevertheless circumscribed by how humans actively engage with their everyday world, for "our explicit [e.g., scientific] thinking about the world is contextualized and given its sense by an *implicit*, largely *unarticulated* background sense of our being in the world"[48] (emphases added). It should be evident that pluralistic robust realism approximates Polanyi's views of explicit and tacit knowledge that was noted above and in chapter 5.[49] A pluralistic realism coupled to our active engagement with the world we inhabit also is consistent with the embodied, action-based cognition advocated by the vision researcher Kevin O'Regan and the philosopher Alva Noë,[50] and with what we know about findings of developmental cognitive neuroscience that have accumulated since at least the 1960s.[51] Consequently, in Dreyfus and Taylor's words, "*pluralistic robust realism* can avoid [epistemological] *reductive realism*, which holds that science explains

47. Hubert Dreyfus and Charles Taylor, *Retrieving Realism* (Harvard University Press, 2015), 154. The first condition sounds more like an epistemological claim than an ontological claim. However, implicit is the notion that corresponding to the many ways of interrogating reality, there are correspondingly separate ways in which reality is constituted of distinct kinds. Moreover, reductive physicalists like E. O. Wilson would not be happy with the third condition.

48. Dreyfus and Taylor, *Retrieving Realism*, 67.

49. See note 44 in chapter 5 and note 16 in appendix 2.

50. Alvin Noë, *Out of Our Heads: Why You Are Not Your Brain, and Other Lessons from the Biology of Consciousness* (Hill and Wang, 2009); J. Kevin O'Regan, *Why Red Doesn't Sound Like a Bell: Understanding the Feel of Consciousness* (Oxford University Press, 2011).

51. Relevant examples are research on visuo-motor development in kittens conducted by Richard Held and Alan Hein, "Movement-Produced Stimulation in the Development of Visually Guided Behavior," *Journal of Comparative and Physiological Psychology* 56, no. 5 (1963): 872–76, and research on development of binocular vision in humans conducted by A. Hohmann and O. D. Creutzfeldt, "Squint and the Development of Binocularity in Humans," *Nature* 254, no. 5501 (1975): 613–14.

all modes of being, and *scientific realism*, which holds that there is only one way that the universe is carved up into kinds . . . , while yet rejecting *deflationary realism's* claim [made, for instance, by postmodernists like Richard Rorty] that we cannot make sense of true statements in science corresponding to the way things are in themselves."[52]

That said about the triad of science, reason, and reality, one can note that another shortcoming of the Enlightenment project, expressed specifically in application of scientific practice, is the inability of providing a scientific basis of morality. Beside the relevant topics dealing with this failure in chapters 3 and 4, a broader historical and philosophical appraisal made by Alasdair MacIntyre amply covers additional reasons for this Enlightenment failure and its aftermath.[53] One of the consequences of the failure, according to MacIntyre, was a turn to utilitarianism for a grounding of morality, proposed initially by Jeremy Bentham and subsequently elaborated by John Stuart Mill. While utilitarianism stressed that the only motives for human action are attraction to pleasure and aversion to pain, thus leading to a maximization of happiness, it is "the polymorphous nature of pleasure and happiness" that makes utility such a problematic criterion or guide for what humans ought to do. For "if someone suggests to us, in the spirit of Bentham and Mill, that we should guide our own choices [of action] by the prospects of our own future pleasure or happiness, the appropriate retort is to inquire: 'But *which* pleasure, *which* happiness ought to guide me?'"[54] (emphases added). By MacIntyre's account, the inability of British utilitarianism and of subsequent American pragmatism (only that which has practical on-the-ground usefulness and applicability lays a claim on anything worthy of philosophical debate and anything resembling truth) to provide answers to this question has facilitated the 20th-century decline of morality into emotivism. As we also saw in chapter 4, the same inability to answer these questions posed to utilitarianism also besets the ongoing neuroscientific quest for the basis of morality. The upshot is that one cannot credit utility or practical results with the ability to ground morality. MacIntyre goes on to explain that "emotivism is the doctrine that all evaluative judgments and more specifically all moral judgments are nothing but expressions of [personal] *preference*, expression of attitude or *feeling*, insofar as they are moral or evaluative in character."[55] Hence, the neuroscientific quest additionally cannot credit individual emotional intuitionism or personal preference with the ability to ground an ethics that is universally applicable. Here, one might note also that utilitarianism's calculus of pleasure/happiness maximization appealed to Darwin him-

52. Dreyfus and Taylor, *Retrieving Realism*, 160.
53. See especially MacIntyre, *After Virtue*, chapters 5–6.
54. MacIntyre, *After Virtue*, 64.
55. MacIntyre, *After Virtue*, 11–12.

self, and that since his time it has been a standard also in later Darwinian evolutionary thinking. But like the attempts of neuroscientists, attempts by present-day Darwinist philosophers and evolutionary psychologists to thwart the naturalist fallacy via a mental alchemy that distills the *Ought* from the *Is* have proven unsuccessful.[56] And so now, as Ronald Osborn further notes, "we are left with a [Darwinian] conception of values based not on reason or morality but on the mere fact of [biologically adaptive] instincts."[57] In a thoroughly Darwinian world, in which *all is* but *naught ought*, one can do no better than contrive to thwart, by delegitimizing, the quest for the moral *ought* elsewhere.

Darwin's enlightened contemporary, Karl Marx, in his own scientistic thinking, was firm in delegitimizing any questions regarding a transcendental moral ought. Such questions were mere cover for decadent bourgeois values. Whereas Darwin undertook to document the evolutionary history of the "descent of man," Marx's task was not only to reveal the history of, but also to actively promote, the revolutionary "ascent of man." To that end, as Voegelin recognizes, Marx's delegitimizing the quest for intelligibility regarding transcendental values was a manifestation of the wider Marxian suppression of reasonable questions. Voegelin also recognizes that Marx was not only a speculative Gnostic but also a Promethean *prophet*. For, similar to Albert Camus's above-mentioned notion of metaphysical rebellion, Voegelin remarks that "a passage from Marx's doctoral dissertation of 1840–1841 takes us further into the problem of [such metaphysical] revolt: Philosophy makes no secret of it. The confession of Prometheus, 'In a word, I hate all the gods,' is its own confession, its own verdict against all gods heavenly and earthly who do not acknowledge human self-consciousness as the supreme deity. *There shall be none beside it* (emphasis added). In this confession, . . . young Marx [23 years old at the time] presents his own attitude under the symbol of Prometheus. . . ."[58] Recalling from the introduction Roy Clouser's definition of the divine, here we also have a clear example of taking human self-consciousness, i.e., human ego, as the divine. The passage thus highlights and summarizes the paradoxical mixture of Marx's anti-theistic and materialist hubris yet, at the same time, his indebtedness to the idealist and prophetic tradition of his Jewish theistic ancestry.[59] One need only go to Exodus 20:3, "You shall not have other gods besides me," repeated in Deuteronomy 5:7 and Isaiah 45:5, to see how YHWH, the jealous God of the ancient Hebrew nation, transmutes into the modern human, the *jealous and cunning* god that, by inclusion,

56. The naturalist or *is*-to-*ought* fallacy, raised already in the 17th century by Hume, was addressed extensively in the early 20th-century philosopher G. E. Moore's *Principia Ethica.*

57. Ronald C. Osborn, *Humanism and the Death of God: Searching for the Good After Darwin, Marx, and Nietzsche* (Oxford University Press, 2017), 44.

58. Voegelin, *Modernity Without Restraint*, 269.

59. Osborn, *Humanism and the Death of God*, 93–99.

is Marx himself. One can credit Marx's social ethic—of Judeo-Christian-Muslim provenance—that focuses on the evils of unfettered capitalism and on alleviating the miseries of the working class. But as diagnosed and documented by Voegelin and separately by Ronald Osborn, Marx allows himself several sorts of knowing and *deliberate* intellectual swindle, in short, violence done to the intellect, that in turn justified and promoted the violence, committed in praxis by his Leninist/Stalinist followers, that first realizes and then stabilizes the proletariat revolution.[60] In the service of such revolution, the ends justify the means and pretty much anything goes, including subjecting the unenlightened masses, the *Lumpenproletariat*, to the political rule of a small cadre of enlightened, authoritarian elites. And of course, as shown by events that unfolded in the preceding century, this applied not only to a brand of revolutionary socialism prefixed by "proletariat" but also to one prefixed by "national."

The union of Promethean and Gnostic strivings for a better human condition thus resulted in some troubled and troubling offspring. The cost of their politically directed outbursts ran in the many tens of millions of human lives. As recent events around the world demonstrate, the recrudescence of authoritarian political rule in the present century is an ongoing danger to constitutional democracy; and since politics is the art of wielding power, it is subject to excessive exercise of the will-to-power and mastery, a power that is crucially and increasingly dependent on technoscientific expertise.

Technoscientism: The Latest Atheistic Ersatz-Religion of Modernity

Humans are occupied predominantly by what is going on in the present and what might occur in the near future. They must provide for themselves and others, engage in their daily work, their assigned tasks and chores, and occasionally they do think of and remember the past and dream of and plan for the

60. For a more detailed analysis and critique of Marx's lack of, and attack on, intellectual integrity, see Osborn, *Humanism and the Death of God*, 83–93; and Voegelin, *Modernity Without Restraint*, 264–77. It is for this reason, among others, that while much of what Terry Eagleton expresses in his writings finds my sympathetic response, I, along with Osborn, *Humanism and the Death of God*, 84, cannot sympathize with his defense of Marxism in his Terry Eagleton, *Why Marx Was Right* (Yale University Press, 2011). As Osborn points out, Eagleton's apologia of Marxism is based on a selective reading of Marx's writings. With Eagleton, I can sympathize with Marx's critique of capitalism and the huge social and economic inequalities it tolerates—if not promotes—and with his overall humanitarian concerns, but my sympathy stops with Marx's advocacy of violent revolution and of the consolidation of the collective power of the proletariat in the hands of a few revolutionary elites. The devastating aftermaths of such revolution and such consolidation of power have been too dramatically demonstrated during the previous century. Perhaps the title of Eagleton's book should have read, more modestly, *Why Marx Was Right—in Part.*

future, before, however, returning to present concerns. So here, too, let's briefly move beyond the past, the historic Gnostic and Promethean technoscientific enterprises discussed above; let's instead look to the future, near and remote, in which Gnostic aspirations of removing the restraints imposed by crude and clueless nature also promise to play a role.

But before doing so, a brief backward look is warranted, some 800 years back, to Dante's *Divine Comedy*.[61] According to Rémi Brague, in it (Line 70, Canto I of the *Paradiso*) Dante introduced the neologism *transumanar*, i.e., to go beyond the human. But to Dante the use of the new word was meant to be "far from being Promethean, . . . [instead it expresses] a process whereby, by obedience to God, one must be lifted to him [Christ] who began by making himself obedient to the point of descending lower than all (Phil. 2:8)."[62] This transformative ascension-by-descension is subscribed to by only a mostly Christian minority of today's transhumanists. Other transhumanists, those inspired by the Gnostic-cum-Promethean ideology, are mainly secular; their aspirations are to establish, without any reliance on God, humanity's self-transcendence beyond every limit so far imposed by nature.

Nietzsche's Will-to-Power and Nihilism

> For some time now, a great many scientific endeavors have been directed at making life also "artificial," toward cutting the last tie through which even man belongs to the children of nature. . . . This future man, whom the scientists tell us they will produce in no more than a hundred years, seems to be possessed by *a rebellion against human existence as it has been given*, a free gift from nowhere (secularly speaking), which he wishes to exchange, as it were, for something he has made himself. There is no reason to doubt our abilities to accomplish such an exchange, just as there is no reason to doubt our present ability to destroy all organic life on earth. The question is only whether we wish to use our new scientific and technical knowledge in this direction, and this question cannot be decided by scientific means; it is a political question of the first order and therefore can hardly be left to the decision of professional scientists or professional politicians.
>
> Hannah Arendt, *The Human Condition*, pp. 2–3

And to their Gnostic and Promethean aspirations, as presciently stated over sixty years ago in the Hannah Arendt epigraph, we can now add a third—namely, the Nietzschean-Zarathustran one, the overcoming of the merely human (menschliches), all too human, by the superhuman (übermenschliches).

61. Dante Alighieri, *The Divine Comedy* (Viking Press, 1959).
62. Brague, *The Kingdom of Man*, 31.

The Gnostic-Promethean drive to rebel against—nay, in recent times to overcome—the natural and the divine can be viewed, following St. Augustine's assessment noted above, as a manifestation of humanity's original sin. It was Nietzsche's vision and wish that this overcoming will have succeeded when Dionysian *eros* triumphs over self-emptying divine *agape*, by activating and unleashing nature's self-serving *libido dominandi*. How versions of this aspiring dream are to be realized is expressed in the fertile imaginations of secular futurologists and not a few scientists with a divinatory bent. According to them, a host of technosciences—AI, cybernetic prosthetics, nanoscience, and genetic engineering, to name just a few—will combine in order to accelerate, and eventually replace, the slow and messy processes of biological evolution by natural selection with a high-speed, high-tech utopia of progressive transhuman evolution and flourishing without end. Should this utopian dream be successfully realized, there is, however, the possibility and risk that most of the emphasis of transhumanism will be placed on the *trans* rather than the human; and, if so, that the *trans*human, the superhuman, will in turn evolve into the *post*human, fully replacing anything that can still be called human.[63]

Let's unpack these less salutary descriptions of the transhumanist promise. Note first that the "promise that science and technology will provide us with more of whatever it is we want more of" dovetails nicely with a feature of what James Hunter and Paul Nedelisky (see chapter 4) refer to as the new science of morality—namely, its degeneration into a science of how to get whatever we want. So, this new, degraded science of morality may contribute, wittingly or

63. My raising the *possibility* of such a dystopic outcome coming to fruition should not be taken as a symptom of a systemic technophobia on my part. Among many other benefits I could mention, I along with others have benefitted appreciably from advances, in medical sciences and technologies and can be genuinely laudatory of and grateful for them. Instead, it should be taken to dispel accusations of alarmism; for it is meant mainly as a bracing splash in the faces of overly optimistic technophiles who blithely sideline, if not dismiss, concerns that are primarily moral and political in nature. Too readily skipping over the moral to the practical concerns, the optimists propose that any practical problems caused by one technology can always be resolved by application of newer ones. One can grant (as we saw above in the case of the use of freon as a refrigerant) that locally applied negative feedback can dampen or even eliminate locally arising problems. But despite such band-aid fixes, the promise of and faith in an ever-increasing technoscientific progress is based on the premise that, at a global level, such progress is endless and whose *unintended* detrimental consequences can always be subjected to countervailing ones produced by intentionally designed negative-feedback controls. But, as our current climate and ecological crises attest, implementation of such controls must contend with the gradually accumulating effects of the reactive forces of nature and with the inertia and active resistance of powerful and morally negligent commercial, economic, political, and social interests. Such human, all too human interests rely on what overall is a positive feedforward system, which competent cyberneticists can tell you might very well lead to ever increasing crashes of progressive transhumanist programs.

unwittingly, to advancing the transhumanist agenda. Moreover, the rarely noticed moral hitch in the transhumanist promise poses a clear problem that few transhuman enthusiasts, in their rush toward their version of utopia, are not willing to address. The problem was already stated years ago by Hans Jonas as follows: "Technologically mastered nature now again includes man who (up to now) had, in technology, set himself against it as its master. . . . But whose power [of mastery] is this—and over whom or over what? Obviously the power of those living today over those coming after them, who will be the defenseless other side of prior choices made by the planners of today. The other side of the power of today is the future bondage of the living to the dead."[64] Note that his warning—had it been possible for other, nonhuman creatures to give it to their yet unborn future generations—is currently already being lived out by the tremendous loss of biodiversity that is plaguing the natural world. Of course, nonhuman creatures mainly living in their briefly extended, moment-to-moment present, can neither make nor heed such long-term warnings about their future demise. We humans, however, who in our living present can *anticipate* prospective events occurring in the distant future, need to heed such warnings and, in *recalling* events from our recent and distant pasts, realize that every innovative technology has the tendency to bring forth, along with its advertised benefits, its unintended and side effects, some of which are injurious to personal and collective well-being. That being so, just as the already apparent harmful effects of today's environmental degradation and global warming produced by the technological exploitation of fossil fuels will be felt more potently by future generations than by us, so too the long-term effects—wished-for ones as well as unwanted incidental ones—produced by today's transhumanist projects will impact future generations most seriously. Transhumanist evangelists tend to promote cyber-, nano-, and biotechnologically enhanced humanity and to readily defend the transhumanist agenda against so-called "bioconservatives,"[65] doing so by minimizing the potential downsides that may be caused by intentional malfeasance and, as noted above, by unintended detrimental side effects.

Add to these concerns the question of who will belong to the caste of transhumanist planners. Taking note of Murray Shanahan's observation that there is a historically invariant and self-perpetuating tendency for power, wealth, and resources to concentrate in the hands of the few,[66] the planners will most likely constitute a class of technoscientific and technomanagerial elites, some of

64. Quoted in Nick Bostrom, "In Defense of Posthuman Dignity," *Bioethics* 19, no. 3 (2005): 211.

65. For examples, see Nick Bostrom, "A Transhumanist Perspective on Human Genetic Enhancements," *Journal of Value Enquiry* 37, no. 4 (2003): 493–506; Bostrom, "In Defense of Posthuman Dignity."

66. Murray Shanahan, *The Technological Singularity* (MIT Press, 2015), 166.

whom are already placed in influential positions of power: Ray Kurzweil at Google; Mihail Roco at the National Nanotechnology Initiative; William Bainbridge, co-director of Human-Centered Computing at the National Science Foundation; and Nick Bostrom at Oxford University's Future of Humanity Institute, to name just four. Recalling the historic ties between the Promethean hate of the gods, Gnosticism, and the roots of metaphysical rebellion described by Albert Camus (see note 5 above), these individuals, among many others, belong to a class of what might be called "rebels with a cause."[67] In this regard, Charles Rubin remarks aptly that

> transhumanism rebels against the randomness of evolution and the mindlessness of a natural tendency to overshoot resources and collapse. . . . But its rebellion is not half as radical as it assumes, for transhumanism builds on the same underlying conception of nature that the Malthusians and Darwinians build on, vociferously rejecting the thought that nature has any inherent normative goals or purposes. While it rejects blind evolution as the future for man, it accepts it as the origins of man. While it rejects a Malthusian future [of the growth of human population catastrophically outpacing available resources], it does so with threatening the same old apocalypse if we do not transcend ourselves, and, in the form of Kurzweil's law of accelerating returns, it adopts a Malthusian sense that mankind is in the grip of forces beyond its control.
>
> Because [secular] transhumanism accepts this account of nature, it is driven [like the ancient Gnostics] to reject nature. Rejecting also any religious foundations of values, then, it is left with nothing but socially constructed norms developed in response to human power over nature, which, given the unpredictable transformative expectations they have for that power as it becomes not-human, ultimately amounts to no norms at all. Transhumanism is a nihilistic response to the nihilism of Malthusians and Darwinians.
>
> The moral lacuna at the heart of transhumanism is why it can advocate the progress of dehumanization so enthusiastically.[68]

This Promethean-Gnostically inspired transhumanism has manifested most noticeably in Ray Kurzweil, whose imagination foresees a day when the human mind that is merely the "software" in the human brain—or at least all the information stored in it—can be "uploaded" from its brain sites, onto an AI supercomputing device that, by retaining it in perpetuity, promises an ersatz-immor-

67. Mark C. Taylor, *Intervolution: Smart Bodies. Smart Things* (Columbia University Press, 2021), 172–73, points ot that at least some of them, like Nick Bostrom, are aware of the potential dangers to the human race raised by uncontrolled, runaway technology, especially in the rapidly developing area of artificial intelligence.

68. Charles T. Rubin, *Eclipse of Man: Human Extinction and the Meaning of Progress* (New Atlantis, 2014), 158–59.

tality to the further evolution of its own supercomputing powers. As pointed out by Mark Taylor, if in the future "information and, by extension, intelligence could be separated from matter and biological bodies, the ancient dream of immortality might become technologically feasible . . . [and] if mind can be uploaded, software engineers will become latter-day Gnostics, who crack the code that enables them to drop their bodies, leave Earth, and rise through the celestial spheres. This is precisely Kurzweil's dream."[69] Moreover, Taylor adds that

> Kurzweil's analysis of the Singularity [occurring when AI's brain emulation creates an intelligence exceeding many fold anything that the brightest human minds are capable of] represents the latest version of the traditional view of technology as an expression of *man's* will-to-power or will to mastery. After mastering death by escaping the body, the next challenge becomes colonizing the universe. Kurzweil predicts [that ultimately] "the entire universe will become saturated with our intelligence. This is the destiny of the universe. We will determine our fate rather than have it determined by current 'dumb,' simple, machinelike forces that rule celestial mechanics." When the universe is saturated with our intelligence, [the philosopher] Heidegger's prediction becomes true: "everywhere *man* turns he sees only himself." Down this path surely lies destruction [of the human race].[70]

Kurzweil's dream seems to manifest both his delusion of grandeur and his unhinging from human—an all too human—reckoning, an unhinging that Nietzsche more than a century ago espoused for "free spirits" like himself.[71] Shanahan reminds us that "as Friedrich Nietzsche said [in his *Daybreak*], above the door of the thinker of the future stands a sign that says 'What do I matter!'"[72] As did Nietzsche, many of today's philosophers consider the human *person*—the deeply and distinctive sensing, thinking, and feeling entity that most of us still refer to and regard as real as anything can be—to be merely an illusory construct. And since Nietzsche's Zarathustra viewed the human self instrumentally, as a mere bridge spanning the abyss that separates the human animal from the superhuman, then, as Shanahan remarks further, "if the transition is harsh [in contrast to the hope that it will be easy], what does it ultimately matter? In ten million years, the fleeting lives of a few apes on a tiny speck of dust in the middle of an ocean of spacetime will be forgotten. [But] the difficulty with this standpoint is that the Nietzschean visionary is a close

69. Taylor, *Intervolution*, 171.

70. Taylor, *Intervolution*, 174.

71. Friedrich Nietzsche, *The Will to Power* (Vintage Books, 1966); Friedrich Nietzsche, *Human, All Too Human* (Cambridge University Press, 1986).

72. Shanahan, *The Technological Singularity*, 163.

73. Shanahan, *The Technological Singularity*, 194–95.

cousin to the Nazi fanatic."[73] And it follows from such nihilistic vision, freed from all transcendent endowment of human dignity and value, that the "triumph of the will"[74] will be realized first in the gradual, but finally in the ultimate destruction of human life and culture.

Kurzweil's dream would pose a threat to the existence of *human* beings as such, for it would spell—to borrow Marilyn Robinson's apt phrase—the death of Adam.[75] Isn't it not only possible but also likely that an AI superintelligence might regard humans as mere biological curiosities to be consigned to one of its zoos or, worse yet, as biological detritus to be eliminated? As expressed by the astronomer Martin Rees,[76] prior to and underneath the current optimism accompanying the secular transhumanist agenda lies the danger that an AI-supported, autonomous Promethean technology learns increasingly to assimilate the Nietzschean will-to-power and thus, beyond good and evil, increasingly detaches itself from all-too-human existential and moral concerns.

For those who are not devotees of the technophilic will-to-power, this prospect can be a source of major existential angst. Christopher Mooney has noted claims made by psychiatrists "that there is serious psychoanalytic evidence for saying that people today are suffering from an unconscious despair, arising on the one hand from fear of becoming an appendage to the machine, and on the other from the sense of having less and less to say about their own destiny. Beneath this unrest is a deep and well-justified fear: that . . . [future steps] in technological progress may bring about the annihilation of the species."[77] And so, as Ronald Osborn explains, "in a world that has fully absorbed the loss of every transcendent source of value or meaning and torn away the masks of *agape* generated for some two millennia in the Western tradition by the story of divine incarnation, compassion for the weak is slave morality. Erotic [Dionysian] desire to dominate and exploit, when purified of lingering doubts and moral compunctions, is good health. Darkness is light. Nietzsche as the feral, inverted gaze of the Enlightenment project, is nihilism's bad conscience."[78] It is pitifully ironic that shortly before he went mad, Nietzsche, the ferocious enemy of *agape*, of pity and compassion, and a remorseless promoter of the will-to-power is said to have embraced out of compassion a horse lying, whipped by its owner, in a street of Turin, Italy. Whether or not this account is true, such an embrace of compassion (in both senses) would have been either the inaugural symptom of his incipient madness or else the last humanly sane thing he could

74. The title of Leni Riefenstahl's 1935 Nazi propaganda film.

75. Marilyn Robinson, *The Death of Adam: Essays on Modern Thought* (Picador, 2005); see especially her introductory chapter and the following one on Darwinism.

76. Martin Rees, *On the Future: Prospects for Humanity* (Princeton University Press, 2018).

77. Mooney, *Theology and Scientific Knowledge*, 195.

78. Osborn, *Humanism and the Death of God*, 158.

have done, thus cancelling out the "insanity"—and the evil[79]—that was his ruinous vainglory and will-to-power.

Theistic Transhumanism and Beyond?

Although the triad of Gnostic, Promethean, and Nietzschean thinking inspired and still inspires much of modernity, including secular transhumanism, there appears to be nothing unorthodox about considering and advocating a transhumanism in theistic traditions. I am not versed on how religious faith traditions, other than the Christian I am familiar with, might approach this issue; I therefore will confine my remarks to that tradition. It is a theological commonplace (i) that creation of the universe is not confined to a one-time event but is also an ongoing process and therefore (ii) that humans themselves, created in the *imago Dei*, the likeness and image of God, can thus be legitimately regarded as the Creator's cocreators. While it has long been held that God creates out of nothing, humans create with the things already put at their disposal by God. Moreover humans, being among God's creatures, are therefore charged with cocreating themselves, most notably by the value-laden, especially the moral, choices they exercise during their lifetimes. Given this charge, each of their lives can be seen as a creative progression guided by a vision of the true, the beautiful and the good, the kingdom of God preached and lived unto death on the cross by his incarnation, Jesus of Nazareth, who is the divine model of the Christian transhuman. However, due to our mortality and our tendency to dawdle and to sin, it is a progressive task that is left unfinished. The finishing, the perfection of human identity, to which each of us is called to contribute, is not left to human means alone but also to the grace of God, whose word speaks each of his creatures out of eternity into time. As our Creator, He is the God not only of history, of the past, but also of the present and the future. He eternally calls the universe and us from the past and present into the future; therefore, our calling is truly a vocation that can be undertaken with hope. In contrast to this, as Mooney has further aptly described,

> the essence of the technological mind is largely a refusal to believe on the basis of hope. Such belief will therefore always remain fragile and insecure. There will always be the suspicion [in the technophilic mind] that the values of individual persons, their desire for community, interpersonal creativity, and preservation of the world of nature can no longer be fostered after so many centuries of [technoscientific] growth. Here is where we must locate the burden of political responsibility and power. For we live in a maximum-risk situation. On the one hand, the responsible use of freedom must focus on this new human capacity to control all governance

79. Ortiz Hill, foreword to *The Roots and Flowers of Evil*, xv.

> decisions. On the other hand, from a religious point of view, relating such prudent decision-making to God's providential design must finally be the work of God's governance, not any human achievement. For [from a Christian viewpoint,] power, as [the theologian] Karl Rahner has said, is something to be gradually modified and absorbed by love. . . .[80]

And so, in our temporality, we Christians look in hope to God who beckons us in each present, each now, toward a future that does not forget or deny the past. Looking into the future beyond our individual lifetimes, the early 20th-century Jesuit paleontologist and geologist Pierre Teilhard de Chardin speculated at length, within a Christocentric teleological framework, on how the human might evolve beyond itself toward what he called the "ultra-human." Teilhard, who was no Luddite, proposed an imaginative account of how evolutionary advances in science and technology could assist this transmutation from human into ultra-human existence.[81] Yet, while from a Christian standpoint one can envision and hope along with Teilhard for a notional convergence of human nature toward the Omega point, the Parousia of the Cosmic Christ who is the lodestar of ultra-human perfection, one might also forgive Teilhard for lapsing imaginatively into an overly buoyant prognosis of humanity's God-destined transformation toward the ultra-human Cosmic Christ. For in contrast to Teilhard's borderline heterodox vision, the orthodox Christian view holds that all humans will encounter at the end of history the judge and redeemer of all, God Incarnate in Christ Jesus of Nazareth, who shared with each of us, except for sin, a *fully human* nature.

80. Mooney, *Theology and Scientific Knowledge*, 215–16.

81. Pierre Teilhard de Chardin, *The Future of Man* (Harper & Row, 1964). Along with being no Luddite, Teilhard also was not a savvy theologian. His reveries of human evolution toward the ultrahuman along with the evolution of Christ the Incarnate Word toward the Cosmic Christ was, according to Jacques Maritain, part and parcel of Teilhard's infatuation with science and his naïve, child-like mysticism that resulted in a form of Christian gnosis that Maritain regarded as theological fiction; see Jacques Maritain, *The Peasant of the Garone: An Old Layman Questions Himself About the Present Time* (Wipf & Stock Publishing, 1968), 116–26.

CHAPTER 9

An Instauration of a Science-Informed Religion and Theology

The haunting obscurity of the question [of human origins] has hardly been illuminated by recent biological, anthropological, and archeological discoveries, whatever success they have had in extending the time span which separates us from an ever more distant past. And it is unlikely that any factual information will ever throw light on the bewildering maze of more or less plausible hypotheses, all of which suffer from the incurable suspicion that their very plausibility and probability may well turn out to be their undoing since our whole real existence—the genesis of the [universe and] the earth, the development of organic life on it, the evolution of man out of the countless animal species—occurred against statistically overwhelming probabilities. All that is real in the universe and in nature once was an "infinite" improbability.

Hannah Arendt, *The Life of the Mind*, vol. 2: *Willing*, p. 202

In its desire to comprehend the universe, the intelligence cannot abandon its search until it has reached the first cause, and one can therefore say, with every show of right, that there is a congenial desire in the intelligence to know that cause. But between that and saying, as St. Thomas [Aquinas] does in effect, that the intelligence desires to know the first cause, not only as the cause of effects which it aspires to understand—as the universal *propter quid*—but in its essence, in and of itself independently of its effects and of its relations to everything else, there is surely an abyss?

The mystical impulse bridges the abyss in a single leap. The mystic discerns the One in the Unifying cause, and when he meets the Unifying cause, he adheres to the one. But can one say that his strength comes to him from the principle which first moved the intelligence to look for the "cause of causes"? Could one even say that the mystical impulse simply continues along the path of reason, that it simply goes further in the same direction? Would it not be better to recognize that the philosopher's reasoning conceals an anagogical dialectic, the inspiration of which is quite different from the general desire to know.

Henri de Lubac, *The Discovery of God*, p. 151

Recent Developments in the Theology of Science

The biological, anthropological, and archeological discoveries that have accumulated since Hannah Arendt published *The Life of the Mind* in the 1970s might have impressed her more than anything that went before. Nonetheless, the crucial point made by her that is still pertinent now is the sheer improbability of human existence in our universe. This is not only due to the mounting evidence that the physical conditions and the values of physical constants must be finely tuned—some extremely finely tuned—in order for any life, let alone intelligent human life, to exist in the universe. As we explore below, the very existence of the universe itself is a mystery that in my opinion has a zero probability of being solved by scientific means alone. It is therefore proper to apply not only philosophical thought to the question as to why anything at all exists but also theological thinking addressing the question as to how the myriad entities in the cosmos relate to divine reality.

In chapters 7 and 8, I argued that scientism in its various manifestations is currently the reigning ideology, belief system, and ersatz-religion of especially many atheistically inclined scientists and scholars. To theistic scientists and scholars, this secular religious belief system is an idolatry, exalting nature or humanity to the level of ersatz-gods. It is also built on the Promethean and Gnostic myths that human technoscience can on its own redeem, repair, and improve the state of nature and us with no need for divine assistance. In response to this challenge, can theists offer a religious and theological view of science that is consistent with their belief in a God who created and sustains the world in which we live? I believe that such a genuine religion—based on faith in a superhuman and supernatural God—and a corresponding theology of science can indeed be offered. It is, however, not an innovation but merely an updated reprise of a longstanding theological tradition. Christian scientists and scholars from several specialty disciplines, among them, Christopher Baglow, Stephen Barr, William Craig, John Lennox, Alister McGrath, Tom McLeish, John Polkinghorne, Robert Spitzer, and Robert Russell, to name just a few, have already contributed significantly to a genuine religious and theological perspective and understanding of science.[1] As such, their thoughtful writ-

1. Christopher T. Baglow, *Creation: A Catholic's Guide to God and the Universe* (Ave Maria Press, 2021). Stephen M. Barr, *Modern Physics and Ancient Faith* (University of Notre Dame Press, 2003); William Lane Craig, "In Defense of Theistic Arguments," in *The Future of Atheism: Alister McGrath & Daniel Dennett in Dialogue*, ed. Robert B. Stewart (Fortress Press, 2008); John C. Lennox, *Gunning for God* (Lion Hudson, 2011); Alister McGrath, *The Twilight of Atheism: The Rise and Fall of Disbelief in the Modern World* (Random House, 2006); Tom McLeish, *Faith and Wisdom in Science* (Oxford University Press, 2014); John Polkinghorne, *One World: The Interaction of Science and Theology* (Princeton University Press, 1986); John Polkinghorne, *Theology in the Context of Science* (Yale University Press,

ings contribute to a viable theology of science. What I find significant is that, for many of them, quantum physics, physical cosmology, and biology play central roles in the development of their thinking. So, below I dare to add my two-cents-worth to a bona fide religion and theology of science that can be theologically supported by physical, cosmological, and biological sciences. The reason for this is that these sciences deal with answering questions concerning not only the nature but also the origin and the fate of the universe and the origin and fate of all life in it. They therefore are relevant to theological concerns regarding the *existence, origin, fate, and meaning* of the universe and of life. To other questions, for instance, those concerned with the *evolution* of the universe and of life, atheistic evolutionists like Daniel Dennett and Richard Dawkins can offer only secondary and penultimate answers that, if not deliberately evading, at least implicitly avoid addressing two ultimate metaphysical questions: *Why is there not nothing, why is there anything at all*? and *What is the origin and end—the goal and meaning—of life*?[2]

In light of the development of modern science, the call for an updated theology of science is not new. The historian of science Joseph Dauben comments on the Roman Church's concerns regarding scientific developments in the late 19th century as follows:

> Pope Leo XIII's attempt to reconcile the new and often perplexing discoveries of science with scripture and with the authorities of the Church encouraged a number of Catholic intellectuals to study the various branches of natural science in detail. . . . Among the first of his pronouncements was the encyclical *Aeterni Patris*, delivered on August 4, 1879. Urged by his brother, the then Cardinal Giuseppe Pecci, Leo XIII sought a renewal of philosophical thought along the lines of a revived Thomism. Seen as an opposing force to political and social liberalism, Leo XIII's new program included several attempts to revitalize and to modernize the thought of the Church by reorganizing the Academy of St. Thomas [founded by his brother in 1859], and by nominating Désiré Mercier (later to become one of the most prominent figures in the neo-Thomist movement), to a chair of Thomism at the [Belgian] University of Louvain.[3]

2009); Robert John Russell et al., eds., *Quantum Cosmology and the Laws of Nature: Scientific Perspectives on Divine Action* (Vatican Observatory Foundation, 1993); Robert J. Spitzer, *New Proofs for the Existence of God* (William B. Eerdmans Publishing, 2010); Robert J. Spitzer, *Evidence for God from Physics and Philosophy: Extending the Legacy of Monsignor Georges Lemaitre and St. Thomas Aquinas* (St. Augustine Press, 2016).

2. For a historical overview of these perennially vexing questions posed to and by philosophers, see Hannah Arendt's *The Life of the Mind*, vol. 1: *Thinking*, 141–49.

3. Joseph Warren Dauben, *Georg Cantor: His Mathematics and Philosophy of the Infinite* (Princeton University Press, 1990), 140–41.

According to Dauben, Cardinal Giuseppe Pecci's urging his brother to revitalize the Church's thought along the lines of an updated Thomism was prompted by his belief that from a historically informed perspective the writing on the wall was "that the Church had to enter the current of modern times or be left behind."[4] In other words, in terms of future sociocultural developments, the Church would become increasingly irrelevant.

From the latter half of the 19th century and still to this day neo-Thomism seems to be the reigning thought informing the Church about engaging with the modern world and its science.[5] Yet, about three decades ago, in his book *Nowa Fyzika i Nowa Theologia (The New Physics and a New Theology)*, the Polish physicist and theologian Michał (Michael) Heller called for an even newer theology of science and of creation. Below I will present and comment on several points of his thinking that I think are worth pursuing. Regarding the relation between the theologies of science and of creation, Heller states that

> on the one hand, the principal research tool of the theology of science should be reflection in the light of the theological truths about creation; on the other hand the theological concept of creation, more than any other theological doctrine, depends on the status of scientific thinking in a given epoch.
>
> The profound philosophical and theological elaboration of the truths about creation, which St. Thomas Aquinas accomplished in the 13th century, was undoubtedly due to his excellent understanding of the natural sciences of the time. It is also necessary to keep in mind that, although St. Thomas had established the distinction and rigorous separation between philosophy and theology, the scientific knowledge of that epoch was frequently subtended by and mixed in with philosophical reflections. So science, even though for the most part implicitly, participated with philosophy in the formulation of theological analyses of creation.[6]

However, it is an empirical and cultural fact that in our present epoch we no longer rely on the Aristotelian science of St. Thomas's time, concerned as it was with logic and antiquated natural sciences of physics and biology, but instead science must now rely on the newer physics and biology that developed during the two centuries prior to the present one. The Church's embrace of neo-Thomism that prevailed in theological thinking from the late 19th through the middle of the 20th century was, as assessed by Heller, not capable of keeping up

4. Dauben, *Georg Cantor*, 141.

5. Dauben, *Georg Cantor*, 141. In the spirit of this revived neo-Thomism, the 20th-century French philosopher Jacques Maritain devoted extensive portions of his major work, *The Degrees of Knowledge*, to the relation between philosophical, metaphysical, and theological thinking and developments in modern physics.

6. Michael Heller, *The New Physics and New Theology* (Vatican Observatory Foundation, 1996), 102.

with developments in the new sciences because of its adherence to Aristotelian scientific and philosophical categories. "Today, in retrospect," notes Heller, "one can state unambiguously that the attempt [of Christian neo-Thomism to dialogue with the new sciences] was doomed to failure and [for which] . . . one can see clearly the reasons. In fact, the [neo-Thomistic] movement was led completely astray by the view of science as Aristotelian, while right from the beginning [near the turn of the 17th century modern] science was remaking itself in the tradition of Archimedes."[7] That tradition was based on creative problem-solving that relied not only on developing new insights about the physical properties of the world through the use of our imaginative and speculative mental powers but also on quantitative experimental measurements testing and verifying the research hypotheses that are logically generated from the insights. These experimental and quantitative aspects of science were alien to Aristotle's purely observational and qualitative approach to science, which, as noted in chapter 6 (see there, notes 15 and 16), was characterized at best by thing-numeracy.

Regarding the creation of the universe and the material and physical entities in it, Heller elaborates in the following cogent remarks that

> the fundamental theological truth concerning the universe is the statement that establishes its creation by God. It is necessary to state right away the tautology that for theologians the universe is all of that which has been created by God. Clearly the universe of science and the universe of theology are not identical. The universe of science is only a part of the universe of theology. This is true not only in the sense that the universe of science contains only that which is defined as the "material world," while the universe of theology goes beyond the domain of the material, but also in the sense that theology can pronounce statements about the "material world" which go beyond [the statements justified by] the empirical method, that is, which does not pertain to the universe of science. Thus, the material world in the theological perspective is, in a sense, richer than the material world as seen in the perspective of the natural sciences. It is precisely here that the possibility arises for a theology of science. As a reflection on the sciences the theology of science would study the consequences of the fact that the natural sciences explore the world created by God. . . . [And so,] if it is correct to say that science is of great value for humanity, then the theology of science should be considered as a subheading of the theology of earthly values. A specific function of the subheading would be, among other matters, to have frequent recourse to the results of the philosophy of science. The philosophy of science . . . examines the boundaries of the possibilities of the natural sciences. On the contrary theology pushes on beyond those boundaries. The awareness that the world has been created by God permits the theology of science to glimpse aspects and dimensions

7. Heller, *The New Physics*, 62.

> of the world which cannot be reached by modern empirical investigations. In other words, the theology of science can look at the boundaries of the empirical domain and, therefore, at the boundaries of the natural sciences, by putting itself in a certain sense on the other side, that is, on the side not accessible to the sciences themselves.[8]

These remarks are very pertinent for several reasons. For one, they can allay some of the concern raised by the religious philosopher Louis Dupré and the Jesuit scholar Michael Buckley (see, above, Dupré's introductory epigraph to part 3). The concern, elaborated by Buckley, is

> that the strategies of theism or religious apologetics in early modernity has led theologians to bracket whatever was of specific religious character or warrant and rely upon the new and prospering sciences for "the first foundations of religion." The implicit but unrecognized premise in such a strategy, building on the new [science of] mechanics, was that the uniquely religious—in all of its experiential, traditional, institutional, and social forms—was cognitively empty, that religion could not secure its own central assertion, and that it had to appeal to other sciences and disciplines for its foundations and even for its methodology. . . . [This reinforces] the basic argument of [Buckley's own book] *At the Origins of Modern Atheism* together with its reading of the dialectic genesis of modern atheism. . . . [Yet obviously] and importantly, [although other] countless social, economic and political influences were formatively at play . . . [the dialectic is what] lent all of these other influences direction and strength. In many ways, modern atheism was the self-subversion of this form of theism.[9]

What is the "uniquely religious" that Buckley is referring to? A sample of answers, given in Buckley's own (but here, slightly modified) words, is that the religious is that by which

> God is experienced or worshipped as a presence and asserted in a real assent. . . ,[10] [that] God is given to human beings in their primordial experience of longing for human happiness, [that] in their experience of human yearning they may come to recognize a desire for a comprehensive, personal love, meaning, and communication . . . [in which] God is given—so vaguely and incomprehensibly—as the focus of these desires . . . , [that] God is given to human beings historically, as part of human history, in Jesus of Nazareth . . . ,[11] [and] that the highest categorical disclosures of

8. Heller, *The New Physics*, 97–98.

9. Michael J. Buckley, SJ, preface to *Denying and Disclosing God: The Ambiguous Progress of Modern Atheism* (Yale University Press, 2004), xi.

10. Buckley, *Denying and Disclosing God*, 37.

11. Buckley, *Denying and Disclosing God*, 68.

> God are the lives of holiness . . . [a holiness that] manifests rather than entails the reality of God as a living presence in the interactions and struggles in which human beings act and are drawn, in which they move toward God in accord with their longings and the structures of their consciousness, and then undergo a response that they may not realize as divine.[12]

From a Christian standpoint, one cannot but agree with these summaries of the truly religious, especially, as I already explained in chapter 1 (see also appendix 2), with their emphasizing the conscious *experience* of the religious yearnings and desires for human happiness, personal love, meaning, and communication with the other, that are summarily experienced as the longings for the Ultimate Other that is God.

Nonetheless, one can here note that Buckley's concerns regarding the historic growth of modern atheism place the responsibility for this growth on historic events that were an inevitable side effect of the concomitant growth of science. In other words, as Buckley notes in reference to Steven Weinberg's condemnation of religion: "It was not the opposition of science to religion; it was much more the endorsement of science [by theologians] that generated modern atheism. It was not because science was indifferent or antagonistic [to religion(?)]; it was because it was too enthusiastically affirmative and comprehensively supportive [of atheism(?)] that atheism emerged."[13] This compact, somewhat puzzling wording—note the bracketed questions]—needs some elaboration and clearing up. I believe what Buckley meant to say is that the endorsement of mechanistic science was not only made available to Enlightenment atheists but also appropriated and incorporated too readily into the thinking of otherwise well-meaning but benighted theists. Hence, science was enthusiastically affirmative and comprehensively supportive not only to atheist thought but also to that of theists. It was in this way that, as also noted above by Buckley, modern atheism was the self-subversion of this form of what I take to be a *scientistically inspired theism*. Yet, this self-subversive form of a too readily accommodating theism is one which the Church—especially after Pope Leo XIII, expressing confidence in the philosophical and theological resources of the Church, issued the encyclical *Aeterni Patris*—does not endorse in its response to the rise of modern atheism. In contrast to the self-subversive accommodation of theology to science, one can invoke Jean Daniélou's introductory epigraph to part 3, where he states that there is a danger of confusing the two regions of scientific and theological reasoning and, therefore, that it is the proper function of scientific criticism to clear up this confusion, but not to pronounce judgments on strictly religious matters. Institutionally, the Church claims to be a repository, protector, and promoter of truth and therefore can

12. Buckley, *Denying and Disclosing God*, 130.
13. Buckley, *Denying and Disclosing God*, 2.

no longer deny scientific truths; but instead, in fully recognizing the institutional, authoritative limits of science, the Church can take them as grist for the development of robust theological thinking.

Hence, additional reasons that Heller's above comments are pertinent is that they importantly draw clear lines between the domains of theology and the natural sciences. The aims and methods of the two domains are governed—to adapt Stephen Jay Gould's phrasing—by non-overlapping magisteria. Additionally, since science is valued by humanity but, as pointed out in chapters 3 and 4, since it can only tell us that, but not why, it ought to be valued, it is most appropriate that this why-aspect of human values remain of concern in the disciplines of philosophy and theology rather than science. Nevertheless, the two separate domains of science and theology can be linked, via philosophy of science, within the capacious domain of general-interest studies—namely, the history of ideas. Finally, in line with Pope Leo XIII's encyclical, Heller's remarks also reflect a deep trust that the truths revealed by the natural sciences of any epoch are not fatal to the truths revealed by philosophical study nor to fundamental truths underlying theological study, such as the existence of a Creator God. It is in the spirit of such research that I offer the following.

A Search for Theologically Relevant Truths in Physics and Physical Cosmology

When it comes to thinking about the timeline of the evolution of our universe, some scientists and physical cosmologists appear to be "hyperallergic" to several important problematic aspects. One is the problem of mathematical infinities that occur when calculations are applied in quantum field theory. Eliminating these infinities can be accomplished by a standard computational procedure, a mathematical "trick" known as renormalization. That said, it should also be noted that an additional reason for the problem of infinite numerical values in the science of physics may be the following. Infinite numbers have found opposition not only in the physical sciences but, since at least the latter half of the 19th century, also in the mathematical sciences themselves. As noted also by Dauben, the German mathematician Georg Cantor, whose life spanned the turn of the 20th century, was among the founders of what is now known as set theory and the first to propose and promote the real existence in mathematics of transfinite numbers, an idea to which some of his contemporary mathematicians and philosophers were strongly opposed. The Catholic philosopher and theologian Constantin Gutberlet, a contemporary and compatriot of Cantor, "realized that the study of infinity had entered a new phase with the appearance of Cantor's mathematical and philosophical studies. The question uppermost in Gutberlet's [theological] mind concerned the challenge posed by mathematical infinity to the unique, absolute infinity of God's existence. It was not long before correspondence [with Gutberlet] over this question began to deepen Cantor's interest in the theological aspects of his theory of transfinite numbers. It was Cantor's claim that instead of diminishing [and therefore challenging] the extent of God's nature and dominion, the transfinite numbers actually made it all the greater."[12] Despite finding opposition among some other theologians, Gutberlet defended "the existence of the [mathematical] absolute infinite . . . and used a ploy reminiscent of [Anglo-Irish bishop and idealist philosopher] Berkeley's use of God as a guarantor of the external world. In short, Gutberlet argued that God Himself ensured the existence of Cantor's transfinite numbers. . . ."[14] (One need not go so far as claiming that the association of the notion of infinity with the notion of God is the primary reason for physicists' aversion to infinite values; nevertheless, this association might be an area of interest in exploring the history behind their aversion to infinities.)

Besides the existence of numerical infinities, physicists and cosmologists are faced with two additional problems, the Anthropic Principle and the Big-Bang singularity (which is accompanied by its own problem of infinities). These two issues relate to the fact that the current best estimate of the age of our universe is about 14.3 billion years. As to the Anthropic Principle, although there are too many versions of it to discuss here, we will rely on the basic definition, offered by the physicist Leonard Susskind, that it is "a hypothetical principle that says that the world [the universe we inhabit] is fine-tuned so that we can be here to observe it."[15] The "we" referred to applies especially to physicists whose theories are meant to explain the empirical observations they make of the physical objects and properties in our world. However, since physicists, like the rest of us, are humans, we need to account for the fact that the evolution of our world to the present took 14.3 billion years, and that the evolution of the living creatures in it required approximately the last 3.5 billion years of its evolution before any life form resembling our distant ancestors, the hominins, appeared; while their first appearance was followed by another two to three million years before *homo sapiens*, modern humans, appeared. At any rate, according to the Anthropic Principle, humans are endowed with a very special status, a status expressed in the belief of a vast number of Christians who relate to God as the most beloved and God-like of all his creatures.[16]

In my opinion, what therefore bothers scientists and cosmologists is that the Anthropic Principle is so easily relatable to religion, to which for assorted reasons many of them are averse. Referring especially to the views of one of his

14. Dauben, *Georg Cantor*, 143.

15. Susskind, *The Cosmic Landscape*, 7.

16. I say "most" beloved, since God loves creation and therefore each one of his creatures; yet the Christian belief is that He especially loved those whom he created in his image.

fellow scientists, Susskind goes on to say that his and other physicists' aversions to religion are due to the fact that perhaps "God did make the world. But scientists—*real* scientists—resist the temptation to explain natural phenomena, *including creation itself*, by divine intervention. Why? Because as scientists we understand that there is a compelling human need to believe—the need to be comforted—that easily clouds people's judgment. It is all too easy to fall into the seductive trap of a comforting fairy tale. *So we [real scientists] resist, to the death*, all explanations of the world based on anything but the Laws of Physics, mathematics, and probability"[17] (emphases added).

These are oversimplified yet strong words, nay fighting words, that certainly cannot apply to all real scientists, past or present. For one, the use of standard tropes such as the "compelling human need to believe [in God]" as expressing the "the need to be comforted" and for humans' tendencies "to fall into the seductive trap of a comforting fairy tale" are already laced with a bias against theistic religions. Such simplified functional characterizations of religion do not apply to many religious scientists or scholars; to name just a few eminent scientists: Clerk Maxwell, who in the 19th century developed the theory of electromagnetic dynamics; the early 20th century physicist Max Planck, who discovered/proposed the quantal nature of the subatomic world; and, more recently, the physicists among the scientists and scholars I listed in this chapter's introduction. It is difficult to believe that the rational judgments of these and many other religious scientists were so easily "clouded" by this overwhelming "need to be comforted," as though satisfying this need was the only or prime motivation for being religious. I suspect also that such needlessly strong and stereotyped debunking of religion gets at something much deeper—namely, an intense aversion to God. Here we might recall some of Thomas Nagel's comments already noted in the introduction, in which he expresses his profound antipathy to God as follows: "It isn't just that I don't believe in God and, naturally, hope that I'm right in my belief. It's that I hope that there is no God! I don't want there to be God; I don't want the universe to be like that. My guess is that this cosmic authority problem [of humbly deferring human authority to the ultimate authority to God] is not a rare condition and that it is responsible for much of the scientism and reductionism of our time."[18] In other words, if God is the author/creator of this world, he wields ultimate knowledge of and authority over the world, an authoritative knowledge that, according to many a scientistically inclined, antireligious scientist, "nothing but the Laws of Physics, mathematics, and probability" can provide. One can agree with Susskind that in the context of modern science all inner-worldly physical phenomena ought to be explainable by only inner-worldly physical processes and properties. The question,

17. Susskind, *The Cosmic Landscape*, 355.
18. Nagel, *The Last Word*, 131.

however, is: To what extent is the very existence and the creation of the physical and natural entities encompassed by the universe, explainable solely by the "real" scientists exemplified by Susskind himself?

Several So-far Inexplicable Physical Phenomena

Here I preface this section by noting that the following arguments are based on what are currently some of the best-established empirical findings and mathematically formalized physical theories and speculations. Limited as they are to the present state of affairs, the current assessment may have to change in view of potential future empirical findings and theoretical developments.

That said, let's now turn to the Big Bang singularity, which raises one of the most puzzling questions posed to physical cosmologists. What current theories cannot answer is what the properties of the universe (such as its temperature, energy density, and size) were in its very earliest stages of evolution, where Einstein's general theory of relativity breaks down. Regressing backwards in time, when the age of the universe gets ever closer to 0 sec (mathematically, 0 is the limit of, say, 10^{-n} sec as $n \rightarrow \infty$), it approaches a singularity. And it is here, in this very short-interval regime, that current quantum physics is applicable. Yet, at what is designated as the origin of the Big Bang, the universe's temperature and energy density theoretically approaches, from a mathematical standpoint, an undesirable infinite value. The Big-Bang singularity also indicates that for the universe there was no "before" the zero-second limit-point of time.

However, the Big Bang initiated the "after" that followed the zero-second limit-point. According to the current inflationary cosmological model, after an extremely brief period following the Big Bang, the very young and tiny universe went through a relatively brief period of exponential hyperinflation that lasted about 380,000 years. This brief period was followed by a longer period of a decelerating inflation until about 7.8 billion years ago; and this longer period of decelerating expansion in turn was followed by a period of a gradually accelerating inflation of the universe that is still going some 6.5 billion later, resulting in the universe's present age of approximately 14.3 billion years. During the past century, physicists and cosmologists have addressed the two following puzzling questions: How can general relativity and quantum mechanics be united in a single and hopefully final theory of physics? And, even if such a theory can eventually be developed, what bearing would it have on our understanding of the origin and the fate of the universe? Up to now, definitive answers to the two questions are still lacking.

Addressing these questions has resulted in a spate of publications on (i) quantum string theory, (ii) quantum loop theory, and (iii) M theory (which appears to be a special application of the prior two theories). Surely noteworthy is the fact that new and elegant mathematics has been developed in these theoretical approaches; despite the mathematical advances, however, these theoretical enterprises have been challenged on several grounds by their critics.[19] That said, one of the ways of eliminating anthropic and theistic implications of the Big Bang singularity is to posit, as some string theorists have done, the existence of a megaverse, also referred to as a multiverse, as Leonard Susskind has done. Here, the number of the megaverse's "pocket universes"—in one of which we presumably live—is taken to be at least as large as 10^{500}, if not infinite. Hence, it is very highly likely, if not certain, that at least one of these pocket universes, e.g., ours, happens to have sufficiently intelligent and technologically advanced creatures in it that are able to make observations and construct theories of its physical properties. Hence also, so the reasoning goes, we need not wonder why, by pure chance, the human species exists in one of these pocket universes any more than why, by equally pure chance, each one of us exists here and now. In other words, we have no need to invoke the theologically relevant Anthropic Principle. Alternatively, one can assume an eternal bouncing or cycling universe, characterized by repeated cycles of expansion followed by contraction as proposed, for example, by Roger Penrose and by Anna Ijjas, Paul Steinhardt, and Abraham Loeb.[20] In both of these proposals, the universe is characterized by endless cycles of contraction followed by expansion, in the latter of which we now happen to live. However, on the reasonable assumption that during any past, sufficiently long, interval of time the average Hubble constant—i.e., the rate at which the cycling universe is expanding—is positive, the mathematical theorizing of Arvind Borde, Alan Guth, and Alexander Vilenkin has discovered a general cosmological constraint, according to which "a cosmological model which is inflating—*or just expanding sufficiently fast*—must be incomplete in null and timelike past directions."[21] Translated into everyday English, whatever the universe's temporal structure, it cannot have existed infinitely into the past and therefore must have had a beginning at some point (at t = 0.0 [null] sec) in

19. See Bernard Carr and George F. Ellis, "Universe or Multiverse?," *Astronomy & Geophysics* 49, no. 2 (2008): 229–33; George Ellis, "Physics Ain't What It Used to Be: Science Is Venturing into Areas Where Experimental Verification Simply Isn't Possible," *Nature* 438, no. 7069 (2005): 739–40; Hossenfelder, *Lost in Math*; Roger Penrose, *Fashion, Faith, and Fantasy in the New Physics and Beyond* (Princeton University Press, 2016); Lee Smolin, *The Trouble with Physics: The Rise of String Theory, The Fall of a Science, and What Comes Next* (Houghton Mifflin & Co., 2007); Peter Woit, *Not Even Wrong: The Failure of String Theory and the Continuing Challenge to Unify the Laws of Physics* (Random House, 2011).

20. Anna Ijjas et al., "Inflationary Paradigm in Trouble After Planck 2013," *Physics Letters B* 723, no. 4–5 (2013): 261–66; Anna Ijjas et al., "POP Goes the Universe," *Scientific American* 316, no. 2 (2017): 32–39; Anna Ijjas and Paul J. Steinhardt, "A New Kind of Cyclic Universe," *Physics Letters B* 795 (2019): 666–72; Anna Ijjas and Paul J. Steinhardt, "Entropy, Black Holes, and the New Cyclic Universe," *Physics Letters B* 824 (2022): 136823; Roger Penrose, *Cycles of Time: An Extraordinary New View of the Universe* (Vintage Books, 2012).

21. Borde et al., "Inflationary Spacetimes Are Incomplete in Past Directions," *Physics Review Letters* 90, no. 15 (2003): 151301.

the past. As further elaborated by Alan Guth, the temporal constraint proposed by Borde et al. holds not only for models of eternal inflation,[22] which are closely related to multiverse cosmologies, but also to bouncing-universe cosmologies.[23] Nevertheless, Ijjas and Steinhardt very recently proposed a revised cycling model of the universe that presumably could be complete or eternal in both the past and future temporal directions.[24] The model was specified (i) by a Hubble parameter for the expansion rate that is characterized by an initial growth followed by a decline during each cycle and (ii) by a cosmic scale factor that grows exponentially from one oscillation to the next in order to counteract the progressive increase of entropy across cycles. However, in line with Borde and coworkers' conclusions, in recent reanalysis of Ijjas and Steinhardt's and Penrose's cycling universe models, William Kinney and colleagues were able to show that, like inflationary cosmologies, the newly proposed cycling-universe models also are past incomplete, and therefore have a null-point beginning.[25] It should be evident that Borde et al.'s constraint, applying to inflationary Big Bang cosmologies, eternal inflation/multiverse cosmologies, and bouncing or cycling cosmologies, signals a clearly relevant message to theology that our universe had a temporal origin.

However, to avoid such dreaded theistic implications, other proposals, some made by atheistically inclined physical cosmologists, attempt to explain, via several bootstrap theories, the spontaneous self-creation of the universe. These proposals apply theoretical notions of quantum mechanics (originally developed to describe the properties of subatomic particles) to the scale of the universe. One expression of these highly questionable proposals resulted, as Stanley Jaki explains it, in "the so-called inflationary theory of the universe as well as in the wide acclaim accorded to them [i.e., the proposals, by their proposers and their scientistic fans], or inversely, in the almost complete absence of protest within and without the scientific community. The core of those claims is nothing less than the spontaneous tunnelling of the entire universe, nay of countless universes, through that infinitely high energy barrier that separates 'nothing' from what really exists. Compared with this robbery on a truly cosmic

22. Alan H. Guth, "Eternal Inflation and Its Implications," *Journal of Physics A: Mathematical and Theoretical* 40, no. 25 (2007): 6811–26.

23. Alan Guth and Paul Gabrielsen, "QnAs with Alan Guth," *Proceedings of the National Academy of Sciences of the United States of America* 111, no. 41 (2014): 14640; Guth et al., "Inflationary Paradigm After Planck 2013," *Physics Letters* B, 733 (2023): 112–19.

24. Ijjas and Steinhardt, "A New Kind of Cyclic Universe"; Ijjas and Steinhardt, "Entropy, Black Holes."

25. William H. Kinney and Nina K. Stein, "Cyclic Cosmology and Geodesic Completeness," *Journal of Cosmology and Astroparticle Physics* 2022, no. 6 (2022): 1–7. See also Kinney et al., "Borde-Guth-Vilenkin Theorem in Extended de Sitter Spaces," *Physical Review D* 109, no. 4 (2024): 043519.

scale the great train robbery [occurring on May 15, 1855, in London] may seem the puniest of petty thefts."[26]

A second attempt to avoid theological implications is to apply theoretical notions of quantum mechanics in a slightly different fashion. Here the purported "nothing" is, in the case of the cosmologist Lawrence Krauss, assumed to be the quantum vacuum, defined as the zero-limited energetic ground state of the universe in which "virtual" particles pop into and out of existence.[27] This quantum-vacuum approach clearly does not resemble the philosophically or theologically assumed literal or absolute nothing. Similar to its "virtual" particles, the quantum vacuum also is a "virtual" or "good-enough" nothing offered by Krauss. The philosopher Daniel Dennett follows suit when he states that the universe, as "we have seen, does perform a version of the ultimate bootstrapping trick; it creates itself *ex nihilo*; or at any rate out of something that is *well-nigh indistinguishable from nothing at all*"[28] (emphasis added). Again as noted by Stanley Jaki, "a cosmologist [like Krauss or a philosopher like Dennett] simply craters to [philosophical] primitivism when he claims that the 'creation' by quantum mechanics of virtual particles out of nothing is only 'slightly different' from emergence out of literally nothing."[29]

A third explanatory version for the existence of the universe without appeal to God, that resembles the one offered by Krauss, has been offered by the string theorist Brian Greene, who states, "To that end [of explaining the existence of the universe], we will need to understand various cosmological details more fully. First up: What drove the primordial nugget to start expanding in the first

26. Stanley L. Jaki, *God and the Cosmologists* (Regnery Gateway, 1989), 127.

27. For examples, see Krauss, *A Universe from Nothing*; Alexander Vilenkin, "Creation of Universes from Nothing," *Physics Letters B* 117, no. 1–2 (1982): 25–28. Although Vilenkin has changed his mind regarding the spontaneous creation of the universe out of nothing (see Spitzer, *Evidence for God*, 61–64), Krauss—perhaps for personal atheist ideological reasons—seems to stick to the spontaneous-creation-out-of-nothing hypothesis. Similar to Krauss and Vilenkin, Maya Lincoln and Avi Wasser, "Spontaneous Creation of the Universe Ex Nihilo," *Physics of the Dark Universe* 2, no. 4 (2013): 196, have more recently proposed a theory of creation out of nothing, in which they define it as follows: "'nothing' is equivalent to an infinite number of simultaneous Nullifying Information Elements (NIEs)—information elements that co-exist simultaneously and cancel [logically oppose] each other." Regarding the quantum nothing or vacuum, Susskind, *The Cosmic Landscape*, 72–73, notes that while "theoretical physicists are used to thinking of the vacuum as flickering in and out of existence so quickly that we cannot detect them under normal circumstances," the "vacuum is not the state of zero energy. It is merely the state of minimum energy." Hence, neither the quantum vacuum nor the infinite number of simultaneous NIEs can qualify as what philosophers refer to an absolute void, which contains nothing whatsoever—not the near-zero energy of the quantum vacuum nor any "nullifying" informational states.

28. Dennett, *Breaking the Spell*, 244.

29. Jaki, *God and the Cosmologists*, 137.

place? Or, in looser language, what ignited the big bang [the initial short-lived super-inflation of the universe]?"[30] One should note immediately that a cosmological detail that Greene does not consider is how this teeniest-tiniest nugget itself came about. Presumably, like Krauss's quantum vacuum, it somehow simply pre-existed the Big Bang.

And a fourth way to avoid theological implications is to develop a cosmological model based on an open, no-boundary universe—a universe with specifically no temporal boundary—proposed by Hartle and Hawking.[31] This approach, however, is also problematic and has been criticized as seriously flawed.[32]

A fifth way, combining elements of Krauss's and the multiverse ways, is to propose cosmological models based on eternal chaotic inflation, according to which, as Stephen Meyer explains, its proponents "postulated [the existence of an] 'inflaton field'—a field that physicists conceived as generating the outward or repulsive pressure of space, causing the universe to expand . . . [and which] would be subject to quantum fluctuations in the energy of the field. As a result, they [the enteral-chaotic-inflation proponents] thought these fluctuations would necessarily produce causally disconnected regions of space—effectively separate 'bubble universes.'"[33] Moreover, the creation of ever newer bubble universes would go on indefinitely into the infinite future. In addition to problems with these theoretical schemes, which will be discussed later, I, along with the astrophysicist Bernard Haisch, find the implications of potentially infinite number of universes bubbling up, as well as those of the many-worlds solution to the observation problem in quantum mechanics,[34] morally reprehensible. Talking specifically of the many-worlds interpretation of quantum mechanics, Haisch protests against this and similar interpretations as follows:

> I personally find this [the hypothesis of infinite alternative universes] absurd and morally repugnant. In those [infinite] alternate universes, decisions are made quite opposite to those I would make in this universe. In any one of these alternate worlds, I might be a serial killer or terrorist, not a scientist. I do not accept that as possible. The Many Worlds interpretation of reality reduces human beings to choiceless, splintered automatons.

30. Greene, *Until the End of Time*, 46.

31. J. B. Hartle and S. W. Hawking, "Wave Function of the Universe," *Physical Review D* 28, no. 12 (1983): 2960–75.

32. See Don N. Page, "Susskind's Challenge to the Hartle–Hawking No-Boundary Proposal and Possible Resolutions," *Journal of Cosmology and Astroparticle Physics* 2007 (2007): 2–20.

33. Meyer, *Return of the God Hypothesis*, 120–21.

34. Bryce S. DeWitt, "Quantum Mechanics and Reality," *Physics Today* 23, no. 9 (1970): 30–35; Hugh Everett, "Relative State Formulation of Quantum Mechanics," *Reviews of Modern Physics* 29, no. 3 (1957): 454–62.

> I cannot believe in a theory that relies on an infinite number of dichotomous existences just to satisfy the requirement that all must be random and purposeless, with all the outcomes possible. Indeed, I think it fair to ask: Isn't the Many Worlds interpretation of quantum mechanics [or the many bubble universes proposed by eternal chaotic inflation] more outrageous than even most spiritual worldviews?[35]

Along with other religious scientists, I can answer his question with an emphatic "Yes; indeed, it is!" While, as noted above, physical cosmologists have had to deal with the Anthropic Principle, something akin to a Morality Principle may also have to play a role in future theorizing by physical cosmologists as well as theologians.[36]

The Problem of Applying Inner-Worldly Physics to the Universe as a Whole

> Human transcendental subjectivity experiences a disjunction between the phenomenon of the universe expected to appear in the manner of ordinary objects and the ego's subjective experience of the universe through a sheer belonging to it in the event of life. Consequently the ego cannot constitute the universe as an "object" whose concept would agree with the conditions of experience of the universe through the ecstatic reference of standing in front [i.e., outside] of it. One has here the intuitive saturation through belonging to the universe which imposes itself by excess and which makes this universe present, but *invisible* (not technically) and incomprehensible. The universe engulfs the ego's intuition to such an extent that any attempt at constituting the universe [as an object] is suspended. *The universe is* visible *in its particular parts and moments but, as a whole, it cannot be* looked at. (emphases added)
>
> Alexander V. Nesteruk, *Consciousness and Matter*, p. 76

35. Bernard Haisch, *The God Theory: Universes, Zero-Point Fields, and What's Behind It All* (Weiser Books, 2006), 136.

36. Instead of simply objecting to multiverse models on the basis of moral and emotional repugnance, Michael Heller, *The New Physics and New Theology*, 88–89, has proposed a rational one grounded in theology—"God exists, therefore . . ."—as follows: "If the Creator had had before him a catalogue of all the [infinite] universes he could create and had wanted to select by chance the one destined to be, the probability that our universe would have been selected is equal to zero. It is difficult to believe that the Creator played at dice, but it is even more difficult to accept that the results of his game [of chance] did not follow the rules for calculating probabilities [since there would be a zero probability of our universe's, and therefore of our, existences]." Heller's argument is based on the mathematical reasoning that an infinitesimally small but positive value will ever *approach* more closely its limiting value of zero as the number of possible universes approaches infinity. That is, given n number of possible universes, the probability of our universe being chosen is $1/n$; hence as $n \to \infty$, $1/n \to 0$.

Besides the problems attending the physical cosmological models discussed above, an even deeper problem with explaining the creation, and thus the existence, of the universe as a whole, has been intuited by several scholars and physicists. As in the above epigraph, the problem is also aptly summarized in the form of a dilemma by the physicist Lee Smolin as follows: "The problem of how to make a theory of a whole universe is thus the problem of how to construct a theory without making any reference to anything that exists, or anything that we might have imagined happened, outside the system we are describing. We must discover a way to speak of the properties *of things in* the universe, the particles, atoms, fields, stars, galaxies, as well as space and time themselves, *without ever referring to something* that is not one of those things, and which hence lies *outside of the universe.* This problem is not new. As long as people have been doing science, there were those who pointed out that a theory of *the whole world must be different in certain respects* from the [world-part] theories people were constructing"[37] (emphases added). Concurring with but going further than Smolin's assessment, the philosopher Roberto Unger, in referring to the laws of nature, states that

> The unified understanding of these laws would then fix the outer limit to our comprehension of nature. There are, however, two grave limitations to this approach to the most general features of reality. [For now, referring to only the first or the two, he continues as follows:]
>
> The first limitation is that its methods are suited to the exploration of parts of nature rather than of the universe as a whole. What one might call the Newtonian paradigm of scientific inquiry studies parts of reality, regions of the universe. In each of these regions, it distinguishes stipulated initial conditions marking out a configuration space within which phenomena change according to laws that can be expressed as mathematical equations. What is an initial condition at one moment may become an explained phenomenon at another. The scientist-observer stands outside the configuration space in the timeless position of God.
>
> This approach fails when it is applied to the universe as a whole. Yet [by referring to what Unger considers to be a triad of irreparable defects in humans' finite existence] it is precisely knowledge about the universe as a whole (rather than about patches of space-time) that we require to defeat or circumscribe speculative groundlessness [one of the irreparable existential defects]. When the subject matter is cosmological rather than local, the distinction between initial conditions and explained phenomena within a configuration of space cannot be maintained. The observer can no longer imagine himself as standing outside the boundaries of the configuration; *there is nowhere outside the universe to stand.*[38] (emphasis added)

37. Lee Smolin, *The Life of the Cosmos* (Oxford University Press, 1997), 14.

38. Roberto Mangabeira Unger, *The Religion of the Future* (Verso, 2016), 8–9.

Three things should be noted here. First, it is important to recall that recourse to extra- or supernatural agents or processes, because of a conventionally adopted methodological rule, is barred from scientific explanation. A second important thing to note is that cosmological theories are theories of the whole universe; and since, as Smolin realizes, they have to be different in certain respects from the theories that scientists have up to now used to explain parts of the whole, they are intrinsically prone to raise pertinent questions. To wit, in what specific respect can what theoretically applies to the observed entities *contained in* the universe be different to what theoretically applies to the universe *as a whole*? This question poses a problem for all scientific theories based on spontaneous creation, that is to say, for what are frequently designated as bootstrap theories of creation, since, as Unger notes, they cannot be verified by evidence obtained by a scientist-observer positioned outside the universe. Third, however, is the fact that Unger fails, or does not want, to acknowledge that while indeed there is nowhere for a scientist-observer to stand outside the universe, the transcendent and eternal omnipresence of God assures that He is present everywhere including "outside" the universe. Therefore, the God hypothesis, as Meyer (2021) argues, may after all be a necessary component in our full *understanding* of the universe's existence.

Related to Smolin's and Unger's dilemmas, and noted in the introduction (see there, note 19), the mathematician William Weiss presents the related argument that the universe as a whole cannot be a physical entity:

1. Premise 1: All things that have physical existence are precisely those things that are contained in the universe.
2. Premise 2: The universe does not contain itself as one of its things.[39]
3. Conclusion: The universe is not a physical entity.

In other words, as humorously implied in figure 9.1, nothing inside the universe can observe the universe as a whole. Hence, the long-sought-after omnivoyant observer of the universe as a whole must be outside the universe. Moreover, if the theory *of* the universe as a whole must be different in certain respects from the physical theories people were constructing of the entities *in* the universe, it remains to be determined what those "certain respects" are. Whatever they are, the universe—being a nonphysical entity—additionally reinforces Unger's argument that our scientific understanding of it as a whole *cannot rely on* observable *physical* evidence. In other words, the universe is not the self-contained entity

39. In set-theoretic terms, Weiss's Premise 2 relates to the Zermelo-Fraenkel (ZF) set theory, whose axioms provide a logical basis for the development of modern mathematical number theory. The ZF axiom of regularity (in conjunction with the axiom of pairing) *disallows* the existence of a set U such that $U \in U$; i.e. that *contains itself* as an element. In other words, $U \notin U$: there can be no universal set that contains itself.

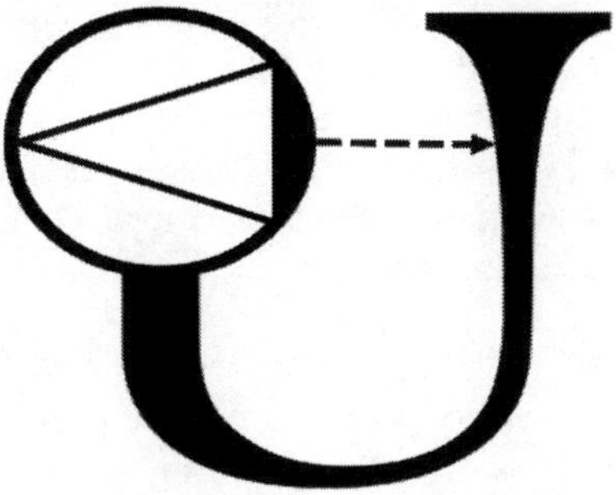

Figure 9.1. A depiction of something in one part of the universe, U, observing an entity in a second *part* of the universe, as indicated by the tip of the arrow.

that the cosmologist Stephen Hawking has proposed in his book *A Brief History of Time*, as follows: "So long as the universe had a beginning, we could suppose it had a creator. But if the universe is really completely self-contained, having no boundary or edge, it would have neither beginning nor end. What place, then, for a creator?"[40] What place, indeed? For, God—and not the universe!—is the *Ipsum Esse Subsistens* (see Thomas Aquinas's *Summa Theologiae*: I, q. 4, a. 2), *the sole self-contained and self-sufficient Being* that surpasses and enfolds all other beings, be they contingent or created. The explanation for the existence of the universe must therefore also rely on the evidence of philosophically, and I dare to add, theologically rational principles. This comports with Stanley Jaki's appraisal (see the introduction, note 22) that the universe is that supreme reality that cannot have within itself the (logical) reason—including a purely scientific reason—for its own existence. The universe, it seems, so long as we view it as an object of scientific study *like any other object within the universe*, will ultimately remain a mystery to us. Regarding this mystery, the remarks made below by the Jesuit scholar Vincent Miceli seem especially pertinent.

> A *problem* is a mental investigation undertaken with respect to an object. A problem bears on something completely *outside the investigator* (emphasis added). Man becomes an observer before a problem, scrutinizing the object from all sides. And there exists a complete answer to the problem that, given enough time and developing enough know-how, man will eventually obtain. Objectified thought solves problems. Man as a person, as a

40. Stephen W. Hawking, *A Brief History of Time: From the Big Bang to Black Holes* (Random House, 1988), 141. Hawking's self-contained universe contradicts Weiss's Premise 2 stating that the *universe does not contain itself* as one of its entities. In set-theoretic terms, Hawking's self-contained universe is as set U such that $U \in U$ and therefore contradicts the set-theoretic axiom of regularity.

> subject, is not involved in the solution or make-up of the problem. Scientific knowledge embodies the problematic approach to things, to objects.
>
> However, when a man is dealing with realities that cannot be objectified [as William Weiss's definition of the universe indicates], he cannot use effectively the [scientific] problematic approach to these realities if he would grow in a valid understanding of them.[41]

So, since the universe does not contain itself and therefore does not have physical existence, is it even possible—given Smolin's and Unger's realizations that a theory of the universe must be different in certain respects from the theories scientists were constructing of its parts—that there is a cosmological theory that can explain the universe's existence in strictly *physical* terms? If not, then, as Weiss and Jaki ask, where are we to seek the theory that accounts for the creation and existence of everything, including the universe itself? Outside the physical universe? If so, what exists outside the physical universe to which such extraordinary and extranatural powers can be attributed? I leave it to the reader to dwell on this question and try to develop a plausible answer. Among other readers, I would like to include Leonard Susskind, who enjoins "real" scientists to resist the temptation to explain what he believes to be natural phenomena, including the natural creation of the universe, by divine intervention.

Along with others, including many other "real" scientists, I believe that, indeed, we must seek an answer to this question outside of physical nature, in the disciplines of philosophy and theology. Although this seems to put a damper on physicists' grand quest for a purely physical theory of the universe as a whole, I would urge the reader to consider the following additional insightful and suggestive remarks, one made by the astrophysicist and theologian, David Alcalde, and the other by the physicist Lee Smolin. Alcalde maintains that "the bottomless mystery of every creature [including the universe as a whole which, after all, was and is continuing to be *created* by God] cannot be avoided by the natural sciences, because [now quoting extensively from the theologian and philosopher of science Michael Hanby] 'at the heart of each thing is the mystery of being, and at the heart of the mystery of being is the mystery of God.' The bottomless character of being is always presupposed by science and it is the continuing positive source of scientific activity. Science can never get at the bottom of reality because it is bottomless. The depth dimension of being 'ensures that the task of the sciences is interminable.' Therefore the idea of a final exhaustive theory of everything [including the universe] 'is ruled out by the nature of being as such.'"[42] And here Smolin pertinently comments that "there may or may not be a God or gods. Yet there is something ennobling about our search for the divine. And also something humanizing, which is reflected in each of the paths people have discovered to take us to

41. Miceli, *The Gods of Atheism*, 15.
42. Alcalde, *Cosmology Without God?*, 76.

deeper levels of truth. Some seek transcendence in meditation or prayer; others seek it in service to their fellow human beings; still others, the ones lucky enough to have the talent, seek transcendence in the practice of an art. [And] another way of [seeking transcendence and] engaging life's deepest questions is science."[43]

So, even if modern science no longer serves merely as handmaiden to theology, I nonetheless take Smolin's latter way of seeking the divine, engaging life's deepest questions by science, to provide a service to the theology of nature. The theologian Christopher Mooney maintains that

> it is important that Christians discern at least some correspondence, some connection between what their theology says about the meaning of the cosmos and the arrival of humans, and of Jesus in particular, and what science has discovered about the survival and development of life over billions of years. . . .
>
> I believe there is such congruity, and that it can be found by reflecting anew on the basic Christian doctrines of creation, incarnation, and redemption. For these teachings all deal with something done to matter, which in turn must mean for Christians that God is not to be found [only] in some sacred sphere, separated from the biological [and physical] world. Rather, God is to be known and God's designs are to be discovered in and through matter, and more specifically in self-reflecting human matter as it has emerged from the evolutionary process.[44]

To this, a theist can respond unreservedly with an "Amen!" (I would also add that creation, incarnation, and redemption point to God's love and mercy, bestowed as it is on all of creation including, of course, humans who are created in his image. But I will leave the working out of these three theologically relevant doctrines to competent experts.) Below I will briefly focus on the theological doctrines of Creation and how modern, scientific cosmology can shed light on it.

Basic Theological Doctrines of Creation

Here are two central theological doctrines: God is not only (i) the creative originator of our universe but also (ii) its creative sustainer, beckoning us not to forget the past while also beckoning the universe and all its creatures into the future.

Creation as an Ongoing Process of Sustaining and Making

Regarding the latter doctrine, a prominent theological doctrine of creation is that it is a work in progress, and while God is responsible for sustaining and furthering the ongoing creation of the entire cosmos, God has charged humans

43. Smolin, preface to *The Life of the Cosmos*, vii.
44. Mooney, *Theology and Scientific Knowledge*, 154.

in their miniscule corner of the cosmos with the task of creating, and lately also repairing, their *Lebenswelt*, the natural, social, and cultural world they inhabit. Our creations and repairs are end products of what the ancient Greeks called ποίησις (*poiesis*), the art or craft of making something new, which in today's world includes the re-making of something broken into something new. An example of the latter, pointed out by the Japanese-American artist Makoto Fujimura, is the Japanese "tradition of *Kintsugi*, the art of taking broken porcelain items—characteristically, items used in serving tea [which in Japan is itself a ceremonial art, called *sadō*]—and, by golden bonding material used for their reassembly, making of them something even more beautiful than before."[45] Fujimura regards God as the supreme Artist and, commenting on God's and humans' role in creation, he remarks that

> when I speak of God as Artist, I am speaking of God not just as the only true Creator—the ultimate Maker, as passages of Genesis describe—but also as the *originator of origins*, the creator of any notion of the Maker. The holiness of God, in this journey, is "otherness" and is set apart from our creativity and imagination. In many ways, we must distinguish between God's creative act and human creativity (what theologians call "Creator-creature distinctions"); but at the same time, the Theology of Making assumes that human creativity echoes God's character and is made in God's image in some way. So when I state "God is THE ultimate Artist," I am not trying to define the original Creator by human terms. I am stating a presupposition up front that the very definition of "art" may need to be redefined by biblical and Godly terms, and that God is the only true Artist that exists."[46]

These remarks resonate with my assessment not only of God as the supreme Artist but also of humans as God-commissioned co-artists.

As such, we humans participate with God in the ongoing creation of our world whenever we discover new technologies that productively and positively contribute to the flourishing of our lives; whenever we care for and repair the harm and suffering done to other humans, to other creatures, and to the well-being of nature; whenever we participate in celebrations that commemorate our past co-creators and their co-creations; whenever we write a poem, a fine novel, compose a new piece of music, paint a new scene or portrait, invent a new dance; and countless other makings.

Since God endows us with free will, each one of us can unfortunately also choose to make things worse than they were by breaking or maltreating God's creations in various physical, social, and spiritual ways. Such destructive actions on our part therefore also affect the making and shaping of us as human persons, for

45. Makoto Fujimura, foreword to *Art and Faith: A Theology of Making* (Yale University Press, 2020), xi.

46. Fujimura, *Art and Faith*, 13.

we as persons are formed most significantly by the ethical and moral choices we enact. At the extremes of such moral formation, the actions of a human person can therefore end up being saintly or demonic. All actions, good or bad, are planned by humans and therefore anticipate future accomplishments. God, as emphasized by theologians like Wolfhart Pannenberg, is not only the God of the ancient Israelites and Christians but also the God of the present and the future.[47] And ever aware of the freedom he gave us by endowing us with the most highly developed conscious mind, he can only beckon, but not force, us to contribute to the well-being of our future world through our productive and life-enhancing tasks. Yet being free, how we respond depends on our choosing to engage either in creative actions that conform to this calling or in destructive actions that defy it.

There is much more, perhaps another book's worth, that can be added to this bare sketch of God's ever creating-by-sustaining the present world, and our ongoing efforts to co-create realities that the future holds only as present possibilities. Yet, instead of going in that direction, I would like to briefly consider the relevance of the deepest past.

Creation of the Universe as a One-Time Origination

I believe in God, the Father almighty, Creator of heaven and earth . . .

So, what do theologians and at least some scientists think about the existence and creation of the universe? We noted above several sound lines of reasoning that point to God's essential relation to the existence of universe. We also noted above that the universe (as well as the ever-inflating multiverse) is past-incomplete and therefore had a beginning. It therefore seems reasonable that some cause or principle transcending the universe created it. The question is: What or Who created it? The Abrahamic religions believe that the answer must be found in a Creator God. In the Christian tradition, this specific belief is encapsulated in the introduction to the Apostle's Creed: "I believe in God, the Father almighty, Creator of heaven and earth. . . . " From further historic elaboration over a few centuries emerged the doctrine stating that God created the universe from or out ot nothing. As noted by the theologian Janet Soskice, ever since "the time [the 4th century CE] of the Cappadocians onwards *creatio ex nihilo* has been, East and West, . . . a foundational teaching of Christian thought."[48] As pointed out by many other

47. On Pannenberg's theology of the future, see Christiaan Mostert, *God and the Future: Wolfhart Pannenberg's Eschatological Doctrine of God* (Bloomsbury, 2002); Pendergast, *The Cosmic Hierarchy*, chapter 6.

48. Janet Soskice, "Why *Creatio ex nihilo* for Theology Today?," in *Creation ex nihilo: Origins, Development, Contemporary Challenges*, ed. Gary A. Anderson and Markus Bockmuehl (University of Notre Dame Press, 2018), 38. The most notable Cappadocians were Basil of Caesarea, Gregory Nazianzus, and Gregory of Nyssa.

commentators, the doctrine of *creatio ex nihilo* encompasses a wealth of current theological speculations regarding how God relates to the world he created.[49] However, many current "academic philosophers and scientists," Soskice further notes, "[might blithely] assume, should they have any views at all, that '*creatio ex nihilo*' just means the big bang theory. They will understand it to be a thesis of cosmic origins at the beginning of time. But *creatio ex nihilo* is not, or not predominantly, a cosmogonic theory happily coincident with [any of several physical cosmologies like] the big bang theory. . . . To put it bluntly . . . *creatio ex nihilo* is *not a teaching about the cosmos* [emphasis added] but about God."[50] Taking exception to this last claim, I propose that while *creatio ex nihilo* is indeed mainly about God, it is also a clear example of how a theological doctrine is clearly relevant to the development of physical cosmological theories.

After all, as we saw above, a number of physical cosmologies putatively requiring no Creator God have been proposed for the "spontaneous" creation of the cosmos out of nothing, by physical cosmologists Alexander Vilenkin, subsequently by Lawrence Krauss, and more recently by Maya Lincoln and Avi Wasser. However, I argue that these cosmological theories have not been successful in describing such spontaneous creation out of nothing, since they *assume a pre-existent state,* whose symmetry is subject to being broken spontaneously by pure chance, be it that of Krauss's quantum vacuum or of Lincoln and Wasser's infinite number of pairwise oppositional informational bits.[51] Indeed, regarding the latter, the physical cosmologists Cláudio Nassif Cruz and Fernando Antônio da Silva argue that Lincoln and Wasser's approach leaves the existence of an infinite number of pairwise oppositional informational bits a total mystery. As one might legitimately ask a cosmologist like Lawrence Krauss about the origin of the quantum vacuum, Nassif Cruz and da Silva therefore ask: "Where do the pre-existing pairwise oppositional informational bits come from?"[52]

49. See Gary A. Anderson and Markus Bockmuehl, eds., *Creation ex nihilo: Origins, Development, Contemporary Challenges* (University of Notre Dame Press, 2018).

50. Soskice, "Why *Creatio ex nihilo* for Theology," 38.

51. As a professed neoatheist, Lawrence Krauss has every reason to propose a Godless creation of the universe from "nothing." His approach to spontaneous *creatio ex nihilo* is basically an elaborate reprise of Vilenkin's earlier paper on the same topic. See also Andrew Davison, "Looking Back Toward the Origin: Scientific Cosmology as Creation *ex nihilo* Considered 'from the Inside,'" and Adam D. Hinks, "What Does Physical Cosmology Say About Creation from Nothing?," (both in Anderson and Bockmuehl, *Creation ex nihilo*, 2018), for the problems attending physical cosmologies in relation to the Creator-God "hypothesis." In contrast to Krauss's proposal, Lincoln and Wasser's may be theologically relevant, assuming that God's Mind contains their pairwise oppositional informational bits.

52. Cláudio Nassif Cruz and Fernando Antônio da Silva, "Cosmology of the Symmetrical Relativity Versus Spontaneous Creation of the Universe Ex Nihilo," *Physics of the Dark Universe* 28 (2020): 5.

Additionally relevant for my theological thinking are three claims made by Nassif Cruz and da Silva: (i) there is a pre-existent fund of information (perhaps encoded in some pre-existent program) that is not, but somehow can act, like physical hardware and (ii) there is a "nothing" that is a pre-existent chaos of infinite entropy. So, even here we again are faced with a mystery raised by yet another question: "Where do *these* two things, information and a chaotic nothing, come from?" Although they provide no satisfactory answer to this question, Nassif Cruz and da Silva nonetheless go on to claim correctly (iii) that the probability of transforming the entropy of the chaos or primordial nothing from infinity to zero (the value theoretically required to "ignite" the temporal origin of the cosmos) is absolutely zero. And as further noted by them, *this is impossible,* since if the probability were zero, the cosmos or universe, *with us in it,* would not exist. This Anthropic-Principle counterargument, however, gives rise to two further, so-far unanswered, questions. The first asks: By what *physical* process could the infinite entropy of the chaotic nothing have been converted to a value of zero at the origin of the universe? The second asks: Since the change in the entropy of the chaos or primordial nothing from infinity to zero is theoretically necessary, how can one reconcile the fact of the zero probability of such a process existing at all with humanity's and the universe's clearly evident existence? Before answering the second and possibly also the first question, we additionally take note, in light of Nassif Cruz and da Silva's argument, of the physicist Michael Heller's following theologically relevant remarks (see also note 36 above): "If the Creator had had before him a catalogue of all the [infinitely possible] universes he could create and had wanted to select *by chance* the one destined to be, *the probability that our universe would have been selected is equal to zero*"[53] (emphases added). What Heller, who is also a Catholic priest and theologian, correctly assumes is that (i) the cosmos we inhabit obviously exists, and in line with Nassif Cruz and da Silva's conclusion, (ii) there is a zero-probability that it *spontaneously* arose by some purely physical process, in other words, one without any nonphysical intervention. Consequently, Heller's conclusion is that a non- and superphysical Power—namely, God—who from (pre- and atemporal) Eternity thought and spoke the cosmos into time freely and *deliberately.*

Creatio ex Nihilo

According to my friend Rabbi Sanford Olshansky, the Hebraic letter beth (ב) follows and consequently "sees in front of it" the first letter of the Hebraic syllabary, the aleph (א), and therefore we are instructed not to ask what comes before. Before what? The א, of course, which in Greek corresponds to the Greek letter alpha (A). In Christian symbology, the Alpha stands for God, who, being

53. Heller, *The New Physics and New Theology*, 88.

eternal, does not have anything "before" him, neither in the causally temporal nor in the logical sense of priority. Yet when we speak of creation of the universe, it also is nearly impossible not to ask what, in some sense, was "before." Therefore, let's dare to ask this question. In answering it, the theologian Andrew Davison, referring to Thomas Aquinas's treatise *On the Eternity of the World*, states that "Aquinas discusses the proper meaning of *priority* when applied to thought about creation. The question, as he sees it, is what the relation of one-after-another means, and what it applies to. Two such relations pertain to creation, he writes: in one respect, creation comes 'after' God; in another, it comes 'after' nothing. If, that is to say, we [instead] ask *what is 'prior' to creation*, we can say *both 'God' and 'nothing'* [emphasis added]. The second response simply reformulates the conviction that creation is *ex nihilo*."[54] One way to interpret the first response is that God exercises not a temporal but rather a strictly logical and causal priority over creation; in other words, God is the eternal uncaused cause of all other causal processes that occur once creation's temporal domain is established. As I read Davison's remarks, "prior" to creation there is God, in the sense of being the eternal and absolute Plenum, the Fullness of Being, the One and the All. This implies that outside of or besides God there is no primal matter that must be given shape, no chaos that must be tamed, no so-called quantum vacuum agitating energetically, and no informational state whose symmetry must be broken; instead, there is absolutely nothing at all.

But this generates the following additional problematic question: What is designated or meant when we use the phrase "absolutely nothing"? When claiming that outside of, or next to, God there is absolutely nothing, we are dealing with the following paradox. Regarding the Christian *creatio-ex-nihilo* doctrine, the Eastern Orthodox scholar Vladimir Lossky explains that

> the very idea of absolute nothingness is contradictory and absurd: to say that nothingness exists [or *is*] is to state a pleonasm, at least unless we are trying awkwardly to express, in this way, the idea that nothing exists outside God; that, indeed, there is no such thing as "outside God." Yet creation ex nihilo does mean just such an act producing something "outside of God"—the production of an entirely new subject, with no origin of any kind either in the divine nature or in any matter or potentiality of being external to God. We might say that by creation ex nihilo God "makes room" for something which is wholly outside of Himself; that, indeed, He sets up the "outside" or nothingness alongside His plenitude. The result is a subject which is entirely "other," infinitely removed from Him, "not by place but by nature" (οὐ τοπῳ, αλλα φύσει), as it is expressed by St. John Damascene.[55]

54. Davison, "Looking Back Toward the Origin," 374. For a related view of creation *ex nihilo*, see also Hart, *The Beauty of the Infinite*, 258–59.

55. Vladimir Lossky, *The Mystical Theology of the Eastern Church* (Crux Press, 2022), 74.

In other words, "nothing" designates a concept of utter emptiness, a total absence of any being at all, but not an actual thing.

All that said, I now venture into theological waters that might be too deep for me. And therefore, if anything I state or claim below is theologically improper or in error, I stand to be corrected by competent theologians. However, I can properly claim that one of Christianity's officially accepted dogma states that whatever exists that is not God was, in its whole substance, created out of or from nothing (*ex nihilo*) by God. Despite this dogma, I am philosophically not convinced of the *ex-nihilo* approach to creation.[56] We have heard or read the phrase *creation out of nothing* (*creatio ex nihilo*) so often that we can easily become convinced that its doctrinal interpretation is unambiguous. But it is not, when we consider the following points.

1. Insofar as God's creation of the world refers positively to a one-time originating event that brought all things in the universe into existence, it follows that "prior" to its creation there "was" from a metaphysical and theological viewpoints—as noted above by Davison's interpretation of St. Thomas's notion of priority—not only God in his Eternal Being but also, from physical as well as metaphysical viewpoints, an absolute absence of any being at all. When these perspectives are combined, one can theologically assert that God created the world *ex nihilo*.
2. Yet, if the *ex-nihilo* stipulation is meant negatively to exclude God's fashioning the cosmos from a preexistent something—the pre- and therefore coexisting chaos proposed, for instance, by Nassif Cruz and da Silva, or some other primeval matter—*creatio ex nihilo* also makes sense. This interpretation of *creatio ex nihilo* goes back to ancient Christianity. For example, relying on a quote from Ian McFarland's book *From Nothing: A Theology of Creation*, the theologian Gary Anderson notes that as early as the 2nd century CE, the bishop Theophilus of Antioch claimed that "God brought everything into being out of what does not exist, so that his greatness might be known and understood through his works."[57] The phrase "what does not exist" is meant, in this case, to exclude any co-eternal primal chaos or matter, and therefor readily translates into the word "nothing." Accordingly, having created the world from what does not exist, God can be seen in this second way as creating it *ex nihilo*.

56. The many historical, philosophical, scientific, and theological contributions in Anderson and Bockmuehl, *Creation ex nihilo*, reveal the many facets to the doctrine of *creatio ex nihilo* that make it hard to pin down its current meaning unequivocally. Consequently, as noted by Soskice, "Why *Creatio ex nihilo* for Theology Today?," 38, some 20th-century philosophers consider the doctrine to be antiquated and unhelpful.

57. Davison, "Looking Back Toward the Origin," 21.

3. Furthermore, since God is not a thing like any of his created entities that have their being in the world, we can conclude that God is a non-thing and, in this specific sense, nothing.

It is this third meaning of *creatio ex nihilo* that I find most congenial for what I will elaborate on below.

Creatio ex Deo in Nihilum

First, I believe that the ancient Greek philosopher Parmenides had it right when he proposed the following metaphysical dictum: οὐδὲν ἐξ οὐδενός (nothing is made from nothing). I therefore subscribe to the following slightly amended, Latinized version of the dictum: *ex nihilo nihil fit* (from nothing, nothing is made). What I, somewhat meekly, dare to propose is that creation—in the sense of a temporal origination of the universe was not from or out of a void, not creation *ex nihilo*, as religious scholars are used to express it. But instead, it was a *creatio ex Deo in nihilum*, a *creation from God*, conceived as a non-thing, of a multitude of things *into that void*. So, what caused this creation? I propose it was the divine creative thought, the Logos or Verbum, existing in the Eternal and Infinite Mind of God.

Can one defend the move from creation *ex nihilo* to creation *in nihilo*? I believe it can be defended using the two following lines of reasoning. First, from a physical cosmological viewpoint, we can assume (i) that the universe contains all that physically exists and (ii) that it will continue to evolve beyond its current state. Regardless of how the universe evolves, one can reasonably ask: What, speaking physically, lies outside or beyond the evolving universe, what "surrounds" it? The answer is that it must be something nonphysical; for if it were some physical existent, it would be (by assumption [i]) a constituent inside the evolving universe. But that contradicts the assumption that it is located outside or beyond the universe. The outside or beyond the universe must consequently be the absence of any and all physical entities. That is to say, the universe is "within"—in the sense that it is surrounded by—an absolute (metaphysical) void, the *absolutum (metaphysicum) nihil*. Second, what keeps the universe "afloat" in the void is, as noted in the prior section, God's sustaining it—and separating it from the void—through his act of continuous creation.

From above, let's recall and take seriously Andrew Davison's metaphysical claim that "prior" to creation (i.e., in eternity) there "was" *God* and *nothing* (outside or beside Him). Then, from a Christian metaphysical and theological standpoint, a hint as to what was initially uttered by God into this nothing, this absolute *nihilo*, is found in the theological prologue of the Gospel of St. John (in my opinion the most philosophical of the four canonical gospels): *in principio erat verbum et verbum erat apud deum et deus erat verbum* (In the beginning was the Word, and the Word was with God, and God was the Word). But the

Verbum, the Word or the Logos of God, is eternally present in and with God in the perichoretic relation that exists between Father, Son, and Holy Spirit. If the creative Logos is spoken forth by God or proceeds from God, one can ask what the Logos proceeds into.

The answer to this question requires addressing two sources of information. One source is the doctrine of divine energies that is especially prominent in Eastern Orthodox theology but also present in in western Christianity. As Vladimir Lossky summarizes, "the doctrine of the [divine] energies, ineffably distinct from the [divine] essence, is the dogmatic basis of the real character of all mystical experience. God, who is [mystically] inaccessible in His essence, is present in His energies, 'as in a mirror'[as expressed by the St. Gregory Palamas]."[58] In other words, we have access to God not in His essence but only as He manifests himself to us in his energies, the effects of which are found not only in our minds' experiences of God but also in our experiencing the physical and natural world outside of us. As Lossky continues, "God has created all things by His energies. . . . [But the divine] energies do not produce the created world by the mere fact of their existence . . . , [and thus] the divine energies in themselves are not the relationship of God to created being, but they do enter in relationship with that which is not God . . . by the will of God. For according to St. Maximus, the will is always an active relationship towards another, towards something external to the subject which acts."[59]

This brings us to the second source of information—namely, the scholar Jordan Wood's historic analyses of Maximus's view of God's creation and incarnation. Wood's analyses and arguments turns out to be a lengthy elaboration on St. Maximus's fundamental assertion that "the Word of God, very God, wills that the mystery of his Incarnation be actualized always and in all things."[60] Particularly relevant to my argument is that, further on, Wood also notes how Maximus, quoting Denys the Areopagite, maintains that "God, from the 'overflow of His intense love for all things, goes out of Himself . . . to be in all according to an ecstatic and superessential power which is yet inseparable from Himself.' That [quote] captures Maximus's underlying conviction . . . [that] 'we consider' that 'all things . . . come from God.' . . . So *creatio ex nihilo* entails an insuperable gap between the nature of God and that of the world, but, simultaneously, that the world's creation is God's coming out of himself—*creatio ex Deo.*"[61] In the context of my present proposal, I take liberty to think of God's Eternal Word or Logos as kenotically speaking Itself out, in a *creatio-ex-Deo* manner, that also

58. Lossky, *The Mystical Theology of the Eastern Church*, 74, 69–70.

59. Lossky, *The Mystical Theology of the Eastern Church*, 72.

60. Jordan Daniel Wood, *The Whole Mystery of Christ: Creation as Incarnation in Maximus Confessor* (University of Notre Dame Press, 2022), 11.

61. Wood, *The Whole Mystery of Christ*, 67.

is a kenotic proceeding *into*,[62] and thereby *in*forming and saturating the universe from its initial creation to its past and ongoing evolution and all physical entities in it, while simultaneously separating and protecting His creation from the negative, counter-creative power of the *absolutum nihil*.

Information Penetrates the Universe, Thereby Displacing the Absolutum Nihil

Very pertinent here is the physicist John Archibald Wheeler's statement—made in perhaps unintendedly theological, yet theologically rich, terms—that everything that exists in the universe owes its existence to a transformation that in the confines of the physicist's laboratory yields

> *it from bit.* Otherwise put, every *it*—every [subatomic] particle, every field of force, even the space-time continuum itself—derives its function, its meaning, its very existence entirely—even if in some contexts indirectly—from the apparatus-elicited answers to yes-or-no questions, binary choices, bits. *It from bit* symbolizes the idea that [beyond the physicist's laboratory] every item of the physical world has at bottom—at a very deep bottom, in most instances—an *immaterial source and explanation* [emphasis added]; that which we call reality arises in the last analysis from the posing of yes-no questions and the registering of equipment-evoked responses; in short, that *all things physical are information-theoretic in origin* [emphasis added] and that this is a *participatory universe*.[63]

Although Wheeler is referring to what is technically known as Shannon information, the particle physicist and theologian John Polkinghorne, in his cosmological theorizing, used information in a slightly different sense of "active information." According to the philosopher Ignacio Silva,

> for Polkinghorne active information is information that is being transferred through an input process. Polkinghorne is clear that God is not the active informational principle, God is not information. Instead, God is the agent that generates that active information and transfers it into the system. If we follow this interpretation of Polkinghorne's ideas, his notion of God's input of information renders God to be a cause among causes. Polkinghorne presents the notion of active information as a new causal category to explain the natural world. Active information, then, is a cause within the natural world. According to information theory there is no need

62. See Bernard Haisch, *The God Theory*, 28–30, for kenotic procession of the world *ex Deo*.

63. John A. Wheeler, "Information, Physics, Quantum: The Search for Links," in *Complexity, Entropy, and the Physics of Information*, ed. Wojciech Hubert Zurek (Addison-Wesley, 1990), 5.

> for any kind of energy exchange for input of information [hence not violating the physical principle of the conservation of energy]. Thus, God introduces this information *as any other natural cause.*[64] (emphasis added)

It seems to me that Polkinghorne's active information therefore implies God's ongoing providential maintenance and guidance of the evolution of an already created universe, but not to creation of the universe per se. Two conclusions can be drawn from Polkinghorne's active-information proposal. For one, since we cannot read God's mind, his actively injecting information from outside the universe into it, a source of uncertainty—let's call it Polkinghorne's Uncertainty Principle—additional to that prescribed by Heisenberg's uncertainty principle can impose itself on quantum theoretical accounts of entities and processes found in the universe. Since Polkinghorne's Uncertainty Principle applies to information and not to physical matter or energy, it does not contravene the physical laws governing the latter. Second, Polkinghorne's active *information* can nonetheless be considered from a Shannon-theoretic viewpoint. Recall from chapter 4 (see there, note 52) that the physicist Shoichi Toyabe and his collaborators demonstrated that a conversion of Shannon information to free energy (energy available to do work) is possible without contradicting the principle of conservation of energy (the first law of thermodynamics). I extrapolate this finding to allow me to talk theologically about God's creation of the universe, in which God, pure Spirit and Mind, decided *in principio* to create the universe by uttering his Word (Be!). Recalling Wheeler's assertion that *all things physical are information-theoretic in origin*, I conjecture that "in the beginning," this in*formative* Logos of God freely created the universe and now continues to sustain it. It did so by endowing the universe with all the super-dense working energy necessary to set off all of its subsequent evolution, which includes, according to recent speculation, its undetectable (dark) energetic and material contents, as well their detectable (visible) counterparts,[65] the latter of which in turn included also that very small portion of the universe's detectable energy and detectable matter that has physically made up and still makes up all living creatures.

Moreover, Divine creation—a still ongoing process—implies that the existence of the universe is contingent. After all, God could have freely decided not to create the universe,[66] and he could decide to no longer maintain its exis-

64. Ignacio Silva, "John Polkinghorne on Divine Action: A Coherent Theological Evolution" *Science and Christian Belief* 24, no. 1 (2012): 21–22.

65. According to physical interpretations consistent with recent astronomical findings, of all of the contents in the current universe about 67% consists of dark energy, 28% of dark matter, and therefore only 5% consists of observable radiant energy and matter.

66. In line with note 64 above, John Wheeler maintained that information provides answers to yes-or-no questions, to binary choices. To the question some of us pose: "Why is there not nothing, why is there anything at all?," God freely chose to answer with "Be" instead

tence—for instance, if the moral evil in the cosmos exceeds its moral good—without his "not-Be " or "no-longer-Be" decision in no way diminishing the infinitely expressive dynamism characterizing the mutual exchange of eternal Trinitarian Love. Since the existence of the universe is contingent, it did not and does not necessarily have to be—a possibility that spites current physicists' and physical cosmologists' continuing struggle to explain its self-sufficient, necessary existence.

The Importance of Time in the Origin of the Universe

What is important to note here also is that time is the first thing, the first moment or event, to be created. Einstein's theory of general relativity mathematically described the universe as a four-dimensional space-time manifold. However, he and, several decades later, the physicist Carlo Rovelli regard time—and its flow from past, through present, to future—as physically unreal, merely a subjective and illusory phenomenon, a psychologically fanciful creation of our consciousness.[67] In contrast to this dismissive assertion, along with the physicist Lee Smolin and the philosopher Roberto Unger, I take time to be not only psychologically but, as manifest in causality, also physically real.[68] In his deliberations regarding possible pretheoretical foundations of physics, Smolin proposes that

1. Time, in its causal manifestation, is fundamental. That is, the process by which current events produce future ones is fundamental.
2. Time is irreversible. The process by which future events are caused from present events can't go backward. Once an event has happened, it can't be made to unhappen.
3. Space is emergent. There is no space, fundamentally. There are events and they cause other events, so there are causal relations. These events make up a network of relationships. Space arises as a coarse-grained and approximate description of the network of relationships between events.[69]

This foundational sketch conforms well to a recent line of thought, relevant to a theology of science and developed by the mathematician and cosmologist Ettore Minguzzi, which dares to ask if God can find a place in physics. Minguzzi answers this question by relating St. Augustine's notions (or quandaries)

---

of "not-Be." However, opposing this strict voluntarist view, from Jordan Wood's reading of Maximus the Confessor one could infer that God's creation of the universe was an inevitable act, since the creation and incarnation were eternally present in his Infinite Mind.

67. Rovelli, *The Order of Time.*

68. Roberto Mangabeira Unger and Lee Smolin, *The Singular Universe and the Reality of Time: A Proposal in Natural Philosophy* (Cambridge University Press, 2015).

69. Smolin, *Einstein's Unfinished Revolution*, 236.

concerning time to the theory of general relativity. Specifically, he tries "to analyze if God can find a place in modern theoretical physics, and if so, to identify the mathematical object that represents it."[70] I will not go into the details of his proposal, which can be found in several of Minguzzi's publications.[71] There has been a mixed response of approbation and pushback to Minguzzi's speculations[72]; and, based on my readings and informal survey of attitudes among scientists whom I personally know, I am skeptical about finding a place for God in the day-to-day goings-on in present-day theoretical physics, or any other natural science. As to future fundamental reconceptualization of physics and natural science, who knows? But I am not doubtful about finding a place for God in a theology that makes productive use of interpretations of current theoretical physics, such as Minguzzi's. That said, in furthering my speculative metaphysical and theological quest, I would like to relate Minguzzi's adoption of St. Augustine's relation of time to causality, since causality plays a key notion also in Smolin's rendition of time. As Minguzzi interprets Augustine, "all . . . times are created by God . . . so that God comes 'before' every time although this 'before' must be understood in [terms of] a causal [logical priority] but not in a temporal way."[73] Furthermore, since this chronology-violating domain—which Minguzzi associates conceptually with the presence of God and which therefore has no "before" and "after"—caused time to exist at the very first instant after the universe began its past and its presently ongoing expansion into the future.

In other words, God is the Uncaused Cause giving rise to time in which all other causal relations occur. Consistent with this is that time manifests, in Lee Smolin's view, in a network of causal relations among events, from which space and all else that eventually comprise the physical cosmos emerge. Therefore, as eternal and infinite uncaused cause, God, as conceived by Minguzzi, is the transcendent, atemporal (and aspatial), eternal (and infinite) domain which violates the chronology characterizing our universe's temporal flow from past through present to future. Moreover, as Minguzzi notes, this chronology-violation, in conjunction with Borde et al.'s previously discussed cosmological constraint, can be related to a singularity that, from a theological standpoint, points to creation by God. It may be more than coincidence that to avoid this theological implication of a chronology-violating region of space-time, the physicist and

70. Ettore Minguzzi, "Can God Find a Place in Physics? St. Augustine's Philosophy Meets General Relativity," *KronoScope* 14, no. 1 (2009): 71–89.

71. Ettore Minguzzi, "Chronology Violations and the Origin of Time," *The European Physical Journal Conferences* 88 (2013): 01003; Ettore Minguzzi, "Augustine of Hippo's Philosophy of Time Meets General Relativity," *Kronoscope* 14 (2014): 71–89.

72. For favorable and critical responses to Minguzzi's theological speculations, see https://fqxi.org/community/forum/topic/522, accessed October 17, 2023.

73. Minguzzi, "Augustine of Hippo's Philosophy of Time," 73.

atheist Stephen Hawking proposed his chronology-protection (or causality-protection) conjecture.[74]

The Importance of Time in the Evolution of the Universe

The origin of the universe marks the beginning of the universe's time-space continuum. Time, of course, is important in ways other than its mere origin. It is within the irreversible flow of time from past, through the present, to future that the universe evolved to the point, some 11 billion years since its origin, of including the origin of life on earth and life's evolution to the present. In many of his published books, Richard Dawkins eloquently described for the nonexpert layperson what is generally involved in our understanding of biological evolution. Dawkins, a member of the tribe of neoatheists, subscribes to and has argued for the neo-Darwinian notion that life evolves gradually when novel biological phenotypes produced by random genetic mutations are winnowed by the process of natural selection, which determines whether or not the phenotypes survive and proliferate as a new species.[75] What he apparently does not realize or will not admit is that initially random *chemical* mutations must incorporate (i) a tremendous amount of information necessary to produce (originate) the first primitive *organic* lifeform composed of *inorganic* atoms and to its subsequent evolution, (ii) the tremendous amount of genetic information that must be stored in RNA and DNA molecules necessary for the construction of the intricately designed protein molecules that make up the micro-machinery of living cells. These in turn contribute their share to the intricately designed organs, the macro-machinery of complex organisms like humans. Neither does he address the problem, identified clearly by the physicist Sara Walker, of how *information*—which, as the physicist Archibald Wheeler maintains, is not a material entity—*can exert causal influence* in a universe that contains physical entities.[76]

Nearly three decades ago, Dawkins published the book optimistically titled *Climbing Mount Improbable*, which describes how, over a sufficiently long time,

74. S. W. Hawking, "Chronology Protection Conjecture," *Physical Review D* 46, no. 2 (1992): 603–11.

75. Dawkins's gradualist view of biological evolution has not gone uncontested by Niles Eldredge and Stephen Jay Gould, "Punctuated Equilibria: An Alternative to Phyletic Gradualism," in *Models in Paleobiology*, ed. Thomas J. M. Schopf (Freeman, Cooper and Co., 1972); and Stephen Jay Gould and Niles Eldredge, "Punctuated Equilibria: The Tempo and Mode of Evolution Reconsidered," *Paleobiology* 3, no. 2 (1977): 115–51, who proposed the existence of "saltatory" punctuated equilibria that opposed gradualist evolutionary approaches. Dawkins pleaded that Gould and Eldredge tone down their advocacy of punctuated equilibria since such advocacy might serve as anti-evolutionary fodder to religious advocates of creation science.

76. See Sara Imari Walker, *Life as No One Knows It: The Physics of Life's Emergence* (Penguin Random House, 2024).

gradual evolutionary changes can eventually—at the summit of Mount Improbable—result in phenotypic speciation yielding new biological creatures, including of course humans.[77] Dawkins, however, could or would not realize that, as one who has very avidly expressed his faith in the power of science, the story ends like a bad dream. For, imagine a person like Dawkins scaling the highest peak of Mount Improbable and pulling himself over the final rock, only to discover that he is greeted by a band of theologians who, having assembled there for centuries, aspire to scale other mountains much higher than Dawkins's Mount Improbable.[78]

Some Comments on Design and Purpose in Nature

Dawkins's view is that complex biological entities such as the human brain merely appear as though they were deliberately designed, when in fact they are merely the unplanned effects of blind chance interacting with the physical laws of nature. However, we now know that the production of complex life forms depends crucially on a tremendous amount of information stored in the structure of DNA. As noted above by Sara Walker, Dawkins does not address the issue of how such information can causally influence the development of complex biological structures, nor does he explain how or when such information arose during the evolution of the universe. Information is embodied or expressed in, but not identical with, complex physical and chemical structures.[79] Hence, information itself is not a physical or material entity. Therefore, if we now add the mathematician William Weiss's stipulations (i) that all physical existents are precisely those that are contained in the universe and (ii) that the universe cannot contain itself, we can conclude that while *information is embodied* in the physico-material structures that are elements contained the universe (much like consciousness is embodied in the biophysically structured organi-

77. Richard Dawkins, *Climbing Mount Improbable* (Norton, 1996).

78. I am here paraphrasing the following felicitous comments of Robert Jastrow, *God and the Astronomers* (Warner Books, 1978), 105–6, regarding science and religion: "For the scientist who has lived by his faith in the power of reason, the story ends like a bad dream. He had scaled the mountains of ignorance; he is about to conquer the highest peak; as he pulls himself over the final rock, he is greeted by a band of theologians who have been sitting there for centuries."

79. See Wheeler, "Information, Physics, Quantum." In this published article, Wheeler's account of how information relates to quantum physics is interesting but also—if not mystery-mongering, then at best—mystifying. First asserting somewhat cryptically on p. 311 that "all things physical are information-theoretic in origin and this is a participatory universe," he also asserts on pp. 313–14 the following most circular and therefore most cryptic of his assertions: "Physics gives rise to observer-participancy; observer-participancy gives rise to information; and information gives rise to physics." One could therefore add "which in turn gives rise to observer-participancy; and so on forever and ever."

zation of our brains), *information*—since it is nonphysical—*is in itself* not an entity in the universe. So, we can ask the following theologically relevant question: What or who is ultimately the nonphysical source of the information embodied in the universe? Since information is embodied in every creative endeavor, another way of phrasing this question is: What or who created and designed the universe we inhabit? Was it pure Chance and Necessity, as the biologist Richard Dawkins has argued?[80] Or was it some Creative Reality inaccessible to biological, biochemical, and any other physical or natural science? If it was some Creative Reality, we are faced with another theologically relevant question: Why and toward what end or purpose was the universe designed and created by this Reality?

One might agree with Leonard Susskind's exhortation (see note 16 above) that all explanations of the natural world should be based on nothing but the laws of physics, mathematics, and probability. However, we noted previously that (i) the best mathematically developed cosmological arguments point to the conclusion that the universe is not past-eternal and therefore had a beginning in time, that (ii) the universe did not arise spontaneously by chance. The above two points therefore indicate strongly that (iii) the universe is not a self-sufficient entity created in and through itself. Together, these three conclusions in turn support the conclusion that (iv) the universe owes its beginning and its continued existence to an eternal cause transcending the temporal order of the universe. This latter conclusion translates readily into the theological doctrine that God created the universe.

Yet it seems to me that this limited view of God as Creator does not go sufficiently beyond the Deist God of the philosophers. However, by adopting the artist Makato Fujimura's approach, we can view God as *the* Ultimate Maker, who *lovingly* designed and crafted the universe into its existent form. And therefore, God conferred *goodness* on its existence—as described in several passages of Genesis and also as in the later works of St. Thomas Aquinas, where he rationally argued that existence per se is a good to be valued. We also can think of God as *THE* Ultimate Artist, who endows creation with *beauty*. Hence, as the Source of Being, Goodness, and Beauty, God is not merely the Creator and Maker of the universe; He also is supremely lovely and lovable.[81] While one need not, in the order of the human rational intellect, go beyond the appropriateness and applicability of physical cosmology to theological *thinking* about God, it is, as St. Thomas Aquinas and Blaise Pascal and many other mystics realized cogently, in the order of the heart, the *ordo* amoris, where our *loving* and *desiring* the presence of God are satisfied. God's Love ultimately satisfies our religious

80. On chance and necessity, see Jacques Monod, *Chance and Necessity: An Essay on the Natural Philosophy of Modern Biology* (Alfred A. Knopf, 1971).

81. See Hart, *The Beauty of the Infinite*; Balthasar, *Seeing the Form*.

quests and validates the truths of theology. As Jean Daniélou put it, "theology is inadequate if it does not end in mysticism, that is, in the living encounter with the living God."[82] As described by the philosopher Michael Mitchell, it is "beauty [that] moves us toward a mystical reality. . . . When a person is enamored with the beautiful, there is a magnetism—a sense of being drawn into or united with something that will consummate the desire by the experience—but the experience itself never brings us fully to the point of consummation. Beauty is the scent of the transcendent reality for which the soul hungers."[83] God has many names; one of them is: the Infinite. It is perhaps for this reason that the religious scholar, David Bentley Hart, could devote hundreds of pages in his treatise to the inexhaustible Beauty of the Infinite.[84]

If, in conclusion, I may elaborate on Daniélou's quote by saying that mystical experience is an encounter with a loving as well as a living God, I would further state that it is only by way of such mystical understanding that the separate magisteria of science and theology, governing respectively the two separate domains of empirico-experiential knowledge (the facts of nature) and of religious-experiential knowledge (the wisdom of love), unite perfectly as the *unifying* truth revealed in the spiritual encounter of God. How so? Here I claim that revelation manifests foremost through our appreciation of the beautiful. In chapter 5 we saw that, of the transcendentals, the this-worldly counterpart of Beauty is most bountifully and immediately accessible to our senses and our minds. And *pace* the misgivings of Sabine Hossenfelder about the role of beauty in science, we also saw in chapter 5 that beauty can serve as a readily available marker inspiring and guiding not only scientists in their inexhaustible and arduous task of uncovering the facts and truths secreted in the natural world, but also religious scholars in their equally arduous and unending task of uncovering the truths hidden in the supernatural realm.

82. Jean Daniélou, *God and the Ways of Knowing* (Ignatius Press, 2003), 168.
83. Mitchell, *Truth Before Logic*, 63.
84. See Hart, *The Beauty of the Infinite*.

APPENDICES

APPENDIX 1

On Neurocognitive and Evolutionary Studies of Mind

A substantial portion of what is covered below is also covered in chapter 1. The reader can therefore choose to skip the material discussed below. On the other hand, since, as a common saying goes, repetition is the mother of learning (by strengthening memory), it might benefit the reader to reacquaint him- or herself with the contents of this appendix.

Fundamental Considerations

> Given consciousness and its causal powers, one could give an evolutionary explanation of why certain mental states would be selected over others in the struggle for reproductive advantage. What cannot be explained is why consciousness exists in the first place. Evolution in particular, and [complex] combinatorial [neural] processes in general, are simply inadequate to explain the hard problem of consciousness. . . .
>
> J. P. Moreland, *Consciousness and the Existence of God*, p. 141

> . . . since within the physicalist paradigm [the philosopher Jaegwon] Kim cannot account for the obviously given intrinsic qualities of our experiences, he denies what he cannot account for. If you want to be a physicalist, you have to deny the obvious.
>
> Benedikt Paul Gōcke, *After Physicalism*, p. 6

To start, we note again that our conscious awareness of objects, events, and states in our external and internal environments, such as trees and hunger, and of our inner cognitive states and faculties, depends on two factors. Most important here is a *global* state of sufficiently high neurological arousal of the neocortex (the most recently evolved part of the mammalian brain) produced by afferent stimulation from what is known as the brain-stem and midbrain reticular systems (the more anciently evolved parts of the brain surrounded by the neocortex). This is supplemented by sufficiently high neural activations produced *locally* in our exteroceptors (the neural systems allowing sensory access to aspects of the external environment such as seeing the colors and tasting the sweetness of ripe fruits) and in our interoceptors (those neural systems monitoring aspects of the internal environment such as lack of nutrients or temperature changes) as well as in the brain regions underlying specific cognitive abilities like attentive reading of a textbook or planning an upcoming road trip. Depending on the state of the reticular activation systems, the state of global cortical neural arousal can be so low as to cause loss of conscious experience altogether, as in deep sleep, anesthesia, or coma. So, states of consciousness can vary on a continuum from none, through drowsiness and normal daily arousal levels, up to hyper-alert level when we, for instance, realize that we are facing imminent threat to our bodily well-being. Moreover, even when global neural arousal is sufficiently high, the neural responses occurring in, say, the retinae of our eyes to the low level of light reflecting from a tree during a starlit night (and a few tens of milliseconds thereafter the neural responses in our visual cortex) may be so weak as to be below the threshold for conscious awareness of the tree; and similarly, stimulation of the internal pain receptors in our leg muscles after a short walk may be too weak for us to consciously perceive any muscle ache in our calves.[1]

One can now ask what, besides sufficiently high global-arousal and local-activation levels, constitutes the neural correlates of consciousness (NCCs). Mental activities and contents don't always register in consciousness; a good portion of them can occur without conscious awareness. For instance, the activity of planning the routes of a bicycle ride on rural roads proceeds at a consciously deliberative level; however, the activity of blinking the eyes when, during a ride, an insect heads rapidly toward one of them is largely, if not entirely, controlled unconsciously, although very shortly after the blinking already has occurred, one of course can become aware of its occurrence. So, mental cognition, our assessment of states, objects, and events in the world can be conscious or unconscious. Since neural circuits are activated strongly both when I deliberate on my upcoming rides and when my eyes blink reflexively, why is it that only some of my brain's neural activity, that correlated with, say, my deliberations, also correlates with conscious awareness, whereas the other neural activity, causing my reflexive blinking, bypasses conscious awareness? Part of the answer lies in the anatomical locations of underlying neural circuitries. My deliberative planning relies heavily (but not exclusively) on neural circuits in the phylogenetically newer frontal areas and the older hippocampal areas of the cerebral cortex. Activation of these circuitries supports, among other abilities, our remembering prior events, in turn allowing us to imagine, anticipate, and predict possible new events, to consider and choose among sev-

1. Nonetheless, we know that local circuits in the sensory neocortex, e.g., the visual cortex, can be strongly activated even while an organism is in a state of deep anesthesia. Thus, no matter how weak or strong, activation of a particular local circuitry that signals a given visuo-cognitive content is by itself not sufficient for that content to be consciously perceived. For conscious perception, the global circuitry of the brain must also be in a resting state of arousal.

eral courses of action in response to these possible outcomes. Consequently, the process of consciously planning is time-consuming and rather slow. In contrast, to avoid a flying insect impacting and possibly damaging the cornea of one of my eyes, the time-consuming cortical neural processes correlated with conscious awareness are at a disadvantage relative to the much faster-responding subcortical system underlying our unconscious instinctive and reflexive abilities to avoid harm. We know that much of this subcortical activity occurs automatically and unconsciously, since it still can guide reflexive impact-avoiding behavior when the portion of the neocortex necessary for consciously registering the approaching object has been damaged or surgically excised.

So, as a first condition, we can say that the activation of specific cortical circuits is necessary for our having correspondingly specific conscious sensory and cognitive contents. Of course, the equally necessary background condition of global neural arousal cannot be neglected. In fact, one can think analogically of consciousness and its contents as akin to the Higgs field whose existence was recently discovered by physicists. Physicists take the Higgs field to confer mass on subatomic particles like the electron (but not on others, like the massless photon). Without it, all particles would be massless. Similarly, the global state of consciousness (for which the brain stem and midbrain reticular arousal systems are crucial) can be considered a unified field that confers consciousness on some but not all cognitive contents.[2] Without the globally aroused state, as in deep anesthesia, all local cortical neural activity that is still recordable in response to an external stimulus would correlate with lack of its registration in consciousness. Exactly if and how a local cortical circuitry is associated with a given conscious content within the larger integrative field of consciousness is not a settled issue; and like mapping the cortical connectome,[3] elucidating the answer to this question within a particular brain—moreover across a vast number of similar, but at the same time distinctly fashioned, brains—remains one of the many pivotal tasks of the cognitive and behavioral neurosciences. Cortical mapping techniques like functional magnetic resonance imaging (fMRI) are already providing some suggestive answers. Yet while current fMRI techniques can tell us, with a spatial resolution finer than a cubic millimeter,

2. Searle, "Consciousness."

3. The neural connectome project is similar to the genome project that has been able to specify the genetic makeup of distinct species of plants and animals, including of course humans. The connectome project seeks to specify all the neural connections between neurons within the nervous systems of organisms. For simple organisms such as the nematode worm *C. elegans*, whose entire nervous system consists of only 302 neurons, an entire connectome has been specified. Currently there are attempts to specify the neural connectome of the more complex mammalian brain, such as that of mice. The existence of about 70 million neurons in the mouse brain already poses staggering problems, and more imposing still will be the difficulty of delineating the neural connectome of the human brain.

where in the brain these local circuits are located, they cannot tell us what these circuits and their activation patterns look like in detail. Currently we can provide only hypothetical models of such activated circuits. Nonetheless, given these and other brain-recording and -modelling techniques, we can already infer, to take just a few examples, something about the neural correlates of consciousness (NCCs) of color, face, and object perception, and of cognitive tasks like searching your memory for a specific item of information. But while these NCCs indicate that cortical neural activities necessarily underly conscious perceptions and cognitions, it is not clear which subset of them, if any, is additionally sufficient to allow us to draw not only correlational but also causal inferences from neural patterns of activity. Cortical stimulation with microelectrodes in patients whose brains are partially exposed during a surgical procedure has resulted in their reporting at times somewhat nebulous at other time more specific, conscious experiences.[4] Results such as these have led some neuroscientists and philosophers of mind to overinterpret them by claiming that the necessity and the sufficiency of cortical activations associated such experiences extends to all other conscious experiences. Other scholars and neuroscientists are more cautious and regard these claims as exercises in interpretive overreach.

Consider the following. Akin to cortical microelectrode stimulation, a knock on the back of the skull can produce a short-lived conscious experience of something like shimmering stars. Do we then conclude that the knock on the back of the head caused the conscious experience? Yes, but only in an indirect, distal way. So, we conclude that some other intermediate and proximal factor(s) must also be involved. The energy in the knock to the back of the skull no doubt was transferred through the skull to the brain, there transiently activating neurons in the primary visual cortex, which might be considered the direct cause of seeing stars. But wrong again, because activation of the primary visual cortex, while necessary, on its own is not sufficient, either, for it must in turn activate neural networks in higher sites in the cortical visual system.[5] However, here again, the best that can be claimed is that activating higher intermediate centers is necessary for conscious visual experience to occur, since their inactivation or destruction leads to blindness of one sort or another. It is therefore reasonable to assume that the integrated activation of a substantial part of the brain might qualify as the sufficient condition. But now a troubling question arises: If the

4. For evidence and discussion of the effects of such stimulation, see Wilder Penfield and Phanor Perot, "The Brain's Record of Auditory and Visual Experience: A Final Summary and Discussion," *Brain* 86, no. 4 (1963): 595–696; and R. Quian Quiroga et al., "Sparse but Not 'Grandmother-Cell' Coding in the Medial Temporal Lobe," *Trends in Cognitive Sciences* 12, no. 3 (2008): 87–91.

5. Francis Crick and Christopher Koch, "Are We Aware of Neural Activity in Primary Visual Cortex?" *Nature* 375, no. 6527 (1995): 121–23; Francis Crick and Christopher Koch. "A Framework for Consciousness," *Nature Neuroscience* 6, no. 2 (2003): 119–26.

neural networks located in distinct anatomical sites are not individually sufficient for consciousness to occur, then how can their interactive totality, itself a globally distributed neural network, be sufficient?[6] What gives the excitation of globally integrated brain circuitry the wizard's elan, the magic of conjuring up consciousness that locally excited networks can't manage to do? In other words, even if such widespread networks are sufficient, one can further ask the more basic question: how is it that a complex neurophysiological event, clearly a bio-*physical* event, gives rise to a *conscious mental* event?

One currently fashionable answer, equally problematized by these questions, is given by the somewhat mysterious property of emergence. Emergence is a property or consequence of the complexity of self-organized systems. For instance, weather patterns, e.g., typhoons, emerge from the complex self-organized system consisting of countless trillions of individual water and air molecules subjected to energetic inputs and top-down physical constraints. Typhoons are windy, wet, huge, and powerful, all of them properties that any of its constituent H_2O and air molecules on their own do not display. Similarly, the liquidity of water or solidity of ice emerges from a self-organized system—again subjected to physical influences and constraints—that is more complex than the individual H_2O molecules that constitute water or ice. While emergence is fine and good when occurring in complex physical systems, it is not clear that emergence can help us to understand the nature of consciousness. By simply extending the concept of emergence used in the physical domains (e.g., that of individual H_2O molecules and that of the liquidity or surface tension of water) analogically to the mental domain, consciousness can too readily be regarded as simply an emergent property of the complex interactive organization of the cortical neural circuitry. The underlying ontological assumption, of course, is that despite its emergence, consciousness remains an entirely physical, neuronal phenomenon. Among some practicing philosophers and neuroscientists,[7] this naturalization of consciousness can easily morph from methodological assumptions grounding an ambitious neuroscientific research program into an ontological assertion. In its strongest form, the naturalization of consciousness is framed in terms of an identity relation: consciousness *is* nothing but (i.e., without remainder) the emergent neural activity expressed via complex cortical circuitry. However, other philosophers and neuroscientists are a bit more skeptical and cautious of such conceptual overreach. In the context of the puzzling

6. Taking recourse to global neural interactions alone to render a sufficient explanation of consciousness is problematic, since such interactions also depend on neural circuitry, although more complex ones than are the local circuitries. That quandary leads some neuroscientists and philosophers to argue that consciousness is an "emergent" property of sufficiently complex neural circuitry.

7. For example, John Searle, "Theory of Mind and Darwin's Legacy." *Proceedings of the National Academy of Sciences USA* 110 (Suppl 2) (2013): 10343–48.

mind-body relation, philosophers like Thomas Natsoulas have pointed out that even physicalists, despite all attempts to explain consciousness fully, must acknowledge the obdurate existence of a residual subjectivity.[8] The subjectivity of consciousness is a *sui generis* mental state or property, i.e., one not reducible to an emergent property or state of the brain's complex biophysical organization. Luis Oviedo, for instance, points out that such emergentist explanation "of some human features [like consciousness] does not help overcome or suppress the mystery surrounding them."[9] Seconding this assessment, the philosopher Michael Silverstein expresses the mysterious aspect of consciousness this way:

> . . . if someone asks how H_2O could possibly possess the [emergent] properties deemed essential to water (such as its liquidity) we can answer their question within an explanation from quantum chemistry. But we cannot answer the analogous question about consciousness and the brain. Accepting the identity theory as a philosophical solution to the mind-body problem does not obviate the need for a scientific explanation of *how* brain states can have consciousness as one of their [emergent] properties, just as in the case of water and liquidity. [He continues by quoting the philosopher David Chalmers that] "in postulating an explanatory 'identity,' one is trying to get something for nothing: all of the explanatory work of a fundamental law, at none of the ontological cost." [And further on, Silverstein states] that the mind-brain identity theory is as yet *not explanatory* the way other identity theories in science are, because it does not tell us *how* mental states can be nothing but brain states. This explanatory gap seems to be insurmountable in principle, because one cannot identify phenomenal-intentional *properties* with objective physical *properties* without falling into [some type of] eliminativism.[10]

This puzzlement raised by the existence of conscious beings in relation to the physical world is evident also in Terrence Deacon's cryptically—one also could say, apophatically—expressed view that inverts "getting something from nothing" in terms of "a 'no-thing' emerging from something":

> Human consciousness—with its features of autonomous causal locus, self-organization, and implicit "aboutness"—epitomises the logic of emergence in its various forms. Like something coming out of nothing, the subjective self is, in effect, a *constitutive absence* for the sake of which new constitutive absence is being incessantly evolved. In this sense, there is some legiti-

8. Thomas Natsoulas, "Residual Subjectivity," *American Psychologist* 33, no. 3 (1978): 269–83.

9. Oviedo, "'Self-Organizing Personhood,'" 145.

10. Michael Silverstein, "In Defense of Ontological Emergence and Mental Causation," in *The Re-Emergence of Emergence: The Emergentist Hypothesis from Science to Religion*, ed. Philip Clayton and Paul Davies (Oxford University Press, 2006), 221.

> macy to the eliminativist claim that there is no "thing" that it is. Indeed this must be so. The locus of self is, effectively, a negative mode of existence, that can act as an unmoved mover of sorts: a non-thing that nonetheless is the locus of a form of inertia—a resistance to change—with respect to which other physical processes can be recruited and organized. Consciousness is not exactly getting something from nothing. It merely appears that way. . . . It is, nevertheless, a form of being that is constituted by what it is not, and yet remains a locus of physical influence. It is the hole at the wheel's hub.[11] (emphasis added)

As we shall see below, this apophatic view of human consciousness bears significantly on related theological views regarding the conscious mind of God.

Philosophical Implications

Eliminativism vs. Panpsychism

Consciousness, a no-thing in a physical universe of things, is the marvelous and mysterious non-stuff that occupies the minds of philosophers like David Chalmers and Michael Silverstein as well as those philosophers of the reductive neural-, functional-, and linguistic-eliminativist bent like Paul and Patricia Churchland, Daniel Dennett, Richard Rorty, and Stephen Stich.[12] For the latter philosophers who, as Silverstein noted above, duly subscribe to some sort of eliminativism, consciousness at bottom is not the physically influential nonthing described by Terrance Deacon but a down-and-out noninfluential nonentity—an epiphenomenal and fanciful "magical mystery show," or the insubstantial "rainbow" overarching the workings of the brain's functional architecture[13]—ultimately no more mysterious than a falling rock, since, like it, consciousness *is* nothing but matter in motion inside the brain, albeit matter that structurally and functionally is highly complex. And rather than posing a

11. Terrance W. Deacon, "Emergence: The Hole in the Wheel's Hub," in *The Re-emergence of Emergence: The Emergentist Hypothesis from Science to Religion*, ed. Philip Clayton and Paul Davies (Oxford University Press, 2006), 149.

12. David J. Chalmers, *The Conscious Mind* (Oxford University Press, 1996); David J. Chalmers, "The Hard Problem of Consciousness," in *The Blackwell Companion to Consciousness*, ed. Susan Schneider and Max Velmans (Blackwell Publishing, 2007); Paul M. Churchland and Patricia Smith Churchland, *On the Contrary: Critical Essays, 1987–1997* (MIT Press, 1998); Daniel C. Dennett, "Quining Qualia," in *Consciousness in Modern Science*, ed. Anthony J. Marcel and Eduardo Bisiach (Oxford University Press, 1988); Dennett, *Consciousness Explained*; Richard Rorty, *Philosophy and the Mirror of Nature* (Princeton University Press, 1979); Silverstein, "In Defense of Ontological Emergence"; Stephen Stich, *From Folk Psychology to Cognitive Science: The Case Against Belief* (MIT Press, 1983).

13. Humphrey, *Soul Dust*; David A. Oakley and Peter W. Halligan, "Chasing the Rainbow: The Non-Conscious Nature of Being," *Frontiers in Psychology* 8 (2017): 1924.

mysterious question, consciousness is an incidental byproduct merely posing scientific puzzles that, as ever promised, will someday be totally solved by the physical and natural sciences. In contrast to these approaches, when addressing the mysterious aspect of consciousness in a physical world, some investigators of consciousness, among them the philosophers Nathaniel Barrett, David Chalmers, Philip Goff, David Griffin, and Galen Strawson, as well as the neuroscientist Christof Koch,[14] have entertained the hypothesis of panpsychism, which states that any physical system that is an integrated organization of parts enjoys some form of what-is-it-like-to-be such a system, be it the proto-consciousness (whatever that may mean) of a subatomic particle (an integrated composite of quarks) or the fully deployed consciousness of an alert human being (whose brain many a neuroscientist exalts to a level of complexity and integrative organization so far unexcelled by anything else known). In other words, the cosmos is through and through a mental/conscious, or at least a proto-mental/conscious, entity.

All this of course introduces new, puzzling questions: How far down the subatomic ladder does panpsychism reach? Are the hypothesized quarks themselves also endowed with a proto-consciousness? Do they have, besides externally specifiable properties, some primitive form of interiority, a what-is-it-like-to-be qualitative existence? If not, how far up the atomic, molecular, cellular, or organic ladder must a physical system evolve before a proto-consciousness edges over the threshold of a certifiable consciousness involving subjective, phenomenal experiences? Can one find it in single-celled organisms? They, after all, are sensitive to (irritated by) changes in the chemical and physical composition of their external milieu. If not there, can one find it in more complex life forms like the nematode *C. elegans*, composed of nearly one thousand cells, of which roughly 30% comprise its primitive nervous system? I will spare the reader the answers to these questions, by stating here my claim—to be elaborated and supported below—that anything like a consciousness involving subjective, phenomenal experiences requires an organism that has evolved a brain

14. Nathaniel F. Barrett, "The Perspectivity of Feeling: Process Panpsychism and The Explanatory Gap," *Process Studies* 38, no. 2 (2009): 189–206; David Chalmers, "Panpsychism and Panprotopsychism," in *Consciousness in the Physical World: Perspectives on Russellian Monism*, ed. Torin Alter and Yujin Nagasawa (Oxford University Press, 2015); David Chalmers, "The Combination Problem for Panpsychism," in *Panpsychism*, ed. Godehard Brüntrup and Ludwig Jaskolla (Oxford University Press, 2016); Philip Goff, *Galileo's Error: Foundations for a New Science of Consciousness* (Pantheon Books, 2010); David Ray Griffin, *Unsnarling the World-Knot: Consciousness, Freedom, and the Mind-Body Problem* (University of California Press, 1998). Christof Koch, *Consciousness: Confessions of a Romantic Reductionist* (MIT Press, 2012); Galen Strawson, "Realistic Monism: Why Physicalism Entails Panpsychism," in *Consciousness and its Place in Nature: Does Physicalism Entail Panpsychism?*, ed. Anthony Freeman (Imprint Academic, 2006).

whose functional architecture is at least as complex as that found no earlier than the evolution of the first mammals.

Fine and good. But what besides a mammalian central nervous system sustains the existence of any psychic entity at all? If the reader is satisfied with the eliminative gambit, the ontological buck stops with neurochemical energy-exchanges occurring in the evolved mammalian central nervous system; therefore, any further, more fundamental, questions need not be asked. If, on the other hand, he bases his account of consciousness on panpsychism or on theism, then, like a pilgrim questing after the holy grail, the ontological buck and the questions move ever farther, if not deeper. In attempts to address the problems inherent in panpsychist or theistic implications posed for physicalism, others have suggested that the human intellect and the physics it generates is not yet sophisticated or imaginative enough to yield an adequate, purely physicalist explanation of consciousness. For example, like the physicist Arthur Eddington before him, Strawson holds that it is a mistake to think we know enough about physical reality to rule out that consciousness can't be physical. Adopting this (now typically applied) deferral to the future, a committed physicalist assumes that the human intellect and its physical theories may eventually evolve to the point that a fully physical explanation of consciousness is forthcoming. Alternatively, alien intellects elsewhere in the universe with brains already much more complex than ours might be able to produce such a physicalist explanation. However, in either imagined case, what is not considered by physicists like Eddington and physicalists like Strawson is that it is just as likely that even the highest evolved humans or the already highly evolved aliens more quickly realize how profoundly insoluble a mystery the existence of consciousness in an otherwise physical reality is.

The Grand Illusion of Panillusionism

We already noted that our senses (primarily vision but, if need be, also audition and touch) are crucial to making the empirical observations that support the scientific acquisition of knowledge of the things, properties, and processes in the universe. This knowledge is also intimately linked to our conscious, higher-level conceptual and cognitive faculties that allow us to theoretically probe into the realm of fundamental particles and their associated fields, the realm of organisms in their natural ecology, or any other contents within any of the larger contexts—such as galactic clusters—distributed throughout the universe. If consciousness is a non-thing or, worse yet, an illusion (as some eliminativists claim), a key question then is: Regarding science as well as our day-to-day lives, to what extent are our conscious apprehension and knowledge true to the objects, events, and states that constitute the entities of our universe and of our lifeworld? One of the most troubling consequences of recent research in cognitive neuroscience and in evolutionary psychology has been a transformation of the no-thing status of consciousness into its illusory double, a transformation promulgated by some scientists who claim that everyday perceptions of the world are through and through nonveridical. This claim's premise (or conclusion) is that not only a few (e.g., the sensory illusions studied by perception researchers like me) but all our perceptions and beliefs based on our observations of the external world are illusory. In fact, as we'll see below, the very ontological status of a world external to the human observer is in serious doubt among some idealistically inclined scholars and scientists. Consequently, since what we know in our daily lives and what scientists know in their professional lives depend crucially on our sense perceptions, the veridicality of mundane as well as scientific knowledge of the world is questionable. Such panillusionism, incoherent and self-defeating though it is, results from the flatlining of reason and intellect. Yet, it is taken seriously by many scientists and academics, and abounds in culturally popularized accounts of all sorts of human cognition, some of which are discussed below.

Most of us are familiar with a variety of visual or optical illusions. For instance, the size of the full moon appears visually larger when it hovers just above the horizon than when it is located at its zenith directly above us. Similarly, a physically vertical line will appear about 2 degrees tilted counterclockwise when it intersects an array of parallel lines tilted clockwise by about 15 degrees. Many other visual illusions, as well as auditory and tactual ones, have been studied by perception psychologists.[15] However, despite their number, perceptual illusions are known—much like visual hallucinations that are produced, for instance, by sensory deprivation and dreams—for what they are—namely, as not corresponding to the objectively measurable properties of external reality. Despite these nonveridical outliers, many, if not all, perception psychologists would argue that the overwhelming proportion of our perceptions are veridical in the sense that they serve a truth-tracking function in relation to a world that exists independently of our perceptions. Otherwise, under the sway of panillusionism, we would have to ask ourselves why a vision researcher interested in the experimental study of visual illusions can, or why she even should, scientifically distinguish between instances of visual illusions and instances of visual veridicalities. With failure to make such distinctions *via consciously experienced observations*, a whole field of past and current visual science—where the study of illusions in fact informs us about underlying perceptual processes, paradoxically helping to render the vast majority of perceptions as close as possible to veridical—is consigned to nonsensical phantasy.

In addition, it is most important to note the following striking and paradoxical fact. It is generally believed among vision scientists that visual illusions are

15. For a host of visual illusions, see Michael Bach, 154 Visual Phenomena & Optical Illusions, accessed October 18, 2023, http://www.michaelbach.de/ot/.

entirely ascribable to properties of, or to how stimuli are processed by, the visual system. But visual illusions are not entirely illusive in this sense. Formal, quantitative analyses of the structural properties of stimuli giving rise to illusory visual perceptions—like the tilt illusion described above—have revealed that a substantial portion of the illusory component can be attributed *to the physical, mathematically describable structures of the visual stimuli themselves* rather than attributing all to an evolutionary "maladaptation" of the visuo-perceptual system. In other words, many of these illusions lie as much, perhaps more, in the objective physical properties of the stimuli themselves as in our visual systems' processes.[16] However, to my knowledge, no experimental work has so far been done to disentangle how much of the physical and mathematically specifiable properties of a stimulus contribute to visuo-perceptual illusion from how much is due to the properties of the visuo-perceptual system. Such work would comprise an entirely new research program that could noticeably impact how philosophers and scientists, especially those inclined toward panillusionism, understand physical reality and its relation to the mental reality of consciousness. However, at present, the truth-tracking function of conscious visual and other sensory experiences is seriously questioned from the perspective of philosophy of mind, cognitive neuroscience, and the science of evolutionary psychology.

Panillusionism is aptly exemplified by an approach to human visual perception known the "multi-user interface" (MUI) theory, or simply the interface theory, of conscious perception proposed by the cognitive neuroscientist Donald Hoffman and colleagues[17] and similarly exemplified by philosopher Daniel Dennett's use of a computer-science metaphor to describe consciousness as a user-illusion, since, from an evolutionary perspective, it serves bodily survival *in the world* but not the search for truth *about the world*.[18] The claim of this approach is that our perceptions, the conscious experiences of the world, are nonveridical (where "veridical" refers to perceptions faithfully corresponding to, or truth-tracking, the events or properties in an objective, mind-independent world). Instead, in the interface theory, they are akin to icons on a computer desktop that communicate between a file, realized in the intricate electronical circuitry of the computer, and a user who is ignorant of

16. Bernt C. Skottun, "Is the Tilt-Illusion in the Stimuli?," *PsyArXiv* (2018); Bernt C. Skottun, "Interference in Tilt-Illusion Stimuli: A Simple Illustration," *PsyArXiv* (2020); Bernt C. Skottun, "A Few Remarks on 'Uncrowding' in Visual Stimuli," *PsyArXiv* (2021); Bernt C. Skottun, "What Is a Visual Stimulus?," *PsyArXiv* (2021b).

17. Donald D. Hoffman, "Conscious Realism and the Mind-Body Problem," *Mind & Matter* 6, no. 1 (2008): 87–121; Donald D. Hoffman and Chetan Prakash, "Objects of Consciousness," *Frontiers of Psychology* 5 (2014): 577; Donald D. Hoffman et al., "The Interface Theory of Perception," *Psychonomic Bulletin & Review* 22, no. 6 (2015): 1480–1506.

18. Daniel Dennett, *From Bacteria to Bach and Back: The Evolution of Minds* (W. W. Norton & Co., 2017).

the complexity underlying the interactive electronic circuitry. In other words, a rectangular icon on the video-screen interface does not veridically manifest the computer file in its icon-independent state (the file that exists as an electronically coded software stored within the computer hardware clearly is not identical to a small rectangle displayed on the computer's screen). As with icons on a computer screen, perceptions are not true to, and do not faithfully render, the intricate information stored in the brain's "hardware" about events, structures, and states of the objective world. From an evolutionary-psychology standpoint, perceptions thus merely serve as useful communication devices between an organism and the environment, thereby promoting its biological, evolutionary fitness, its ability to survive and reproduce, without conveying a veridical representation of a mind-independent, objective world. Surprisingly, this notion is not as novel an insight as Hoffman et al. or Dennett might want to believe; for it is a rehashed version of Aristotle's understanding of perception—as conveyed by philosopher John Cottingham—that "we have the perceptual faculties we have so that we might protect our bodies [thereby increasing our reproductive fitness], not so that we might know [the truth about] the world."[19] In this sense, not only are the illusions familiar to perception psychologists nonveridical but so are *all* our perceptions. The MUI approach claims to be noncommittal regarding any ontological appeal to the existence of an objective world[20]; the existence of such a world is—too conveniently, in my view—neither affirmed nor denied. All of science, including the science of perception—so the promoters of the MUI approach assert—can happily proceed with or without the world's objective existence. This assertion, however, runs counter to the fact that most natural scientists attempt to explain how empirical observations, ultimately based as they are on *subjective* conscious experiences, relate to objects, events, and properties that reside in what is deemed to be an *objectively* observable, external world.

A consequence of assuming the validity of the MUI theory of conscious perception is that several baffling puzzles and questions arise. Following the icon-on-the-desktop analogy, if all perceptions that exist are illusory, then *of* what or *about* what are they perceptions? In other words, if they are illusory, how can they designate anything outside themselves that itself is a reality, i.e., a non-illusory entity such as a real computer file instantiated in the hardware of a computer? It seems that what has stealthily crept into the MUI theory of conscious perception through its backdoor is the intuition of a non-illusory real world that can be perceived, that includes real biologically evolving humans, computers, computer icons, and the like, and that—most importantly for our daily commerce in our *Lebenswelt* and for doing science—exists independently

19. Cottingham, *In Search of the Soul*, 166.
20. Hoffman, "Conscious Realism."

of the so-called illusory perception of it. Without this, pursuing any scientifically objective, third-person account of what we sense to be a real, out-there world is neither worthwhile nor possible. During the last three to four decades, even several hundreds of scientists and scholars around the world—among them physicists, neuroscientists, cognitive scientists, and philosophers—have spent huge amounts of effort and time investigating the nature of human conscious perception. Why would they engage in these investigations so arduously and lengthily if—as the MUI theory holds—all conscious perceptions and consciousness itself were mere illusions, i.e., not real entities? The answer is that, in the context of J. P. Moreland's remark made below in appendix 2 (see footnote 20), it bears to note that although one relates to the external world at best as an indirect or critical realist, in relation to consciousness and its contents, one can be a *direct realist*. In other words, we can be absolutely certain that our private experiences, including our conscious perceptions, are undeniably presented to us, in unmediated direct fashion, as *real*, or even more so, than anything else.

Beyond considering the above problems raised by the MUI theory of perception, we can address the important matter regarding the truth-tracking function of perceptions. Supporting the MUI theory is the fact that computational simulation studies[21] show that models of perception based on reproductive fitness outdo models based on truth-tracking. Yet this does not imply that human truth-tracking abilities fail to contribute to reproductive fitness. It only shows that human truth-tracking ability *might* be merely an evolutionary byproduct or spandrel that does not add to reproductive fitness. However, to rule out this possibility we need only look at the special case of scientific truth-tracking. Due to the undeniable fact that the application of especially the science-based medical and agricultural technologies have supported the geometrically accelerating increase of the worldwide human population over the last century, it is no longer possible to deny that scientific truth-tracking can contribute substantively to the reproductive fitness of humans.

Moreover, although MUI theory claims to be neutral vis-à-vis an objective, mind-independent world, from an ontological standpoint we can ask: In what type of reality can any kind of biologically adaptive function evolve—in a mind-independent type or, as noted above, in an incoherent mind-dependent one? The early evolution of the cosmos predated biological evolution of living microbes by a total of 13.5 billion years, before rudimentary nervous systems that could support anything like a conscious mind first appeared. If so, then from a current scientific perspective, during that vast stretch of time did or didn't the cosmological and biological evolutions occur in a world that was mind-independent? For the reader finding difficulty in coping with such puzzles

21. For the reader interested in a recent simulation study, see Prakash et al., "Fitness Beats Truth in the Evolution of Perception," *Acta Biotheoretica* 69, no. 3 (2021): 319–41.

or questions raised by the proposition of the MUI or other approaches to panillusionism,[22] I offer a different view of perceptual consciousness.

Consciousness: Veridical, Yet Superficial

> . . . their eyes merely glide over the surface of things and see "forms."
>
> Friedrich Nietzsche, *On Truth and Lies in a Nonmoral Sense*, p. 21

What is proposed in this section may be just as nonsensical as panillusionism. For in not only a metaphoric but also a literal sense, I claim as a main thesis that *our lives proceed experientially on the surface of reality.* It is the experienced surface of reality that begs all sorts of questions—be they artistic, philosophical, theological, scientific, practical, or theoretical—regarding the deeper significance, the existential meaning behind or below surface appearances. In making my claim, I ask the reader to bear patiently with my delving more deeply into how and why visual observations/perceptions of the world (and therefore much of our knowledge of the world, including scientific knowledge) carry with them an intrinsic "superficiality," the overcoming of which is nonetheless one of the prime motivations for engaging in deeper investigations of the world we inhabit. As an analogue of what I mean, consider the scientific disciplines of solid-state physics. The keyboard on which I am typing the present sentence is a physical structure that is solid. Therefore, any study of its components by solid-state physicists takes for granted that solid states exist as real entities in the external world; why else should we study them? Nonetheless, the solid-state physicist, who tries to explain their solidity and impenetrability, has recourse to deeper levels of physical analysis offered by what is known about forcefields and their associated subatomic particles studied by quantum physicists and chemists. Although the lower-level microscopic quantum world is fundamental to the macroscopic solid-state world, one is not justified in claiming that the higher-level phenomena such as the impenetrability studied by solid-state physics are illusory, unless one takes the epistemically and ontologically reductive stance, unwarranted on strictly scientific grounds, that all physical phenomena are reducible to quantum ones, and therefore that all of the higher-level physical phenomena exhibited by solids are illusory. In other words, the solidity of my keyboard and its components are perceptually exhibited by the hardness, impenetrability, and opaqueness of their surfaces without, however, exhibiting or negating the deeper, hidden reality that only trained quantum physicists can experientially penetrate. As this example shows,

22. Additional reasons for skepticism regarding the validity of the interface theory of perception, and replies to these reasons by Hoffman et al., can be found in *Psychonomic Bulletin & Review* 22 (2015): 1507–76.

science is indeed a way to delve more deeply into what at first glance appears to be a superficial reality.

But recall that the natural sciences depend on empirical observations, and that these are first and foremost private and subjective observational experiences or perceptions of the world. In addition to this main claim, we can now fill in details of its corollary claim that *all perceptions are superficial.* I will justify this claim by focusing on my research specialty, visual perception and cognition. I start with the profound intuition articulated by the philosopher of art John Hyman, in his book *The Objective Eye.* He states that "there is an *intrinsic tie between color and sentience,* as there is between smell or taste and sentience, *which does not exist between sentience and shape*"[23] (emphases added). Shortly thereafter, he elaborates that "[one] cannot see the shape [i.e., the form] of a banana except by seeing its spatial boundaries, however fleeting and uncertain this experience may be. And [one] cannot see its spatial boundaries *except* by seeing the differences of color that make it visibly distinct from its surroundings"[24] (emphasis added). Hyman's phenomenological distinction between boundaries of objects and their surface properties such as color makes intuitive sense. This philosophic intuition can be given scientific backing. In the field of visual cognition, color is regarded as the premier example of a surface feature (examples of other surface features are achromatic brightness levels, textures, and shadings). And in philosophy, the perceptual experiences of colors have been taken as the prime examples of qualia. That noted, a related view of the importance of surface features such as colors to our understanding of visual consciousness and perception are expressed most explicitly by Stephen Grossberg's claim, based on his formal mathematical model of human vision, that "surfaces are for seeing."[25] Since standard definitions of "sentience" and "seeing" refer to conscious awareness, Hyman's intuition and Grossberg's model assert that our visual perception of shape depends crucially on conscious awareness of surface properties such as color. Without going into great detail, the increasingly sophisticated models of human vision proposed by Grossberg and his collaborators[26] incorporate what is called the boundary-contour system (BCS),

23. John Hyman, *The Objective Eye: Color, Form, and Reality in the Theory of Art* (University of Chicago Press, 2006), 17.

24. Hyman, *The Objective Eye*, 18.

25. Grossberg, "Filling-In the Forms," 19.

26. Stephen Grossberg, "3-D Vision and Figure-Ground Separation by Visual Cortex," *Perception & Psychophysics* 55, no. 1 (1994): 48–121; Stephen Grossberg and Gurumurthy Swaminathan, "A Laminar Cortical Model for 3D Perception of Slanted and Curved Surfaces and of 2D Images: Development, Attention, and Bistability," *Vision Research* 44, no. 11 (2004): 1147–87; Yongqiang Cao and Stephen Grossberg, "A Laminar Cortical Model of Stereopsis and 3D Surface Perception: Closure and da Vinci Stereopsis," *Spatial Vision* 18, no. 5 (2005): 515–78.

which is responsible for the processing of the boundary of a visual form, and the feature-contour system (FCS), which is responsible for processing the surface features that fill-in in the region surrounded by the contours of visual two- and three-dimensional structures. These two systems are more than hypothetical entities; their underlying neurophysiological distinctions have been carefully documented in studies of primates such as macaques,[27] whose visual system is anatomically very similar to that of humans.

Grossberg further argues that the BCS's processing of contour can occur fully at the unconscious, i.e., nonvisible, level, in that "a boundary that is completed within the segmentation system (denoted BCS) does not generate visible contrasts within the BCS. In this sense, *all boundaries are invisible* [original emphases]. *Visibility* [i.e., conscious vision] *is a property of the surface filling-in system (denoted FCS)*"[28] (emphases added). My own work has experimentally confirmed that, without (the FCS) filling in the surface features, visual boundaries per se register only at the nonconscious (BCS) level of visual processing.[29] Furthermore, it has been shown that the filling-in process normally occurs rapidly, at most within a few to a few tens of milliseconds, but, under very special experimental conditions, it can be shown to require upwards of two seconds.[30] Similar to the distinction between linguistic surface structure, i.e., the audible or visible arrangement of words, and linguistic deep structure, i.e., the conceptual and semantic bases underlying that arrangement, the "language" of visual perception—and other perceptions, as I have argued elsewhere[31]—consists of the registration of superficial features of objects on which the conscious perception of their deeper formal features depends. So much for my brief justification of the claim that all perception crucially depends on its being first and foremost superficial. In this sense and as epigraphically summarized above by Nietzsche's quote, insofar as objective empirical science ultimately depends on subjective perceptual experiences of nature, the first step in the entire process of doing science is to, so to speak, experientially set foot on the surface of reality. And as far as religion also is intimately and more importantly tied to subjective experiences, it also initially moves on the surface of reality. Reality in its widest and deepest sense, toward

27. Daniel J. Felleman et al., "Modular Organization of Occipito-Temporal Pathways: Cortical Connections Between Visual Area 4 and Visual Area 2 and Posterior Inferotemporal Ventral Area in Macaque Monkeys," *Journal of Neuroscience* 17, no. 9 (1997): 3185–3200.

28. Grossberg, "3-D Vision and Figure-Ground Separation," 59.

29. Bruno Breitmeyer et al., "Unconscious Priming by Forms and Their Parts," *Visual Cognition* 12, no. 5 (2005): 720–36.

30. Bruno G. Breitmeyer and Jane Jacob, "Microgenesis of Surface Completion in Visual Objects: Evidence for Filling-Out," *Vision Research* 55, no. 5 (2012): 11–18; V. S. Ramachandran and R. L. Gregory, "Perceptual Filling In of Artificially Induced Scotomas in Human Vision," *Nature* 350, no. 6320 (1991): 699–702.

31. Breitmeyer, *The Visual (Un)Conscious*, chapter 10.

which both scientific and religious experiences are aimed, will continue to entice yet ever remain frustratingly elusive to our full understanding.

There are further implications of the fact that the contours of bounded regions in visual space can define the shape of forms whose surfaces are filled in by features such as color, achromatic variations of brightness and shadings, chiaroscuros, highlights, and textures. Visual forms are spatially extended in the visual field, and their spatial transformations, e.g., change of shape, size, or location, can be specified quantitatively by geometrical formulae. In terms used by the 17th-century French philosopher Rene Descartes, they corresponded to physical entities that he called *res extensae* (spatially extended things). As such, their physical properties can be subjected to scientific analysis by observing and measuring them. So, from an objective scientific standpoint these properties, the *res extensa*, were things in the external world, and thereby acquired the status of being of primary interest to science. In contrast, Descartes considered entities like color, brightness (but also hunger, thirst, taste, smell, pain, and itch) to correspond only to internal, subjective sensations, that belonged entirely to the subjective realm of *res cogitans* (things merely subjectively thought or felt); hence, since they had no objectively measurable referents in the external world, they were of a secondary interest. It was maintained, for instance by Descartes's near contemporary, Galileo, that these *res cogitans* were not within the scope of scientific physical analysis, but remain open to philosophical and phenomenological methods of studying the human mind. Shortly thereafter, the English philosopher John Locke introduced the terms "primary qualities" and "secondary qualities"[32] to distinguish between the properties of the external, worldly entities and the merely internal, subjective properties of sensation. In *An Essay Concerning Human Understanding*, Locke makes explicit that "ideas of primary qualities are resemblances; of secondary, not. From whence I think it easy to draw this observation,—that the ideas of pri-

32. Some scholars have argued that the primary-secondary distinction was first introduced not by Locke, but by Locke's contemporary, the Irish philosopher, physicist, and chemist Robert Boyle. For a look at the historic priority of making the distinction, see Laura Keating, "Un-Locke-ing Boyle: Boyle on Primary and Secondary Qualities," *History of Philosophy Quarterly* 10, no. 4 (1993): 305–23. However, on p. 305 of her article, Keating states, "It is widely accepted among commentators on Locke that his distinction between primary and secondary qualities is taken from Robert Boyle, who is credited with introducing the 'primary-secondary' terminology. A careful reading of Locke and Boyle, however, brings this accepted view [namely, that Locke's distinction between primary and secondary qualities is taken from Robert Boyle, who is credited with introducing the 'primary-secondary' terminology] into doubt, at least given how Locke is presently understood. As a step toward overthrowing this view, it will be shown that the two interpretations of Boyle that are given by those who hold the accepted view are mistaken." Unless I have sorely misunderstood the quoted passage, the only way that I can interpret it is that not Boyle, but Locke, introduced the "primary-secondary" terminology.

mary qualities of bodies are *resemblances* of them, and their [the bodies'] patterns do really exist in the bodies themselves, but the *ideas produced in us by these secondary qualities have no resemblance* of them at all. *There is nothing like our ideas, existing in the bodies themselves*"[33] (emphases added). The distinction was already evident in rudimentary form in the thinking of the ancient Greek natural philosophers Democritus and Epicurus; and in addition to Galileo and Descartes, it became a standard distinction for several other philosophers and scientists, such as Robert Boyle and Isaac Newton. The distinction between primary and secondary qualities, without explicitly naming it as such, made eminent sense in the early days of modern science. Yet, as early as Locke's time, the validity of the distinction was debated and criticized by the Scottish philosopher David Hume and the Anglo-Irish philosopher Bishop Berkely, in turn reasserted by the Scottish philosopher Thomas Reid, and by present-day philosophers.[34]

The following quote from James Van Cleve summarizes what, I believe, is the key objection Hume and Berkeley raised regarding Locke's distinction: "What Berkeley and Hume are asking is a question of which the following is a more concrete instance: could an object have [a primary quality like] shape without having any *sensuous* [secondary qualities like] color or texture to fill its boundaries and differentiate it from its surroundings? To that question, their answer is no."[35] I fully endorse Van Cleve's answer to the question and extend the critique inherent in it as follows. First, insofar as color is a surface feature of visual objects, all that was said in the prior sub-section affirms that the correct answer to the question has to be, not only on philosophic but also on scientifically theoretical and empirical grounds, a definite no. For we noted that the conscious registration (i.e., perception) of the primary quality of an object's shape/form cannot occur without first the filling-in and conscious registration of its color or other surface feature; and therefore, the shape of an object is as much in the mind—as much a subjective perceptual impression—as is its color, a conclusion previously argued in § 10 of Berkeley's *A Treatise Concerning The Principles of Human Knowledge*.[36] A similar critique of the primary-secondary distinction is expressed in § 122 of Hume's *An Enquiry Concerning Human*

33. John Locke, *An Essay Concerning Human Understanding* (Penguin, 1997), chapter 8, ¶ 15.

34. For current views of the primary-secondary quality distinction, see Lawrence Nolan, ed., *Primary & Secondary Qualities: The Historical and Ongoing Debate* (Oxford University Press, 2011).

35. James Van Cleve, "Reid on the Real Foundation of the Primary-Secondary Quality Distinction," in *Primary & Secondary Qualities: The Historical and Ongoing Debate*, ed. Lawrence Nolan (Oxford University Press, 2011), 293.

36. George Berkeley, *A Treatise Concerning the Principles of Human Knowledge* (Dover Publications, 2003), 10–11.

Understanding.[37] In contrast to Hume and Berkeley, Reid argued that the primary-secondary quality distinction is valid. In fact, argues Reid, in Section 6.8 of *An Inquiry into the Human Mind on the Principles of Common Sense*, that one possibly could "perceive the visible figure of bodies, without having any sensation or impression [of surface color] made upon his mind."[38] Here again, all that was said in the prior sub-section provides strong philosophic as well as scientific grounds that Reid's modal (it-is-possible-that) argument cannot apply in our real world, where one cannot perceive a shape without its surface qualities such as color.

From all that was said in the previous sub-section, we can note further that the perceptual filling-in of surface features is the *sine qua non* of the conscious registration of the object's contours comprising its shape. Hence, one can argue that the conscious registration of surface features is *prior*—temporally on empirical grounds[39] and logically on philosophic grounds—to the conscious registration of shape features, which also *follows* on both grounds. From the standpoint of visual perception and, thus, importantly, from the standpoint of scientific observations, this priority of secondary surface qualities, such as color, confers on them a primacy that Locke's so-called "primary" shape qualities can no longer claim. In effect, we could invert Locke's distinction as follows: An object's *perceived surface qualities* (e.g., color, achromatic brightness, and texture) *are primary* while its *perceived contour qualities* (e.g., its shape, size, and spatial location) *are secondary*.[40]

Theological Implications

We can summarize all the above as follows. The traditionally-termed secondary perceptual qualities are as real as primary ones. Both manifest perceptually in first-person, visual, and other sensory experiences that correspond to—in Locke's words, have resemblances to—the measurable properties of objects in

37. David Hume, *An Enquiry Concerning Human Understanding* (Hackett Publishing, 1993), 106.

38. Thomas Reid, *An Inquiry into the Human Mind on the Principles of Common Sense* (Edinburgh University Press, 1997), 100–101.

39. Colin W. G. Clifford et al., "A Paradox of Temporal Perception Revealed by a Stimulus Oscillating in Colour and Orientation," *Vision Research* 43, no. 21 (2003): 2245–53; Konstantinos Moutoussis, "Asynchrony in Visual Consciousness and the Possible Involvement of Attention," *Frontiers in Psychology* 3 (2012): 314; Konstantinos Moutoussis and Semir Zeki, "Functional Segregation and Temporal Hierarchy of the Visual Perceptive Systems," *Proceedings: Biological Sciences* 264, no. 1387 (1997): 1407–14; Paola Viviani and Christelle Aymoz, "Colour, Form, and Movement Are Not Perceived Simultaneously," *Vision Research* 41, no. 22 (2001): 2909–18; S. Zeki and A. Bartels, "The Asynchrony of Consciousness," *Proceedings of the Royal Society of London B* 265, no. 1405 (1998): 1583–85.

40. For possible extension of these claims to sense modalities other than the visual sense, see Breitmeyer, *The Visual (Un)Conscious*, 164.

the world, whose existence is independent of our subjective experiences. (For example, the subjectively perceived differences between a blue flower and its green leaves under daytime viewing do correspond to corresponding measurable differences between the wavelength composition of the light reflected from the surfaces of the flower's petals as compared to that of its leaves.) The traditionally-regarded primary qualities are the subjectively experienced form or shape qualia that point to or resemble the objective shape properties of objects, while the traditionally-regarded secondary qualities are the subjectively experienced surface qualia pointing correspondingly to their physical surface-reflectance properties. It is these correspondences between our conscious experiences and the world so experienced which allows us to objectively differentiate the rare visual error and illusion from the vastly preponderant experiences of reality and veridicality. Hence to repeat, the formal, unconsciously processed shape properties can manifest consciously as *formal shape qualia* only by virtue of the *stuff* of consciousness realized in the prior filling-in of the *surface qualia* of color, brightness, shading and texture. The composites of these two types of qualia comprise the rich and varied contents of visual consciousness. The manifold contents of visual and other sensory consciousness serve as hints at the overall richness of consciousness that includes also memorial, imaginative, emotional, aesthetic, ethical, scientific, and religious experiences.

Regarding the latter experiences, human consciousness becomes theologically significant. Here I agree with J. P. Moreland's appraisal of the importance of consciousness:

> Consciousness is ontologically basic for theism since it characterizes the fundamental being. The appearance of finite consciousness qua finite requires explanation and theism may employ the resources of its basic ontological inventory (e.g. [the infinite] consciousness of God) for that explanation. But consciousness *per se* is ontologically basic. Not so for a naturalist though he or she may treat consciousness as pretheoretically basic [and for a reductive physicalist who may treat consciousness as a nonentity, nonreal and merely epiphenomenal]. According to naturalism, consciousness is emergent, derivative or supervenient, and both its finitude . . . and intrinsic nature require explanation.[41]

Seconding this assessment of consciousness, John Cottingham notes correctly that theism

> posits a source or ground of all being that is somehow *mind-like*: consciousness is taken to be at the heart of reality. The theistic picture tends to be discarded or ignored by the majority of contemporary philosophers

41. Moreland, *Consciousness and the Existence of God*, 29.

> [and scientists], but it seems perverse to dismiss it from consideration should it turn out to fit rather well with certain aspects of reality that cannot in integrity be denied. And it appears from what has been said so far, that it is at least no worse equipped to accommodate the irreducible reality of consciousness than either the expedient of downgrading it as somehow illusory, or the panpsychist expedient on construing it as a mysterious intrinsic property of the physical world.[42]

In other words, when making an inference from evidence to the best explanation, for the theist the evidential existence of creaturely *finite* consciousness is more readily explainable on the *basic* premise of God's *infinite* consciousness than a naturalist or physicalist can explain the existence of *finite* consciousness on the basis of natural/physical processes. Try as they can, natural explanations of human consciousness have failed due to *lack* of any credible evidence, despite claims otherwise.[43] Besides its being an attribute of the fundamental being, another reason that consciousness is ontologically basic to theism is that all religions inherently rely on consciousness as source of religious experiences, beliefs, and practices.

But is consciousness ontologically basic only to theism? Or is it also basic to science? Charles Taliaferro offers the following answer:

> What is it to [scientifically] observe things? At least initially, this seems to involve conscious episodes and sensations, and it therefore seems to rest the notion of the physical upon some notion of consciousness, a notion that is ordinarily classified as mental. The idea of a public object as an object that can be observed involves a psychological notion and, as a result, the analysis of the physical is left dangling until we have understanding of its nature. Far from the analysis of the physical being conceptually more basic or lucid than the mental, it seems the former cannot be any more basic than the latter.[44]

Hence, science, by relying on empirical observations, rests primarily on the personal conscious experiences of individual scientists and derivatively on the interpersonal consensus that these individual experiences allow.

42. Cottingham, *In Search of the Soul*, 83.

43. See Dennett, *Consciousness Explained*, which, based on the critiques of several fellow naturalist philosophers and neuroscientists, might better be titled *Consciousness Still in Need of Explanation*. Dennett does, however, provide a fair explanation of the many mechanistic and functional processes that underly and *support* conscious perceptions and cognition, while leaving the mystery of consciousness unsolved. The meaning of "support" ought not be confused with the meaning of "be."

44. Agreeably presaging J. P. Moreland and John Cottingham noted above, Charles Taliaferro, *Consciousness and the Mind of God* (Cambridge University Press, 1994), 95, further states that "theism does not so much displace neurophysiology as provide it with an underlying metaphysical account within which to understand both the mental and the physical."

In view of the fundamental nature that consciousness plays in theology, it pays to recall Terrence Deacon's mystifying, apophatic description of consciousness (see note 11 above) as a hole at the wheel's hub, a form of being that is constituted by what it is not, and yet remains a locus of physical influence. But then we can ask: In relation to (i) the physical cosmos comprised of natural entities and (ii) the theologically correct understanding of God as the *nonphysical* non-thing, is God therefore also a specifiable entity in the cosmos (such as that of the hole at a wheel's hub)? In one sense He is—namely, that from a theological standpoint, he is believed to be present in one way or another to *each individual* human being and to every other localizable nonhuman entity. Isn't God therefore an immanent non-localized, *ubiquitous* presence in the cosmos and thus able to influence it? If yes, one can see Deacon's construal of a non-thing that individual human consciousness *is* as the theologically analogous and apophatic non-thing that God *is,* in contrast to all material things that exist in the physical cosmos. In that regard consciousness comes as close to being a divine attribute as no material or physical attribute can be. This theologically correct view of God is seconded by David Bentley Hart's view (see chapter 5, note 5 above) and by Moreland's view of God as a spiritual "substance qua conscious, self-aware agent."[45] It is for this reason that a theist, as compared to an atheist like Tim Crane or a religious naturalist like Chet Raymo (see the introduction), finds it hard to *directly* discern nature's sacredness. For, relative to the theist's directly targeting her religious impulse on the God who creates and sustains nature and endows it with discernable evidence of His existence, both Tim Crane and Chet Raymo seem to misdirect the religious impulse toward nature. Thus, both the atheist and the theist can admit that nature *reveals* something of the sacred and divine, however, without the theist taking nature to *be* divine or holy. To the theist, nature cannot be considered inherently sacred; to him or her it is only indirectly sacred—namely, by virtue of its being a part of God's good creation. In contrast, by taking nature to be necessarily or essentially sacred, the religious atheist or naturalist reverts to something like a pagan version of polytheistic nature worship or to a Spinozian pantheism and its cognate pannaturalism.

Like some philosophers and scientists, I am a qualia realist.[46] I can therefore endorse what the philosopher Charles Taliaferro refers to as phenomenal realism,[47] with the addendum that I subscribe to a critical phenomenal realism. By that I mean that our phenomenal experiences—mindful also of some perceptual illusions—are part of a capacious reality, without their necessarily always corresponding objectively to physical reality. That said, I agree heartily with both

45. Moreland, *Consciousness and the Existence of God*, 153.

46. See Edmond Wright, ed., *The Case for Qualia* (MIT Press, 2008); Breitmeyer, *The Visual (Un)Conscious*, 171.

47. Taliaferro, *Consciousness and the Mind of God*, 49.

Taliaferro and Moreland in that one must take first-person or subjective experiences seriously and trust them unless and until serious reasons are offered to mistrust them.[48] As I argued above, the existence of rarely experienced errors and illusions in vision and other sense modalities do not provide sufficient reason to distrust all sensory appearances. That sort of skepticism carried to an extreme is epistemically crippling. For, if that sort of skepticism would win the day, then one need rely on only this extreme skepticism to justify one's distrusting the truthfulness of any scientific assertions at all. Unfortunately, we often see this sort of skepticism prevalent among current, anti-science evangelicals and populists.

Implications of Developmental and Evolutionary Approaches to the Study of Consciousness

Here, along with relevant material covered in chapter 1 (pp. 63–74), the aim of this section is to develop further an understanding of the human mind not only when its capabilities are deployed with fully conscious awareness but also when it is able to function at unconscious levels of processing. The last four decades have witnessed the burgeoning of new, extended approaches to biological research that, as noted above, were covered in chapter 1, pp. 63–74. There, in the context of the eco-devo-evo approach to the development of visual consciousness,[49] we also discussed what William James hypothesized to be the confused and differentiated feel, the what-it-is-like-to-be, of an infant's mind confronting its strange, new external environment at and shortly after its birth.[50] As to the qualitative types of consciousness of a healthy adult human, it is endowed with a highly differentiated sensory consciousnesses corresponding to their various modalities toward not only external sources of stimulation (e.g., the visual, auditory, tactual, gustatory, and olfactory senses) but also those internal and bodily sensations such as hunger and thirst and the proprioceptive and kinesthetic sensations produced when moving one's legs, arms, and hands. Helen Keller, for instance, lacked visual and auditory consciousness but compensated for this lack by enhancing her conscious awareness of her surroundings through the internal and the tactual, proprioceptive, and kinesthetic senses. Regarding quantitative aspects of conscious experiences, they can vary in intensity or magnitude, depending on the level of focused attention allocated to the

48. Taliaferro, *Consciousness and the Mind of God*, 49; Moreland, *Consciousness and the Existence of God*, 153.

49. Ehab Abouheif et al., "Eco-evo-devo: The Time has Come," in *Ecological Genomics: Ecology and the Evolution of Genes and Genomes*, ed. Christian R. Landry and Nadia Aubin-Horth (Springer, 2014); Brian K. Hall, "Evolutionary Developmental Biology (Evo-Devo): Past, Present, and Future," *Evolution: Education and Outreach* 5, no. 2 (2012): 184–93.

50. James, *The Principles of Psychology*, 488.

external source of the experience as well as on the intensity of the physical, sensory stimulation, which can vary from next to none when, for example, an acoustic source has a physical stimulation-level so low that we cannot hear it at all to a level that, like a jackhammer at a nearby construction site, is very high and we would prefer not being exposed to.

The Eco-Devo-Evo Approach to the Study of Consciousness as State and Consciousness as Trait

These examples, illustrating a distinction between qualitative types and quantitative levels of consciousness, allow us to distinguish further between consciousness as a variable state, hence referred to as state-consciousness, and consciousness as a variable trait, hence referred to as trait-consciousness.[51] The philosopher John Searle characterized consciousness as that which one's mind loses when in a coma or in state of general anesthesia and which one regains when one recovers from either.[52] Here he was referring to state-consciousness as well as an underlying biological state that depends on the existence of what is referred to as the neural-activation or -arousal system, some of whose properties were already listed above. This system consists of various regulatory subcortical sites, whose collective neural output is relatively high during the waking state and all but eliminated during the state of deep sleep or anesthesia. In the normal, daily cycle of life, the subcortical activation/arousal system is under the influence of neurohormonal changes that in turn are influenced by diurnal body rhythms. During waking states, the output of the subcortical arousal system projects globally to the brain's neocortex, where it activates the various local and regional interactive neural networks specialized to process specific types of sensory information and/or generate appropriate responses to the processed information.

It is also here, at the cortical level, that the interactive neural processing supports the existence of trait-consciousness. That is to say, the local and regional interactive networks are known to support the processing of distinct types of information that are consciously expressed as distinct types of phenomenal experience. Visual experience, supported by its regional interactive neural networks, is qualitatively different from other sensory experiences (such as the olfactory one) that are supported each by their own neural networks. For example, in normal humans the experienced color of a rose blossom is nothing like its experienced scent. Furthermore, within a sense modality, such as vision, we can experientially distinguish between different sensations, such as the color, shape, and motion of, say, a bouncing ball. Correspondingly, in the cortical visual system that supports these distinct qualitative experiences, there are cor-

51. See Breitmeyer and Stoerig, "Neural Correlates and Levels," 37–39.
52. Searle, "Consciousness."

respondingly distinct neural networks that can respond even more distinctly to (i) the subtle variations of the shape or form of a stimulus, (ii) the rich variety of colors and shadings, (iii) the many speeds and directions of motion, and many other variable properties of a stimulus. It is these aspects of a consciously apprehended, seen stimulus that give rise to the nearly endless number of qualia comprising the rich diversity of experiences that comprise visual trait-consciousness. It is trait-consciousness, by adding a bonus property/trait to cognitive contents, that renders these contents visible in their experienced qualitative richness. The upshot of this supports my claim, as explained in chapter 1, that the qualia-rich contents of conscious experiences is *necessarily* supported by the neocortex—and it alone.[53] This claim applies to not only the sense-based consciousnesses but also to the qualia-rich what-it-is-like-to-be aspects of any other types of trait-consciousness—be it emotional, memorial, reflective, fantasy-filled, dream-filled, and whatever else.

The Ontogenetic Development of Human Consciousness

In view of the distinction between state-consciousness as a globally aroused condition and trait-consciousness as a property of local and specific perceptual and cognitive contents, let's try to reconstruct the developmental characteristics of these two types of consciousness. I concur with William James's epigraph that a human infant's mental life has a feel to it of a "great blooming, buzzing confusion." In other words, when not asleep, the infant clearly is aroused and alert, and therefore avails itself of state-consciousness. However, it is largely, if not totally, devoid of the trait-consciousness necessary for distinct, qualia-rich mental contents. To understand why this is so, we must take into account several important properties characterizing the infant's brain. First, at and shortly after birth much of an infant's development, which is necessary for the acquisition of cognitive and behavioral skills allowing it to thrive in its immediate environment, is no doubt guided by genetic factors. Second, the newborn is born with a brain whose neurons exceed greatly in number those that will eventually populate the adult brain. These two properties are the necessary givens at birth. Third, some of the immediate maturational post-birth growth, being genetically guided, can proceed without environmental influences. Yet fourth, the development of all sorts of perceptual, cognitive, affective, and behavioral skills depends not only on growth of the brain's neurons along with the sprouting of their axonal and their dendritic branchings, all of which eventually become part of the adult brain, but also and counterintuitively on the pruning and elimination of the remaining neurons. Fifth, both the retaining and the

53. I emphasize the importance of the neocortex, because, as argued in chapter 1, pp. 64–70, only it can support the superabundant and qualia-rich experiences that humans can have.

pruning of neurons shortly after birth to suitably match behavioral and cognitive skills to a particular ecological niche depends on environmental factors.

These environmental factors present in the infant's lifeworld, in its physical, behavioral, social, and cultural manifestations, exert an influence equal to or greater than the influence of nature on its post-birth development. Shortly after birth, all sorts of nurturing encounters with objects and events in its lifeworld exert powerful influences which cause billions of the brain's neurons to survive and sprout exuberantly to form complex neural networks, and which cause other neurons and their immature axonal and dendritic sproutings to be eliminated. This selective growth and pruning, as explained in chapter 1, have serious and long-lasting consequences. As also explained in chapter 1, it implies, moreover, that diverse cultures with their correspondingly different visual ecologies, may induce developmental differences that in turn cause differences between the visual perceptions of individuals in these cultures.[54]

A normally nurtured, unimpeded course of development depends on the infant brain's neural sprouting and the subsequent, environmentally influenced formation of complex neural networks. These include the networks that eventually support the processing of the distinct features of external objects and events in each of equally distinct sensory modalities, but also those that integrate those distinctive features and modalities to form a unified conscious experience of the world. It is not until development of such distinctive, yet increasingly integrative processing occurs that a unified consciousness of the world can in turn develop, eventually allowing for the emergence of the qualia-rich experiences characterizing a fully developed trait-consciousness.

It is for this reason that the infant's underdeveloped functional neuroanatomy is, in my opinion, inadequate for supporting the qualia-rich experiences characterizing a full-blown trait-consciousness, thus leaving the infant with a feel of what James referred to as "one great blooming, buzzing confusion."

En Route to Evolutionary Development of Human Consciousness

What applies to the post-birth ontogenetic development of consciousness also applies to its phylogenetic, evolutionary development described by George Mashour and Michael Alkire in chapter 1 (see pp. 63–74). However, as I argued there, the consciousness of the earliest reptiles some 315 Mya and the species in their later evolutionary trajectory probably did not approach that of the earliest mammals appearing a few Mya after the appearance of reptiles and certainly not in those mammals' later evolutionary stages of, say, primate, let alone human, evolution. What distinguishes a chimp's and a human's from the reptile's brain is that neural processing depends in reptilic brains on rudimentary, three-layered

54. Phillips, "Cross-Cultural Differences"; Marshall H. Segall et al., *The Influence of Culture*.

cortical structures known as archicortex, whereas neural processing in the mammalian brain depends on the more complex, six-layered neocortex. The visual system of reptiles—like that of their evolutionary neighbors, the amphibians—is geared to respond instinctively to a limited number of stimuli, including prey, predator, and movement in the environment. These types of visually guided, reflexive behaviors need not be accompanied by conscious experiences. For instance, rattlesnakes wait until after sunset when the desert's ambient temperature can fall to less than 40° Fahrenheit, before they hunt for small mammals whose bodies, at a temperature exceeding 90° Fahrenheit, radiate infrared heat waves. Do rattlesnakes consciously experience anything like the distinct, detailed images that we can experience via an infrared camera? I doubt it.

Similarly, monkeys that are missing the part of their neocortex known as the primary visual cortex and therefore, like the rattlesnake, lack conscious, qualia-rich visual experiences, can nonetheless master what is known as an open field test, by avoiding and negotiating around obstacles as they locomote through the field.[55] In other words, without being consciously aware of the obstacles, they evince a visual capacity that paradoxically has been named "blindsight,"[56] an anomalous kind of ability to unconsciously detect the presence of stimuli and objects in the field of view without consciously experiencing them.

Setting aside these visual deficits, we can move on to consider the progressive phyletic differentiation of primates toward the class of hominins, who appeared as early as 6–7 Mya. These ancient hominins no doubt had a fully functioning state-consciousness and a functionally adequate trait-consciousness. About 2.5 Mya, during the Lower Paleolithic period, a new hominin species known as *homo habilis* made its appearance on the evolutionary timeline. The initial crude ability of *homo habilis* to manufacture stone tools was subsequently refined during the Acheulean period starting about 1.7 Mya, and, as described in chapter 1, the refinement no doubt relied on several complex cognitive skills and attributes. After another 1.4 My, anatomically "modern" *homo sapiens* first began its evolutionary journey about 300 Kya, a time that was 200,000 years past the beginning of the Middle Paleolithic period. Recent archeological studies confirm that some types of highly developed symbolic behavior already existed in *homo sapiens* at that time.[57] And there is general agreement among scientists and scholars that the ability—like that of modern humans—to engage in truly human symbolic behavior, was present in the Upper Paleolithic period no later than around 60 Kya.

55. Humphrey, "Vision in a Monkey."

56. Weiskrantz et al., "Visual Capacity in the Hemianopic Field."

57. Berwick and Chomsky, *Why Only Us*; Clottes, *What Is Paleolithic Art?*; Lewis-Williams and Clottes, "The Mind in the Cave"; Tripp et al, "Art, Paleolithic." For an extensive review of research on prehistoric humans' symbolic behaviors, see von Petzinger and Nowell, "A Place in Time." See also chapter 2 of Barry Cooper, *Paleolithic Politics*.

APPENDIX 2

The Roles of Conscious and Unconscious Mind in Religion and Theology

While Michael Polanyi limited the application of his problem-solving analysis to natural science, technology, and mathematics, there is no reason to exclude other cultural practices from its applications. After all, "technology" and "poetry" have their semantic roots in the Greek terms *tékhnē* and *poiesis*. The former refers to art or craft, and the latter, to making, creating, or bringing forth. Artists and craftspeople, who make, create and bring forth, are also faced with problems posed in their practices that call for creative and novel solutions. Think, for instance, of the rediscovery of linear perspective by early Renaissance artists like Alberti, Brunelleschi, and Masaccio that added a realistic appearance of three-dimensional depth to their two-dimensional paintings.[1] Or think of Brunelleschi's architectural craftmanship with which he had to overcome the many practical obstacles and conceptual problems facing the construction of the massive dome crowning Florence's Cathedral of Santa Maria del Fiore.[2] The problems posed to the artists were how to render on a two-dimensional canvas more realistic depictions of the three-dimensionality of the world, and the volumetric properties of objects in it, in a better way than the prior, pre-Renaissance painters did; and to the architect, how to construct the multi-ton dome, from its base to its apex, without its collapse onto the cathedral's floor about three hundred feet below.

Likewise, theologians familiar with sacred art, Scripture, and doctrine no doubt also rely on the mind's unconscious as well as conscious states to creatively contribute to their study of religious experiences, doctrines, and practices. Descriptions of such states, including sleep-, dream-, and vision-induced ones, are found in the Old and New Testaments of the Christian Bible. A problem with many of these scripturally-based descriptions is that it is difficult, if not impossible, to historically check on their veracity, since often these descriptions are made by scribes who were not themselves the experiential subjects of

1. Samuel Y. Edgerton, *Renaissance Rediscovery of Linear Perspective* (Harper & Row, 1976).

2. Ross King, *Brunelleschi's Dome: How a Renaissance Genius Reinvented Architecture* (Walker & Co., 2000).

these states, and whose intent was not directed so much to rendering factual accounts of historic events as it was to rhetorically persuade individuals and groups to renew and maintain their religious faith. Nonetheless, subsequent religious practitioners—St. Teresa of Avila, St. John of the Cross, and many other monastics, including those practicing non-Christian religions—have left evidence in their writings of having directly experienced such states.[3]

In a comparable way, there is nothing to prevent contemporary theologians who reflect on and struggle with the meaning and relevance of ancient doctrines and dogmas when dealing with novel problems posed by contemporary culture, e.g., the troubles and travails attending the LGBT community or those attending biomedical ethics, from unconsciously as well as consciously generating novel insights regarding the ancients' contemporary impact. These contemporary theologians have the important task of rendering ancient doctrines and traditions relevant and inspirational to modern believers. And there is the perennial mystery facing any theologian or serious religious practitioner as to why dreadful evils are allowed to afflict humans and other sentient creatures in the world, given that God is considered to be all-loving, all-knowing, and all-powerful. The problem that evil poses to theologians and philosophers of religion, on the assumption of an omnipotent, omniscient, and omnibenevolent God, is known as the theodicy problem. However, like the problem posed by the existence of subjective, conscious minds in a physical universe, the theodicy problem, the problem of the existence of evil in a world created by God, eludes an airtight logical solution, and no doubt will continue to do so. Perhaps all that one can say here from a theological perspective is that humans are created in the image of God, but, as sentient creatures, they are biologically destined to suffer pain and loss but also to exult with joy and delight. Placing talk of God within a theologically and scientifically informed context, the theologian Christopher Mooney correctly avers that natural acts can be "designated as 'evil' only insofar as they bring misery to self-conscious humans; in themselves they simply represent the normal workings of physical and biological processes and are therefore unavoidable. To be religiously [and, for atheists, morally] scandalized at this is to presume that God's creation of matter over billions of years is wholly anthropocentric in character with purposes for no other creature but the human."[4] Yet one of the factors I believe to be legitimately at the heart of such

3. St. Teresa of Avila, *The Way of Perfection* (Cosimo Classics, 2007), 161; St. John of the Cross, "The Ascent of Mount Carmel," in *The Collected Works of St. John of the Cross*, trans. Kieran Kavanaugh and Otilio Rodriguez (Institute of Carmelite Studies, 1991).

4. Mooney, *Theology and Scientific Knowledge*, 172. The philosopher Luke Russell, *Evil: A Very Short Introduction* (Oxford University Press, 2022), also argues that natural catastrophes such as pandemics, floods, or tsunamis, which cause death and suffering, do not qualify as genuine evils. In other words, truly evil events are morally evil and therefore must result from deliberate human action intended to cause suffering.

anthropocentric concerns is the fact that human consciousness, and especially human self-consciousness, has evolved to such widened and heightened levels, that the pains we suffer and the joys we experience are felt more intensely and deeply than those suffered and enjoyed by other sentient creatures.[5] Relevant to the religious and theological searches for meaning in, and possible solutions to, animal and human suffering are especially the biological and medical sciences. Cornelius Hunter argues that natural biological evolution can solve the problem posed to theology by the existence of natural evils in that "Darwin's theory of evolution was very much the solution to the problem of natural evil—a theodicy. The problem has confounded thinkers for centuries. They needed to distance God to clear him of any evil doings [to sentient creatures and especially to humans with their heightened consciousness]. Natural selection, operating blindly on a pool of biological diversity, according to Darwin, could produce nature's carnage and waste."[6] So, instead of blaming God for evolution's carnage and waste of sentient creatures, one can say from a theistic perspective that the pertinent investigations performed by natural science further the theological understanding of God by furthering also our understanding of how a heightened consciousness relates in a *natural* way to pain and suffering.

Referred to by some as the "queen of the sciences," theology is the beneficiary of relevant scientific discoveries; and since natural science is a self-correcting undertaking, then, as Christopher Mooney sees it, one of the gifts of science to theology is that "theology [rather than being error-proof] is also corrigible."[7] And therefore, to paraphrase the philosopher Jean-Pierre Dupuy,[8] science is doing theology in spite of itself and in defiance of the objections by many scientists to this appraisal of science. Especially from the perspective of atheist scientists, such a complaisant relation of natural science to theology and religion is considered to be rubbish. But to theists, the metaphysically relevant truths of nature, such as the above explored by scientists, in turn serve as pointers to a treasure, a reality greater than, yet including, nature. The theological explorations of this more inclusive and farther-reaching reality may in several ways be analogous to the ways, covered in the prior appendix, by which scientists conduct their empirically limited explorations of nature. To wit, consider the ideational discoveries made by the founders of religious movements—let's call them "proto-theologians"—and subsequently refined by latter-day theologians. Like Michael Polanyi's assessment of scientific research, we could say that all those theologians are also motivated by heuristic cravings, which,

5. Anders, *The Evolution of Evil*.

6. Cornelius G. Hunter, *Darwin's God: Evolution and the Problem of Evil* (Wipf & Stock Publishers, 2001), 16.

7. Mooney, *Theology and Scientific Knowledge*, 98.

8. Dupuy, *The Mark of the Sacred*, chapter 2: "Science, A Theology in Spite of Itself."

like our bodily appetites, imply the existence of something actual that has the properties required to satisfy us. Moreover, here also—once more paraphrasing Polanyi—the theological strivings are realized with the humbling assumption that they originate or create nothing, but merely reveal what was latently present not only in individual minds but also in the immense archival records of centuries of prior theological work. In line with this assumption, subsequent efforts have resulted in heartening conceptual discoveries that do bear the mark of reality in their being pregnant with implications for future theological developments. Thus, in these analogous ways, we are not dealing with only the fertile scientific understanding of nature; additionally, we are dealing with a flourishing understanding of the extranatural reality that is the all-inclusive Infinite, i.e., with a reality writ-large, that includes, yet transcends, nature.

But, like the scientists and the theologians among us, the finite and fallible beings that all humans are must heuristically struggle and wrest from the latent cognitive contents in our unconscious minds novel arrangements that surface into our conscious minds and there comprise the discovery, the explicit new knowledge, about the world we inhabit. Here I insert a German saying which goes as follows: *Wenn der Mensch macht, der Gott lacht* (When humans make/create, God laughs). This can be taken in two ways: God laughs joyfully along with humans when they humbly accept and fulfill each of their tasks in cocreating the world they inhabit; or God, ever confronted with human pride, is amused by hubristic attempts to lay claim to His creative abilities. In either case, though, we can be assured that there is only one mind in which the distinction between the unconscious realms of deep latent knowledge and the realms of conscious brought-to-the-surface knowledge plays no role. It is, in other words, a mind in which the splendor of surface knowledge and the profundity of interior knowledge are one and the same. This mind is the Infinite Mind of God, eternally comprehending and directly and fully illuminating the beauty and truth of the natural and divine realms. To paraphrase the theologian Bernard Lonergan, God can be regarded as the supreme and unrestricted act of understanding,[9] an understanding that, going beyond mere knowledge, is wisdom realized in four levels of conscious intentionality or directedness: the empirical, the intelligible, the rational, and the communally and morally responsible.[10] A theistic standpoint allows us to see that not only theologians but also scientists—even atheistic ones like the brilliant physicist and cosmologist Stephen Hawking—take on the task of humbly struggling for some understanding, some glimpse of God's mind.[11]

9. Bernard Lonergan, *Insight.*

10. Mark T. Miller, *The Quest for God and the Good Life: Lonergan's Theological Anthropology* (The Catholic University of America Press, 2013).

11. Hawking, *A Brief History of Time.*

Mind's Contributions to Philosophical Theology in Relation to Science

I ask you the reader to look around when you are outdoors and notice the objects in your visual compass, their locations relative to each other, their continuous change of location as they move, their assorted colors, sizes, and shapes. Notice also how the book you are now reading feels in your hand. Is it a thick or a thin book, heavy or light, a hardbound copy that has a matte look and whose binding's texture feels slightly rough, or a slick paperback copy with a binding that looks shiny and feels smooth? You might even bring it close to your face and smell the paper on which its text is printed. Yes, this medley of sensations pleases many a reader who, like me, prefers to read books printed on paper pages rather in the format of e-books whose pages appear as various digitized displays on electronic devices. Then reflect a bit, and notice further that the medley of visual, tactile, and olfactory experiences are part and parcel of your *conscious* mind. Then also notice a marvelous aspect of the conscious mind: it itself can recursively become the object of further conscious reflection, a reflection that can prompt philosophic and scientific curiosity about the nature and properties of consciousness.

An unfortunate consequence of the logical positivism and stimulus-response behaviorism that prevailed during the first half of the prior century—which was preceded by a reductive empiricism and pragmatism—was that scientific research engendered by such curiosity, research on the conscious mind, on art and aesthetic experience, on religion and religious experience, and of the phenomenology of the sensory experiences, like those described above, were scrupulously avoided for decades in the human sciences. After all, because such experiences are inherently tainted with a subjectivity that hides its inner realm from public inspection, how could they become meaningful topics for objective scientific research that inherently relies on publicly observable properties and processes? Fortunately, the reductive positivistic/behaviorist outlook is now all but passe. With the "cognitive revolution" of the 1960s, which opened psychological research to areas beyond behaviorist constraints; and later, with the dramatic progress of instrumentation and techniques used in the human brain sciences that has become evident especially since the 1980s, the merger of the cognitive and the brain sciences can aptly be called "cognitive neuroscience." This dramatic change in outlook over the last few decades spurred psychological, neuroscientific, sociological, anthropological, evolutionary, and archeological methods of research that also were increasingly applied to the study of consciousness, the arts, and religion.

Neuroscience, however, has been an active field of study since the 19th century. Then, much of what was known about the human brain depended on diagnosing and classifying brain diseases or injuries and on assessing their mental and their behavioral consequences. These neurological deficits manifested via observable symptoms—e.g., the inability to visually recognize common objects or understand words, and the loss of short-term memory. These deficits could in some cases be related to histologically determined neuronal damage and to gross anatomical damage in specific sites in the brain found during post-mortem analysis. Human neuroscience since then has established a strong track record of steadily improving noninvasive brain-measurement techniques, such as electroencephalography (EEG), magnetoencephalography (MEG), computer (x-ray) tomography (CT), positron emission tomography (PET), functional magnetic resonance imaging (fMRI), functional near-infrared spectroscopy (fNIRS), and on rare occasions, with the permission of patients undergoing brain surgery, even some recordings of single- and multi-cell responses. The use of any of these methods with living humans has allowed investigators to measure, with different degrees of temporal and spatial resolution, when and where in the diseased as well as the healthy brain measurable neural indicators are found during various cognitive or behavioral tasks. Although these brain-recording techniques have been crudely criticized by some skeptical cognitive scientists as a "new phrenology," they have, in my opinion, added genuine knowledge to the field of cognitive neuroscience by revealing ever new and more detailed findings, thereby refining our theoretical understanding of how the human brain's functional and anatomical organization relates to various behavioral, perceptual, emotional, and cognitive phenomena.

Nevertheless, the rapid developments and apparent successes of these lines of research have resulted, in recent years, in—to use Raymond Tallis's apt expression[12]—a neuromanic proliferation of newly defined domains of research. Besides the well-established life sciences of neuroanatomy, neurobiology, neurochemistry, neuroendocrinology, and neuropharmacology, new fields have emerged, including neurocognition, neurophilosophy, neuroeconomics, neurolinguistics, neuroethics, neurojurisprudence, neuroaesthetics, neuro-art-history, neurotruistics, neuroagapics, neuro-literary-criticism, and, yes, even neurotheology.[13] The number of publications that have resulted runs into many tens or a few hundreds. Sharing Tallis's views, other observers of the neuromania afflicting neuroscientists have noted tersely that neurons only do two things: they respond to and emit electrochemical signals; hence, singly or collectively, they neither think, ponder ethical dilemmas, have conscious experiences, make aesthetic, moral, or juridical judgments, or evaluate and optimize economic decisions; nor do they talk of or love God. Nonetheless, the "manic" research in the fields of neuroscience raises two important questions. From an epistemological standpoint, can explanations of the workings and products of the

12. Tallis, *Aping Mankind.*

13. I have expanded Tallis's list of neuro-areas of study.

human mind be replaced by explaining the processes and neural activity patterns of the human brain? If so, then from the ontological standpoint, is it legitimate to infer that the human mind is nothing but these processes; in other words, can phenomena like consciousness, religion, and art be reduced to merely the functional or behavioral realizations of the outputs of complex neural circuitries in the human brain? To answer this question adequately, more than the perfunctory "Of course they can!" typical of neuro-reductive scientists and philosophers is required.

Excepting periods of coma, deep sleep, and deep anesthesia, humans can subjectively experience a world containing an extremely rich array of objects and events. While consciousness *per se* is a *global state* of alertness and arousal, each of our specific subjective experiences, say of a bird's song, its association with musical phrases in Beethoven's Pastoral Symphony (No. 6), and the internal sensation of pleasure they elicit, constitute the *local contents* of consciousness. So, in addition to being a global neurological state, what I will refer to as state-consciousness, one can also think of consciousness as a *trait* of specific mental contents, what I will refer to as trait-consciousness. State-consciousness is state of global arousal, activating extensive cortical neural networks, without which no trait-consciousness can be ascribed to specific and local mental contents. Much in the way that the air we breathe is essential to our physical existence, consciousness is essential to our psychic and spiritual existence and, as such, to how we practice and experience science, art, religion, the spectrum of emotions, and many other facets of our lives. We live simultaneously within not only a biosphere (in which air, material sustenance, and an opportune ecology around us are essential to our existence) but also within a noosphere[14] (a mental sphere, in and to which consciousness and its contents are essential to our psychological and spiritual sustenance).

In his book *God and the New Physics*, Paul Davies claims that we will understand the mystery of mind when we also understand the mystery of time.[15] Implied is an intimate relation between time and consciousness as part of the deep structure of reality. Long ago St. Augustine, in chapter 15 of his *Confessions*, anticipated the mystery of time by answering the question "What is time?" as follows: "Provided that no one asks me, I know. If I want to explain it to an inquirer, I do not know."[16] He might have given that same answer if he were asked, "What is consciousness?" A more recent version of this puzzling state is Michael Polanyi's claim that we know more than we can say.[17] Similarly, despite our intuitive understanding of consciousness, its clear univocal definition as a

14. Pierre Teilhard de Chardin, *The Phenomenon of Man* (Harper Collins, 1976).
15. Paul Davies, *God and the New Physics* (Simon & Schuster, 1984).
16. St. Augustine, *Confessions*, 230.
17. Polanyi, *The Tacit Dimension*.

psychic phenomenon is difficult to pin down; and no adequate explanation of consciousness has yet been made, despite the fact that, by the title of one of philosopher Daniel Dennett's books, some might think that he has done so.[18] And this complication in turn creates difficulties for knowing what it is that the neuroscience of consciousness is about. Despite these conceptual complexities, the neurosciences have made appreciable progress in specifying what are known as the neural correlates of consciousness (NCCs).[19] However, even though current research efforts have not yet been able to adjudicate which of several theoretical specifications of NCCs may be preferable, and despite our failure to clearly understand consciousness conceptually (via clear definition), my guess is that each of us intuitively knows *that* it is and thereby *what* it is by way of our *direct* personal acquaintance with it. The philosopher J. P. Moreland expresses this intuitive knowledge of consciousness by way of personal acquaintance as follows. "Some and, perhaps, all mental states are constituted by self-presenting properties. I can be [consciously] aware of the external, physical world only by means of my mental state, but I need not be aware of any mental states by means of anything else. In diverse ways, a self-presenting property presents to a subject the intentional object of that property and the self-presenting property itself. . . . For example, it is by way of a sensation of red that one is aware of the color of the apple [i.e., the intentional object], *but one is not aware of the sensation of red by way of another sensation.* The red sensation makes the apple's surface present to one by virtue of one having the sensation; but the sensation also presents itself directly to one without another intermediary"[20] (emphasis added). In other words, our acquired knowledge of the properties of the world and its objects is not direct; it is a *mediated* knowledge by way of *what* our sensory apparatus passes into our consciousness, but the sensory *what,* as such, constitutes *directly* acquired, unmediated epistemic contact with the contents of consciousness. If so, then it follows that in relation to the external world one can be (at best) an indirect or critical realist, whereas in relation to consciousness and its contents, one can be a direct realist.

18. Dennett, *Consciousness Explained.*

19. To speak of neural correlates of consciousness is to acknowledge that while a given neural activation is a *necessary* support of conscious experience, of itself it is not *sufficient.* There may be many other necessary neural activations supporting conscious experience. If neuroscientists were to discover the minimal set of necessary neural activations for consciousness to occur, they might then define this set of activations as the sufficient neural cause of consciousness. Yet despite this possibility, to my and many other neuroscientists' understanding, how a strictly neural and therefore *physical* activation pattern can cause a *mental* event would still remain a mystery. Other neuroscientists and some philosophers, by adopting a neural-identity approach, deny such mystery by asserting that, instead of causing consciousness, this minimal set of necessary neural activation patterns *is* consciousness.

20. Moreland, *Consciousness and the Existence of God,* 40–41.

The Relation Between Consciousness, Time, and the Sacred

Yet in the context of the present book, a brief yet pertinent observation can be made for the time being. I tend to agree with the aforementioned claim made by the physicist Paul Davies that we will understand the mystery of conscious mind only when we understand the mystery of time. I tend to agree with this claim in the following ways. First, if time, according to physicists Albert Einstein and Carlo Rovelli, is merely a mental illusion rather than a reality,[21] then, considering the close relationship between consciousness and time, perhaps a whole tribe of philosophers, cognitive scientists, and neuroscientists may be justified in their belief that consciousness, the bearer of psychological time, also is illusory. However, along with the physicist Lee Smolin and the philosopher Roberto Mangabeira Unger, I take time to be real[22]; and in view of the intimate relation between time and consciousness, I also take consciousness to be real in two senses, (i) that it is part of a reality more comprehensive than the physical one and (ii) that it presents to us objective, truth-bearing aspects of nature's spatiotemporal realities. I should note here that although I have an intuition *that* a greater reality than nature exists, I have no clear conception of *what* that reality is like, other than that it includes the reality investigated scientifically by physicists.

That said, let's accept the mysterious existence of conscious mind and explore how it bears on our understanding of the mystery of time. Time is taken to be a unidirectional dimension of reality composed of a realized past, an elusive and transient present, and a realizable future. Yet when we reflect carefully on conscious experiences of the past and of the future, we note that our conscious experiences of both are in fact in the present moment, the phenomenal now.[23] So, from an experiential/phenomenological standpoint, only the present is directly experienced as the phenomenal now. The current conscious memory of anything is not *in* the real past but only *of* this past. For this of-the-past experience exists only by virtue of the now's brief memorial retention of some property of the past. Similarly, we are not conscious of anything *in* the future,

21. Rovelli, *The Order of Time*.

22. Lee Smolin, *Time Reborn: From the Crisis in Physics to the Future of the Universe* (Mariner Books, 2013); Unger and Smolin, *The Singular Universe*.

23. This description, informed primarily by my understanding of philosophic analysis of temporality, is based on Edmund Husserl, *On the Phenomenology of Internal Time-Consciousness* (Indiana University Press, 1964). Even if Bergson, *The Two Sources*, is correct in asserting that the immediate past survives as a memory in the present, thus constituting the temporal interval which is the *durée* (duration), the *durée* itself, relying as it does on *retention*, seems not to include Husserl's *protention* which phenomenally anticipates the future. For an insightful comparison of Husserl's and Bergson's takes on time, see Rafael Winkler, "Husserl and Bergson on Time and Consciousness," in *Logos of Phenomenology and Phenomenology of the Logos. Book Three*. Analecta Husserliana, vol. 90, ed. Anna-Teresa Tymieniecka (Springer, 2006).

because we exist not in the future but again only in the now as it is represented in our consciousness, where also our anticipatory protention *about* the future exists. The *experience* of the now is given to consciousness *directly* without intermediary experiences, much like—following Moreland's phrasing (see note 20 above)—the sensation of, say, red presents itself directly to our consciousness without any intermediary sensation. In other words, our experience of the now does not present itself indirectly in consciousness via any other experience. In contrast to the present, the past and future are experienced *indirectly*—on the one hand, *via intermediary* experience of memorial retentions and, on the other, via anticipatory protentions that reside *in the phenomenal now*.

Yet in our active and distracted day-to-day existence, we don't experience the now as static presence but instead as flowing through time. The now, although directly apprehended, also remains phenomenally embedded in this flow. Nonetheless, there are rare occasions during deep meditation, during contemplative prayer, and in spontaneous mystical states, which allow one to shed all remnants of memorial and anticipative consciousness and experience the now as decoupled from the experienced flow through time, thereby manifesting in an awareness of a timeless now, in other words, in an awareness of the Eternal. On these rare occasions, one begins to tread on hallowed ground, the bedrock on which a mysterious and sacred presence is experientially revealed.

I and Thou: From First-Person, I-It to Second-Person, I-Thou Encounters

Some attribute such sacred presence to nature. Yet nature, the object of modern scientific study, is difficult to relate to personally without something like the polytheistic personhood found in ancient pagan religions. But however much we are cognizant of and thankful for the gifts that nature bestows on us, and however much nature can mediate the religious experience of the sacred, nature in itself is not the object of such experience.[24] That object is what the religious scholar Rudolf Otto has described as the *mysterium tremendum et fascinans*, the immediate presence to us of the divine or holy.[25] Indeed, the mysteries of nature are bountiful sources of ideas that advance scientific study; yet their sum constitutes a *non plus ultra*, a limit which the natural mysteries revealed to scientists cannot transcend. The divine and holy, the *mysterium tremendum et fascinans*, differs from nature in that it is totally other, totally transcends nature, and nonetheless fully comprehends nature. What is this Other, this mysterious and holy presence, that one encounters on holy ground? An answer to this question has been fashioned—successfully in my opinion—by the Jewish mystic and

24. Fingelkurts and Fingelkurts, "Is Our Brain Hardwired," 294–95, 308.
25. Otto, *The Idea of the Holy*.

scholar Martin Buber, in his book *I and Thou*.[26] As compared to the impersonal I-It encounter that is the basis of natural science, the personal I-Thou encounter between humans and God takes place on sacred ground, but also, because humans are fashioned in the image of God, the encounter can also take place on common sacred ground between humans themselves.

How Religion Relates to Science by Way of Consciousness

Although above we noted some differences and possible sources of tension between religion and science, the fact is that a more positive way they relate to each other is that each can become an object of research for the other.

Religion: A Subject for Scientific Research

Religion has been studied by psychologists and sociologists for over a century. In the last several decades, as we saw in chapter 1, it also has interested the cognitive sciences, the neurosciences, and the discipline of evolutionary psychology.[27] Since religious experiences, like other experiences, are mediated by the brain's neuronal processes and mechanisms that have evolved over millions of years, our understanding of them can in principle be enhanced by various heterophenomenological, third-person approaches aided by what we know about our brains' structural and functional properties and the evolutionary and sociocultural impacts on them.

Regardless of how they may be inspired, religious experiences are systematically relatable to measurable bodily states and events. To deny this is to deny that these experiences are contents of consciousness and that these contents have their neural and bodily correlates. The existing psychological and neuroscientific literature on religious practice and experience is immense, and doing justice to a thorough review or a meta-analysis of all this published work would itself require a separate book-length monograph. Despite this lack of thorough review, what cannot be questioned is that spiritual and, more specifically, religious practices, beliefs, and experiences are accompanied by measurable bodily states and responses. Besides specific areas in the central nervous system, such as the frontal, temporo-parietal, limbic, and thalamic areas of the brain covered in chapter 1, the sympathetic and parasympathetic nervous systems (parts of the peripheral nervous system) as well as the hormonal endocrine system have

26. Martin Buber, *I and Thou* (Charles Scribner's Sons, 1970).

27. Readily accessible overviews of past and recent work on the relation of neuroscience and of evolutionary and cognitive psychology to religion can be found in Robert A. Emmons and Raymond F. Paloutzian, "The Psychology of Religion," *Annual Review of Psychology* 54, no. 1 (2003): 377–402; Fraser Watts, "Religion and the Emergence"; Fraser Watts, *Psychology, Religion, and Spirituality: Concepts and Applications* (Cambridge University Press, 2017).

been shown to register signatures of religious beliefs, of practices such as prayer and meditation, and of experiences such as visions or the feelings and encounters of the numinous and divine.[28] Moreover, we know that cognate quasi-religious experiences can also occur after ingestion or inhalation of pharmacological agents, stimulation of specific brain areas, or in extreme physiological states such as those produced during epileptic seizures and near-death episodes. And we also know that these types of experiences have marked effects on brain function.[29]

While experimentally and pathologically induced brain- and body-related markers of "spiritual" and "religious" experiences are real, what is of greater interest are experiences that arise during states not induced by drugs, electromagnetic stimulation of the brain, or physiological extremes. There are experiences that arise spontaneously in pedestrian, everyday settings or after the disciplined, oft-repeated prayer and the rigorous spiritual practice of, for example, mystics and monastics.[30] However, there also are less forceful, milder forms of religious experience; for instance, the sense of divine support during periods of

28. For relevant findings and reviews, see Fingelkurts and Fingelkurts, "Is Our Brain Hardwired"; Kapogiannis et al., "Cognitive and Neural Foundations"; Newberg, "The Neuroscientific Study"; Fred H. Previc, "The Role of the Extrapersonal Brain Systems in Religious Activity," *Consciousness and Cognition* 15, no. 3 (2006): 500–539; Urgesi et al., "The Spiritual Brain"; and Yaden et al., "Neuroscience and Religion."

29. For effects of pharmacological agents, see Ismael Apud, "Pharmacology of Consciousness or Pharmacology of Spirituality? A Historical Review of Psychedelic Clinical Studies," *The Journal of Transpersonal Psychology* 48, no. 2 (2016): 150–67; Michael J. Winkelman, "The Mechanisms of Psychedelic Visionary Experiences: Hypotheses from Evolutionary Psychology," *Frontiers in Neuroscience* 11 (2017): 539. For experiences during near-death episodes, see Enrico Facco and Christian Agrillo, "Near-Death Experiences Between Science and Prejudice," *Frontiers in Human Neuroscience* 6 (2012): 209; Dean Mobbs and Caroline Watt, "There Is Nothing Paranormal About Near-Death Experiences: How Neuroscience Can Explain Seeing Bright Lights, Meeting the Dead, or Being Convinced You Are One of Them," *Trends in Cognitive Sciences* 15, no. 10 (2011): 447–49.

30. See Fingelkurts and Fingelkurts, "Is Our Brain Hardwired." Anecdotally, during my quasi-agnostic early adulthood, I had two such spontaneous extraordinary experiences, the first lasting nearly two hours. Both experiences were accompanied by what I can describe as an intensely blissful serenity (a peace that surpasses understanding) in which I experienced every object or thing as endowed with a superabundance of meaning, significance, and beauty that expressed its distinctive and perfectly fitting now-and-here thusness; all this accompanied by a prevenient sense very fittingly expressed by the medieval anchoress and mystic Julian of Norwich, *Showings* (Paulist Press, 1978), 305, as follows: "And there it will truly be made known to us what he [God the Father] means in the sweet words when he says: All will be well, and you will see it yourself, that every kind of thing will be well." I also know an individual who confided to me that he had a very intense, profound and, in his words, "knee-buckling" religious experience that literally floored him for some time and led to a conversion from his previous semi-lapsed faith to a fully flourishing one.

spiritual suffering and distress, the sense of deliverance from such distress and suffering, the sense of divine consolation during periods of loss and grief, and the fleeting minor epiphanies or theophanies many have felt in sacred settings or in private moments of distress-free serenity and rest. What is the significance of such experiences? And how do neuroscientific findings relate to them? Is their experiential significance ultimately reducible to, and found in nothing but, mere neurological states and events, as some neuroscientists and neurophilosophers are wont to claim about any and every experience? Are they merely illusions or delusions reinforced by the powerful sociocultural forces affecting our brains? Or, as theologians and religious practitioners believe, are they something *sui generis*; something real that, beyond such reductive ontologies, make *bona fide* epistemic claims to truth? A fitting description of the problems posed by these questions is given by the philosopher Hugh McCann:

> A believer may feel that the experiences are veridical, but a skeptic might think they are simply a common illusion to which religious people are in certain circumstances subject.
>
> At present, I don't see how to resolve this issue in a way that is usefully scientific. It is, for example, no good treating claims of encounters of the divine as hypotheses. Those who have such experiences are not offering us a claim that there is a God as a hypothesis. They are not inferring that there is a God any more than a person looking at her hand infers that there is a hand before her. They are reporting what they allege to be their *direct experience*. What then are we to say? Should such reports be declared uniformly illusory? Surely not on the basis that ordinary empirical experience—experience with the usual five senses—has shown that so-called mystical experience cannot be veridical. Such claims would be straightforwardly question-begging as to what kinds of experiences we may trust. . . .
>
> [This is] important because I believe that the broader range of religious experience constitutes the heart of the matter when it comes to explaining the phenomenon of religion. What holds religion in place is not arguments for the existence of God, . . . external signs and wonders, . . . the childlike tendency to believe parents or Sunday school teachers, the Kantian sense of the sublime. . . . Rather, it is the compelling nature of religious experience that holds things in place.[31] (emphasis added)

McCann rightly notes, *pace* the neoatheists Jerry Coyne, Richard Dawkins, and Victor Stenger, that existence claims about God are clearly not empirical claims, in the sense of scientifically testable hypotheses. If God's existence were a scientifically testable hypothesis, he would have to be just another inner-worldly entity, like an asteroid or, as in pantheism, he would have to be identical with all that is in the physical cosmos.

31. McCann, "Getting Scientific About Religion," 124–25.

One can quibble with McCann's placing such great, loadbearing emphasis on religious experience; it is after all the rich symbolic experiences found regularly not only in religion but in all kinds of settings—e.g., public rituals, ceremonies, feasts, commemorations, and celebrations—which contribute to holding things in place. Yet, one can agree that it is generally nonroutine, powerful experiences of the divine that have inspired individuals, the founders of religions and religious sects, the prophets and mystics, to write sacred scriptures and develop religious doctrines and traditions. Either way, while McCann's emphasizing the importance of and epistemic problem posed by such experiences is felicitous, we are left with addressing the "compelling nature of religious experience." Is such experience as compelling as the empirical evidence of the senses on which valid claims to knowledge of scientific research is based?

To address this question, we can revert to material discussed above in relation to hetero- and autophenomenology. Here again we can explore a further relation between science and religion. Let us recall (i) that scientific evidence is initially based on the direct subjective perceptual experiences of each scientist and (ii) that the evidence is consensually validated by agreement regarding the core significance of the individual experiences. Does this also comport with religious experiences? As long as we keep in mind that scientific experience bears distinctly on physical ontology, whereas religious experience bears likewise on mystical ontology, I believe it does. In line with McCann, one could draw the following parallels between how a set of trained scientists and, say, a set of trained mystics arrive at their interpretation of experiential evidence.[32]

1. Both science and religion are based on experiential evidence.[33]
2. Experiences of the divine are as forthrightly given in the private consciousness of each mystic as are the observational experiences of nature in the private consciousness of each scientist. (Here it is important to note that directly experienced observations of science often only indirectly support the existence of physical entities and their properties. An example is the warping of space predicted by Einstein's theory of general relativity. To evaluate this prediction, the astronomer Arthur Eddington's 1919 *observation* of the disparity between the recorded positions of stars during an eclipse of the sun, relative to their recorded position under non-eclipse control conditions, allows one to *infer* but not directly

32. Also relevant here are the thoughts on how science and religion relate to each other of B. Alan Wallace, "The Intersubjective Worlds of Science and Religion," in *Science, Religion and the Human Experience*, ed. James D. Proctor (Oxford University Press, 2005), 309–27.

33. Noting that science was more broadly understood in the late Middle Ages, one could further note that the spiritual practices of St. John of the Cross were experientially tried and assessed, in that sense experimental, and were expressions of what was, in his words, the "science of love."

observe the warping of space and the consequent lensing effect produced by a massive body, in this case, our sun. Nonetheless, a competent astronomer or astrophysicist must trust, first, his or her own private observation and interpretation of the recorded disparities; and second, the similar private observations and interpretations of other involved scientists. Together they constitute the consensual weight of evidence that bears on the validity of the prediction. Likewise, directly experienced mystical experiences only indirectly support the existence of God. For God does not allow direct, face-to-face encounter with a mystic [Exodus 33: 20–23]; but his presence can be experienced indirectly.)

3. A mystic's and a scientist's experience, though private and interior, is taken by each to point to a realm that is independent of his or her private and interior realms of consciousness; and
4. From the methodological standpoint assumed by science, the material, physical universe is the only reality that is independent of and transcends the private and interior realm of consciousness; whereas,
5. In contrast to natural science, from the standpoint assumed by mystical method, practiced for instance by St. John of the Cross in his "science of love," the existence of an independent extra- or super-physical realm transcends not only the private, interior realm of consciousness but also the reality that is the material, physical universe.

Now, one could argue, as might any practicing scientist, that the factual truth about the external material world that the observational experiences point to can be satisfactorily confirmed by replication and consensual validation of other scientists. For instance, consider again the discovery of the Higgs boson by the team of many physicists at the CERN particle smasher and detector in Switzerland. A competent physicist, one with sufficient intelligence and experience to discern the pattern of particle tracks replicated and registered by two separate detectors, can agree with other competent physicists that these tracks, as well as the Higgs boson to which they point by way of theoretical inference, exist. Note that, were you one of many sufficiently intelligent but non-expert individuals at CERN at the time, you could agree that these registered tracks exist, yet you would not be able to render an expert judgment on or interpretation of what these empirical facts point to, in other words, what the theoretical significance of these scientific facts is. Since the significance of confirmatory observations is not to be found in their brute existence, their facticity is already theory laden, so that rather elite, highly intelligent, and trained individuals must make the interpretations of these observations. Fine and good.

But can such replication, consensual confirmation, and interpretive context find parallels in the religious experiences of mystics? Although it might be met with derisive hoots and howls from skeptical scientists and philosophers, the thesis here put forward for consideration is that on procedural and epistemic grounds there are such parallels in religious experiences. In, for instance, the Christian tradition,[34] one could cite a group of elite and religious practitioners, highly disciplined and trained in the contemplative methods they use, who have *experienced* the highest illumination, which they *interpret* from their theological standpoint as their having been mystically united with ultimate or highest reality, i.e., with the Divine.[35] To paraphrase the words of St. John of the Cross, the union is experienced as the living flame of love, but only after gradually and assiduously "ascending Mt. Carmel" to its summit.[36] Let us assume that a set of elite, highly trained, and disciplined practitioners of Christianity exists, each having successfully ascended to such spiritual summit. (The practitioners would most likely be found in Christian monasteries, convents, and hermitages around the world.) These practitioners have each had their private, interior experience of such an apical illumination. In principle, I also take it that they could communally, i.e., heterophenomenologically, agree on having attained this summit of experiences by criteria that they share; and, in their theologically interpretive context, they could therefore agree that their consensually affirmed interior states reflect an experiential union with ultimate reality, which in the Christian tradition is—as Thomas Aquinas would phrase it—what we call God.

Several possible objections might come to mind. One objection is that not everyone can have these most profound and at the same time highest of religious experiences and thereby contribute to these mystics' consensually agreed-upon assessments. But this objection is not decisive in denying to religious experiences what is allowed in scientific experiences. These inabilities found in the vast majority of humans cannot be a criterion of demarcation between the what of religious mystical experience and the what of scientific observational experience. As discussed in the introduction, Richard Lewontin clearly notes the esoteric methods and language employed in science that are not accessible to the ordinary human. It is, therefore, a fact that all sorts of individuals—due to lack of talent, intelligence, or training—also are incapable of discerning the physical, theory-laden experiences as factual experimental observations, nor of consensually deciding on the proper theoretical interpretation of such observations.

34. I limit myself to the Christian mystical tradition with which I am most familiar. Similar experiences of union with ultimate reality and the divine may be found in other traditions: e.g., in Sufi Islam, the experience of Al-Haqq; and in Hinduism and Buddhism, the experience of samadhi, luminous mind, satori.

35. Besides John of the Cross, through the centuries many other Christian mystics have attained the summit state of religious experience, an illumination of union with the divine. To name just a few: St. Paul the Apostle, Augustine of Hippo, Gregory of Nyssa, Symeon the New Theologian, Denys the Areopagite, Thomas Aquinas, Gregory Palamas, Meister Eckhart, Julian of Norwich, Teresa of Avila, Blaise Pascal.

36. St. John of the Cross, "The Ascent of Mount Carmel."

Another objection is that, in the case of science, claims based on scientifically obtained experiences are made about the existence of the physical world of matter in motion that is external to and transcends the experience; whereas, in the case of religion, claims based on religiously obtained experience are made about the existence of a realm that transcends not only such experience but also the material physical world as such. But that objection is also undecisive from a purely methodological and procedural standpoint—unless, of course, you additionally subscribe to a question-begging metaphysical claim that only matter, and the physical forces that move and transform it, truly exist; i.e., unless whatever "faith" or trust you have in the validity of your objection already presumes that the universe is all there is.

A third objection is that the experiences of divine illumination in the Abrahamic traditions, or, say, of attaining luminous mind or samadhi in the Hindu tradition, are inherently too private, therefore making it impossible for anyone else to check on their status or significance. Hence, these experiences are different from I and you experiencing and agreeing on a pattern of tracks recorded in a particle collider. Even if you and I had each attained his/her apical spiritual experience, there is no way for me to know via an objective outside referent (like the particle tracks that are directly accessible to me and to you) that your experience of divine illumination is equivalent to mine. Indeed, that is so. However, here it pays to be reminded of what—thanks to Daniel Dennett—we referred to above as heterophenomenology, the ability to communicate and compare indirectly via symbolic means (language or art) what each of our private conscious experiences are like. Recall that, according to Dennett, heterophenomenology is "a method of phenomenological description that can (in principle) do justice to the most private and ineffable subjective experiences, while never abandoning the methodological scruples of science." It follows that, first, like other private and ineffable experiences, the conscious mystical experiences of religious practitioners can be assessed and compared as to their content and replicability. And second, no replication is ever fully exact; nor need it be. In the human sciences, cognitive psychology, for instance, besides relying on exact replication, one can also rely on what is known as convergent replications. Here a given cognitive property or process, for example, the information storage capacity of visual working memory, can be obtained/measured through several distinct methodological and procedural implementations, all of which converge to nearly the same value of the capacity, despite their quantitatively covarying somewhat with systematic methodological variations of the inputs (e.g., individual features of stimuli such as their color, shape, spatial location, or size). Similarly, in each religious tradition, one mystic's experience, when subjected to heterophenomenological methods, need not replicate exactly every nuance of the experience of another mystic. Each might result from a distinctive method of recollecting and focusing one's mental faculties—

e.g., dwelling on God's love in one case, centering on a sacred image in the other, or meditative prayer in a third—to attain the ultimate state of spiritual illumination or enlightenment which, as St. Teresa of Avila put it, "will be recognized by those who know it from personal experience."[37] Here Henri Bergson remarks relevantly that we

> . . . must first note the fact that mystics generally agree among themselves. This is striking in the case of Christian mystics. To reach the ultimate identification with God, they go through a series of states. These may vary from mystic to mystic, but there is a strong resemblance between them. In any case the path followed is the same, even admitting that the stopping places by the way are at different intervals. They have the same terminal point. In the descriptions of the final state we find the same expressions, the same images, the same comparisons, although the authors were generally unknown to each other. . . . [Later, in response to the possible objection of skeptics that the resemblances can be explained by the fact] that all Christian mystics have lived on the Gospels, that they all received the same theological teaching, . . . [Bergson goes on to say that] this would be to forget that, if the resemblance of the visions is indeed explainable by a common religion, these visions occupy but a small place in the lives of the mystics; they are soon left behind, and treated as they had been merely symbolical [interpretations]. [But to what reality do these symbols point? Bergson answers that] . . . their deep-seated agreement is a sign of an identity of intuition which would find its simplest explanation in the actual existence of the Being with whom they believe themselves to hold intercourse. So much the more so, then, if we consider that the other [non-Christian] mysticisms, ancient or modern, go more or less far, stopping at this or that stage, but all point [symbolically] in the same direction.[38]

The fact that heterophenomenological comparison of these states may reveal some idiosyncratic differences does not invalidate their converging on essentially the same phenomenological event, divine illumination. In fact, as much as experiences of convergent observational replication in scientific research increase our confidence in the validity of what the experiences signify about scientifically studied reality, so also can the convergent replications of religious experiences increase our confidence regarding the validity of experiences about religiously explored reality. (However, despite this agreement, there is a difference between the observational experiences of science and the religious experiences of mystics. The physicist Ian Hutchinson correctly points out that only the exact, natural sciences can claim to yield interpretations of observational findings with the highest degree of pre-

37. Teresa of Avila, *The Way of Perfection*, 161.
38. Bergson, *The Two Sources*, 246–47.

cision and clarity or, alternately, the lowest degree of ambiguity, and therefore with the more exacting replicability by others,[39] a degree of interpretative and linguistic clarity that, in my opinion, cannot be attained with the religious experiences of mystics.)

Finally, given that religious illuminations point to a common referent, a fourth objection a critic might raise is that such illuminations do not correspond to anything real. Well, if what is meant by "real" is whatever can be empirically observed and physically measured, then, yes, the illuminations point to nothing that is real. My only response here is that perhaps the critic ought to broaden his conception of reality. The *number* 12 also is not accessible as a concrete physical, hence a sensorially observable and measurable entity, although the *numerals* "12" and "XII" are. But a mathematician would not hesitate to say that her experience of and with the numeral "12" concretely points to a particular abstract entity, a number, that is part of mathematical reality, which in turn points to and is part of a reality more capacious than that accessible only to the empirical sciences.

The crucial issue therefore is not so much one of consensually agreed upon method or procedure; instead, it is one of interpretive context, commitment, trust, and what is meant by "reality." In both science and religion, it is trained experts who have privileged access, on one hand, to scientific observational particulars concerning the physical entities in the universe and, on the other hand, to religious experiential particulars concerning the divine realm of God.[40] A scientist's knowledge must rely on a commitment to trust that his own private observational experiences point to the existence of physical entities, against which he can test the experiences (and the attendant theoretical interpretations) of other trustworthy scientists. And you and I, who are not expert in most sciences, can in turn augment our knowledge of the physical universe by committing to trust, without an in-depth understanding, in the observational judgments of the scientists who are experts in their respective fields. Similarly, a religious person who desires to grow in her knowledge of God can rely on her own limited religious experiences and knowledge, which she can assess against the additional evidence of trusted religious practitioners such as Teresa of Avila, Catherine of Siena, Hildegard von Bingen, and Julian of Norwich, whose apical religious experiences are revelations of the ultimate and transcendent reality that is God. Consequently, on these methodological and procedural grounds, there appears to be to me no reason why religious truths, when compared to

39. Hutchinson, *Monopolizing Knowledge.*

40. By a religious expert, I don't mean a theologian familiar with church dogmatics, who might never have had a mystical experience of highest illumination, i.e., being in union with ultimate or highest reality. A theologian's expertise is in a scholarly realm and is primarily intellectual and not experiential.

the way scientific truths are gleaned from research into nature, cannot be gleaned from seeking God.[41]

Besides the aforementioned differences between the degrees of conceptual and linguistic clarity regarding the theological evaluations of religious experiences and the theoretical evaluations of scientifically produced experiences, there are several additional differences between science and religion that are noteworthy. The chief difference, as William Franke sees it (and with which, based on the above, I can agree), is not so much "that they have separate domains or are grounded in separate epistemological faculties. Such distinctions are always artificial wherever the essential human vocation and drive to know as such is [sic] at issue. . . . What separates science and religion—and even then, not in their essential core, but only in their most common manifestations—is simply that that their interests differ."[42] This difference is one of motivation and goal that accompanies every research problem in most any field of study. For "science is interested in what can be objectively known and manipulated, whereas religion is interested in what transcends our control and what we [can know and] can relate to only through means other than objective knowing, for example, by worship, ritual devotion, love, commitment, and engaged actions."[43] Perhaps a way to rephrase this is to say that natural scientists train their intellects to actively probe into the natural realm in order to reveal its secrets, its inexhaustible facts and truths, whereas religious mystics, after learning to still their intellect, train their hearts in stillness and patient receptivity to the presence of the sacred.

As to more specific differences between science and religion, let's look more closely at the ways of knowing scientifically vs. religiously. Scientific objective knowledge is attained by developing as clear, unambiguous, and impersonal an account of the what and how of the natural and physical world as can be. It does so by methodologically bracketing the first-person autophenomenological experiences of scientists: their frustrations, apprehensions, and disappointments; their tension-filled anticipations of results; and their relief and joy of discovery when the outcome of research rewards all their hopes and dissolves their doubts. We can ask if religion likewise can bracket, let alone do without, the many and varied personal what-it-is-like experiences of ourselves and of the spiritual world we indwell. The answer here is: most unlikely. For religious individuals, firsthand experiences of beauty, good, joy, admiration, success, love, hope, and peace can rarely if ever be univocally separated from firsthand experi-

41. Wider discussions of the stages and varieties of religious experience, their significance and their interpretations can be found in James, *The Varieties of Religious Experience*; Luigi Giussani, *The Religious Sense* (McGill-Queen's University Press, 1997); Howard Wettstein, *The Significance of Religious Experience* (Oxford University Press, 2012).

42. Franke, *On the Universality of What Is Not*, 357.

43. Franke, *On the Universality of What Is Not*, 357.

ences of their respective counterparts of ugliness, evil, suffering, contempt, failure, hate, despair, and hostility. Pairwise, opposites such as these are inseparable in their implicated connection to each other, and combined, they contribute analogically to the substance and sustenance of not only secular but also religious life. David Bentley Hart, in his inimitable way, describes that "analogy sees that the interminable slippage of language is not simply devolution into the flux of ontological univocity, . . . but [is instead] the gesture of donation, the thematic variation and elaboration that is the very form of presence, the immediacy of the mediate, set free by the God who is his own mediation, his own response."[44]

Since God mediates his presence to each of us via the personal encounter between a mortal I and the eternal Thou, one can also make the case for why solitude, a respite from the obligations of communal life, provides a most private and personal setting for developing the loftiest as well as the profoundest religious insights and revelations. Yet given this fundamental difference between the univocity that science strives for and the ambiguity of analogical mediation that is God's gift to religion—a difference that at times can manifest as opposition and conflict between science and religion—there are always similarities that bind them: the ultimate reliance, common to science and religion, on personal, first-person autophenomenology and the human calling and motivation to seek truth, knowledge, and understanding.

A second difference that clearly does distinguish science from religion is the interpretive contexts within which experiences are given coherent meaning. In one case, the context of a communally validated interpretation is provided by a scientific theory or research paradigm that can explain experiences of the natural world; in the other case, the context of a communally validated interpretation is found in a theological paradigm that can explain religious experiences of the divine domain. We must note that different religions adopt different theological interpretive contexts. However, that fact should not be taken as a differentiating between religion and science, for in science there often exist several distinct theorical models that can interpret and account for the same observations, a feature known as the observational indeterminacy of theories. Such indeterminacy is a sign that further research must be undertaken to obtain new types of observations and measurements that can minimize (or eliminate) the indeterminacy. Similarly, different religions can be considered as manifestations of the indeterminacy of their respective theological differences. Without divine intervention, theological indeterminacies might not be resolvable and therefore persist as a sore point in interreligious dialogue.

Thus, a third difference is the distinct advantage that science has here over religion in that the competing theoretical models can, in principle, be eliminated one by one via a series of clear empirical tests until their observational

44. Hart, *The Beauty of the Infinite*, 316.

outcomes disconfirm all but one model. However, this surviving theoretical model is not a final truth-bearing account. Its truth-bearing nature is ever provisional; while it has increased its proximity to some sort of final truth, it cannot attain identity with it, a feature of scientific theoretical accounts that the philosopher Karl Popper called *verisimilitude*.[45] For that reason, science is ever progressive; ever new theoretical models stimulate ever new empirical tests. In contrast, religions are more tightly bound to tradition and tend to be conservative. While in science one can take Arthur Eddington's 1919 astronomical observations confirming Einstein's theoretical prediction that space is warped by massive objects as one example of a decisive, unambiguous test, to my knowledge no such decisive tests as yet exist allowing one to clearly opt for one of the competing theologies offered by differing religions. Yet is it not possible that, in a distant future project—perhaps one examining and comparing the fruits (unpalatable as well as palatable) accumulated over time when distinct religious are put into practice—an impartial agnostic historian of religions may discover some critical indicators, among a range of weak to strong ones, that can be used to point at least to on-the-ground, existential truth-bearing rankings of religions and their theologies?

The differences between the respective interpretive contexts within which scientific and religious knowledge are acquired bespeak a yet deeper difference. The scientific understanding of reality, while it is limited by its explanations of the natural world, certainly claims to go beyond the everyday experiences of the lifeworld all of us inhabit. But although religious understanding of reality also goes beyond these same everyday experiences, it additionally claims to be informed by a reality that is larger than that targeted by the natural sciences. A denial of such larger reality, illegitimately inspired by methodological constraints imposed on science, is itself an act of faith resting on a priori metaphysical presuppositions that support this methodology. Short of such metaphysics, there is nothing about science that by and of itself recommends the denial of a larger reality accessible to religious experience. While the methodologically limited reality explored by the natural sciences certainly affects religious worldviews, as expressed for instance in recent theologies of nature,[46] the reality

45. Karl R. Popper, *Conjectures and Refutations* (Routledge, 1972).

46. Among notable 20th- and 21st-century scholars and theologians who have taken a serious look at how the science of nature relates to theology of nature and to religion are Ian Barbour, George Ellis, Nancy Murphy, Wolfhart Pannenberg, Arthur Peacocke, John Polkinghorne, and Robert Russell. See Barbour, *Religion in an Age of Science*; Ellis, "Physics Ain't What It Used to Be"; Ellis, *How Can Physics Underlie the Mind*; Wolfhart Pannenberg, *Toward a Theology of Nature: Essays on Science and Faith* (Westminster/John Knox Press, 1993); Peacocke, *Theology for a Scientific Age*; Polkinghorne, *One World*; Polkinghorne, *Theology in the Context of Science*; Robert John Russell et al., eds., *Quantum Cosmology and the Laws of Nature: Scientific Perspectives on Divine* Action (Vatican Observatory Foundation, 1993).

accessible to religious experience is more commodious and accommodates the transcendent realm, in addition to the richness of the everyday lifeworld in which the natural world explored by the natural sciences is embedded.

Science: A Subject for Theological Study

A millennium ago, theology, encompassing several concurrent disciplines, was considered the queen of what was then considered to be the sciences. From among these disciplines, three areas of study stood out in medieval cathedral schools and universities: metaphysics, the trivium (the "forensic sciences" consisting of grammar, rhetoric, and logic), and the quadrivium (the "mathematical sciences" consisting of arithmetic, geometry, astronomy, and music). The training acquired from all three areas of study—excepting the study of music (i.e., harmony, which required the mathematical sciences)[47]—was relevantly applied in the contentious disputes between Galileo, promoting the Copernican heliocentric worldview, and his rivals, defending the Aristotelian/Ptolemaic worldview. A few decades later, the purview of theology and its attendant metaphysics—metaphysics considered as first philosophy—was to be circumscribed by the new experimental science promoted by Francis Bacon's *Novum Organum*, published in 1620. Bacon argued that metaphysics and first philosophy are distinct. Accordingly, the function of first philosophy was no longer to be assumed by metaphysics but instead by natural philosophy.[48] Because it has presumably separated from metaphysics and has replaced natural philosophy, its progeny, present-day science, occupies for some of its practitioners and admirers the pinnacle of philosophy, the basis of all legitimate knowledge.

Yet many other science practitioners, philosophers, and theologians would disagree. The modern sciences, ranging from the physical to the human ones, have become areas of study for a sizable number of theologians. Aware of Darwin's legacy, they might no longer promote anything like the natural theology

47. Aspects of musical harmony are related to mathematics. In the 6th century BCE, the Greek philosopher Pythagoras of Samos established the physics behind musical intervals in mathematical terms by determining the separations between the frequencies of pleasant-sounding, harmonious notes. The notes could be produced by plucking a taught string whose length was varied systematically. These musical intervals comprise the musical harmonic system taught by music theorists to this day. The influence of Pythagorean discoveries, conveyed over the centuries, became evident in medieval cosmologies. In these cosmologies, the movements of celestial bodies were regarded as forming harmonies, the "music of the celestial spheres." Around the turn of the 17th century, Johannes Kepler's mathematical work, under the sway of Platonic/Pythagorean harmonies, led to his discovery of the laws of planetary motions around the sun.

48. Jürgen Klein and Guido Giglioni, "Francis Bacon," in *The Stanford Encyclopedia of Philosophy*, ed. Edward N. Zalta (Fall 2020), https://plato.stanford.edu/archives/fall2020/entries/francis-bacon.

that was promoted early in the 19th century by the English clergyman William Paley. Paley argued and concluded that, just as finding an artifact such as a watch while strolling in nature leads one to infer the watch was purposely designed by an intelligent agent, so was a natural object like, say, a tiny house cricket designed by the intelligent agency of God. In other words, if purposeful intelligent design is denied and therefore if the likelihood of a found watch having been assembled from its parts by unintelligent, blind chance is extremely low, then, similarly, so is the likelihood of assembling the complex functional anatomy of a field cricket—allowing it to hop, fly, stridulate, and seek nutrients, prey, and a mate—also extremely low. In both cases, the extremely low likelihoods support the inference that an intelligent and purposeful designer has created both assemblages. Although this inductive inferential argument is problematic, to this day it finds support from intelligent design (ID) advocates.[49] However, some theologians no longer subscribe to such natural theology; instead, they subscribe to a theology of nature not by concluding but by *assuming*, as a preamble to faith, that nature is first and foremost God's creation, and they explore God's order and artistry in nature on that basis. As arduously laid out by philosopher of science and religion Michael Hanby, since nature is part of God's creation, a theology of nature is implicitly embedded in the natural sciences; for without God the Creator, argues Hanby, there is no creation and therefore no science of anything.[50] For this reason, theology of nature, informed by the practices and findings of the natural sciences and especially the neurosciences and evolutionary ones, is assuming increasing importance, although unfortunately, many traditional theologians remain oblivious to their significance.

49. For example, mathematician and philosopher William Dembski and philosopher of science Stephen Meyer, both at the Discovery Institute, are proponents of ID.

50. Hanby, *No God, No Science.*

Bibliography

Aarts, Bas, Sylvia Chalker, and Edmund Weiner. *The Oxford Dictionary of English Grammar*. Oxford University Press, 2014.

Abouheif, Ehab, Marie-Julie Favé, Ana Sofia Ibarrarán-Viniegra, Maryna P. Lesoway, Ab Matteen Rafiqi, and Rajendhran Rajakumar. "Eco-evo-devo: The Time Has Come." In *Ecological Genomics: Ecology and the Evolution of Genes and Genomes*, edited by Christian R. Landry and Nadia Aubin-Horth. Springer, 2014. https://doi.org/10.1007/978-94-007-7347-9_6.

Aczel, Amir D. *Why Science Does Not Disprove God*. HarperCollins Publishers, 2014.

Albertson, David. *Mathematical Theologies*. Oxford University Press, 2014.

Alcalde, David. *Cosmology Without God: The Problematic Theology Inherent in Modern Cosmology*. Wipf & Stock, 2019.

Alcorta, Candace S., and Richard Sosis. "Ritual, Emotion, and Sacred Symbols: The Evolution of Religion as an Adaptive Complex." *Human Nature* 16, no. 4 (2005): 323–59. https://doi.org/10.1007/s12110-005-1014-3.

Amit, Elinor, and Joshua D. Greene. "You See, the Ends Don't Justify the Means: Visual Imagery and Moral Judgment." *Psychological Science* 23, no. 8 (2012): 861–68. https://doi.org/10.1177/0956797611434965.

Anders, Timothy. *The Evolution of Evil*. Open Court, 1994.

Anderson, Gary A. "*Creatio ex nihilo* and the Bible." In *Creation ex nihilo: Origins, Development, Contemporary Challenges*, edited by Gary A. Anderson and Markus Bockmuehl. University of Notre Dame Press, 2018.

Anderson, Gary A., and Markus Bockmuehl, eds. *Creatio ex nihilo: Origins, Development, Contemporary Challenges*. University of Notre Dame Press, 2018.

Antonello, Pierpaolo, and Paul Gifford, eds. *Can We Survive Our Origins: Readings in Rene Girard's Theory of Violence and the Sacred*. Michigan State University Press, 2015.

Antonello, Pierpaolo, and Paul Gifford, eds. *How We Became Human: Mimetic Theory and the Science of Evolutionary Origins*. Michigan State University Press, 2015.

Appiah, Kwame Anthony. "What is a Science of Religion?" *Philosophy* 93, no. 4 (2018): 485–503. https://doi.org/10.1017/S003181911800030X.

Apud, Ismael. "Pharmacology of Consciousness or Pharmacology of Spirituality? A Historical Review of Psychedelic Clinical Studies." *The Journal of Transpersonal Psychology* 48, no. 2 (2016): 150–67.

Arendt, Hannah. *The Human Condition*. University of Chicago Press, 2018.

Arendt, Hannah. *The Life of the Mind*. Vol. 1, *Thinking*. Vol. 2, *Willing*. Mariner Books, 1978.

Arnaldez, Roger. *Three Messengers for One God*. University of Notre Dame Press, 1994.

Ashworth, William B., Jr. "Catholicism and Early Modern Science." In *God & Nature: Historical Essays on the Encounter Between Christianity and Science*, edited by David C. Lindberg and Ronald L. Numbers. University of California Press, 1986.

Atran, Scott. *In Gods We Trust: The Evolutionary Landscape of Religion*. Oxford University Press, 2002.

Augros, Michael. *Who Designed the Designer?: A Rediscovered Path to God's Existence*. Ignatius Press, 2015.

Augustine. *Confessions*. Oxford University Press, 2008.

Ayala, Francisco J. *Darwin's Gift to Science and Religion*. Joseph Henry Press, 2007.

Azzopardi, Paul, and Alan Cowey. "Is Blindsight like Normal, Near-Threshold Vision?" *Proceedings of the National Academy of Sciences* 94, no. 25 (1997): 14190–14194. https://doi.org/10.1073/pnas.94.25.14190.

Baggini, Julian. *The Possibility of Free Will: Freedom Regained*. University of Chicago Press, 2015.

Baglow, Christopher T. *Creation: A Catholic's Guide to God and the Universe*. Ave Maria Press, 2021.

Baillargeon, Reneé, Peipei Setoh, Stephanie Sloane, Kyong-Sun Jin, and Lin Bian. "Infant Social Cognition: Psychological and Sociomoral Reasoning." In *The Cognitive Neurosciences*, 5th ed., edited by Michael S. Gazzaniga and George R. Mangun. MIT Press, 2014.

Balaguer, Mark. "Free Will, Determinism, and Epiphenomenalism." *Frontiers of Psychology* 9 (2018): 2623. https://doi.org/10.3389/fpsyg.2018.02623.

Ball, Philip. "Triumph of the Medieval Mind." *Nature* 452, no. 7189 (2008): 816–18. https://doi.org/10.1038/452816a.

Barbour, Ian. *Religion in an Age of Science*. HarperCollins Publishers, 1990.

Barnes, Michael Horace. *Stages of Thought: The Co-evolution of Religious Thought and Science*. Oxford University Press, 2000.

Barr, Stephen M. *Modern Physics and Ancient Faith*. University of Notre Dame Press, 2003.

Barrett, Justin L. *Born Believers: The Science of Children's Religious Belief*. The Free Press, 2012.

Barrett, Justin L. "Exploring the Natural Foundations of Religion." *Trends in Cognitive Sciences* 4, no. 1 (2000): 29–34. https://doi.org/10.1016/s1364-6613(99)01419-9.

Barrett, Justin L. "Is the Spell Really Broken? Bio-Psychological Explanations of Religion and Theistic Belief." *Theology and Science* 5, no. 1 (2007): 57–72. https://doi.org/ 10.1080/14746700601159564.

Barrett, Justin L. "The Relative Unnaturalness of Atheism: On Why Geertz and Markússon are Both Right and Wrong." *Religion* 40, no. 3 (2010): 169–72. https://doi.org/10.1016/j.religion.2009.11.002.

Barrett, Nathaniel F. "The Perspectivity of Feeling: Process Panpsychism and The Explanatory Gap." *Process Studies* 38, no. 2 (2009): 189–206. https://doi.org/10.2307/44798486.

Bartley, W. W., III. “Logical Strength and Demarcation.” In *Rationality in Science and Politics.* Boston Studies in the Philosophy of Science 79, edited by Gunnar Andersson. Springer, 1984. https://doi.org/10.1007/978-94-009-6254-5_5.

Bartley, W. W., III. “Theories of Rationality.” In *Evolutionary Epistemology, Rationality, and the Sociology of Knowledge,* edited by Gerald Radnitzky and W. W. Bartley III. Open Court, 1987.

Batchelor, Stephen. *Buddhism Without Beliefs: A Contemporary Guide to Awakening.* Penguin Group, 1998.

Batson, C. Daniel, David A. Lishner, Amy Carpenter, Luis Dulin, Sanna Harjusola-Webb, E. L. Stocks, et al. “As You Would Have Them Do unto You: Does Imagining Yourself in the Other’s Place Stimulate Moral Action?” *Personality and Social Psychology Bulletin* 29, no. 9 (2003): 1190–1201. https://doi.org/10.1177/0146167203254600.

Baumard, Nicolas, and Pascal Boyer. “Explaining Moral Religions.” *Trends in Cognitive Sciences* 17, no. 6 (2013), 272–80. https://doi.org/10.1016/j.tics.2013.04.003.

Bellah, R. N. *Religion in Human Evolution: From the Paleolithic to the Axial Age.* Harvard University Press, 2011.

Bergson, Henri. *The Two Sources of Morality and Religion.* University of Notre Dame Press, 2013.

Bering, Jessie M., and David F. Bjorklund. “The Natural Emergence of Reasoning about the Afterlife as a Developmental Regularity.” *Developmental Psychology* 40, no. 2 (2004), 217–33. https://doi.org/10.1037/0012-1649.40.2.217.

Berkeley, George. *A Treatise Concerning the Principles of Human Knowledge.* Dover Publications, 2003.

Berkovich-Ohana, Avina, Yair Dor-Ziderman, Joseph Glicksohn, and Abraham Goldstein. “Alterations In the Sense of Time, Space, and Body in the Mindfulness-Trained Brain: A Neurophenomenologically-guided MEG Study.” *Frontiers in Psychology* 4 (2013): 912. https://doi.org/10.3389/fpsyg.2013.0091.

Berridge, Kent C., and Morton L. Kringelbach. “Pleasure Systems in the Brain.” *Neuron* 86, no. 3 (2015): 646–64. https://doi.org/10.1016/j.neuron.2015.02.018.

Berwick, Robert C., and Noam Chomsky. *Why Only Us: Language and Evolution.* MIT Press, 2016.

Biederman, Irving, and Edward A. Vessel. “Perceptual Pleasure and the Brain: A Novel Theory Explains Why the Brain Craves Information and Seeks It Through the Senses.” *American Scientist* 94, no. 3 (2006): 247–53. https://www.jstor.org/stable/27858773.

Bishop, Jeffrey P., M. Therese Lysaught, and Andrew A. Michel. *Biopolitics After Neuroscience: Morality and the Economy of Virtue.* Bloomsbury Publishing, 2022.

Blackmore, Susan. “Living Without Free Will.” In *Exploring the Illusion of Free Will and Moral Responsibility,* edited by Gregg D. Caruso. Lexington Books, 2013.

Blackmore, Susan J. *The Meme Machine.* Oxford University Press, 1999.

Blackwell, Richard J. *Galileo, Bellarmine, and the Bible.* University of Notre Dame Press, 1991.

Blom, Philipp. *A Wicked Company: The Forgotten Radicalism of the European Enlightenment.* Basic Books, 2010.

Bloom, Paul. "Religion is Natural." *Developmental Science* 10, no. 1 (2007): 147–51. http://dx.doi.org/10.1111/j.1467-7687.2007.00577.x.

Borde, Arvin, Alan H. Guth, and Alexander Vilenkin. "Inflationary Spacetimes Are Incomplete in Past Directions." *Physics Review Letters* 90, no. 15 (2003): 151301. https://doi.org/10.1103/PhysRevLett.90.151301.

Bostrom, Nick. "In Defense of Posthuman Dignity." *Bioethics* 19, no. 3 (2005): 202–14. https://doi.org/10.1111/j.1467-8519.2005.00437.x.

Bostrom, Nick. "A Transhumanist Perspective on Human Genetic Enhancements." *Journal of Value Enquiry* 37, no. 4 (2003): 493–506. http://www.nickbostrom.com/ethics/enhancements.html.

Bower, T. G. R., J. Broughton, and M. K. Moore. "The Development of the Object Concept as Manifested by Changes in the Tracking Behavior of Infants Between 7 and 20 Weeks of Age." *Journal of Experimental Child Psychology* 11, no. 2 (1971): 182–93. https://doi.org/10.1016/0022-0965(71)90074-9.

Boyer, Pascal. "Gods and Mental Instincts That Create Them." In *Science, Religion and the Human Experience*, edited by James D. Proctor. Oxford University Press, 2005.

Boyer, Pascal. "Paleolithic Art: Awesome—but Not Religious." International Cognition and Culture Institute. February 24, 2009. Accessed June 5, 2022. http://cognitionandculture.net/blog/pascals-blog/paleolithic-art-awesome-mdash-but-not-religious.

Boyer, Pascal. "Religion: Bound to Believe?" *Nature* 455, no. 7216 (2008): 1038–39. https://doi.org/10.1038/4551038a.

Boyer, Pascal. *Religion Explained: The Evolutionary Origins of Religious Thought.* Basic Books, 2001.

Boyer, Pascal. "Religious Thought and Behaviour as By-Products of Brain Function." *Trends in Cognitive Sciences* 7, no. 3 (2003): 119–24. https://doi.org/10.1016/S1364-6613(03)00031-7.

Boyer, Pascal, and Brian Bergstrom. "Evolutionary Perspectives on Religion." *Annual Review of Anthropology* 37, no. 1 (2008): 111–30. https://doi.org/10.1146/annurev.anthro.37.081407.085201.

Brague, Rémi. *The Kingdom of Man: Genesis and Failure of the Modern Project.* University of Notre Dame Press, 2018.

Breitmeyer, Bruno G. "In Support of Pockett's Critique of Libet's Studies of the Time Course of Consciousness." *Consciousness and Cognition* 11, no. 2 (2002): 280–83. http://dx.doi.org/10.1006/ccog.2002.0555.

Breitmeyer, Bruno G. "Problems with the Psychophysics of Intentions." *Behavioral and Brain Sciences* 8, no. 4 (1985): 539–40. https://doi.org/10.1017/S0140525X00044915.

Breitmeyer, Bruno G. *The Visual (Un)Conscious & Its (Dis)Contents.* Oxford University Press, 2014.

Breitmeyer, Bruno G. "What's All the Free-Will Ado About?" *Psychology of Consciousness: Theory, Research, and Practice* 4, no. 3 (2017): 330–33. https://doi.org/10.1037/cns0000132.

Breitmeyer, Bruno G., and Jane Jacob. "Microgenesis of Surface Completion in Visual Objects: Evidence for Filling-Out." *Vision Research* 55, no. 5 (2012): 11–18. https://doi.org/10.1016/j.visres.2011.12.010.

Breitmeyer, Bruno G., and Haluk Öğmen. *Visual Masking: Time Slices Through Conscious and Unconscious Vision*. 2nd ed. Oxford University Press, 2006.

Breitmeyer, Bruno, Haluk Ogmen, Jose Ramon, and Jian Chen. "Unconscious Priming by Forms and Their Parts." *Visual Cognition* 12, no. 5 (2005): 720–36. https://doi.org/10.1080/13506280444000472.

Breitmeyer, Bruno G., and Petra Stoerig. "Neural Correlates and Levels of Conscious and Unconscious Vision." In *The First Half Second: The Microgenesis and Temporal Dynamics of Unconscious and Conscious Visual Processes*, edited by Haluk Öğmen and Bruno G. Breitmeyer. MIT Press, 2006.

Brielmann, Aenne A., and Denis G. Pelli. "Beauty Requires Thought." *Current Biology* 27, no. 10 (2017): 1506–13. https://doi.org/10.1016/j.cub.2017.04.018.

Brielmann, Aenne A., and Denis G. Pelli. "Intense Beauty Requires Intense Pleasure." *Frontiers in Psychology* 10 (2019): 2420. https://doi.org/10.3389/fpsyg.2019.02420.

Brooke, John Hedley. *Science and Religion: Some Historical Perspectives*. Cambridge University Press, 1991.

Broom, Donald M. *The Evolution of Morality and Religion*. Cambridge University Press, 2003.

Brosnan, Sarah F. "Why an Evolutionary Perspective Is Critical to Understanding Moral Behavior in Humans." In *Challenges to Moral and Religious Belief: Disagreement and Evolution*, edited by Michael Bergmann and Patrick Kain. Oxford University Press, 2014.

Brosnan, Sarah F., and Frans B. M. de Waal. "Monkeys Reject Unequal Pay." *Nature* 425, no. 6955 (2003): 297–99. https://doi.org/10.1038/nature01963.

Brown, Montague. *Restoration of Reason: The Eclipse and Recovery of Truth, Goodness, and Beauty*. Baker Academic, 2006.

Buber, Martin. *I and Thou*. Charles Scribner's Sons, 1970.

Buckley, Michael J., SJ. *Denying and Disclosing God: The Ambiguous Progress of Modern Atheism*. Yale University Press, 2004.

Bulbulia, Joseph. "The Cognitive and Evolutionary Psychology of Religion." *Biology and Philosophy* 19, no. 5 (2004): 655–86. https://doi.org/10.1007/s10539-005-5568-6.

Camus, Albert. *The Rebel: An Essay of Man in Revolt*. Vintage Books, 1956.

Cao, Yongqiang, and Stephen Grossberg. "Laminar Cortical Model for 3D Perception of Slanted and Curved Surfaces and of 2D Images: Development, Attention, and Bistability." *Spatial Vision* 18, no. 5 (2005): 515–78.

Carr, Bernard, and George F. Ellis. "Universe or Multiverse?" *Astronomy & Geophysics* 49, no. 2 (2008): 2.29–2.33. https://doi.org/10.1111/j.1468-4004.2008.49229.x.

Cavanaugh, William T. *The Myth of Religious Violence.* Oxford University Press, 2009.

Chalmers, David. "The Combination Problem for Panpsychism." In *Panpsychism,* edited by Godehard Brüntrup and Ludwig Jaskolla. Oxford University Press, 2016.

Chalmers, David J. *The Conscious Mind.* Oxford University Press, 1996.

Chalmers, David. "Panpsychism and Panprotopsychism." In *Consciousness in the Physical World: Perspectives on Russellian Monism,* edited by Torin Alter and Yujin Nagasawa. Oxford University Press, 2015.

Chandrasekhar, S. "The General Theory of Relativity: 'Why It Is Probably the Most Beautiful of All Existing Theories.'" *Journal of Astrophysics and Astronomy* 5, no. 1 (1984): 3–11.

Chudek, Maciej, and Joseph Henrich. "Culture-Gene Coevolution, Norm-Psychology and the Emergence of Human Prosociality." *Trends in Cognitive Sciences* 15, no. 5 (2011): 218–26. https://doi.org/10.1016/j.tics.2011.03.003.

Chudek, Maciej, Rita Anne McNamara, Susan Birch, Paul Bloom, and Joseph Henrich. "Do Minds Switch Bodies? Dualist Interpretations Across Ages and Societies." *Religion, Brain & Behavior* 8, no. 4 (2018): 354–68. https://doi.org/10.1080/2153599X.2017.1377757.

Churchland, Paul M., and Patricia Smith Churchland. *On the Contrary: Critical Essays, 1987–1997.* MIT Press, 1998.

Clayton, Phillip. "How Radically Can God Be Reconceived Before Ceasing to Be God? The Four Faces of Panentheism." *Zygon* 52, no. 4 (2017): 1044–59. https://doi.org.10.1111/zygo.12368.

Clayton, Phillip, and Arthur Peacocke. *In Whom We Live and Move and Have Our Being: Panentheistic Reflections on God's Presence in a Scientific World.* William B. Eerdmans Publishing Co., 2004.

Clifford, Colin W. G., Derek Henry Arnold, and Joel Pearson. "A Paradox of Temporal Perception Revealed by a Stimulus Oscillating in Colour and Orientation." *Vision Research* 43, no. 21 (2003): 2245–53. https://doi.org/10.1016/S0042-6989(03)00120-2.

Clottes, Jean. *What Is Paleolithic Art?: Cave Paintings and the Dawn of Human Creativity.* University of Chicago Press, 2016.

Clottes, Jean, and David Lewis-Williams. *The Shamans of Prehistory: Trance and Magic in the Painted Caves.* Harry N. Adams, 1998.

Clouser, Roy A. *The Myth of Religious Neutrality.* University of Notre Dame Press, 1991.

Cohen, Arthur A. *The Tremendum: A Theological Interpretation of the Holocaust.* Continuum, 1993.

Cohen, Michael A., Cole Dembski, Kevin Ortego, Clay Steinhibler, and Michael Pitts. "Neural Signatures of Visual Awareness Independent of Postperceptual Processing." *Cerebral Cortex* 34, no. 11 (2024): 1–15. https://doi.org/10.1093/cercor/bhae415.

Collingwood, R. R. *The Idea of History.* Oxford University Press, 1956.

Collins, Andrew. *Göbekli Tepe: Genesis of the Gods*. Bear & Company, 2014.
Collins, Francis S. *The Language of God: A Scientist Presents Evidence for Belief*. Free Press, 2006.
Confer, Jaime C., Judith A. Easton, Diana S. Fleischman, Cari D. Goetz, David M. G. Lewis, Carin Perilloux, and David M. Buss. "Evolutionary Psychology: Controversies, Questions, Prospects, and Limitations." *American Psychologist* 65, no. 2 (2010): 110–26. https://doi.org/10.1037/a0018413.
Consolmagno, Guy, and Christopher M. Graney. "The Galileo Myth." *America*, September 18, 2020.
Conway, Paul, and Bertram Gawronski. "Deontological and Utilitarian Inclinations in Moral Decision Making: A Process Dissociation Approach." *Journal of Personality and Social Psychology* 104, no. 2 (2013): 216–35. https://doi.org/10.1037/a0031021.
Cooper, Barry. *Action into Nature: An Essay on the Meaning of Technology*. University of Notre Dame Press, 1991.
Cooper, Barry. *Paleolithic Politics: The Human Community in Early Art*. University of Notre Dame Press, 2020.
Cooper, John W. *Panentheism: The Other God of the Philosophers*. Baker Academic, 2006.
Cottingham, John. *In Search of the Soul: A Philosophical Essay*. Princeton University Press, 2020.
Coyne, George V., SJ. "The Church's Most Recent Attempt to Dispel the Galileo Myth." In *Church and God*, edited by Ernan McMullan. University of Notre Dame Press, 2005.
Coyne, Jerry A. *Faith vs. Fact: Why Science and Religion Are Incompatible*. Viking Press, 2015.
Coyne, Jerry A. "Of Vice and Men: The Fairy Tales of Evolutionary Psychology." *The New Republic*, April 3, 2000.
Craig, William Lane. "In Defense of Theistic Arguments." In *The Future of Atheism: Alister McGrath & Daniel Dennett in Dialogue*, edited by Robert B. Stewart. Fortress Press, 2008.
Crane, Tim. *The Meaning of Belief: Religion from an Atheist's Point of View*. Harvard University Press, 2017.
Creanza, Nicole, Oren Kolodny, and Marcus W. Feldman. "Cultural Evolutionary Theory: How Culture Evolves and Why It Matters." *Proceedings of the National Academy of Sciences USA* 114, no. 30 (2017): 7782–89. https://doi.org/10.1073/pnas.1620732114.
Crick, Francis, and Christopher Koch. "Are We Aware of Neural Activity in Primary Visual Cortex?" *Nature* 375, no. 6527 (1995): 121–23. https://doi.org/10.1038/375121a0.
Crick, Francis, and Christopher Koch. "A Framework for Consciousness." *Nature Neuroscience* 6, no. 2 (2003): 119–26. https://doi.org/10.1038/nn0203-119.
Daniélou, Jean. *God and the Ways of Knowing*. Ignatius Press, 2003.
Dante Alighieri. *The Divine Comedy*. Viking Press, 1959.

Darley, John M., and C. Daniel Batson. "From Jerusalem to Jericho: A Study of Situational and Dispositional Variables in Helping Behavior." *Journal of Personality and Social Psychology* 27, no. 1 (1973): 100–108. https://doi.org/10.1037/h0034449.

Darwin, Charles. *The Descent of Man*. Penguin Classics, 2004.

Dauben, Joseph Warren. *Georg Cantor: His Mathematics and Philosophy of the Infinite.* Princeton University Press, 1990.

David, Marian. "The Correspondence Theory of Truth." In *The Stanford Encyclopedia of Philosophy*, edited by Edward N. Zalta. Summer 2022. https://plato.stanford.edu/ archives/sum2022/entries/truth-correspondence.

Davies, Daniel. "Reason, Will, and Purpose." In Anderson and Bockmuehl, *Creation ex nihilo*.

Davies, Paul. *God and the New Physics*. Simon & Schuster, 1984.

Davison, Andrew. "Looking Back Toward the Origin: Scientific Cosmology as Creation *ex nihilo* Considered 'from the Inside.'" In Anderson and Bockmuehl, *Creation ex nihilo*.

Dawes, Gregory. *Galileo and the Conflict Between Religion and Science*. Routledge, 2016.

Dawkins, Richard. *The Blind Watch Maker: Why the Evidence of Evolution Reveals a Universe Without Design*. W. W. Norton & Co., 1986.

Dawkins, Richard. *Climbing Mount Improbable*. W. W. Norton & Co., 1996.

Dawkins, Richard. *The God Delusion*. Houghton Mifflin, 2006.

Dawkins, Richard. *The Selfish Gene*. Oxford University Press, 1976.

Deacon, Terrance W. "Emergence: The Hole in the Wheel's Hub." In *The Re-emergence of Emergence: The Emergentist Hypothesis from Science to Religion*, edited by Philip Clayton and Paul Davies. Oxford University Press, 2006.

Decety, Jean. "The Neuroevolution of Empathy and Caring for Others: Why It Matters for Morality." In *New Frontiers in Social Neuroscience*, edited by Jean Decety and Yves Christen. Springer, 2014. https://doi.org/10.1007/978-3-319-02904-7_8.

De Cruz, Helen, "Religion and Science." In *The Stanford Encyclopedia of Philosophy*, edited by Edward N. Zalta & Uri Nodelman. Fall 2025. https://plato.stanford.edu/archives/fall2025/entries/religion-science.

De Cruz, Helen, Maarten Boudry, Johan De Smedt, and Stefaan Blancke. "Evolutionary Approaches to Epistemic Justification." *Dialectica* 65, no. 4 (2011): 517–35. https://doi.org/10.1111/j.1746-8361.2011.01283.x.

De Cruz, Helen, and Johan De Smedt. *A Natural History of Natural Theology: The Cognitive Science of Theology and Philosophy of Religion*. MIT Press, 2015.

de Duve, Christian. *Genetics of Original Sin: The Impact of Natural Selection on the Future of Humanity*. Yale University Press, 2010.

de Lubac, Henri, SJ. *The Drama of Atheist Humanism*. Ignatius Press, 1995.

Del Noce, Augusto. *The Crisis of Modernity*. McGill-Queen's University Press, 2014.

Dennett, Daniel C. *Breaking the Spell: Religion as a Natural Phenomenon*. Penguin Books, 2007.

Dennett, Daniel C. *Consciousness Explained*. Little, Brown & Co, 1991.

Dennett, Daniel C. *Darwin's Dangerous Idea*. Touchstone, 1995.

Dennett, Daniel C. *Freedom Evolves*. Viking Press, 2003.

Dennett, Daniel C. *From Bacteria to Bach and Back: The Evolution of Minds*. W. W. Norton & Co., 2017.

Dennett, Daniel C. "Quining Qualia." In *Consciousness in Modern Science*, edited by Anthony J. Marcel and Eduardo Bisiach. Oxford University Press, 1988.

de Unamuno, Miguel. *The Tragic Sense of Life*. Dover Publications, 1954.

de Waal, Frans B. M. *Good Natured: The Origins of Right and Wrong in Humans and Other Animals*. Harvard University Press, 1996.

de Waal, Frans B. M. "Putting the Altruism Back into Altruism: The Evolution of Empathy." *Annual Review of Psychology* 59, no. 1 (2008): 279–300. https://doi.org/10.1146/annurev.psych.59.103006.093625.

de Waal, Frans B. M., and Stephanie D. Preston. "Mammalian Empathy: Behavioural Manifestations and Neural Basis." *Nature Reviews Neuroscience* 18, no. 8 (2017): 498–509. https://doi.org/10.1038/nrn.2017.72.

de Waal, Frans B. M., and Stephen A. Sherblom. "Bottom-Up Morality: The Basis of Human Morality in Our Primate Nature." *Journal of Moral Education* 47, no. 2 (2018): 248–58. https://doi.org/10.1080/03057240.2018. 1440701.

DeWitt, Bryce S. "Quantum Mechanics and Reality." *Physics Today* 23, no. 9 (1970): 30–35. https://doi.org/10.1063/1.3022331.

Diessner, Rett, Ravi Iyer, Meghan M. Smith, and Jonathan Haidt. "Who Engages with Moral Beauty?" *Journal of Moral Education* 42, no. 2 (2013): 139–63. https://doi.org/10.1080/03057240. 2013.785941.

Dirac, P. A. M. "The Evolution of the Physicist's Picture of Nature." *Scientific American* 258, no. 5 (1963): 45–53. https://www.jstor.org/stable/24936146.

Dover, Kenneth James. *Greek Popular Morality in the Time of Plato and Aristotle*. University of California Press, 1974.

Downes, Stephen M. "Evolutionary Psychology." In *The Stanford Encyclopedia of Philosophy* (Spring 2021 Edition), edited by Edward N. Zalta. Spring 2021. https://plato.stanford.edu/archives/spr2021/entries/evolutionary-psychology.

Draper, John William. *History of the Conflict Between Religion and Science*. Cambridge University Press, 2009.

Dreyfus, Hubert, and Charles Taylor. *Retrieving Realism*. Harvard University Press, 2015.

Dubay, Thomas, SM. *The Evidential Power of Beauty*. Ignatius Press, 1999.

Dupré, Louis. *Religion and the Rise of Modern Culture*. University of Notre Dame Press, 2008.

Dupuy, Jean-Pierre. *The Mark of the Sacred*. Stanford University Press, 2013.

Dutton, Dennis. *The Art Instinct: Beauty, Pleasure, and Human Evolution*. Bloomsbury Press, 2009.

Eagleton, Terry. *Radical Sacrifice*. Yale University Press, 2018.

Eagleton, Terry. *Why Marx Was Right*. Yale University Press, 2011.

Edgerton, Samuel Y. *Renaissance Rediscovery of Linear Perspective*. Harper & Row, 1976.

Edmundson, Mark. *Self and Soul: A Defense of Ideals*. Harvard University Press, 2015.

Eldredge, Niles, and Stephen Jay Gould. "Punctuated Equilibria: An Alternative to Phyletic Gradualism." In *Models in Paleobiology*, edited by Thoms J. M. Schopf. Freeman, Cooper and Co., 1972.

Ellis, George. *How Can Physics Underlie the Mind?: Top-Down Causation in the Human Context*. Springer, 2016.

Ellis, George. "Physics Ain't What It Used to Be: Science Is Venturing into Areas Where Experimental Verification Simply Isn't Possible." *Nature* 438, no. 7069 (2005): 739–40. https://doi.org/10.1038/438739a.

Ellul, Jacques. *The Subversion of Christianity*. William B. Eerdmans Publishing Co., 1966.

Embry, Charles R., and Glenn Hughes, eds. *The Eric Voegelin Reader: Politics, History, Consciousness*. University of Missouri Press, 2017.

Emmons, Robert A., and Raymond F. Paloutzian. "The Psychology of Religion." *Annual Review of Psychology* 54, no. 1 (2003): 377–402. https://doi.org/10.1146/annurev.psych.54.101601.145024.

Engler, Gideon. "Aesthetics in Science and in Art." *British Journal of Aesthetics* 30, no. 1 (1990): 24–34. https://doi.org/10.1093/bjaesthetics/30.1.24.

Evans, E. Margaret. "Cognitive and Contextual Factors in the Emergence of Diverse Belief Systems: Creation Versus Evolution." *Cognitive Psychology* 42, no. 3 (2001): 217–66. https://doi.org/10.1006/cogp.2001.0749.

Everett, Hugh. "Relative State Formulation of Quantum Mechanics." *Reviews of Modern Physics* 29, no. 3 (1957): 454–62. https://doi.org/10.1103/RevModPhys.29.454.

Facco, Enrico, and Christian Agrillo. "Near-Death Experiences Between Science and Prejudice." *Frontiers in Human Neuroscience* 6 (2012): 209. https://doi.org/10.3389/fnhum.2012.00209.

Fantoli, Annibale. *The Case of Galileo: A Closed Question?* University of Notre Dame Press, 2012.

Fantoli, Annibale. "The Disputed Injunction and Its Role in Galileo's Trial." In *The Church and Galileo*, edited by Ernan McMullin. University of Notre Dame Press, 2005.

Fechner, Gustav Theodor. *Elemente der Psychophysik*. Leipzig: Breitkopf und Härtel, 1860. Accessed August 18, 2023. https://www.projekt-gutenberg.org/fechner/epsypht1/chap004.html.

Felleman, Daniel J., Youping Xiao, and Evelyn McClendon. "Modular Organization of Occipito-Temporal Pathways: Cortical Connections Between Visual Area 4 and Visual Area 2 and Posterior Inferotemporal Ventral Area in Macaque Monkeys." *Journal of Neuroscience* 17, no. 9 (1997): 3185–3200. https://doi.org/10.1523/JNEUROSCI.17-09-03185.1997.

Feyerabend, Paul. *Against Method*. Verso, 1984.

Feyerabend, Paul. "Galileo and the Tyranny of Truth." In *The Galileo Affair: A Meeting of Faith and Science. Proceedings of Cracow Conference*, edited by

George V. Coyne, Michał Heller, and Józef Życiński. Vatican Observatory Foundation, 1985.

Feyerabend, Paul. *Wissenschaft als Kunst*. Suhrkamp, 1984.

Feynman, Richard P. *The Meaning of It All: Thoughts of a Citizen-Scientist*. Basic Books, 1998.

Fingelkurts, Alexander A., and Andrew A. Fingelkurts. "Is Our Brain Hardwired to Produce God, or Is Our Brain Hardwired to Perceive God? A Systematic Review on the Role of The Brain in Mediating Religious Experience." *Cognitive Processing* 10, no. 4 (2009): 293–326. https://doi.org/10.1007/s10339-009-0261-3.

Finocchiaro, Maurice A. "Myth 8. That Galileo Was Imprisoned and Tortured for Advocating Copernicanism." In *Galileo Goes to Jail: And Other Myths about Science and Religion*, edited by Ronald L. Numbers. Harvard University Press, 2009.

Finocchiaro, Maurice A. "Science, Religion, and the Historiography of the Galileo Affair: On the Undesirability of Oversimplification." *Osiris* 16 (2001): 114–32. https://www.jstor.org/stable/301982.

Fischer, John Martin, and Mark Ravizza. *Responsibility and Control: A Theory of Moral Responsibility*. Cambridge University Press, 1998.

Flack, Jessica C., and Frans B. M. de Waal. "'Any Animal Whatever': Darwinian Building Blocks of Morality in Monkeys and Apes." *Journal of Consciousness Studies* 7, no. 1–2 (2000): 1–29.

Fox, Michael D., Abraham Z. Snyder, Justin L. Vincent, and Marcus E. Raichle. "The Human Brain Is Intrinsically Organized into Dynamic, Anticorrelated Functional Networks." *Proceedings of the National Academy of Sciences USA* 102, no. 27 (2005): 9673–78. https://doi.org/10.1073/pnas.0504136102.

Franke, William. *On the Universality of What Is Not: The Apophatic Turn in Critical Thinking*. University of Notre Dame Press, 2020.

Frankl, Victor. *Man's Search for Meaning*. Beacon Press, 1984.

Frankl, Victor. *Man's Search for Ultimate Meaning*. Perseus Books, 2000.

Freud, Sigmund. *Moses and Monotheism*. Vintage Books, 1955.

Freud, Sigmund. *Totem and Taboo*. W. W. Norton & Co., 1990.

Fried, Itzhak, Roy Mukamel, and Gabriel Kreiman. "Internally Generated Preactivation of Single Neurons in Human Medial Frontal Cortex Predicts Volition." *Neuron* 69, no. 3 (2011): 548–62. http://dx.doi.org/10.1016/j.neuron.2010.11.045.

Fuentes, Augustín. "Human Evolution, Niche Complexity, and the Emergence of a Distinctively Human Imagination." *Time & Mind* 7, no. 3 (2014): 241–57. https://doi.org/10.1080/1751696X.2014.945720.

Fuentes, Augustín. "Hyper-Cooperation Is Deep in Our Evolutionary History and Individual Perception of Belief Matters." *Religion, Brain & Behavior* 5, no. 4 (2015): 284–90. https://doi.org/10.1080/2153599X.2014.928350.

Fuentes, Augustín. "Putting Evolutionary Theory to Work in Investigating Human Nature(s)." In *Verbs, Bones, and Brains*, edited by Augustín Fuentes and Aku Visala. University of Notre Dame Press, 2017.

Fujimura, Makoto. *Art and Faith: A Theology of Making*. Yale University Press, 2020.
Fuller, Steve. *Science*. Acumen Publishing Ltd., 2010.
Funkenstein, Amos. *Theology and the Scientific Imagination: From the Middle Ages to the Seventeenth Century*. Princeton University Press, 1986.
Gaukroger, Stephen. *The Emergence of a Scientific Culture: Science and the Shaping of Modernity 1210–1685*. Oxford University Press, 2006.
Gaukroger, Stephen. *The Failures of Philosophy: A Historical Essay*. Princeton University Press, 2020.
Gazzaniga, Michael S. *Who's in Charge?: Free Will and the Science of the Brain*. HarperCollins Publishers, 2011.
Gervais, Will M., and Ara Norenzayan. "Analytic Thinking Promotes Religious Disbelief." *Science* 336, no. 6080 (2012): 493–96. https://doi.org/10.1126/science.1215647.
Ghasemi, Omid, Onurcan Yilmaz, Ozan Isler, Jenny Terry, and Robert M. Ross. "Reflective Thinking Predicts Disbelief in God Across 19 Countries." *Psychonomic Bulletin & Review* 32, no. 4 (2025): 2220–29. https://doi.org/10.3758/s13423-025-02691-9.
Gibson, Eleanor J. "Exploratory Behavior in the Development of Perceiving, Acting, and the Acquiring of Knowledge." *Annual Review of Psychology* 39, no. 1 (1988): 1–41. https://doi.org/10.1146/annurev.ps.39.020188.000245.
Gibson, Eleanor J. *Principles of Perceptual Learning and Development*. Appleton-Century-Crofts, 1969.
Gillespie, Michael Allan. *Nihilism Before Nietzsche*. University of Chicago Press, 1995.
Gilley, Sheridan, and Ann Loades. "Thomas Henry Huxley: The War Between Science and Religion." *The Journal of Religion* 61, no. 3 (1981): 285–308. https://doi.org/10.1086/486872.
Gilson, Étienne. *History of Christian Philosophy in the Middle Ages*. Sheed and Ward, 1980.
Gingerich, Owen. "The Copernican Revolution." In *Science & Religion: A Historical Introduction*, edited by Gary B. Ferngren. Johns Hopkins University Press, 2002.
Gino, Francesca, Shahar Ayal, and Dan Ariely. "Contagion and Differentiation in Unethical Behavior: The Effect of One Bad Apple on the Barrel." *Psychological Science* 20, no. 3 (2009): 393–98. https://doi.org/10.1111/j.1467-9280.2009.02306.x.
Girard, René. "Animal Scapegoating at Çatalhöyük." In *How We Became Human: Mimetic Theory and the Science of Evolutionary Origins*, edited by Pierpaolo Antonello and Paul Gifford. Michigan State University Press, 2015.
Girard, René. *Deceit, Desire, and the Novel: Self and Other in Literary Structure*. Johns Hopkins University Press, 1966.
Girard, René. *The Girard Reader*. Crossroads Publishing Co., 1996.
Girard, René. *The Scapegoat*. Johns Hopkins University Press, 1986.
Giussani, Luigi. *The Religious Sense*. McGill-Queen's University Press, 1997.
Göcke, Benedikt Paul. Introduction to *After Physicalism*, edited by Benedikt Paul Göcke. University of Notre Dame Press, 2012.

Goff, Philip. *Galileo's Error: Foundations for a New Science of Consciousness*. Pantheon Books, 2010.

Gould, Stephen Jay. "Nonoverlapping Magisteria." *Natural History* 106, no. 2 (1997): 16–22. https://doi.org/10.53763/fag.2014.11.95.

Gould, Stephen Jay, and Niles Eldredge, "Punctuated Equilibria: the Tempo and Mode of Evolution Reconsidered." *Paleobiology* 3, no. 2 (1977): 115–51. https://doi.org/10.1017/S0094837300005224.

Gould, Stephen Jay, and Richard Lewontin. "The Spandrels of San Marco and the Panglossian Paradigm: A Critique of the Adaptationist Programme." *Proceedings of the Royal Society London B* 205, no. 1161 (1979): 581–98. http://www.jstor.org/stable/77447.

Graeber, David, and David Wengrow. *The Dawn of Everything: A New History of Humanity*. Farrar, Straus and Giroux, 2021.

Graney, Christopher M. *Setting Aside All Authority: Giovanni Battista Riccioli and the Science Against Copernicus in the Age of Galileo*. Notre Dame University Press, 2015.

Graney, Christopher M. "Stars as the Armies of God: Lansbergen's Incorporation of Tycho Brahe's Star-Size Argument into the Copernican Theory." *Journal for the History of Astronomy* 44, no. 2 (2013): 165–72. https://doi.org/10.1177/002182861304400203.

Greene, Brian. *Until the End of Time: Mind, Matter, and Our Search for Meaning in an Evolving Universe*. Vintage Books, 2021.

Greene, Joshua D. "Beyond Point-and-Shoot Morality: Why Cognitive (Neuro)-Science Matters for Ethics." *Ethics* 124, no. 4 (2014): 695–726. https://doi.org/10.1086/675875.

Greene, Joshua D. "The Cognitive Neuroscience of Moral Judgment and Decision-Making." In *The Cognitive Neurosciences V*, edited by Michael S. Gazzaniga. MIT Press, 2014.

Greene, Joshua, and Jonathan Cohen. "For The Law, Neuroscience Changes Nothing, and Everything." *Philosophical Transactions of the Royal Society B* 359, no. 1451 (2004): 1775–85. https://doi.org/10.1098/rstb.2004.1546.

Greene, Joshua D., Sylvia A. Morelli, Kelly Lowenberg, Leigh E. Nystrom, and Jonathan D. Cohen, "Cognitive Load Selectively Interferes with Utilitarian Moral Judgment." *Cognition* 107, no. 3 (2008): 1144–54. https://doi.org/10.1016/j.cognition.2007.11.004.

Greenway, Tyler S., and Justin L. Barrett. "Evolutionary Developmental Psychology of Children's Religious Beliefs." In *The Oxford Handbook of Evolutionary Psychology and Religion*, edited by James R. Liddle and Todd K. Shackelford. Oxford University Press, 2021.

Griffin, David Ray. *Panentheism and Scientific Naturalism: Rethinking Evil, Morality, Religious Experience, Religious Pluralism, and the Academic Study of Religion*. Process Century Press, 2014.

Griffin, David Ray. *Unsnarling the World-Knot: Consciousness, Freedom, and the Mind-Body Problem*. University of California Press, 1998.

Grossberg, Stephen. "3-D Vision and Figure-Ground Separation by Visual Cortex." *Perception & Psychophysics* 55, no. 1 (1994): 48–121. https://doi.org/10.3758/BF03206880.

Grossberg, Stephen. "Filling-In the Forms: Surface and Boundary Interactions in Visual Cortex." In *Filling-In: From Perceptual Completion to Cortical Reorganization*, edited by Luiz Pessoa and Peter De Weerd. Oxford University Press, 2003.

Grossberg, Stephen, and Gurumurthy Swaminathan. "A Laminar Cortical Model for 3D Perception of Slanted and Curved Surfaces and of 2D Images: Development, Attention, and Bistability." *Vision Research* 44, no. 11 (2004): 1147–87. https://doi.org/10.1016/j.visres.2003.12.009.

Guggisberg, Adrian G., and Anais Mottaz. "Timing and Awareness of Movement Decisions: Does Consciousness Really Come Too Late?" *Frontiers in Human Neuroscience* 7 (2013): 385. https://doi.org/10.3389/fnhum.2013.00385.

Guth, Alan H. "Eternal Inflation and Its Implications." *Journal of Physics A: Mathematical and Theoretical* 40, no. 25 (2007): 6811–26. https://doi.org/10.1088/1751-8113/40/25/S25.

Guth, Alan, and Paul Gabrielsen. "QnAs with Alan Guth." *Proceedings of the National Academy of Sciences of the United States of America* 111, no. 41 (2014): 14640. https://doi.org/10.1073/pnas.1417149111.

Guth, Alan H., David I. Kaiser, and Yasunori Nomura. "Inflationary Paradigm After Planck 2013." *Physics Letters B*, 733 (2023): 112–19. https://doi.org/10.1016/j.physletb.2014.03.020.

Guthrie, R. Dale. *The Nature of Paleolithic Art*. University of Chicago Press, 2005.

Haidt, Jonathan. "The Emotional Dog and Its Rational Tail: A Social Intuitionist Approach to Moral Judgment." *Psychological Review* 108, no. 4 (2001): 814–34. https://doi.org/10.1037/0033-295X.108.4.814.

Haidt, Jonathan. "The New Synthesis in Moral Psychology." *Science* 316, no. 5827 (2007): 998–1002. https://doi.org/10.1126/science.1137651.

Haisch, Bernard. *The God Theory: Universes, Zero-Point Fields, and What's Behind It All*. Weiser Books, 2006.

Hall, Brian K. "Evolutionary Developmental Biology (Evo-Devo): Past, Present, and Future." *Evolution: Education and Outreach* 5, no. 2 (2012): 184–93. https://doi.org/10.1007/s12052-012-0418-x.

Hallett, Mark. "What Does the Brain Know and When Does It Know It?" In Caruso, *Exploring the Illusion of Free Will and Moral Responsibility*.

Hamer, Dean. *The GOD Gene: How Faith Is Hardwired into Our Genes*. Doubleday, 2004.

Hamlin, J. Kiley. "Context-Dependent Social Evaluation in 4.5-Month-old Human Infants: The Role of Domain-General versus Domain-Specific Processes in the Development of Evaluation." *Frontiers in Psychology* 5 (2014): 614. https://doi.org/10.3389/fpsyg.2014.0061442.

Hamlin, J. Kiley. "The Origins of Human Morality: Complex Socio-Moral Evaluations by Preverbal Infants." In *New Frontiers in Social Neuroscience*, edited by Jean Decety and Yves Christen. Springer, 2014. https://doi.org/10.1007/978-3-319-02904-7_10.

Hamlin, J. Kiley, Tomer Ullman, Josh Tenenbaum, Noah Goodman, and Chris Baker. "The Mentalistic Basis of Core Social Cognition: Experiments in Preverbal Infants and a Computational Model." *Developmental Science* 16, no. 2 (2013): 209–26. https://doi.org/10.1111/desc.12017.

Hanby, Michael. *No God, No Science?: Theology, Cosmology, Biology*. Wiley-Blackwell, 2017.

Harris, Sam. *The End of Faith*. W. W. Norton & Co., 2004.

Harris, Sam. *Free Will*. Free Press, 2012.

Harris, Sam. *The Moral Landscape: How Science Can Determine Human Values*. Free Press, 2010.

Hart, David Bentley. *The Beauty of the Infinite*. William B. Eerdmans Publishing Co., 2004.

Hart, David Bentley. "The Devil's March: Creation *ex nihilo*, the Problem of Evil and a Few Dostoyevskian Meditations." In Anderson and Bockmuehl, *Creation ex nihilo*.

Hart, David Bentley. *The Experience of God*. Yale University Press, 2013.

Hartle, J. B., and S. W. Hawking. "Wave Function of the Universe." *Physical Review D* 28, no. 12 (1983): 2960–75. https://doi.org/10.1103/PhysRevD.28.2960.

Hatina, Meir, and Meir Litvak, eds. *Martyrdom and Sacrifice in Islam: Theological, Political and Social Contexts*. I. B. Tauris, 2017.

Haught, John F. *Christianity and Science: Toward a Theology of Nature*. Orbis Books, 2007.

Hawking, Stephen W. *A Brief History of Time: From the Big Bang to Black Holes*. Random House, 1988.

Hawking, S. W. "Chronology Protection Conjecture." *Physical Review D* 46, no. 2 (1992): 603–11. https://doi-org.ezproxy.lib.uh.edu/10.1103/PhysRevD.46.603.

Hawking, Stephen, and Leonard Mlodinow. *The Grand Design*. Random House, 2010.

Hebb, Donald O. *The Organization of Behavior: A Neuropsychological Theory*. Wiley and Sons, 1949.

Heilbron, John L. *Galileo*. Oxford University Press, 2010.

Held, Richard, and Alan Hein. "Movement-Produced Stimulation in the Development of Visually Guided Behavior." *Journal of Comparative and Physiological Psychology* 56, no. 5 (1963): 872–76. https://doi.org/10.1037/h0040546.

Heller, Michael. *The New Physics and New Theology*. Vatican Observatory Foundation, 1996.

Heschel, Abraham J. *The Prophets*. Harper & Row, 1962.

Hiller, Jacob M., and Li-Quin Fan. "Laminar Distribution of the Multiple Opioid Receptors in the Human Cerebral Cortex." *Neurochemical Research* 21, no. 11 (1996): 1333–45. https://doi.org/10.1007/BF02532374.

Hincks, Adam D. "What Does Physical Cosmology Say About Creation from Nothing." In Anderson and Bockmuehl, *Creation ex nihilo*.

Hitchens, Christopher. *God Is Not Great.* Hachette Book Group, 2007.

Hobart, Michael E. *The Great Rift: Literacy, Numeracy, and the Religion-Science Divide.* Harvard University Press, 2018.

Hoffman, Donald D. "Conscious Realism and the Mind-Body Problem." *Mind & Matter* 6, no. 1 (2008): 87–121.

Hoffman, Donald D., and Chetan Prakash. "Objects of Consciousness." *Frontiers of Psychology* 5 (2014): 577. https://doi.org/10.3389/fpsyg.2014.00577.

Hoffman, Donald D., Manish Singh, and Chetan Prakash. "The Interface Theory of Perception." *Psychonomic Bulletin & Review* 22, no. 6 (2015): 1480–1506. https://doi.org/10.3758/s13423-015-0890-8.

Hohmann, A., and O. D. Creutzfeldt. "Squint and the Development of Binocularity in Humans." *Nature* 254, no. 5501 (1975): 613–14. https://doi.org/10.1038/254613a0.

Honderich, Ted. "Determinism, Incompatibilism and Compatibilism, Actual Consciousness and Subjective Physical Worlds, Humanity." In Caruso, *Exploring the Illusion of Free Will and Moral Responsibility.*

Hossenfelder, Sabine. *Existential Physics: A Scientist's Guide to Life's Biggest Questions.* Viking Press, 2022.

Hossenfelder, Sabine. *Lost in Math: How Beauty Leads Physics Astray.* Basic Books, 2020.

Hoyt, Sarah F. "The Etymology of Religion." *Journal of the American Oriental Society* 32, no. 2 (1912): 126–29. https://www.jstor.org/stable/i355419.

Hughson, Thomas, SJ. *Neanderthal Religion? Theology in Dialogue with Archeology.* Wipf & Stock, 2024.

Hume, David. *An Enquiry Concerning Human Understanding.* Hackett Publishing, 1993.

Humphrey, N. K. "Vision in a Monkey Without Striate Cortex: A Case Study." *Perception* 3, no. 3 (1974): 241–55. https://doi.org/10.1068/p030241.

Humphrey, Nicholas. *Soul Dust: The Magic of Consciousness.* Princeton University Press, 2011.

Hunter, Cornelius G. *Darwin's God: Evolution and the Problem of Evil.* Wipf & Stock Publishers, 2001.

Hunter, James Davison, and Paul Nedelisky. *Science and the Good: The Tragic Quest for the Foundations of Morality.* Yale University Press, 2018.

Hurme, Mikko, Mika Koivisto, Antti Revonsuo, and Henry Railo. "Early Processing in Primary Visual Cortex Is Necessary for Conscious and Unconscious Vision While Late Processing Is Necessary only for Conscious Vision in Neurologically Healthy Humans." *Neuroimage* 150 (2017): 230–38. https://doi.org/10.1016/j.neuroimage.2017.02.060.

Husserl, Edmund. *On the Phenomenology of Internal Time-Consciousness.* Indiana University Press, 1964.

Hutchinson, Ian. *Monopolizing Knowledge: A Scientist Refutes Religion-Denying, Reason-Destroying Scientism.* Fias Publishing, 2011.

Hyman, John. *The Objective Eye: Color, Form, and Reality in the Theory of Art.* University of Chicago Press, 2006.
Ijjas, Anna, and Paul J. Steinhardt. "Entropy, Black Holes, and the New Cyclic Universe." *Physics Letters B* 824 (2022): 136823. https://doi.org/10.1016/ j.physletb.2021.136823.
Ijjas, Anna, and Paul J. Steinhardt. "A New Kind of Cyclic Universe." *Physics Letters B* 795 (2019): 666–72. https://doi.org/10.1016/j.physletb.2019.06.056.
Ijjas, Anna, Paul J. Steinhardt, and Abraham Loeb. "Inflationary Paradigm in Trouble After Planck 2013." *Physics Letters B* 723, no. 4–5 (2013): 261–66. https://doi.org/10.1016/j.physletb.2013.05.023.
Ijjas, Anna, Paul J. Steinhardt, and Abraham Loeb. "POP Goes the Universe." *Scientific American* 316, no. 2 (2017): 32–39. https://www.jstor.org/stable/10.2307/26047449.
Irenaeus. *Scandal of the Incarnation: Irenaeus Against the Heresies.* Ignatius Press, 1990.
Irons, William. "Religion as a Hard-to-Fake Sign of Commitment." In *Evolution and the Capacity for Commitment,* edited by Randolph Nesse. Russell Sage Foundation, 2001.
Jablonka, Eva, and Marion J. Lamb. *Evolution in Four Dimensions: Genetic, Epigenetic, Behavioral, and Symbolic Variation in the History of Life.* MIT Press, 2014.
Jack, Anthony I., Abigail J. Dawson, Katelyn L. Begany, Regina L. Leckie, Kevin P. Barry, Angela H. Ciccia, and Abraham Z. Snyder. "fMRI Reveals Reciprocal Inhibition Between Social and Physical Cognitive Domains." *Neuroimage* 66 (2013): 385–401. https://doi.org/10.1016/j.neuroimage.2012.10.061.
Jack, Anthony Ian, Jared Parker Friedman, Richard Eleftherios Boyatzis, and Scott Nolan Taylor. "Why Do You Believe in God? Relationships Between Religious Belief, Analytic Thinking, Mentalizing and Moral Concern." *PLOS ONE* 11, no. 3 (2016): e0155283. https://doi.org/10.1371/journal.pone.0149989.
Jaeger, Werner. *The Theology of the Early Greek Philosophers.* Wipf & Stock, 2003.
Jaki, Stanley L. *God and the Cosmologists.* Regnery Gateway, 1989.
Jaki, Stanley L. *The Origin of Science and the Science of Its Origin.* University of Chicago Press, 1978.
Jaki, Stanley L. *Patterns or Principles and Other Essays.* Intercollegiate Studies Institute, 1995.
Jaki, Stanley L. *The Road of Science and the Ways of God.* University of Chicago Press, 1978.
Jaki, Stanley L. *The Savior of Science.* Regnery Gateway, 1988.
James, William. *The Principles of Psychology.* Dover Publications, 1950.
James, William. *The Varieties of Religious Experience.* Random House, 1936.
Jaspers, Karl. *The Origin and Goal of History.* Routledge, 2021.
Jastrow, Robert. *God and the Astronomers.* Warner Books, 1978.
Jo, Han-Gue, Thilo Hinterberger, Marc Wittmann, and Tilmann Lhündrup Borghardt. "Spontaneous EEG Fluctuations Determine the Readiness Potential: Is

Preconscious Brain Activation a Preparation Process to Move?" *Experimental Brain Research* 231, no. 4 (2003): 495–500. https://doi.org/10.1371/journal.pone.0155283.

Joas, Hans. *The Power of the Sacred: An Alternative to the Narrative of Disenchantment.* Oxford University Press, 2021.

John of the Cross. "The Ascent of Mount Carmel." In *The Collected Works of St. John of the Cross.* Translated by Kieran Kavanaugh and Otilio Rodriguez. Institute of Carmelite Studies, 1991.

Johnson, Dominic. "What Are Atheists for? Hypotheses on the Functions of Non-Belief in the Evolution of Religion." *Religion, Brain & Behavior* 2, no. 1 (2012): 48–99. https://doi.org/10.1080/2153599X.2012.667948.

Joseph, R. "The Limbic System and the Soul: Evolution and the Neuroanatomy of Religious Experience." *Zygon* 36, no. 1 (2001): 105–36. https://doi.org/10.1111/0591-2385.00343.

Julian of Norwich. *Showings.* Paulist Press, 1978.

Kamteka, Rachana. "Situationism and Virtue Ethics on the Content of Our Character." *Ethics* 114, no. 3 (2004): 458–91. https://doi.org/10.1086/381696.

Kant, Immanuel. *Beantwortung der Frage: Was ist Aufklärung?: und andere kleine Schriften.* Henricus-Edition Deutsche Klassik GmbH, 2019.

Kaplan, Grant. *René Girard, Unlikely Apologist: Mimetic Theory and Fundamental Theology.* University of Notre Dame Press, 2016.

Kapogiannis, Dimitrios, Aron K. Barbey, Michael Su, Giovanna Zamboni, Frank Krueger, and Jordan Grafmana. "Cognitive and Neural Foundations of Religious Belief." *Proceedings of the National Academy of Sciences USA* 106, no. 12 (2009): 4876–81. https://doi.org/10.1073/pnas.0811717106.

Kastrup, Bernardo. *The Idea of the World: A Multi-Disciplinary Argument for the Mental Nature of Reality.* Iff Books, 2019.

Keating, Laura. "Un-Locke-ing Boyle: Boyle on Primary and Secondary Qualities." *History of Philosophy Quarterly* 10, no. 4 (1993): 305–23. http://www.jstor.org/stable/27744071.

Kelemen, Deborah. "Are Children 'Intuitive Theists'?: Reasoning About Purpose and Design in Nature." *Psychological Science* 15, no. 5 (2004): 295–301. https://doi.org/10.1111/j.0956-7976.2004.00672.x.

Kelemen, Deborah. "The Scope of Teleological Thinking in Preschool Children." *Cognition* 70, no. 3 (1999): 241–72. https://doi.org/10.1016/S0010-0277(99)00010-4.

Kelemen, Deborah, and Cara DiYanni. "Intuitions About Origins: Purpose and Intelligent Design in Children's Reasoning about Nature." *Journal of Cognition and Development* 6, no. 1 (2004): 3–31. https://doi.org/10.1207s15327647jcd0601_2.

Kierkegaard, Søren. *Fear and Trembling.* Penguin Books, 1989.

Kierkegaard, Søren. *The Sickness unto Death.* Penguin Books, 1986.

Kihlstrom, John F. "Time to Lay the Libet Experiment to Rest: Commentary on Papanicolaou." *Psychology of Consciousness: Theory, Research, and Practice* 4, no. 3 (2017): 324–29. https://doi.org/10.1037/cns0000124.

King, Pamela Ebstyne, and Boyatzis Chris J. "Religious and Spiritual Development." In *Handbook of Child Psychology and Developmental Science: Socioemotional Processes*, vol. 3, edited by Michael E. Lamb and Richard. M. Lerner. John Wiley & Sons, 2015.

King, Ross. *Brunelleschi's Dome: How a Renaissance Genius Reinvented Architecture.* Walker & Co., 2000.

Kinney, William H., Suvashis Maity, and L. Sriramkumar. "Borde-Guth-Vilenkin Theorem in Extended de Sitter Spaces." *Physical Review D* 109, no. 4 (2024): 043519. https://doi.org/10.1103/PhysRevD.109.043519.

Kinney, William H., and Nina K. Stein. "Cyclic Cosmology and Geodesic Completeness." *Journal of Cosmology and Astroparticle Physics* 2022, no. 6 (2022): 1–7. https://doi.org/10.1088/1475-7516/2022/06/011.

Klein, Jürgen, and Guido Giglioni. "Francis Bacon." In *The Stanford Encyclopedia of Philosophy*, edited by Edward N. Zalta. Fall 2020. https://plato.stanford.edu/archives/fall2020/entries/francis-bacon.

Klemm, W. R. "Free Will Debates: Simple Experiments Are Not So Simple." *Advances in Cognitive Psychology* 6 (2010): 47–65. https://doi.org/10.2478/v10053-008-0073-5.

Koch, Christof. *Consciousness: Confessions of a Romantic Reductionist.* MIT Press, 2012.

Kohlberg, Lawrence. *Stages in the Development of Moral Thought and Action.* Holt, Rinehart & Winston, 1969.

Krauss, Lawrence M. *A Universe from Nothing: Why There Is Something Rather Than Nothing.* Free Press, 2012.

Kringelbach, Morten L., and Kent C. Berridge. "A New Understanding of How The Brain Generates Pleasure Could Lead to Better Treatment of Addiction and Depression—and Even to a New Science of Happiness." *Scientific American* 397, no. 2 (2012): 40–45. https://www.jstor.org/stable/26016035.

Kuhn, Thomas S. *The Copernican Revolution: Planetary Astronomy in the Development of Western Thought.* Harvard University Press, 1992.

Lakeland, Paul. *The Wounded Angel: Fiction and the Religious Imagination.* Liturgical Press, 2017.

Laland, Kevin N. *Darwin's Unfinished Symphony: How Culture Made the Human Mind.* Princeton University Press, 2017.

Laland, Kevin N., Jeremy R. Kendall, and Gillian R. Brown. "The Niche Construction Perspective: Implications for Evolution and Human Behavior." *Journal of Evolutionary Psychology* 5, no. 1 (2007): 51–66. https://doi.org/10.1556/jep.2007.1003.

Laland, Kevin N., John Odling-Smee, and Marcus W. Feldman. "Niche Construction, Biological Evolution, and Cultural Change." *Behavioral and Brain Sciences* 23, no. 1 (2000), 131–75. https://doi.org/10.1017/S0140525X00002417.

Laland, Kevin, Tobias Uller, Marc Feldman, et al. "Does Evolutionary Theory Need a Rethink?" *Nature* 514, no. 7521 (2014): 161–64. https://doi.org/10.1038/514161a. This article represents one side of a debate. See also Wray et al. below.

Larson, Greger, Philip A. Stephens, Jamshid J. Tehrani, and Robert H. Layton. "Exapting Exaptation." *Trends in Ecology and Evolution* 28, no. 9 (2013): 497–98. https://doi.org/10.1016/j.tree.2013.05.018.

Leat, Susan J., Naveen K. Yadav, and Elizabeth L. Irving. "Development of Visual Acuity and Contrast Sensitivity in Children." *Journal of Optometry* 2, no. 1 (2009): 19–26. https://doi.org/10.3921/joptom.2009.19.

Lehner, Ulrich L. *The Catholic Enlightenment: The Forgotten History of a Global Movement.* Oxford University Press, 2016.

Leknes , Siri, and Irene Tracey. "A Common Neurobiology for Pain and Pleasure." *Nature Reviews Neuroscience* 9, no. 4 (2008): 314–20. https://doi.org/10.1038/nrn2333.

Lennox, John. *God's Undertaker: Has Science Buried God?* Lion Hudson, 2009.

Lennox, John C. *Gunning for God.* Lion Hudson, 2011.

Lewis, Michael E., Mortimer Mishkin, Evgeni Bragin, Roger M. Brown, Candace B. Pert, and Agu Pert. "Opiate Receptor Gradients in Monkey Cerebral Cortex: Correspondence with Sensory Processing Hierarchies." *Science* 211, no. 4487 (1981): 1166–69. http://www.jstor.org/stable/1685240.

Lewis-Williams, David. *Conceiving God: The Cognitive Origin and Evolution of Religion.* Thames & Hudson, 2010.

Lewis-Williams, David J., and Jean Clottes. "The Mind in the Cave—The Cave in the Mind: Altered Consciousness in the Upper Paleolithic." *Anthropology of Consciousness* 9, no. 1 (1998): 13–21. https://doi.org/10.1525/ac.1998.9.1.13.

Lewis-Williams, David, and David Pearce. *Consciousness, Cosmos and the Realm of the Gods.* Thames & Hudson, 2009.

Lewontin, R. C. *Biology as Ideology: The Doctrine of DNA.* Harper Perennial, 1993.

Lewontin, R. C. "Facts and the Factitious in Natural Sciences." *Critical Inquiry* 18, no. 1 (1991): 40–153. https://doi.org/10.1086/448627.

Libet, Benjamin. "Unconscious Cerebral Initiative and the Role of Conscious Will in Voluntary Action." *Behavioral and Brain Sciences* 8, no. 4 (1985): 529–39. https://doi.org/10.1017/S0140525X00044903.

Libet, Benjamin, Curtis A. Gleason, Elwood W. Wright, and Denis K. Pearl. "Time of Conscious Intention to Act in Relation to Onset of Cerebral Activity (Readiness-Potential)." *Brain* 106 (Pt 3) (1983): 623–42. https://doi.org/10.1093/brain/106.3.623.

Lightman, Bernard. "Victorian Sciences and Religions: Discordant Harmonies." *Osiris* 16 (2001): 343–66. https://www.jstor.org/stable/301992.

Lincoln, Maya, and Avi Wasser. "Spontaneous Creation of the Universe Ex Nihilo." *Physics of the Dark Universe* 2, no. 4 (2013): 195–99. https://doi.org/10.1016/j.dark.2013.11.004.

Lindberg, David C. "Galileo, the Church, and the Cosmos." In *When Science & Christianity Meet,* edited by David C. Lindberg and Ronal L. Numbers. University of Chicago Press, 2003.

Lindberg, David C. "Science and the Early Church." In *God and Nature: Historical Essays on the Encounter Between Christianity and Science*, edited by David C. Lindberg and Ronald L. Numbers. University of California Press, 1986.

List, Christian. *Why Free Will Is Real*. Harvard University Press, 2019.

Locke, John. *An Essay Concerning Human Understanding*. Penguin, 1997.

Logan, Robert K. "The Extended Mind Model of the Origin of Language and Culture." In *Evolutionary Epistemology, Language and Culture*, edited by Nathalie Gontier, Jean Paul van Bendegem, and Diederik Aerts. Springer, 2006.

Lokhorst, Gert-Jan. "Descartes and the Pineal Gland." In *The Stanford Encyclopedia of Philosophy*, edited by Edward N. Zalta. Winter 2021. https://plato.stanford.edu/archives/win2021/entries/pineal-gland.

Lonergan, Bernard. *Insight: A Study into Human Understanding*. University of Toronto Press, 1992.

Lossky, Vladimir. *The Mystical Theology of the Eastern Church*. Crux Press, 2022.

MacIntyre, Alasdair. *After Virtue*. University of Notre Dame Press, 1984.

MacIntyre, Alasdair. *Ethics in the Conflicts of Modernity: An Essay on Desire, Practical Reasoning, and Narrative*. Cambridge University Press, 2016.

MacIntyre, Alasdair. *The Task of Philosophy*. Cambridge University Press, 2006.

MacIntyre, Alasdair. *Three Rival Versions of Moral Enquiry: Encyclopaedia, Genealogy, and Tradition*. University of Notre Dame Press, 1991.

Maoz, Uri, Gideon Yaffe, Christof Koch, and Liad Mudrik. "Neural Precursors of Decisions That Matter—an ERP Study of Deliberate and Arbitrary Choice." *eLife* 8 (2019): e39787. https://doi.org/10.7554/eLife.39787.

Marbach, Eduard. "No Heterophenomenology Without Autophenomenology: Variations on a Theme of Mine." *Phenomenology and the Cognitive Sciences* 6, no. 1 (2007): 75–87.

Maritain, Jacques. *Art and Scholasticism*. Cluny Media, 2020.

Maritain, Jacques. *The Degrees of Knowledge*. University of Notre Dame Press, 1998.

Maritain, Jacques. *The Peasant of the Garone: An Old Layman Questions Himself About the Present Time*. Wipf & Stock, 1968.

Maritain, Jacques. *Science and Wisdom*. Charles Scribner's Sons, 1940.

Marr, David. *Vision: A Computational Investigation into the Human Representation and Processing of Visual Information*. W. H. Freeman, 1982.

Martí, Africa Pitarch, João Zilhão, Francesco d'Errico, et al. "The Symbolic Role of the Underground World among Middle Paleolithic Neanderthals." *Proceedings of the National Academy of Sciences USA* 110, no. 33 (2021): e2021495118. https://doi.org/10.1073/pnas.2021495118.

Mashour, George A., and Michael T. Alkire. "Evolution of Consciousness: Phylogeny, Ontogeny, and Emergence from General Anesthesia." *Proceedings of the National Academy of Sciences USA* 110 (Suppl 2) (2013): 10357–64. https://doi.org/10.1073/pnas.130118811.

McCann, Hugh J. "Getting Scientific About Religion." In *The Future of Atheism: Alister McGrath & Daniel Dennett in Dialogue*, edited by Robert B. Stewart. Fortress Press, 2008.

McCarraher, Eugene. *The Enchantments of Mammon: How Capitalism Became the Religion of Modernity*. Harvard University Press, 2019.

McCauly, Robert N. *Why Religion is Natural and Science Is Not*. Oxford University Press, 2011.

McFarland, Ian A. *From Nothing: A Theology of Creation*. Westminster John Knox Press, 2014.

McGrath, Alister. *The Twilight of Atheism: The Rise and Fall of Disbelief in the Modern World*. Random House, 2006.

McLeish, Tom. *Faith and Wisdom in Science*. Oxford University Press, 2014.

McMullin, Ernan, ed. *The Church and Galileo*. University of Notre Dame Press, 2005.

Mele, Alfred R. *Free: Why Science Hasn't Disproved Free Will*. Oxford University Press, 2014.

Meristo, Marek, and Luca Surian. "Infants Distinguish Antisocial Actions Directed Towards Fair and Unfair Agents." *PLOS ONE* 9, no. 10 (2014): e110553. https://doi.org/10.1371/journal.pone.0110553.

Merritt, Maria. "Virtue Ethics and Situationist Personality Psychology." *Ethical Theory and Moral Practice* 3, no. 43 (2000): 65–83. https://doi.org/10.1023/A:1009926720584.

Meyer, Stephen C. *Return of the God Hypothesis: Three Scientific Discoveries That Reveal the Mind Behind the Universe*. HarperCollins, 2021.

Micelli, Vincent. *The Gods of Atheism*. Sophia Institute Press, 2022.

Midgley, Mary. *Evolution as a Religion: Strange Hopes and Stranger Fears*. Routledge, 1985.

Midgley, Mary. *Science as Salvation: A Modern Myth and Its Meaning*. Routledge, 1994.

Miller, Alexander. "Realism." In *The Stanford Encyclopedia of Philosophy*, edited by Edward N. Zalta. Winter 2021. https://plato.stanford.edu/archives/win2021/entries/realism.

Miller, Christian. "Social Psychology, Mood, and Helping: Mixed Results for Virtue Ethics." *Journal of Ethics* 13, no. 2 (2009): 145–73. https://doi.org/10.1007/s10892-009-9046-2.

Miller, Jeff, Peter Shepherdson, and Judy Trevena. "Effects of Clock Monitoring on Electroencephalographic Activity: Is Unconscious Movement Initiation an Artifact of the Clock?" *Psychological Science* 22, no. 1 (2011): 103–9. https://doi.org/10.1177/0956797610391100.

Miller, Mark T. *The Quest for God and the Good Life: Lonergan's Theological Anthropology*. Catholic University of America Press, 2013.

Minguzzi, Ettore. "Augustine of Hippo's Philosophy of Time Meets General Relativity." *Kronoscope* 14 (2014): 71–89. https://doi.org/10.1163/15685241-12341292.

Minguzzi, Ettore. "Chronology Violations and the Origin of Time." *The European Physical Journal Conferences* 88 (2013): 01003. https://doi.org/10.1051/epjconf/20135801003.

Mitchell, Michael B. *Truth Before Logic: Finding Wisdom with G. K. Chesterton in a World Blinkered by Scientism*. Wipf & Stock, 2024.

Mobbs, Dean, and Caroline Watt. "There Is Nothing Paranormal About Near-Death Experiences: How Neuroscience Can Explain Seeing Bright Lights, Meeting the Dead, or Being Convinced You Are One of Them." *Trends in Cognitive Sciences* 15, no. 10 (2011): 447–49. https://doi.org/10.1016/j.tics.2011.07.010.

Monod, Jacques, *Chance and Necessity: An Essay on the Natural Philosophy of Modern Biology*. Alfred A. Knopf, 1971.

Mooney, Christopher F., SJ. *Theology and Scientific Knowledge: Changing Models of God's Presence in the World*. University of Notre Dame Press, 1996.

Moore, G. E. *Principia Ethica*. Dover Publications, 2004.

Moore, M. Keith, Richard Borton, and Betty Lee Darby. "Visual Tracking in Young Infants: Evidence for Object Identity or Object Permanence?" *Journal of Experimental Child Psychology* 25, no. 2 (1978): 183–98. https://doi.org/10.1016/0022-0965(78)90076-0.

Moreland, J. P. *Consciousness and the Existence of God: A Theistic Argument*. Routledge, 2008.

Morsella, E. "The Function of Phenomenal States: Supramodular Interaction Theory." *Psychological Review* 112, no. 4 (2005): 1000–1021. https://doi.org/10.1037/0033-295X.112.4.1000.

Morsella, Ezequiel, Stephen C. Krieger, Sergio Rizzo-Fontanesi, and John A. Bargh. "The Primary Function of Consciousness in the Nervous System." *Annual Review of Biomedical Sciences* 9 (2007): 37–40. https://doi.org/http://dx.doi.org/10.5016/1806-8774.2007v9p37.

Mostert, Christiaan. *God and the Future: Wolfhart Pannenberg's Eschatological Doctrine of God*. Bloomsbury, 2002.

Moutoussis, Konstantinos. "Asynchrony in Visual Consciousness and the Possible Involvement of Attention." *Frontiers in Psychology* 3 (2012): 314. https://doi.org/10.3389/fpsyg.2012.00314.

Moutoussis, Konstantinos, and Semir Zeki. "Functional Segregation and Temporal Hierarchy of the Visual Perceptive Systems." *Proceedings: Biological Sciences* 264, no. 1387 (1997): 1407–14. http://www.jstor.org/stable/51041.

Nagel, Thomas. *The Last Word*. Oxford University Press, 1997.

Nagel, Thomas. *The View from Nowhere*. Oxford University Press, 1986.

Nagel, Thomas. "What Is It Like to Be a Bat?" *The Philosophical Review* 83, no. 4 (1974): 435–50. https://doi.org/10.2307/2183914.

Nassif Cruz, Cláudio, and Fernando Antônio da Silva. "Cosmology of the Symmetrical Relativity Versus Spontaneous Creation of the Universe Ex Nihilo." *Physics of the Dark Universe* 28 (2020): 1–15. https://doi.org/10.1016/j.dark.2020.100525.

Natsoulas, Thomas. "Residual Subjectivity." *American Psychologist* 33, no. 3 (1978): 269–83. https://doi.org/10.1037/0003-066X.33.3.269.

Nesteruk, A. V. "The 'Hard Problem' of Consciousness Elucidated Cosmologically: The Saturated Phenomenality of the Universe Versus Its Object-like Constitution." In *Consciousness and Matter: Mind, Brain, and Cosmos in the Dialogue Between Science and Theology*, edited by Kirill Kopeikin and Alexei V. Nesteruk. Wipf & Stock, 2024.

Newberg, Andrew B. "The Neuroscientific Study of Spiritual Practices." *Frontiers in Psychology* 5 (2014): 215. https://doi.org/10.3389/fpsyg.2014.00215.

Nietzsche, Friedrich. *The Gay Science*. Vintage Books, 1974.

Nietzsche, Friedrich. *Human, All Too Human*. Cambridge University Press, 1986.

Nietzsche, Friedrich. *On the Genealogy of Morals: A Polemic*. Oxford University Press, 1996.

Nietzsche, Friedrich. *The Will to Power*. Vintage Books, 1966.

Noë, Alvin. *Out of Our Heads: Why You Are Not Your Brain, and Other Lessons from the Biology of Consciousness*. Hill and Wang, 2009.

Nogbri, Brent. *Before Religion: A History of a Modern Concept*. Yale University Press, 2013.

Nolan, Lawrence, ed. *Primary & Secondary Qualities: The Historical and Ongoing Debate*. Oxford University Press, 2011.

Norenzayan, Ara. *Big Gods: How Religion Transformed Cooperation and Conflict*. Princeton University Press, 2013.

Norenzayan, Ara, and Will M. Gervais. "The Origins of Religious Disbelief." *Trends in Cognitive Sciences* 17, no. 1 (2013): 20–25. https://doi.org/10.1016/j.tics.2012.11.006.

Norenzayan, Ara, Azim F. Shariff, Will M. Gervais, Aiyana K. Willard, Rita A. McNamara, Edward Slingerland, and Joseph Henrich. "The Cultural Evolution of Prosocial Religions." *Behavioral and Brain Sciences* 39 (2016): e1. https://doi.org/10.1017/S0140525X14001356.

Numbers, Ronald L., ed., *Galileo Goes to Jail: And Other Myths About Science and Religion*. Harvard University Press, 2009.

Oakley, David A., and Peter W. Halligan. "Chasing the Rainbow: The Non-Conscious Nature of Being." *Frontiers in Psychology* 8 (2017): 1924. https://doi.org/10.3389/fpsyg.2017.019.

O'Regan, J. Kevin. *Why Red Doesn't Sound Like a Bell: Understanding the Feel of Consciousness*. Oxford University Press, 2011.

Ortiz Hill, Claire. *The Roots and Flowers of Evil in Baudelaire, Nietzsche, and Hitler*. Open Court, 2006.

Osborn, Ronald C. *Humanism and the Death of God: Searching for the Good After Darwin, Marx, and Nietzsche*. Oxford University Press, 2017.

Ostler, Teresa. "Heinz Werner: His Life, Ideas, and Contributions to Developmental Psychology in the First Half of the 20th Century." *The Journal of Genetic Psychology* 177, no. 6 (2016): 231–43. https://doi.org/10.1080/00221325.2016.1245520.

Otto, Rudolf. *The Idea of the Holy*. Oxford University Press, 1958.

Oviedo, Luis. "'Self-Organizing Personhood' and Many Loose Ends." In *Verbs, Bones, and Brains*, edited by Augustín Fuentes and Aku Visala. University of Notre Dame Press, 2017.

Page, Don N. "Susskind's Challenge to the Hartle–Hawking No-Boundary Proposal and Possible Resolutions." *Journal of Cosmology and Astroparticle Physics* 2007 (2007): 2–20. https://doi.org/10.1088/1475-7516/2007/01/004.

Pannenberg, Wolfhart. *Toward a Theology of Nature: Essays on Science and Faith.* Westminster John Knox Press, 1993.

Papanicolaou, Andrew C. "The Myth of the Neuroscience of Will." *Psychology of Consciousness: Theory, Research, and Practice* 4, no. 3 (2017): 310–20. https://doi.org/10.1037/cns0000116.

Pascal, Blaise. *Pensées*. Penguin Books, 1966.

Paxton, Joseph M., Leo Ungar, and Jonathan D. Greene. "Reflection and Reasoning in Moral Judgment." *Cognitive Science* 36, no. 1 (2012): 163–77. https://doi.org/10.1111/j.1551-6709.2011.01210.x.

Peacocke, Arthur. *Theology for a Scientific Age: Being and Becoming—Natural, Divine, and Human*. Fortress Press, 1993.

Pederson, Olaf. *Two Books: Historical Notes on Some Interactions Between Natural Science and Theology*. Vatican Observatory Foundation, 2007.

Pendergast, Richard J. *The Cosmic Hierarchy: God's Plan for the Evolution of the Universe.* Crossroad Publishing Co., 2020.

Penfield, Wilder, and Phanor Perot. "The Brain's Record of Auditory and Visual Experience: A Final Summary and Discussion." *Brain* 86, no. 4 (1963): 595–696. https://doi.org/10.1093/brain/86.4.595.

Penrose, Roger. *Cycles of Time: An Extraordinary New View of the Universe.* Vintage Books, 2012.

Penrose, Roger. *Fashion, Faith, and Fantasy in the New Physics and Beyond.* Princeton University Press, 2016.

Peoples, Hervey C., Pavel Duda, and Frank W. Marlowe. "Hunter-Gatherers and the Origin of Religion." *Human Nature* 27, no. 3 (2016): 261–82. https://doi.org/10.1007/s12110-016-9260-0.

Phillips, William L. "Cross-Cultural Differences in Visual Perception of Color, Illusions, Depth, and Pictures." In *Cross-Cultural Psychology: Contemporary Themes and Perspectives*, edited by Kenneth D. Keith. Wiley-Blackwell, 2019.

Pike, A. W., D. L. Hoffmann, M. García-Diez, et al. "U-series Dating of Paleolithic Art in 11 Caves in Spain." *Science* 336, no. 6087 (2012): 1409–13. https://doi.org/10.1126/science.121995.

Pinker, Steven. *Enlightenment Now: The Case for Reason, Science, Humanism, and Progress*. Viking Press, 2018.

Pinker, Steven. "Science Is Not Your Enemy: A Plea for an Intellectual Truce." *The New Republic*, August 6, 2013.

Pockett, Susan. "If Free Will Did Not Exist, It Would Be Necessary to Invent It." In Caruso, *Exploring the Illusion of Free Will and Moral Responsibility*.

Poehlman, T. Andrew, Tiffany K. Jantz, and Ezequiel Morsella, "Adaptive Skeletal Muscle Action Requires Anticipation and 'Conscious Broadcasting,'" *Frontiers in Psychology* 3 (2012): 369. https://doi.org/10.3389/fpsyg.2012.00369.

Pohling, Rico, and Rhett Diessner. "Moral Elevation and Moral Beauty: A Review of the Empirical Literature." *Review of General Psychology* 20, no. 4 (2016): 412–25. https://doi.org/10.1037/gpr0000089.

Polanyi, Michael. *Personal Knowledge: Towards a Post-Critical Philosophy*. University of Chicago Press, 1958.

Polanyi, Michael. *The Tacit Dimension*. Doubleday, 1966.

Polanyi, Michael, and Harry Prosch. *Meaning*. University of Chicago Press, 1975.

Polkinghorne, John. *One World: The Interaction of Science and Theology*. Princeton University Press, 1986.

Polkinghorne, John. *Theology in the Context of Science*. Yale University Press, 2009.

Popper, Karl R. *Conjectures and Refutations*. Routledge, 1972.

Popper, Karl R. *Objective Knowledge: An Evolutionary Approach*. Oxford University Press, 1979.

Popper, Karl R., and John C. Eccles. *The Self and Its Brain: An Argument for Interactionism*. Springer, 1977.

Powell, Lynda H., Lila Shahabi, and Carl E. Thoresen. "Religion and Spirituality: Linkages to Physical Health." *American Psychologist* 58, no. 1 (2003): 36–52. http://dx.doi.org.ezproxy.lib.uh.edu/10.1037/0003-066X.58.1.36.

Prakash, Chetan, Kyle D. Stephens, Donald D. Hoffman, Manish Singh, and Chris Fields. "Fitness Beats Truth in the Evolution of Perception." *Acta Biotheoretica* 69, no. 3 (2021): 319–41. https://doi.org/10.1007/s10441-020-09400-0.

Previc, Fred H. "The Role of the Extrapersonal Brain Systems in Religious Activity." *Consciousness and Cognition* 15, no. 3 (2006): 500–539. https://doi.org/10.1016/j.concog.2005.09.009.

Priest, Stephen. "The Unconditioned Soul." In *After Physicalism*, edited by Benedikt Paul Göcke. University of Notre Dame Press, 2012.

Putnam, Hillary. "The Depths and Shallows of Experience." In Proctor, *Science, Religion and the Human Experience*.

Pyysiäinen, Ilkka. "The Cognitive Science of Religion." In *Evolution, Religion, and Cognitive Science: Critical & Constructive Essays*, edited by Fraser Watts and Léon Turner. Oxford University Press, 2014.

Pyysiäinen, Ilkka, and Marc Hauser. "The Origins of Religion: Evolved Adaptation or By-Product?" *Trends in Cognitive Sciences* 14, no. 3 (2010): 104–9. https://doi.org/10.1016/j.tics.2009.12.007.

Quiroga, R. Quian, G. Kreiman, C. Koch, and I. Fried. "Sparse but Not 'Grandmother-Cell' Coding in the Medial Temporal Lobe." *Trends in Cognitive Sciences* 12, no. 3 (2008): 87–91. https://doi.org/10.1016/j.tics2007.12.003.

Raatikainen, Panu. "Gödel's Incompleteness Theorems." In *The Stanford Encyclopedia of Philosophy*, edited by Edward N. Zalta. Spring 2022. https://plato.stanford.edu/archives/spr2022/entries/goedel-incompleteness.

Radnitzky, G., and W. W. Bartley, III, eds. *Evolutionary Epistemology, Rationality, and the Sociology of Knowledge*. Open Court, 1987.

Ramachandran, Vilayanur S. Foreword to Pessoa and De Weerd, *Filling-In: From Perceptual Completion to Cortical Reorganization*.

Ramachandran, V. S., and R. L. Gregory. "Perceptual Filling in of Artificially Induced Scotomas in Human Vision." *Nature* 350, no. 6320 (1991): 699–702. https://doi.org/10.1038/350699a0.

Ramachandran, Vilayanur S., and William Hirstein. "The Science of Art: A Neurological Theory of Aesthetic Experience." *Journal of Consciousness Studies* 6, no. 6–7 (1999): 15–51.

Rand, Ayn. *The Virtue of Selfishness*. Signet Classics, 1963.

Raymo, Chet. *When God Is Gone Everything Is Holy: The Making of a Religious Naturalist*. Sorin Books, 2008.

Rees, Martin. *On the Future: Prospects for Humanity*. Princeton University Press, 2018.

Reid, Thomas. *An Inquiry into the Human Mind on the Principles of Common Sense*. Edinburgh University Press, 1997.

Renfrew, Colin, and Michael J. Boyd, eds. *Death Rituals, Social Order and the Archeology of Immortality in the Ancient World: "Death Shall Have No Dominion."* Cambridge University Press, 2016.

Revonsuo, Antti. *Inner Presence: Consciousness as a Biological Phenomenon*. MIT Press, 2006.

Richard, Jocelyn M., Daniel C. Castro, Alexandra G. DiFeliceantonio, Mike J. F. Robinson, and Kent C. Berridge. "Mapping Brain Circuits of Reward and Motivation: In the Footsteps of Ann Kelley." *Neuroscience and Biobehavioral Reviews* 37, no. 9/Pt A (2013): 1919–31. https://doi.org/10.1016/j.neubiorev.2012.12.008.

Richardson, Robert C. *Evolutionary Psychology as Maladapted Psychology*. MIT Press, 2007.

Richerson, Peter J., Robert Boyd, and Joseph Henrich. "Gene-Culture Coevolution in the Age of Genomics." *Proceedings of the National Academy of Sciences USA* 107 (Suppl 2) (2010): 8985–92. https://doi.org/10.1073/pnas.0914631 10.

Robinson, Daniel N. *Consciousness and Mental Life*. Columbia University Press, 2008.

Robinson, Daniel N. *Praise and Blame: Moral Realism and Its Applications*. Princeton University Press, 2002.

Robinson, Daniel. "Still Looking: Science and Philosophy in Pursuit of Prince Reason." In *Neuroscience & Philosophy: Brain, Mind, & Language*, edited by Maxwell Bennett, Daniel Dennett, Peter Hacker, and John Searle. Columbia University Press, 2007.

Robinson, Howard. "Qualia, Qualities, and Our Conception of the Physical World." In *After Physicalism*, edited by Benedikt Paul Göcke. University of Notre Dame Press, 2012.

Robinson, Marilyn. *The Death of Adam: Essays on Modern Thought*. Picador, 2005.

Rochat, Phillipe. "Five Levels of Self-Awareness as They Unfold Early in Life." *Consciousness and Cognition* 12, no. 4 (2003): 717–31. https://doi.org/10.1016/S1053-8100(03)00081-3.

Rochat, Phillipe, and Tricia Striano. "Perceived Self in Infancy." *Infant Behavior & Development* 23, no. 3 (2000): 513–30. https://doi.org/10.1016/S0163-6383(01)00055-8.

Roche, Mark William. *Beautiful Ugliness: Christianity, Modernity, and the Arts*. University of Notre Dame Press, 2023.

Rodríguez-Hidalgo, Antonio, Juan Ignacio Morales, Artur Cebrià, et al. "The Châtelperronian Neanderthals of Cova Foradada (Calafell, Spain) Used Imperial Eagle Phalanges for Symbolic Purposes." *Science Advances* 5, no. 11 (2019): eaax1984. https://doi.org/10.1126/sciadv.aax1984.

Rorty, Richard. *Philosophy and the Mirror of Nature*. Princeton University Press, 1979.

Rosenberg, Alex. *The Atheist's Guide to Reality: Enjoying Life Without Illusions*. W. W. Norton & Co., 2011.

Rossano, Matt. "The African Interregnum: The 'Where,' 'When,' and 'Why' of the Evolution of Religion." In *The Biological Evolution of Religious Mind and Behavior*, edited by Eckart Voland and Wulf Schiefenhövel. Springer, 2009. https://doi.org/10.1007/978-3-642-00128-4_9.

Rossano, Matt J. *Supernatural Selection: How Religion Evolved*. Oxford University Press, 2010.

Rossano, Matt J. "Supernaturalizing Social Life: Religion and the Evolution of Human Cooperation." *Human Nature* 18, no. 3 (2007): 272–94. https://doi.org/10.1007/s12110-007-9002-4.

Rovelli, Carlo. *The Order of Time*. Riverhead Books, 2018.

Rowland, Wade. *Galileo's Mistake: A New Look at the Epic Confrontation Between Galileo and the Church*. Arcade Publishing, 2003.

Rowthorn, Robert. "Religion, Fertility and Genes: A Dual Inheritance Model." *Proceedings of the Royal Society B* 278, no. 1717 (2911): 2519–27. https://doi.org/10.1098/rspb.2010.2504.

Rubin, Charles T. *Eclipse of Man: Human Extinction and the Meaning of Progress*. New Atlantis, 2014.

Ruse, Michael. *Darwinism as Religion: What Literature Tells Us About Evolution*. Oxford University Press, 2016.

Russell, Luke. *Evil: A Very Short Introduction*. Oxford University Press, 2022.

Russell, Robert John, Nancy Murphy, and C. J. Isham, eds. *Quantum Cosmology and the Laws of Nature: Scientific Perspectives on Divine Action*. Vatican Observatory Foundation, 1993.

Ryle, Gilbert. *The Concept of Mind*. University of Chicago Press, 2000.

Sacks, Jonathan. *Not in God's Name: Confronting Religious Violence*. Schocken Books, 2015.

Santayana, George. *The Sense of Beauty*. Dover Publications, 1955.

Schaler, Jeffrey A. *Peter Singer Under Fire: The Moral Iconoclast Faces His Critics*. Open Court, 2009.

Schellenberg, Susanna. "Experience and Evidence." *Mind* 122, no. 487 (2013): 699–747. https://doi.org/10.1093/mind/fzt088.

Schmidt, Klaus. *Sie Bauten die Ersten Tempel: Das Rätselhafte Heiligtum der Steinzeitjäger*. Verlag C. H. Beck, 2006.

Schneegans, S., T. Straza, and J. Lewis, eds. *UNESCO Science Report: The Race Against Time for Smarter Development*. UNESCO Publishing, 2021.

Schweizer, Bernard. *Hating God: The Untold Story of Misotheism*. Oxford University Press, 2011.

Scotti, Dom Pascal. *Galileo Revisited: The Galileo Affair in Context*. Ignatius Press, 2017.

Searle, John R. "Consciousness." *Annual Review of Neuroscience* 23, no. 1 (2000): 557–78. https://doi.org/10.1146/annurev.neuro.23.1.557.

Searle, John. "Theory of Mind and Darwin's Legacy." *Proceedings of the National Academy of Sciences USA* 110 (Suppl 2) (2013): 10343–48. https://doi.org/10.1073/pnas.1301214110.

Segall, Marshall H., Donald T. Campbell, and Melville J. Herskovits. *The Influence of Culture on Visual Perception*. Bobbs-Merrill, 1966.

Shanahan, Murray. *The Technological Singularity*. MIT Press, 2015.

Shapiro, Lawrence, and Shannon Spaulding. "Embodied Cognition." In *The Stanford Encyclopedia of Philosophy*, edited by Edward N. Zalta & Uri Nodelman. Fall 2024. https://plato.stanford.edu/archives/fall2024/entries/embodied-cognition.

Shea, William R. "Galileo and the Church." In Lindberg and Numbers, *God & Nature: Historical Essays on the Encounter Between Christianity and Science*.

Shea, William R., and Mariano Artigas. *Galileo in Rome: The Rise and Fall of a Troublesome Genius*. Oxford University Press, 2003.

Shenhav, Amitai, David G. Rand, and Joshua D. Greene. "Divine Intuition: Cognitive Style Influences Belief in God." *Journal of Experimental Psychology: General* 141, no. 3 (2012): 423–28. https://doi.org/10.1037/a0025391.

Silva, Ignacio. "John Polkinghorne on Divine Action: A Coherent Theological Evolution." *Science and Christian Belief* 24, no. 1 (2012): 19–30.

Silverstein, Michael. "In Defense of Ontological Emergence and Mental Causation." In *The Re-Emergence of Emergence: The Emergentist Hypothesis from Science to Religion*, edited by Philip Clayton and Paul Davies. Oxford University Press, 2006.

Skinner, B. F. *Beyond Freedom & Dignity*. Alfred A. Knopf, 1972.

Skottun, B. C. "A Few Remarks on 'Uncrowding' in Visual Stimuli." *PsyArXiv* (2021). https://doi.org/10.31234/osf.io/rp5bd.

Skottun, B. C. "Interference in Tilt-Illusion Stimuli: A Simple Illustration." *PsyArXiv* (2020). https://doi.org/10.31234/osf.io/qw3dt.

Skottun, B. C. "Is the Tilt-Illusion in the Stimuli?" *PsyArXiv* (2018). https://doi.org/10.31234/osf.io/mwxvd.

Skottun, B. C. "What Is a Visual Stimulus?" *PsyArXiv* (2021). https://doi.org/10.31234/osf.io/3tfnq.

Slingerland, Edward. *What Science Offers the Humanities: Integrating Body and Culture*. Cambridge University Press, 2008.

Smart, J. J. C., and J. J. Haldane. *Atheism and Theism*, 2nd ed. Blackwell Publishing, 2003.

Smith, Barbara Herrnstein. *Natural Reflections: Human Cognition at the Nexus of Science and Religion*. Yale University Press, 2009.

Smolin, Lee. *Einstein's Unfinished Revolution: The Search for What Lies beyond the Quantum*. Penguin Press, 2019.

Smolin, Lee. *The Life of the Cosmos*. Oxford University Press, 1997.

Smolin, Lee. *Time Reborn: From the Crisis in Physics to the Future of the Universe*. Mariner Books, 2013.

Smolin, Lee. *The Trouble with Physics: The Rise of String Theory, The Fall of a Science, and What Comes Next*. Houghton Mifflin & Co., 2007.

Snow, Charles P. *The Two Cultures and the Scientific Revolution*. Cambridge University Press, 1959.

Soloviev, Vladimir Sergeyevich. *The Heart of Reality: Essays on Beauty, Love, and Ethics*. University of Notre Dame Press, 2003.

Sommers, Tamler, and Alex Rosenberg. "Darwin's Nihilistic Idea: Evolution and the Meaninglessness of Life." *Biology and Philosophy* 18, no. 5 (2003): 653–68. https://doi.org/10.1023/A:1026311011245.

Soon, Chung Sion, Marcel Brass, Hans-Jochen Heinze, and John-Dylon Haynes. "Unconscious Determinants of Free Decisions in the Human Brain." *Nature Neuroscience* 11, no. 5 (2008): 543–45. https://doi.org/10.1038/nn.2112.

Sosis, Richard. "The Adaptationist-Byproduct Debate on the Evolution of Religion: Five Misunderstandings of the Adaptationist Program." *Journal of Cognition and Culture* 9, no. 3 (2009): 315–33. https://doi.org/10.1163/156770909X12518536414411.

Sosis, Richard, and Jordan Kiper. "Religion Is More Than Belief: What Evolutionary Theories of Religion Tell Us About Religious Commitments." In *Disagreement and Evolution*, edited by Michael Bergmann and Patrick Kain. Oxford University Press, 2014.

Soskice, Janet. "Why *Creatio ex nihilo* for Theology Today?" In Anderson and Bockmuehl, *Creation ex nihilo*, 2018.

Sperry, R. W. "The Problem of Central Nervous Reorganization After Nerve Regeneration and Muscle Transposition." *The Quarterly Review of Biology* 20, no. 4 (1945): 311–69. https://www.jstor.org/stable/2809110.

Spitzer, Robert J. *Evidence for God from Physics and Philosophy: Extending the Legacy of Monsignor Georges Lemaitre and St. Thomas Aquinas*. St. Augustine Press, 2016.

Spitzer, Robert J. *New Proofs for the Existence of God*. William B. Eerdmans Publishing, 2010.

Sreenivasan, Gopal. "Errors About Errors: Virtue Theory and Trait Attribution." *Mind* 111, no. 441 (2002): 47–68. https://doi.org/10.1093/mind/111.441.47.

Stark, Rodney. *Discovering God: The Origins of the Great Religions and the Evolution of Belief*. HarperCollins Publishers, 2007.

Steane, Andrew. *Faithful to Science: The Role of Science in Religion*. Oxford University Press, 2014.

Stenger, Victor J. *God: The Failed Hypothesis*. Prometheus Books, 2007.

Stewart, Ian. *Why Beauty Is Truth*. Basic Books, 2008.

Stich, Stephen. *From Folk Psychology to Cognitive Science: The Case Against Belief*. MIT Press, 1983.

Strawson, Galen. "Realistic Monism: Why Physicalism Entails Panpsychism." In *Consciousness and its Place in Nature: Does Physicalism Entail Panpsychism?*, edited by Anthony Freeman. Imprint Academic, 2006.

Striemer, Christopher L., Craig S. Chapman, and Melvyn A. Goodale. "'Real-time' Obstacle Avoidance in the Absence of Primary Visual Cortex." *Proceedings of the National Academy of Sciences USA* 106, no. 37 (2009): 15996–16001. https://doi.org/10.1073/pnas.0905549106.

Susskind, Leonard. *The Cosmic Landscape: String Theory and the Illusion of Intelligent Design*. Little, Brown & Co., 2005.

Suter, Renata S., and Ralph Hertwig. "Time and Moral Judgment." *Cognition* 119, no. 3 (2011): 454–58. https://doi.org/10.1016/j.cognition.2011.01.018.

Tallis, Raymond. *Aping Mankind: Neuromania, Darwinitis and the Misrepresentation of Humanity*. Acumen, 2011.

Tarlow, Sarah, and Liv Nilsson Stutz, eds. *The Oxford Handbook of the Archaeology of Death and Burial*. Oxford University Press, 2013.

Tartaglia, Angelo. *A Physicist's Journey Between Science and Faith: Friends or Foes?* Cambridge Scholars Publishing, 2023.

Taylor, Charles. *A Secular Age*. Harvard University Press, 2007.

Taylor, Mark C. *Intervolution: Smart Bodies. Smart Things*. Columbia University Press, 2021.

Teilhard de Chardin, Pierre. *The Future of Man*. Harper & Row, 1964.

Teilhard de Chardin, Pierre. *The Phenomenon of Man*. Harper Collins, 1976.

Teresa of Avila. *The Way of Perfection*. Cosimo Classics, 2007.

Tett, Robert P., and Hal A. Guterman. "Situation Trait Relevance, Trait Expression, and Cross-Situational Consistency: Testing a Principle of Trait Activation." *Journal of Research in Personality* 34, no. 4 (2000): 397–423. https://doi.org/10.1006/jrpe.2000.2292.

Thurman, Howard. *Temptations of Jesus*. Friends United Press, 1978.

Tinbergen, Niko. *The Herring Gull's World*. Collins, 1953.

Tooby, John, and Lea Cosmides. "Conceptual Foundations of Evolutionary Psychology." In *The Handbook of Evolutionary Psychology*, edited by David M. Buss. John Wiley & Sons, 2005.

Toulmin, Stephen. *Cosmopolis: The Hidden Agenda of Modernity*. University of Chicago Press, 1990.

Toulmin, Stephen. *Return to Reason*. Harvard University Press, 2001.

Townsend, Mark, Virginia Kladder, Hana Ayele, and Thomas Mulligan. "Systematic Review of Clinical Trials Examining the Effects of Religion on Health." *Southern Medical Journal* 95, no. 12 (2002): 1429–34. https://doi.org/10.1097/00007611-200212000-00015.

Toyabe, Shoichi, Takahiro Sagawa, Masahito Ueda, Eiro Muneyuki, and Masaki Sano. "Experimental Demonstration of Information-to-Energy Conversion and Validation of the Generalized Jarzynski Equality." *Nature Physics* 6, no. 12 (2010): 988–92. https://doi.org/10.1038/nphys1821.

Tribus, Myron, and Edward C. McIrvine. "Source Energy and Information." *Scientific American* 225, no. 3 (1971): 179–90. https://www.jstor.org/stable/10.2307/24923125.

Trimble, Walker. "Seed and Law: Neuroscience and Virtue Ethics in Christian Anthropology." In Kopeikin and Nesteruk, *Consciousness and Matter: Mind, Brain, and Cosmos in the Dialogue Between Science and Theology.*

Tripp, Alison, Genevieve von Petzinger, and Amanda Cooke. "Art, Paleolithic." In *Encyclopedia of Global Archaeology*, vol. 1, edited by Claire Smith. Springer, 2018. https://doi.org/10.1007/978-3-319-51726-1_657-2.

Tse, Peter Ulric. *The Neural Basis of Free Will: Criterial Causations.* MIT Press, 2013.

Tse, Peter Ulric. *A Neurophilosophy of Libertarian Free Will.* Oxford University Press, 2024.

Turner, Frank Miller. *Between Science and Religion: The Reaction to Scientific Naturalism in Late Victorian England.* Yale University Press, 1974.

Turner, Frederick. *Beauty: The Value of Values.* University of Virginia Press, 1991.

Udías, Agustín. *Jesuit Contribution to Science: A History.* Springer, 2014.

Underwood, Bill, and Bert Moore. "Perspective-Taking and Altruism." *Psychological Bulletin* 91, no. 1 (1982): 143–73. https://doi.org/10.1037/0033-2909.91.1.143.

Underwood, Lynn G. "Ordinary Spiritual Experience: Qualitative Research, Interpretive Guidelines, and Population Distribution for the Daily Spiritual Experience Scale." *Archiv für Religionspsychologie/Archive for the Psychology of Religion* 28, no. 1 (2006): 181–218. https://doi.org/10.1163/008467206777832562.

Unger, Roberto Mangabeira. *The Religion of the Future.* Verso, 2016.

Unger, Roberto Mangabeira, and Lee Smolin. *The Singular Universe and the Reality of Time: A Proposal in Natural Philosophy.* Cambridge University Press, 2015.

Urgesi, Cosimo, Salvatore M. Aglioti, Miran Skrap, and Franco Fabbro. "The Spiritual Brain: Selective Cortical Lesions Modulate Human Self-Transcendence." *Neuron* 65, no. 3 (2010): 309–19. https://doi.org/10.1016/j.neuron.2010.01.026.

Valsiner, Jaan. "Heinz Werner: A Differentiation Theory of Development." In *Portraits of Pioneers in Developmental Psychology*, edited by Wade E. Pickren, Donald A. Dewsbury and Michael Wertheimer. Psychology Press, 2012.

Van Cleve, James. "Reid on the Real Foundation of the Primary-Secondary Quality Distinction." In *Primary & Secondary Qualities: The Historical and Ongoing Debate*, edited by Lawrence Nolan. Oxford University Press, 2011.

Van de Vondervoort, Julia W., and J. Kiley Hamlin. "Evidence for Intuitive Morality: Preverbal Infants Make Sociomoral Evaluations." *Child Development Perspectives* 10, no. 3 (2016): 143–48. https://doi.org/10.1111/cdep.12175.

Van der Lugt, Mara. *Dark Matters: Pessimism and the Problem of Suffering.* Princeton University Press, 2021.

Van Huyssteen, J. Wentzel. "From Empathy to Embodied Faith? Interdisciplinary Perspectives on the Evolution of Religion." In Watts and Turner, *Evolution, Religion, and Cognitive Science: Critical and Constructive Essays.*

Van Wolkenten, Megan, Sarah F. Brosnan, and Frans B. M. de Waal. "Inequity Responses of Monkeys Modified by Effort." *Proceedings of the National Academy of Sciences USA* 104, no. 47 (2007): 18854–59. https://doi.org/10.1073/pnas.0707182104.

Vargas, Manuel. "If Free Will Doesn't Exist Neither Does Water." In Caruso, *Exploring the Illusion of Free Will and Moral Responsibility.*

Vessel, Edward A., G. Gabrielle Starr, and Nava Rubin. "The Brain on Art: Intense Aesthetic Experience Activates the Default Mode Network." *Frontiers in Human Neuroscience* 4 (2012): 66. https://doi.org/10.3389/fnhum.2012.00066.

Vickers, Geoffrey. "Rationality and Intuition." In *On Aesthetics in Science*, edited by Judith Wechsler. MIT Press, 1978.

Vilenkin, Alexander. "Creation of Universes from Nothing." *Physics Letters B* 117, no. 1–2 (1982): 25–28. https://doi.org/10.1016/0370-2693(82)90866-8.

Viviani, Paola, and Christelle Aymoz. "Colour, Form, and Movement Are Not Perceived Simultaneously." *Vision Research* 41, no. 22 (2001): 2909–18. https://doi.org/10.1016/S0042-6989(01)00160-2.

Voegelin, Eric. *Modernity Without Restraint.* Vol. 5. University of Missouri Press, 2000.

von Balthasar, Hans Urs. *The Glory of the Lord: A Theological Aesthetics.* Vol. 1, *Seeing the Form.* Ignatius Press, 2009.

von Petzinger, Genevieve, and April Nowell. "A Place in Time: Situating Chauvet within the Long Chronology of Symbolic Behavioral Development." *Journal of Human Evolution* 74 (2014): 37–54. https://doi.org/10.1016/j.jhevol.2014.02.022.

Walker, J. M., W. D. Bowen, L. A. Thompson, J. Frascella, S. Lehmkuhle, and H. C. Hughes. "Distribution of Opiate Receptors Within Visual Structures of the Cat Brain." *Experimental Brain Research* 73, no. 3 (1988): 523–32. https://doi.org/10.1007/BF00406610.PMID:2852119.

Walker, Sara Imari. *Life as No One Knows It: The Physics of Life's Emergence*. Penguin Random House, 2024.

Wallace, B. Alan. "The Intersubjective Worlds of Science and Religion." In Proctor, *Science, Religion and the Human Experience*,.

Watts, Fraser. *Psychology, Religion, and Spirituality: Concepts and Applications.* Cambridge University Press, 2017.

Watts, Fraser. "Religion and the Emergence of Differentiated Cognitions." In Watts and Turner, *Evolution, Religion, and Cognitive Science; Critical and Constructive Essays.*

Weddle, David L. *Sacrifice in Judaism, Christianity, and Islam.* New York University Press, 2017.

Wegner, Daniel. *The Illusion of Conscious Will.* MIT Press, 2002.

Wegner, Daniel M. "The Mind's Best Trick: How We Experience Conscious Will." *Trends in Cognitive Science* 7, no. 2 (2003): 65–69. https://doi.org/10.1016/S1364-6613(03)00002-0.

Wegner, Daniel M. "Précis of *The Illusion of Conscious Will.*" *Behavioral and Brain Sciences* 27, no. 5 (2004): 649–92.

Weinberg, Steven. *The First Three Minutes.* Basic Books, 1993.

Weinberg, Steven. "The Future of Science, and the Universe." *New York Review of Books.* November 15, 2002.

Weiskrantz, Lawrence. *Consciousness Lost and Found: A Neuropsychological Exploration.* Oxford University Press, 1997.

Weiskrantz, Larry. "Is Blindsight Just Degraded Normal Vision?" *Experimental Brain Research* 192, no. 3 (2009): 413–16. https://doi.org/10.1007/s00221-008-1388-7.

Weiskrantz, L., E. K. Warrington, M. D. Sanders, and J. Marshall. "Visual Capacity in the Hemianopic Field Following a Restricted Occipital Ablation." *Brain* 97, no. 1 (1974): 709–28. https://doi.org/10.1093/brain/97.1.709.

Weiss, William A. R. "An Introduction to Set Theory" (course notes). 2014. https://www.math.toronto.edu/~weiss/Set_Theory.pdf.

Wellman, James K., Jr., ed. *Belief and Bloodshed: Religion and Violence Across Time and Tradition.* Rowman & Littlefield, 2007.

Werner, Heinz J. "The Conception of Development from a Comparative and Organismic Point of View." In *The Concept of Development: An Issue in the Study of Behavior*, edited by Dale B. Harris. University of Minnesota Press, 1957.

Westfall, Richard S. *Essays on the Trial of Galileo.* Vatican Observatory Foundation, 1989.

Westman, Robert S. *The Copernican Question: Prognostication, Skepticism, and Celestial Order.* University of California Press, 2011.

Westman, Robert S. "The Copernicans and the Churches." In Lindberg and Numbers, *God & Nature: Historical Essays on the Encounter Between Christianity and Science.*

Wettstein, Howard. *The Significance of Religious Experience.* Oxford University Press, 2012.

Wheeler, John A. "Information, Physics, Quantum: The Search for Links." In *Complexity, Entropy, and the Physics of Information*, edited by Wojciech Hubert Zurek. Addison-Wesley, 1990.

Wheeler-Barclay, Marjorie. *The Science of Religion in Britain, 1860–1915.* University of Virginia Press, 2010.

White, Andrew Dickson. *A History of the Warfare of Science with Religion in Christendom.* Prometheus Books, 1993.

White, Curtis. *The Science Delusion: Asking Big Questions in a Culture of Easy Answers.* Melville House, 2013.

Wiebe, Donald. *The Learned Practice of Religion in the Modern University.* Bloomsbury Academic, 2021.

Wieseltier, Leon. "Crimes Against Humanities." *The New Republic.* September 3, 2013.

Wightman, Gregory J. *The Origins of Religion in the Paleolithic.* Rowman & Littlefield, 2015.

Wiker, Benjamin. "Science and the Natural Law." In *God's Grandeur: The Catholic Case for Intelligent Design*, edited by Ann Gauger. Sophia Institute Press, 2023.

Williams, Richard N. Introduction to *Scientism: The New Orthodoxy*, edited by Richard N. Williams and Daniel N. Robinson. Bloomsbury Press, 2015.

Wilson, Edward O. *Consilience: The Unity of Knowledge*. Vintage Books, 1999.

Wilson, Edward O. *The Social Conquest of Earth*. W. W. Norton, 2013.

Wilson, Edward O. *Sociobiology: The New Synthesis*. Harvard University Press, 2000.

Winkelman, Michael J. "The Mechanisms of Psychedelic Visionary Experiences: Hypotheses from Evolutionary Psychology." *Frontiers in Neuroscience* 11 (2017): 539. https://doi.org/10.3389/fnins.2017.00539.

Winkler, Rafael. "Husserl and Bergson on Time and Consciousness." In *Logos of Phenomenology and Phenomenology of the Logos. Book Three.* Analecta Husserliana, vol. 90, edited by Anna-Teresa Tymieniecka. Springer, 2006. https://doi.org/10.1007/1-4020-3718-X_6.

Wittgenstein, Ludwig. *Philosophical Investigations*. Blackwell Publishing, 2001.

Wittgenstein, Ludwig. *Philosophical Remarks*. University of Chicago Press, 1975.

Wittgenstein, Ludwig. *Tractatus Logico-Philosophicus*. Routledge & Kegan Paul, 1974.

Woit, Peter. *Not Even Wrong: The Failure of String Theory and the Continuing Challenge to Unify the Laws of Physics*. Random House, 2011.

Wood, Jordan Daniel. *The Whole Mystery of Christ: Creation as Incarnation in Maximus Confessor*. University of Notre Dame Press, 2022.

Woods, Thomas E., Jr. *How the Catholic Church Built Western Civilization*. Regnery Publishing, 2005.

Wray, Gregory A., Hopi E. Hoekstra, Douglas J. Futuyma et al. "Does Evolutionary Theory Need a Rethink? *Nature* 514, no. 7521 (2014): 161–4. https://doi.org/10.1038/514161a. This article represents one side of a debate. See also Laland et al. above.

Wright, Edmond, ed. *The Case for Qualia*. MIT Press, 2008.

Yaden, David Bryce, Jonathan Iwry, and Andrew B. Newberg. "Neuroscience and Religion: Surveying the Field." In *Religion: Mental Religion*, edited by Niki Kasumi Clements. Macmillan Publishers, 2016.

Zeki, Semir. *Inner Vision: An Exploration of Art and the Brain*. Oxford University Press, 1999.

Zeki, S., and A. Bartels. "The Asynchrony of Consciousness." Proceedings of the Royal Society of *London B* 265, no. 1405 (1998): 1583–85. http://www.jstor.org/stable/51443.

Subject Index

Author Index